Keep It Old-Time

Billy Craighead at a program at the public library in Fulton, Missouri, January 2018, with Heinrich Leonhard on guitar and Kathy Gordon on bass. From a family of fiddlers and musicians, Billy's forte is fiddling two-steps and waltzes for dancers. (Photo by Margot McMillen)

Keep It Old-Time

Fiddle Music in Missouri from the 1960s Folk Music Revival to the Present

Howard Wight Marshall

Cheers!
Howard Marshall.

UNIVERSITY OF MISSOURI PRESS
Columbia

University of Missouri Press, Columbia, Missouri 65211
Printed and bound in the United States of America

Library of Congress Cataloging-in-Publication Data

Names: Marshall, Howard W., author.
Title: Keep it old-time : fiddle music in Missouri from the 1960s folk music revival to the present / Howard Wight Marshall.
Description: Columbia : University of Missouri Press, 2022. | Includes bibliographical references and index.
Identifiers: LCCN 2022013716 | ISBN 9780826222695 (hardcover)
Subjects: LCSH: Folk music--Missouri--History and criticism. | Old-time music--Missouri--History and criticism. | Fiddle tunes--Missouri--History and criticism. | Fiddlers--Missouri.
Classification: LCC ML3551.7.M68 M36 2022 | DDC 781.62/130778--dc23/eng/20220525
LC record available at https://lccn.loc.gov/2022013716

∞™ This paper meets the requirements of the American National Standard for Permanence of Paper for Printed Library Materials, Z39.48, 1984.

Typeface: Garamond

For Henry Glassie,
my teacher and mentor at Indiana University's Folklore Institute,
who taught me the great joy of chasing tradition down to the people
who carry it on.

Contents

Snapshot of a jam session, the lifeblood of old-time fiddling. *Left to right*: George Crigler (guitar, Paris), Henry Wells (fiddle, Glasgow), Olen Wells (guitar), and Bill Stearns (a guitarist, fiddler, bass player, Fayette, and cousin of Olen Wells). (Courtesy of Mike Wells)

Preface

Tradition is the comforting sound of a distant waterfall that helps us negotiate the cluttered, noisy, trails we travel.

—Jackson Pollock, 1950

Keep It Old-Time and its companion pieces, *"Play Me Something Quick and Devilish"* and *Fiddler's Dream*, represent a lifelong fascination with the world of music and the people who make it.

"Old-time" means music played in an old-fashioned style or in a style of earlier times. *Keep It Old-Time* is an invitation, like a favorite book from college days many years ago, Jim Deetz's *Invitation to Archaeology*. Perhaps readers will become interested in exploring the layers of tradition and time that help give meaning to our lives.

Acknowledgments

I appreciate the University of Missouri Press for supporting this project, and in particular director David Rosenbaum. Special thanks to Tom Adler, who reviewed the first draft of the manuscript and made valuable suggestions for improvement, and to David Cavins, who provided the technical work and production for the companion CD. As with the previous two volumes, Annette Wenda provided outstanding work as copy editor. Financial support for publication was provided by the Missouri Humanities Council.

Many people helped me with advice, assistance, and inspiration, and I thank Thomas A. Adler; Aaron Albrecht; Paul Anastasio; Kenny Applebee; Bob Atchison; Harvie Atterberry; Trustin Baker; Cathy Barton; Sue Ann McMahan Benedict; Katie Benyo; Thayne Bradford; Michael Breid; Kyle Brown; Jack and Mae Burlison; Leroy Canaday; Annette Calton Wood; Bob Carlin; Kim Carr; Robert Carroll; Robert Cathey; David Cavins; Dennis Coelhoe; Van Colbert; Thomas Coriell; Hillis and Jane Crowell; Tess and Maria Cuevas; Terry Cunningham; Rusty and Dory Dutton; Pat Elliott; Larry Ellis; James Eoppolo; Hannah, Norm, Tricia, and Benjamin Farnum; Ed Fedrizzi; Joe Fedrizzi; Paul Fotsch; Sean Franzel; Michael Fraser; Darrell P. Friend; Amber Gaddy; Judy Gaff; Spencer Galloway; Heather Roberson Gaston; Cecil Goforth; Gene Goforth; Kathy Gordon; Sharon Graf; Dan Grotewohl; John Hartford; Mike Hartgrove; Warren Helton; Julie Henigan; Lonnie and Charlene Hoppers; Win Horner; Travis Inman; Gerald Jones; Kelly and Shirley Jones; Mona Jones; Billy Lee; Brad Leftwich; Heinrich Leonhard; C. J. Lewandowski; Art Logan; Junior Marriott; Gordon McCann; Jim McCarty; Jim McGreevy; Ed and Blanche McKinney; Sarah McMahan; Mike Mendelson; Rod Moag; Darryl Muhrer; Verle Muhrer; Benton Naylor; Jim Nelson; Robin Netherton; Roger Netherton; Joe Newberry; Jim Orchard; Malcolm Owen; Joe Palmer; Dave Para; Dale and Mary Ruth Pauley; Dan William Peek; Stacy Phillips; Russ Ravert; Frank Ray; Ron Raymer; David Rees; Marc Rennard; Ralph Rinzler; Bill Rogers; Teresa Romans; Jim Ruth; Geoff Seitz; Jason Shaw; John Shaw; John Shewmaker; Richard Shewmaker; Bill Shull; H. K. Silvey; Amy Skillman; Larry Sledge; Roosevelt (Sonny) Smith; John G. Stewart; Alita Stoneking; Laine Sutherland; Tom Verdot; Charlie Walden; Mike Wells; Tom West; John P. Williams; Phil and Vivian Williams; Mark Wilson; Musial Wolfe; Lyn Wolz; and Bud, Matt, and Allen Wyatt.

I thank the staff at the State Historical Society of Missouri and, in particular, Laura Jolley, Sara Przybylski, and Gary Kremer. I am grateful to David Cavins for help with digital photography, sound recording digitization and CD production, and website assistance. Tune transcriptions were provided by Amber Gaddy, Sharon Graf, Brad Leftwich, Richard Shewmaker, and Matt Wyatt.

Some of the material grew from articles in such journals as the *Missouri Historical Review*, *Fiddler Magazine*, *Missouri Folklore Society Journal*, *Devil's Box*, *Old-Time Herald*, and *MSOTFA Quarterly* (Missouri State Old Time Fiddlers Association).

I also thank family members Sandy Marshall of Toronto; John and Katie Marshall of Golden Valley, Minnesota; Holly Roberson and John Goldstein of Berkeley, California; Heather and Gareth Gaston of Charlottesville, Virginia; and Kathe, Eliot, Aurelia, and James Jordan of Berkeley, California, for encouragement and ideas. As always, my patient wife and first reader, Margot Ford McMillen, provided significant advice and encouragement from start to finish.

I owe much to the scholars, teachers, and mentors who helped me understand what counts in our work and how to think about it, namely, Henry Glassie, Archie Green, Osmund Overby, and Ralph Rinzler.

Keep It Old-Time

Musicians say the best music happens when the recorder is off or absent. An impromptu session on the porch of the Fest Hall during Bethel Fiddle Camp week in the early 2000s. *Left to right*: fiddle instructors John White (here playing his mandolin), Dwight Lamb and Jim Lansford (*right*, fiddle), and Jordan Wax on guitar (Wax lives in New Mexico and performs with a "conjunto" called Lone Piñon). (Photo courtesy of John White)

Introduction

If I should ever die, God forbid, let this be my epitaph: "The only proof he needed for the existence of God was music."

—Kurt Vonnegut, *A Man without a Country* (2005)

Keep It Old-Time celebrates the cultural heritage and community of people who make traditional fiddle and dance music. This is the third book to treat the subject, roughly from the early 1960s to the present, and also speaks for a variety of aspects of the continuing evolution of traditional music in the Midwest and the state of Missouri, and ranges throughout much of the United States. This book builds on my first two. *"Play Me Something Quick and Devilish"* (2012) covered the period from Missouri's earliest European settlements (French) in the mid-1700s to the World War I years and 1920s. *Fiddler's Dream* (2017) picked up the saga in the 1920s and wound down in the 1960s. The frame of this volume is the 1960s to the present.

Keep It Old-Time opens with the Folk Music Revival of the 1960s. In thinking about the youngsters into fiddle and string-band music in the 1960s and 1970s, in almost every case they "got into fiddling" in high school or college, wanting to learn and *perform* the music—often under the influence of revival musicians, from Pete Seeger to Bob Dylan to Peter, Paul & Mary and Silly Wizard. Many became fascinated by the lore and history behind the music, inspired by older generations of collectors and scholars in Missouri and the Ozarks, such as Henry Belden (ballads and folksongs), R. P. Christeson, Vance Randolph, or John Hartford (or scholar-writers, such as Breandán Breathnach in Ireland), Archie Green, Sam Bayard, Sandy Ives, and Henry Glassie,[1] or by meeting people like Mike Seeger, Joe Hickerson, and Ralph Rinzler.

These books span several approaches in documenting and conserving cultural expression and grassroots history, from ethnography, ethnology, and popular culture to American studies, anthropology, cultural and social history, cultural geography, and folklore and folklife studies. As an adventure in multidisciplinary thinking, perhaps the simplest label is history in its broadest sense. I was lucky to be able to do graduate studies at Indiana University's Folklore Institute (1970–73), an institution where fresh ways of thinking about heritage were being developed. Like other young people who loved folk music and eventually developed academic careers, music has remained vital in my life, alongside my focus on material culture, vernacular architecture, and historic preservation.

This is not a book of scholarly analysis of music; others do that better. Rather, it represents decades of hanging out with fiddlers, playing the fiddle, and the curatorship and contemplation that ensue from these adventures. But that doesn't mean that there are no theories or opinions here, even if they aren't articulated in academic

The Raggedy Grass String Band's fiddler was Warren Elliott (d. 2010) in the late 1960s. A farm boy from Audrain County, by age twelve he was fiddling for square dances. In the 2000s, Warren performed with a second version of the band. *Left to right*: Scott Dunwoody (bass, guitar), Dan William Peek (banjo), Elliott (violin, guitar), Fred Dunwoody (guitar). Fred filled the band's hillbilly comic stereotype, performing in the guise of his alter ego, Hector from Huckleberry Holler. I bought my first violin, a bedraggled Sears Roebuck instrument, from Warren in 1968, price five dollars. (Photo by Joy Peek, 2007)

language. Many of the endnotes are informational, providing documentation and guides for readers. I am not very interested these days in trying to define "old-time," or parsing regional fiddle styles, because they are endlessly complex, evolving things. One example where I tiptoe out on the diving board is in attempting to write about modern "Texas"/"Contest Style" fiddling as opposed to "old-time" contest fiddling; I am well acquainted with both styles.

The companion CD that comes with this book gives readers and listeners samples of tunes performed by many of the fiddlers discussed. Taken together with CDs in *"Play Me Something Quick and Devilish"* and *Fiddler's Dream*, the three recordings—more than eighty different fiddlers—constitute a fair representation of the depth and variety of repertoires and styles in Missouri (and, I suggest, in the broader Midwest). Selections are meant not as a "hall of fame" but as examples among many interesting fiddlers, past and present.

As with previous books, several tunes are included in notated (transcribed) form. In this case, the performances are by Cleo Persinger, transcribed by Richard Shewmaker (Columbia); Lee Stoneking, transcribed by Brad Leftwich (Bloomington, Indiana); Mike Hartgrove, transcribed by Amber Gaddy (Columbia); Matt Wyatt, transcribed by Wyatt (Independence); and Travis Inman, transcribed by Sharon Graf (Springfield, Illinois).

It is worth remembering that many fiddle tunes have been written out, composed, and published for hundreds of years in places such as Scotland, where there is a long tradition in musical literacy in the fiddle community. As Charlie Walden notes, transcriptions play an important role in keeping alive and available the way a tune was composed or first published, and this provides us with the essential, "correct," core of a melody through time.[2]

In 2019 Hillis Crowell asked me what my book is about. My answer was not complicated. I'm interested in people who play music, mostly as amateurs and by their own motivations, for their family, a dance, a contest, a jam session, or simply for their own amusement sitting in the kitchen on a quiet afternoon. I let the recorder run in our visits, because it is important to put flesh on the bones of local history, and all the little details in our conversations about 1940s fiddle sessions, and your love of jazz, your memories of Charlie Cook, will be of interest in archives of the future, well beyond this book.

Bythel Friend was from Goodman, near the Oklahoma border, and toured and performed on radio with a western swing dance band, the Oklahoma Ramblers, in the late 1940s. Growing uncomfortable with the high life of traveling musicians, Friend left the Ramblers, returned to Missouri, and pursued a career as an Assembly of God minister. In contrast to many people in the Ozarks, Reverend Friend saw no problem with playing his fiddle in church services. "The fiddle got the blame for what the booze was doing." (Bythel Friend, September 20, 2006; courtesy of Friend)

Oral history has problems, of course. Memories and retellings of stories may have inconsistencies and even errors of fact, and sometimes a story tells more about the person asking the questions than about the person being interviewed. But oral history is helpful in bringing grassroots history and underrepresented information about the past to the broader record. If a detail or a date may be forgotten, the essence of a person's narrative has a kind of truth that lasts.

The exact brackets of the Folk Music Revival (or Folk Song Revival) and "the sixties" decade are unclear and not precisely congruent. The long decade—opinions differ as to when it began and ended—was a complex and troubling time in American society, a time of change and evolution, an undeclared unpopular war, and problems that still rattle our world. For present purposes, I think of the 1960s as bracketed from around 1960 (with President John F. Kennedy's election) to 1975 (the bitter end of the Vietnam War). This was a troubled yet in many ways marvelous period in US history, for a lot of different reasons. Think of the emotions ping-ponging back and forth between terrible events and marvelous advances—the Cold War and the Bay of Pigs, JFK, Miles Davis, the free-speech movement, Volkswagens, *Bonnie and Clyde*, the Beatles, the Beach Boys, Ken Kesey, *2001: A Space Odyssey*, the Watts riots, civil rights legislation, the Peace Corps, the Berlin Wall, Charles Manson, Apollo 11, *Star Trek*, Walmart, Kent State, *Bob and Ted and Carol and Alice*, Vietnam, RFK, MLK, *Sesame Street*.

The revival and its hootenannies and folk festivals attracted people especially in cities and cosmopolitan areas. Later phases included the maturing bluegrass music scene, the string-band movement, the evolution of fiddlers' associations, and the proliferation of fiddle contests.

Jim Ruth (violin) and Heinrich Leonhard, Columbia, ca. 1974. (Courtesy of Jim Ruth)

The Folk Music Revival was largely focused on solo and group singing of traditional songs as well as newly composed songs, including topical and protest songs. The revival of old-time instrumental music and growth of bluegrass fiddling came toward the end of the 1960s and took off in the 1970s. Folk festivals set the pattern, stressing popular "commercial" stars with lesser-known regional as well as local names.[3] In Fincastle, Virginia, bluegrass and country music promoter and songwriter Carlton Haney, along with Ralph Rinzler, pioneered the multiday bluegrass festival.

This was a time of energy and excitement for traditional music of all kinds. The banjo was the darling in the sixties, but the violin reclaimed prominence in the seventies.

Roosevelt (Sonny) Smith was a welcome participant in country music sessions and shows in the Chillicothe-Brookfield area of north Missouri. Born in Seminole, Oklahoma, Smith was a World War II veteran and developed a career as an electrician and carpenter. Like most harmonica players, Smith played a Hohner Marine Band. (Photo by Howard Marshall, November 2002)

Columbia, Missouri, is offered as an example of college-town folk-music activity, where coffeehouses and restaurants were attractive to musicians. Previously, in the 1960s, there were perhaps five or six young fiddlers in Columbia, and then, all of a sudden, in the 1970s as many as fifteen young fiddlers could be found passing through the Chez coffeehouse on Saturday nights.

The seventies also witnessed new interest in square dancing and the growth of New England–style contra dancing. Relatively unknown lines of academic research grew into significant fields of study—folklore, cultural geography, historical anthropology, dialectology, American studies, and more—creating new ideas of understanding cultural heritage, particularly of what we call "the people who have been left out of the history books." A lot of this work was inspired by the nation's bicentennial celebrations and some rethinking and rediscovery of what lies beneath the sometimes elitist and partial narratives of formal received history.

Lucky were the older musicians "discovered" and given exposure and introduction to new audiences. The enthusiasm often went both directions. Older fiddlers like Taylor McBaine, Lena Hughes, and Art Galbraith gained wider respect, just as young people were inspired to study and learn directly from them. A remarkable number of young people embraced fiddle and banjo playing, and many musicians had a serious commitment to documentation and study of the music and musicians they admired.

Accompaniment for the Fiddle

The "second," "backup," or "rhythm" accompaniment is crucial in old-time fiddling. Accompaniment can elevate fiddle music to joy or reduce it to rubble. The standard instruments we see as fiddle backup in Missouri are guitar and five-string and four-string banjo, the venerable old-time fiddle-band trio sound; in bluegrass, add the mandolin, bass and, sometimes, resophonic guitar. We have become narrow in what we expect to see for rhythm backup. To the old-time dance fiddler, virtually any rhythmic assistance is welcome—sticks, bones, jugs, cellos, reed organs, accordions, tubas, bagpipes, pianos, autoharps, tin whistles, sousaphones, harmonicas, cornets, washboards, ukuleles, banjo ukes, saxophones, harps, didgeridoos, flutes, hammered dulcimer, mountain dulcimer, hurdy-gurdy, xylophones, and anything else that works. Appropriateness is about context and the players. Appropriateness is also about sensitivity and awareness of the unwritten codes that make an impromptu jam session fun.

Playing second fiddle is a good thing, and the old custom is edging back into usage after being shunted aside in modern times by fiddle accompaniment such as "twin fiddle," "the bluegrass chop," and other devices. The expression "playing second fiddle" implies one melody dominated by another, as in an orchestra performing in the second violin section with different music from the "first violins." And playing second fiddle in old-time music is a satisfying skill. The seconder provides accent and chords and sometimes melody doubling. Among practitioners in Missouri were Johnny Bruce, Leroy Canaday, Pete McMahan, Charlie Pashia, Joe Politte, Lonnie Robertson, Nile Wilson, and members of the Helton family. Charlie Walden and McMahan's "Marmaduke's Hornpipe" stands the test of time as an example of fiddle seconding on *Now That's a Good Tune*, as does Roger Netherton and Rachel Eddy's "Half Past Four" (*Roger Netherton*). The effect can sound much like the resonant, surging sounds of chords on a reed organ or accordion.[4]

The sixties was a great age for young people to discover the banjo, but by the late sixties and early seventies, interest began to shift; while continuing to like bluegrass styles, young people were gravitating to brands of melodic claw-hammer five-string

A jam session in Pickard Hall on the University of Missouri campus in Columbia, with a variety of instruments. *Clockwise from bottom*: Knox McCrory (harmonica, back to camera), Kenny Applebee (guitar), John Williams (violin), Alan Jabbour (Washington, DC, violin), Howard Marshall (violin), Musial Wolfe (reed organ), Russ Ravert (guitar, *center*), Jim Ruth (banjo), Joel Chrisman (violin), Tom Verdot (violin), and Kathy Gordon (bass), September 2000.

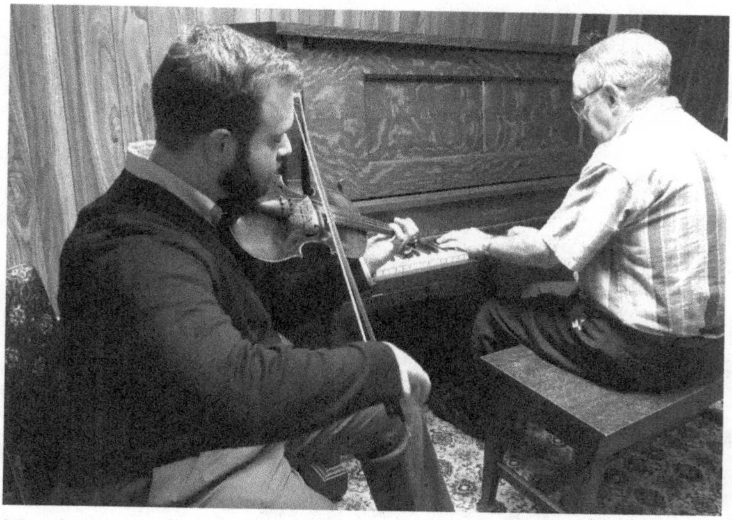

Musial Wolfe backs fiddler Aaron Albrecht on his Gulbranson player piano (set in nonmechanical mode), Boonville. Through the years, Wolfe advised other pianists such as Debbie Young and Carrie Watson on the spare, driving backup style traditionally preferred by fiddlers in Missouri. (Photo by Howard Marshall, 2019)

Guy Craighead of Fulton played tenor guitar backup at dances, fiddle contests, and over WOS-AM radio with fiddler Vee Latty. (Photo by Mike DeSantis, *Fulton Sun Gazette*, October 13, 1984)

Sims family musicians. *Left to right*: Jesse Sims, violin; his cousin Porter Sims, five-string banjo; and Ruby Christopher Ray (Porter's son), resophonic guitar, ca. 1940. The men played for dances in Boone County in the thirties and forties. (Courtesy of Ron Ray)

Van Colbert of Willow Springs teaches a banjo workshop at the annual Ozark Heritage Music Festival in West Plains. Colbert developed a personal style he considers "Ozark" and uses the terms "frailing" and "claw-hammer" to explain it, acknowledging the influence today of the so-called Round Peak style from the North Carolina piedmont—a banjo style once regional but now international; however, unlike many modern clawhammer players, Van does not match a fiddler's melody: "I'm more into a *rhythm*, keeping a good rhythm for the fiddlers, and drive. Put in some melody notes if I know the melody of it, but I mainly play the *chords*, behind 'em. (Photo by Howard Marshall, June 2013)

Harvie Atterberry, a great-nephew of the Callaway County fiddler Clark Atterberry, with his Oscar Schmidt five-string banjo, a popular brand during the Folk Music Revival, mail-ordered from Sears Roebuck in the 1960s. Harvie's old-time down-picking style makes good fiddle accompaniment. He and his wife, Joyce, led a country music band called the Front Porch Pickers and were regulars at bluegrass festivals and fiddle contests. (Photo by Howard Marshall, 2019)

radiating across the country from festivals, fiddlers' conventions, jam-session tapes, and records from the southern Appalachians. Young banjoists were on hand around Columbia, a magnet college town for young musicians, in the early 1970s, such as Tom Verdot, Bill Rogers, Joel Chrisman, Jim Ruth, Kevin Sanders, Ken Mietus, Rob Golan, Joe Newberry, and Cathy Barton. Some people played both banjo and violin, and most banjo players and fiddlers were adept at playing guitar and other instruments as well. So, in the early 1970s, the violin returned from the wings of the Folk Music Revival to center stage.

Some fans would say that banjo is more important than fiddle in bluegrass music. In the massive growth of 1960s and 1970s bluegrass and bluegrass festivals, the thrilling playing of pioneers like Earl Scruggs and Don Reno put banjo center stage; fiddle music, on the other hand, while also experiencing new ideas, had been around for centuries and was a bit slower to catch the attention of the legion of young fans.

Jim McGreevy in a jam session, Kansas City, 2008. McGreevy came to Kansas City from Oklahoma in 1960 to start a career as a chemist. His exposure to old-time and bluegrass fiddling in the Kansas City area is linked to jam sessions at the Kansas City old-time fiddlers club. "That's where several of us went to learn to play *backup for fiddle players*, and to try to hone our minimal skills on mandolins and guitars and banjos while staying out of the way of the fiddlers." Jim has performed for many years with Kansas City bands, the Bluegrass Association (which included fiddler Lyman Enloe), and the Bluegrass Brigade (which included fiddlers Bob Cartmill, Don Montgomery, and Rusty Dutton). (McGreevy, January 6, 2017; courtesy of McGreevy)

Some influential young bands did not include a fiddler, such as the Greenbrier Boys and the Country Gentlemen.

Within any region's broad style, there are as many personal variations as there are players. In a letter from Pete McMahan in 1976:

> If I was a writer, I could write a book on old time Missouri fiddling and fiddlers who I have had the honor to know and play in competition with. In my own mind and

Lynn Wells plays at the Fourth of July contest in Boonesboro, 2007. Junior Marriott (*left*) and Lynn's younger brother Mike Wells (also a fine fiddler) on guitar. Lynn and Mike are two children of champion Dewey Eugene (Gene) Wells and nephews of the great left-handed fiddler Henry Wells. Lynn often plays his father's and uncle Henry's composition "Combination Waltz" in contests. (Photo by Kay Allen)

my own recognition of good fiddle playing I think that Missouri has had and still has the best fiddlers in the United States. I mean *old* time fiddlers, not the modern style which is nice to listen to but far from traditional. There is a hell of a lot of difference. I have heard fiddlers play tunes in competition and at jam sessions that put so many notes in the tune that it distorted it so badly you could not tell what they are playing if they hadn't told you the name of the tune. And to me that is not fiddling. And that is the kind of fiddling that wins the National Oldtime Fiddlers' Contest. And I think that is a shame.

[Listen to track 1 on the companion CD to hear Henry Wells play his version of "Bill Cheatem."]

Contests

Fiddle contests have been around since colonial times, were prolific during the 1920s, and returned in the 1950s and 1960s after decline during the Great Depression and World War II years. For many people, seeing a contest is their first exposure to live fiddle music. In the 1960s and 1970s, fiddlers' associations tried to sort out rules. People became more interested in questions of fairness and propriety; adjudication eventually moved from audience applause (the famous Applause-O-Meter gadgets) to panels of ostensibly more fair and knowledgeable judges.

The 1960s and 1970s were still dominated by old-time contest fiddling exemplified by players like Dean Johnston, Jake Hockemeyer, Pete McMahan, Cleo

Persinger, and Cyril Stinnett, as well as younger-generation counterparts such as John Griffin and Charlie Walden.

The end of the sixties and early seventies marks a horizon when we saw the rise in popularity of two increasingly nationalized superstyles of fiddling. On the one hand, there was the approach to contest fiddling in the southern Appalachian region (particularly North Carolina and Virginia) and southeastern United States that was popularized through recordings and festivals. Many young fiddlers across the country adopted these "mountain" or "Appalachian" styles and tunes. Generally speaking, these fiddle styles were the seeds of old-time fiddle styles carried westward in nineteenth-century pioneer days.

Contest Style

In this book, "Contest Style" (with capital letters) denotes Texas-derived contest-style fiddling that became dominant in the 2000s in fiddle contests in Missouri and west of the Mississippi River.[5] This subject appears throughout much of this book, since Contest Style permeates the great majority of contest stages today.

Contest Style fiddling was invented to win fiddle contests. Old-time fiddling is generally for dancing; the performance emphasis is on rhythm, and the focus is on the dancers. Contest Style fiddling is generally *listening music* for people seated in an audience; the performance emphasis is on melody, and the performance emphasis is on the solo fiddler.

Contest Style is contest music developed by several creative fiddlers in Texas in the 1950s and 1960s (with palpable roots in earlier decades). This innovative, attractive style was grounded in old-time fiddle styles that had evolved through time, especially across the American South and Southwest. A crucial element was numerous repetitions of the tune after stating its core and with each repetition displaying creative variations on the old melodies; the more creative variations a fiddler could imagine without losing sight of the core melody, the better. Influences and quotations from early jazz and western swing became essential to this Texas-derived Contest Style, and this approach to contest fiddling proved tremendously successful. Contest Style became a national superstyle, no longer confined to its evolutionary region of Texas and the Southwest. It is now a global style.

This Texas-derived contest style was widely referred to as "Texas style" as it began to be influential far beyond its hearth, through LP records with titles such as *Texas Hoedown* and *Texas Fiddle Favorites*, spotlighting this distinctive improvisational, highly melodic contest and jam-session fiddling. Such records helped cement the term "Texas style" for what Texans such as Major Franklin, Orville Burns, and Benny Thomasson were doing.[6]

In the 1970s, this Texas-derived contest style was becoming influential and encouraged at the National Oldtime Fiddlers' Contest at Weiser, Idaho, and it was promulgated in the Southeast by such powerful fiddlers as J. T. Perkins of Alabama and Randy Howard of Nashville. Many people familiar with the Weiser contest, the nation's largest, even if primarily a western-states contest, began using the term "Contest Style" as well as "Texas style" for this posh music, exemplified in the Junior and Open Divisions at Weiser.

Contest Style became predominant at Weiser. Some fiddlers there, or others familiar with the Weiser event, began calling it "Weiser style"—even though fiddlers from the state of Texas as well as ethnomusicologists notice differences the general public may not.[7]

Today many Missouri fiddlers use "Texas style" interchangeably with "Weiser style." But note that contest style (lowercase) may apply to competition performance styles in regions with their own special "contest styles," such as New England, the southern Appalachians, and maritime Canada.

People noticed the difference between old-time and Contest Style fiddling. As California old-time fiddler Kenny Hall quipped, "Texas style makes 'Leather Britches' sound like perma press."[8] Few people appreciated that historic old-time "Texas style" fiddling and its fancier child, Contest Style, are not the same. According to Drew Beisswenger, "Modern contest fiddling gives Texas style a bad name."[9]

If you want to know what baroque music is, pull up Vivaldi or Handel on the Internet. If you want to know what modern jazz is, look for Dave Brubeck and Miles Davis. If you want to know what Contest Style fiddling is, search on the Internet for the Texas State Championship Fiddlers' Frolics in Hallettsville and the National Oldtime Fiddlers' Contest in Weiser, Idaho, and take a seat.[10]

In Missouri, just as in many other states, the tug-of-war for stylistic dominance in fiddle contests has favored the Texas-derived Contest Style more and more. However, old-time fiddlers continue to be successful in contests, keeping strong the music of Pete McMahan, Cyril Stinnett, and other old-time contest champions. Fiddlers will always have choices; they embrace the musical style that fulfills their imaginations and emotions.

Perhaps old-time fiddlers imagine that the struggle for stylistic dominance in the big coliseum of fiddle contests is still to be decided or that audiences, contest judges, and audiences decided the outcome twenty years ago. However, old-time fiddlers continue to do well against Contest Style fiddlers in contests, and they are devoted to their music just as much as the are Contest Style players. Change happens. What will future changes bring?

A Note on Backup Guitar in Contest Fiddling Today

"Over the past few decades Texas contest-style fiddling has made inroads into most regions of North America, and wherever it goes, so goes its partner, Texas-style rhythm guitar."[11] Guitar is the most common accompaniment in contests. Its influence on how the fiddling sounds is important, and its influence can be subtle or bold. Most listeners cue on the fiddler's performance and may barely notice the backup. But the guitar backup (a.k.a. rhythm or seconding) is exceedingly important in how the fiddling comes out.

The most important difference in backup-guitar styles is whether the guitarist employs open chords or closed chords. Both styles are traditional and can be heard on early 78-rpm fiddle records of fiddlers and string bands. Most fiddlers prefer one or the other guitar style.[12] As often discussed, in old-time and bluegrass fiddling, the prevailing backup-guitar style is generally called "straight chord," using open-chord shapes and relatively few chords—what some call "three-finger chords." In a nutshell, the strings in open chords tend to ring out, while closed chords tend to create a percussive thump.

Closed-chord backup involves the player using jazz-based chord shapes and bar chords, creating a heavy, moving rhythm. The chords tend to be numerous and travel up and down the neck in different shapes and are like the "comping" (accompaniment) guitar styles in jazz and western swing. This backup style in 4/4 time (for breakdowns and rags) emphasizes the "backbeat"—like in jazz, boom-CHUCK, boom-CHUCK. In contrast, backup in old-time (and bluegrass) fiddling places the rhythmic emphasis on the first and third beats of a measure: BOOM-chuck, BOOM-chuck.

The closed-chord guitar playing is linked to Contest Style fiddling and can be called "contest guitar style." Perhaps more important than the fiddle style we are calling Contest Style is the absolutely crucial role of a fiddler's guitar accompaniment. Contest Style fiddling is powered by lavish guitar accompaniment, backup in which guitarists play numerous and fast-changing closed chords and jazz-influenced moves, instead of the plain-Jane open chords of typical old-time and bluegrass fiddle accompaniment.

A guitarist's seconding style has a strong bearing on the music. The fiddler may or may notice. "Soldier's Joy" with an open-chord guitar player will sound different—although the fiddler may play the tune the same way—than it sounds with a closed-chord player. I find it fascinating that a seasoned expert fiddler tends to perform his or her tunes in a fiddle contest (or at a square dance, for that matter) the same way, whether he or she is backed up by an old-time, spare, straight-chord guitar player or a modern Contest Style guitar player. What that says is that many fiddlers can present their tunes the way they want, whatever backup-guitar style is being provided. They "tune out" the backup and still perform well.

Other fiddlers, of course, are apt to be distracted by accompaniment that feels wrong, and thus they underperform. Some people change their fiddling according to the backup. As Junior Marriott, champion fiddler and master guitar accompanist in various styles, once said, "Different guitar players will make you play differently."[13] What this also implies is that a fiddler may bring two or three or more guitarists to the microphone, which can help produce a wall of sound, or a "groove," that helps a fiddler do well, and perhaps camouflage flubs. Many people have commented on swing guitar in contemporary contest fiddling, as well as the style's debt to the kind of "groove" that characterizes western swing bands like the Bob Wills organization.

The two customs, open-chord and closed-chord guitar backup, are not an either-or choice and not diametrically opposed. Many guitarists focus on one of them but can shift to the other. In contests, the closed-chord swing guitar style has supplanted other styles in many locations across the country—a source for debate and grumbling among musicians from the open-chord school.[14]

To hear the difference, for old-time straight-chord guitar backup, listen to "Brenda's Reel" on the companion CD, by fiddler Richard Shewmaker with Aaron Albrecht on guitar. For Texas-derived Contest Style fiddling and its swing-based closed-chord guitar backup, listen to "Dusty Miller" on the companion CD, by fiddler Alita Stoneking with Tom Weisgerber on guitar.

Many young people came to "folk music" thanks to the Kingston Trio. They were part of the calypso fad sparked by Harry Belafonte in the 1950s and soon broadened their horizons. Bob Shane and Nick Reynolds played Martin guitars (Reynolds, tenor guitar), and, in this 1959 iteration, Dave Guard plays his Vega five-string "Pete Seeger" long-neck banjo. (Cover, *Here We Go Again*, Capitol ST1258, 1959).

The Folk Music Revival of the 1960s and 1970s—and the Fiddle

1

The U.S. is smack in the middle of a folk-music boom.
—"Folk Music Frenzy," *Time*, July 11, 1960

Precisely when revivals start is muddled by opinion, forgetfulness, and opaque documentation. Interpretations depend upon when a person was born, within what cultural traditions and social milieu, and their experiences. A great deal of scholarship is devoted to the subject.[1] This chapter considers the Folk Music Revival in the United States in the era of the 1960s and 1970s and its offspring, the string-band movement and instrumental Folk Music Revival that took off in the 1970s.

The revival reaches back to folklore collectors in the 1920s and 1930s,[2] as well as the 1940s' parallel renewal of interest in square dancing, topical songwriting, and a looking inward in American society during the World War II years. The focus was primarily on singers and composed "protest songs" in which performers such as Woody Guthrie and the Weavers addressed politics, government, current events, and such issues as the rights to unionize among coal miners and migrant farmworkers, the anti-nuclear-arms movement ("Ban the Bomb"), the free-speech movement, civil rights, and, in the 1960s, the military draft and Vietnam War.

Many of the early leaders of the Folk Music Revival were balladeers, well educated, liberal, and urbane. But people found common cause. Woody Guthrie and Pete Seeger, for example, were different in background but alike in music and politics. At the same time, the Library of Congress made efforts to make their field recordings of folk music available. Many of the young, urban, educated folksong aficionados explored archives in the Library of Congress, and historic recordings and documents became sources for popular (and popularized) versions of authentic folk music.

Folk music broke into pop culture in the 1950s with the Kingston Trio and, on the other end of the stylistic scale, the New Lost City Ramblers (NLCR). The Folk Music Revival began to show cracks in the hull only a decade later, when Bob Dylan "went electric" at the 1965 Newport Folk Festival, seeming more rock-and-roller than Woody Guthrie disciple.[3] To others, Dylan playing an electric guitar proved the inherent engines of change and heralded the emerging genre of folk rock. If the Folk Music Revival lost energy in the later 1960s and through the 1970s, it gave birth to the string-band movement and the singer-songwriter movement that continue. The Folk Song Revival did its work well and truly, and only pieces of the counterculture zeitgeist persist.

The revival was linked to protest politics, antiwar songwriting, and the hippie movement, even if many young participants were uninterested in societal rumblings and global issues. The sixties era also brought go-go boots, *Dr. Strangelove*, Apollo 11,

Laugh-In, rock and roll,[4] the Beatles, Truman Capote, *2001: a Space Odyssey*, Dave Brubeck, pop art, bell-bottom trousers, and the Age of Aquarius.[5]

A hootenanny is an informal concert of individual performers and groups hosted in a coffeehouse, community hall, college cafeteria, or any of many other sociable public spaces (most of them small and intimate), featuring musicians who sign up with the host or emcee to receive a position in the lineup. Musicians of all ages and levels of experience are given a slot of time (a "set") and perform in front of a microphone in front of an audience. A cover charge may or may not be collected but is usually collected if a popular or famous musician is on the bill. Typically, a basket or hat is passed around the audience for donations for the musicians (with or without a deduction for host expenses), and typically the audience orders food and drink while the show ensues. Hootenannies popped up everywhere from the 1940s into the 1970s. They tended to feature singing more than instrumentals. Performers often invited the audience to sing along. Just as an aspiring young bluegrass banjo picker could get performance experience and exposure in bluegrass-festival campground pickin' sessions, hoots gave experience and exposure to singers and instrumentalists.

According to the album notes for a 1963 LP by the Knob Lick Upper 10,000: "Like the legendary Wabash Cannonball, the word 'hootenanny' now rumbles across America at a rate of speed that guarantees it will soon be out of sight. Yes, Virginia the hucksters have hooted the nanny into a T-shirt, a television show, a questionable concert and, least likely of all, a shoe. [But] hootenanny after all (and all else) is a simple circumstance. And folk music is at least as American as jingles and slogans."[6]

Protest songs and music began to be quietly suppressed by the recording industry and media outlets during what Pete Seeger called the "Frightened Fifties" amid Red Scare fears and the infamous House Committee on Un-American Affairs hearings mounted by ultraconservative politicians.[7] Seemingly apolitical folk music (at least on the surface), such as Harry Belafonte's 1950s calypso hits, had subtle messages.[8]

As the Vietnam War grew larger and more troubling to Americans, Barry McGuire's 1965 protest song "The Eve of Destruction" made it to number one on the *Billboard* pop music charts: "The Eastern world, it is explodin' / Violence flarin', bullets loadin' / You're old enough to kill but not for votin' / You don't believe in war, what's that gun you're totin'?" A year later, those who disliked "The Eve of Destruction" had their answer song, the ultrapatriotic "Ballad of the Green Berets," written and performed by Sergeant Barry Sadler, a wounded Vietnam combat veteran. "Ballad of the Green Berets" made the *Billboard* number one in 1966.[9]

Commercial folk groups like the Kingston Trio, Brothers Four, and New Christy Minstrels drew us to guitars and banjos and singing folksongs—and incidentally were crucial in the survival and spread of homemade music among young people. Epitomized by the Kingston Trio and the New Christy Minstrels, both of them on the West Coast, the groups tended to be politically conservative or neutral, "clean-cut" in repertoires and performance styles, as well as projecting what was called "collegiate" and "Joe college" imagery. Their popularity was in part generated in coffeehouses and at concerts at colleges, in tandem with record contracts in California and New York and spots on TV variety shows. This nonthreatening seam of the Folk Music Revival was promoted on Top 40 radio and *The Ed Sullivan Show* on TV, and this kind of music as entertainment reached far and wide. Critics and scholars may consider groups like the Kingston Trio to be usurpers or worse, compared to politically active predecessors like the Weavers or contemporaries like Joan Baez and Bob Dylan. However, the Kingston Trio respected the roots of the music and did not claim to be anything more than students who liked to sing and entertain. It was the pleasure of the music and charm of the young men that attracted people. Their appreciation of backstories to "Tom Dooley" and "M.T.A." would come eventually. The music was convivial. We wanted to sing along. We wanted a banjo.

Through records available at any record shop, people might find their way to what was thought to be more authentic, "noncommercial," folk music. Much of the protest music "went underground"—enhancing the allure of the lifestyle—and continued in bohemian/beatnik and counterculture venues in campus coffeehouses, hip bookshops and music stores, summer camps, small venues, and, perhaps most important, festivals.[10]

Over on Music Row, kingpins of country music wanted in on the money being made by Folk Music Revival labels as well as wanting to capitalize on the surprising popularity of bluegrass music. Nashville projects could be brilliant or shambles. One such project, George Jones and Melba Montgomery's *Blue Grass Music Hootenanny* (United Artists, UAS 6352, 1964), was saved from the dustbin by adding A-list session musicians (bluegrass banjoist Curtis McPeake, resophonic guitarist Shot Jackson, and fiddler Tommy Jackson). Some albums like that sprang from jam sessions backstage at the Grand Ole Opry and were accepted by fans in good fun. More successful in the crossover game were projects that went the other direction: old-time, bluegrass, and hillbilly-style fiddlers made upmarket "country and western" albums. Many of these fiddlers were pioneers in country music, such as Tommy Jackson, Howdy Forrester, and Chubby Wise, and their Nashville country records fared well. Hard-core old-time and bluegrass fans, collectors, and scholars, whose purist and protective tendencies were offended by electric instruments and studio tweaking of fiddling, could "tune out" the sounds they disliked.[11]

Lester Flatt and Earl Scruggs and the Foggy Mountain Boys were, arguably, the most popular and successful of bluegrass pioneers who tried to appeal to a wide crossover audience. Their push into the commercial country music market and at the same time the folk market was only modestly successful. On LPs in 1968 they tried to be more relevant, with covers of Pete Seeger's and Bob Dylan's revival anthems, such as "Where Have All the Flowers Gone" (Seeger), "Mr. Tambourine Man," "Don't Think Twice, It's All Right," "Blowin' in the Wind," and "It Ain't Me Babe" (*Changin' Times*, Columbia CS 9596). On *Nashville Airplane* (Columbia 8741), they covered hits such as "Folsom Prison Blues" (Johnny Cash), "Gentle on My Mind" (Glen Campbell), and Dylan's "Like a Rolling Stone" and "The Times They Are a-Changin'." Certainly, the times *were* a-changing, but staunch bluegrassers were not amused. Such recordings devalued the Flatt and Scruggs brand and factored in their breakup in 1969.

Flatt wanted to stay pure bluegrass and did so with his new band, the Nashville Grass; Scruggs wanted to have more fun and experiment with rock and roll, which he did in a band with his sons, the Earl Scruggs Revue.

More interesting were projects launched by youngsters teasing boundaries and enjoying themselves. A genre began to emerge (or clash) in 1964 with "the British Invasion," led by the Beatles, but change was not wholesale. The Beatles' rock and roll embraced folk-music elements and acoustic guitars. The relative purity and instrumental simplicity and ballad-like mood of many of the Beatles' hits appealed to the same kids who were into folk music. The Charles River Valley Boys' 1966 LP, *Beatle Country*, was a delightful project of Lennon and McCartney songs worked up bluegrass style.[12] Some groups created "newgrass," such as the New Grass Revival (led by former teenage fiddle champion Sam Bush).[13] Further out in the Milky Way was mandolinist David Grisman's "Dawg" music, a fusion of progressive bluegrass, folk, and jazz of the Django Reinhardt–Stéphane Grappelli school.

The underground folk-music scene, emerging from poetry and socially aware standup comedy of beatnik coffeehouses, had become sufficiently commercialized and popularized that record companies were issuing albums by groups looking like well-mannered college kids (many of the folk groups *were* well-mannered college kids). The protest and antiestablishment essence in the lyrics may have remained, but the buffed performances and packaging suggested that these youngsters were nice, polite, patrons of barbershops and JCPenney, and certainly not druggies or members of the Communist Party USA. Syndicated television featured shows such as *The Smothers Brothers Comedy Hour*, *Hootenanny*, and *The Glen Campbell Show*. Banjo pickers appeared on *Ed Sullivan*, fiddlers on *Ted Mack's Amateur Hour*. Folk music and most protest songs got spruced up and professionalized.

The string-band movement of the later 1960s through the 1970s was less political. It's early phase emphasized rediscovering and performing music of the classic string bands and fiddlers of the 1920s era. More nostalgia than protest, they projected their politics more in attire, buttons on jackets, and attitudes than by singing protest songs. A string-band fiddler in "old-timey" music was more likely to be "against" contemporary pop music than deeply involved in radical politics and protest.

Fiddle music in a Hollywood movie could be corny and ridiculous, but the sixties also began to see increasingly accurate film delineations of traditional music. *Dillinger* producers found authentic string musicians to play "Turkey in the Straw" and "Red River Valley" at a platform dance scene in Oklahoma. *The Long Riders* featured a saloon band composed of young California pickers Mitch Greenhill (guitar), Bill Bryson (banjo), and Tom Sauber (violin). In *The Outlaw Josey Wales*, actor Sheb Wooley fiddles for a Texas settlers' dance, and two authentic tunes of the Civil War era are in the soundtrack, "Irish Washerwoman" and "The Rose of Alabama." In *McCabe and Mrs. Miller*, another revisionist western, Brantley Kearns fiddles "Mississippi Sawyer," "Ta-ra-ra Boom De-ay!," "Listen to the Mockingbird," "Beautiful Dreamer," and "Sugar in the Gourd," appropriate for the late 1800s.[14]

On television, authentic fiddlers worked on *Hee Haw*, but not, to my knowledge, on *The Ed Sullivan Show*. TV executives seemed to draw a line: studios tended to send fiddlers to jobs where hillbilly-themed shows were developed that reinforced supposedly funny stereotypes of rural music and life; used costuming from minstrel stage, vaudeville, and Grand Ole Opry comedy; or reflected Nashville glitz. Lawrence Welk's TV orchestra included violinists and banjoists who could fiddle a respectable hoedown or strum a tenor-banjo rag or pick bluegrass when the script indicated.[15]

Success enjoyed by folk and bluegrass performers in movies and television helped loosen the recording industry to regional and ethnic performers and unrecognized performers. Labels began producing LPs of fiddle music in the context of old-time string-band music and bluegrass, the path blazed by independents such as Rounder Records (whose policies ensured that performers secured creative rights to their recordings). Folkways, Flying Fish, American Heritage, County, Voyager, Bay, Philo, and others brought music of cultural regions and ethnic communities to attention. New York and Los Angeles major labels reflected their supposed audiences; the New Lost City Ramblers appeared on Vanguard (the folksingers' urbane label), Bill Monroe and His Blue Grass Boys on Decca. Collectors such as Charles Faurot and Richard Nevins brought little-known and well-documented musicians and fiddle music to the public. Compilations were released of 78-rpm records from the 1920s and early 1930s, such as Harry Smith's 1952 *Anthology of Folk Music*, and old-time fiddle music was celebrated in Alan Jabbour's *American Fiddle Tunes* set with history and analysis.[16]

The Folk Music Revival Ends, and Keeps on Keepin' On

The revival crested in the early seventies (or in the late sixties, depending on whom you ask), and by the late seventies it and the hippie movement had mostly fizzled out. What goes up must come down. The action had shifted to the West Coast, particularly California and the orbits of Portland and Seattle, and other epicenters, among them San Francisco and the university town Berkeley across the Bay, as well as various parts of the Los Angeles basin and metro area and on down Highway 101 to San Diego's Mission Beach. San Francisco and the Bay Area often get the limelight in the popular media, perhaps because the age of the "freaks" and psychedelia was preceded by the Beat generation and the emergence of coffeehouses there.

The Beatles split up in 1970. President Nixon resigned in the summer of 1974. US troops in Vietnam came home. The folksong movement waned; an easy target for satirists, some called it "the great boom" and "the Great Folk Scare."[17] But through this period, undercurrents of nostalgia and searching led many young people to the "old-timey music."

String-Band Redux

The string-band movement, or revival, begins in the same space as the Folk Music Revival and in many ways was part of it. The time is the late fifties, sixties, and seventies, and the locales for the most part are big cities (New York City and the San Francisco Bay Area receive the most credit) and college and university towns and campuses. Their inspirations came more from 1920s hillbilly records, Grand Ole Opry broadcasts, and bluegrass music, and the principal instruments were banjos and violins. The group that showed the way was the New Lost City Ramblers.

The New Lost City Ramblers was founded in New York City in 1958 by multi-instrumentalist Mike Seeger (younger half-brother of Pete Seeger). Mike played five-string banjo, guitar, mandolin, violin, autoharp, and other instruments in many styles and typically replicating music on the old 78-rpm records. In its first iteration, the NLCR included the New York City–born photography teacher, artist, photographer, guitarist, and singer John Cohen (a Yale graduate) and New York City–born mathematician-cum-banjoist, fiddler, and singer Tom Paley (also a Yale grad), Ivy Leaguers and avid devotees of old and mostly rural southern string-band and blues music.[18] Seeger, Paley, and Cohen were pied pipers in New York. When Paley left the NLCR in 1962, New Englander Tracy Schwarz took his chair, and the band continued evolving as professionals, recording artists, teachers, and mentors. Schwarz proved an excellent new bandmate.

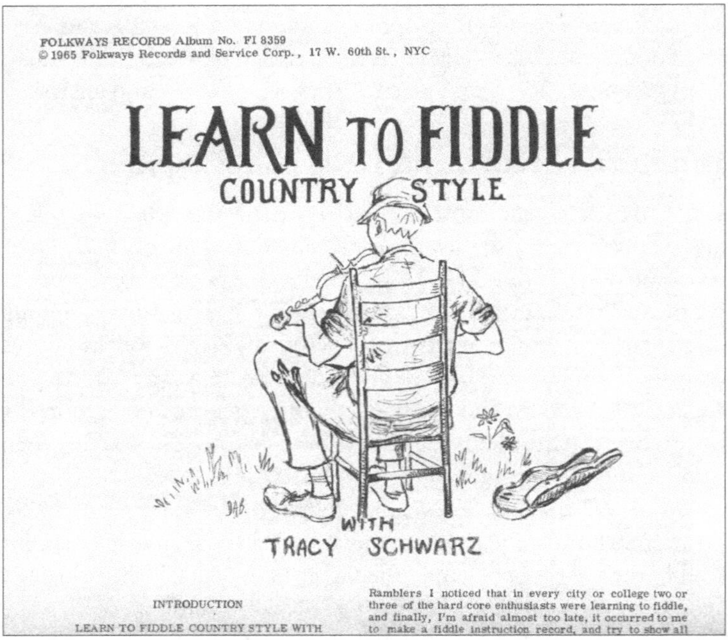

Tracy Schwarz noticed aspiring fiddlers at festivals and decided to create a congenial tutor to help beginners, *Learn to Fiddle Country Style*. Schwarz suggests listening to recordings by Eck Robertson, Lowe Stokes, Doc Roberts, and Charlie Bowman and more modern players such as Arthur Smith, Chubby Wise, Georgia Slim, Benny Martin, Tommy Jackson, Paul Warren, and Kenny Baker. (Courtesy of Tracy Schwarz, July 1974)

These erudite gentlemen had a knack for curating and re-creating an authentic old-time sound, and their dedication to historical research was infectious. They helped situate in the lexicon the terms "old-timey" (the category under which 78-rpm string-band records were marketed) and "old-time." They faithfully interpreted and gave new life to string-band music that had flourished on early recordings and radio programming. As Cohen recalled, they promoted the older musicians who made the 78s as artists and individuals rather than as "sources" or "informants."[19] Aware of the importance of how one presents oneself and thus one's music, the Ramblers decided not to dress as rumpled hillbillies, setting a different image of old-time musicians. For appearance at the Gate of Horn in Chicago in 1960, they were required to dress "respectable." "So we thought about what an old-time country farmer would wear if he had gone to town to perform in a show, and decided to dress our best, rather than in blue jeans or work clothes. We studied old photographs and early rural performers . . . and came up with white shirts, ties, and differing vests as our garb."[20]

The Ramblers' influence was significant, thanks to keenly produced records and a heavy schedule of campus concerts, festivals, and gigs on the coffeehouse circuit. They appealed to a new community of aficionados, squares as well as hippies, and sent many people foraging in flea markets and attics in search of old 78s and their grandfather's dusty violin. According to Lyle Lofgren, "As we tried to learn how to perform the material, we used the records and concert appearances of the New Lost City Ramblers on the proper way for non-traditionalists to perform traditional music. They showed us that it was possible to be respectful, knowledgeable, creative, and sophisticated toward a tradition, all at the same time. What marvelous mentors!"[21] Those still around from the Old Days can recognize an NLCR recording being interpreted by younger musicians who may or may not be aware that they inherit gold from the Ramblers. But this is the way of the folk process. Its masters would not have it any other way: We hear music, we become enchanted, and we try to tease it out for ourselves. We make the music our own as it flows on down the line.

In 1963, Tom Paley, Artie Rose, and Roy Berkeley formed the Old Reliable String Band, and their LP of replications of early string-band 78s was prized. The Holy Modal Rounders, with fiddler Pete Stampfel, was another influential young group making old music. LPs of bands like these were not easy to find, and they were treasured. They connected musicians around the globe, as old-time and string-band music worked its way into the seams of popular music. Band names often played off names from the 1920s and 1930s ("Hillbillies," "Mountaineers," "Ramblers," "Boys," "Hill Toppers," "Rounders," "Hotshots"). Many old-time band names were inside jokes or puns that referenced iconic places, presenting a loose, sangfroid persona that contrasted with the typically stern and sober, though evocative, names of most bluegrass bands.

The New Lost City Ramblers were influential in the emerging string-band revival. Others were there, too, a bit later, such as the Hollow Rock String Band and the Fuzzy Mountain String Band out of the Raleigh-Durham–Chapel Hill, North Carolina, area of college campuses in the mid-1960s, and, in the 1970s, the Highwoods

Stringband. These and other revival string bands represented a shift away from the Kingston Trio–style "commercial" folk groups built around singing.

The Hollow Rock String Band's album *Traditional Dance Tunes* befitted the group's austere tone and curated ethnographic sources. Alan Jabbour, fiddler and leader, a scholar interested in the workings of tradition, recognized and stressed the values of home recordings and learning fiddle tunes directly from older performers still alive, in their own communities.[22] Following Jabbour's model, the Fuzzy Mountain String Band emphasized local and regional music, drawing on field recordings, including Jabbour's tapes of fiddler Henry Reed along the West Virginia–Virginia border.[23] In rather sharp contrast, the rollicking hippies of the Highwoods were unconcerned with seminars or scholarly research; they titled their albums *Fire on the Mountain* and *Feed Your Babies Onions.*

Other bands included the Arkansas Sheiks, in the San Francisco Bay Area, founded by Grinnell College students fiddler Mike Drayton and pianist Karana Drayton, who were interested in the history of the music and carried tunes of Iowa and Missouri with them when they went west. In the Central Valley, there was the Sweet's Mill String Band; in San Diego, it was the bluegrass-oriented Scottsville Squirrel Barkers; in Utah, the Deseret String Band carried on the spirit of the Fuzzy Mountain String Band; in Illinois, there were the Allen Street String Band and the Indian Creek Delta Boys; and in Indiana were the Plank Road String Band and Rain-Crow Countryside Band. In Missouri, there were groups such as the Raggedy Grass String Band and the Little Dixie Hoss Hair Pullers in Columbia, in St. Louis the Missouri Corn Dodgers and Cousin Curtis and the Cash Rebates. Some band names gave humorous references to earlier bands, sometimes with musicians who liked frolic, mind-bending supplements and beverages, and staying up all night—like their heroes back in the 1920s such as the Fruit Jar Drinkers, Dr. Humphrey Bate and His Possum Hunters, Dr. Smith's Champion Hoss Hair Pullers, and Gid Tanner and His Skillet Lickers.

The mood of the 1960s did not completely evaporate. There continues to be popularity of young musicians writing and performing folk music, usually called singer-songwriters. Topical songs and protest singing—music with a message—are important in America's musical crazy quilt. Discourse continues.[24] New generations have also continued to discover and rediscover various kinds of fiddling, with genres as strong as ever—bluegrass, Irish and Celtic fiddling, Appalachian fiddling, western swing, and varieties of ethnic and old-time fiddling.

Yesterday's young people who started out in the 1960s as distracted students may today be considered authentic old-time fiddlers, ballad singers, clog dancers, or banjo pickers. Their personal self-identification can decide whether one is, or is not, considered worthy by an arts council to be awarded folk-master status or be invited to perform in a prestigious folk festival.

Books appeared on the history and culture of old-time fiddling, such as Marion Thede's *Fiddle Book* and Krassen's *Appalachian Fiddling.* At Middle Tennessee State, Charles Wolfe studied old-time fiddling, helping produce LPs of Art Galbraith and writing on fiddle music in numerous articles and his book *The Devil's Box: Masters*

The Gaslight Square entertainment district of St. Louis, 1964, boasted a thriving and raucous assortment of generally seedy coffeehouses, nightclubs, sidewalk cafés, and restaurants around the intersection of Olive and Boyle. Famous entertainers received early exposure here, from the Smothers Brothers to Miles Davis, Jerry Lee Lewis and Barbra Streisand to George Carlin. Heavily gentrified, its old Victorian buildings razed, the nightspots gone, today the district is upscale and known as the Central West End. (State Historical Society of Missouri, George McCue Collection 019902)

of Old-Time Fiddling. Magazines appeared with documentary and analytical essays, including *Old-Time Music*, *Mugwumps*, and the *Devil's Box*.[25] These developments in documentation and understanding of traditional music by fans as well as academics led to the term "fiddle scholars" for this global community of interested people.

New York City was an important place for the folksinging movement of the Folk Music Revival, most visible in Greenwich Village postbeatnik coffeehouses with stages and jam sessions, hootenannies, and concerts. The Village, along with events like the Berkeley Folk Festival in California and the University of Chicago Folk Festival, and other places (many following the lead of the Newport Folk Festivals) brought traditional music genres like old-time fiddling and bluegrass music to big cities and "the North"—meaning just about everywhere outside the southeastern United States.

People today are sometimes more interested in artistic expression as part of the processes of evolution and change, and that helps explain why many young people are not interested in the history of a fiddle tune or a fiddler—they are more interested in how the music is performed in different places in different styles (which may, in time, lead them to history!). Many newcomers seem to regard folk music and roots music to be simply part of the all-encompassing genre called world music. "World music" makes us look outward rather than look inward. Looking globally is not necessarily a good sign for the health of local traditions inherited from former times and burnished through generations.

Indiana University graduate student Miles Krassen plays Appalachian and Irish fiddle tunes with Tommy Harlan (guitar) and Dave Molk (pennywhistle), busking on Kirkwood Avenue in downtown Bloomington, near campus, 1972. Krassen wrote valuable books about Appalachian old-time, klezmer, and Irish styles of music. Krassen took his MA at Indiana and his PhD at the University of Pennsylvania, and he taught religious studies at Smith College, Oberlin College, and Naropa University. (Courtesy of Miles Krassen)

"Who're You Calling a Revivalist?" and Other Term-Paper Topics

Folk festivals were where the ideas of scholars and purists encountered ideas of festival promoters more concerned about finances than about authenticity. Debate continues about who's authentic and who isn't, who or what ensemble makes the best performance to represent a region, culture, or musical style.[26] Most people outside the academy had little interest in splitting hairs; they just liked the music. But academics and purists are often in charge of funding, so they became more influential in festivals. And people became aware of ways in which local grassroots musicians and their traditions could be changed, for good or ill, by academics and public-sector specialists.[27]

Studies of old-time fiddling and string-band music often came from people involved in one way or another, and universities began to appreciate or at least tolerate students who petitioned to write theses or dissertations on the subject. Their work encouraged acceptance of folk music as legitimate research.[28] Academic journals became more open to folk music. Incisive essays appeared as album notes on LP records, sometimes providing documentation available nowhere else. "Hillbilly scholars" and "fiddle scholars" found a place in academic literature. Graduate projects continued addressing themes related to old-time fiddling and string-band music, as well as the frequently exasperating topic of fiddle contests.

But often, in their considerations of festival administrators and grants agencies, the scholars and purists could be high-handed in dealings with traditional musicians, especially if the musicians were considered revivalists. The scholars and purists preferred folk musicians who were born into the tradition (this is less problematic today). The scholars and purists were, in a sense, gatekeepers. Overly purist folklorists and others began to be called "the folk police" and "the fiddle police."

California fiddle champion and fiddle scholar Gus Garelick wrote about an experience in "My Encounter with the Folk Police." Garelick was in Washington over the Fourth of July weekend, when the Smithsonian Institution's Festival of American Folklife was in full swing on the National Mall. He knew that the charismatic fiddler, mandolinist, and folksinger Kenny Hall and other fellow California musicians and friends were on the schedule.

> I ran into western swing guitar legend Frank Hicks, jamming with Kenny Hall and about a dozen other fiddlers and old-time musicians I knew from northern California. I grabbed my fiddle and joined in the jam.
>
> But then something very unexpected happened. At the height of the jam, a festival official came over and told the California delegation to head for the stage and do a show. I just followed the crowd, ready to continue the jam in front of an audience. But it wasn't that simple.
>
> The official who had arranged for the California delegation to fly to Washington for the festival did not know who I was. She stopped me from getting on stage and began a very uncomfortable interrogation.
>
> She wanted to know who I was, what I was doing there, why I knew these fiddlers, and why I didn't have a badge. I thought of the classic line from *The Treasure of the Sierra Madre*: "I don't have to show you any stinkin' badge," but I thought better of it. This official was not in the mood. So I tried to explain that I was a fiddler from California and had won top honors that year in the California State Old Time Fiddling Championship. I knew all these folks, from contests and get-togethers around the state; these were all friends of mine.
>
> It looked like it might be OK, but then she asked if I had grown up with this style of music (which I had not), and where I had grownup and what kind of work I did. Explaining that I was a schoolteacher in San Francisco and had grown up in Detroit, studying classical violin—none of this helped.[29]

As Garelick discovered, being "born into the tradition" was high on most festival staffers' (and academics') criteria for who was and who (they thought) was not an authentic "tradition bearer" ("source musician"). That criterion was commonplace in earlier days of the Folk Music Revival and festival movement (and in bluegrass music, too). Happily, the old notion that one has to be born into a tradition to be legitimate is no longer widely accepted, just as we now recognize that an authentic old-time fiddler is as likely to wear a suit and tie as overalls or plow shoes—*notwithstanding* the fact that fiddlers or ballad singers born into families nourishing these traditions are, usually, good candidates for our attention and documentation.

Telling an old-time fiddler or singer of now older generations that he or she is a revivalist can start a complicated conversation. People in their sixties and older years remember the revival and how it could be difficult to be taken seriously as a fiddler if one was an outsider, especially an outsider of a different ethnic, social, academic, or economic "class." As it turned out, a great many of today's acknowledged old-time fiddling masters did not grow up with the music but came to the music as young people inspired by a New Lost City Ramblers album or a chance hearing of a fiddler at a festival, or even on *Hee Haw* on network TV.

Most scholars use "revivalist" to apply to newcomers from outside a realm of traditional life who, in a sense, discover its attractions and become devotees and promoters of the part of the tradition that fascinates them. Young people and students from cities such as Chicago and New York ventured mostly south to immerse themselves in collecting, recording, and performing old ballads, banjo playing, argot of the countryman, fiddling, crafts, and other aspects of old and seemingly moribund backwoods lifestyles and customs. Many revivalists were Romantics and did not notice disconcerting aspects of "the old days" such as poverty and racial discrimination. Often, people in the communities were also revivalists—is "conservationist" a better term?—seeking old traditions or keeping alive traditions of their own places.

Fiddlers learned to highlight "authenticity"—confirming chapters of their lives rather than parts that suggest change, urbanity, higher education, travel, and musical sophistication. It seems as though operating a moonshine still was preferable to a circuit judge in one's grant application. Performers who wished a spot at a festival learned to speak about how Grandpa fiddled "Sally Goodin" at square dances rather than sat in the violin section in the town's orchestra, how their ballads or tunes were the last leaves of ancient minstrelsy from the days of yore. Ironically and unfortunately, the idea remains strong among many people that there are carriers of isolated, unaffected "pure" folk fiddle music that happily defies the rust of time. But bad news for the purists: by the 1960s, few people in the Midwest qualified as the sort of isolated, uneducated, inward-looking rural folk depicted on TV shows or celebrated in festivals and seminar rooms.

The schism between the devoted, self-directed amateur collector working with his or her own resources and academics and collectors working with official credentials and institutional support has been an ongoing one since the early days of the Folk Music Revival. Rivalries and suspicions were apparent on both sides of the hall. The self-made collectors and "revivalists" were often considered merely Romantics or popularizers by credentialed scholars and public-agency professionals. Likewise, academics were often considered ivory-tower theorists and fussbudgets with no mud on their L. L. Bean khakis and Clark's desert boots. Both sides, the keen amateurs and the keen scholars, wrote articles and books and produced documentary recordings. Significant contributions continue to appear from both camps. Some were people comfortable both in the academic seminar and in the popular folk festival. Scholars such as Archie Green, who taught at the University of Illinois, published landmark books and inspired the creation of the American Folklife Center in the Library of Congress in the heady mid-1970s post-Watergate and post-Vietnam era.

Unbeknownst to (or shunned by) many scholars, many so-called amateurs and revivalists were deeply knowledgeable about cultural heritage behind the music and, like R. P. Christeson and Art Galbraith, were library patrons and readers of scholarly publications. The thin bundling board between the academic world and the nonacademic world is getting more rickety, at least in part due to new forms of digital media, such as free-for-all Internet worlds like FIDDLE-L, FiddleHangout.com, Facebook, and the rest, where, in cyberspace, questionable pronouncements of the ill-informed hobbyist, the crank, and the trickster, adrift from the moorings of fact, can seem as valid as the scholar.

In the big yellow tent backstage, St. Louis musicians Geoff Seitz and Jim Nelson play a tune while waiting in line to go onstage to compete at the Galax, Virginia, fiddlers' convention in 1985; Geoff won first place in the Old Time Fiddle division. In line behind them for their turn to compete in the contest are Reid Miller (*left*) and Ashley Carder (*right*) of South Carolina. (Courtesy of Jim Nelson)

String Bands and College Towns 2

The country's come to town.
—Rod Moag, 1967

A typical folk group of high school or college students in 1960 or 1962 covered Kingston Trio hits and recordings by performers such as Joan Baez, the Highwaymen, the Brothers Four, Rooftop Singers, the Limeliters, the Seekers, the New Christy Minstrels, and Peter, Paul & Mary. These groups tended to be conservative and clean-cut in performance styles, perhaps what was called "collegiate" and "Joe college," in their general appeal and images. Many were primarily singers and entertainers, rather than instrumentalists, and few if any groups featured the fiddle.

While they may have started out at a hootenanny or coffeehouse gig, the lucky few gained global popularity by being "discovered" by major record labels and professional management that landed them on Top 40 radio with abundant sales, concert tours, and appearances on television shows. Before long, the growing community of purist scholars and musicians interested in more academic and ethnographic ("authentic," perhaps) local and regional traditional music tagged them as "popularizers" and "commercial" folk groups.

"Kumbaya" (from Joan Baez) was still "in," and this communal hymn had not yet attached the cynicism and satire that following generations of post–civil rights movement and post–Vietnam War *Saturday Night Live* skits would heap upon it.[1] Just as today, most fiddlers in Missouri tended to keep their politics mostly to themselves; the music was the thing. String-band music and old-time fiddling were by their nature, in contrast to folksinging, less political. String-band fans and fiddlers across the spectrums of age, class, and politics could meet and interact in coffeehouses, jam sessions, and hootenannies.

With increasing electrification changing music in Nashville and LA studios, fiddles were often pushed aside by pedal steel guitars, not to mention growing dominance of rock and roll and rock-influenced country music. A few stars, like Porter Wagoner and Ray Price, bucked the trend by keeping fiddling on their records, and western swing kept fiddles up front. And fiddle contests were gradually undergoing a little-noticed rejuvenation in the 1960s thanks to the development of fiddlers' associations.

There were several kinds of aspiring young fiddlers who knew about traditional old-time music. These groups could be characterized as people devoted to Appalachian old-time music, those devoted to old-time music long established in Missouri (a small group at first), those devoted to bluegrass, those devoted to "Nashville" country music, those interested in early minstrelsy and vaudeville, and those devoted to Irish ("Celtic") fiddling. Most fiddlers liked more than just one or two of these categories (and some categories overlap). There were smaller pockets in Missouri too, such as Cajun fiddling, jazz, and western swing.

Geoff Seitz, St. Louis

In Missouri's sprawling metro areas of Kansas City and St. Louis, numerous young people became active in the Folk Music Revival. One of these was fiddler and violin maker Geoff Seitz, whose hometown of Lemay is in the St. Louis County region of Missouri and southern Illinois. Today Lemay is engulfed in the St. Louis metro area; the old family farms disappeared to make way for shopping malls.

Involved in the fiddle and dance community since his youth in the 1970s, Geoff Seitz jokingly calls himself "the last of the great Lemay fiddlers." He had some classical training, but his "real love is old-time fiddle music" and he "sought out and visited many great Midwestern fiddlers such as R. P. Christeson, Joe Politte, Charlie Pashia, Taylor McBaine, Pete McMahan, Bob Holt, Dwight Lamb, Charlie Walden, as well as many others, and learned many tunes from them over the years."[2]

The Casalone-Seitz farm was founded by Geoff's mother's father, Dominic Casalone, in Lemay along Gravois Creek ("grah'voy") area. The family raised strawberries and tomatoes for local markets. Geoff's father, Frank Herman Seitz, descended from German immigrants who came to St. Louis in the middle 1800s. Frank Seitz was a fiddle and mandolin player. Geoff's mother, Mary Casalone Seitz, was born in 1915 in Monfiletto, Italy, in the Asti area of the Piedmont, and came to America when her father brought family members over and established the produce farm.[3]

Born in December 1954, Geoff graduated from St. Louis University High School and began college at the University of Missouri at St. Louis in 1973. He played drums and piano, but had not yet tried to play his father Frank's instrument—the violin. At the university Seitz met fiddler Chris Germain, who fired Geoff's interest. Geoff learned to play acoustic bass so he could perform with (and learn from) an old-time string band, Cousin Curtis and the Cash Rebates, with fiddler Les Lewis; Rich Hibbs, banjo; Curtis Buckhannon, mandolin; and Dennis Buckhannon, guitar. Seitz's interest in fiddling was whetted further in 1974 at the Galax fiddlers' convention, where he saw fiddlers playing a range of styles, from bluegrass and country to old-time. He decided to focus on old-time fiddle styles and repertoire.[4] Geoff was impressed with Christeson's first tune book and learned tunes from it, and later he learned tunes from Charlie Walden's cassette, *Traditional Fiddle Music of Missouri*, with piano backup by Emily Buckhannon, who had learned from Christeson.[5]

Seitz fiddles for square dances as well as contra dances and enjoys both. Geoff also played drums and fiddle in a renowned blues band from St. Louis called the Leroy Pierson Band.[6] The band was the Saturday-night mainstay at the Broadway Oyster Bar throughout the 1980s. The US Information Agency asked the Leroy Pierson Band to represent America on a nine-country tour of the Middle East, including Iraq, Sudan, Yemen, and surrounding countries. In a cultural exchange in Bahrain, the band met a group of men singing traditional pearl-diving music; in turn, Seitz played a fiddle tune for the group.

Seitz has fiddled in numerous contests, from Missouri to Galax, Virginia, and Clifftop, West Virginia, and he also serves as a contest judge. Seitz won first place at

Galax in 1985 playing "Marmaduke's Hornpipe" (learned from Bill Driver's version printed in Christeson), and in 1993 he took first at Clifftop. A favorite of Geoff's, "Marmaduke's" is on *Good Old Days Are Here.* Seitz talks about contests in an *Old-Time Herald* article. "Geoff believes the successful contest fiddler is the person who can handle his emotions in front of the audience and judges and stay in control. He uses deep breathing to gain this control prior to going on stage. Also, he believes you should play what you know best. Often, he will pick out his contest tunes several weeks before an event and practice them thoroughly. He will also practice scales to maintain intonation."[7]

Geoff's style reflects early interest in Appalachian fiddling, but it also draws inspiration from Midwest and Missouri fiddlers, from northerners Cyril Stinnett and Nile Wilson to Ozarker Bob Holt and bluegrass fiddler Gene Goforth. Seitz plays unusual tunes, including several from Missouri's Old French District,[8] and his version of Joe Politte's "Louisiana Hornpipe" is on the companion CD with *"Play Me Something Quick and Devilish."* Seitz has composed several fiddle tunes. "Gravois Creek Pump" is on the companion CD in this book. A waltz, "Rose of Sharon" was written for the closing of a St. Louis production of the play *Grapes of Wrath.*[9] Geoff plays old-time guitar and backs Bob Holt (and plays fiddle on several tracks) on the Field Recorders Collective project.[10]

The Ill-Mo Boys is probably Seitz's best-known band, and the name references the interstate region.[11] The band formed in 1985 and includes Seitz, violin; Jim Nelson, guitar; and Curtis Buckhannon, mandolin. Their approach is spare and clean, and the project includes vocals as well as instrumentals. The Ill-Mo Boys cover a broad array from classic 78s of bands such as southeast Missouri's Grinnell Giggers to Fiddlin' Sam Long, Bob Wills and the Texas Playboys, and revivalist bands of the 1960s such as Stu Jamieson's Boys. They play a number of tunes from southern Illinois fiddlers and groups such as the Allen Street String Band.

The Farmertones represented an interesting lark. Geoff and some friends provided an old-time string-band soundtrack for a reality TV series, *The Farmer Wants a Wife.*[12] Locations ranged across the country, and the setup was an eligible, young, attractive, and wealthy man presented with an enthusiastic brace of eligible, young, attractive, big-city women.[13] The hope is that sparks of romance will fly and perhaps lead to a lasting relationship when the bachelor picks the girl of his dreams from the applicants, none of whom know much about farming. In 2008, the young farmer farmed impressive acreage in the Mississippi River bottoms of Portage des Sioux in north St. Louis County. While packaged music plays through most episodes, for a square dance the producers sought local musicians to play what global audiences would hear as rural music—old-time string-band music. Enter Geoff Seitz, Dennis and Curtis Buckhannon, Dave Landreth, and Marc Rennard. Just in time for the airing, the group recorded an album of fiddle tunes called *The Farmertones, Old Time Stringband Music.* Seitz was also in an NBC miniseries movie, *A Will of Their Own,* about women's suffrage. A moment depicts a barn dance, set in the nineteenth century, in which Seitz, Nelson, Rennard, and Landreth play "Ways of the World" from Geoff's *Good Old Days Are Here.*

Ill-Mo Boys promo photo. *Left to right*: Curtis Buchanan, Geoff Seitz, and Jim Nelson. (Ravetta Photography, St. Louis; courtesy of Geoff Seitz)

Geoff traveled an indirect route to violin making. He planned to complete college, but events got in the way. In 1977 he was traveling and playing fiddle music—busking—in the Northwest, before his senior college year. He was playing his father's violin. In Spokane, Washington, the poor emergency repair job that Geoff had done on the violin failed. Suddenly without a usable fiddle, he found Glenn T. Stockton's shop in Spokane. This was a turning point in Geoff's life. He watched while Stockton repaired the violin and was fascinated by the work, the shop, and Mr. Stockton, a welcoming and genial man. "It was then, Seitz says, that he decided, 'I'm not trying to fix anything ever again before I learn how to fix it properly.'"[14]

Back in St. Louis, Geoff decided to drop out of the university and head back to Spokane. He convinced Stockton to take him on as an employee—at first janitor and gofer—via the Comprehensive Employment Training Act, a federal program that paid half a person's salary if he or she was learning a trade. He stayed two years and was eventually allowed to learn violin repair and, finally, violin building as Stockton's apprentice. In 1978 Seitz made his first violin (using rock maple from an old tabletop he found in an antique shop). In 1979, Seitz opened a shop in Spokane, managed the strings department in a music store, and took classical violin lessons with Helen de la Fuente. During this time, Geoff learned additional violin-making and -repair skills from Armin Barnett in Seattle.

Back again in St. Louis, Seitz worked on violins in his house for a few years and then opened a storefront in 1987. Seitz's violins and violas are based on Old Masters but are his own designs and patterns. His violins can take hundreds of hours to complete, using maple for the backs, bouts, and necks from Minnesota and Wisconsin as well as Sitka spruce from Alaska and Michigan for tops. Like other violin makers of my acquaintance, Geoff likes to build violins from old overlooked wood, such as century-old flooring from a derelict barn he used in a viola. In 1986, Seitz was featured in a juried exhibition by the Best of Missouri Hands organization and more recently in a traveling exhibition by Lisa Higgins and Debbie Bailey of six violin makers in the Traditional Arts Apprenticeship Program (TAAP) program.

> If you start manipulating the shape or the look of it too much, it starts moving away from being a violin and it starts to become something else—"violin-like." What comes to mind are these electric violins they've come out with now with these really wild colors and really weird body styles. Well, you play them like a violin and you have a sound if you have an amplifier. But in essence they're something different. A real violin is an acoustic instrument, and you just play it—you don't need any stuff around. . . . See, the violin is an old technology. It's been around for hundreds of years. So the technology peaked in, like, 1705. It's never really gotten better than Stradivari and all those Italian guys. It [a modern violin] could be as good, but it never got better than that. So the trick is to make something that kind of achieves that art form. It doesn't have to sound exactly like a Stradivari, but it should at least be in that target.[15]

Portrait of Geoffrey Seitz by Erik Lunsford. "'This business is based on a real old-fashioned style of business,' says Seitz. 'One could take my business and just go back a hundred years and plunk it right down.'" (Quoted in the *St. Louis Post-Dispatch*, April 5, 2009; courtesy of Geoff Seitz)

On the perennial question "Is it the wood or the varnish?" Geoff takes a different turn. Paraphrased, "If it was just the wood and the varnish, then all those early violins would be excellent violins, but they are not. It's the *workmanship* more than the materials." What was the secret of the Old Masters? "The *workmanship*."[16] The mark of a great violin, apart from its sound, is "an ineffable artistic beauty. 'It has kind of a uniqueness to it,' he says. 'It does something to you when you look at it, like a painting does. It will move you a little bit.'"[17]

Seitz has developed YouTube videos to discuss his violins and invites violinists to sample their quality. One of the personal touches he brings is ornamental engraved decoration. He describes his violins as "a combination of a European tradition with a little bit of American art."

Geoff has trained staff to take care of most of the repairs that keep a violin shop busy. In contrast to the 1970s when Seitz and many other young people were seeking careers in crafts and trades outside "the establishment," finding young people who want to learn violin repair or become apprentices is difficult; the training is lengthy and financial rewards modest. Violin making is "a very competitive field, so sometimes, it gets down to how some people will order a violin from me because they know my artwork, and they want a violin from me. After the famous 17th century luthier Antonio Stradivarius died, his family found 90 violins laying on tables in the shop. Even the greatest violin maker on earth couldn't sell all his stuff."[18]

Geoff Seitz lives in the farmhouse where he grew up and plays dances, conducts fiddle workshops, performs at festivals, and records an occasional project. Seitz studied with Kansas City jazz fiddler Claude Williams in the Traditional Arts Apprenticeship Program in 1984–85. A decade later, Geoff participated again in TAAP, as a master violin maker with apprentice Gregory Krone.

Seitz mentors young fiddlers. Understanding the challenges they face in locating recordings that encourage learning, Geoff issued a cassette in 1994, *Fiddle Tunes Fast and Slow*, in which he plays tunes newcomers are expected to know, "Liberty," "8th of January," "Soldier's Joy," "Mississippi Sawyer," "Old Joe Clark," "Sourwood Mountain," "Arkansas Traveler," and "Devil's Dream."[19]

Listen to track 2 on the companion CD to hear Geoff Seitz play his composition "Gravois Creek Pump."

Columbia, Missouri, for Example

Cultural ideas and fashions percolate into Missouri hinterlands via the state's two big funnels, St. Louis on the east and Kansas City on the west. One could make a case for St. Louis being the earliest and most important in the Folk Music Revival in the 1960s, the string-band revival of the 1970s, and continued interest in old-time fiddle music.[20]

Columbia is the site of the state university's flagship campus as well as two private liberal arts colleges, Stephens College and Columbia College (formerly called

Christian College). Another half-dozen private colleges, junior colleges, and military schools are within an hour's drive. Columbia is the seat of Boone County, in the north-central part of Missouri, a few miles above the hilly north bank of the Missouri River and some thirty miles from the state capital (Jefferson City) and the Ozarks region to the south. While geologists say that parts of Boone County are in the physiographic Ozarks, the older culture, politics, and heritage reflect the region's Little Dixie identity and not Ozark identity. To some degree, Columbia stirs together "town" and "gown" populations.

People formed clubs to sponsor concerts and host informal performances in homes. Some who liked old-time fiddling, ballad singing, and banjo music were so-called campus radicals and activists concerned about social justice, human rights, and the ill-fated Vietnam War, but most students tended to keep their politics to themselves. People of whatever politics were drawn together by homemade music at coffeehouses, bluegrass festivals, folk festivals, hootenannies, and jam sessions.

The Boone Folk University Club included people active in politics, protest movements, and the counterculture. The club presented concerts, workshops, and celebrations with traditional musicians who reflected the era's growing interest in the rural community and folk arts. Some of the house concerts showcased local campus-town groups, and others reflected members' research in locating traditional musicians in the region. Among leaders of the Folk U Club was Verle Muhrer, a doctoral student in philosophy at the university, who later moved to Kansas City and taught at Metropolitan Community College (Penn Valley) for many years. Muhrer was among graduate students, teaching assistants, and faculty active in the anti–Vietnam War movement and underground politics, raising the community's awareness of political and social issues.

Folk U events featured people such as old-time banjo player and farmer Frankie Fullington in house concerts, and there were public concerts in the Hall Theatre near campus (a former vaudeville and movie house) showcasing Cleo Persinger, who a few years before had won the National Oldtime Fiddlers' Contest in Weiser, and bluegrass fiddler and singer Billy Lee of Wright City. Fullington played fiddle tunes and folksongs on banjo in an archaic drop-thumb five-string banjo style.[21] Concerts presented samplers of the range of traditional music being made—not only Missouri fiddlers, but also well-known bluesmen such as Sleepy John Estes from Tennessee, who had recorded for Victor Records in 1929.

The Boone Folk University Club membership included Keith and Kathy Cunningham. Keith Cunningham, born in Illinois and son of Methodist ministers, came to Columbia for his master's in English, and his wife, Kathy, is a photographer. They lived in an apartment near the Wabash rail yards in Moberly. Keith taught English and creative writing at the high school and served effectively as the school's far-out but cool hippie teacher-writer. Keith and Kathy were staples of the underground community in the Columbia area and its small enclave in Moberly and took part in the Boone Folk University Club's activities. In their rambles, which included April trips to the Arkansas Folk Festival in Mountain View, the Cunninghams recorded

Darryl Muhrer (Spike Bones) at one of the bluegrass jam sessions organized by Barry Gainor in Columbia, September 2019. Percussion with scoured-clean lengths of animal ribs (sheep, pigs, cattle) or wood is an ancient and universal form of making rhythm and a staple in minstrelsy and vaudeville and excellent accompaniment for fiddling. He became a student of Percy Danforth (Ann Arbor, Michigan), who created a revival of bones playing. Darryl created "The Bones Show" (interpreting the period 1840 to 1940) and for many years traveled and performed. (Photo by Howard Marshall)

old-time pre-bluegrass-style banjo players and ballad singers. In Clifton Hill, west of Moberly, they had "discovered" banjoists such as Olen Fox and Frankie Fullington. Keith and Kathy created their own private-label record company to issue recordings of musicians they noticed in Missouri and Arkansas; their company, Shoe String Tapes, issued boxed five-inch-reel tapes of musicians, including Fullington, and a tape of the Raggedy Grass String Band.[22]

There were several hangouts and music spots. Many nourished an underground insider atmosphere where cliques of friends of similar politics and pastimes gathered. The environment developed in the mid-1960s as the coffeehouses and smoky cafés that added interesting hues to the landscape around the university campus shifted from the beatnik days to the livelier period of hippies and freaks. The Agora House on South Ninth was more postbeatnik beanery than performance venue but welcomed the folk-music crowd. The emergent counterculture of hippies was, in small-town Missouri, only superficially connected to the beatniks. The Harris Café, two blocks north, typically featured jazz players such as guitarist Lyle Harris; one of the town's influential folksingers, Lee Ruth, performed there. In the area on South Ninth Street, Breisch's Cafeteria often featured live music, too.

Lee Ruth in a parking lot pickin' session at Bill Monroe's Bluegrass Festival, Bean Blossom, Indiana, June 1972. He was an influential performer and teacher bringing attention to diverse guitar styles as a folksinger, composer, and band member. During the folk boom, Lee traveled to New York's Greenwich Village and San Francisco, performing in folk clubs where musicians' pay consisted of donations in a basket passed from table to table. Ruth is among the Columbia area's most creative and respected folk-music elders, one of the first to perform at the Chez coffeehouse when it opened in 1964, and a late-night radio show on community radio station KOPN. (Photo by Howard Marshall)

One of the performance opportunities was at the Ivanhoe Restaurant, next to the university campus. The Chez coffeehouse in the Presbyterian Church had opened in 1964, but it seemed to be something of a hippie hangout and did not serve beer. So a restaurant had an opportunity to host hootenannies and string bands.

Folk clubs replicated the look and vibe of famed clubs and coffeehouses in New York and San Francisco. Founders of these places tended to be laid-back devotees, and their places evolved as much into hangouts and social centers as effective businesses. The Coronado Club, dating to the 1920s, was on old Highway 40 (now Business Loop 70 East) and offered a variety of music, from jazz to folk and country. Rock-and-roll nightclubs near campus occasionally took a night off from kids dancing the twist to bands such as Moberly's Krazy Kats and stage concerts by touring folk groups such as Kansas City's Brewer & Shipley. One of these was the International Club ("I Club") downtown. For country-music fans, there were nightspots and dance halls where live music, including touring stars from Nashville, was on offer; customers there tended to comprise an older and more conservative patronage, with country-and-western bands and old-fashioned couple dances (two-steps, waltzes) with cocktails and beer. Most students could not get past the doorkeeper's examination of driver's licenses.

Club owners usually relied on a network that brought in traditional music from somewhere else. Thus, the usual approach to the music remained searching out and bringing in traditional music of someplace else. Thus, authentic old-time fiddlers and ballad singers around the corner were, for the most part, unknown, especially in the early 1960s. Fortunately, some young people were looking for banjo pickers, fiddlers, and ballad singers closer to home.

Fiddle Scholars

A lot of people in the music scene became self-made genuine experts. There are, of course, fiddle scholars with academic credentials in fields such as folklore, musicology, music, ethnomusicology, anthropology, and American studies, whose vetted scholarly publications add greatly to our knowledge; academics in apparently unrelated fields like psychology, the arts, and architecture also become experts.

On the other hand, many fiddle scholars have worked alone or outside academe and may or may not publish their research (such as R. P. Christeson, Ira Ford, Art Galbraith, Kelly Jones, and Billy Lee). Important contributions came from staff in public and private agencies, from arts and humanities councils, and from libraries, museums, and festivals. All these fiddle scholars were interested in music makers and their stories. Various collectors and musicians passed through Missouri, making contributions and taking with them their knowledge of Missouri fiddling. Mike and Karana Drayton were students at Grinnell College in Iowa and made valuable recordings of north Missouri fiddlers such as Pearl Sivetts of Unionville.[23] Mike Seeger visited and recorded Lena Hughes and learned her archaic style of finger-picked parlor guitar and banjo music. In the eighties, young fiddle scholars and prominent musicians Brad Leftwich, Linda Higginbotham, and Kenny Jackson visited and recorded Lee Roy Stoneking.[24]

Among recent academic studies are those of Holly Hobbs, Mark Bilyeu, and Judy Warner. From Columbia, Hobbs wrote her master's thesis at Indiana University, "Women of Old-Time Music: Tradition and Change in the Missouri Ozarks." Bilyeu is from a family of fiddlers documented by Vance Randolph and Gordon McCann and wrote a master's thesis at Missouri State University on "Durang's Hornpipe." Arkansas fiddler Judy Warner wrote her thesis at the University of Arkansas at Little Rock on Ozark fiddling in Missouri and Arkansas, her goal to help keep the region's fiddle music "from being lost into the vast sea of new styles that are out there."[25] Julie Henigan is among Missouri musicians with a scholarly portfolio. Widely traveled and versatile, Julie performed with Kim Lansford and Barbara Weathers as the Missouri Girls. Henigan's interests include Ozark fiddlers and session traditions in Ireland.[26]

The zest among the college crowd and parallel growth of academic studies (especially folklore, musicology, anthropology, American studies, and cultural geography) for fiddle and dance music was important in widening recognition that local and regional music was worthy of attention. Arts councils and festivals began funding local music in previously ignored places.

Old School: R. P. Christeson and John Hartford

There had been collectors and young musicians in the 1950s, of course, doing research and making home recordings of figures in old-time fiddling. For fiddlers and historians today, the best-known names among these foresighted individuals were R. P. Christeson and John Hartford. Christeson in the 1940s and 1950s, and Hartford in the 1950s, sought out authentic old-time fiddlers and recorded them, well before doing so became popular avocations or professions in the 1960s and 1970s. Although active in their Missouri research much earlier, Christeson and Hartford both emerged on the national stage in the 1970s—Christeson in retirement in Missouri as author and Hartford in California as songwriter, recording artist, and performer.

Christeson, from Dixon in the central upper Ozarks, was an excellent old-time fiddler and piano and reed-organ accompanist for fiddling. He became famous for visiting and recording a number of Missouri fiddlers in the 1940s, such as Bill Driver, and for notating tunes that in the 1970s and 1980s were published by the University of Missouri Press in two volumes as *The Old-Time Fiddler's Repertory*. Christeson's published commentaries and interactions with scholars, amateur historians, and youngsters in the 1970s and 1980s show how sharp an observer and listener he was, as well as revealing an even sharper tendency toward blunt criticism of anything he viewed as foolish, "ivy towerish" (overly academic), or just plain wrong in the academic studies of fiddle music and history as well as in the efforts of others to play the fiddle and banjo music he remembered.

When Christeson retired from the US Department of Agriculture in 1986, he and Joan moved to Missouri and were living in retirement in Auxvasse, in Columbia's arc of small towns. Bob, or "R. P." as most called him, became the "dean of Missouri fiddling," thanks to mentoring young fiddlers and fiddlers scholars such as Bill Shull, Emily Buchanan, and Charlie Walden and thanks to wide use of his tune books.[27] What few knew until the late 1980s documentary *Now That's a Good Tune* is that Christeson was still fiddling, jig dancing, and playing piano accompaniment well into his eighties.

If Christeson was a straitlaced son of sturdy Ozark pioneers, John Hartford was a full-on city-bred, puckish hippie who gloried in the company of rural and small-town musicians.[28] Once he got to Southern California, Hartford (née Harford), who grew up in St. Louis, found financial success as a young songwriter and performer. In the 1960s, Hartford appeared on TV shows such as *The Smothers Brothers Comedy Hour* and *The Glen Campbell Show*, where his instrument was the five-string banjo, which he had taken up in high school after hearing Earl Scruggs at a concert north of St. Louis.

Hartford often said that his composition "Gentle on My Mind," made into a hit record by Glen Campbell in 1977, made him so much money that, in effect, he could do what he wanted for the rest of his life.[29] In California, Hartford was drawn to "newgrass" and experiments at the edge of tradition, and he helped forge that genre. But before all that, as a youngster "ate up with fiddling," while still in St. Louis, in the late 1950s Hartford sought out and made recordings of Missouri old-time and bluegrass fiddlers in Missouri on a reel-to-reel Wollensak.

Hartford had a lifelong devotion to fiddle history and music, and later in life he became active in the community of fiddle scholars and collectors. He made CD copies of his 1950s recordings of fiddlers such as Gene Goforth, Cleo Persinger, and Walter Alexander, which he happily shared with younger musicians and fans such as Jim Nelson, who, in turn, with John's blessing, shared copies with others. Hartford had been an artist since boyhood and dropped out of Washington University as a freshman art student. Later, his artful hand-drawn transcriptions of tunes in the now defunct journal the *Devil's Box* helped spread the music. His hand-drawn transcriptions of his composed fiddle tunes were issued posthumously.[30]

Rod Moag

Columbia occasionally had a faculty member interested in bluegrass, old-time fiddling, and string-band music. Dr. Rodney Moag was one of these. Born in 1936 in Wyoming County, New York, at age five Rod was enrolled in the New York State School for the Blind, where learned piano, music theory, and various instruments in school dance bands and orchestras. There he also formed his first bluegrass band, the Oldtime Hay Balers. Rod bought his first Bob Wills record in 1945—"Roly Poly" / "Spanish Two-Step"—and played it on the wind-up Victrola his grandfather had given him and fell in love with western swing. He performed in the late 1950s on radio in Batavia, New York, with Charley Elwell as the Pickin' Partners and played fiddle in country bands. He listened to Grand Ole Opry and National Barn Dance radio shows. Rod competed in his first fiddle contest in 1955 in western New York and took second place playing "Ragtime Annie" and "Over the Waves."

Rod graduated from Syracuse University and earned a PhD at Wisconsin, where he specialized in South Asian languages. At Wisconsin, playing mandolin and singing tenor, he fronted bluegrass groups the Front Porch Backsteppers and the Bluegrass Hoppers with banjoist Don Gale (from St. Louis), guitarist Jerry Wicentowski, and fiddler Earl Spielman.[31] While in Madison, Rod traveled to Nashville and recorded six original songs, accompanied by Hank Williams's fiddler Jerry Rivers.

Moag came to Columbia in the late 1960s to teach South Asian languages at the university (he is fluent in Hindi and Malayalam, as well as Italian, Spanish, Portuguese, German, and Russian) and began playing bluegrass and old-time country music around the area. Rod is a walking encyclopedia of the history of fiddling, country music, and bluegrass with a massive record library. He performed with various ad hoc and pickup bands at bluegrass festivals. I met Rod at a bluegrass festival in Centralia

Rod Moag (*left*) with Charley Elwell—the Pickin' Partners—ca. 1957, Batavia, New York. In this studio portrait, Moag plays a Gibson "Les Paul" electric guitar and Elwell a Martin D-28 acoustic guitar, examples of fine guitars. (Courtesy of Rod Moag and Robert Carroll)

in 1968, and we enjoyed a jam session backstage; later, we teamed up and performed at a few festivals and gigs as a "brother duet" (he, mandolin; me, guitar) in the style of the Monroe Brothers, the Delmore Brothers, and the Blue Sky Boys.[32]

Moag entered and judged some fiddle contests in the area.[33] He left Columbia in 1975 for a Fulbright at the University of the South Pacific in Fiji and published a book on the dialect of Hindi spoken by the East Indian community. In 1978, Rod moved to the University of Michigan for several years and then took a position in Asian studies at the University of Texas in 1988. For several years, he attended the Bob Wills Day festival in Turkey, Texas, and, one year, competed in the fiddle contest, playing "Cincinnati Rag" and "Whistling Rufus." He recorded several CDs with such fiddle luminaries as Johnny Gimble, Buddy Spicher, Billy Contreras, and Byron Berline and hosted a radio show called "Country, Swing, & Rockabilly Jamboree" for twenty-five years on Austin's KOOP 91.7 FM and participated in the local fiddle club.[34] In 2004, Rod published a history of early bluegrass in Texas in the *Journal of Texas Music History* and was elected to the Western Swing Hall of Fame in 2015.[35]

Jim Lansford was a fiddle scholar who made a career in music in the Ozarks, his adopted home, in the 1980s. He played violin, mandolin, guitar, and banjo and performed in Branson and Silver Dollar City country-music shows, taught fiddle at Bethel Fiddle Camp, and for eight years was a member of the Skirtlifters. Kim Lansford is from Kansas City and moved to Springfield for college and took up hammered dulcimer and began performing at Silver Dollar City. (Cover, *Old-Time Herald* 7, no. 1 [1999])

Dancing of Divers Kinds

Providing for social dancing has long been the raison d'être for much of the fiddle music we inherit, and the fiddler has remained at the forefront in dance traditions. In the 1960s and 1970s, the rediscovery and reinvigoration among young people of old-time dancing and old-time fiddling went hand in hand.

There were two broad kinds of square dancing that continued to be popular and that continue apace. There was the older kind of square dance, often held in barns, community halls, one-room schoolhouses, and private homes, with live bands and a potluck dinner. If there were alcoholic beverages, these were usually consumed quietly outside. Children and beginners were welcome. Many a child fell asleep in a corner while mom and dad danced or played music. Young people became involved in the old-time dances, and, with luck, they would hear fiddlers and make connections. Old-time square dances customarily featured a caller who was a member of one of the pairs in a square of eight people. Each square had its own caller and danced whatever figures they wanted. The band may or may not have needed a sound system. The musicians played vigorous square-dance tunes and included occasional waltzes and perhaps a schottische, jig, polka, or varsouvienne. Bands may or may not have been paid. Bands were often ad hoc and could include beginners alongside veterans who knew the music and were the ensemble's glue. Bands played requests and "Happy Birthday" when asked, and just about any tune the band felt like playing, the people danced to it. Organization and rules were minimal.

Somewhat in contrast, there was "association" or "federation" square dancing, which also continues today. Callers were in a musicians union as well as professional organizations and brought a record player and commercial records, using a sound system at the front of the hall or stage. The tune list was discussed with the dancers' leadership. Dancers often were members of clubs such as the United Square Dancers of America, Inc., or the Missouri Federation of Square 'n Round Dance Clubs, Inc. The groups have classes, newsletters, dues, conventions, and abundant rules. The organizations usually ask that dancers attire themselves in cowboy or western ranch-life costumes. Dancers sometimes have taps on their shoes or wear professional tap-dancing shoes (some old-time jig dancers also do this). Today's "clogging groups" seen at county fairs and other events are an offshoot. The Missouri group's number-one goal is "to promote square dancing as a recreational activity of the highest standard."[36] Association dancing promotes the "western" style of square dancing instead of traditional midwestern styles and figures, and recordings used may include rock-and-roll hits and electronic ersatz versions of old-time fiddle tunes such "Turkey in the Straw." Among the organized clogging clubs, "Cotton-Eyed Joe" (a Bob Wills and the Texas Playboy hit record from 1947) is a favorite for their choreographed routines.[37] Association and federation square-dance callers do not seem interested in dancing to live, authentic old-time fiddle music.

New England Contra Dance Comes to Missouri

St. Louis was and continues to be important in traditional dancing—perhaps especially contra dancing—which flourished there and carried across Missouri to emerging contra and "country" dancers. An evolution of old traditions that parallel the evolution of old-time square dancing, contra dancing primarily of New England was transplanted into St. Louis and college towns in the 1960s and 1970s.

An active group is the Mid-Missouri Traditional Dancers (MMTD) of Columbia. The group enjoys various kinds of dance, from contra, including Irish dancing, English Morris dancing, and two-step "mixers," to square dancing. A typical MMTD dance, held most Fridays in a hall in Columbia, includes old-time square dances interspersed with contra dances and a waltz or two. Many of the dances feature music by experienced contra-dance string bands, and from time to time the group has asked local old-time fiddlers to play. The requirements of fiddling for contra dances, often with steps and moves from books that need certain tunes, differ from those of the old-time, freewheeling square dance where the fiddler plays largely whatever he or she wishes, as long as dancers can dance, with the caller calling traditional moves.[38] Contra dancers have national organizations, such as the

Country Dance and Song Society, which publish dance figures, including newly composed dances and matching tunes.

We still like the old maxim that "without dancing there would be very little fiddle music." However, in the 2000s, many young fiddlers have never played for a dance or even been to a dance. Instead, they perform in contests, bluegrass bands, festival shows, and private jam sessions. They find satisfaction but may never feel what it is like to be a fiddler trying to make people want to dance.

Tom Verdot, Violin Maker, Contra-Dance Fiddler

Tom Verdot is a violin maker, fiddle scholar, banjoist, and fiddler who founded one of Missouri's A-list bands specializing in music for contra dancers. He was born in Jefferson City in 1947.

Tom Verdot's paternal ancestors were French.[39] Typical of Victorian-era history books describing the Missouri French, Goodspeed's 1889 tome includes Osage County's French Village and repeats familiar stereotypes that would give today's scholars and French Missourians a good laugh: "The jolly French spent their days in revelry, only needing a few hours a week for necessary duties. The tri-weekly dance was a cardinal feature of their life, in which the Indian brave and maiden were welcome.

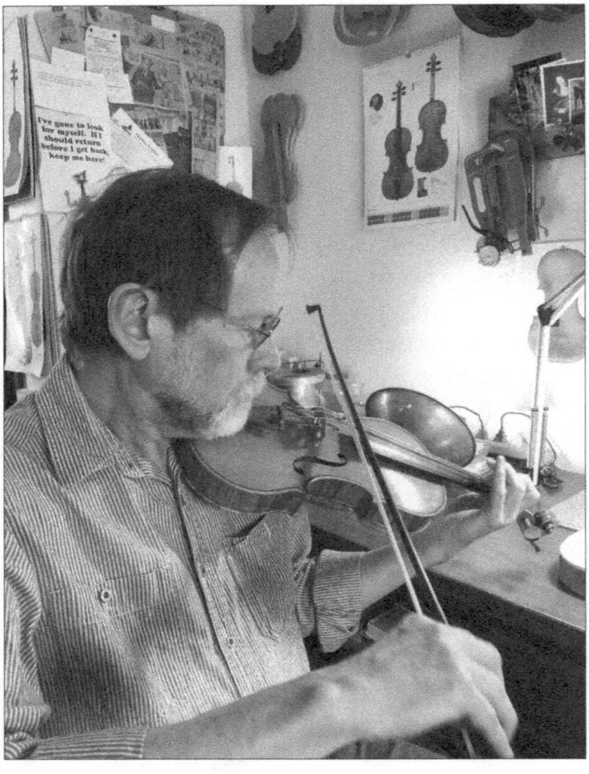

Tom Verdot plays a violin he built. (Photo by Howard Marshall, March 2019)

This French community was far more moral and refined than late generations are accustomed to considering them. The Fourth of July was celebrated with the inevitable dance."[40]

Verdot received classical violin training in elementary and high school in Jefferson City. As he gravitated toward old-time music as a teenager, he began playing fiddle tunes and traditional five-string banjo music—especially old-time and ragtime music—from various archival sources and recordings as well as tunes in the local tradition. A scholarly bent, and love of history, led Verdot to become knowledgeable about the culture and people behind the music. Tom's violin skills brought a full scholarship to study at the University of Missouri, and he moved to Columbia in 1967. He found time to continue playing old-time fiddle, banjo, and guitar. The academic ways of the university did not agree with Tom, and he dropped out after a semester and moved to Hermosa Beach, California. He worked in the Los Angeles area off and on for several years, taking various jobs. In the thriving LA folk-music landscape, he was able to see a variety of revival luminaries perform at the Ash Grove and other clubs.

By 1972, the lifestyle was wearing thin, and he began to feel cramped by the stresses of daily life in a massive urban area. The beach was nice, but "I was forty-two miles from the nearest piece of open ground." As he recalled, "It was fun to be there when I was twenty." But eventually, "It got old; I came back." Tom returned to Jefferson City and began working in the shoe-repair shop that his father, Elmer Verdot, operated on East Miller Street. Tom made custom-designed and period-correct shoes for historical reenactors and in 1973 or 1974 enrolled in Lincoln University. He accumulated credits for a history major but did not graduate. He worked for his dad for several more years and, when his father retired, assumed operation of the shop.

Verdot was inspired to build violins after he had taken a violin to a local repairman, with poor results; he thought he could do a better job. He began accumulating books and articles about violin making and decided to seek training at a school that taught Old World and Old Master theory and method. In 1990 Tom began traveling to New Hampshire for summer classes in violin repair and building at the University of New Hampshire's Craftsmanship Institute. In 1991, he closed the shoe shop and decided to "do fiddles full time. And I never looked back." He studied in New Hampshire six summers with luthiers Karl Roy and Hans J. Nebel, German masters trained in famed schools and shops in the alpine village of Mittenwald, Germany. Roy, "a patient but demanding teacher," had been director of the Mittenwald School of Violin Making and trained Verdot in the "Mittenwald style" of violin construction.[41] Tom began handling stringed instrument maintenance for Jefferson City schools, building violins, and performing in the traditional music community. He moved to Columbia in 2000, realizing that most of his clients were in the Columbia area, and set up his own violin shop.

Verdot makes one or two violins or violas a year, taking time when he can between repair and restoration jobs. If he were able to work full-time, he says it would take two and a half weeks to bring a new violin or viola to the point of being "in the white"—ready for varnish. Regarding restoration, something clients do not always understand:

> *Restoration* is an often-overused term. I sometimes am presented with "Grandpa's" fiddle which was "restored" at the local piano/drum/guitar store by attaching a new bridge blank with no fitting and a new set of baling wire strings. If the person hasn't already spent more on this "Strad" than it is worth, it now needs a set-up, possibly some repairs & a good bath.
>
> If I use the term "restoration" I mean one or more extensive repairs to a badly damaged or heavily worn old instrument. This would include a sagging top, sound post patch, neck graft, warped ribs, edge doublings or replacements, etc. Often one violin can need all of the above to put it back into playing condition. Almost anything can be done but a good deal of the determination depends on the cost to value ratio of the item at hand.[42]

Tom has little use for the majority of homemade violins from self-taught makers. He does have high regard for some of the instruments made by the Rodier firm in Kansas City, founded by three French Canadian brothers in the 1910s, and he also gives high marks to violins made by Frederick James Buckley, a St. Louis maker active in the early 1900s.[43] Among contemporary luthiers in Missouri, Tom points to Gregory Krone, who trained at the Violin Making School of America in Utah and apprenticed with Geoff Seitz.[44]

Tom knew Jefferson City fiddler and self-taught violin and guitar maker Jim Gilmore. A brakeman on the Missouri Pacific Railroad, Gilmore learned from a library book in the 1950s after his favorite violin (a gift from his father) was stolen. Jim tried to continue fiddling with a poor-quality fiddle and decided he could make a better instrument himself, which he did, using measured drawings of a Stradivarius. He enjoyed the process of carving, graduating, and "tap tuning" violin tops to get just the right tone. A nephew of fiddler Tony Gilmore, Jim was a jolly character and mainstay of sessions and contests from the 1940s into the 1990s. He liked to experiment with different kinds of wood. "I remember one in particular that he showed me. The back of it was plain wood, and it was all stained and really ugly. And he said, 'Yeah, my wife was cuttin' up vegetables, I looked at her and she dropped the breadboard and it kind of *rang* [when it hit the sink] and I thought, gee, that sounds pretty good,' so he took the breadboard and made a fiddle out of it. But it had grease stains and stuff in it, it was terrible, absolutely terrible. But I have seen a couple of his fiddles that I thought were perfectly acceptable."

Tom has been a violin-making teacher in the Traditional Arts Apprenticeship Program. In 2016 his student was luthier Will Scherer of Columbia,[45] and in 2020 Verdot worked with Vanessa Markley of Boonville, who had classical violin training and attended Bethel fiddle camp.

Tom Verdot never liked fiddle contests. He responded to a post from fiddle teacher Donna Hébert in October 2003 on the FIDDLE-L Internet discussion list, in which

Hébert wrote, "Contests encourage people to play by the rules, and yet music is one of the few places in life where you can 'call your own tune.' I know it's the American way, but I don't believe fiddling (or music at all) is best served by being a competitive sport." Verdot responded:

> I'm in total agreement. I've never played a contest, turned down the one offer to judge one & always joked that I wanted to know what I was getting paid before the gig. Seriously speaking, I think contests are the ruination of fiddle playing or any other art form. Rather than developing a style of one's own, many try to play the way the "state champ" plays. In Missouri this means that super slick Texas style that has displaced traditional styles which can seldom do well in contests these days. It's a sad loss of a strong tradition (I'm happy to say that there has been a backlash to all this). Why not have a "convention" instead, split the available money evenly & have a good tune swap? The better players will be recognized with a nod from their peers & no one will be crying sour grapes.[46]

Tom has performed with a number of bands. The first band that Tom "really felt comfortable with" was called Out of the Ordinary (an "ordinary" was a tavern in former times) in the 1980s, with Barbara and Denny Duff of Camdenton. They presented programs at historic sites and played for dances. In the mid-1990s, Verdot began focusing on nineteenth-century popular music and minstrel-era fiddle and banjo music and in 1995 played fiddle and banjo with the Skirtlifters. Verdot had met Skirtlifters founder Clarke Buehling in San Francisco in 1968 (Buehling later settled in Fayetteville, Arkansas). Tom retired from the Skirtlifters in 2014, tired of travel to performances and rehearsals. Verdot's commercial recordings include a ragtime CD with the Skirtlifters and a project on music of the Santa Fe Trail historical era with Mark Gardner and the Muleskinners.[47]

Verdot performs in the rotation of fiddlers and bands that play for the Mid-Missouri Traditional Dancers as well as for old-time-style square dances.

> So, you know you are going to have to play [each number] for a *while*. My solution to that [to having to play a tune for as long as the specific dance lasts] is, you can take a tune, and do what jazz musicians do, which is to twist it around and go fifteen different directions and then finally circle back to it. Well, sometimes that works out okay.
>
> But you can also do *medleys*. I *like* doing medleys, because you can do things like, start with a jig and then go to a reel. Because you set up a *pattern*, and then, even though you're keeping exactly the same tempos—one-two-three, one-two-three [6/8 jig time], one-two, one-two with a hornpipe or a reel—things that somebody who's otherwise a fine fiddle player needs to adapt to, are the *length of a dance*. I recommend medleys. As a dancer, it's nice to hear a tune *change*.

Verdot plays tunes from "the page" as well as by ear. "I learn tunes listening and I learn tunes reading. I have no preference. So, sometimes I have paper in front of me,

32 Bar Tenders: "Impromptu dancing is wildly encouraged." *Left to right*: Tom Verdot, Marcie Maguire, Rebecca Logan, and Thom Howard (with mandolin and a guitar made by David Cavins of Columbia). The band plays a variety of dance tunes from different traditions, with some original reels, jigs, and waltzes, as well as swing, ragtime, and klezmer. Tom formed the group in 2000. (Courtesy of Tom Verdot)

but usually it's just as a jumping-off point. And I don't feel attached to a certain way to play a time."

> And the other thing is getting a solid "four potatoes" for the *dancers*, so they know [that the dance is about to start]. Fiddlers need to really punch that out. You have to indicate what the tempo is going to be for the dancers. I think that's the roughest thing for fiddlers who are not used to playing for dancers. So I'm fine playing contra dances. But you do have that down time when they're instructing between dances. It depends less on the caller than it does on the crowd. If you have a bunch of beginners, probably best to keep it fairly simple and do dances that can get 'em going fairly quickly; Jim Thaxter does a great job at that.

Listen to track 3 on the companion CD to hear Tom Verdot's "Polka Medley."

The Chez, a Coffeehouse

"There was no other place even remotely like it in the area. It was just a product of the times and the people that came through there," said Lee Ruth.[48] "For me, living at the Chez was a wonderful experience I'll never forget. I made lasting friendships and continued to frequent the place for many years after my residency there. Those times are gone now and so is the Chez," said Spencer Galloway.[49]

Most coffeehouses around campuses in the 1960s adopted the "underground" laid-back atmosphere of the beats and hippies, even while many of their patrons and performers were far from being beats and hippies. There were hootenannies and open-mike evenings, bluegrass as well as old-time music and occasionally a bit of swing, some guitar-strumming ballad singers, and every variety of string-band music one could want. Coffeehouses were informal schools of music, where aspiring pickers and singers could meet and learn from experienced players, touring professionals, and from each other. The sense of belonging nourished the sharing, in an air of the excitement of discovery and experimentation.

St. Louis had venues such as Music Folk in Webster Groves. There was also a coffeehouse in Kirksville east of the campus of Northeast Missouri State University (now Truman State), in Warrensburg, and another north of the Central Missouri State University campus (now University of Central Missouri); these were similar spots where young people gathered to hear folk music. In Kansas City there were places such as the Twelve Plus One, and the Vanguard, which opened in 1963 at Forty-Third and Main, near museums, the Art Institute, and the University of Missouri–Kansas City campus. Stan Plesser owned the Vanguard Coffee House.

> At this time the coffee house circuit had passed its peak, but there was really good talent in it," Plesser said several years later. "So, I began booking people into the club and things started happening. The people who were still doing the coffeehouse thing were in it because that was their life, music was their life, and there was no other way for them to go. I loved that club," Plesser said in 2008. "The audiences were great and listened so well. I would never even put in a cash register. I just put in a cash drawer so there wouldn't be any noise.[50]

Most college or university towns by the late sixties had at least one such place. Columbia, for example, had several. The coffeehouse with the most lasting influence was the Chez Chandelle. The Chez (pronounced "shay") was created by the First Presbyterian Church on Hitt Street downtown. It welcomed everyone and asked nothing more of patrons but common courtesy.[51] The Chez welcomed those who were too young for the restaurant-taverns and young people looking for a user-friendly performance space and a comfortable place to "hang." Church leadership had a public service and ecumenical bent; efforts were made to "reach" and "relate" to young people (many of whom were presumed to be rebellious in one way or another). The Chez was within walking distance of three institutions of higher learning—the University of Missouri two blocks south, Christian College (now Columbia College) four blocks north, and Stephens College, a block east. The Chez opened in 1964, found its footing, and became a zone with special identity in the traditional music scene.

"Folk was a way of communicating in a non-threatening way what was important in life."[52] The Chez was a safe place for young folk musicians and aspiring musicians, some still high school age and some who simply appreciated the ease of a laid-back cosmopolitan "bistro" (they mostly served coffee, tea, and ice cream in the beginning) where alcoholic beverages were not served. Parents could feel good about their teenagers there. The space was also used for open forums and discussions of issues in society, student art, and an occasional indie film.

Joint Effort: Recorded Live at the Chez echoed the variety of performers in the late 1960s. Cover art by Debbie Richards captures the "psychedelic" and "underground" surrealist graphic art of the age. There was no fiddle music on the album, released just before the old-time fiddling boom of the early 1970s. Much of what made the revival enticing was its emphasis on traditional musicians as a community, and the Chez was a community. The 1970 LP documents a kind of rearview parting of the sixties folk scene.

The coffeehouse included an old upright piano, ice cream parlor–style chairs and tables, and stools at the soda fountain–style counter. There was a small stage under the west window painted as stained glass by Stephens College art students. Lumber was scavenged for the interior walls from a derelict Boone County barn, installed by Fred Dittrich and Spencer Galloway.

Spencer Galloway moved to the Chez as a resident in the summer of 1969. One of his innovations was hosting occasional "pay gigs," when "special performers were brought in and an admission charged at the door (fifty cents or a dollar)." "The standard procedure was that I would make up a flyer which residents would plaster all over campus. We'd paint a banner to hang outside the Chez on the day of the performance. That was the extent of our publicity, but it seemed to work. We always had a good crowd and performers seemed satisfied with their take."[53]

There were spartan quarters in the back where college students roomed free in exchange for helping operate the coffeehouse as "Chez keepers." When Dave Para was a resident "Chez keeper," his job included arranging and managing some of the weekend music and hoots, but he says he was really there to hear and play folk music and, as it turned out, to meet his future bride and lifelong musical partner, Cathy Barton, who was a student at Hickman High School. Dave and Cathy looked back to their time onstage, unpaid, at the Chez as a pivotal phase in becoming professional musicians. "I have great sentimental feelings about the Chez, not only because we met there and started singing together, but because we were both nurtured musically there," Cathy said. "The Chez nurtured performance."[54]

The "Dave Crowder tapes" helped increase interest in string-band music in Columbia. Crowder was not a Chez regular, and left Columbia when graduate work at the university was finished, but his tapes of jam sessions were circulated and helped steer enthusiasts to the older local fiddlers.[55] Crowder had accumulated taped copies of classic 78s of southern string bands and home recordings of Chapel Hill–area musicians, and he also had a stash of tapes of Irish fiddlers.[56] Crowder recorded fiddle sessions at the Crane and Nichols auto-repair shop at 11 North Fifth Street in Columbia. Wayne Crane had sung and played fiddle and guitar with the Country Boys on Saturday-morning broadcasts over KFRU-AM radio. Crane placed well in contests, such as in a contest at Oak Towers in Columbia in March 1974, taking third place, behind Dale Pauley and Jake Hockemeyer.

In the beginning, Crane's garage sessions were invitation-only and held at Ozzie Gentry's house, but moved to the auto shop when one too many cigarette butts found their way into the Gentry family's living-room carpet.[57] Regulars included fiddlers such as Cleo Persinger, Taylor McBaine, Jim Gilmore, Dale Pauley, and Crane, as well as guitarists Allen Boggs, N. C. Ficklin, Carl Richardson, Otto Palmer (a multigenre guitar genius who performed with the Tunemasters country-and-western band on KOMU-TV), and Taylor McBaine's high school–student son, Frank McBaine. Ozzie Gentry served as the gregarious host. Music included country songs and fiddling of various styles and repertoires, with helpings of swing and western swing. Electric guitars and electrically amplified violins were welcome.

In addition to cassette copies of his Crane's garage tapes, Dave Crowder shared cassettes of 78 rpm string-band records with Jim Ruth and Spencer Galloway. Galloway recalls that Crowder gave him a cassette of some of the historic 1920s and 1930s southern string-band records. "That was kind of a seminal moment for us."[58] Another inflection point was when Bill Rogers came back to Columbia.

Spencer Galloway, a Curator of Tradition

As the 1960s merged into the 1970s, certain of the young folksingers took up old-time fiddling—an unexpected new phase of the Folk Music Revival. One of these people was Spencer Galloway of Fayette, Missouri.

Galloway was born in Warrensburg in 1947 and moved with the family to Kansas City in 1956. His parents were Glenn Andrew and Myra Elizabeth Sinclair Galloway. Spencer's uncle played mandolin. Glenn Galloway sang and yodeled and loved to listen to the Grand Ole Opry on Saturday nights. Spencer's grandfather Andrew Galloway was a fiddler.

As a child in Warrensburg, Spencer was given piano and then tap-dancing lessons. In junior high school after the family moved to Kansas City, he played trumpet. "I wasn't any good at any of them."[59] At around sixteen, he "found the guitar" and began trying to learn to play. After graduating from Center High School in Kansas City in 1965, Spencer enrolled in Metropolitan Junior College, where he was a student of Ray Lawless, author of *Folksingers and Folksongs in America*, and became aware of a wide range of traditional music.[60] Spence took classes for three years but left without graduating; he took summer courses each year and was unfazed by not graduating. "Well, I got a good education." He moved to Columbia in 1968 and enrolled in photojournalism at the University of Missouri; after two years, he dropped out and in 1971 was hired as a paste-up artist at the *Columbia Daily Tribune*. Working in Columbia, Galloway was able to stay part of the fiddle and string-band community, and a deferment kept him out of the military draft. The Vietnam War was still raging. Due to a clerical glitch after his first semester at junior college, he was reclassified 1A and ordered to report for his physical, but the error was corrected and his student deferment reinstated and extended. "That providential glitch gave me an extra semester of deferment which carried me through to the first lottery drawing." He was not drafted because his birth-date number was drawn too far down the list in the lottery.[61]

Spencer headed for the Chez his first week in Columbia and in 1969 moved in and became a "Chez keeper." He helped redecorate the interior of the café and performance space, learned how to cook residents' meals, and generally supervised things. Galloway reorganized the weekend entertainment by auditioning Friday- and Saturday-night performers, such as Lee Ruth, Jerome Wheeler, and Steve Hutchins. Weekend nights remained "open mike" (microphone) nights. "We developed a pretty reliable stable of credible talent and never had any trouble filling slots." Spencer had been among the folksingers performing at the Chez (and appears on the Chez LP),[62] but switched his musical energies to old-time fiddle and banjo.

Spencer Galloway in the front parlor of his 1860 home in Fayette on a December afternoon, 2018. (Photo by Howard Marshall)

How did Columbia's burst of interest in old-time fiddling and banjo playing in the early 1970s come about? Just a few years before, in the late sixties, the focus had been on bluegrass, folksinging, and bluegrass banjo. According to Galloway, "It just happened. Spontaneous generation."

While initially most of the fiddling was influenced by Appalachian and southern fiddling styles and repertoire of the classic string bands on old records, some people realized that Columbia was in a region abundant with fiddling, with its own traditions and heroes. "I was always kind of torn between old-timey style fiddling and this Missouri-style stuff. And it took me a long time to warm up to Missouri style. And I think it's hard to play both styles—well, it is for *me*. The Missouri style of fiddling is more sophisticated—and you've got slurs going across the bar line, and stuff like that, and more sophisticated and complicated bowing."

Bill Shull (1950–2022) was an early advocate of Missouri fiddle styles and repertoire, and Spencer and Bill drove around the area to visit fiddlers on "collecting trips." It was not hard to notice that Appalachian fiddling, with was popular across the United States, was not the same as central Missouri fiddling. Galloway, Jim Ruth, Rob Golan, and others had learned Appalachian and southern fiddle music from the old 78s, but when the youngsters played "old-time stuff" learned from Appalachian recordings around older fiddlers like Taylor McBaine, they "just didn't know what to make of it. They never listened to Appalachian stuff and old-time." Jim Ruth seconded the point: "For most people, it [Appalachian-style fiddle] was just a little too raw-sounding for what they consider music. But if you're the right kind of person, it hits you right in the gut."[63] Galloway remarks that the string bands that he, Jim, Rob Golan, Al Cranis, Heinrich Leonhard, and Dave Para put together had to travel to

Illinois or Indiana, or "St. Louis, at least," to be appreciated when they played their old-time Appalachian repertoire and style.

Galloway traveled to Illinois and Indiana, meeting musicians such as Garry Harrison and his band the Indian Creek Delta Boys. Harrison impressed Galloway because "he eschewed the usual Appalachian style, drawing his repertoire from fiddlers he'd collected around his home in Charleston, Illinois." In Bloomington, Indiana, he met young musicians such as Brian "Hawk" Hubbard and Dave Moke and the Easy Street Stringband. In New Harmony, Indiana, Spencer met Dillon Bustin and was invited to the Indiana Fiddlers Gathering at the Tippecanoe Battleground. "Bustin was kind of the impresario of several festivals; he said, 'I can't pay you, but I'll see that you get some gas money.'" Galloway went to Battleground, and the Hoss Hair Pullers were booked there several years.

Galloway thinks of himself as a dance fiddler. He enjoyed contra dances, "but they were just so *slow* [taking so much time to teach the contra-dance moves and walk them through while the band sits]." Some square dances they played went over well, and some did not. "We [the Missouri State Old Time Fiddlers Association] tried to have a dance here at the old Boone County fairgrounds, with Peter [Lippincott] calling, but, boy, it didn't go over at all.[64] The old-timers just didn't like having a *common caller* [one caller for all the dancers]—they were used to having somebody call in the *square* [a caller in each set of dancers], and they were used to the cornmeal on the floor, and all, and so it was pretty much a disaster." Recalling another event, he said, "I think the *worst* dance I ever played for—just about every year, we'd go down and play a show at Arrow Rock [during the fall Craft Festival] and then in the evening play a dance. And they had different callers. One time they had this caller in from Kansas City. And we were sitting there after we'd eaten, and we were just fooling around, playing. And he came up, and we said, 'Oh, don't worry, don't worry, we'll play faster than this for the dance.' And he said, 'Oh, *no—that's* too *fast*!' And it was just *agony* to play at that slow speed."

"Contests Seem to Be Dying Out and I'm Not Really Sorry to See Them Go"

Galloway was especially interested in fiddlers such as Taylor McBaine and Jake Hockemeyer, leading contest fiddlers in the area. He played in contests and came into contact with other styles, especially the increasingly popular "Texas" Contest Style fiddling.

Fiddle contests are not for everyone, but contests are where older interesting fiddlers competed and hung out, so Galloway participated. When the state contest moved from Columbia to Sedalia around 1990, Galloway, Pete McMahan, and Taylor McBaine drove together. That evening, there was a major contest in Clinton with a $500 first prize, so they added a side trip on the way back to Columbia. Fifty fiddlers showed up. "I was lucky to get ninth or tenth place. I considered myself *real* lucky."

He continued: "I have really mixed feelings about contests, though. In a way they're good—they popularize fiddling to a broader audience. But a lot of fiddlers I've known just polish their contest material to the exclusion of anything else. Anyway, I'm not really a contest fiddler. I'm a dance fiddler, really."

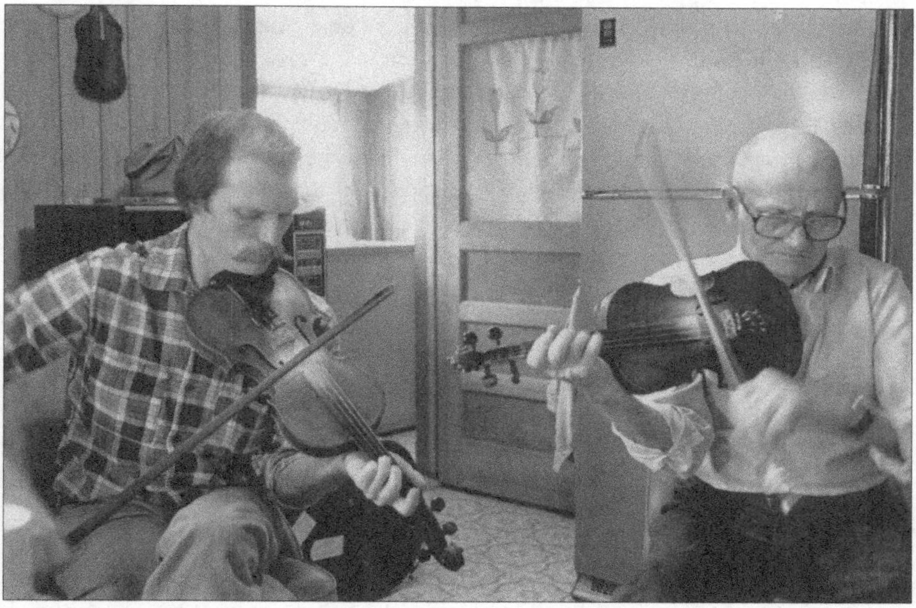
Spencer Galloway and Jake Hockemeyer, in Jake's kitchen in Mokane, 1985. (Photo by Howard Marshall)

Studies with Jake

In 1985–86, Galloway partnered with Jake Hockemeyer in the Traditional Arts Apprenticeship Program.[65] In the application, Galloway wrote of his love of traditional music, his extensive research, and his archive of historic recordings and photographs. He wrote of his desire to "become a better fiddler from what I learn and thereby become a conduit to preserve and pass along Mr. Hockemeyer's unique Mid-Mo style. Second, I hope to gain a better understanding of the origins and development of the Mid-Mo fiddle style and to forge a link through my master to area fiddlers such as Cleo Persinger and Vee Latty."

Hockemeyer played Little Dixie "hornpipe" style and was a contest champion and one of Missouri's best-known fiddlers. He was left-handed and played "backward" or "over the bass," and it was difficult for Galloway (right-handed) to figure out what Jake was doing.

A half hour of fiddling taped at a Callaway County fish fry circa 1965 became the ultimate Hockemeyer recording, copied from reel-to-reel to cassette tape to homemade CDs and passed among fans and fiddlers, a précis of Hockemeyer's depth and power in his prime.[66] Adding interest to the recording is Russ Orchard's electric-guitar accompaniment—common in Missouri fiddling at the time but eventually cast aside as purists, fiddle contests, and folk festivals frowned on electric-guitar backup as being, in their opinion, not old-time enough. According to Galloway, "When I was an apprentice, somebody gave me that fish-fry tape. And I took it down to Jake [at one of their Thursday lessons], and I put it on Jake's cassette machine. And I said, 'Jake, who is that?' And he said, 'Oh—I don't know, I'm not sure, I don't think I quite know.' And Frances, his wife, said, 'Why you old fool, that's *you*!" And Jake said, 'Damn, I never knew I was that good.'"[67] Jake liked the tape so much that he asked Spencer to "run it off." He couldn't wait for Spencer's next visit, so two days later he drove to Spencer's farm north of Columbia to pick it up.

Many of Jake's contest tunes are on the fish-fry tape: "Liverpool Hornpipe," "Durang's Hornpipe," "Fisher's Hornpipe" (in F), "Coming Down from Denver," "Marmaduke's Hornpipe," "Grey Eagle," "Fiddler's Waltz," "Leather Britches," "Devil's Dream," "Red Apple Rag," and "Twinkle Little Star." When Spencer queried Jake about his favorites—a different batch from his contest pieces—Jake replied, "Echoes of the Ozarks," "Billy in the Low Ground," "Black Velvet Waltz," "Dry and Dusty," "Fiddler's Waltz," "Dill Pickle Rag," "Clarinet Polka," "Sugar Tree Stomp," "Clark's Waltz," "St. Anne's Reel," "Too Young to Marry" ("Lead Out"), "Cowboy Waltz," "Cotton Eyed Joe," "Old Joe Clark," "Westphalia Waltz," and "Liberty."[68]

Hockemeyer did not play many waltzes, unusual for central Missouri fiddlers, but he played his waltzes with authority. While one could expect a German American fiddler of his generation to play some Germanic melodies, he did not, other than the universally popular "Jenny Lind Polka" (apparently of Bohemian roots but composed by Anton Wallerstein in 1843)[69] and a midwestern schottische or two, such as "D and A Schottische" ("Rochester Schottische") and "Flop-Eared Mule" ("Detroit Schottische").

The Hockemeyer-Galloway partnership was unusually successful, musically and "culturally." Hockemeyer was in his sixties and suffering from advancing debilitating arthritis; Galloway was thirty-seven. Jake knew his fiddling days were limited and was ready to accept a capable and knowledgeable student. Spencer wrote all sorts of information in his journal (notebooks), from Hockemeyer's life story and family history and documentation of his repertoire with annotations and sources to Jake's folk wisdom and sayings. Galloway would sometimes ask about an incident or story, and Jake would say, "You shut that thing off [tape recorder] and I'll tell ya.'" Then, on the drive home, Spencer would stop and write in his journal. "I just wanted to get Jake's words down while they were still fresh in my mind."

Spencer explained "Jake's style" in his journal, a crisp and important outline of the old-time central Missouri and Little Dixie manner of playing: "I. Melodically full. A. Notey construction. B. Variation without sacrificing melody line. II. Rhythmic. A. Danceable. B. Pattern licks add to strong beat. III. Lack of ornamentation and embellishments. A. Minimum of vibrato.[70] B. Few slides. C. No triplets."

What was Hockemeyer like as a teacher? Like many fiddlers, Hockemeyer focused on playing tunes for the student and did not try to explain complicated bowings and variations. "You had to *learn*. He didn't teach. You talked to him and you played with him and you recorded with him. You went home and tried to learn it [listening to the recording]." This is the tried-and-true custom by which many traditions are learned and conveyed from one person to another.

Spencer took his Martin D-28 guitar to lessons to accompany Jake, playing straight chords. At one lesson, Columbia guitarist John G. Stewart (accustomed to backing up fiddlers) drove to Mokane with Galloway so Jake could play pop tunes and two-steps like "South" with Stewart's swing-style backup and chord progressions.

Galloway prospered at the *Columbia Daily Tribune* in various positions from design to assistant editor and department supervisor. In 1977 he was burned out and quit, but later returned part-time. Spencer helped bring attention to traditional musicians in Missouri and helped steer reporters and photographers to likely subjects and stories. He saw into print articles and photographs about concerts, fiddle contests, festivals, and musicians. Spencer did some of his own photography and supplied archival photos from his collection to illustrate reporters' articles. He created the logo for the Missouri State Old Time Fiddlers Association and designed and oversaw production of MSOTFA newsletters and other materials. He designed publications for the Missouri Cultural Heritage Center, including the sixty-four-page booklet, logo, and LP set *"Now That's a Good Tune": Masters of Missouri Fiddling*, a finalist for two Grammy Awards, and designed Margot McMillen's *Our Missouri* educational magazine for young people.[71] Galloway retired from the *Tribune* in 2006.

After retiring, Galloway focused on music, snooker, and collecting stamps, kerosene lamps, art, books, and furniture, "just a lot of useless stuff." Spencer Galloway is the kind of person who contributes significantly to the study, conservation, and appreciation of this music and the people behind it. Spencer and his wife, Rebecca, play music at various programs, with him playing mandolin mostly (some violin) and her on guitar. They sing old folksongs and enjoy laid-back, informal music making together. "I'm just a kid who snuck in the side door of the theater, and the movie's in the third reel of a four-reeler, and the usher ain't caught me yet."

Bill Rogers Comes Back to Columbia

According to Spencer Galloway, "It's funny the small events that things turn on."[72] In 1970, Bill Rogers returned to Columbia from California. Galloway had just designed a poster for the Chez, featuring his Martin D-28 guitar learning against a stool on the coffeehouse stage. Based on his recollections from 1966–67, Bill Rogers said he had "written off the Chez as just a Kingston Trio place" where young people just copied commercial folksongs, but that D-28 on the poster tipped Bill that this coffeehouse might offer more. He knew that elite guitar was favored by seasoned amateurs well as professional folk, bluegrass, and country musicians; its image implied that a more interesting level of music might be on offer at the Chez. And Bill was right. Checking out the Chez, he met bluegrass banjoist Kevin Sanders, Galloway, and others. "Obviously, the music scene in Columbia was changing since I left in '67."[73]

Bill Rogers's presence was, as Galloway recalls, "the catalyst" in the move away among some musicians from "folk music" and bluegrass to old-time string-band music. A banjo player in several styles, Bill played fiddle, too. Kevin Sanders had been playing bluegrass banjo, but after hearing Bill Rogers play frailing and clawhammer style on his open-back five-string, Kevin bought an open-back five-string banjo and started learning Bill's old-time styles. Deciding to play fiddle, in 1971 Galloway bought his first violin, a secondhand Czech-made John Juzek instrument, from Rogers, and "the rest is history."

Rogers was born in Columbia in 1944 and moved to and from town for many years. In Columbia in 1970, he says:

> I headed to the Chez, where I found, among others, the late Kevin Sanders, a solid bluegrass banjo player; Spence Galloway, who was playing guitar and singing. We hit it off well. Later, I met Jim Ruth, already a skilled flat-picker and bluegrass banjo player, who'd made his own banjo. He was beginning to play clawhammer, so there was a commonality there. I was trying to learn fiddle, never succeeded, though, but Jim and I did play some fiddle and banjo stuff. Over the next four years there was interaction among various players. Cathy Barton was doing her thing, though most of the Chez crowd did not play much music with her. Dave Para showed up in that time frame too.
>
> The music we played evolved to more old-time than bluegrass pretty quickly. I did play some attempted bluegrass with Rod Moag, and, for one year, a psychology grad student named John James, who was a good singer, passable mandolin player, but maybe a tad too friendly with John Barleycorn. We would put together ad hoc groups to play the Chez off and on. A sociology PhD student, already on the faculty at Western Illinois, named Ken Mietus, played old-time fiddle and sang a bit, and he joined us on occasion. Kevin Sanders left for grad school, and Mietus went back to WIU before I left in 1974. I finished my course work and took my comps, returning to CA in the summer of '74 to find a job and get started on research.
>
> I returned, newly married to a fellow history grad, in 1979, but didn't play all that much music in the ensuing six years. I did play off and on with Jim, Spencer, Joe Newberry, and Rob Golan. Newberry, of course, would turn out to be the one among us to become a successful professional musician. In those days, Joe was working on his guitar and banjo playing, but was already a fine singer, which set him apart from the other locals except for Cathy Barton.[74]

Rogers had tapes of the revival string band featuring Walt Koken, the Busted Toe Mud Thumpers. Rogers met Koken in Ithaca, New York (born in Columbia, Missouri), in 1965 and in 1969 recorded Koken with the band in San Francisco in 1969. By 1969, Bill recalls that Koken's distinctive, driving clawhammer banjo style had "really matured." "Walt's banjo playing was unbelievable, still with the reckless verve

Bill Rogers with his Essex banjo, a Grand Concert model (made 1912–15), Lodi, California. (Photo by Bryan Caldwell, June 2019)

of youth, but complete mastery of the fretboard and his incomparable right hand." The Koken tape was Jim Ruth's "major connection with Walt, since Walt was nowhere near Columbia and moving into playing fiddle with the Highwoods."[75] Koken played Scruggs-style bluegrass, too, but it was his clawhammer banjo playing that captured people's attention.[76]

Koken was born in Columbia in 1947 while his father was a graduate student at the university. The Kokens are an old St. Louis family with German roots. Walt's family moved to places such as Oswego, New York, where Walt went to high school and where his father bought Walt his first banjo in 1959, a tenor. He then found a five-string, and, studying the Pete Seeger book, began learning five-string styles. He played tenor banjo with a New Orleans–style or riverboat jazz band and then shifted to the Virginia "mountain music" clawhammer five-string banjo style of Wade Ward, whose 1920s 78-rpm records were being reissued in the 1960s.[77]

After high school, Koken moved to Webster Groves in the St. Louis metro area where his maternal grandfather, George Hawkens, lived. In the fall of 1963, Walt was a sixteen-year-old freshman honors student at the university in Columbia and a fraternity pledge. Koken played "Pete Seeger and Earl Scruggs–centric" banjo and sang folksongs. "I was a source of entertainment (usually late-night) for guys in the house, and for some friends of my sister who lived off campus, but that was all. My plans to follow up academics, learn Spanish so I could sing Mexican songs and become a chemist or something, were dashed initially by my 'adviser' who made me take German because I was interested in chemistry, and who somehow bamboozled me out of taking my honors course, and finally because it was party time at the frat house whenever possible, and so I was asked to take a semester off at the end of the year due to an embarrassingly low grade point average."[78] Dropping out, Walt returned to Webster Groves and soon began his adventures in string-band music.

Koken played in bands in Ithaca and then San Francisco, where he helped form the Fat City String Band. Back in Ithaca in 1972, this band evolved into the Highwoods

Stringband, the influential revivalist group that hit the national stage in 1971 at the Smithsonian Institution's Festival of American Folklife at the Union Grove fiddlers' convention in North Carolina.[79] The band became a staple at fiddlers' conventions, contests, and folk festivals. The Highwoods set a high bar for vigorous musicianship and spirited interpretation of Appalachian music and the classic string bands of the 1920s and 1930s being discovered on old 78-rpm records. The Highwoods was a rollicking gang of cosmopolitan kids with a hippie lifestyle and lighthearted performances.[80]

The Chez launched the careers of many young players. In its time, it was a hotbed of youngsters playing old-time fiddle and banjo, echoing the wave of interest across the United States. Fred Dittrich, a Chez regular and folksinger (today an advocate of Irish button-box accordion), recalls seeing eight fiddlers there one evening in the early seventies. But time passes. The action began to thin in the late 1980s. The Chez was shuttered in 1999. Most of the characters who made the place the stuff of legends had moved on, just as the coffeehouse idea itself seems to have drifted away. The vibe was gone. By the 1980s, there was no longer a critical mass of young people lugging guitars and banjos and fiddles to the Chez; the keepers and patrons had graduated, started families, moved on.

The door was gently closing on the headiest days of the Folk Music Revival. A new phase was coming. Publishing his first book of fiddle tunes in 1975, Christeson was "discovered" by young fiddlers as well as the Missouri Folklore Society. His *Old-Time Fiddler's Repertory* tune books, valued especially by those who read violin music in the old-time fiddle movement, helped bring worldwide recognition to old-time fiddle styles and repertoires of the Midwest (mostly Nebraska and Missouri), a region where scant attention had been paid. The numerous other fiddlers left out of the Christeson books needed no discovering, of course; they made their own way, as they had done for generations, performing in sessions, leading square dances, competing in contests, joining opry shows and bluegrass bands, making records, and, occasionally, "making it"—becoming well known and earning a living—in Nashville or Los Angeles.

Ken Mietus graduated from high school in Chicago in 1959, the era when the Kingston Trio and other folk groups were popular on LP records and Top 40 radio stations. He came to Columbia in the fall of 1970 to obtain a PhD at the university. In 1972, he joined the faculty at Western Illinois and retired as professor emeritus in 2008. "My brief time in Columbia was among the most enjoyable periods of my life. As I recall, it was Kevin [banjoist Kevin Sanders] who came up with the name King Mietus and the Golden Dixie Hotshots. Therein lies a tale."[81]

> I can understand some confusion about who exactly comprised the membership of the Golden Hotshots as it informally evolved over the course of several months. It's genesis began in the back "rehearsal" room of The Chez Coffeehouse in the Fall of 1970. Jim Ruth, a neighbor of mine heard me playing 5-string banjo on the front porch of my house and invited me to join him one weekend at the Chez coffeehouse.
>
> I was new to Columbia and was happy to meet some local musicians who shared my

Residents of the Chez, fall 1980. *Left to right*, front: Mochalis Alimin, Joe Newberry (banjo), Louise Solarzano, and John Murdock (violin); rear, *left to right*: Bob Atchison (with violin), Becky Backhues, Bruce Everly, ecumenical minister Ed Church (who oversaw operation of the Chez), and Heinrich Leonhard. Solarzano and Backhues were the first women allowed to live at the Chez. (*Columbia Daily Tribune*, September 28, 1980; courtesy of Spencer Galloway, Dave Para, and Bob Atchison)

interest in folk and old timey music (I was a big New Lost City Ramblers fan). That evening I met a variety of very talented musicians and spent an hour or so jamming with an assortment of people. After a while, a small group consisting of myself, Jim Ruth, Kevin Sanders, and some other fellows whom I can't specifically recall were asked by the MC if we would like to take the stage and play a few tunes. We readily agreed.

The MC asked us what the name of our "group" was. This took us by surprise, since we had barely known one another for more than a few hours. We took the stage, played several tunes and were well received by the audience.

Over the months, a core group of Jim, Kevin, and I played sets at the Chez and were joined on stage by a variety of different personnel, including Bill Rogers, Spence Galloway and whoever wished to join in. There was never a fixed list of musicians—it was largely whoever was available at the time. I was one of the vocalists and primarily played 5-string and guitar, some autoharp, and a *very* small amount of fiddle.

In the Summer of '72 (although it might have been '71—my memory does not serve me very well after nearly 50 years) Kevin dropped by my house, excited to inform me that we were entered as contestants in the upcoming Boone County Fair talent contest. He informed me that we were billed as "King Mietus and the Golden Dixie Hotshots." I was a bit taken aback, and amused, that he had expropriated my name without asking me ahead of time. I asked him, "How did you come by that name?" He gleefully replied that he "always wanted to be in a band called King Midas and the Golden Dixie Hotshots." Fair enough.[82]

The crowd seemed to enjoy us and as things turned out, we won first prize in the talent contest and, as part of that privilege, we were to represent Boone County in the upcoming Missouri State Fair. Because of prior commitments, some of us were unable to make it to that event and we suggested that the second-place winner, a youngster about 12 years old who had a pretty slick magic act, serve in our stead. I have a vague recollection of Jim Ruth telling me that the kid with the magic act won first place at the State Fair. I like to believe that that was indeed true.[83]

Kevin Sanders was among the youngsters whose journey into banjo playing began by being attracted to the music of Doug Dillard—a jolly and charismatic character and well known in his native Missouri. Kevin mastered Dillard's picking style (a version of Earl Scruggs's style) and the nationally popular repertoire of the Dillards band

Ken Mietus, Macomb, Illinois, 1969, when Ken was a graduate student in sociology at Western Illinois University. His banjo was a Vega ("Pete Seeger") long-neck bought in 1962 at Sid Sherman Music in Chicago. (Photo by Terry Dosset; courtesy of Ken Mietus)

and participated in festivals.[84] Sanders then gravitated from bluegrass to old-time styles and the string-band movement in the early 1970s as his tastes changed along with those of many of his musician friends. Best known as a versatile banjo player, Sanders also played harmonica, mandolin, and fiddle.

From Raytown, Sanders learned five-string banjo from Lonnie Hoppers and performed at Kansas City–area folk clubs and coffeehouses such as the Twelve Plus One, while still in high school. He attended the University of Missouri–Kansas City for two years and then transferred to the University of Missouri in Columbia as a psychology major. In Columbia, Kevin became a resident of the Chez and performed in several groups. Clawhammer banjo players such as Rogers and Ruth inspired Sanders to shift to the Appalachian clawhammer-style banjo, and he made the transition skillfully. In order to partake fully in the clawhammer community, Sanders put aside his stellar-quality ODE resonator banjo and obtained a rehabbed banjo (of poor quality) but of the open-back type favored by old-timey musicians.

Sanders graduated and moved east to pursue a master's degree in sociology at the New School for Social Research in New York City, where he met people such as Ray Alden (a pupil of Tommy Jarrell), and then returned to Columbia. Although immersed in the string-band community around the Chez and traveling to festivals, Kevin was restless and around 1974 moved to Seattle to study toward a PhD at the University of Washington. He played music in the local string-band community, performing with the Last Chance Boys. He took a job in journalism on the *Seattle Times*, married, and settled down with his wife and children.[85]

Kevin Sanders at the Knob Noster bluegrass festival, August 1971. "Hair length doesn't matter as Kevin Sanders of Columbia demonstrates a banjo 'lick.'" Sanders, from Raytown in the Kansas City metro area, was one of the 1960s banjo enthusiasts who switched from old-time string-band banjo styles to bluegrass; his principal bluegrass mentor was Lonnie Hoppers. (Photo by Spencer Galloway)

The Little Dixie Hoss Hair Pullers, 1979, at a festival in Lafayette, Indiana. *Left to right*: Dave Para, Spencer Galloway, Jim Ruth, and Rob Golan. (Courtesy of Rob Golan)

"Dance music is what it's all about" is a familiar remark when Spence Galloway talks about being a fiddler with the Little Dixie Hoss Hair Pullers in the seventies and eighties. He enjoyed playing for dances more than playing in contests or performing onstage with a band. He liked the conviviality of playing for dancers and enjoyed fiddling for contra dances, such as those in St. Louis for the Childgrove Country Dancers. The dancers liked old-time square dancing, too, and squares were intermixed with the contra dances. "It's just more fun to play a dance, it's just—energy."[86] The St. Louis dances were typically held at the Odd Fellows Hall in University City, which could be, especially depending on the weather, a long drive from Columbia; the Hoss Hair Pullers eventually tired of the trek and retired from the Childgrove group's bullpen of fine bands, where fiddlers such as Bill Stewart guaranteed good dances.

Jim Ruth, Musician and Scholar of Old-Time Music

Jim Ruth was born in Appleton, Wisconsin, in 1950 and began playing music at age four—rock-and-roll melodies on a ukulele. He was fascinated with the banjo sounds on Kingston Trio records. Jim's family moved to Overland Park, Kansas, and to Columbia in 1962. Jim's father had a woodshop and machine shop at home, and Jim built three five-string banjos there while in high school. The one he played most often was the last of the three, with a heavy brass Gibson Mastertone–like tone ring. Jim gave his first banjo to his brother Lee when Lee's Vega Ranger was stolen around 1970. When Lee recovered the Vega and gave the banjo back, Lee had taken a plastic label maker and punched out "Agnew" and stuck the label on the peg head (this was during the scandalous term of Vice President Spiro Agnew). Jim took the "Agnew" neck off and installed it on a 1920s Stromberg Marimbaphone tenor pot that he obtained from Bill Rogers in trade for a photographic enlarging lens.

Jim graduated from Hickman High in 1969 and studied at the University of Missouri for a year as a geology major. He took a position in the composing department at the *Columbia Daily Tribune* in 1973 and was let go in 1991 due to technological changes in newspaper printing. In 1995, Jim went to work for John Griffin, as Griffin was developing Old Standard Wood in the rural Millersburg community east of Columbia. Ruth became John's chief employee, the company's point man working with customers around the world searching for quality woods for construction of musical instruments, particularly guitars and mandolins.

> I learned banjo on my own at first by using just a thumb. Then Lee taught me a basic frailing style which he probably learned from the Seeger book as well as by listening to records. I could never make sense of tablature. I needed to hear a piece played. Meanwhile I started three-finger picking and slowed the Scruggs records down to 16 RPM. I was able to pick up a lot of playing secrets that way. I never owned the Scruggs book. That came out several years after I had learned the basics on my own. Lee had a good LP collection of bluegrass and old-time music so I got to hear the right stuff.[87]

Ruth was taken with melodic bluegrass banjo as developed particularly by Bill Keith, on LPs such as Bill Monroe's *Bluegrass Instrumentals* compilation. Jim could play Earl Scruggs style, but preferred what Bill Keith was teaching—as well as the young Oklahoma phenomenon Alan Munde, who was creating sparkling interpretations of fiddle tunes and bluegrass standards. Jim worked out Keith-style interpretations of fiddle tunes such as "Sailor's Hornpipe" (a.k.a. "College Hornpipe")[88] and composed tunes in the Keith-melodic style—"Fishing Reel," "Huckleberry Finn," and his version of the theme for the 1968 TV sitcom *The Ghost and Mrs. Muir* (with an added second part) that he called "Muir's Hornpipe."

Jim has been performing in different styles since the 1960s and impressed listeners with his laser focus and knowledge of traditional acoustic music. Jim sampled most of the instrumental old-time and bluegrass music that was out there, and then, in deliberate phases, naturally curious, he drew on several distinct kinds of traditional music. He also played mandolin and worked out brilliant solo guitar playing in the general manner of Doc Watson, Dan Crary, and Clarence White.

Jim's guitar flat-picking followed the trend toward working out fiddle tunes. In 1972, Jim won third place in the national flat-picking championship in Winfield, Kansas. His prize was a fine Mossman guitar, built by the S. L. Mossman shop in Winfield, one of the first small shops to compete in quality with Martin dreadnaught guitars. "I had a batch of tunes practiced up and I didn't make any mistakes that I remember. I played 'John Henry,' 'Other Side of Baker,' and an Irish reel medley, 'The Pigeon on the Gate' / 'Sligo Maid.' That [Irish medley] might have cost me a place. Judges were Norman Blake, Dan Crary and Byron Berline. Later in the evening the winners came back on stage and each played a couple tunes. I played 'Cherokee Shuffle' and 'Crazy Creek.'"[89]

Around that same year, Jim started playing fiddle, learning from masters such as Taylor McBaine. He also learned Appalachian styles like those of Henry Reed, Tommy Jarrell, the Kimble family, and Frank George. Jim recalls that he and his friends played the popular and widespread Appalachian fiddle repertoire, easily available on records and at festivals. The Appalachian fiddling "got some of us really into fiddle music and cleared the way for us to properly appreciate our local fiddlers in good time, though we always knew they were great players. Bill Rogers was more centered around early bluegrass and Appalachian fiddle music but certainly appreciated local fiddlers. Before Bill Rogers arrived, I had played a bit with fiddler John White which whetted my appetite for claw-hammer duets with fast fiddling." He recalls:

> Sometime in the late '60s I was picking with Lee down on campus. A fellow walked up with a fiddle case and asked if he could play a few tunes with us. It was John White and when he launched into Mississippi Sawyer, I found I could claw-hammer it fast enough to keep up with him. I was hooked on claw-hammering with fast dance fiddlers after that. Eventually I tried it with Taylor McBaine and then of course a few years later Cathy Barton really put the frailing style with the local fiddling.[90]
>
> But when I heard the Koken tapes I realized that was something I wanted to pursue. Of course, I had heard good banjo-fiddle duets on County and Folkways records. And I had heard Dan Peek's nice frailing banjo and Jim Olin's also.
>
> Olin told me about County Records in the late '60s and I soon ordered up a bunch of old-time LPs and heard a lot of the great claw-hammer players of the Blue Ridge. But for percussive drive and melody Hobart Smith was the one I was fascinated by, though I did try to emulate the Round Peak banjo style to some extent. Bill Rogers had a nice LP collection also.[91]

Jim began to adopt and adapt to his playing the driving, percussive, down-stroke clawhammer styles of Appalachian banjo players like Hobart Smith, Fred Cockerham, and Kyle Creed. This was a defining moment. In the seventies, for all practical purposes, he put his melodic Keith-style bluegrass on the shelf and devoted himself to percussive, melodic clawhammer. Jim's goal in playing clawhammer is to "mirror the fiddle as close as I can in phrasing without losing the basic claw-hammer lope and drive."[92]

In the early 1970s, Jim became interested in Irish fiddling as that movement gained adherents across the country. Again, Bill Rogers played a role, introducing Jim Ruth to Irish fiddling through records by the Dubliners. "John Sheahan played some fiddle medleys with Barney McKenna on tenor banjo. Still great stuff. Then in about 1973 John Maguire of New York City sent a tape of nearly all the Michael Coleman 78s." Jim took up Irish fiddling and became a devotee. Many people were fascinated by the various sectors of the string-band revival, but few are the musicians who were able to immerse themselves in different genres and become proficient at them all—melodic bluegrass banjo, bluegrass flat-pick guitar, old-time Missouri fiddling, Appalachian clawhammer banjo, and Irish fiddling.

These days, Jim plays banjo at dances in the Springfield–Reeds Spring area with Kim Lansford; Nathan Lee McAlister of Neosho; Pete Howard of Fayetteville, Arkansas; and Barb Weathers of Springfield. On some occasions, Jim plays banjo with Pete Howard and Barb Weathers as the James River Scraphounds. Now in his sixties,

Jim Ruth's music has two principal foci, clawhammer banjo and Irish fiddle. "In a nutshell, I have never been a performer, just a back-porch player who lives for those somewhat rare times when everyone is in the same zone and somehow playing better than they would on their own."[93]

The Little Dixie Hoss Hair Pullers

As newspaper columnist Forrest Rose wrote, "The Little Dixie Hoss Hair Pullers keep a rough tradition full of resonant life by eschewing the musical mainstream."[94] The first band was called the Boone County Ham Hands; old-fashioned Boone County ham is justly famous and was served in the best restaurants and at political rallies. The group included Jim Ruth (violin), Kevin Sanders (clawhammer banjo), and Spencer Galloway (mandolin). Al Cranis sometimes sat in on guitar. After Sanders left town, Jim Ruth took over the banjo duties, Spencer played fiddle, and Heinrich Leonhard played guitar.

Ruth says, "The Ham Hands went to Galax in 1974 and 1975 in those two different forms. After that Rob Golan joined up, and we were the Little Dixie Hoss Hair Pullers with double fiddles by Spence and Rob. That would have been around 1976. Sometimes Dave Para played guitar with the Pullers, sometimes Heinrich."[95] Galloway suggested the name "Hoss Hair Pullers" "after the Ozark string band, 'Dr. Smith's Champion Hoss Hair Pullers,' who cut a few sides for Victor in the late 1920s. The name stuck and we became 'The Little Dixie Hoss Hair Pullers.' Our specialty was playing two fiddles in octaves, similar to the Carter Brothers and Son records."[96]

In 1974, the Boone County Ham Hands trekked to Galax, Virginia, to partake of the massive old-time and bluegrass music festival and compete in the Old-Time Band division of the contest. Al Cranis was unavailable for the trip, so Galloway (who had been playing mandolin with the group) took over guitar duties, playing what he calls a "scruffy cross-picking style" on his small Martin guitar. Kevin Sanders handled old-time banjo; Jim Ruth was on fiddle. There seemed to be drunks everywhere at Galax, especially in the parking lot. "You could look out across there and it looked like a bunch of zombies comin' at you."[97] Galloway and the others heard and met some of the top Appalachian-style fiddlers and banjoists, including influential fiddlers of the era, such as Tommy Jarrell. "We travelled to Galax in '74 (I think, anyway it was the year Nixon resigned) and again the following year. Tommy Jarrell took to calling me 'Jesse James.' I was quite surprised and pleased the second year, when Tommy remembered me and said, 'Well, look here, it's Jesse James.'"[98]

Galloway recalls the excitement of the Galax fiddlers' convention and visits with Sanders, Ruth, and Ray Alden at the home of fiddler Tommy Jarrell, but did not enjoy the jam-session style there, in which masses of musicians latch onto a popular tune and the lead instruments (violins, banjos, mandolins) all play the melody at the same time, a custom that accrues a groove but, for those unfamiliar with the custom, seems to roll on indefinitely. "Galax was a weird scene. You'd walk around and there'd be a group of people playing 'Sally Ann.' Musicians would come and others would wander off. There was a constant turnover, but you could come back an hour or two later and they'd still be playing 'Sally Ann.'"[99]

The Ham Hands went back to Galax in 1975 with altered membership. The band now was composed of Galloway playing violin, with Jim Ruth (clawhammer banjo) and Heinrich Leonhard (guitar).[100] In 1976, the Little Dixie Hoss Hair Pullers consisted of Galloway and Golan (fiddles), Ruth (clawhammer banjo), and Leonhard (guitar). "Our bread and butter was playing in octaves. We'd play in cross-tuning, and one [violin] would play high and one go low and then we'd switch off. Sometimes we'd play half one way and then the other. These were basic tunes (pentatonic scale) and we were pretty loose and fluid." Golan and Galloway held their violins "down" on their chests, as some of the old-timers did (especially when posing for a photograph or calling a square dance).

Among the festivals and fiddlers' conventions the Hoss Hair Pullers took part in was the 1981 Tennessee state fiddle championships in Clarksville. This was an event typical of many in the South and Southeast, where there were many divisions of competition, including classes for both old-time bands and bluegrass bands, old-time as well as bluegrass banjo players, dancers, and more. As Jim Ruth recalls:

> Cathy Barton won the old-time banjo contest. Then she joined the Rebel Yellers stringband to help them place high in the band contest. Dave Para, myself, Spencer Galloway and Rob Golan played as The Little Dixie Hoss Hair Pullers. We did not make the second round. Golan and the Rebel Yellers were friends so Rob might have been slightly miffed they stole this great banjo player from our neck of the woods and bested his band. And I did not place in the banjo contest either. Pete McMahan won the senior fiddle title so between him and Cathy they made a good showing for Central Missouri musicians. It was a fun weekend we still talk about all these years later.[101]

Rob Golan

In 1974, Rob Golan came to the University of Missouri to study archaeology from Fairfax, Virginia, where he had been friends with Piedmont bluesman John Jackson. Though never entirely becoming a "Missouri fiddler," Rob knew Boone County's masters and developed a fondness for their waltzes that he has maintained ever since. Golan met Spencer Galloway and Jim Ruth, and they formed the Boone County Ham Hands, which became the Little Dixie Hoss Hair Pullers.[102] Golan visited Pete McMahan often and learned Pete's "Clark's Waltz" and "Waltz of Shannon," among other tunes. Galloway recalls that these became Golan's favorite contest waltzes and that "Rob placed sixth in the open division of the State Contest in, I think, 1980, largely on the strength of his waltzes."[103] After Golan left Columbia in 1981, the Little Dixie Hoss Hair Pullers became a trio—Galloway, violin; Jim Ruth, banjo; and Dave Para, guitar. Heinrich Leonhard often filled in for Para. Galloway remembers:

Without Rob, the "Pullers" soldiered on as a trio. But it just wasn't the same. Our trademark had been the double fiddles played in octaves. We played the Battleground Fiddlers Gathering successfully again in the mid-'80s and had a sort of reunion at the Big Muddy festival in the early '90s. I was probably a better fiddler by then, with the onus completely on me. But that was all. By this time, things were wearing thin. The hassle of taking off work and travelling three or four hundred miles for very little money was taking its toll. It had just ceased to be as much fun. The Hoss Hair Pullers, like so many other bands of the time, simply drifted into obscurity.[104]

Listen to track 4 on the companion CD to hear the Little Dixie Hoss Hair Pullers' version of "Jimmy Shank."

St. Louis was fertile ground for old-time fiddling and old-time string-band music, with groups such as the Original Mound City String Band, the Ill-Mo Boys, and the Missouri Corn Dodgers.[105] The Original Mound City String Band featured fiddler Kevin Kegin, banjoist Larry Sugarman, and Gail Heil on guitar, and they performed Missouri tunes as well as classics from 78s,[106] and they won fourth in the string-band division at the 1977 Tennessee state fiddle championships in Clarksville. The group disbanded when Sugarman entered medical school at the University of Missouri. Gail Heil later formed a duo with Bob Bovee.

The Missouri Corn Dodgers appeared at festivals and fiddlers' conventions. The members were Bob Abrams (violin, guitar, mandolin), Julia Hager (guitar, vocals), Jim Olin (Julia's husband, banjo, violin, vocals), and, on occasion, Steve Mote, all expert in the history behind their music.[107] They won first in the string-band division at the Second Annual Mid-Tennessee Old Time Fiddlers' Convention in Clarksville in 1972, and their 1975 LP, *The Missouri Corn Dodgers*, included tunes indicating immersion in old 78s, Appalachian music of the revival, and tunes picked up at festivals and fiddlers' conventions.[108] The Corn Dodgers often introduced tunes by stating catalog numbers of reissue LPs from which they learned the tunes—"Now we're gonna play a tune that we learned off of County record five-fourteen—*Hell Broke Loose in Georgia*."[109] Such was the popularity of reissues of 1920s and 1930s string-band 78s that the audience gives a knowing chuckle when they hear the catalog number. Mote played bowed cello on the album, just as bowed cello is on the original record from 1932. The *Corn Dodgers* album includes titles from Missouri fiddlers in Christeson's *Old-Time Fiddler's Repertory*, such as a medley of "Liverpool Hornpipe" and "Missouri Quickstep" (better known as "Rachel").[110] The group ceased with the death of Jim Olin in 1980. Today, Julia (Hager) Olin is executive director of the National Council for the Traditional Arts, and Bob Abrams is a luthier in New Hampshire, where he builds bouzoukis, citterns, and octave mandolins.

In Columbia, John Murdock and Charlie Walden rose to the top of the pack of young fiddlers in contests. Chris Brashear became immersed in bluegrass and jazz and recorded with Perfect Strangers and other bands.[111] Some who played fiddle were known more for performing on multiple instruments in folksinging groups (for example, Paul Fotsch with "Paul and Win") than for fiddling. Bob Hagan was drawn to bluegrass and country music and performed for the most part on mandolin and fiddle with the Rooster Creek Boys in Fulton on weekly KFAL-AM radio shows.

Paul Fotsch grew up in a Swiss German family in St. Louis. Paul first heard fiddle music in a square-dance class in elementary school. As a teenager, he played Kingston Trio songs. Paul came to Columbia in 1967 and graduated from the university with a forestry degree in 1971. After graduation, Fotsch bought a mandolin and began playing bluegrass, and a year later, "I acquired a fiddle and never looked back. I'm still drawn to Appalachian style string band music. Missouri fiddling's not bad."[112]

Paul and folksinger Win Grace (née Horner) of Columbia began performing together in 1974 as Paul and Win. A Columbia native, Win took her BA at Denison University in 1971 with a major in theater arts and minors in French and dance. Adding additional instrumentation to their performances, Paul began playing fiddle (in addition to mandolin and guitar), and Win played autoharp. Win added accordion in 1978. By the late seventies, Paul was playing fiddle in performances, with Win playing accordion, with the keyboard side playing the fiddle tune melody and the bass side providing chords and bass runs. Win comments on their penchant for playing what she describes as "Appalachian string band style of playing where all the instruments except possibly bass and guitar (although guitar can join in too) play the fiddle tune melodies simultaneously. I love the sound! Also, I confess that I am just not a backup player type of woman, could never be content with that role, so for that reason I could play lead and backup at the same time on the accordion, with fake fiddling on the keyboard side and fake bass runs and guitar chords on the bass side."[113]

Win and Paul married and had two daughters; Leela and Ellie became skilled dancers and musicians with abundant stage charisma. As the Grace Family, the quartet toured, recorded seven albums between 1984 and 2006, and appeared at festivals. Paul's festival style of fiddling was a good match for Win's accordion playing, Leela played old-time five-string banjo, and Ellie played mandolin.[114] The two girls performed clog dance routines and taught a variety of traditional dance and went to college and pursued separate paths in recording, songwriting, and entertainment. Ellie took up fiddling, received an MFA in dance from Smith College, and lives in Kansas City. Leela directs and teaches at the Rose City Folk School in Portland, Oregon.[115]

For the most part, in the later phase of the Folk Music Revival and string-band movement, it was young people who got involved, and eventually the music and heritage of an older generation of fiddlers were recognized and encouraged and found new audiences and fans. Young people wanted to learn from those they considered more authentic traditional players whose music appeared to be untainted by modernity—Taylor McBaine, Art Galbraith, Cyril Stinnett, Uncle Bunk Williams, Lee Stoneking. Upon understanding the scope of the old-timers' styles, repertoires, and personal histories, most of the colorful elders who had seemed to the youngsters to be rather unsophisticated and musically primitive turned out to be educated, sophisticated, knowledgeable about other musical traditions, and capable of spinning out all sorts of stereotype-busting music, from Sousa marches to ragtime tunes, Tin Pan Alley

Paul Fotsch and Win Grace (née Horner), ca. 1980, Boone County. (Photo by Walter Bargen; courtesy of Win Grace)

hits, and parlor piano songs, with as much enthusiasm and skill as they spun out the square-dance breakdowns and waltzes so loved by the collectors. Time and experience teach the scholar as well as the student that the fiddler's world is rich and complex, once we take time to listen and learn.

Fiddlers came forward not only because of the young people's interest in hearing and learning from senior players, but also because of fiddlers' associations, contests, festivals, and opportunities presented by arts council programs and festivals that proliferated in the sixties and seventies and well into the eighties. Folk-music aficionados and scholars and collectors did their work well. The spirit of the revival years flourishes today among younger generations of fiddlers and banjo pickers and among relatively recent genres of music making such as the singer-songwriter. Another new but connected community of singers and instrumentalists has evolved in recent decades in cyberspace and another new community with the home-school movement.

In some ways, the Folk Music Revival is over. As Julie Henigan notes, the scaffolding that supported folk music as a viable entity in the music world (and business) is no longer as strong; there is less opportunity to find and learn directly from old-timers, and, with that loss, there is less opportunity for young people to "immerse themselves not only in the music but the culture that surrounded the old-time tradition."[116]

It is hard for a learner to perceive whether a certain YouTube performance of "Billy in the Low Ground" is genuine traditional music. The pearls of traditional music that people worked so hard to find and learn in 1965 or 1975 are now a digitized ocean of immeasurable volume, shepherded if not owned on someone's computer or Internet entity. The lack of context on most Internet sites and in YouTube videos is troubling, just as it was in the 1960s when someone handed us a tape of tunes with nothing about the musicians or tunes; in my opinion, it is important and relevant that we learn and think about the cultural and historical backgrounds from which music springs—the who, what, when, where, how, and why.

Pete McMahan (*left*) and Taylor McBaine pose while warming up for a fiddle contest, 1990. As Marc Drye said to me, this is "a photo that captures them both perfectly. Even their hats are perfect. The cap for Pete, and the town hat for Taylor." (Photographer unknown; print courtesy of Sarah McMahan)

Pete & Taylor, Two among the Masters 3

Fiddling makes me feel *real* well. Boy, I'm telling you. And when I see someone I *helped* a little bit enjoy it—that makes me *happy*.

—Taylor McBaine, *Country Missouri Fiddling*

The first time I heard Taylor McBaine, I thought he was the best fiddler I ever heard. He was *awesome* when he was younger. He had *drive*. He was a hornpipe fiddler. He played just as smooth as butter.

—Travis Inman, 2019

Taylor McBaine never lost the excitement of learning, and his generosity and friendly teaching style made him a sought-after "old-timer." His style was representative of the hard-driving, precise style in the Little Dixie region that he learned as a child from mentors and colleagues such as Daniel Boone Jones and Cleo Persinger. As Taylor said, "Fiddling—that's my pan of berries!"

McBaine was perhaps the most influential of older fiddlers who mentored the youngsters at the Chez, happily guiding them into the complex world of Missouri old-time fiddling. His style defined the Little Dixie fiddling he learned as a child in the early 1900s. McBaine played backup guitar and piano and could take a turn as accompanist; he thought fiddlers should also be able to accompany other fiddlers (a tradition that needs emphasis today) and took time to share backup-guitar technique with youngsters such as Polly Pastoret, Dave Para, and Heinrich Leonhard.

McBaine was born in a log cabin in the Brown's Station rural community north of Columbia, not far from the Boonslick Trail that had brought his ancestors from Kentucky in the early 1800s. Some family members favor the pronunciation "mack BAYN," but the more common pronunciation "mick BAYN" is also used.[1] Generally old-stock American and Scotch-Irish, like many Missourians, McBaine also had some Native American blood, in his case Cherokee.[2] His father, Henry Lee McBaine, was a coal miner. His mother, Annie Lee Medley Woodsmall McBaine, kept a garden and reared five children. On the east side of the home was Uncle Sherd Davis's log house, on the other side Uncle Richard's. On the east and north were the farms of the fiddling Morris brothers, Ernie, Dave, and George.

McBaine learned to play violin as a child from his father, Henry Lee McBaine, and his uncles Frank and Richard McBaine—especially Richard. The children were encouraged to sing and play instruments. As a child still crawling on the floor, Taylor was given a violin by his uncle Richard McBaine, and Taylor dragged the violin around and treated it as other children treated teddy bears.[3] By five, he was fiddling his father's and uncle's tunes, such as "Getting Upstairs with the Monkeys,"[4]

"Boatsman," "Miss McCloud's Reel" (a.k.a. "Take a Chaw Tobacco, Uncle John," "Uncle Joe"), "Run Boy Run," and "Buckeye Reel" ("Buckley's Reel"). He often spoke of how, in the stillness of evenings, his father and Uncle Richard would sit on their porches (Richard's farm was adjacent), and Taylor could hear them "talk to each other with their fiddles," by playing tunes back and forth.

At five McBaine was performing at Wayne Allen's music store on Tenth Street in Columbia. Allen specialized in pianos and built guitars of his own design from spruce soundboards from derelict upright pianos.[5] Allen would perch McBaine on a small red chair on top of a grand-piano lid in the front window, and "I'd sit there sawing away!"[6] In 1917, the family moved to Columbia, and, as a teenager in the mid-1920s, McBaine began playing at church services (the family was Methodist), schoolhouse pie suppers, and dances with guitarist and violinist Alfred Rice, who lived a few miles from the McBaine farm and played fiddle in jam sessions in the area. Rice helped Taylor to develop a classical-like bow grip and use the length of the bow in long, smooth strokes.

Taylor played his first dance for pay, with his own band, at the Happy Holler restaurant and dance hall (later known as Moon Valley) in Columbia in the mid-1920s, heyday of the Jazz Age and social dancing. Happy Holler was frequented by the range of citizenry, from college kids and flappers to farmers, coal miners, and the town's upper crust; Taylor enjoyed the scene. "McBaine's band" usually included a guitar, tenor banjo, and piano, familiar for the time in Missouri.[7] A snare drum or a small drum set was sometimes included; the "round dance" and waltz couples did not notice the drums, but square dancers often complained.

Taylor McBaine, 1989. (Photo by Julie Youmans, Missouri Cultural Heritage Center)

At house dances ("splinter kickers"),

> They just stacked all the furniture in one room. They'd empty up usually two rooms. Most all the houses had a double door or a sliding door that slides in the wall. It was a big wide door—and that would make a big dance room. So we'd sit in the middle of the big wide door. And there we'd sit and play, and they'd dance in those two rooms. A lot of people had these dances in order to make a little money. They [guests] didn't have to pay to get in, but they'd have to pay if they danced. If you gave a dance at your home, you or someone of your family would run the floor [supervise the dancing and collect money from dancers]. I remember they gave around a quarter [in the 1920s]. Then you danced and if you wanted to dance a waltz or something else, they'd play two or three waltzes during the evening and they were free. Everybody did square dancing then. The host provided late evening "supper" of sandwiches and drinks. Many people in Columbia had dances at that time. People just wanted to kick up their heels, you might say.[8]

Taylor did not attend high school. Taylor married Mildred Neal in 1933, and he set the violin aside when they began raising their two children. His first paid work was truck farming in about 1933, making $4 a week for Ira Walls, who provided garden produce to markets and restaurants. After two years, McBaine needed more income and looked for a new job. Times were hard in the midst of the Great Depression.

McBaine found work as a lasting machine operator at the Hamilton-Brown Shoe Factory, paying enough to build to a house. When the factory had to lay off workers, McBaine recalled going to the county courthouse when the Works Progress Administration started hiring, to see if he could get work. The WPA administrator selected men and sent them to work sites for two or three days' wages. Taylor's mother had bought him a new white shirt, leather jacket, and dress trousers for Christmas, and he wore them to the courthouse, hoping to impress the WPA that he was a proper and reliable young man. He needed a job but did not appear "raggedy." McBaine sat in the hallway and was passed over repeatedly. He finally asked the "boss man" why his name was not called. The boss said, "Heck, look at you, you don't need no job, you're doing fine!" Taylor told the man, "You're right about that, I don't need no job if *that's* how it's gonna be." The shoe factory eventually reopened, and McBaine went back to work, until it closed permanently in 1939. He then worked at Neal's coal mine, a drift-type "deep mine" where McBaine ran equipment as a "top man" outside the shaft, happy not to be working underground.[9]

While working at the mine, in 1939 McBaine found his real career. The university was hiring, and he went to "the hiring place" and, not seeing anyone in charge, sat until someone noticed him. Eventually, a man came in and surveyed the group of men, looked at Taylor, and asked him if he knew anything about electricity. Taylor said, "Heck no, but I can learn!" McBaine stared that day, earning around $12 a week; when he retired thirty-five years later in 1975, he was earning $25,000 a year. "I loved the University. That was my life."

McBaine won his first fiddle contest at fifteen in 1925, upstairs in the Lupus general store, across the Missouri River west of Columbia: his prize, a new pair of overalls. But from the late 1930s until the late 1960s, McBaine was busy making a living, helping rear a family, and only rarely could go to contests. McBaine returned to contests at the insistence of Cleo Persinger and Pete McMahan. In 1965 or 1967, Taylor happened to see Pete (recently returned from several years in Arizona) in a hardware store, and Pete urged him to come to a fiddle contest he was organizing at a chili supper at the high school in Harrisburg. Taylor told Pete he did not have a violin, and Pete said, "You can borrow mine."[10] He agreed to drive to Harrisburg and give it a whirl; with McMahan's violin, McBaine won the contest, $50 cash and a trophy.[11]

Through the ensuing years, McBaine was a consistent top finisher in contests large and small, tackling big stages with the same zest as a local contest at a strip mall or old settlers reunion. McBaine did not travel to big competitions in distant locations.

"I appreciate it when I win. But I really go to have a good time. And I think most of the fiddlers feel that way. Because, well—you see your friends. You play with eight or ten guys, you know, and that's a lot of fiddlin'. And those jam sessions [before and after contests], that's where the fiddlers really have their good times. When the *blood* starts is when they get on *stage*, you know, to play, 'cause you got to satisfy the *judges* then."[12] McBaine disliked the politics of contests and jealousies that can cloud the fun, and he disliked increased tempos at which square-dance tunes were often played. At a jam session with Wayne Crane: "Boy, this contest fiddling will ruin you, y'know, I can tell you that. Because you don't play nothing but contest music. [You] play too fast."[13] On another occasion, he spoke about how a fiddler with the skills to rise to the peak of the totem pole may lose friends by doing so; if you win too often, "Pretty soon people will start hating you."[14]

McBaine enjoyed visiting and often played at retirement centers, rest homes, and hospitals, as well as countless sessions, election-year picnics, and wedding receptions. His grin and raspy voice were well known, and he could get nursing-home residents out of seats and wheelchairs and dancing, albeit haltingly, to "Five Foot Two" and "Four Leaf Clover." Taylor invented generic band names, such as the Down Home Boys,[15] but often his appearances were billed as "Taylor McBaine and Friends."

In the 1970s, McBaine was a fixture at the Chez coffeehouse, meeting young musicians and sharing music. Living in or near Columbia meant that fiddlers could be the subject of stories by students in journalism classes and other courses, and McBaine appeared regularly in the *Columbia Missourian* (produced by the journalism school), the *Maneater* (the university's student paper), and the *Columbia Daily Tribune*.[16]

Several of his colleagues produced LPs in the 1970s, but McBaine did not feel that he merited his own "record." But, persuaded by Charlie Walden, he relented in 1987 when the Missouri State Old Time Fiddlers Association issued *Boone County Fiddler* with guitar backup by John G. Stewart and bass by Forrest Rose, two of the region's best musicians who were fans and friends of Taylor's. McBaine was in declining health and grew weary with the recording session, but his fiddling is well represented on this recording and he was proud of it.

McBaine provided "Valley Forge" / "Grey Eagle" for Cathy Barton and Dave Para's 1992 *Ballad of the Boonslick*[17] and was featured at festivals from Massachusetts to California, typically performing with Barton and Para.[18] In 1992, McBaine opened the Big Muddy Folk Festival in Boonville with backup by his "kids" Cathy and Dave, and Taylor performed with them on *Pepper and Friends* TV shows. Lois Gandt, with help from Cathy Barton, produced videotapes for the educational television service at the university, *Taylor McBaine: Country Missouri Fiddling* and *Ballads, Bones and Fiddle Tunes*.[19] Charlie Walden has posted videos of a number of McBaine's fiddle contest appearances on YouTube, and in 2019 Walden made available a digital album from a 1975 jam session called *Fiddlin' 75*.[20]

Taylor McBaine with Cathy Barton and Dave Para at an annual Arrow Rock crafts festival in 1983. (Photo by Sam Griffin, *Columbia Missourian*)

Student musicians and fans beat a path to Taylor's door, and he would sometimes cook a meal for them. He loved to cook and had some unusual old recipes, such as squirrel heads (brains) and gravy. One of the university students, Chris Germain, liked the idea of squirrel heads and gravy so much that he made up a fiddle tune to honor the dish—"Squirrel Heads and Gravy."[21]

Taylor McBaine in his bedroom, where he practiced, ca. 1975. Here he plays along with a tape recording—a familiar activity for musicians for enjoyment as well learning and practice. He was an ear musician, but he learned from the page when he wanted to sort out a tune. (Photo by Ann Yow, University of Missouri photojournalism graduate student; courtesy of Taylor McBaine)

Many violins passed through Taylor McBaine's parlor. He enjoyed the occasional swap and the lore of violins and violin makers. He had two favorites, an Amati-model German-shop violin from Alfred Rice and a 1912 American violin supposedly made by an Ohio luthier named Brussard (or Broussard) that he bought from luthier Jack Roberts and that had belonged to a local fiddler Pee Wee Shocks. The Amati was his "number one." As told and retold by McBaine, he and his friend Rice had driven down to Rolla to survey violins on offer at Henry Thompson's music store. Thompson was a well-known fiddler, classical violinist, and contest fiddler and judge, and he was considered by some to be a "sharp trader." Rice and McBaine took their favorite violins along, for comparison with what the shop had on display and for the jam session that often ensued on such visits. Thompson gave Rice's Amati a once-over inspection, liked what he saw, and offered Rice a large sum of money for it. "Alfred, name your price." Rice said no. Thompson doubled his offer. Rice said he'd think about it. "Okay, Alfred, but I want that fiddle." On the drive back to Columbia, sensing that the Amati was a great violin, McBaine asked Rice if he'd take $50 for it. Rice said, "No, Taylor, but I'd take *sixty!*"—and the Amati went home with Taylor.

What makes a good fiddle? "Ease of playing. It's like a pair of shoes—if it don't fit you, you aren't going to play it very well."[22] Each of McBaine's violins was loud, just as violins played by McMahan and Persinger, with volume enough to be heard in the midst of a dance or from a stage in the days before modern amplification.

Taylor McBaine, Mentor

McBaine's personality made him an ideal teacher. He was from the "patient and supportive" school of instruction. He taught in the Traditional Arts Apprenticeship Program (1984–85), with Julie Carton from Marshall and Barbara Dutton of Columbia and with adult students Steve Young of Harrisburg (1991–92) and Marc Drye of Columbia (1992–93, 1993–94). Being labeled a "master fiddler" amused Taylor, but he took pride in the recognition and respect that came with the limelight. "I'm not a teacher, but I help a lot of people—and I can teach you technique."[23]

McBaine spent many evenings at the Youngs' home near Harrisburg, where there would be a sumptuous dinner, visiting, and music, with Steve, Taylor's fiddle student, and Debbie at her piano. Taylor sometimes asked Debbie to play a tune he wanted to learn, pulled from one of Steve's tune books. Debbie was adept at playing old-time piano backup and was Delia White's piano apprentice in TAAP in 1993–94. Steve and Debbie were active at square dances, with Steve a caller and Debbie often part of the band. Steve refurbished a portable reed organ like the one Christeson played in the 1940s, and Debbie played the instrument in jam sessions. The Youngs took the organ to a 1993 fiddle contest in Fulton, where Taylor was to compete; the contest was billed as a "traditional" contest, and they thought reed organ would be a nice accompaniment, as so often in former times. Debbie backed Taylor and the audience enjoyed the music, but a Columbia newspaper columnist made light of the "wheezy" old pump organ and its player; that was Debbie's first and last fiddle contest.

The ineffable thing called "drive" is important. According to McBaine:

> I like to put *drive* in whatever I'm playing on the fiddle. If I can hear it before I play it. That's what you've gotta do, because if you play by ear, you got to know what's going to come out of there before it gets there. Now you can take a violinist who plays violin real well. And give him a hornpipe out of a hornpipe book and he'll play it *just exactly* like it's written. But an *ear musician* [who would] hear him play it—first thing you know, when the ear musician plays it there's some *feeling* going there. You gotta have *drive* and no one can put *drive* on a piece of paper.[24]

McBaine was keenly interested in bowing. He had known many fiddlers who had "good notions" about how to play fiddle but never figured out how to "handle" the bow, the fiddler's handwriting. "You can take a cheap fiddle and a good bow and make pretty good music. But you take a good fiddle and a *cheap* bow, and you can't do very well."[25] He disliked "choppy, messy" bowing. He wanted it smooth. He often asked pupils to play a basic, solid waltz, such as "'Over the Waves,' a good tune to get your bowing straightened out. Start out about eight inches from your frog." He was careful about up bows and down bows and avoided putting in too many notes. "Get those little, short licks *out.* Get those two pickup notes with one quarter bow. Always start with an up bow. Keep the bow down on the strings, don't lift it up. Whenever you lift the bow up, you get an unwanted note." "Keep that bow going 'round and 'round, like that." "The important part of your bow is from the middle on up." "Most tunes end on a down bow." "If you have your bow out there waving at the stars, it doesn't look as good to the judges. That's part of the 'presentation' of your tune."

McBaine understood that fiddlers should develop their own styles. "Once you get the foundation, it doesn't make any difference—you're playing *your style.* Who am I to change your style, see. You don't want to play like *me*, see, you want to play like *you.* If you try to play after [like] everybody, pretty soon you can't play anything well."[26] He taught by the "one note, one bow" method: one note for each bow stroke helps one pull a clean, distinct melody; more elaborate bowings come later. To help develop smooth bowing, tuck a tennis ball or a Ping-Pong ball under your right arm (bowing arm) and practice. This helps you learn to keep your arm down and keep your shoulder steady and helps develop limber arm and wrist movement.[27]

McBaine was adamant about learning to use the little finger of the noting hand to reach high notes as well as to make "primes" (two strings bowed together, the lower string fingered in exact tune with the open string above it). Proper use of the little finger distinguished a competent and knowledgeable player, and playing primes is characteristic of the style that McBaine mastered and taught.

McBaine generally disliked putting "caps" (ending flourishes) on tunes but advised adding one in situations where you feel you have made mistakes. A cap helps resolve and clear up a tune's presentation; when he used one, he preferred the time-honored "shave and a haircut—two bits." McBaine's version was "Match in the gas tank—boom boom!"

Taylor played "The Flower Song" (in F) as a bowing exercise, a light classical piece that involves elaborate, precise bowing, with string crossings and arpeggios. He often used it as a teaching tune with students (some of whom had classical training). He also enjoyed playing light classical and popular music; Dvořák's "Humoresque" was a favorite, memorized from radio and records (and probably from his friend Alfred Rice).[28] In addition, he recommended an exercise in which the player draws the bow in the key of G from low to high, "like going up the stairs on a piano."

McBaine enjoyed elaborate hornpipes, two-steps, and playing in the flat keys of F, B-flat, and E-flat. His style was marked by accent and drive honed from years playing for square dancers at house parties. He played loud and full-speed ahead.[29] A penciled scrap of paper ("cheat sheet") in his fiddle box dated 1992 named some favorite tunes, "Billy in the Low Ground," "Sugar in the Gourd," "Liverpool Hornpipe," "Whisky before Breakfast," "Grey Eagle," "Forked Deer" (pronounced "FOR-kid deer"), "Marmaduke's Hornpipe," "Wake Up Susie," "Ragtime Annie" (with the third part in G), "Mississippi Sawyer," "Hooker's Hornpipe," "Red Fox Waltz," "Rose of Sharon," "Bonaparte's Retreat," "Down Yonder," "Red Wing," "Golden Slippers," and "Missouri Waltz."[30] Titles in a typical set at contests in the late 1980s and early 1990s were "Dance around Molly," "Fifty Year Ago Waltz," and "Jack of Diamonds." His smooth bowing and authority were especially impressive in waltzes.[31]

Marc Drye was Taylor McBaine's last student. A Polaroid photo of Marc and Taylor at McBaine's home, ca. 1993. In short order, Drye began giving fiddle lessons to beginners. (Photo by Nancy Jones; courtesy of Marc Drye)

Marc Drye

A devoted pupil, Drye taught American history at Mineral Area College in Park Hills for many years and grew up on the family cattle farm near Ozark, Missouri. Marc's great-grandfather was William McHenry, a fiddler who traveled with the family vaudeville show. "I never heard my great grandpa or other relatives play the fiddle because they were long gone. Therefore, I had to find the names of these old tunes by talking to the remaining relatives. Then I listened to those tunes as played by Taylor McBaine and others. I was originally drawn to learning the fiddle because I had always heard that my great-grandpa who had the minstrel show was a great fiddler." When Marc decided to learn, his mother found an old Klotz (Kloz) in the newspaper want ads. "No one knew at the time that it was a Klotz or that it was possibly made in the 1840s. John Griffin discovered that when he took my violin apart to restore it."[32]

During his apprenticeships with McBaine, Marc drove him to contests, sessions, county fairs, and festivals and kept a journal about his experiences. Marc was completing his second apprenticeship when McBaine died in May 1994.[33]

Drye wrote about one of his rambles with McBaine in March 1993, not long after Taylor's wife died. Taylor had visibly declined, and his health, stamina, and fiddling capacities were waning.

Taylor Visits Hallsville Church

When I go over to Taylor's house I have to knock loudly on the door because sometimes he is asleep. That is what I did today, but no Taylor showed up right away. I knocked again and waited and pretty soon the door swung open and there was Taylor. His hair was kind of sticking up and he said, "I was watching the Andy Griffith Show!" (Which means he fell asleep.)

It didn't take Taylor long, however, to get out his fiddle. He moved the newspapers off the wooden chair for me to sit on and he sat on the piano stool. He had on his navy-blue suit pants, brown house shoes, a white long-sleeved shirt, and his bright red suspenders. Those red suspenders are his trademark. He will say to people, "Know why I wear *red* suspenders?" And they'll say, "No," and he will say, "Well to hold up my pants of course!"

The first thing Taylor asked me today was another standard question of his, "Are you in tune?"

"I think so," I said, but I kind of doubted it.

Both of us got our "A" tuning forks out, and tapped them, and listened to the "A strings. Taylor tapped his tuning fork on the piano stool and I tapped mine on my knee.

"They misplaced me wrong at Boonville," Taylor said all of a sudden.

"What did you say?" I asked.

"Judges. I had a strike against me cause Pete played ahead of me, and you don't want two good fiddlers playing back to back."

Taylor was talking about the fiddle contest that we went to last week at Boonville. Taylor's main competitor, Pete McMahan, played right before Taylor played. Pete is a good friend of Taylor's, but Taylor always hates to lose a fiddle contest. He was the "champion fiddler" at the State Fair one year.

We talked about the contest some more, and Taylor said, "Whenever you get up there to play at a contest, you just have to say to yourself, 'I'm playin' as good as anyone else out here today,' and sometimes you are."

Taylor was very happy tonight, in general, even though he got "misplaced" at Boonville. We played several tunes. I played what I could of "Boil the Cabbage Down," and Taylor said, "Yeah, you know that." Then he played a new part to the tune and said, "That's an F note," and he pointed to my finger with his fiddle bow to show me which finger I should be pressing down.

"Not that one!" he said, "I'm going to cut that finger off if you don't stop using it!" Just kidding me.

Pretty soon Taylor said, "Well, if we're going to that church, we better get started."

I didn't know where Taylor was talking about going, but that was usual for us. We would drive around and visit with people whether they wanted to be visited with or not.

Taylor said, "Let's go see Steve and Debbie. They'll be surprised to see us 'cause I didn't tell them we was coming out there."

Today is Wednesday, so Steve and Debbie Young had choir practice at the Hallsville Baptist Church, which is only about twenty miles north of Columbia on Route B. Like many other drives that Taylor and I have taken, it began raining as we drove off in the dark.

The Hallsville church is one of those modern churches that has the same look as a ranch-style house. It's a one-story, red-brick, layout with winding halls. I turned my old Buick into the parking lot and parked up close to the door as Taylor advised. Taylor hopped right out into the rain, almost before the car was stopped, without his hat or coat, and made a beeline for the door. I could hear him say, "Wooooooooooo" as puddles of cold water went over the tops of his shoes. March hadn't warmed up much yet.

As I entered the church, I wondered if I should have changed out of my overalls. That's my uniform as an equipment operator for the City of Columbia. Just then I spotted Taylor taking a right turn down one of those winding church hallways.

Steve and Debbie Young are a nice couple that have a little daughter named Sarah. Steve is learning to play the fiddle too. We started talking about fiddling, but Taylor wasn't interested. He was talking to the little kids, kindergarteners, who had made toy fishing poles and paper fish. Those children really gathered around Taylor. A little boy and a little girl showed their fish to Taylor and he helped them put the fish on their lines with paperclips.

Soon the choir director herded everybody into the sanctuary, and Taylor and I went along. The "stage" of that church was interesting. They had built fake rocks for the program they were practicing. Maybe the singers were supposed to be singing by the tomb of Jesus. Easter is around the corner.

After a while, Taylor was ready to go, so we slipped out and headed home. The old Buick rolled along with a dependable hum and the rain was letting up. Taylor was smiling.

I asked Taylor one of my fiddle questions, "Did you ever play a tune called 'Bully of the Town'?"

"Oh yeah," he said, "I played it at a lotta dances. That bully of the town! A man gets off a train. He's lookin' for that bully of the town. But the bully of the town ain't nowhere to be found. I'm lookin' for that bully of the town."[34]

Listen to track 5 on the companion CD to hear Taylor McBaine's version of "Rachel."

Pete McMahan. (Photo by David Rees, *Columbia Daily-Tribune*, September 8, 1981; courtesy of Spencer Galloway)

Pete McMahan

"My first memory of Pete McMahan was almost 20 years ago outside the Missouri State Fiddle Contest. A group of younger fiddlers was gathered in the parking lot amid empty fiddle cases and whiskey bottles. This group had recently emerged from the building where the contest was held and an effort was being made to work ourselves into a competitive fiddling frenzy. We knew what we were up against—we had just heard Pete play. After struggling through several tunes, one of the group lowered his fiddle in disgust saying, 'It's no use, he can't be beat,'" said John Griffin.[35] According to Spencer Galloway, "I'll tell you, the first time I stumbled into that hall, in Boonville, and heard Pete in there. God! That guy is so polished! So perfect! I still like Jake's fiddling better but, as far as just being just *on*, Pete was *something*."[36]

For some fifty years, Pete McMahan was the old-time fiddler par excellence in conserving and performing touches, the rolling, flowing, driving, old-time fiddle style many people associate with Missouri contest fiddling in one of its golden ages, the mid-1900s to 2000, the year he died.

The music of Pete McMahan (pronounced MACK-muh-han) was well regarded across the archipelago of regional styles in North America, from old-time square-dance breakdowns, church hymns, and folksongs to swing and big-band music, bluegrass, and his specialty, "dressed-up" tunes for the contest arena. Twenty years after his passing, fiddlers keep going back for inspiration to his four 1970s LPs (reissued on CD as *50 Old-Time Fiddle Gems*).[37]

Phil Nusbaum, Minnesota Arts Council folklorist, recalls, "I remember Pete, from my Iowa days, as a 'Missouri Fiddler,' code for a very good player, compared to the locals. In his case, the accolades were true. Like other Missouri players I encountered, he was able to play many types of tunes, and he was the boss of the tune when he was playing. In other words, he played the tune, the tune didn't play him. Also, he was in no hurry to finish a tune once he began playing it. Music, for him, was not a race to get the tune over with, but a means of expression. It is amazing that the distinction exists, but it does."[38]

McMahan's family was Ulster Scots (Scotch-Irish). He often remarked, "I am Irish, but I'm not an Irish fiddler. All I play is 'Irish Washerwoman.'"[39] His McMahan (a.k.a. McMahon) line in America began in 1734 when James and Susannah McMahan, Protestants from County Cavan in Ulster, arrived in the North Carolina colony from Cork on Ireland's south coast. James and Susannah McMahan brought seven children with them. Family members in next generations moved across the Blue Ridge into Kentucky or Tennessee and then farther west to Missouri and often farther west.

Most of the first settlements here were by British-background farmers from bluegrass Kentucky, middle Tennessee, and piedmont and tidewater areas of Virginia and the Carolinas, who, in some cases, brought enslaved people with them to work their hemp and tobacco holdings. Pete McMahan respected the African American fiddlers he heard at dances and jam sessions and over WOS-AM radio as a child, such as Bill

Katon, Ola Gathright, Bill Driver, and Howard Cave—descendants of slaves who had remained after the Civil War and emancipation to make homes in south Callaway County.[40]

The family farm was part of John Fox McMahan's land grant, in creek-cut forested hills interspersed with small prairies. Most families here had modest acreage and focused on cattle raising and did not engage in large-scale commercial crop production; better terrain and soil for agriculture are some twenty miles north.[41] During the Great Depression, economic crisis forced many subsistence farmers into poverty, and Pete's family was among them. Pete remembered the drought year of 1936, watching a farmer, tears running down his face, driving starving cattle into the Missouri River, hoping someone downriver would be able take them in. Pete and his siblings grew up hard and poor. At fifteen he found a job to help with family finances as a laborer in a limestone quarry at St. Charles. Small of stature, but strong, Pete was proud of being able to load more and heavier rocks than his fellow quarrymen.

Pete's mother, Dorothy, and several sisters played violin as well as guitar, and his sister Dorothy played backup guitar. All of Homer and Dorothy McMahan's eight children were jig dancers. His mother played reed organ and specialized in playing backup for fiddlers at dances and house parties. A large, jolly lady and a good dancer, Pete's mother was also a popular accompanist for fiddlers in the community. Pete was a solid guitar accompanist for fiddling and played tenor banjo as a young man. Pete did not chord the tenor banjo as most others did. Rather, he tuned the four-stringer like a violin and picked out melodies with a flat pick. He listened to radio programs with fiddle music, such as the Grand Ole Opry on WSM in Nashville, WOS in Jefferson City, and KFRU in Columbia.[42] He sang tenor in the Methodist church choir. He had a good singing voice and a memory for lyrics and songs of all sorts.

Pete spoke of long nights playing backup guitar for his older cousin Herman Boone, one of many descendants of Daniel Boone and his sons in this area, pioneers in exploration and settlement of eastern and central Missouri. Herman Boone fiddled at dances in places such as Crane's Store in Williamsburg, along US 40 in eastern Callaway County—the new highway that followed the course of the trail west established by the Boone pioneers. The tunes Herman played reflected the familiar dance repertoire, "Soldiers Joy," "Mississippi Sawyer," "Sugar in the Gourd," "Leather Britches," waltzes such as "Cowboy Waltz," "Peekaboo Waltz," "Goodnight Waltz," and waltzes from local fiddlers such as "Stars and Stripes Waltz" and "Crystal Stream Waltz" ("But not the way they play it now!").[43]

Earl Willis of Mineola knew Herman Boone well, and Willis took local fiddle tunes in his repertoire when he migrated to Oregon in the 1930s. "Herman Boone—he was a real fiddler—he was first cousin to Nolan—'course they're second cousins of mine. Herman was a very fine fiddler, but he never did play in contests. We got him to go one night to a county contest, and he played 'Wild Irish Rose.' Never heard it played any more beautiful in my life, and when he played it, you could-a heard a pin drop in that whole building. Naturally he got first prize. Naturally he did."[44]

McMahan spoke of the frustrations playing dance after dance. "Sometimes they'll get on a square dance and they'll just run you in the weeds." Elsewhere he stated, "A genuine old-time square dance—it was something to watch, they jig-danced to every step of it. It's hard work to play for a square dance . . . one set might last 15 minutes you know. You made a dollar or dollar and a half a night, playing from dark till daylight." He continued: "All they wanted was time. You could play 'Nearer My God to Thee' and if you played it in square dance time, they'd dance to it."[45]

Down in Little Dixie with Clark Atterberry

According to his great-nephew Harvie, Clark Atterberry "had the reputation of being one of the best fiddle players in that part of the county. And every one of them kids played some kind of music instrument, and he was the best one of the thirteen."[46]

In his formative years, Pete McMahan encountered two fiddlers whose music gave him the inspiration to learn. One was radio fiddler and champion in Columbia George Morris, whom Pete would meet when he moved to Columbia in 1937. But years before, the fiddler who first kindled Pete's imagination was a plug-tobacco-chewing south Callaway County farmer named Clark Atterberry.

Plat books locate Atterberry's farm of about eighty acres on a branch of Little Tavern Creek, a tributary of the Missouri River and a few miles northeast of Portland, near the Montgomery County line. The McMahan farm was just across the county line in Montgomery County, near a different branch of Little Tavern Creek.[47]

Allie Clark Atterberry went by "Clark," did not attend school, and apparently could not read or write. He lived on the farm and was a jack-of-all-trades. According to Harvie Atterberry, Clark and his eight brothers were "timber people" and made money by making and selling railroad ties; they felled massive white-oak trees in the forest with cross-cut saws, sawed out thick planks, and then hewed the planks into railroad ties with broad axes. They freighted the ties on horse and mule wagons several miles down to Portland, on the new railroad line that ran along the bottomland on the north edge of the Missouri River.[48] They sold the ties to the Missouri Kansas and Texas Railway for ten cents each, as the KATY was building a new track along the north side of the river from Kansas City east to St. Louis. The Atterberrys also derived cash income by such jobs as repairing harness, hauling crops to grain mills and railroad spurs, and mending and sharpening plows on their blacksmith forges at their farms. Clark Atterberry married Elizabeth Sieckmann, and their children were Golda Mae and Gerald (Butch) Atterberry.[49] Mrs. Atterberry's brother-in-law Bill Sieckmann was also a fiddler, and he and Clark enjoyed discussing and debating the fine points of fiddle music.

Atterberry performed on AM radio WOS in Jefferson City, some fifty miles away, on weekend evening broadcasts of live string-band music in the 1920s. Ray Moseley, whom Atterberry had taught to play guitar, was Atterberry's usual accompanist. Most of the dances Atterberry and Moseley played were held in barns around Portland and Readsville, and in the 1930s they played a dance somewhere in Callaway, Boone, Montgomery, or Cole County almost every Saturday night. Jack Drullinger (a.k.a. Drollinger) was the area's best square-dance caller and often called dances for Atterberry and Moseley.

Clark Atterberry with guitarist Ray Moseley, ca. 1965. (Courtesy of Charlie Walden)

Pete's parents encouraged their children to make music and were especially fond of the fiddle, which had long been entertainment in the family. From the McMahan house less than two miles away, Pete could hear "old man Atterberry"—who would have been thirty or thirty-five at the time—fiddling on the front porch in the evenings. Pete's first memory of dance music was Clark's fiddling, with Pete's mother providing rhythm on her reed organ. Clark's great-nephew Harvie Atterberry remembers that "Uncle Clark said he never played with nobody who could keep time like Pete's mother could" (and Pete recalled that Clark and his mother "danced beautifully together").[50] Watching Clark Atterberry and his mother playing music was a treasured memory for McMahan. "I wasn't over four or five when they started having those dances. I had an old gallon syrup bucket and I sat right down between that old man's legs and I stayed right there. And I didn't care if they stayed till six o'clock in the morning, I stayed right there and listened to him play."[51]

Pete learned fiddle on a three-quarter-size violin that his grandfather gave him. At six years old, Pete liked to sit in the kitchen on a chair, noodling out tunes. His feet did not reach the floor. He liked to practice with his eyes closed, and one day he lost his balance and fell, crashing to the floor—right on top of the violin, smashing it into "a hundred pieces." His mother and father forgave him, and Pete continued practicing with a violin one of his older sisters played in school and offered to share. Pete's first fiddle tunes and songs—he sang them if they had lyrics—were "Rye Whiskey" and the vaudeville silly song from Tin Pan Alley "Ta-ra-ra Boom De-ay."

Rye whisky, rye whisky, rye whisky I cry,
if I don't get a rye whisky, I surely will die.
Jack of diamonds, jack of diamonds, I know you of old,
you robbed my poor pockets of silver and gold.
If the ocean was whisky was and I was a duck,
I'd dive to the bottom and never come up.

I'll tune up my fiddle, I'll rosin my bow,
I'll make myself welcome, wherever I go.
Beef steak when I'm hungry, rye whisky when I'm dry,
if a tree don't fall on me, I'll live till I die.[52]

A bit later, Pete's first waltz was "Cowboy Waltz," a favorite in Missouri. Pete learned by ear and did not have formal violin lessons; he often said he would have benefited from violin lessons, but family finances made it impossible.

Clark Atterberry had two violins, a $7.95 German-shop violin ordered from a Sears Roebuck catalog and an old German-shop copy of a Stainer. McMahan recalled that Clark could make the cheap Sears Roebuck fiddle (which he carried in a flour sack) sound like the Stradivarius on which it was modeled and that it was the loudest fiddle he'd ever heard. Playing a "loud fiddle" was desirable when a fiddler would perform without amplification, endeavoring to be heard above square-dance calls, jig-dancing feet, and the general din of merrymaking. McMahan was fascinated by Atterberry, who could play fiddle at a dance and turn in his chair, shift the violin from under his chin, and visit with people while he kept right on playing.

Atterberry played some tunes and songs in an open violin tuning often called "discord" in this region (cross-tuning or scordatura). So young McMahan learned tunes in discord from Atterberry such as "Pretty Polly" and "Black Sally Goodin."[53]

Pete often spoke of dances in his childhood during the Jazz Age, Prohibition, and the Great Depression. Outlawed liquor and other intoxicants, drawn and distilled from field, orchard, and garden, seemed to be everywhere. Most of it was homemade corn whiskey in mason jars or stoneware jugs and known by various names—poteen, white lightning, moonshine, white liquor—and typically sold quietly behind dance halls. Some people made peach brandy, and some German-speaking families made wine. Corn liquor, peach brandy, and homemade wine generally went for twenty-five cents a jar or bottle. Prohibition law did not stop the river of whiskey, wine, and beer. If anything, the law's quixotic revenue enforcement officers, who tried to stop the making and distribution of the outlawed alcoholic beverages, just added to the allure of illicit drink. Dance halls and speakeasies flourished. Booze, fistfights, scuffles, and phone calls to the sheriff's office were as much a part of dance halls and honky-tonks as the cornmeal scattered on the dance floor and the haze of cigarette smoke.[54]

Homer McMahan was a hardworking farmer, a harsh parent, and an alcoholic.[55] Pete and his older brother Frank (who went by "Jim") would pilfer whiskey from their father's cupboard and get drunk. Pete and Frank became notorious as a team of scrappers in tavern brawls, which they often instigated. Pete continued drinking through his growing years and through service in World War II. His experiences in combat during the war added weight on a young man already drinking too much. Alcoholism cost Pete dearly, but eventually he won the struggle with addiction and went on to family life, a stable and respectable working career, and recognition as a teacher and champion old-time fiddler.

Clark Atterberry spent his last three years in a nursing home, suffering from Alzheimer's disease. In 1970, shortly before Clark died, Pete went to pay his respects. Clark told Pete that he disliked the fact that Pete renamed an old waltz he taught Pete forty years before—"Clark's Waltz." It was one of Atterberry's favorite tunes, but Atterberry would play it without mentioning its title. Pete loved the tune and called it "Clark's Waltz" in the custom of remembering tunes with lost titles by naming them in honor of the person from whom they are learned.[56] The waltz is a local one that Atterberry learned from a fiddler named Crews or Kruse.

> "Clark's Waltz?" Uncle Clark learned it from a man named Crews.
>
> Marshall: How do you spell that?
>
> Atterberry: Don't ask *me*. Well, that's what Uncle Clark called it, "Crews Waltz," because he didn't remember the *name* of it, or the guy never did tell him. Way I understood it, when he was young, he was learning to play, slippin' around and standing behind [fiddlers]. They had a lot of *platform* dances, and what-not, and he'd stand right behind the musicians, or sit right behind 'em and *listen*. In fact, a lot of the tunes that learned to *play* and did play, he learned from an old black man [Bill Katon]. He learned a lot of them tunes sittin' behind Bill Katon. He couldn't write 'em down because he couldn't read or write, so he just done it by *memory*.[57]

On his last visit to see Clark Atterberry, as Clark was near death, he asked Pete to play a tune. After Pete played something, Clark said: "Pete, you play just like I do," and Pete replied, "'I should, you gave me the inspiration to learn to play.' He was a fine old man."[58]

Pete's First Contest, and Moving to Columbia

In 1934 at fifteen, McMahan entered his first contest. He heard about the competition to be held in a theater in St. Charles (where he was working in the stone quarry). At his older sister Dorothy's urging, Pete signed up and won first place. The prize was a bushel of groceries.

In the late 1930s (Pete remembered the year as 1937, 1938, and 1939), he left the farm and moved some fifty miles northwest to Columbia, a growing regional hub at the intersection of US 40 and US 63, the college town and seat of Boone County. There were jobs there, and he went to work for twelve dollars a week as a carpenter for Ed Swearingen, whose firm erected prefabricated tract houses. In Columbia, a galaxy of fiddlers, styles, and tunes greeted Pete. "I never saw so many *good* fiddlers." He began playing dances, competing in contests, and picking up skills, experience, and repertoire. He polished complex hornpipes and reels in F and B-flat he learned from Cleo Persinger, Ed Tharp, Aaron Oliver, brothers Jones and Buck Cuno, Emmett Heath, Jim Gilmore, Jim Gilpin, Nolan Boone, Taylor McBaine, Charlie Cook, and brothers Dave and George Morris.

Pete was particularly impressed with and challenged by George Morris. Morris had a KFRU radio show with his New Blue Goose String Band and was a proud coon hunter and "loafer" who liked whiskey. Pete marveled that George managed to do nothing other than play the fiddle and go hunting, leaving others to work the old family farm north of Columbia. Pete considered George Morris to be the best player in this community of particularly strong players. Morris could present demanding melodies with smooth, driving bowing and perfect double-stops in upper positions on the violin. "That old man could play hornpipes running out his ears in B-flat." In this part of Missouri, playing in the flat keys of F and B-flat was admired, so Pete became "a B-flat fiddler." The predilection for flat keys was not exclusive to the Little Dixie region, but concentrated there, in part due to the relatively higher rate of violin knowledge and musical literacy in and around the many college and university towns in central Missouri.

In Morris's youth in the 1920s, 1930s, and 1940s, he butted heads in contests with Daniel Boone Jones, Doc Hill, Ed Tharp, Aaron Oliver, and other top players. Taylor McBaine and Jake Hockemeyer used to say, "If George doesn't win, it's crooked" and "George could play you anything you asked him to play." Actually, Morris lost regularly to the lesser-known Ed Tharp in the 1940s and 1950s, and some considered Tharp the superior player. And like Morris and McMahan, Tharp and others enjoyed playing old favorite "semipopular" tunes for the two-steps (fox-trots) at dances, such as "My Dear," "The Sheik of Araby," and "Twelfth Street Rag."[59]

World War II

In December 1941, Pete was twenty-one and working at a Sheffield Steel plant in Kansas City when the Japanese air service made the surprise attack on the US naval base at Pearl Harbor. For a while, Pete continued working at the plant (steel production was a priority in the war effort) but was drafted into the Army in 1943. He was sent to Fort Meade, Maryland, for training and then boarded a troop ship to North Africa for the Allies' campaign to reverse German army successes there. He was part of the Allied invasion of Sicily and continued on to Italy, and he often remarked, "I walked the length of Italy carrying a full field pack."

One of Pete's narratives focused on violins found by American soldiers after a battle with German forces. Remembered at different times with different details, after the Germans retreated, troops in his unit rummaged through an abandoned "castle," picking up souvenirs, and found violins. Pete obtained two (or perhaps three) of them. One of the violins was good quality, and Pete played it in country-music shows and dances during breaks as the war was ending. At the end, in May 1945, Pete was in the Alps serving guard duty on the Austrian-Italian border; his unit was charged with "catching Nazis." Pete volunteered to stay in Italy another six months in order to continue fiddling in a dance band of GIs entertaining Allied troops. What happened to the fiddles? Pete recalled bringing them home and selling them in Columbia; in another variation, Pete sold one of the violins to a Nebraska fiddler at a contest in Yankton, South Dakota.

Sergeant Pete McMahan, US Army, 1945. Among his decorations was the Combat Infantry Badge with two battle stars. (Courtesy of Sarah McMahan)

At war's end, McMahan became friends with an impoverished family in an Alpine village. Each day Pete carried half of his hot meal to the gate of his compound and handed it to the family's nine-year-old daughter. At the request of the child's mother, Pete submitted Army paperwork to adopt the child, but the request was denied. As he was boarding a troop train to leave the village in the summer of 1945, to show their affection, the child's mother presented Pete with a baked chicken—the family's last chicken—for the journey. Back in the States at Newport News, Virginia, Pete was given a forty-five-day furlough before reporting to his final period of duty (serving temporarily as a cook) at Camp Carson, Colorado. McMahan was discharged November 12, 1945.

On furlough in Columbia in the summer of 1945, McMahan won his first big fiddle contest, held at the armory downtown. Pete remembered how good it felt when he heard Ailene Thornton lean over to her husband, Herb, and remark, "Damn, he's *good*, ain't he!" Pete was ready for some contest fiddling. "I just come back from overseas. And Herb and Ailene Thornton seconded for me [plectrum banjo, piano], and I won first place. I was so drunk, I couldn't stand up in front of the microphone, I had to sit down in a chair to play."[60] He played "Money Musk" (in A), "Favorite Hornpipe" (B-flat), and "Zig Zag Hornpipe" (in F), three difficult tunes he had learned from George Morris and had heard Ed Tharp and Cleo Persinger play in contests and sessions before the war. These were favorite contest pieces of Morris's, and this was the first time Pete was able to beat him.

According to Hillis Crowell, "To *win*, George would play a real nice breakdown, but what he would really kill the people and judges with is a tune called 'Marchéta.' It's a waltz. And when George played that, the judges just had to give it to him. He just slayed 'em."[61] As Morris came off the stage that night at the armory, with his second-place prize, and passed McMahan coming up the steps, Morris said, "You little son-of-a-bitch, I'd rather play against anybody but you." George Morris changed from friendly elder to bad-tempered competitor. Pete McMahan had arrived. Despite this memory, which McMahan shared with a wry smile, he always acknowledged the influence of Morris's style and repertoire and passed on "George Morris tunes" such as "Morris Hornpipe" and the radio-show theme tune "Taters."[62]

Pete McMahan plays a dance with Herb and Ailene Thornton, Columbia, ca. 1950. Herb was known for playing tenor and plectrum four-string banjo, and here he plays a plectrum. In this period, four-string banjo and piano were McMahan's favorite accompaniment. (Courtesy of Pete McMahan)

McMahan often remarked that he would have appreciated the chance to have violin lessons, but his lack of skill at reading violin music did not faze him. He had picked up fundamental musical literacy from his mother's reed-organ playing, and he had learned to sing tenor lines in church hymnals. In his later years teaching at fiddle camps, Pete was able to tell pupils what precise note was to be fingered.

Herb and Ailene Thornton's Dance Band

In the 1940s into the 1960s, social dancing was widely popular. Getting cleaned up and going out to a club on Friday or Saturday night was a familiar pastime and entertainment, and many bands came together to provide the music.

Places where people danced seemed to fall into two basic types. In small-town and rural Missouri, people of means and of the professional class for the most part danced in hotel ballrooms, restaurant rooms, stylish nightclubs, and members-only country clubs. Other people, for the most part, danced at taverns of sundry kinds and in clubs and halls, some of which required membership, such as the Elks, Moose, American Legion, and VFW (Veterans of Foreign Wars). Fancier venues typically featured posh orchestras and jazz combos playing pop music and Great American Songbook favorites, with little or no square dancing or old-time fiddling; there the principal dances were fox-trot (two-step) and waltz, with an occasional Charleston, jitterbug, or "Mexican hat dance" mixed in. The second category of venues tended to attract country people and blue-collar working people and to hire bands that featured country music and fiddling mixed in with pop hits. People would dance waltzes, fox-trots, and square dances, with a schottische, polka, varsouvienne ("Put Your Little Foot"), or jig if the mood suited.[63]

Some of the popular couple-dance types have passed from sight, such as the one-step, popular in the ragtime era before World War I. The one-step has the feeling of a nineteenth-century minstrel tune from the vaudeville stage (imagine a cakewalk) and of a bouncy ragtime dance. Numerous variations existed, some having dancers moving in spirited pairs dancing on the balls of their feet, while other versions have the dancers moving their feet in a walking or sliding motion. Tin Pan Alley compositions for the one-step were published in the early twentieth century, and high-style dance teachers and performers helped popularize the dance. The one-step was the most popular dance, along with the fox-trot, at Governor Frederick Gardner's inaugural ball at the Governor's Mansion in Jefferson City in January 1917.[64] But fashion is fickle. By the 1950s the one-step was on the way out.[65]

McMahan played in combos for dances, including dances with musicians he would later hire when he was in charge. "Pete's band" featured his fiddle work, along with guitar, bass, and B-flat tenor saxophone played by Lenny Northup (leading to Pete's continued sorting out of the flat keys). Pete liked F and B-flat so much that he enjoyed arranging familiar tunes in those keys. He sang with his band, too, covering hit songs on the country and pop charts.

One of the best bands was Herb and Ailene Thornton's combo. Pete learned pop and swing tunes from his bandmates, especially young trumpeter Hillis Crowell. The Thornton band changed in instrumentation as players came and went, but often featured two guitars, tenor or plectrum banjo, two violins, an electric bass, piano, and B-flat trumpet. It was a "hot" band, with Hillis Crowell (a spunky high school kid playing trumpet solos), the area's best swinging guitarists, and two fiddlers trading off on leads—Pete McMahan and Charlie Cook.

The Thornton band was strictly instrumental and played vintage hits like "Sweet Georgia Brown," big-band tunes such as Glenn Miller's 1940s "Tuxedo Junction" and "String of Pearls," Bing Crosby songs such as "I've Got a Pocketful of Dreams,"[66] and movie songs like Gene Autry's "When It's Nighttime in Nevada" and Roy Rogers's "Along the Navajo Trail." In old age, at a session or riding along in a car, without hesitation Pete could sing or recite lyrics to pop hits from a half century before. He liked pop songs and big-band music and commented that the "uptown music" was "a far cry from old man Atterberry's 'Pretty Polly.'"

Hillis Crowell

Born in Columbia in 1933, Hillis Crowell played backup piano for fiddlers in his youth and later became a well-known jazz trumpeter and pianist. By "jazz," Crowell means, essentially, the Great American Songbook of big-band and swing music of the 1930s and 1940s, rather than the modern jazz becoming popular in the 1950s. Left-handed and self-taught, he played B-flat clarinet, piano, tenor banjo, violin, and his favorite instrument, trumpet. In the third grade, when the school board made its periodic visits at his school, Hillis would be summoned to a piano to play boogie-woogie for the guests. Hillis's father, Humphreys County (H. C.) Crowell, was an old-time banjo player and fiddler who came to Columbia from Waverly, Tennessee, around 1920 to attend the university. H. C. married and began rearing a family; needing steady income, he dropped his university studies and went to work as a mechanic at a gas station and eventually became successful as the owner of his own stations.[67]

H. C. Crowell hosted sessions at the family home on North Rangeline featuring some elite fiddlers—George Morris, Ed Tharp, and Luther Caldwell (H. C.'s favorite). H. C. took part, too, fiddling his favorite square-dance tunes such as "Ragtime Annie." Crowell invited the best accompanists to his music parties and would ask them to come to the house early so they would be tuned up and ready when the fiddlers arrived. Accompanists included Herb Thornton (tenor and plectrum banjo); Herb's wife, Ailene (piano); guitarists N. C. Ficklin (who played a Gretsch hollow-body electric guitar), Eddie Rule, and Claude Baker; and Jimmie Reeder (bass). Too young to play in the sessions, Hillis watched and listened to see "who was doing what." He particularly observed Ailene Thornton's backup. A few years later, he applied what he had learned, playing piano accompaniment for Luther Caldwell (before and after Caldwell lost his right arm in an accident); Caldwell was versatile, known for swing fiddling.[68] When backing up fiddlers, "All I did was second. You don't do a lot of piano *playing*. No melody at all," essentially providing "bass"—boom-chuck, boom-chuck—with little or no sustain pedal.

Crowell sessions provided fine chicken dinners. George Morris was always there. Morris, the region's most famous celebrity fiddler, "was big in stature, he had eyebrows as black and bushy as you could get 'em, and had a *beautiful smile* to him. But he was always a gentleman. And when Dad would have these set up, my mother, who was five-two and weighed a hundred and twenty pounds—and with five children—she cooked fried chicken until I thought she was gonna die. But George Morris said, '*Missus Crowell*, you've got the finest chicken I believe I've ever eaten.' That was part of it. The guys came for an evening and they played till they finally decided, well, I guess we'll go home."

Hillis had a paper route, delivering the *Columbia Daily Tribune* on his bicycle. His route included downtown Columbia. Among subscribers was Cope Ashlock, whose violin shop was upstairs at 915 East Broadway. Each week as Crowell brought the paper, he would pause to watch Ashlock work on violins. A highly regarded luthier and repairman for Cleo Persinger, Taylor McBaine, Billy Craighead, and others, Ashlock was also something of a character and not everyone got along with him. But Hillis Crowell and the fastidious bachelor violin maker Ashlock became friends. "For some reason, he took a liking to me. Instead of just delivering his paper and walking out, every time I would stop and we would just talk about things in general. We got along great. I always called him by his first name, 'Cope.' He was a fine man and I respected him and really like him."

Each week, Hillis's eyes would be drawn to an old red violin laying in a display case alongside others for sale. Cope noticed the boy pausing in front of the case and studying the violins. Hillis did not have enough savings to buy a violin and said nothing about the red fiddle he admired in the case, and, in any event, he was left-handed. A few weeks later, when Hillis came upstairs to deliver the paper, he noticed the red violin was missing and mentioned it to Ashlock. Ashlock mumbled something unintelligible, went to his back room, and returned with a violin. "Here's the red fiddle," he said. Ashlock had disassembled the violin and converted it to a left-handed instrument.[69] "I realized then that he wanted me to have that fiddle. We discussed the price. Ashlock said, 'The price is thirty dollars.' I remarked that I don't have thirty dollars but that I would be willing to pay it off over time. I was lucky to make three dollars a week. I paid him some cash each week until it was paid off." Crowell kept the red fiddle, but his creative energies were drawn elsewhere.

A high school student and focused on trumpet and piano studies, Hillis did not have much time for the fiddle, but as an ear musician and fast learner he worked out several tunes. His models were the fiddlers he admired and observed rather than recordings. The first tune he worked out was "Black Mountain Rag," as he had heard Pete McMahan play it many times in the Herb and Ailene Thornton dance band. McMahan played "Black Mountain Rag" in the key of A and did not retune his violin to an A chord as many fiddlers do, so Hillis played it that way too, in concert tuning. Other "first tunes" he figured out were "Listen to the Mockingbird" (complete with "rocking the bow" and imitation birdcalls), "Beaumont Rag" (in the key of F, learned from listening to Junior Perkins fiddle it in jam sessions), and "Biling [Boil] the Cabbage Down," a commonplace breakdown most fiddlers play.

In high school in 1948–49, Hillis played tenor banjo in a hillbilly string band with his classmates guitarist Bobby Joe Caldwell, Joe Daly (mandolin), Harold Crane (guitar), John Willingham (three-quarter-size upright bass), and Tom Wirt (fiddle).

They took wood-shop class under Vinton Decker, a teacher interested in music who played guitar, and two of the boys built solid-body electric guitars for their projects. The boys called their group the Melody Ramblers and won a string of talent shows. "We had the dangdest hillbilly band you ever heard, kids who couldn't read music." They were invited to audition for the *Ted Mack Old Gold Amateur Hour*, a nationally syndicated radio show. Auditions were held at the Municipal Auditorium in Kansas City, and the boys did well in the competition. Hillis recalled:

> I'll tell you a quick one. We were rehearsing on a Friday afternoon, everyone was around the place, talking and carrying-on, musicians, and everything. And we were standing around talking, and Ted Mack happened to walk by, and about that time, someone asked Joe Daly, "Where do you live?" And he said, "Uh, Eighth and Plumb." "Eighth and Plumb?" asked Ted. "Yeah," Daly said, "eight miles out and plumb back in the brush." And Mack stopped, and he laughed and said, "We're gonna use that tonight on the air." And we did. And they had *Joe say* it. And of course the whole place laughed.

Members of the Kiwanis Club drove the boys to Kansas City for the auditions. Winners were decided by telephone calls from listeners across the United States. The Melody Ramblers took second place, losing to "a guy who sang just like Frank Sinatra."

During senior year in high school (1951) and in 1952 while a first-year student at the university, Crowell played trumpet in Herb and Ailene Thornton's dance band. The core members were Herb and Ailene Thornton (plectrum and tenor banjo, piano), Junior Perkins (guitar), Eddie Rule (substitute guitar), Lionel (Lenny) Northrup (B-flat tenor saxophone), Jimmy Reeder (upright bass), Hillis Crowell (trumpet), and Charlie Cook and Pete McMahan (violins; they alternated nights). Hillis loved the work and the challenge of performing on a bandstand with Charlie Cook and Pete McMahan. "I would say, in my opinion, that those were two of the finest fiddlers that *I* played with. Back then, those guys were unbelievably good, in my opinion. Pete McMahan was one of the best breakdown fiddlers that I ever heard. And Charlie Cook was leaning toward the more smooth, waltz-type and ballad-type of music. And I'll tell ya, it was really nice to be playing with *those* guys."

Crowell was amazed that the dancers—they danced both square dances and round dances—accepted a trumpet in what was essentially a country string band. "Who would ever want to hear a B-flat trumpet played with that group. It doesn't make any sense, but, Howard, it went over like *crazy*. I was playing songs that those guys knew but had never played, 'Tuxedo Junction,' 'Sundown,' 'Sugar Blues,' and some others, in B-flat. We were playing night clubs and beer joints around Columbia like crazy. It was a terrific band. I sometimes felt like the Pied Piper of Hamlin. You blow your horn and the dancers will follow you."

Playing trumpet in a dance band in unpredictable nightclub venues was quite an experience for the teenager.[70] Crowell's first gig with the Thornton band was at the rough-and-tumble Bright Lights on US 40 in Columbia (later renamed the Bambi Club and finally the Rebel Room). The first thing the manager told the band was, "When they start fighting, just keep playing!"[71] Hillis's mother and father agreed to let their son play music in such places not only because the band members said they liked his trumpet playing but also because they knew the band members would look out for the lad. On a typical dance evening, Hillis's mother would drive him to the club and come back and retrieve him around eleven, when the dance wound down.

The Thornton band played everything from Hank Williams hits and honky-tonk to swing and big-band music. There were nightspots everywhere, nice and not so nice, with names such as Jug Head's, Dozier's Station, Breezy Hill, the Top Hat, the Show Boat, Reed's Lake, Bell's Tavern, Andy's Corner, Cavalier Club, Bellamy Springs, the Pinnacles, the Chicken Coop, the Pow-Wow Lounge, and Brite Lights. Old-time banjo player Walter Mountjoy remembered Andy's Corner as "the toughest place around here" in the late 1930s and early 1940s: "I was never in it—because my nose was too tender."[72] Pete's favorite clubs were the Brite Lights and Breezy Hill, where he thought the music was properly appreciated by both clientele and management.

Eventually, Crowell left the Thorntons to play jazz piano. "I had been so struck by what was going on in jazz—I call it the 'jazz world'—I'm talking *Big Band stuff* in the thirties and forties. I was taken aback by Stan Kenton, who had a terrific orchestra and played some wonderful music, but he had a *certain chord structure* that I use to this day. It got me to a point where I finally, reluctantly, had to leave the string band music behind. But I never forgot it."

At a session with Hillis Crowell; the music was a mix of big-band standards and old-time fiddle tunes, with Hillis pausing now and then to comment on Stan Kenton's jazz chords. Hillis Crowell, piano; Dale Pauley, violin. (Photo by Howard Marshall, 2020)

Crowell graduated from Hickman High in 1951 and the following fall enrolled in the University of Missouri, planning to become a dentist. But learning that dental chairs and most dental instruments were right-handed (today, they are ambidextrous), he focused instead on business. Business courses did not suit him, so Hillis became a trumpet major in the music department. On the side, he played piano in campus-town jazz bands such as Eddie Sigeloff's group and George Kratz's Kollege Kats Kombo (Crowell later bought the band name when Kratz graduated from the university), playing dances and fraternity and sorority formals and parties as well as evenings in local spots.

People often ask Hillis if he made any real money playing jazz piano for campus dances and clubs with combo. Yes, he answers, with a hint of a smile. While he was paying $120 per semester for his university tuition, he was making $50 a night, usually three nights a week, fronting a jazz band.[73]

Crowell graduated from the university in January 1956. Knowing he would be subject to the draft, he enlisted in the Army. A few months before, a sergeant at Fort Leonard Wood (ninety miles south of Columbia) had filled in on bass with Hillis's jazz band. Crowell mentioned to him that graduation was approaching and that he was planning to enlist. Crowell knew he would go to Fort Wood for basic training. The sergeant told Hillis to contact him when he arrived at Fort Wood and arranged for Hillis to audition for the post band on both trumpet and piano. The intent was to keep Hillis in the band at Fort Wood for the duration of his service. However, shortly after the audition, Crowell received orders transferring him to Fort Dix, New Jersey, where the Army's band training program was located. Hillis contacted the sergeant to find out what happened to the plan for him to stay at Fort Wood—which would have made it possible for Crowell to travel to Columbia for gigs. "He said, 'you scored too highly on your test—you scored a 95 and a 96 out of 100,'" so Hillis was selected for special music training at Fort Dix.

At Fort Dix, Crowell auditioned for the Army's prestigious United States Military Band at West Point and placed at the top of the auditions. Transferred to West Point, he spent the remainder of his two years' enlistment performing in the band for presidents and dignitaries from around the world who were given tours and ceremonies. He spent most of his spare time and evenings playing jazz piano, from combos for officers' club dances to gigs off-base. Crowell was promoted to Specialist 3, and as his enlistment was expiring, he was offered promotion to sergeant if he would stay in the Army. His reply? "I'm not a fighter, I'm a lover."

Back in Columbia, Crowell returned to the university and received a master's degree in secondary education. Hillis married Jane Vandenberg, a Stephens College graduate, in 1959, and continued playing jazz as responsibilities allowed. Hillis worked in administrative positions at the university from 1969 to 1977 while working toward his PhD. After leaving the university in 1977 (and unable to finish his dissertation to complete his PhD), Crowell established an insurance office and, after thirty-five years in the business, retired in 2019.

Crowell's red violin was recently refurbished by the Wyatt Violin Shop, and he says he is working to "get back" into fiddling by relearning "Listen to the Mockingbird."

Charlie Cook

The Thorntons liked having two fiddlers. The other fiddler on the stand most nights with Pete McMahan was another great player, Charlie Cook.[74] The spirit of Charlie Cook moves phantom-like through chitchat among older musicians. Cook was born on a farm near Huntsdale in the tobacco- and hemp-growing Missouri River hills of Boone County and worked as a maintenance man on the University of Missouri campus, fifteen miles away. A swing guitarist and fiddler, he specialized in pop tunes and waltzes but was also a master of hard-driving breakdowns.[75] He was creative, with smooth, perfect double-stops and the flat keys common in the dance-band repertoire. Listening to home recordings of 1950s house parties, it is clear that Cook's breakdown fiddling was just as excellent as his waltz fiddling.

In the Thornton band, Cook fiddled waltzes and two-steps and McMahan played the breakdowns for square dances, and they sometimes played twin fiddle together. Both men were heavy drinkers. On nights when McMahan was too intoxicated to perform, Columbia fiddler Bill (Junior) Perkins would sometimes be called to sit in, covering McMahan's role. It was not easy for the band when McMahan or Cook was drinking during gigs. Crowell recalls, "I've been on the bandstand [when Cook was drunk], and I don't see how Charlie could stand on the bandstand and *fiddle*, but he *did*. There were times when we weren't sure what he was gonna *do*. The whole band was kinda *watching* him. But he made it through. And I don't know how many times we went through that."[76]

McMahan often acknowledged the quality of Cook's untitled waltzes, "Charlie Cook's G Waltz," and "Charlie Cook's A Waltz" (Cook may have learned the latter from fiddler Buzz Dailey of Huntsville).[77] Pete, Cleo Persinger, Leroy Canaday, and others also learned Cook's "Flowers from Heaven" (B-flat), and it became a contest standard. Pete took in Cook's B-flat waltz, personalized it, and added parts and his own special touches. Pete played "Flowers from Heaven" in June 1968 at the National Oldtime Fiddlers' Contest, introducing the tune to an influential audience; however, instead of "Flowers from Heaven," Pete titled it "Charlie Cook's B-flat Waltz" at Weiser. Ed Tharp and Taylor McBaine typically called it "The B-Flat Waltz" without referencing Cook, the composer.[78] Charlie Cook died in 1960 in an automobile accident, too soon to be part of the fiddlers' association movement and reinvigorated contest world and too soon to have a place among fiddlers lionized by young fiddlers and collectors in the late sixties and seventies.[79]

Listen to track 6 on the companion CD to hear Charlie Cook's "Flowers from Heaven."

Pete and Sarah

McMahan's first marriage ended in divorce in 1951. Later that year, Pete met Sarah Ronimous at the Wigwam Café in Columbia.[80] Sara was a waitress and soon to be divorced. Pete was still drinking and driving trucks, hauling freight between Columbia and Kansas City. Sarah was the daughter of Cecil and Anna Ronimous. Charles Cecil (CC) Ronimous was part Cherokee and a well-known fiddler and dancer in the Harrisburg area of northern Boone County.[81] Ronimous may have also played old-time banjo. A World War I veteran, CC was a farmer, restaurant cook, and University of Missouri grounds maintenance worker, and he enjoyed playing fiddle at home and at dance parties with friends. The family raised sheep and sold barbecue mutton at dances. Pete and Sarah married in 1953.

Sarah was a dancer and liked the hard-core old-time fiddle style Pete played. "Pete was a rough fiddler. What I mean is that he'd get *down*, and you could *dance to it*."[82]

Pete used to laugh about Alcoholics Anonymous "giving up on me." He said he was drinking a quart of bourbon a day. Pete went through drinking relapses for several years, disappearing for three or four days on a spree, staying with friends, coming home when he sobered up. Sarah held the family together during these episodes.[83]

In 1954, Pete and Sarah moved to Williams, Arizona, where Pete took a well-paying job driving trucks and working on road repairs for General Tire Company. It was hard work. Pete was on call twenty-four hours a day to service wheels and tires on trucks and heavy equipment. Pete all but stopped playing fiddle, but he did make an occasional appearance, such as performing on an Arizona television program. Contests were being revived in the Southwest, but work and family responsibilities prevented Pete from taking part.

The McMahans moved back to Missouri in 1965 and settled in Harrisburg. Pete went to work at McKnight Tire in Columbia, handling tires on trucks and earth-moving machinery on the on-call repair truck. When they heard Pete and Sarah were back, Cleo Persinger and Taylor McBaine came to their house and talked him into picking up the fiddle again, and Pete began going to sessions with Taylor and Cleo, rotating the location among their homes. According to John Griffin, "For me, Pete's delivery of his music is more full of life and emotion than any other fiddler I have ever heard. He is the best."[84]

Pete acquired the violin that would become his "number one" in 1965. He was hosting a session in the basement of his home in north Columbia with Taylor McBaine, Lyman Enloe, Cleo Persinger, Jack Roberts, and Kansas City fiddle jockey and fiddler "Long John" Journagin. Journagin would bring a few violins, bows, and cases when he traveled to music parties, in case a trade or sale might develop. Journagin handed a violin to McMahan, saying, "Pete, give this one a try." Pete liked it immediately. "The first time I put my fingers on it, I fell in love with it." Pete remarked, "He knew I liked the fiddle. I played it all night. They got ready to go home and I asked him what he wanted for it, and he wanted a hundred and fifty dollars. He wanted me to keep it and pay the dollars when I could." Enloe offered to take up a collection to buy the violin for Pete (they told Pete he could pay them back later), but Pete refused what might look like charity. Journagin left the violin with Pete to "try out." "And finally he called me and said he'd be down here on Saturday and he needed a new set of tires for his car and he'd trade me the fiddle for a set of tires and fifteen dollars cash. And of course he knew I worked at McKnight Tire. I got the tires wholesale and I paid for them by the week. And I wouldn't trade this fiddle for any. It's been pretty good to me. I've made a dollar or two with it."[85] When asked what makes a good violin, McMahan would answer in one word: tone. But he also valued volume; in an interview in 1996 with Jenn Stecker for KBIA radio in Columbia, Pete said his violin "bawls just like a bull."

McMahan loved the violin and brooked no criticism of it. In 1972, Dale Pauley was barbering at Fenton's shop in Columbia (Dale regularly cut Pete's hair before the Pauleys moved to Arizona in 1976). One day, Pete came in and asked Dale, "Did you hear me on KFAL this morning?" Pete's first *Missouri Fiddlin'* LP had just come out, and Ron Lutz was playing it on his Fulton radio show. Dale replied yes. Pete asked, "What'd you think?" Joking, Pauley quipped, "Well, it'd be pretty good if that guy had a decent fiddle to play on." Pete blew his top and said words to the effect of "There ain't nobody anywhere has a better fiddle than mine!"[86]

Dozens of violins passed through McMahan's hands, found at flea markets, auctions, attics, sessions, and trades in parking lots at contests. People sometimes gave him a violin when a closet or attic was cleaned out. To pay bills, Pete sold violins, bows, and cases and continued to check antique malls, flea markets, and want ads for violins and bows that could be bought cheap and reconditioned by his friend Jack Roberts or, in later years, by John Griffin.

McMahan retired. The company had no retirement plan. Pete had only his Social Security and veteran's benefits, and the bits of cash brought home from a contest became more important. In 1993, Pete and Sarah sold their home and acreage and moved to an apartment in Columbia, where two of their daughters worked. In 1998, Pete was moved to the Williamsburg nursing home. In frail health, Pete felt that he was the last of a line and often repeated a familiar comment heard from many older musicians in their decline: "All the old timers are gone and I'm the only one that's left." John Williams was there in Pete's final days—the high school kid who was McMahan's last student. "What we have around here in this part of Missouri we call the Little Dixie style. I'm strictly an old-timer, I am an old man, and I go by the old ways, I play the old music." When McMahan died in February 2000, there was no public announcement, wake, or funeral, but the news spread through the fiddle community and memorials appeared in newspapers and magazines.[87]

Listen to track 7 on the companion CD to hear Pete McMahan's version of "Sugar in the Gourd."

Pete McMahan at a street fair in downtown Columbia with Jack Deck, who played a 1960s Gibson RB-250 banjo. Deck, who passed away in 1990, was born in Iowa, grew up in northwest Missouri, and moved to Marshall (Saline County) in 1965. A Korean War veteran, University of Missouri graduate, and professional stock-market trader, Jack was known to most people as a country guitarist and fiddler; he appears on McMahan's third LP and the documentary *"Now That's a Good Tune."* (Photo by Howard Marshall)

Vesta Johnson with Frank Reed and John Philbrick at Missouri Fiddlers and Country Music Association event, St. Louis, ca. 1970. (Courtesy of Vesta Johnson)

Voluntary Associations and Fiddle Contests 4

The Missouri Fiddlers and Country Music Association began in 1974 with the concept of preserving and promoting Old-Time fiddle & country music. This type of music is a "handed down from generation to generation" art form. Our main objective is to ensure that this music is continued into the future. We feel this is necessary because of the link to our past from which these songs have evolved. Old Time Music helps us remember our roots and tradition which are sometimes lost in today's world.

—Missouri Fiddlers and Country Music Association (2021)

Fiddlers' associations flowered in the South in the early 1900s when associations evolved to promote and administer fiddle contests. Built around fiddle contests, like the contests themselves, fiddlers' associations have tended to be sprinkled with contradictions, jealousies, factions, and the occasional shouting match.

Among groups in Missouri during the Folk Music Revival in the 1960s were the Missouri Old-Time Fiddlers' Association (a.k.a. Mid-West Fiddlers), the Missouri Fiddlers and Country Music Association, the Missouri State Old Time Fiddlers Association, the State of the Ozarks Fiddlers' Association, and bluegrass-oriented groups such as the Missouri Area Bluegrass Committee, the Tri-State Bluegrass Association, the Society for the Preservation of Blue Grass Music of America, the Kansas City Blue Grass Music Club, and the Heart of America Bluegrass and Oldtime Music Club. Other groups formed with a wider scope that included many forms of folk tradition, such as the Missouri Folklore Society (revived after decades on hiatus) and the Missouri Friends of the Folk Arts in St. Louis, which focused on the St. Louis area and upper eastern Ozarks and helped lead in rediscovery and documentation of regional cultural traditions, showcased in programs such as the Frontier Folklife Festival.[1]

Some groups enjoyed support from new public agencies, such as the National Endowment for the Arts, National Endowment for the Humanities, National Council on the Traditional Arts, Missouri Arts Council, and Missouri Humanities Council, along with new interest among existing institutions such as the State Historical Society of Missouri, the Missouri Historical Society, and universities, art galleries, county historical societies, libraries, and museums. From 1982 to 1993 the Missouri Cultural Heritage Center at the University of Missouri developed statewide programs of documentation and presentation, such as the Traditional Arts Apprenticeship Program and Missouri Folk Arts Program, now part of the university's Museum of Art and Archaeology. There are archives of recordings, journals, ephemera, and collectanea of all kinds in many Missouri institutions. The Gordon McCann Collection of Ozark Fiddle Music at Missouri State University is one of the best. The Missouri State Old Time Fiddlers Association collections and those of the Missouri Folklore Society and the Missouri Cultural Heritage Center are archived in the State Historical Society in Columbia and its branches.[2]

Associations were significant movers in revitalizing contests, to one degree or another reflecting enthusiasm for cultural revitalization at dances, hootenannies, and folk festivals of all kinds, as well as new interest in documenting vernacular music. Fiddlers' conventions of earlier times served as patterns, celebrations built around a desire for musicians and their families and friends to have get-togethers to share music, victuals, and memories.

Missouri Old Time Fiddlers' Association, 1962

The Missouri Old Time Fiddlers' Association was the state's first such group.[3] Cleo Persinger was president and Jake Hughes the secretary-treasurer. Early supporters were prominent fiddlers such as Jake's wife, Lena Hughes, as well as Gene Wells, Forrest Ellifrits, Johnny Bruce, Joe Grable, Cyril Stinnett, and Taylor McBaine, contest fiddlers in central and northwest Missouri. The organization was inspired by what Persinger and the Hugheses saw as great success at the National Oldtime Fiddlers' Contest in Weiser in 1963,[4] and they knew about other big contest festivals such as those in Union Grove, North Carolina; Galax, Virginia; Atlanta, Georgia; as well as contests in Texas at Athens, Hallettsville, and Crockett. The new organization was optimistic about increasing interest in old-time fiddling, and they knew their organization could help. Several hundred fiddlers signed up for membership in Missouri, nearby states, and beyond.

The Missouri Old Time Fiddlers' Association was concerned with finding ways to nourish "authentic old-time fiddling styles." The group organized dances, public jam sessions, school programs, and contests, with newsletters and an event calendar. Their weekend fiddlers' conventions were conceived as campouts in parks and campgrounds. People brought tents and camping trailers and set up for several days of music, dancing, and visiting. The campouts featured fiddle contests, groups of musicians were invited to entertain, and there were spaces for dancing in front of the stage. Young people and families were especially welcome.

The Hugheses were aware of rising interest in bluegrass as well as the attractive "national contest" in Weiser, Idaho—where Texas-style and progressive contest styles were evolving and growing in influence. Jake Hughes was blunt and obdurate in his opinions. As Richard Blaustein notes, Jake complained about encroachments of "bluegrass and Texas fiddling upon fiddling contests in Missouri."[5] Unbeknownst to Jake and his colleagues in the mid-1960s, bluegrass fiddling and straight-chord backup-guitar style would prove to be more compatible with their conservative interpretation of old-time fiddling than the emerging Texas/Contest Style.

Voluntary associations invariably involve some disharmony among members about goals and procedures as well as how to construct mission statements. Some Missouri Old Time Fiddlers' Association members disagreed about whether to try to keep contests "old-time" as they understood that term—that is, whether to keep bluegrass and Texas-style contest fiddlers from dominating contests. Other members accepted the fact that all sorts of styles were heard in competitions despite stated rules and that administrators could not and should not try to legislate what fiddlers could fiddle in their contests. Cleo Persinger favored a broad view of these things. Jake and Lena Hughes wanted to fortify their conservative vision of "old-time."

Johnny Bruce of Bosworth, Missouri, has a tune with Lena Hughes, playing her 1950s Gibson RB-100 five-string banjo. At a jam session at Lena's home in Ludlow, prior to playing for the dance at nearby Tina, February 23, 1991. (Photo by Howard Marshall)

Listen to track 8 on the companion CD to hear Johnny Bruce's version of "Leather Britches."

Lena Hughes

Lena Hughes seemed to be everyone's favorite banjo accompanist as well as a celebrated guitarist and champion fiddler. She traveled to contests, sessions, and dances to play backup banjo for fiddlers such as Cleo Persinger, Dwight Lamb, Cyril Stinnett, Lonnie Robertson, Johnny Bruce, Lyman Enloe, Amos Chase, and her brother Casey Jones. Lena competed as a fiddler in numerous contests, several times at the National Oldtime Fiddlers' Contest in Weiser, winning the Ladies Division in 1963. Jake and Lena's first trip to Weiser was in June 1962. Lena played banjo in a prebluegrass finger-picking style often called "parlor banjo"—excellent for fiddle backup. Parlor banjo, related to "classical" banjo styles of the late 1800s and ancestor of bluegrass banjo, in north-central Missouri was exemplified in the playing of people such as Alva Lee Hendren (Madison), Rolly (Rattler) Pogue (Huntsville), and Lena Hughes, its best-known proponent.[6]

Lena was born on a farm in the Tinney (Tinney's) Grove community near Braymer in Ray County. Hers was a large family peppered with musicians and dancers. Lena's father, John Henry Jones (Scotch-Irish and Cherokee), was a popular dance fiddler who also played reed organ and guitar accompaniment. John Henry Jones enjoyed teaching and always said that you should, after you have the basics, "play it like you want to play it." Lena learned to accompany fiddlers on guitar first, and then her father taught her to "follow" fiddlers on five-string banjo. Her finger-picking parlor guitar style was like her banjo style; her 1960s LP, *Lena Hughes, Queen of the Guitar Pickers and Her Flat Top Guitar*, influenced players such as Mike Seeger and John Renbourn.[7]

Lena's brother Casey Jones was a "hornpipe-style" fiddler. Lena remembered Casey's first fiddle contest, in Iowa, in 1928 or 1929 when Casey was eighteen. Jake and Lena drove him to the contest, and Casey got third place; the following year Casey won first and was hired as a regular performer on KMA radio in Shenandoah.

Contests in Salisbury, 1967, and Lexington, 1968, Signs of Things to Come

Salisbury is a farm town in Chariton County on the north bank of the Missouri River in central Missouri. A major contest in Salisbury was created by Jake and Lena Hughes, Cleo Persinger, and other members of the Missouri Old Time Fiddlers' Association, to help celebrate the town's centennial celebration. The four-day event was promoted heavily in the *Salisbury Press-Spectator* and announcements mailed to numerous fiddlers. It was billed as the biggest fiddle contest ever held in the Midwest; one of its features was a Missouri state championship division.

The *Press-Spectator* reported on small local contests in the region to generate interest in the big event in August. The paper ran a photo story around Renick fiddler George Skaggs. "A Real 'Old Fiddler. Over 90 and still fiddlin'—George Skaggs of Renick who said he's going on 91, played his fiddle for a while at the Centennial Bar-B-Q here Sunday afternoon. He said he has been playing since he was 12 or 13 years old but he hasn't used the microphone and amplifier that were attached to his fiddle Sunday."[8] Lena Hughes, Cyril Stinnett, Cleo Persinger, and Iowa's Dwight Lamb had competed in the national contest at Weiser the previous June and helped advertise the Salisbury Centennial Old Time Fiddler's Contest.

In early August, the paper started running promotions. "Salisbury Old-Time Fiddlers' Contest. Biggest Old-Time Fiddlers' Contest Ever Held in the Midwest. August 17–18–19. 150 FIDDLERS—Judges from 5 states, FIDDLERS from 8 states. Plenty of seats—reserved seats also available. Attend anytime, doors open and fiddlers start playing each day at 9:00 a.m. Night contest at 8:00 p.m. Held in S. H. S. Auditorium. Special Drawing for TV set Saturday night."

> Fiddlin' Starts Thursday in Big Contest Here. An old time Fiddlers Contest which is being billed as one of the "Biggest ever held in the Midwest" will begin at Salisbury High School on Thursday and continue for three days. According to Dr. W. W. Leatherwood, who is head of the event, entries have already been received from ten states and many more are expected. The contestants will start arriving Wednesday and will register Wednesday and on Thursday morning. The "Fiddlin" will start on Thursday at 10:00 a.m. and will continue each day through Saturday night when the finals will be held. . . . Record-keeping, standings etc. will be handled by Mrs. Leatherwood. Mrs. Elmer Spellman is in charge of food service in the school cafeteria for contestants and spectators. On Saturday night a portable television set will be given away as a door prize. The winner must be present. Reserved seats will be sold for the Saturday night performance only. General admission tickets will be available for all other sessions.[9]

The organizers offered a serious purse—$1,700 total—and the contest attracted national champions who had won or placed high at state contests as well as at Weiser and other major contests. The fiddlers did not number 150 as predicted, but there were dozens who took part. California, Idaho, Kentucky, Kansas, Oklahoma, Nebraska, Tennessee, Iowa, and Arkansas were represented. Among the fiddlers were Uncle Dick Hutchison from Oklahoma (born in McDonald County, Missouri), who won the Senior Division; Herman Johnson (the Oklahoma champion who would win at Weiser a year later), who was eliminated before the final round; and several young hotshots, such as Van Smith from Idaho (1965 and 1966 national junior champion at Weiser), Sam Bush from Kentucky (1967 junior champion at Weiser), and Iowa's Kirk Brandenberger.[10] Most of the rules followed those promoted by the national contest at Weiser. But while the Salisbury contest rivaled the major contests in Missouri in the 1920s, none of the major newspapers in Kansas City or St. Louis covered the proceedings.

The judges were Loyd Wanzer from Idaho, Kelley Kirksey from California, Bud Meredith from Kentucky, Ken Copeland from Iowa, and Casey Jones from Missouri. Kirksey, Meredith, and Wanzer had won or placed high in national contests at Weiser and touted as "expert fiddlers and past winners in national contests."[11] All but Copeland had been successful fiddlers or judges at Weiser. Although all were well acquainted with Contest Style, their scoring favored older regional fiddling that clearly qualified as "old-time" to Missouri audiences and fiddlers. Bluegrass fiddling, considered "old-time" music, was fine, too. Fiddlers drew numbers for the order of competition. There was a sound system. No electric amplification devices were allowed to be fixed to instruments. Contestants played a hoedown, waltz, and a tune of choice in each round. "Only old time tunes of danceable quality in existence before 1910 were allowed," a nod to the event as part of the town's celebration of history but also, some thought, a guarantee that no one would play "modern" music. Two accompanists were permitted.

As at Weiser, judges were sequestered in a separate room wired for sound, which supposedly would prevent favoritism. Judging criteria were smoothness, rhythm, and tone quality. Scoring was cumulative through the several rounds. Also following Weiser rules, no tune could be played more than once during all rounds by the same fiddler. "Orange Blossom Special," "Mocking Bird," and "Black Mountain Rag" were banned—exhibition pieces that had accrued a false reputation as being "trick tunes."

> The rhythm was contagious, and whether or not old-time fiddling is your particular cup of tea, one could not help but notice the quiet toe tapping and the nodding of heads to the beat of the tunes that came from the platform. But the real heart of the contest was to be found in the halls backstage. Here contestants watched closely the lists of winners posted after each elimination, and then walked quickly away to arrange for accompanists and practice for the next round. While courteous to this interviewer, it was evident that Sammy Bush, a 15-year-old high school sophomore from Bowling Green, Kentucky who placed sixth in the open contest, was more anxious to practice for the final round than to answer questions for anybody's paper. Sammy was the not the only fine young fiddler. Twelve-year-old Kirk Brandenberger from Keokuk, Ia. played well and Tim Rued came all the way from Santa Rosa, California with his grandfather, Kelley Kirksey, one of the judges, just to play in Salisbury's contest. Between rounds another group of young men who call themselves "The Kaw Valley Boys" from Lawrence, Kansas entertained. The group composed of Jim Hale, lead guitar, Dave Warner, banjo, and Chuck Stearman, mandolin.[12]

When the final tallies at Salisbury were sorted out, Lena Hughes won the Ladies Division. Second place went to Elaine Grove of Omaha, Nebraska, a violinist in the Omaha Symphony with degrees from Northwestern University and the University of Nebraska who had recently taken up "the fascinating art of fiddling as a hobby" and found it "a new challenge."[13] Third place was won by Ida Mae Green of Lexington. The Senior Division was won by Dick Hutchison, followed by Lena Hughes (women could compete in other divisions), Ben Drake (Humboldt, Nebraska), Herman "Sac River" Jones (El Dorado Springs, Missouri),[14] Melvin Oster (Norborne, Missouri), and Dean Smith (Anderson, Missouri). Cyril Stinnett won the Open Division, followed by Dwight Lamb, Pete McMahan, Jake Hockemeyer, Lonnie Peerce (Louisville, Kentucky), Sam Bush, Van Smith, and Forrest (Frosty) Lamb (Bloomfield, Iowa). Fiddlers could compete both in their age division and the Open Division.

Fiddlers who saw Stinnett's performances at Weiser were not surprised, but for some fiddlers accustomed to winning contests, the brilliance of the unassuming, dour farmer in striped overalls was a shock. Cyril did not say much to people at Weiser and usually would say nothing at all to people he did not know or respect. Just before the contest began, as Cyril was listening to Pete McMahan warm up, Cyril mumbled to Pete, "If I couldn't play any better than that, I'd quit." Pete laughed; he knew that was a halfhearted attempt by his laconic friend to "psyche him out" just before Pete went onstage.[15]

Like other contests, Salisbury had a Trick Fiddler Division, a concession to those who wanted to blaze away with the outlawed crowd-pleasers. Kirk Brandenberger won this division as well as the youngest fiddler award. The oldest fiddler award went to Albert Spray (Winigan, Missouri; Delbert's father). The fiddler coming from the farthest distance was Tim Rued from Northern California. Pete McMahan won the "Best Liked Fiddler" trophy.[16]

Salisbury was the first big Missouri contest modeled on Weiser. There were five judges, sequestered. (The tradition in Missouri was, and generally continues to be, seating the judges where all can see them, in front of or near the stage or in the audience.) As the contest ensued, the top and low scores from the judges (in each performance or round played by a fiddler) were nullified, with only the three other judges' scores being totaled. Throwing out high and low scores was another device thought to help defeat favoritism; skeptics doubt that this makes much difference, but it constitutes an attempt at more fairness in the adjudication process.

The rules stipulated that tunes must date to at least the year 1910. The idea was that old-time fiddle tunes are antiques. So, like a buggy whip at an antique shop, fiddle tunes should be at least fifty years old. The rule was impossible to enforce, and such a rule causes consternation and arguments that are incapable of being resolved on the spot. But such a rule makes people think the fiddlers are performing *really old* old-time music.

The Salisbury contest was a success, and the town continued to have periodic contests on a local scale in following years. Competitions were held in July 1977 and 1978 at the city park, as were several contests in the 1990s in conjunction with the town's Salisbury Steak Festival.

Impressed with success at Salisbury, in 1968 the Missouri Old Time Fiddlers' Association inaugurated a new state and national contest. They picked Lexington as the location, on the Missouri River east of Kansas City, and, like Salisbury, Lexington was largely modeled on the National Oldtime Fiddlers' Contest at Weiser. During this time period, contests like Lexington and Weiser meant national contest: in the sense that anyone was welcome to compete, from any state, and not that the event was going to endow a national title, but national champions were declared anyway.

Lexington in 1968 was another contest that led to shifts in contest performance and repertory. Held in early August, Lexington's "state and national" old-time fiddling contest attracted contest fiddlers from distant places, just as at Salisbury a year earlier. Fiddlers were also enticed because these big Missouri events had the implied approval of the National Oldtime Fiddlers' Association.

The *Lexington Advertiser-News* of July 31, 1968, reflected the gravity of the event: "Registration will begin tomorrow for what the Chamber of Commerce hopes will be more than 100 old-time fiddlers vying for $1,750 in prize money in the state and National Old-Time Fiddlers Contest to be held here through Sunday."[17] The whole town got involved. The Lions Club spruced up the town park and built spaces for campers and trailers, added picnic tables, and installed restrooms with running water in new shelter houses. Church groups and clubs planned to sell meals, motels prepared to be sold out, people rented out rooms in their homes, and National Guard troops volunteered to direct traffic.

The contest was held in the high school gym August 2, 3, and 4. On Friday and Saturday, elimination rounds were held, and finals were all day Sunday, with the final playoff at 8:00 p.m. There were three divisions, open (any age), senior (age sixty and up), and ladies. A Missouri state champion as well as a national champion were to be anointed, and fiddlers in the Open Division were allowed to compete for both titles. Trophies were given for "Best Trick Fiddling," "Most Congenial Fiddler," "Best Liked Second" (accompanist), fiddler coming from the farthest distance, youngest fiddler, and oldest fiddler.

The Open Division awarded a first prize of $500 and a trophy, just as Weiser and just as at Salisbury in 1967. Half the prize money was provided by the Chamber of Commerce and half by "the Missouri National Old-Time Fiddler's Association"—Jake and Lena Hughes's Missouri Old-Time Fiddlers' Association.

Loyd Wanzer of Caldwell, Idaho, the popular former champion at Weiser, whose LP records were enjoyed in Missouri, won three prizes—best trick fiddling, most congenial competitor, and fiddler traveling the longest distance. Oldest fiddler trophy went to L. E. Whited of Meadville, Missouri (age ninety-nine). Kirk Brandenberger, who would go on to become a well-known bluegrass fiddler and music producer, won youngest fiddler. Fred Stoneking (then living in Blairstown) won best accompanist. Senior Division winners were J. A. (Jim) Gilmore (Jefferson City), first place; Jess B. Arthur (Rolla), second; Nolan Boone (Mexico), third; Lena Hughes, fourth; Ray Miller (St. Joseph), fifth; and Seth Allen (Valley Falls, Kansas), sixth.[18] Dick Hutchison of Disney, Oklahoma, a well-known former champion who won the senior crown at Salisbury in 1967, did not place in the finals.

Ida Mae Green of Lexington, who had won third place at Salisbury, won the Ladies Division. Others doing well in the Ladies Division were Carol Hascall (Independence), second; Lena Hughes, third; Pamela Kruse (Concordia), fourth; and Florence Jeffries (Hale), fifth place.

In the Open Division, Herman Johnson did not make the finals at Salisbury in 1967, but he won at Lexington in 1968. Just two months before, he had made his first trip to Weiser and was crowned national champion. He would be virtually invincible in contests from 1968 on. In Lexington, he won both the Missouri state title and the national champion title. The Missouri state championship and other top prizes going to outsiders did not set well with some in the Missouri contingent. Pete McMahan and Fred Stoneking were among those critical of what they saw as "progressive"-style performances pushing the envelope too far from what was considered old-time fiddling in Missouri.

Other contest fiddlers from outside Missouri came back in 1968 for the Open Division. While Johnson took first place, second was Sam Bush; third, Lonnie Peerce; fourth, William A. (Bill) Long (Montana); fifth, Jim Gilmore; sixth, Fred Stoneking; seventh, Cyril Stinnett; eighth, Pete McMahan; ninth, Nolan Boone; tenth, Ida Mae

Green; eleventh, Loyd Wanzer (Idaho); and twelfth, Leroy (Roy) Cowan (Oklahoma). That roster includes prominent fiddlers at the Weiser national contests—Johnson, Bush (1967 and 1968 national junior champion), Long (Montana state champion), Wanzer (a national champion), and Cowan.

After Salisbury in 1967 and Lexington in 1968, many Missouri contest administrators fortified their rule that only Missouri residents were allowed to compete for Missouri state champion, a rule codified by the Missouri State Old Time Fiddlers Association in 1982. The question of admitting nonresidents to compete for Missouri state champion continues to be debated. Some state contests offer separate divisions for nonresidents, which partly solves the quandary.

The Mid-West Fiddlers' Association, 1969

A splinter group called the Mid-West Fiddlers' Association evolved in 1969 and 1970 when Missouri Old Time Fiddlers' Association leadership argued over the goals of the group.[19] Persinger wanted to concentrate on supporting fiddle contests and developing their new state contest at Lexington. The Hugheses were more interested in supporting square dances and presenting school programs to educate young people and their teachers about Missouri's fiddle heritage. Jake and Lena formed a new group, the Mid-West Fiddlers' Association, with members from surrounding states but focused on central and northwest Missouri. The Hugheses hoped their group would become Missouri's official branch of the National Oldtime Fiddlers' Association (NOTFA).[20]

The idea of a regional organization was worthy, but the group failed to get off the ground. Despite enthusiasm generated by the Mid-West Fiddlers' Association (sometimes confusingly referred to as the Missouri Old Time Fiddlers' Association), the organization did not have a strong administrative core and did not develop mechanisms to build and keep people's interest.

Persinger's group helped administer contests for small communities. One of these was an October 1967 event in Sumner (Chariton County) in conjunction with the village's annual Goose Festival. "The Wild Goose Capital of the World," Sumner is a prairie community of about 150 people near Swan Lake National Wildlife Refuge, a major attraction for wildlife fans and seasonal goose and duck hunters. One of the services rendered by fiddlers' groups is the deceptively simple chore of mailing out announcements to an ample mailing list. Often, the promoter has the foresight to follow up the announcements with phone calls (today, emails and the Internet) to encourage people to attend. The typed postal card sent out by the 1967 Sumner administrator, fiddler Francis Kepner (Rothville), included the necessary details and a reminder of the rules—"no more than two seconds"; fiddlers will play three tunes, a breakdown, waltz, and tune of choice; "Orange Blossom Special," "Black Mountain Rag" and "Mocking Bird" are barred; fiddlers draw numbers for the order of competition; and "no entries accepted after drawing." At Sumner, contestants who had contact microphones attached to their violins were allowed to use them—but "all will use same amplifier." Despite the small purse and remote location, Sumner contests, held in 1967 and several following years, attracted some of Missouri's top contest fiddlers and champions.

Without Persinger, the Missouri Old Time Fiddlers' Association melted away. Jake and Lena Hughes's upstart Mid-West Fiddlers' Association also withered as the couple grew older and experienced health problems. These two foundational fiddlers' associations are generally forgotten, but they helped chart the way.

Other big contests were happening in Missouri. The Boone County Fair restarted its annual fiddle contest in Columbia in 1968, continuing its legendary career.[21] The fair had supported contests since 1947, when it was revived after World War II, and this contest was considered by many fiddlers to be a state contest and the state's most competitive contest of the era.[22] In 1957, the contest had been canceled for several years when the fair decided to put their budget to bringing in country music stars from the Grand Ole Opry. By 1968, however, Nashville shows had become too expensive, and the fiddle contest was brought back. Boone Countians claimed that they preferred old-time fiddling at the county fair because a county fair is "a rural fair stressing country living."[23] The Boone County Fair contest again became one of Missouri's best, under the management of Glen Whitesides and others who knew fiddle music and dance. Unfortunately, the fair lost its contest around 2004 in a familiar scenario: after its original leader, Whitesides, died, effective administration ended. In its final year, arguments broke out among fiddlers, accompanists, and judges over new confusing rules, misunderstandings about whether fiddlers would have to pay to play (fiddlers hate doing that), and other snafus that made for a poor contest and disappointed audience.[24]

A successful contest depends on the ingenuity, organizational skills, dedication, and goodwill of a small group of people. Often an individual got inspired to launch a contest, as with Cecil Windsor in Boonville in the 1960s. Windsor was a fiddler and well-known citizen, and he had support from his Odd Fellows Lodge, which meant not only that friends of lodge members would support lodge events but also that spouses of lodge members (or another local group) could be recruited to set up the obligatory refreshment stand. Throughout its four-decade run, the Boonville contest, held each March around St. Patrick's Day, was considered the "season opener" for contest fiddlers, and with spring around the corner, fiddlers were ready to dust off their violins and come to Boonville, the seat of Cooper County. The judging quality was not always admired, but most fiddlers (with notable exceptions) did not stress out over how the winners were ranked. Windsor passed away in the 1990s, and members of his family and lodge members kept the contest going several more years. But without Cecil Windsor's charm and organizational skills, after forty-five years the Boonville contest folded in 2009.

Beginning in 1969, several annual contests were held in St. Joseph at the East Hills Mall, a retail center that opened in 1965 next to the recently completed Interstate 29 from Kansas City to Des Moines. These were events organized like festivals, with the parking lot given to visitors for campers and jam sessions. The contest was another that billed itself as a state contest. Winners at the 1971 contest included some of the usual top competitors, with McMahan, Stinnett, and Nolan Boone the top three in the Open Division. In 1971, women were still typically invited to play in the Ladies Division, and here they included Carol Hascall, Sandra Bates, and Vesta Johnson. In the Senior Division, however, women were allowed to compete, and Lena Hughes won, followed by Ray Miller and Russell Smith. Dr. James Gray, age eighty, received a trophy as the contest's oldest fiddler.[25]

In the late 1970s, another state contest was hosted by the Missouri Old Time Fiddlers' Association, in the farm town of Graham in northwest Missouri—the backyard of champion Cyril Stinnett as well as first-rate local fiddlers such as Joe Grable. As Ed Fedrizzi writes, "People would come a long way to hear Cyril."[26] It is interesting that the Missouri Old Time Fiddlers' Association sponsored several contests informally called a "state contest." They did not plan to have a single overarching state contest, but instead designated several that way. Calling the event a state contest certainly helped in promotion and tended to attract many of Missouri's top contest fiddlers. Perhaps the group imagined that, in due course, one of their trial state contests would evolve and become truly a statewide competition.

Joe Grable, from Dearborn (near St. Joseph), was a strong supporter of fiddlers' associations and fiddle contests. Here, Joe poses with his 1913 Joseph Geiger violin (made in St. Joseph) and wearing his Missouri State Old Time Fiddlers Association ball cap. (Courtesy of Ed Fedrizzi)

Joe Grable's grandson Joe Fedrizzi is carrying on his grandfather's enjoyment of fiddle contests and has become a frequent top finisher. Fedrizzi plays his grandfather's violin. After the contest at Sedalia's Trail's End Days contest in 2015, Joe plays a tune for the audience with Travis Inman (*left*, guitar, one of the judges) and Junior Marriott. Joe graduated from Kansas State University with a music degree in 2016 and is director of bands at North Platte High School. (Photo by Howard Marshall)

Listen to track 9 on the companion CD to hear Joe Fedrizzi's "Goodnight Waltz."

Missouri Fiddlers and Country Music Association, 1974

According to the Missouri Fiddlers and Country Music Association, "Fun and entertainment are also a large part of what we do, and through these events and activities you'll meet lots of nice and friendly people. Many of our members aren't musicians, just plain ol' folks enjoying and rediscovering some of the good old songs we all love to hear! Our doors are open to the public and our passion for Old Time Music can be shared by all."[27]

After the demise of the Missouri Old Time Fiddlers' Association and Mid-West Fiddlers, in 1974 Steve and Vesta Johnson, Frank Reed, John Philbrick, and others set up the Midwest Fiddlers and Country Music Association. They welcomed country music (and singing) and dancing as well as old-time fiddling.[28] The MF&CMA did not claim to represent the whole state or region, but rather represented the St. Louis metro area and surrounding territory in eastern Missouri and southern Illinois. Based in Kirkwood, the group developed monthly meetings and dinners, performed at fairs and festivals, and sponsored and participated in dances, jam sessions, and carry-in dinners in towns with members such as St. Charles, Houston, Jonesburg, New Florence, Eureka, Cuba, Ste. Genevieve, and Potosi. School programs were supported with Missouri Arts Council grants.

Like other groups, they seek to "preserve and promote" the music they see as a "link to the past," a musical culture jostled and considered vulnerable in the modern world. "MF&CMA members lend instruments to beginners and offer lessons, and Vesta Johnson and her grandson Steve Hall were instructors at the Bethel fiddle camps. Events sometimes include contests, and members sometimes administer contests for other groups, such as the Montgomery County Old Threshers Association's annual festival."

Their contest rules were conceived by R. P. Christeson and Virgil Smith, and they did not follow the "Weiser model" gaining traction in the 1970s. Judges are not sequestered but seated in front of the stage. Rules allow one or two backups "who will not play the melody or be so loud as to drown out the fiddler. This could cause the loss of points or disqualification." The emcee usually takes time to read the rules before the contest starts.

In 1998, the MF&CMA created a new annual contest at the historic Stovall's Grove country tavern and dance hall ("Home of Country Music Since 1935") in west St. Louis County. The contest was inspired by Vesta Johnson along with her daughter Lois Amburn and grandson Steve Hall. Fiddlers were encouraged to stay after the contest, enjoy a free barbecue meal, and participate in the dance and stage entertainment; however, most fiddlers today are uninterested in playing for dancers. The Stovall's Grove contest and other events were not held during the COVID pandemic.

After Cleo Persinger's death in 1971, the Boone County Fair contest sponsor, Sunrise Optimist Club, initiated a traveling "loving-cup" trophy in his memory, awarded to each year's champion and passed to the next winner the following year. Names engraved on the Cleo Persinger Challenge Trophy: Taylor McBaine in 1971 and 1972, Gene Wells in 1973, and Pete McMahan in 1974 and 1975. The trophy was retired after the 1975 contest. The presentation of loving cups is a long tradition. (Courtesy of Sarah McMahan)

Empire Building Fiddle Contests in the 1960s and 1970s

5

During the past few years there has been a phenomenal revival of interest in old-time fiddlers' contests.

—Thomas Spencer and Stephen Davis,
"On the Popularity of Old-Time Fiddlers' Contests"

In the 1920s Jazz Age and Roaring Twenties, contests enjoyed a surge, thanks to the creation of live radio, records, and the heyday of newspapers, social dancing, and small-town boosterism. Contests were an ingredient in the era's pleasure-seeking and post–World War I rejuvenation. In the tougher years of the Great Depression that followed, and then during the World War II era, the number of contests shrank. As peace came and times improved in the late 1940s and 1950s (the Korean War notwithstanding), fiddle contests came back.[1] This chapter looks at fiddle contests in the 1960s and 1970s, an era of enthusiastic expansion, offering some history and personalities in the drama who made the contest scene and fiddlers' associations interesting.

In the Midwest, fiddlers present three tunes: a "hoedown" (breakdown, reel, hornpipe played as a reel) in square-dance time, a waltz, and a "tune of choice"—which may be any kind of tune, and usually this is another hoedown. A few contests required the tune of choice to be something other than another hoedown or waltz, such as a schottische, march, rag, polka, two-step, air, or jig. Tune-of-choice rules vary, and fiddlers are often confused by them. Bill Shull codified the interpretation of the Missouri State Oldtime Fiddlers' Association in 1996: "The most typical practice is to have each fiddler play three tunes: a 'hoedown' or 'breakdown'; a waltz; and a 'tune of your choice' (which could include another waltz or breakdown). The 'tune of your choice' could also be any traditional piece, including polka, jig, quadrille, etc., but many contests would not accept these latter tunes."[2]

Waltzes began to be required in the 1950s to add variety and as a device to help judges compare fiddlers. It is often said it is harder to play a waltz well than a hoedown. Jim McGreevy, who judged contests from the 1970s on, recalls, "So many of the old-time fiddlers were *great* in the breakdowns, but not so strong in the waltzes. So, some of the organizers of these contests said, 'Let's put a waltz in there and find out who the really *good* fiddlers *are*.'"[3]

In Missouri, a few contests continued from the 1950s, and many more were inaugurated by the fiddlers' associations and bluegrass associations that appeared in the 1960s and 1970s, especially during the nation's bicentennial era (the middle 1970s). In these years, we saw a welcome rise of interest in local and family history and ethnic and minority communities, as well as creation of public-funded arts and humanities agencies, folk museums, and celebratory festivals of many kinds. Festivals, genealogy clubs, local history museums, academic programs in folklore and folklife searching to study and understand old ways of life, and fiddlers' associations and contests proliferated. The years around the bicentennial were a prime time for evoking heritage and drawing attention to nearby history and historic preservation.

Most fiddlers of my acquaintance have a competitive spirit when performing their art, but not many are really "contest fiddlers." They may enjoy watching a contest, or they may dislike the whole business. Many fiddlers take to contests not because they seek adrenaline-pumping rivalry to claim a trophy and a bit of cash—although others thrive on that. Many go to contests because they are social events, perhaps part of a community fish fry or county fair. Fiddlers who do not like contests have various and good reasons, such as "Who needs the stress? I don't have anything to prove. I'm a dance fiddler, not an exhibitionist. I'm not good enough."

Many contest fiddlers have a love-hate relationship with contests. Competitions of any kind play upon traditions, skills, beliefs, egos, politics, misunderstandings, and tribal self-interest. Fiddlers contend not only for prizes but also for prestige, respect, and territorial dominance. Wanting to perform under klieg lights in front of microphones, judges, and distracted audiences in order to "beat" one's peers implies a type-A personality, long practice, and razor-sharp focus. Contests can bring out passions and festering resentments. Very few do it for the money. "At a contest, a fiddler walks off the stage to a chorus of boos. Another contestant tries to console him by saying, 'It wasn't that bad, I heard some applause out there.' The first fiddler replies, 'Yes—the applause was for the booing.'"[4]

Missouri is home to many styles of music. Generally, the more successful contest fiddling styles became the most popular for contest fiddlers. The styles fell into loose and confusing groups labeled by such terms as bluegrass, old-time, Little Dixie, Ozark, festival style, Contest Style, and others.[5] The styles that judges noticed and awarded were most likely to be imitated.

Questionable results are commonplace because of the strong likelihood of subjective and biased adjudication. Judges are not neutral and may have gotten their appointments because they knew the organizers. They may have little understanding of what makes for a superior performance. So, as they say, "A fiddle contest is a crapshoot." The same top-drawer contest fiddlers may win week after week, but just who will snag the first-place money on any given day depends on a certain amount of good old-fashioned luck. Such vagaries of the game are why most contest fiddlers try not to get too concerned about rules or judging or who wins and who loses. Dale Pauley recalls Jimmy Gilmore telling him decades ago at a contest, "Don't take this fiddling too seriously!"[6] Good advice.

Nixa: From Local to Regional to State Contest

Contests in the Ozark town of Nixa from around 1946 to 1982 offer an example of the ups and downs of fiddle contests and changing times. Organized by former mayor Finis Gold and sponsored by the American Legion post, the Nixa contest was in an auspicious location, near the regional capital of Springfield with its country music radio and television programs, close to the expanding country music opry and tourism industry at Branson, and an area with plentiful fiddlers. Proximity to the oprys and country music media guaranteed an audience; it also meant that Nixa would attract some of the area's professional and semiprofessional "Branson fiddlers."[7]

Nixa was among many fiddle contests revived and picking up fans in the post–World War II and post–Korean War years. In October 1954, the contest attracted twenty-five fiddlers, while fifteen hundred spectators "rocked the Nixa high school auditorium."[8] Lloyd Trantham from Ozark (a few miles east of Nixa) won the Senior Division with "Oklahoma Blues" and "The Wagner," with second place to Emanuel Wood and third to Kenneth Butler. Delbert Butler won the "under 40" class. The door prize was a new washing machine. "Specials" inserted as breaks in the competition were provided by Springfield country radio and TV musicians Slim Wilson, Speedy Haworth, and Haworth's mother, "Aunt Martha." In 1957, administrators decided to claim the whole multistate Ozarks region, and the newspaper announced that an "Ozark Grand Champion Fiddler" would be crowned.[9] On October 16, 1958, the *Christian County Republican* announced that there would be no entry fee and that the first fifteen fiddlers to register would receive $2.50 "to show." After the contest, the newspaper announced that the American Legion was changing the event from an Ozarks regional contest to a Missouri state championship, and in 1959 Nixa began being promoted as "The Annual Missouri State Old Fiddlers Contest."[10]

In the late 1960s, Nixa's state contest reverted to being primarily for the nearby area within the Ozarks. One factor was the development of numerous new contests in central and northern Missouri, including major contests such as those at Lexington, Salisbury, and Graham. Contests with fuzzy or bad rules or unsure administration had a hard time getting top fiddlers to travel from distances to participate. Fiddlers began looking more to their own areas, where they might be more comfortable and better known and travel expenses moderate—factors that continue to affect contest participation.

A problem at Nixa was that the contest began to be "owned" by several charismatic or exceptionally skilled fiddlers. Dominance by the same performers year in and year out discourages others from competing, and audiences may get bored. At Nixa in 1969, Alvin "Red" Periman of Cassville began a decade-long reign, punctuated by wins by Dean Johnston and others. In 1969 there was no ad for the contest, but results were mentioned in the *Nixa Enterprise.*[11] Red Periman's daughter Geneva was his guitar second. There were thirty-one contestants. Second place was Barbara Childress (Bolivar) and third Donnie Wright, who was in town performing with Dave Drennon's opry. Wright played "Arkansas Traveler," "Black Mountain Rag," and "Wednesday Night Waltz" in both the 1968 and the 1969 contests.[12] These crowd-pleasing tunes were played countless times in contests in the 1970s, and "Black Mountain Rag" would eventually be banned by many contests as fiddlers' associations began to focus on rules. Nixa instituted a rule that the first-place winner could not win the following year, so Periman skipped competing in off years.

In 1970 there were announcements for Nixa's annual Missouri State Old Fiddlers Contest, but no results were published.[13] In 1971, the paper advertised the event and later ran a small notice naming winners; Red Periman took first place and the state championship, with daughters Geneva and Brenda playing guitar accompaniment.[14] For several years, only three places were awarded. In 1972, an ad in the paper included some of the rules: "One accompanist permitted for each contestant. Electric amplifiers will be permitted. Entry fee $1.50. Last year's winners cannot compete this year."[15] In 1976, there was an ad for the contest and a notice of the outcome: "Periman Takes First in Nixa's State Fiddlers Contest."[16] Newspapers in following years have similar reports, with some years unreported. In 1977, the advertisement included the "fiddling cowboy" cartoon figure associated with the National Oldtime Fiddlers' Association and contest in Weiser, Idaho.[17]

In 1979, Dean Johnston won first, Kelly Jones second, and Leland Thrasher (Fair Grove) third. The contest had been moved from October to November, just before the Thanksgiving holiday.[18] The Nixa state contest continued for two more years. In November 1981, the paper carried a small ad for the "33rd Annual Missouri State Fiddlers Contest," but no results were reported.[19] Gordon McCann tape-recorded the 1981 event; Dean Johnston won the state title again, second went to Dennis Essary (Willard), and third to Art Galbraith.[20]

Nixa held their last state championship in November 1982.[21] The demise of the contest was hastened by a familiar pattern. Founder and leader Finis Gold was in failing health, and without his leadership or a dedicated successor, community support flagged.[22] Word spread along the fiddlers' grapevine that the contest was moribund. Old hands were not surprised.

The Nixa rules were problematic, and confusion about rules detracts from a contest's success and public image, and arguments over rules can speed loss of support. Nixa did not resolve the thorny issue of whether to allow "professionals" in the contest. Some contests tried to define a professional as a musician who made at least half his or her income through music, but that settled nothing and people had a point in questioning letting "Branson fiddlers" compete, whose profession is performing music in the country music business six or seven nights a week. But contests have always been a venue for talented fiddlers anticipating careers, and only very seldom does a full-time professional show up in an amateur contest. It would be difficult and confrontational for administrators to attempt to cross-examine fiddlers to ascertain whether a fiddler makes 50 percent of his or her income through some aspect of music.

Ineffective judging and administration were problems at Nixa and important factors in its cancellation. Poor judging was obvious. Often judges lack enough knowledge and experience, but compounding that problem at Nixa were administrators' and judges' favoritism and cronyism, plain to see when winners' names were called. Michael Breid, who played guitar for Art Galbraith in Nixa contests, recalls that Galbraith knew the contest was "rigged" (but performed anyway). "I think fiddlers 'saw the light' eventually, and started staying away, and the Nixa contest folded."[23] In

Dean Johnston won the Open Division at Nixa in 1967 and thus the Missouri state championship. Rules at Nixa allowed one accompanist. Dean was a popular instructor in the Missouri Traditional Arts Apprenticeship Program (in which he taught Mike McCluey) and at Bethel fiddle camp. His brothers, Don, Bud, and Gary, played guitar and fiddle, and the four entertained at fairs and events in the Lamar area. Gary's sons, Beau and Tad, are fiddlers, carrying on the family tradition. Dean called himself "a Model T fiddler in a Cadillac world." (Photo by Kathryn Jones, Missouri Cultural Heritage Center, 1986)

addition, Finis Gold insisted on a quirky procedure of requiring that each contestant play one tune, then step to the side of the stage while the other contestants did the same thing, having to wait for one's turn to play one's next tune—a unique procedure that vexed and distracted contestants. Fiddlers are not likely to go back to a contest with habitually questionable judging, unacceptable rules, or odd gimmicks.[24]

Nixa had a good run. But once a contest declines and dies, it is difficult for it to be revived. Customs and accumulated knowledge are seldom written down to guide future volunteers. The key to keeping an event going depends on administrators having the foresight to find and train fresh talent so that retiring leaders can hand over the reins when the time comes. Unfortunately, such planning seldom happens.

Further Notes on Fiddle Contest Adjudication

As Billy Lee liked to say, "Contests? They're crooked. Old Doc played 'Pop Goes the Weasel' behind his back and between his legs—and won."[25] Contest judging is analyzed and debated ad infinitum. And it is an important subject.

It is difficult to secure qualified judges. Some fiddlers believe that fiddlers who compete in contests should be willing to help judge when asked to do so; others refuse requests to help. Few fiddlers want to help judge because they prefer to roll the dice as a contestant or sit and enjoy the show. Who wants to risk the abuse that can be flung at judges from musicians who say they have been "stiffed," or, perhaps more often, arguments and complaints from disgruntled parents, grandparents, or friends? Illinois fiddler and judge Randy Smith of McComb, Illinois, joked: "Surviving Fiddle Contests. Rule 6 for judges: Park near the stage."[26]

Some sports have unimpeachable judging. Olympic swimming races and downhill skiing have digital timing devices that cannot play favorites. Other sports have notoriously questionable judging; Olympic figure skating and dressage have human judges who seem unable to resist filling out score sheets to boost favorite skaters and riders or favor certain nations for transparent political reasons. Television commentary of Olympic figure skating at the 2108 Winter Games sounded like comments heard at fiddle contests: "She had a lower base value in the technical part of her program." "She had perfect technique but lacked expression." "Her mistakes were probably due to nerves." "She makes it look so easy." "They have the same teacher."[27]

A fiddle-contest judge is usually considered qualified if he or she is a fiddler or accompanist or if he or she has credibility among fiddlers. Age is important because people feel that judges need experience to be sufficiently knowledgeable. Judges typically are paid small sums and sometimes paid nothing at all. Contests have seen a modicum of professionalization in judging, as opposed to the older way based on audience response. And judges may have their own contest going—seeing if one's scores will be sufficient to help favorite fiddlers make it into the top finishers, and no one would deny that judging is a subliminal business. As Pete McMahan often said, "You don't have to beat the other fiddlers, you have to beat the judges." But after some seventy years competing in fiddle contests, in the late 1990s McMahan had become sufficiently jaded about judging that he told young Matt Wyatt to just ignore what the judges might want to hear and "play whatever you want to play."[28] And in a similar vein, this old advice also remains worthy: play tunes you can play in your sleep.

Judges fill out score sheets and reward points on "*Tone,* which means in tune, pleasing tone, *Timing*, good tempo, rhythm and beat, and *Execution*, oldtime sound, solid performance, good overall"—criteria listed in the 1980s by the Missouri State Old Time Fiddlers Association. Judges usually sit at a table in front of the stage, where all may see that they are doing their job. While some contests conceal judges in a room or area furnished with a sound system (a method promulgated by the National Oldtime Fiddlers' Association), many believe this is unnecessary, works poorly, and perhaps may be counterproductive to fairness.

In the 1950s and 1960s, prizes settled into a pattern of trophies (ribbons, loving cups, belt buckles, plaques, clocks, certificates, and the like) and cash. Among the nicest prizes in more recent decades were clocks made by Jack Morrow of Annada. Jack's daughters, Patty and Mary Jane, put on a competition at the AppleFest in Clarksville. Jack Morrow, a luthier and machinist, made clocks in different shapes, with brass badges. One year, it was apple-shaped clocks to reflect the AppleFest theme, one year it was steamboats, and eventually Jack settled on clocks in the shape of violins. On the other end of taste, Musial Wolfe once won a fiddle contest trophy made from an (empty) beer can.

Some judges say they admire familiar and comparatively simple tunes played brilliantly, but score sheets prove that most judges award extra points for more difficult tunes in the contest repertoire performed brilliantly.[29] Many a fiddler has stumbled when trying to copy a champion's impressive, well-studied setting of an already big tune, meaning one of the fifteen or so "big tunes" that one hears the top-drawer contest fiddlers play, contest after contest. Yes, it is complicated. As Drew Beisswenger notes, Bill Shull spoke to the problems of judging in terms of the old-time styles versus modern Contest Style: "Shull argues that good old-time fiddling should be judged based on musicianship and technique rather than on the 'rusticity' of the music"[30]—implying that Shull, an authority and practitioner of older Midwest fiddle styles, gives no added points if a fiddler presents a rare, quirky, or regional fiddle tune that may be a favorite in the area (say, a jig or schottische). And Shull was right on that point; the fiddler who simply plays the best that day—all else being equal—should win. But the itchy question still irritates some people: Should a modern Contest Style fiddling and repertoire be rewarded in a contest that is advertised as "old-time" fiddling? To make things even more complicated, note that "Contest Style" is often called "Texas style." So, the discussion (argument) can become circular, and we're back to fussing about "What is old-time fiddling?"

What makes a good contest tune? The scene has changed since the days when solid old-time square-dance tunes won contests. Now, old-time fiddling has become listening music for seated audiences and judges, and only rarely is it for dancing. Short answer? Play one of those fifteen "big" contest tunes, or play what Junior Marriott, Matt Wyatt, Travis Inman, John Williams, or Trustin Baker plays, if you can handle those tunes well. Or buy "Mark's book" and see what you can come up with by studying Stacy Phillips's detailed transcriptions of Mark O'Connor's contest winners.[31]

It is remarkable that many fiddlers really do not seem to care who wins. All this is why contests that many fiddlers enjoy the most tend to be small ones where prize money is modest and contestants do not feel that reputation, prestige, ego, and grocery money are on the line. But it is important to remember that some contest fiddlers depend on prize money to help with expenses of daily life.

Fun and Games

Funny business can take place at contests, on- and offstage. Jealous contestants may pull gags before the contest starts. One familiar ploy I have encountered is for a fiddler to interrupt another fiddler with a concentration-breaking question or comment just as the fiddler is getting ready to go onstage. A fiddler may invite a competitor to have a drink or beer or two as they are visiting in the parking lot or warming up (a more effective trick in former times when many musicians were known to drink too much). A more subtle game is for the trickster to stand near or right behind a fiddler warming up and pretend it's a jam session (or not pretend) and fiddle along—while being just slightly out of tune or out of rhythm, causing consternation among the target fiddler and accompanists who try to quickly retune or figure out what has gone amiss.

Fred Stoneking saw it all in the capricious yet exciting world of fiddle contests. A lot of shenanigans can happen, providing the stuff of legends:

> Fiddlers will play a lot of tricks on each other so that they can win. If someone knows that a contestant's apt to beat him he might take him out and give him a drink. If he accepts that first one, then the other guy'll try to fill him up as much as he can. After that, when the poor fiddler gets on the mic he'll be bound to make a mistake. I saw a guy one time who had been nipping pretty heavy and he played "Bill Cheatem" for his hoedown and he done a good job, too. And then he announced some other piece for his tune of choice, but, when he started to play, by George, it came out "Bill Cheatem" again. And he did a good job that time too, but, needless to say, he got blackballed.
>
> There's a couple of Missouri fiddle players, both of them top-notch. I love them both for their fiddling ability, but I'm afraid they used to be crooks. They'd meet up at these contests, and one guy'd say, "Boy, Joe, you sure got a good sounding fiddle, and you got a good bow there, too." Old Joe'd say, "Yeah, John," and he'd talk about how much money he had paid for it. Then John would say, "Well, let me borrow that now. I just want to play it a little bit to see what it is like." While Joe wasn't looking, John'd run his hand through his hair, get a little hair oil on his hand and rub that bow down. Eventually John'd hand it back to Joe, but he didn't know that Joe was doing the same thing to him. At this one contest I went to, I remember both them boys getting up to the microphone and [their bows] just going "ssss, ssss." They were both dandy fiddle players, but there were always playing these pranks on one another.
>
> I'm afraid not all the judges are totally honest either. I've been a judge in a contest where the head judge started telling who was going to win before they even started the contest: "This guy's gonna win, that guy's over there's gonna get second" and so on down the line. And, by gum, it actually turned out to go that way. Thinking about the score sheet I had turned in, I imagine that the headmaster must have been a whiz at juggling figures.[32]

Sometimes an accompanist might pull a trick on a fiddler if the accompanist wants someone else to win the contest. Dale Pauley experienced a clever maneuver when a backup he did not know personally tried to sabotage his performance in a contest in Utah in the 1980s. The guitarist was there to back up a friend. Walking around, searching for a someone to back him up, Pauley observed that the guitarist in question was a good one by listening to him with fiddlers jamming and warming up. Dale asked the fellow to play backup. When Dale got onstage and launched into his first tune, the guitarist started playing off rhythm to try to throw Pauley off his performance. The judges, however, knew the guitarist, saw what was happening, and did not deduct points. Pauley won the contest anyway.[33]

The Mockingbird's Last Call?

The Missouri Farmers Association Oil Company (MFA) enjoyed huge membership in the post–World War II era when Missouri still had a vast number of small family farms. The company was looking for a public relations project. Fiddlers such as Columbia's Bobby Joe Caldwell were often hired to entertain at openings of MFA Oil dealerships. Fiddle music was a sentimental emblem of rural life, in spite of increasing urbanization and loss of family farms through the growth of agribusiness. A big new fiddle championship seemed like a good idea.[34]

To frame the contest as a significant statewide affair, MFA set up three rounds of competition—local, regional, and state. Round-one contests were held in towns with MFA Oil distributorships willing to sponsor them, such as Freeburg, Fulton, Hannibal, Mexico, Moberly, and Union—not surprisingly, towns in rural counties known for their fiddlers. The contests typically took place at spring MFA membership meetings and served as banquet entertainment for company employees and guests. Winners in round one were invited to round-two "district" contests billed as "gateways to the State Contest." The company covered travel expenses for fiddlers chosen for the five district playoffs. Some of the same towns held both round one and round two. District winners and four runners-up were then invited to Columbia for the grand championship in November.

The MFA contest was advertised as statewide, but this was marketing hype. Most people understood that the claim of being a statewide championship was P. T. Barnum advertising. St. Louis and Kansas City were left out, as well as large swaths of low-population rural counties in northern and southern Missouri. Despite ignoring fiddlers in left-out areas, the contest brought out many of Missouri's premier contest fiddlers.

Anyone could sign up for round one. For round two, invited fiddlers received written invitations to the district rounds from MFA contest administration. In the districts, five fiddlers were selected to go to Columbia for the grand finale later in the year. Leroy Canaday's form letter came from MFA manager R. A. Young, April 5, 1961, reminding fiddlers that they were to play a waltz, a hoedown, and "a third number of your own choosing," and that "you will be expected to furnish your own accompaniment, limited to two accompanists." MFA director of sales promotion Clay Davis wrote to congratulate fiddlers who won their districts, informing them that they were invited to compete for "Champion Fiddler of the State of Missouri" in downtown Columbia at the luxurious Missouri Theatre, two blocks from the university campus, on November 20, 1961. The date coincided with MFA's annual meeting and fell just before the Thanksgiving holiday. MFA Oil paid contestants' expenses to Columbia. Young wrote contestants again in September, reminding them of the contest and asking for a photo for publicity in the company newsletter.

Rules were mailed in early November, and a following letter from Kirk Dodge stated the arrival date and time and urged fiddlers to observe contest rules. "Prizes to be awarded are as follows: State Champion-trophy plus $100; First runner up-trophy plus $50; Second runner up trophy plus $25; Third runner up-trophy plus $15; and

At the MFA district playoff at Fulton, April 1961. First place, Leroy Canaday (*center front*); *clockwise around him, left to right*: Lyle Crow (Paris), Knight Kinsey (California), George Bent (Vandalia), John Hager (Jefferson City, third place), Tom Clark (Perry), Paul Shikles (Russellville), Dale Pauley; center is Buck Cuno (Fulton, second place). Earlier in April 1961, Canaday previously won round one in Moberly. (Courtesy of Dale Pauley)

fourth runner up-trophy plus $10. Checks will be sent to the winners following the contest. Trophies will be sent to winners after imprinting of winner's name. 5. Contestant trip expenses will be paid by the company. All of the above rules will be explained to you in advance of the contest so that there will be no misunderstanding."[35]

These communications gave voice to the three-tunes-per-round rule that had become customary, as well as the no-more-than-two-accompanists rule. How many backups a fiddler could have was an ongoing debate, but questions of what style of fiddling would be expected were not as relevant as they would become in later decades. Letters to fiddlers also discussed the panel of four judges. MFA obtained an applause-o-meter electronic device as a secondary judging device to measure audience response (an unpopular and unfair method of adjudication). Further, stage antics would result in lower scores from the judges.

The five district champions who met in the finals in Columbia in November 1961 were Leroy Canaday (Randolph County), LeRoy Haslag (Osage County), Maurice Evans (Caldwell County), Earl Morgan (Greene County), and Dick Logan (Johnson County). Canaday played "Devil's Dream," "Wednesday Night Waltz," and

"Black Mountain Rag." Judges' tallies resulted in a tie with LeRoy Haslag, another fiddler skilled in presentation of polished exhibition pieces. In the playoff, Canaday and Haslag played the same crowd-pleasers—"Orange Blossom Special," "Listen to the Mockingbird," and "Westphalia Waltz." When the scores were in, Canaday and Haslag were deadlocked again. To solve the impasse, the judges did something strange. Rather than ask the fiddlers to play one more tune to break the tie, the judges told the emcee to have the boys draw straws to decide who would have first place. Canaday drew the long straw and was crowned Missouri state champion, much to the chagrin of Haslag, who never forgot this bizarre and unfair method of selecting the winner. Haslag did not compete in the contest in 1962 and generally quit contests but enjoyed a career on the Ozark Opry.[36]

Ray Young mailed letters of appreciation. Those who came in behind first place were thanked and congratulated, and MFA checks were enclosed to cover travel expenses. Canaday received letters of congratulation from his pastor Rev. Charles Hendrickson, elected officials, and others. Ralph Houchins, manager of the National Life and Accident Insurance Company in Nashville, wrote a congratulatory letter dated March 5, 1962, inviting Canaday to the Grand Ole Opry: "I hope that we will have the opportunity to hear you play and appear on our radio station, WSM in Nashville, Tennessee." Leroy talked it over with his wife, Betty, but misgivings about flirting with "the big time" in a big city for a young married musician caused him to turn down the offer. Canaday was also invited to audition for Roy Acuff's Smoky Mountain Boys road band, working out of Nashville, another chance to "follow the fiddle" to the country music capital; again, Canaday thought long and hard and declined.

Nell Gross wrote about Leroy Canaday and the 1961 state contest for the *St. Louis Globe-Democrat*. Her article conveys the mood of the event and the time, but neglects to mention the deadlock with LeRoy Haslag and the drawing of straws for the championship.

> You could almost smell the sulfur and see the flames as "Devil's Dream" hoe-down flashed from Canaday's fiddle. Fast and foot-stomping, hot as Beelzebub's blazes, it burned an impression on a panel of judges at the recent State Champion Old-Time Fiddlers Contest in Columbia, Mo.
>
> But it was Canaday's encore, "Listen to the Mocking Bird," that won him the championship. With eyes closed, lips parted, emotion lining his rusty-freckled face, the gaunt country fiddler drew his freshly rosined bow. Sweet, shrill, tender twitterings warbled and whistled down the strings. Through his fluttering fingers and peck-peck-pecking bow, "Mocking Bird" soared aloft.
>
> The term "old" fiddler doesn't always insinuate age. (Canaday, for example, is 33.) It's more likely to mean "old fashioned," or that he plays "in the old style."
>
> What precisely is fiddling? In the words of Leroy Canaday, "It's a gift."
>
> It's also a special way of playing the violin, and the special kind of music that is-played. The instrument's no different from one used on the concert stage, but there all similarity ends.

Second-place winner LeRoy Haslag (*left*) with first-place winner Leroy Canaday after the MFA state contest, Columbia, 1961. (Courtesy of LeRoy Haslag)

Like Canaday, most old fiddlers are self-taught and don't read music (even when they can). Individualists, they weave their own interpolations and alter, add, subtract at whim.

"Every fiddler has his own way of playing 'Mocking Bird'," Canaday said in explanation. "Depends on what birds he's got in his locale. I put in a bob white and whippoorwill; hear 'em a lot around here."

"Fella picks up his fiddle," Canaday explained, "gets to playin' 'round and makes himself up a tune. Next fella thinks maybe he can do it better, changes it here and there. Folks keep making changes till it finally gets to be the one way everybody likes."

Some fiddlers' tunes, like "Mocking Bird," were pop songs in their day. That number was composed by Septimus Winner who lived from 1826 to 1902 . . . under the pseudonym of "Alice Hawthorne:" it whistled up $3,000,000 in sales.

Canaday's rendition of it netted $100 as first prize in the contest. But more important to him was the title it bestowed--"Missouri Champion Old Fiddler."[37]

At a contest Canaday entered around 1964 in the brick schoolhouse in Higbee, a coal-mining town south of Moberly, he planned to display the same crowd-favorite winners. But when he got to the registration table, he was informed that fiddlers would not be allowed to play "Black Mountain Rag," "Orange Blossom Special," or "Listen to the Mockingbird." His best contest tunes were outlawed by the "old fiddlers' association" (Mid-West Fiddlers) founded by Cleo Persinger, Jake and Lena Hughes, and friends. The newly formed fiddlers' associations (influenced by the National Oldtime Fiddlers' Contest) were blackballing those exciting "trick and fancy tunes." Cross-tuning (scordatura), employed in "Black Mountain Rag," was also now banned. In the heat of the moment, Canaday fiddled "Devil's Dream" and "my waltz" ("Wednesday Night Waltz"); he could think of nothing he wanted to play for his third tune and played "Mockingbird" and, playing the banned tune, finished far down the list. This experience deeply vexed Canaday, and he stayed away from contests for years. "Fiddle contests were a lot more fun before they had fiddlers' associations."[38]

The MFA contests were held just two years, but they had an impact in the contest community. There were efforts to find better judges, eliminate applause-o-meters, and create score sheets that could emphasize qualities in fiddling. As it happened, the early 1960s was when Missouri fiddlers began going to big western fiddling expos, such as the so-called national contests in Truth or Consequences, New Mexico, and Weiser, Idaho, and bringing home some new notions about how contests could be run. The MFA contests were among the last in Missouri where fiddlers were allowed to play flashy exhibition pieces like "Listen to the Mockingbird," "Orange Blossom Special," and "Black Mountain Rag."[39] Despite how people love to hear a good fiddler take off on "Listen to the Mockingbird" and other exhibition pieces, those tunes began to disappear from repertoires for public performance. Whether banning tunes by labeling them mistakenly as "trick tunes" is a good idea or bad idea is still discussed six decades after Leroy Canaday and LeRoy Haslag echoed the mockingbird's calls off the crystal chandelier of the Missouri Theatre.[40]

Dick Logan

An email in 2016 from Art Logan of Appleton City to the Missouri Traditional Fiddle and Dance Network website brought Dick Logan into this book. Logan wrote, "I would like to see my dad, Richard 'Dick' Logan mentioned. He was quite the fiddler in the '60s and on. He finished 3rd in 1961 to Leroy Canaday and was 1st in Clinton to get to the finals beating out Lee Stoneking and Frankie Hickson among others to advance to the finals. Played all over the Midwest and even in the '70s won a contest or two."[41]

In 1844, Dick Logan's great-great-grandparents Ernest H. Lauging and Clara Elizabeth (Eliza) Lauging came to St. Charles County, Missouri, from the village of Buer in the Kingdom of Hanover in Lower Saxony. They brought their children, Caroline, Mary, and Franz Henry. From the 1830s through the 1840s, many German-speaking immigrants came to the St. Louis and St. Charles area and farther into Missouri, adding important ingredients here as across the United States—the waltz (known since colonial times but popularized extensively), schottische, polka, and related couple dances and dance tunes.[42] In the early 1900s some of the Laugings anglicized the name as "Logan." In Cole Camp cemeteries, there are gravestones in the Lutheran and Catholic cemeteries with the name spelled both ways. The name change may have happened during the World War I era, when many German Americans stopped using German in public places, newspapers, schools, and church services.

Dick Logan's parents were Frederick William (Fred) Logan and Martha Eichelberger Logan. Fred Logan served in the US Army during World War I and after the war settled on a farm a few miles north of Knob Noster in eastern Johnson County.[43] Richard Charles (Dick) Logan was born on the Knob Noster farm. He caught the "fiddle bug" as a teen and was given the basics by a gentleman on a neighboring farm. Dick was, as far as can be known, the first in the family to be a fiddler. He did not play the old German dance tunes that one might have expected.

Logan was drafted into the US Army in 1951 during the Korean War and spent 1952 and 1953 in the Forty-Third Infantry Division's signal corps. He was assigned to the Augsburg base in Bavaria, where the shoulder-patch emblem of his signal corps unit was a grape leaf. Years later, Logan named his family band's record label Grape Leaf Records. While in Germany, he bought a Stainer-model violin that he played in jam sessions and a country band in off-duty time. According to Art Logan: "The sergeant in the barracks noticed him carrying the fiddle case. And the sergeant said, 'What d'ya *got* there?' Dad says, 'That's my new fiddle.' And the guy says, 'Well, I know you play my kind of music because you didn't call it a *violin*.' And so, Dad said, from *then on*—that sergeant had a country band and Dad got to play at all the dances there on the base."

Dick Logan at the Army base in Augsburg, Germany, in 1952 or 1953, with the Stainer-copy violin acquired there. Due to his fiddling ability and support from his sergeant, Logan enjoyed comfortable duty and was promoted to corporal. (Courtesy of Art Logan)

After the Army in 1953, Logan returned to Knob Noster and started a career as a carpenter. He married Doris Myrick in 1954 in Miami, Oklahoma, a businesswoman who would operate her own bookkeeping and tax service and insurance firm in Knob Noster for many years. The Logans had three children, Art, an insurance agent in Appleton City; Jane, who made a career in law enforcement and lives in Knob Noster; and Paul, a truck driver.

Dick Logan started playing fiddle music at dances and absorbed country and western swing music from radio and records. He enjoyed a variety of music but was uninterested in pop music. According to Art Logan, "He liked Bob Wills, he played the western swing. He played old-time country *hoedowns* and waltzes. But when it came to the newer kind of stuff, he didn't play any of that. Now, he did some *polkas*, they'd get him to do 'Beer Barrel Polka,' and he had another one. You couldn't be around a German beer fest and not play a polka or two." Logan did not read violin music but knew that being able to read music has its place. "Dad's statement to me one time was, 'You know, I'm not knocking reading music, it's nice if people can.' But he said, 'In my mind, reading the music is like painting by number.' And you know, I had to think about it awhile, but it sunk in. In other words, it's your painting that someone has put there in front of you, okay, and in *his mind* if you *hear the song* and play it, it becomes *yours*. Because, if you're not reading the music and you're playing it from what you *hear*, it's *your song*."

Logan was attracted to bluegrass music and adopted bluegrass repertoire and performance techniques. He was a proficient harmony ("twin fiddle") fiddler. He preferred not to label his fiddling. If someone asked what style he plays, he would say, "I play fiddle music that I like to hear." Logan played a long-bow style with drive, precision, and plentiful double-stops. For his bluegrass performing, he figured out the requisite backup skills and stagecraft.

Among his favorite tunes for the many two-steps (fox-trots) at dances was "Darktown Strutter's Ball," a vaudeville hit from 1917. Logan liked "Spanish Two-Step," "San Antonio Rose," "Faded Love," and other Bob Wills tunes for two-steps. For square dances, his favorites were "Bill Cheatem," "Ragtime Annie," and "Fire on the Mountain." "'Bill Cheatem' and 'Fire on the Mountain' were *guaranteed* to last until our fingers were sore! He had a clear favorite when he played a waltz, 'Over the Waves'—I can never remember *ever* that he didn't play that at a dance." Dick Logan was the kind of fiddler who would keep the tune going until the last dancer retired from the floor. "There would always be *one guy* who wouldn't quit *dancing*. And Dad was one of those fiddlers that, as long as there was somebody who still had enough *air*, he'd play! Them *barn* dances, *they was something*."

Dances in barns were popular in the spring and autumn. Families had fed most if not all of their winter hay to the livestock and had their barns cleared out and ready for spring planting. A barn dance was a popular elixir as people emerged from winter and welcomed springtime. Per Art Logan, "Along about March or April, as long as it didn't get too cold, and we'd get a nice Saturday night—buddy, *we'd be there*! A farmer would just call up. This one guy, Jesse McMullen, he would call Dad and say, 'Dick—the *loft's clean*.' Boy, I'd hate to hear that!—It'd be the spur of the moment. You know, he might call Friday, and the dance would be Saturday night, but you know what, there'd still be thirty-forty people there—they'd just be wandering up the steps to the hayloft. But that was *entertainment* back then."

Concordia, famed for its German personality, has an annual fall festival (beer festival), and the Logans played there many years at one of the two bars facing each other on Main Street. Dancers in Concordia were particularly fond of "Put Your Little Foot" and the polkas "Little Brown Jug" and "Beer Barrel Polka." To add interest in dances that might last an extended length of time, Dick Logan would fiddle two tunes in the same key as a medley, such as "Down Yonder" and "Old Spinning Wheel." He would play each tune twice through, transition to the next tune and play that through twice, and then return to the first tune and play it twice. A circle dance (sometimes called a whistle dance) was formed with two circles, one for men, and one for women inside the men's circle. They circled in opposite directions, moving to the music. "When a fellow with a whistle or some type of horn or bell, whistled. You grabbed the closet person in other circle and then it was couples until the whistle blew again."

There was very little jig dancing (individual step dancing or clogging) at these dances, but some people did jig dance alone and apart from the square or while dancing in the square. Jig dancers danced the longest of anyone during square dances, but this did not faze Logan. "I can't think of any time that a guy outlasted Dad. We might get to the point where I was exhausted [playing rhythm]. But as far as the guy out there on the floor—if Dad had his way, it'd just be *him* [the dancer] and the *fiddle*. He usually played four to five minutes for a square dance, sometimes longer, close to eight minutes. And we're just going, 'It's time to quit'!"

For many years, Logan played the Stainer he brought home from Germany, using it in the MFA contests in 1960s and during the years the children were growing up. He also had a German shop-made Maggini copy acquired in the early 1980s, which he acquired due to his admiration for the Springfield radio fiddler Lonnie Robertson, who played a Maggini. Logan had a DeArmond detachable contact violin pickup attached to his violins' tailpieces, when amplification was needed at a busy dance.[44] When repairs were needed or a new bridge cut for a violin, or when a bow needed new hair, he relied on Bob George of Kansas City and Chris Burford of Leeton. Logan preferred Black Diamond strings, in part because Black Diamonds were heavily marketed to fiddlers, old-time, jazz, swing, and bluegrass musicians, and sets for violin, banjo, mandolin, and guitar could be found inexpensively at drugstores and bargain barns and other local businesses.

Logan was particular about the kind of accompaniment he preferred, especially in fiddle contests. Lucky enough to have children with a knack for music, Dick encouraged Art, Jane, and Paul to learn to play mandolin and guitar so they could "second" for him in contests. "Dad figured out that it was easier to *train* his seconds than it was to *obtain* his seconds. So, from then on it was my sister and I, normally, because fiddlers contests would only let you have *two seconds*. Jane was one of the *better* rhythm guitar players that I was ever around. And I think my dad *ingrained* in her that *timing is everything*. Timing, timing."

Dick Logan usually placed among winners and often took first. His favorite contest was part of the Midwest Old Threshers Reunion at Mount Pleasant, Iowa, where there were activities for families and a campground. The Logans traveled to Mount Pleasant in the mid- and later 1960s. Fiddlers with bands typically entered the fiddle contest, and their bands were invited to perform a set onstage at some point during the festival. Dick Logan would usually finish in the top five; he enjoyed the family-band performances and campground sessions more than the few minutes fiddling in the contests.[45] Among Missouri contest fiddlers Art Logan remembers were Fred Stoneking and Dude Fellows ("Fellers"), a performer on KWTO in Springfield (Dude always performed wearing house slippers). In the Logan family's territory, the top contest players and bluegrass fiddlers Art remembers were Stoneking, Lyman Enloe, Joe McIntyre, Larry Ellis, and Kelly Jones.[46]

Finalists at the 1961 MFA state contest at the Missouri Theatre in Columbia. *Left to right*: first place, Leroy Canaday; second, LeRoy Haslag; fourth, Maurice Evans; third, Dick Logan; and fifth, Earl Morgan. (Courtesy of LeRoy Haslag)

Bluegrass music is an ensemble experience. As their skills developed, and as they saw bluegrass bands, Jane, Art, and Paul became interested in working out tunes and songs in addition to accompanying their father's fiddling, and "the Logan Family" band was born. They became more involved in bluegrass festivals than fiddle contests. Festivals were a lot more fun.

Dick Logan appreciated quality instruments and bought or traded for quality instruments as the children advanced. A fine instrument inspired them to practice, and "name-brand" instruments played by professionals added credibility. Paul played a

Gibson RB-250 "bowtie" Mastertone five-string banjo, Jane played a Martin 0-18 guitar, and Art played a 1914 Gibson "A" model mandolin.[47] Dick obtained the Martin and the Gibson mandolin in Kansas City, trading a "little Gibson" guitar (LG model) and some cash.[48] Paul got his start on the five-string banjo from Jack Deck, in Marshall. In addition to performances at bluegrass festivals, the Logans competed in the band contests that often were part of bluegrass festivals. Art Logan tells a story about a festival at Knob Noster operated by Herman Smith. Smith brought in major stars, including Bill Monroe and the Blue Grass Boys. At age nine or ten, Paul was getting attention as a local prodigy, picking banjo like Earl Scruggs. At Smith's festival in 1969 or 1970:

> We were playing there in Knob Noster. 'Course, since we were local, we got to play the opening stuff. At the end of the day, Herman had everybody that played up on the stage. 'Course, my family was all towards the back, just leaning against the stage. All of the big names were at the front. But all of a sudden it was kind of like *Moses parting the water*—all these people started moving aside. Next thing you know, here come *Bill Monroe* with a microphone, weaving his way back through the crowd and sat down in front of my brother. Well, my brother kind of perked up *then*, and finished the song, and then Bill grabbed him and pulled him up to the front, he said, "Young man, what's your name, and how old are you?" And Paul told him and Bill says, "Well, we're going to let you start this next song out, and why don't you just pick us a song and let's *go*!" Well, at the time, being *kids*, no one knows [we did not know] the *politics of music*. Or my brother would never have played an Earl Scruggs song with Bill Monroe! They hadn't made up yet. But Paul says, "Well, let's just do a little bit of "Foggy Mountain Breakdown." "Well," Bill said—"Okay, son."[49]

In spying Paul with his banjo, Monroe was acknowledging young people and tipping his hat to a local family band. Paul Logan had a memorable experience with the eccentric Father of Bluegrass Music that day, and Monroe responded graciously to the youngster's innocence.

By 1970, fans were asking the Logans if they had records for sale. For groups like this as well as individual fiddlers, it was common to invest in recording and pressing a few hundred records 45s or LPs to sell at concerts, festivals, and other appearances, as well as to promote in mail-order catalogs and on local radio shows. Dick Logan and the kids loaded up the station wagon and headed down to Concord, Arkansas. Dick made arrangements with Wayne Raney to hire Rimrock Records for a recording session and for manufacture of 45-rpm records.[50] Raney encouraged Dick to record something different in addition to covers of popular Flatt and Scruggs favorites and others. Logan fiddled his composition "Grape Leaf Rag," and that was the "something different" Raney wanted to hear. Raney believed that "it's always good to have something that you wrote" as well as tunes fans know. Raney urged Logan to copyright "Grape Leaf Rag" and helped with the necessary paperwork.

The Logan family at Wayne Raney's Rimrock Studio, Concord, Arkansas, 1970. *Left to right*: recording engineer Zyndall Raney (Wayne's son, who volunteered to sit in and add bass to the session); *kneeling, front*, Dick Logan; Paul (age ten or eleven), banjo; Art (age fifteen), mandolin; Jane (age fourteen), guitar. (Courtesy of Art Logan)

The band generally ceased performing in the mid-1970s. Dick Logan retired from carpentry around 1995 but continued to work on an occasional building job and found more time to hunt quail, deer, and raccoons. Advancing age did not end his fiddling; he continued to play music informally with Art, Jane, and others. A few years after his father's death in 2008, Art Logan decided to try to revive the contests once held in west-central Missouri. With friends, and largely self-financed, in 2010 Logan hosted the first of four Dick Logan Memorial Youth Fiddling Competitions in Appleton City in conjunction with a youth bluegrass festival. Conscious of the importance of bringing children into the music, Art conceived the contest just for young people, and the age limit was eighteen. There were two preliminary rounds and a final round. The purse was ample, and awards were presented to the youngest fiddler and the fiddler coming the farthest distance. In 2010, the contest had eight fiddlers, including Hannah Farnum, an outstanding young player with the Farnum Family band in the Branson area. The contest was off to a good start, but in 2011 and 2012 only two fiddlers showed up.[51] In 2014 Art tried one more time and organized the Fourth Annual Dick Logan Memorial Youth Fiddling Competition, but there was little support in the community and the contest ended.

Listen to track 10 on the companion CD to hear Dick Logan's "Grape Leaf Rag."

Cleo Persinger, a Patriarch

Cleo Persinger, a name often encountered in these books, was grand champion at the National Oldtime Fiddlers' Contest in Weiser, Idaho, in 1964. Cleo was the son of Frances and Albert Persinger, a lumberyard laborer. Cleo's grandfather Wood Persinger came to Boone County from Kentucky as a young man in the mid-1800s and farmed in the Shaw community east of Columbia. Cleo's father, Albert, and his great-grandfather Joseph were fiddlers, and a great-great-grandfather was a concert violinist.[52] Cleo was orphaned at age one, when his father died, and he was taken to Mr. and Mrs. Edgar T. Thurston and grew up on the Thurstons' prosperous farm in the Blackfoot community near Midway, west of Columbia.

Cleo learned to play the flowing, intense, largely single-string "hornpipey" Little Dixie fiddle style from his foster father, Edgar Thurston, and from Dr. William Dow Hatton.[53] "Doc" Hatton was a horse-and-buggy physician in Columbia who enjoyed giving music lessons to young people, and he gave Cleo several violin lessons at the Thurston farm. Persinger did not learn to read violin music, however, and continued to be an ear musician. As a young man, he played for square and round dances several nights a week at taverns and nightclubs, sometimes swapping fiddle jobs with his friend Gene Wells from next-door Howard County.

Persinger's fiddling exhibited a curious tendency to drop or add a beat or two in certain tunes, and some of his friends, such as Taylor McBaine, may have picked up this quirk from Cleo. Cleo was fascinated by the violin and violinists, and he experimented with different bridges, strings, sound posts, and setups in search of improved sound. He enjoyed buying and trading violins and was a regular at Cope Ashlock's violin shop in Columbia. Cleo's friend luthier Jack Roberts took care of most repairs Cleo needed. Persinger liked a loud fiddle, and he owned violins in which he had enlarged the lower terminal holes of the F-holes with a pocketknife in hopes of inducing enhanced volume.

Cleo entered his first contest at fifteen and lost, but he was hooked on the challenge and excitement. In the vernacular of fiddlers, he enjoyed "butting heads" with other fiddlers. Persinger's long list of mentors and peers included dance and contest fiddlers such as Luther Caldwell, Charlie Cook, Daniel Boone Jones, Tony and Jim Gilmore, Charlie Jackson, Taylor McBaine, Pete McMahan, George Morris, Aaron Oliver, Junior Perkins, Ed Tharp, and Gene and Henry Wells and other Wells fiddlers. Older fiddlers still remember Cleo's special versions of dance tunes and contest pieces as well as obscure local melodies. His fiddling influenced fiddlers such as McBaine, McMahan, Dale Pauley, John Hartford, and Mike Hartgrove.

Around 1960, Jim Chancellor (Texas Shorty) and his father, Robert, drove to Cleo Persinger's farm near Columbia to visit and play music. Robert Chancellor and Persinger had become acquainted previously. Jim Chancellor was well known among many Missouri fiddlers, in part because of his much-admired 45-rpm records. The Chancellors stayed overnight, and a fiddle session was held that included Pete McMahan and Dwight Lamb (who drove down from Iowa). "Cleo lived in a rural home, and I recall having a very pleasant evening there. The significant thing I remember was the syrup buckets. Cleo had positioned them along the eves of his home because he liked the sound of raindrops falling on the top of the buckets."[54]

Persinger was a strong promoter of all things fiddle and liked contests—the bigger, the better. In 1953, he helped organize a contest billed as a "state fiddle contest" in Midway. The contest drew players from around Missouri but did not accrue enough support to be repeated.[55]

In June 1964, Cleo and his wife, Lillian, along with several other Missouri fiddlers, drove seventeen hundred miles west to the "Northwest Mountain" contest in Missoula, Montana, and then on to the National Oldtime Fiddlers' Contest in Idaho. At Missoula, Persinger played, in various rounds, "Fiddler's Hoedown" (a.k.a. "Boone County Rag"),[56] "Bill Cheatem," "Devil's Dream," "Rose Waltz," "Marmaduke's Hornpipe," "Charlie Cook's G Waltz," "Durang's Hornpipe," and "Grey Eagle." Byron Berline took first place at Missoula; second place, Almon Manes; third place, Loyd Wanzer; fourth place, Vivian Williams; and fifth place, Cleo Persinger.

At the following week's contest in Weiser, in the penultimate round, Persinger played "Leather Britches," "Parish Hornpipe," and "Flowers from Heaven" for his waltz. In the final round he played "Arkansas Traveler," "Coming Down from Denver" and "40 Years Ago Waltz." He received a trophy and $400 for first place and the grand champion title. The *Columbia Tribune* ran a story about Persinger's victory under the headline "Nation's Top Fiddler."[57] Just as at Missoula, Mrs. Persinger accompanied her husband on guitar (open-chord style, with a thumb pick), and Lena Hughes seconded with her plunky parlor-style five-string banjo.

Cleo returned to Weiser in 1965 to defend his title, playing "Jack Rabbit in the Cabbage Patch," "Sally Goodin," "Fiddler's Hoedown," "Grey Eagle," "Sunflower Waltz," "Red Apple Rag," "Coming Down from Denver," "Black Velvet Waltz," "Leather Britches," "Arkansas Traveler," and "Flowers from Heaven." This time, the championship went to Byron Berline.

John Hartford visited and recorded a number of fiddlers in the late 1950s and early 1960s. Hartford was still living in St. Louis and was engrossed in old-time and bluegrass fiddling as well as bluegrass banjo; he was also on the verge of dropping out of Washington University and heading for California. Hartford made trips to the Columbia area and organized a fiddle session at the Persinger farm in 1961, which he recorded on his reel-to-reel "school-house Wollensak."[58] Years later, Hartford included his transcription of one of Persinger's contest tunes, "Coming Down from Denver on a Trip from Galway Here and There" for a *Devil's Box* article. The long title was

Persinger's; he announced the tune by joining together three alternate titles he knew: "Coming Down from Denver" (the standard Missouri title), "Trip to Galway," and "Here and There" (the title Nashville fiddler Tommy Jackson used on a 1960 LP, *Square Dance Festival*). Announcing the tune that way always got a chuckle from the audience.[59]

Listen to track 11 on the companion CD to hear Cleo Persinger's version of "Buckeye Reel."

Persinger commanded the stage. He dressed well, typically in a white dress shirt, slacks, and suspenders. He was a gregarious and engaging person. Persinger eagerly attended a concert by classical violinist Albert Spalding in the Missouri Theatre in

Buckeye Reel

As played by Cleo Persinger

Transcribed by Richard Shewmaker

"Buckeye Reel" as played by Cleo Persinger, ca. 1960, an obscure breakdown, played by Ed Tharp, Taylor McBaine, as well as Pete McMahan and George Morris (who called it "Buckley's Reel"). (Transcription by Richard Shewmaker)

Columbia. Persinger loved classical music and bought a seat in the middle of the front row. An enthusiastic University of Missouri journalism student, Harold Hopkins, arranged for Persinger to visit Spalding in his dressing room after the concert, and the two musicians hit it off. Spalding handed Persinger his Guarnerius to examine; handing it gently back to the maestro, Cleo commented, "'I'm a violinist of sorts, myself,' he said with a quiet dignity. 'My father paid $2.50 for my violin more than fifty years ago.'"[60]

> Persinger will never forget one fiddle contest. That was in August, 1936, during the drought, when his entire crop was ruined by the scorching sun. "Things were going pretty tough for me then," he recalls. "I heard about a fiddlers' contest to be held at Mexico, Mo. I had to borrow a dollar from my mother to pay for my own and my wife's admission to the gate. There were twenty-two fiddlers playing. The first prize was $25, and there was a special prize of $10 for the best rendition of "Arkansas Traveler." I had read somewhere that the famous violinist, Fritz Kreisler, read a newspaper before his performances to quieten his nerves. I picked up a newspaper, my wife and I put it between us, and we read right up to the time my name was called. Then I went out and played for all I was worth."
>
> Mr. Persinger carried off both prizes for a total of $35—big money in those days. The winnings carried him and his family through to Christmas, and for a year after that, he won first prize in every contest in which he participated.

Persinger's favorite tunes when I saw him fiddle in the late 1960s were "Leather Britches," "Sally Goodin," and "Devil's Dream," ironclads and crowd-pleasers played in many styles. His "money tune" was "Sally Goodin," and he would save this if he was in a contest with two rounds so that he could bring it out in the finals. He played some unusual tunes, such as "Black Foot Waltz," named for the rural neighborhood near Midway where Cleo grew up.[61] Hartford transcribed Persinger's versions of "Boone County Rag" and "Darkie's Curly Hair," based on his home recordings in the 1960s.[62] Among other local and unusual tunes Persinger played is "Going across the Prairie."[63] As Spencer Galloway writes, Persinger's repertory "consisted mainly of hoedowns and waltzes common to the region. Like most of the better Central Missouri fiddlers, he played with confidence in the difficult 'flat' keys of F and B-flat." Typical of top fiddle players in our state, Persinger not only played complex hornpipes in F and B-flat but also played a number of tunes he brought back from journeys to major fiddle contests in Canada as well as Montana, Idaho, and New Mexico.

The only known commercial recording of Persinger is on a 1970 LP produced by the National Oldtime Fiddlers' Association, a sampler of contest fiddlers and "folk music" from that year's festival; *Oldtime Fiddling and Other Folk Music Weiser, Idaho, 1970* included Persinger's "Barber Shop Rag," from one of Persinger's 1960s years at the contest. In 2020, Charlie Walden made a number of Persinger tunes from Persinger's deep repertoire available on the Internet.[64]

Dale Pauley (*left*) and Cleo Persinger at a fiddle contest held as entertainment at the annual meeting of the MFA Oil Company, Columbia, 1961. (Courtesy of Dale Pauley)

In his fifties, perhaps bored with overseeing the farm, Cleo took a custodian job at the university in nearby Columbia. He was an avid reader with a curious mind and enjoyed being around the campus for its intellectual atmosphere and youthful hubbub. It was while he was sweeping out classrooms at the end of a day when students remembered first meeting Cleo; one of these "discoveries" led to Persinger being featured in a Boone Folk University Club concert at the Hall Theatre.[65]

Lords of the Strings

The 1960s was an exciting time. Cleo Persinger, Lena Hughes, and Cyril Stinnett had won national championships at Weiser, and Persinger had started a fiddlers' association. Old-time fiddling was coming back after a lackluster 1950s when fiddling was under the shadow of commercial country music and rock and roll and the uncertainty of how old-time fiddling would jell with bluegrass.

After returning to Columbia from Arizona, Pete McMahan focused on contests instead of fiddle jobs in nightclub dance bands. He was successful immediately, competing at major regional contests and the Weiser national contests. At Weiser and other contests outside Missouri, for many people McMahan's fiddling became synonymous with "Missouri fiddling." The financial rewards of doing well in contests were useful, but, "if you tried to make a living at playing contests, you'd starve to death."[66]

The year 1966 was McMahan's first at Weiser; that year, Cyril Stinnett won first place."[67] In 1968, Pete made it through to the finals and played "Sally Goodin," "Charlie Cook's B-flat Waltz," and "San Antonio Rose." This set was well chosen: "Sally Goodin" was the old breakdown favored by champions, the Cook waltz was an unusual tune that could catch judges' attention, and "San Antonio Rose" was the Bob Wills western swing hit. Pete won fourth place that year.

McMahan judged contests. He often said that fiddlers who play in contests should be willing to take a turn at the thankless chore of adjudication. "Judging's a complicated job, compounded by whether it's [advertised as] an *old-time* fiddle contest or just a fiddle contest. Not every good fiddler makes a good judge. You have to give each tune its merits. You can't judge a tune high just because you like the tune." What makes a competent judge? He did not believe that one has to be a fiddler to be a good judge; if a person was an experienced accompanist for fiddling, that person should be able to judge competently, and he supported nonmusicians being judges in cases of individuals with extraordinary knowledge. Pete often said he would rather have an old-time jig dancer judge his performance than a classical violinist from the symphony.

As a judge, Pete often remarked that a certain fiddler could play all the notes and know all about music but lack drive, snap, and accent in his or her bowing. He said many times that, when you are fiddling in a contest, look at the feet of the audience and judges—if they are tapping their feet, you have a good chance of doing well. "You're not playing the fiddle unless you can make people want to dance." Pete had strong opinions about what is "old-time," what is acceptable, and what merits praise. But it is more complicated. Sometimes his score sheets seemed to contradict his comments about the importance of authentic old-time styles in contests billed as old-time contests. When asked about this, he would say that, whatever styles were heard, he gave the best scores to the "best fiddlers." What Pete meant by that (the same comment made by other judges) is that when he judged, he focused not on style but on *performance*. Pete wanted it "clean." He had little use for players whose tunes were overly decorated with "whinkerdinks," even while he may have given high points on his judge's sheet; "'Course I don't like it, but you've got to judge it when you judge it [in a contest]."[68] Technical virtuosity wins.

"Whinkerdinks" is a derogatory term McMahan used for what he considered unnecessary and distracting fancy licks or unwanted improvisations, creative leaps that detract from a tune's flow, integrity, and quality—or simply just "too many notes." Among other terms fiddlers use for things that they feel do not belong in fiddling include "trash" (Taylor McBaine), "gingerbread," "embroidery," "fizzlegigs," "junk," "extras," and "dog shit" (Gene Goforth). But one person's whinkerdinks may be another person's artistry.

Anecdotes, jokes, and legends abound about contest judging, and most of the narratives contain a bit of humor and focus on a misunderstanding or misfortune befalling a champion. One of these concerns McMahan, a perpetual winner or top finisher in the 1980s and early 1990s contests. Pete happened to miss the annual contest in Boonville in March 1985; the date sometimes conflicted with fiddlers' conventions in Arkansas and Oklahoma as well as the Tennessee state contest in Clarksville. In 1985, Pete was at Clarksville. After the first round, while the emcee was raffling off sacks of Always Save dog food, they announced the "callbacks" (fiddlers chosen by the judges to compete in the final round). Boonville always had callbacks, bringing the top several contestants to the stage for another tune.[69] Fiddlers called back knew they were going to win a prize, but did not know where they would rank in the final tally. The emcee called out to the finalists, "Report backstage and get ready," and "Pete McMahan" was announced, along with Johnny Bruce, Travis Inman, and other familiar names. The emcee seems to have been studiously reading down the list of finalists and, not seeing Pete's name, assumed that the scorekeeper forgot to write it down. Pete McMahan could make the callbacks in a fiddle contest without even being there.

One factor in McMahan's enjoyment of contests was the luxury (most of the time) of having top-drawer accompaniment. Sometimes a guitarist such as Charlie Daugherty (Tina) would make the trip with Pete to contests in Athens, Alabama, and Kentucky state contests at Rough River Dam. Daugherty played open chords in Pete's preferred old-time backup style, as did Fred Stoneking, Joe Stevens, Charlie Brattin, Truman Sorenson, and others he appreciated. McMahan often said some version of, "I don't like people playing choke chords with me. I like to hear all the strings *ring*."[70] Truman Sorenson, a trucker and cheerful Norwegian American from Lengby, Minnesota, knew Pete from Yankton and other contests and came to Harrisburg to drive Pete to some of the contests at Clarksville, Tennessee, and Athens, Alabama, as well as a few Missouri contests.[71]

McMahan called his dressed-up contest style "semiprogressive," and he would adjust his performance to be more effective when competing with Texas-style and Contest Style players—which he called "progressive" fiddlers. His melody on certain tunes does sound like Texas contest versions, but, as Bill Shull notes, "what he does with it" is strictly old-time, hard-driving, central Missouri style.[72] One of Pete's semiprogressive tunes is "The Waltz of Shannon," which he learned from a Texas Shorty record (Shorty had learned it from an LP by Canadian champion Al Cherny, a fiddler also admired by McMahan).[73] Pete was blunt in saying that his way of dressing up a tune for a contest was "not really old-time" but also said it was not "Texas style" contest fiddling either. "People who say I play Texas style are crazier than hell."[74] In 1975, Pete wrote:

> The Missouri style of fiddling is quite different from styles over the United States. It is referred to as *long bow style*. By long bow I mean that the bow is used in long

strokes instead of the short choppy strokes. It makes the notes a lot more clear and distinct and the tone smooth and rolling.

In fiddling, timing of tunes is very essential. They should be played in a danceable time. If a tune is not played so it can be danced to it isn't played right. That is what the original fiddle was used for here in Missouri. Square dance was about the only dance around here when I was young and a square dance done by some of the older people around Missouri is something worth watching. It is beautiful.[75]

Pete McMahan with Joe Stevens of Montgomery City on the cover of Pete's second LP, *Missouri Fiddlin' No. 2*. In the 1970s, Pete often wore western outfits at contests and programs, sometimes the $300 western suit Sarah had bought in the 1960s. Pete liked western shirts, a Stetson Open Road hat, and cowboy boots; the reason he liked cowboy boots is that he could stomp rhythm while he fiddled. Joe Stevens played hard driving, open-chord backup that enhanced Pete's fiddle style. (Courtesy of Sarah McMahan)

Ed Carnes of Nashville is among Texas/Contest Style champions who knew Pete and contemplated Pete's style in insightful comments after watching a video of McMahan at Bethel fiddle camp in 1997 (posted by Charlie Walden):

I would not say all of Pete's playing was "Old Time" vs. "Contest" style—although those terms mean different things to different people. If you listen to Pete's version of "Tom and Jerry" and then listen to Benny Thomasson's version—you will see vast

> similarities and Pete's version was definitely a "Contest" version. I would definitely NOT classify Pete as an "Old Time" fiddler only. Pete was a very well-rounded player who could play in many styles, whatever suited him, and I think his "main" style was one of his choosing, heavily influenced by the fiddlers in the Missouri area where he grew up and lived. I myself am a "Contest" Style fiddler but even in my heyday I did not take Pete for granted because he would whip you when he was "on." I don't like the Old Time and Contest labels. Good fiddling is good fiddling regardless of the label [smile emoticon].[76]

Carnes articulates the supposed contradiction in McMahan between his old-time and his contest fiddling, and we are reminded that highly skilled fiddlers can shift from style to style to suit the occasion, if they want to do so.[77]

Pete used to say, "Playing for dances will ruin your contest fiddling." But he would also say, on other occasions, that fiddling in contests ruins your *dance* fiddling, because you tend to forget how dancers and callers want the music. Taylor McBaine used to say it this way: "Boy, this contest fiddling will ruin you. Because you don't play nothing but contest music."[78] These are complex notions, and debated. The demands and varieties of one's experience are different when one plays for dancers, who care only about rhythm. McMahan was bemused by some of the Texas-style contest players' slowing down tunes, making them undanceable—in central Missouri at least. And this does not apply to the national contest at Weiser, where time limits force players to speed up and shorten their tunes to avoid time penalties.

Among episodes that have become apocryphal in the McMahan saga is an exchange related by Ed Carnes that implies the tensions over the ascendance of Contest Style in contests advertised as "old-time." The setting was a contest where Pete was visiting with the Oklahoma Texas-style champion Ace Sewell sometime in the 1970s or early 1980s.[79] Sewell and McMahan were visiting, and Sewell remarked, "In this day and age, a tune's got to come out even." McMahan replied, "Well, you guys play it so slow you can't dance to it." To which Sewell answered, "I'm not here to dance. I'm here to fiddle."

The term "Little Dixie style" has worked reasonably well for players like McMahan, Taylor McBaine, Cleo Persinger, and others. Pete told a story to illustrate his brand of Little Dixie fiddling in comparison with progressive and Texas-based Contest Style, and the story reflects the importance of "making people want to dance." He took part in a major competition at the Orpheum Theatre in Memphis, Tennessee, in 1980. Preliminary rounds were played, and competitors making it through were whittled down. Pete made the final cut of ten and drew the last number. All the other fiddlers, including Nashville professional and champion Randy Howard (born in Georgia) and Texas champion Terry Morris (the eventual winner), were what Pete called progressive. Referring to Howard, Pete said his "music was beautiful, artistic, but progressive fiddlers play too slow to dance to and most of them don't have drive."[80]

Pete thought Randy Howard's style was so far out that "it's past progressive—it's *super-progressive*." When McMahan came onstage as the last contestant, the auditorium was packed. He struck up "Grey Eagle," stomped his cowboy-booted right foot, and people just couldn't sit still. By the time Pete finished, people had gotten out of their seats and were jig dancing and buck dancing in the aisles.[81] Howard's waltzes were spectacular, and Pete knew he needed to "play the fire out of" a big breakdown to best Howard in the contest to take second place behind Terry Morris. And he did so.[82] Pete often spoke of this contest as one of his favorites—and where he was in top form and competing with celebrated champions.

Pete won and judged many years at the Minnesota state contest in Cotton, making friends who still speak of his engaging personality as well as his fiddling. South Dakota's Great Plains contest in Yankton was developed in the 1970s by Wilbur Foss and his associates based on Missouri contests and advice from Bill Kearns, Bill Eddy, and McMahan. Wilbur arranged for the governor to declare a "Pete McMahan Day" and appoint Pete an honorary citizen. Pete did not like to lose to a player whose skills he considered inferior, but this was inevitable in the politics and vicissitudes of adjudication. Pete would say, "He may have won, but he sure didn't *beat* me." According to John Griffin: "Occasionally, Pete will win something less than first place. I have known of some less than talented fiddlers using these occasions to rub Pete's nose in his defeat. Some strutting rube, encouraged by his victory will say to Pete, 'Well Pete, how does it feel to get beat?' 'Oh, not too bad,' says Pete, 'I've even been beat by *good* fiddlers before.'"[83]

McMahan could ignore a wisecrack or dumb remark, and he could also bluntly criticize fiddlers he did not know as well as those he knew well. Bob Cathey of Hallsville recalls an occasion in 1982 at the state contest in the Stephens College auditorium in Columbia. An eager teenager, Bob was going to contests to meet and learn about fiddling from masters of the craft. Bob was standing in a cluster of people listening to Pete warm up in the hallway. "I was a young kid, around 13, I guess. It was backstage at Stephens College and he was there, in a small group of musicians, and was asking them what they thought he should play for the contest. For some unknown reason, I said, 'St. Anne's Reel,' to which he replied, 'You can't win no damn fiddle contest playing *that* tune, boy!' That was my one and almost only conversation with him. Funny now, but at the time—not so much."[84] Bob knew what Pete failed to articulate in that snap at the enthusiastic teenager: to place at the top, Pete thought fiddlers needed to present "contest tunes" that judges were conditioned to reward.

John Griffin absorbed stories Pete told and spoke about his musical life in April 2000, a few months after Pete's death:

> Pete's fiddling, like most people's fiddling, was a reflection of what they are. If you look at Pete's life, where he grew up, the things he did in his life, you can understand his fiddling a lot better. He had such good drive, and time. A lot of people worry about a string of notes that make the tune, and Pete could extract some of those and still get the flavor of the tune, and then would add the beat. It was a great beat, great time, strong. There was no decoration, no flowery notes, jazz, blues, bluegrass-type of runs in his playing. Everything he did was directed at the *roll* of the music.

His bowing was very strong. On one end of the spectrum there's the *tone* you get out of the instrument. And at the other end of the spectrum, where I think most fiddlers reside, is the tune, and to get the tune in the early stages of your fiddling you have to slough over a lot of notes, and it's a light bowing, to get the speed, and you have a lot of notes thrown together with one bow. And somewhere in the middle there, and maybe towards the tone end of the spectrum, versus the notey end of the spectrum, is *Pete*.

His tone that he got out of the instrument was, he could pick up a cheap chunk of crap fiddle, and it was still consistent what he got out of it. He had that talent, and he was doing it with his bow. He just had a real strong bow arm. He was after that tone, and he was after that timing. And at the same time, he didn't Tex-a-fy the tunes or adopt some other style of fiddling. In some of his tunes you could hear a little of the Texas lilt in there. Some of the older Texas fiddlers had that roll, but they didn't extract notes like Pete did, they put more in. He had a real jump to it [in his bowing].

I don't have much of Pete [on recordings], but what he taught me, not only about fiddling but about living, what he taught me on the fiddle, I have good memories of the things we did together. He was a good guy, besides being a good fiddler. He had one hell of a work ethic. And that has something to do with what he was able to do on the fiddle.

He said he never practiced. But he did. Every time you thought he was "playing," you know [in a contest or session], he was *practicing*, he was working on it, all the time. In other words, he didn't get a set thing to play except a few tunes at contests. He didn't get a set thing to play and then go home and play it over and over and over again. When he was jamming, he was practicing.

You take that background, and you can maybe understand that contests were a job for Pete. He had a lot more fun with Kenny Applebee [guitar accompanist] or Forrest Rose [bass accompanist] playing for Cultural Heritage Center programs, not contests—I never saw him so relaxed.

He'd tell you what he thought. At the most politest, he'd just walk off. His judgement of music was good, he could listen to somebody, what they were doing wrong. He knew if they were hopeless.

It's kind of a hard thing to write, but you are what you play. You are what you live, but you can hear it, that's the personality. If they get good enough, with ninety percent of people, there's nothing there. But Pete, he was so good, you could hear everything. Pete was one of the few guys, you could feel the breeze and smell the flowers, and it was real good.

As Pete said, "Us old-timers, a lot of the tunes we play, nobody plays them but us, and if we don't teach 'em to someone, they'll be lost."[85] McMahan's style is carried on by people such as John Griffin, Charlie Walden, Travis Inman, and John P. Williams. Pete knew they would take what he had to offer and make it their own. "No two fiddlers play the same tune exactly alike. If they did, there wouldn't be anything to like." "If you don't make mistakes, you're not doing anything. Don't *exactly* copy *anybody*. If you know a tune in your *mind*, you can play it."[86]

The Pete McMahan that strangers met at contests far from Missouri seemed a different person from the reserved, austere McMahan back home. Brad Solon, a young fiddler from Rapid City, South Dakota, met Pete at the Great Plains Championships in Yankton. Solon found Pete to be congenial and generous. McMahan was often on the judging panel at Yankton, and during breaks in the contest he would step behind the building, where fiddlers were getting ready for their rounds, and light a cigarette. As Solon recalls:

> One time we were in the back behind the building in Yankton and Pete was out for a smoke in his crooked cowboy hat, and I was playing "Leather Britches." I don't know who was there playing the guitar. Pete grabbed my bow and fiddle and he said, "you're playing it wrong—*look here*" and he showed me a different bowing and I was like "WHAT?" I thought that was nuts. He gave me back my fiddle and told me to practice it and get it right, so I did. In a just a short time I had to go in the building and play on stage—so I played "Leather Britches" doing what showed me. Afterwards he came out in the back to have another smoke and he threw his hat on the ground and gave me a hug!
>
> Then he probably offered to buy my fiddle! He always took my fiddle—he was always playing someone's fiddle to see what it was like—then he would offer me a little more $ than last time. He did that for several years. I never knew if he was serious! He was sure a fun guy, too. And why did he enjoy Yankton so much? He was there almost every year. At Yankton in the old days, he showed me more than anyone I ever met.[87]

I think one of the reasons Pete liked fiddle contests at places such as Rough River, Kentucky; Clarksville, Tennessee; Athens, Alabama; Yankton, South Dakota; and Weiser, Idaho, so much is that people he met there treated him as an honored guest, and he and Sarah made lasting friends. It was like a fresh start.

Weiser, Idaho, and the Popularization of Modern "Contest Style" Fiddling

"Weiser" is shorthand for the National Oldtime Fiddlers' Contest, a multiday festival held each June since the 1950s in the southwestern Idaho farming town.[88] For contest fiddlers, Weiser became the Matterhorn. One cannot easily grasp the changes in contest fiddling in Missouri, or anywhere else, without some consideration of the pervasive influence of Weiser in the global fiddling community.

Modern Contest Style fiddling evolved in the western United States. Contests billed as "national" were held for years in Truth or Consequences, New Mexico, bringing fiddlers (mainly from Missouri west), with the majority from Texas, New Mexico, and Arizona.[89] But Truth or Consequences contests ended in the 1960s. In early June 1964, a Northwest Mountain Fiddlers Contest was held in Missoula, Montana, attracting fiddlers throughout western states and east as far as Missouri. Two young men new to Northwest contests, Jim Chancellor of Texas and Byron Berline of Kansas, brought their attractive, newish Contest Style—new to most people at Missoula, that is—to everyone's attention. The Texas-based Contest Style (often called "Oklahoma/Texas style" at the time) was only beginning its slow march toward dominance in much of the fiddle-contest world; most people at Missoula in 1964 had never heard it, and some "old-time" diehards resisted its charms.

Some interesting things happened at Missoula in 1964. Jim (Texas Shorty) Chancellor, three-time Texas state champ, winner of the "World Championship" at Crockett, and a pupil of Benny Thomasson, was expected to do well.[90] Of the Texas players who had given shape and formulas to the modern Texas Contest Style in the previous generation, many of them friends of McMahan, Pete said, "Texas style, most of it, the older fiddlers, they added stuff to it, but you could *always recognize it* when they played it. Benny Thomasson was the best hand [an originator of style] I have ever heard. You could always tell what Benny was playing."[91] Vivian and Phil Williams remembered the event, during a time when there was "a lot of acrimony" between contest fiddlers presenting Texas style and old-time dance fiddlers who thought the Texas approach was unsuitable for dancing (and perhaps just too fancy) and therefore not old-time. The contest was billed as an old-time fiddle contest. Chancellor was cut in the first round by Mom Ruth, one of the judges. "We were listening just outside the judges' room at that moment. Mom Ruth said 'Hell, that ain't old time fiddling, that's modern.'"[92] First place went to Berline, who performed his strong bluegrass-inflected style. Berline chose old-time tunes for his rounds, picked old-time/bluegrass accompaniment, and mixed in a bit of "Texas," and his appealing style resulted in a sound quite acceptable to all the judges.[93] The emerging Texas- and Oklahoma-based Contest Style had not yet risen to prominence and acceptance in the Northwest.

The week following the June 1964 contest there, fiddlers there packed up and traveled down to Weiser.[94] Weiser had held contests since pioneer days and began advertising regional contests in 1953 to celebrate western heritage and help revitalize square dancing and fiddling in the region, and to bring business and visitors. In 1963, Weiser administration started calling it the National Oldtime Fiddlers' Contest. At that time, "national" *did not mean* that the winners were the best fiddlers anywhere; "national" meant that everyone was welcome to compete, no matter what state or country they were from. The contestant pool and the music began to change. Within twenty-five years, Weiser was attracting ten thousand visitors to the farm town of some fifty-three hundred. Hundreds of fiddlers signed up in many classes of competition, and a great many more came not for the contest but for jam-session reunions in the various dominions in the campgrounds (with names like "Tin Town," "Stickerville," and "the football field") focusing on music such as Appalachian, western swing, Cape Breton, bluegrass, Irish, jazz, and classic country songs in addition to the evolving Contest Style.[95] Weiser found itself in the happy position of eclipsing other "national" contests as the biggest and thereby, presumably, the most prestigious championship (in the West, at least). The impression encouraged today is that whoever wins the Grand National Division at Weiser is champion of the world.[96]

Lena Hughes's 1963 portrait in the Hall of Fame exhibition in Weiser, Idaho. That year, Lena won first place in the National Ladies Division. Lena's husband, Jake, played old-time five-string banjo accompaniment for her. Lena played banjo accompaniment for several fiddlers at Weiser.

Looking back, the global Contest Style associated with Weiser and Texas had evolutionary markers. Key years include 1968 and 1979 and key names, such as Herman Johnson and Mark O'Connor.[97] Although known back home as an almost-unbeatable contest fiddler, Herman Johnson was unfamiliar to most people in 1968. He was already well known in Missouri, having competed at the big contest in Salisbury in 1967 and returning to win first at the big contest in Lexington in 1968. But at Weiser, Johnson's sweep through the rounds to become national champion was unexpected and electrifying. As Johnson said, you had to come up with something different to win.[98] Johnson's stunning, clean style and flawless technique, based on Texas contest fiddlers, nourished the seeds that became today's virtuosic Contest Style. It is "the first really hard-core 'Texas/Contest' style (or whatever we've decided to name it!) to show up at Weiser. Starting with 1968, EVERYONE who won [the Grand National Division] at Weiser played some variety of Texas/Contest style."[99] Johnson's guitar accompanist was Ralph McCraw, playing open-chord guitar backup; closed-chord, swing-based backup style had not yet become standard among top contest fiddlers at Weiser.

In 1979, teenager Mark O'Connor, from the state of Washington and a pupil of Barbara Lamb and Benny Thomasson, dominated the Grand Nationals. O'Connor had been competing at Weiser since age eleven in 1972, winning and progressing through the younger age divisions to win the Grand Nationals (open to age) in 1979.[100] In 1973 at thirteen he won the Grand Masters fiddle contest in Nashville (another contest considered by some to be the most important in the world). O'Connor took things beyond other fiddlers in terms of improvisation, ornaments, and swing and performed with great precision. O'Connor's celebrity encouraged participation of more and more children and young people, especially girls and young women (who now outnumber male fiddlers at Weiser). Conservative old-timers may have groaned at O'Connor's extravagant improvisations and decorations: "He plays too fast." "He puts in too much extra stuff." "No rhyme or reason to it."[101] One Weiser regular for fifty years, fiddle scholar Phil Williams, often articulated what he considered O'Connor's deleterious influence on the Weiser contest:

> In my opinion the death knell of the Weiser contest was the Mark O'Connor years. By that time a number of good Northwest fiddlers had shifted to "Sally Gooden" (a.k.a. "Sally Goodin")," etc. [Contest Style winners year after year] in the contest. Mark, however, got to the young fiddlers and showed them that if they wanted to win the contests, they needed to follow his lead. The fiddle teachers needed to keep their young students happy, and, even more important, make them "stars" to their parents to keep them coming back for lessons. The junior divisions in this period were nearly 100% folks trying to imitate Mark note for note. There was something of a joke going around Weiser that, as a judge for the junior division, one had only to follow the "score" in the Mark O'Connor books and see if the fiddler actually hit all the "right" notes.[102]

Again, Phil Williams:

> So, at Weiser, like many contests around the country, there was a serious mix of "apples & oranges" at the fiddle contests, lots of acrimony among fiddlers from the different style groups, and lots of confusion for the audiences. The practice of many contests, like Weiser, to pick judges from the "top" placers in the previous years' contests simply exacerbated the situation by assuring that the judges would be Contest Style players, who dedicated their talents to contest winning [and who were] not familiar with many of the other old-time fiddle styles of North America, and especially not familiar with the nuances of these styles that distinguish the great players in these styles from the rest.
>
> It is commonly understood among old-time dance-style fiddlers that, at Weiser, a mediocre "contest" style fiddler easily can beat the very best fiddler in the world playing in a "non-contest" style. This has driven away from the Weiser contest virtually all the great fiddlers in other styles.[103]

Mark O'Connor's performances were so exciting that he influenced countless fiddlers everywhere, whether they admit it or not and whether they know it or not. O'Connor won Weiser four times, 1979, 1980, 1981, 1984.

Many of the champions at Weiser became respected teachers and built a self-propagating network. Violin teachers began having their pupils memorize notations and recordings of specific winning performances, copying as best they could renditions of contest tunes as performed by Contest Style champions such as Benny Thomasson, Mark O'Connor, Terry Morris, and Dick Barrett.[104]

Because so many contests have moved toward the Texas/Contest Style fiddle and swing guitar sound, audiences, administrators, and judges are now "trained" to think that Contest Style is superior to old-time, regional, and ethnic styles of performance, repertoire, and backup. Phil Williams summarized the emotions of many Weiser fans and fiddlers about the increasing professionalism there and across the nation's contest landscape: "Technical virtuosity took over as the criterion of excellence."[105] How could it be otherwise? Contest fiddling is listening music, not dance music, and, after all, it's a competition.

Contest Style has been the engine for what some feel is disruptive change in the fiddle and dance heritage of many places across the United States and Canada. Contest Style (Texas style, progressive style, Weiser style) and its swing-based guitar accompaniment became prevalent as winners and crowd-pleasers. However, Contest Style is perceived by some people as an incursion into regional, ethnic, and older customs of old-time fiddling rather than a natural evolution over time. Abrupt change can be shocking. From the 1960s on, conservative old-time fiddlers and what were seen as purists began to urge contest administrators and judges to "keep it old-time" but with precious little success.

Fiddlers inclined toward old-time southeastern United States, Appalachian, and bluegrass styles gravitated east to Galax, Virginia, or Union Grove, North Carolina. Those focused more on Missouri and midwestern styles and the emerging Contest Style tended to steer west to Weiser, Idaho. Today, "Galax style" and "Weiser style" (Texas-based, nationalized Contest Style) are, broadly taken, prevalent contest styles across the continent. In Missouri, in the center of the United States, eastern styles (Galax) and western styles (Weiser/Texas) bumped into each other. Western styles of contest performance, epitomized by today's Grand National Championship players at Weiser, have exerted a far stronger impact on *contest* fiddling in Missouri.

In the 1990s, several Missourians competed at Weiser, most of them advocates of Contest Style, such as Junior Marriott, Matt Wyatt, Billy Ward, Alita Stoneking, and Cody Marriott. In the 2000s, young fiddlers competing at Weiser have included Justin Branum and Richard Shewmaker. All except Shewmaker performed their take on national Contest Style.[106]

(Illustration facing first page of Chapter 6) Crewel embroidery, farmer with a fiddle, a Sears Roebuck kit that Mary Ruth Pauley obtained in Tucson, Arizona, ca. 1978, and embroidered by her mother, Margaret Pace, back in Boone County, Missouri.

Dale Pauley—"Let's Play that Uptown Stuff"

6

All I know, I taught myself.

Dale Pauley was a regular at fiddle contests and jam sessions for decades, but his first love was always swing and pop music. Born September 14, 1931, Dale was a son of Altie Argalus Pauley and Oneita Henry Pauley. Dale's grandparents were James Samuel (J. Sam) Pauley and Virginia Crane Pauley, southern Boone County families. J. Sam was a farmer and county commissioner and played fiddle music.[1] Dale's forbearers came from Kentucky in the early 1800s. Dale says the Pauleys are "English."[2]

Dale Pauley, age two or three, with his child-size violin, Deer Park, Missouri, 1932–33. Between Jefferson City and Columbia, Deer Park was formed in the 1880s and named for a deer preserve in the area owned by a prosperous judge. The village was rubbed out by expansion of US 63 in the 1960s. Dale composed a fiddle tune called "Deer Park Stomp." (Courtesy of Dale Pauley)

Altie Pauley farmed in the Deer Park community in Boone County and played fiddle tunes from the popular and swing music repertoire of radio and records. "He didn't play many hoedowns. Mostly he played old stuff like 'Up a Lazy River' and stuff like that, old popular tunes." Altie's preferred accompaniment was guitar and piano (he played piano, too) with neighbors and cousins. Although he was born into a musical family, no one in particular taught Dale to play music, and he generally taught himself as a teenager in junior high school in Columbia. And while most fiddlers of his generation started out playing backup piano, banjo, or guitar behind fiddlers, this was not the case with Dale.

Charlie Cook inspired Dale to play fiddle. One summer day, perhaps in 1945, Dale was at a music party in a park behind the city power plant in Columbia.[3] There, Dale heard Charlie Cook, who was famous for smooth fiddling, elaborate waltzes, and swing music and played in a popular dance band. "I thought he had to be about the best around." Soon after hearing Charlie Cook, Dale borrowed a violin from guitarist George LaRoe and started working. "I didn't know anything." A year or so later, in Ashland, Dale traded a shotgun for a violin.[4] "I traded a shotgun for it, to Jimmy Pauley—you know he was a State Rep at one time, he was in my class in high school. And he had an old fiddle he wanted to trade for that *shotgun* [a double-barrel, twelve-gauge hammer gun], so I traded him."

Dale Pauley graduated from Hickman High School in 1950 and took a job with Boone County Oil Company in Columbia. He was drawn to popular music and swing, and among fiddlers playing pop and swing were his friend Bobby Joe Caldwell, George Morris, Jim Gilmore, Henry Thompson, Jake Hockemeyer, and Pete McMahan, excellent swing and popular music fiddlers as well as old-time fiddlers and contest fiddlers. Eventually, Pauley absorbed some old-time square-dance tunes, necessary for participation in fiddle contests and most dances. Dale was not interested in bluegrass music. He exaggerates when he quips, "I don't know anything about bluegrass," but we get the point. "Bluegrass is a whole different ball game,"[5] with all its fills and special licks that take a fiddler to a different place from the old-time and swing music that Pauley favors.

Korea

In January 1952 in the midst of the Korean War, Dale Pauley was drafted into the US Army for a standard two-year hitch. He took basic training at Fort Ord, California, and was transferred to Camp Cooke (now Vandenberg Air Force Base) at Santa Maria, where he was assigned to the Illinois Forty-Fourth Division National Guard training combat in Korea. Pauley was trained as a machine gunner. At Camp Cooke, Dale met soldiers who played music, and they formed a string band to entertain at off-hours events. They played swing, western swing, and the popular repertoire from radio and records, but they did not play dances. Instruments were provided by the special-services unit and checked out to band members for practices and performances.

Pauley shipped out to Japan for final training and staging for Korea. Dale was pulled from the infantry and sent to "med school" to become a combat medic. In January 1953, he graduated from Medical Aidman training at Camp Eta Jima, the former Japanese naval academy at Hiroshima. "Med school lasted for six weeks of first-aid training. But you don't learn much in six weeks." Pauley was than assigned to the Third Infantry Division.

Pauley's job in Korea was driving an ambulance for an aid station serving an antiaircraft unit. Pauley's ambulance got the wounded to the aid station, from which

Private Dale Pauley in a band at Camp Cooke, early 1952. Some wear cowboy outfits, others civilian clothes. Instruments (*from left*): mandolin, electric archtop guitar, acoustic guitar, electric lap steel guitar (a recently developed instrument), acoustic bass, and violin. (Courtesy of Dale Pauley)

wounded soldiers could be transferred farther from the front lines to a mobile Army surgical hospital.[6]

Pauley was in Seattle when the war ended in July 1953, and in January 1954 he was posted to Camp Carson, Colorado, where he was discharged at the rank of sergeant. Dale took a train to Columbia, and on January 17 married his fiancée, Mary Ruth Pace, in the home of her parents, Ansel and Margaret Pace, at their farm east of Deer Park.

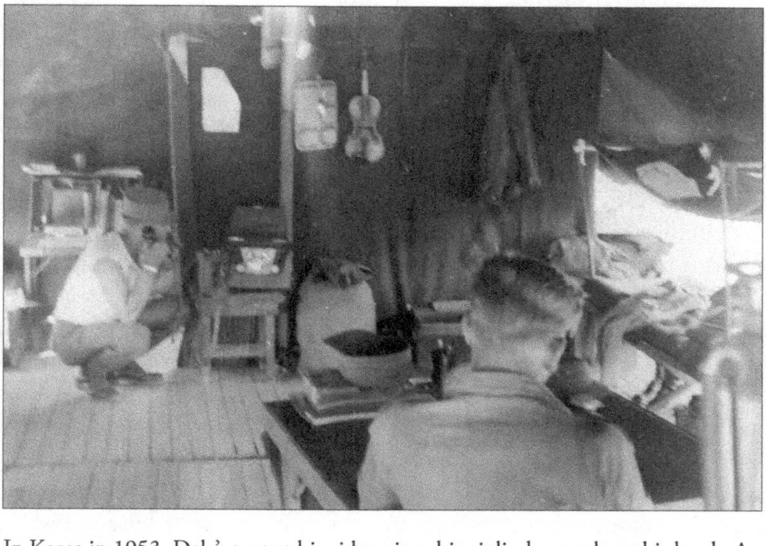

In Korea in 1953, Dale's tent at his aid station; his violin hangs above his bunk. A colleague was sent to a rear base, and Dale asked him to bring a violin back, and he did so (price: forty dollars). When his tour of duty was complete and he received orders for Seattle, Dale padded the violin in a duffel bag and shipped it home to Deer Park; the duffel bag was lost, the violin never found. (Courtesy of Pauley)

Columbia

Dale and Mary Ruth settled in Columbia. Dale was twenty-two and looking for a career. He was not interested in farming. He happened to be getting a haircut at Ralph Fenton's barbershop on North Providence Road, and Fenton asked him what he planned to do. Dale said he didn't have any idea, and Fenton said, "Why don't you go to barber school, we need barbers." Barbers were in demand, with the many veterans coming home and with expansion of the University of Missouri and growth of Columbia. Dale and Mary Ruth moved to Kansas City, and Dale enrolled at Molar Barber College. The prospect of being part of a small, friendly business suited Dale.

Barbers served two-year apprenticeships, and, back in Columbia, Pauley served under Blackie Chilcott at the Campus Barber Shop. Chilcott was "first chair" (the privileged location in the window of the shop). Nick McNeff was second chair, Pauley third chair, Joe Burnett fourth chair (whom Dale considered the shop's best barber), and Gene George fifth chair. The shop was in a block of small businesses called Campus Towne, in the center of the University of Missouri campus and across the street from the administration building. When the university continued to expand in 1980, Campus Towne was scheduled for demolition and the shop moved a few blocks north to the other side of campus. After ten years with Chilcott, Pauley moved to Don Fenton's shop on North Providence Road, where he worked third chair for twelve years.

In 1956, Pauley acquired his favorite violin, made by Jesse L. Sims. "Jess" Sims was a farmer, clock maker, and fiddler who built violins and repaired stringed instruments. From a large family of musicians, Sims lived north of Columbia in the Hallsville area and hosted music parties at his clock shop. Fiddlers who attended, such as Pauley, Taylor McBaine, and John White, remembered clocks of all kinds ticking away and a few striking while they played fiddle music. Based on a Stradivarius model, Sims built the violin in 1956 and sold it to Dale for $150. The Jess Sims violin is Dale's number one, and his other favorite is a German-made Guarnarius-model violin he inherited after his father's death in 1978; Altie Pauley bought the Guarnerius, used, from Cope Ashlock sometime before 1930 for $175.

Pauley won his first trophy in a major contest held in the north Missouri railroad town of La Plata in 1957. Mary Ruth remembers that the sculpture on the trophy looked like a naked man—a classical pose of a muscular, handsome young man holding up a laurel wreath. She jokes, "I never saw a fiddler that looked like that, did you?"[7] Dale was playing well that day and took first place, beating Pete McMahan. After the contest, which McMahan expected to win, McMahan walked over to Dale and said in a friendly tone, "The only reason you won is you're better lookin' than I am!" Pauley knew that was a compliment, coming from McMahan, who hated to lose a contest. "He wasn't mad or anything. Like I say, I just got lucky, because I couldn't *beat* Pete any day of the week."

Dale competed with Henry Thompson in a number of contests. Thompson, a Rolla music-store owner, was an early adopter of Contest Style fiddling. His wife was a music teacher in Iberia. Henry had classical violin training and played his hoedowns and waltzes with broad classical vibrato. Dale and Mary Ruth considered Henry Thompson a fine fiddler and one who did not get his due from some of the contest fiddlers. "I always liked Henry's fiddling. He was playing some of that Texas stuff before anybody else. And he didn't mind putting some of that hokum in." According to Mary Ruth, "He played the most beautiful waltzes you ever heard. He was one of the best, but he didn't win a lot. Because there was a lot of the old purists that didn't like that [Thompson's classical-sounding playing]! And they didn't like that up into the *eighties*."[8]

In many of these fiddle contests, Pauley's guitar seconding was provided by one or two of his old friends from Ashland, guitarists George LeRoe, George Phillips, and Derwood Garrett. Sometimes Pauley was accompanied by Columbia guitarist Carl Richardson, who was one of the stalwart players happy to accompany anyone needing help. In the sixties and seventies, Dale and Mary Ruth sometimes picked Carl up in their car (he did not drive) and took him to contests. Richardson was known for his spare, rock-solid rhythm, traits appreciated by fiddlers. "I'll tell you, you start a tune, and he'd get *with you*, and he'd never fall behind or speed up or anything, he'd stay right with you on that same beat all the way through."[9]

In the 1950s and early 1960s, contest winners were often determined by audience applause. Selecting contest winners by the apparent enthusiasm of audiences was an old custom but not a fair one. Mary Ruth Pauley remembers, "We had a standing joke that whoever had the most relatives would win."[10] Later in the 1960s, applause and applause-o-meters were replaced with panels of judges when fiddlers' associations searched for ways to improve contest judging.

Third Place Won With Borrowed Fiddle

A borrowed fiddle helped Dale Pauley, left, 210 Monroe St., win third place in the 10th annual fiddle contest sponsored by the Columbia Odd Fellows last night at Hickman.

Henry Thomson, center, Iberia, won $50 and a trophy for his first-place effort while J. A. Gilmore, Jefferson City, received $25 for second place.

Pauley, a barber, came to the contest without his fiddle but with the urge to compete. At the last moment, he borrowed an instrument from Jack Deck of 1111 East Walnut St., another competitor, and won $15.

Other finalists were Cleo Persinger of Columbia, last year's winner, and Dewey Wells of Fayette. Approximately 500 watched a total of 18 performers; proceeds were given to the American Cancer Society.

Dale Pauley played in the tenth annual Odd Fellows Lodge contest in Columbia, March 23, 1957, with a violin borrowed from Jack Deck. *Left to right*: Pauley (third place), Henry Thompson (Iberia, first place), and Jimmy Gilmore (Jefferson City, second place).

Dale competed in the MFA Oil Company competitions in 1960 and 1961. In 1961 he won the first elimination round, but did not win the second round and thus was not invited to compete in the grand championship in Columbia in November. At the 1961 Boone County Fair contest, Pauley won first place, playing "Orange Blossom Special," "B-flat Waltz," and "Draggin' the Bow."[11] "Orange Blossom Special" and "Draggin' the Bow" feature hokum bowing. Some feel that a dash of hokum spices up a tune; others consider it trick fiddling and inappropriate in contests. It is usually accepted that hokum bowing (fast single, double, or triple "shuffle bow" licks) is permissible in contests, as long as the hot stuff is inherent in the original tune or early recordings, such as "Draggin' the Bow," a country rag from the 1930s. Most old-time fiddlers in Missouri of my acquaintance play hokum in "Draggin' the Bow" as well as the quintessential Missouri breakdown "Marmaduke's' Hornpipe." "Hokum is one of the first things I learned. It was easy for me."[12]

Arizona and Colorado

Dale and Mary Ruth moved to Tucson, Arizona, in 1976, and Dale opened a one-chair barbershop, Dale's Shearing Shed. He was soon working long days, and the business prospered.

Barbershops are compatible social venues for informal music sessions, and Dale hosted weekly jam sessions. Pauley conducted the sessions. No electrical instruments allowed, with a lot of styles and repertoires welcome. Although the emphasis was on instrumental fiddle music, an occasional country or bluegrass song would be performed. The privilege for starting a tune passed clockwise around the circle, and other fiddlers in the circle did not play while the person was playing his or her tune. Dale and Mary Ruth met fiddlers and other musicians from all over the area, and several seasoned group players formed the core of Dale's sessions.

Backup in Arizona included banjo (four- and five-string) and other instruments. Guitar was the favorite, played both old-time open-chord guitar style and closed-chord swing guitar style. The regular banjoist at Dale's sessions played tenor player with a New Orleans–style jazz band. Pauley liked tenor banjo backup with its chunky, rhythmic chording.

There was plenty of music—jam sessions, potluck dinners with sessions, and fiddle events put on by individuals, service clubs, and chapters of the Arizona Old Time Fiddlers' Association. Arizonans were early advocates of voluntary fiddlers' associations and hosted numerous contests and a state fiddle championship (with a division for nonresidents). Dale's first contest in Arizona was in Safford in 1976, sponsored by the eastern Arizona branch of the association, where the fiddling contest was entertainment at a rodeo.

Pauley recalls that old-time was still the prevailing style in Arizona contests in the 1970s, but says that Texas Contest Style "was *on its way*." Pauley felt welcome among fiddlers in Arizona and Colorado in the 1970s and 1980s and found that his articulate, driving, clean central Missouri/Little Dixie style worked well among southwestern fiddlers. Dale liked the more moderate pace at which most southwest fiddlers played hoedowns.

Dale's contest tunes typically were "Polk County Breakdown," "Arkansas Traveler," "Sally Goodin," "Billy in the Low Ground," "Cincinnati Rag," "Beaumont Rag," and "Westphalia Waltz." Like most contest fiddlers, he had a "money tune," and his was "Tom and Jerry"; like Cleo Persinger did back in Missouri, Dale would hold this back in preliminary rounds and perform it in the final round or in a runoff when he was tied with another player. Pauley developed a reputation as a contest fiddler, winning at contests in Arizona, New Mexico, Utah, and Colorado.

At Rodeo Week in Tucson in 1985, Dale won the contest, and this contest included a category for the fiddler who offered the best performance of "Arkansas Traveler," a tune every fiddler is expected to know and a tune with a title reminiscent of the pioneer days. Pauley won first in this division, too. This contest also included a division specifically for professional musicians, and in this division brothers Brian and Bruce Wurst took first and second.[13]

Dale Pauley, first place, with fellow winners at the North American Championship in Gallup, New Mexico, June 30, 1988. Michelle Kuhlman (*center*) took second, Chad Partington third place. Dale's trophy states that the contest is "The National Old Time Fiddlers North America Championship (All Star)." (Courtesy of Dale Pauley)

Pauley participated in a competition called the Super Bowl of Fiddling in Cortez, Colorado. Held at the county fairgrounds in July 1987, this was one of several contests in the West under the aegis of the National Oldtime Fiddlers' Association, devised in 1983 by NOTFA leaders with the hopes of bringing all styles of fiddling together in a major southwestern contest. They encouraged participation by regional and ethnic fiddlers, with something for everyone.[14] The Super Bowl of Fiddling was timed to follow the National Oldtime Fiddlers' Contest in Weiser so that it could attract fiddlers who had been at Weiser a week or so before. The NOTFA link required administrators to adhere to NOTFA rules and procedures, and, if they agreed, these contests were anointed as "sanctioned" by the national organization. Contest contestants received a Certificate of Award from NOTFA.[15] Among top winners in 1987 at Cortez were fiddlers prominent in modern Texas-style contest fiddling such as Bart and Marilyn Trotter, Dale Morris, Ken Sloan, and Jeff Wiley. There were three age divisions for children. In other divisions (Adult, Senior, Senior-Senior), old-time fiddling was still prominent among top finishers (Dale Pauley took first in the Adult Division). There were three rounds in the grand championship division, in which fiddlers from other divisions could compete.

Dale and Mary Ruth had misgivings about some of the NOTFA-enforced rules at Cortez. They did not like the three-minute time limit for a fiddler's round. Three minutes is not enough time to present satisfactorily or fully three fiddle tunes; with a minute per tune, "You have to leave a lot out." They also did not like "hiding" judges away from the stage. Sequestering judges sounds good to audiences and gives an impression of impartiality because judges do not see the players or hear their names when announced, but sequestering fools very few judges. Mary Ruth comments, "These judges been around a little while, they know who's up there playing." Hiding the judges also denies judges the ability to watch fiddlers perform for the audience—thus missing an element in what makes a great contest fiddler, the ability to entertain. Savvy fiddlers figure out how to play to the judges. "I knew all those judges, and you kind of get to know what they *like*—and what they *don't' like*." Dale remembers a judge at contests in Green River, Utah, who would "cut you down" (knock off points on the score sheet) "if you didn't start with an umm-um-a-umm-uma ('potatoes') and end with a traditional shave-and-a-haircut tune ending."[16]

The 1987 Super Bowl of Fiddling was one of the competitions where administrators were aware of the widening gap between contest fiddlers playing old-time and bluegrass styles and those performing Contest Style (Texas-based, swing-influenced, progressive styles). The Open Division and Grand Championship classes were where Texas and progressive fiddling was going to rule. Dale was impressed with the Texas fiddling and agreed that just about anything should be allowed in the Open and Grand Championship Divisions, no matter how distant from old-time or bluegrass fiddling their creative improvisations take the music. Pauley feels that the modern contest fiddling is fine in the Open Division, but there are limits on his acceptance of it. "In the open division, whatever they want to do—*let* 'em *do it*. But sometimes in Texas, fiddlers there, you can't hardly make out what they're playing, it's so far out."

What happened at Cortez in 1987 will sound familiar to some fiddlers today. There was an Open Division and an "Old-Time" Division. The old-time class was meant to be a place for styles other than Contest Style, but the two divisions did not hold. The top Contest Style fiddlers were, in most instances, performing at such a high level of technical skill yet with audible foundations in old-time fiddling that they were able to divide into groups: one group entered the Open Division, and the other entered the Old-Time Division. Contest Style champions Bart Trotter and Dale Morris won the Open Division and the Old-Time Division, respectively.

In 1988 at the Super Bowl of Fiddling, Dale Pauley won first in the Adult Division. The Open Division was won by Monte Gaylord of Oklahoma. Karla Shivers of New Mexico won the Old-Time division, while Hughie Smith of California placed second; Missouri's young Jamie Maddux won third place, and her sister Mindy (Bob Walsh students) placed third in the Juniors. The judges included Ken Sloan, Roscoe White, and Herman Johnson. Pauley remembers with a smile that Johnson complimented him on his version of "Martin's Waltz." The Super Bowl of Fiddling eventually ended, due to a combination of overworked volunteers and diminishing funds for prize money and expenses.

In 1988 Dale retired from barbering and closed the Shearing Shed. He and Mary Ruth had a motor home and enjoyed traveling the contest circuit. In the Southwest and West, fiddlers' associations encouraged camping and helped people with needs and arrangements. After Dale retired, they decided to live in the motor home as they drove to contests along the Colorado River in Arizona, Utah, and Colorado. Fiddlers' association newsletters listed contests, so they planned accordingly. Dale was fortunate; Mary Ruth is an avid reader who loves conversation, does not play a musical instrument, but was never bothered by being a "fiddle widow." Mary Ruth: "You were talking about music. We always laughed and said, 'we have his, hers, and *music*'—Dale plays one kind, the kids were in rock-and-roll, and I like orchestras and Frank Sinatra."

> I always went with him to contests. And I'm a big blabber, and I always visit with people, and if they don't introduce themselves, I make 'em! And I read a lot. And there are people who follow, who love the music and they love to sit and visit. That's what they're there for, the party. And one time we were sitting out in south Arizona, in the Dragoon Mountains, and you had to go over a fence to get to the outhouse. Some of these contests were in some really *interesting places*! And this old couple was sitting behind me [watching the fiddle contest] and she says, "I need to go the bathroom," and he says, "Well, ya gotta go across that *barb war* fence." And I turned around and said to him, "Where are you from?" and he said "north Missouri" and I said, "I thought so—my father says *barb war* too."[17]

Pauley likes to trade and checks flea markets, yard sales, and music shops. While visiting in Sikeston, Missouri, in the 1980s, Dale traded for two Barcus-Berry electric violins. "I went into this store, sign said 'TV repair, music instruments.' A bunch of old junky fiddles hanging on the wall. He [the proprietor] said, 'Would you be interested in a couple of electric fiddles,' and I said, 'Yeah—I might.' So, I had just bought an old Winchester Model 97, and I showed him, and he wanted that gun. So, I traded him for those Barcus-Berrys, one of them was a four-string and one was a five-string." Dale sold the four-string Barcus-Berry in Tucson and kept the five-string.

After about a year, the Pauleys' motor-home adventures brought them to Cortez, Colorado, and the aforementioned Super Bowl of Fiddling. They liked Cortez, a region with four seasons (Dale did not like southern Arizona summers), and they bought a house. The Pauleys enjoyed the living conditions and the heritage and prehistory of the Four Corners region. They joined the Mesa Verde area fiddlers' association.

Pauley judged a few contests in Arizona and Colorado. His favorite was the New Mexico state contest in Truth or Consequences, where judges were welcomed, provided for, and respected. Dale represented Arizona, and the two other judges represented Colorado and New Mexico. Among NOTFA activities to promote contests was certification of judges, and many of the judges in the region secured this. One could be certified and issued an identity card. On the face of it, this was a good thing. Dale liked the certified-judge concept and would like to see some sort of process in Missouri to try to help contests hire judges with legitimate experience and respect among audiences and musicians.

Home

In 1992 Mary Ruth and Dale left Cortez and returned to Missouri, where their children and grandchildren lived and where they wanted to spend their later years. In addition, Cortez living conditions had changed for the worse, in their view, with the opening of Ute Mountain Casino, a major gambling and tourism center. The casino produced a real-estate boom, and many new residents and visitors shifted the town's character.

Back in Missouri, the Pauleys bought a farm at Gravois Mills, an upper Ozarks town in Morgan County on one of the north-side arms of the Lake of the Ozarks. Later in 1992 they moved to a house on the lake, in the Rocky Mount community. In 1999 they moved to a new house in the Seven Oaks subdivision in Columbia. Dale and Mary Ruth returned to visit in Arizona and Colorado on several occasions, and Dale competed in several fiddle contests.

Dale got back into contests and music parties, and he joined a country band, Just Us, led by Tyree Crane (guitar), with Tyree's wife, Patty Crane (piano); Gene Spencer (lead guitar); Steve Mossman (bass); and various drummers. They played pop and swing music for dances, their principal venues VFW and American Legion halls an hour or so from Columbia. Dale often played the Barcus-Berry electric violin, and he was with Just Us for eight years.

In 2002 Pauley had heart bypass surgery and returned to fiddling with Just Us, but he found that the physical commitment of fiddling long evenings was too much. Dale brought in his friend Bobby Joe Caldwell to take over the fiddle duties (other fiddlers filled in with Just Us at different times, including Travis Inman and Kelly Jones).

At a 2007 fiddle contest at Boonesboro, Pauley competes in the Senior Division, with accompanists Junior Marriott (guitar) and Kathy Gordon (bass). (Photo by Kay Allen)

In dance bands, Pauley was often asked to add new titles to his repertoire, and people made requests. One of the tunes he fiddled every week with Just Us is "Orange Blossom Special." "I played that thing every week! Eight years!"[18] "OBS" is still just as big an audience pleaser as it was seven or eight decades ago, a fiddler's extravaganza and smash hit on Grand Ole Opry radio broadcasts in the late 1930s. The tune has been recorded by a multitude of fiddlers of all persuasions in a bewildering number of styles, including early settings by gifted fiddlers Chubby Wise, Tommy Magness, and Art Wooten.[19]

"Orange Blossom Special"? This showboat tune is the bane of most fiddlers, even though some thoroughly enjoy it. Most fiddlers do not even think it's an authentic fiddle tune, but something more like a fireworks display on the Fourth of July. "OBS" is among exhibition pieces considered trick tunes, outlawed in fiddle contests in the 1960s. Before the ban, Dale Pauley had "OBS" shined up well enough that it helped him win at least one major contest (Boone County Fair, 1961). As we have seen, "OBS" was so popular in the 1960s that the top two fiddlers in the 1961 MFA state contest (Leroy Canaday and LeRoy Haslag) both presented it in preliminary contest rounds.[20] The piece may seem nothing more than a boiling stew of hot sauce and hokum, without musical substance or merit, fluff to be tossed off for the hoi polloi in noisy taverns. Most fiddlers playing a dance or show rue the inevitable moment when someone yells, "Play 'Orange Blossom Special'!" (In fairness, "The Devil Went Down to Georgia" is equally disliked by fiddlers.) But not all fiddlers dislike "OBS." Ozark Opry fiddler LeRoy Haslag enjoyed watching audiences react to the exciting music. Dale Pauley was burned out on "OBS" through years working with Just Us; today he will not play the tune. "I had to play 'Orange Blossom Special' every time we played for a dance and when I quit, I said I'd never play it again."[21]

By the time the Pauleys moved back in 1992, contests had undergone changes. Some of the old champions and leaders of the community had passed or retired, such as Gene Wells (d. 1981), Cyril Stinnett (d. 1986), Lee Stoneking (d. 1989), Bob Walsh (d. 1990), and Jimmy Gilmore (d. 1991), and his mentors such as Charlie Cook had died well before. Texas-based Contest Style and swing-style guitar music increased in popularity.

What is the future in terms of old-time fiddling? Mary Ruth Pauley: "Well, these kids are not only extremely talented, they have fabulous musical *educations*." Dale Pauley: "Look at Richard Shewmaker!" Mary Ruth Pauley: "And look at Kyle Pudenz. Look at the Quebe Sisters. Oh my gosh, the talent those people have just blows your mind." Howard Marshall: "Any advice for young fiddlers, Dale?" Dale Pauley: "I'm not a *teacher*." Kids today have better access to a thorough musical education, a luxury that few people of Dale's generation enjoyed. What should youngsters today do to learn to play *fiddle* music? Mary Ruth and Dale answer, "Education!" (Mary Ruth) and "Get some help" (Dale), neatly putting in a nutshell the time-honored paths to being an old-time fiddler.

Dale Pauley's music these days is heavily laced with elegant, smooth waltzes, rags, and western-swing pieces. With advancing age, he plays fewer fast breakdowns, but keeps a few of his contest winners reasonably in hand in his inactive repertoire such as "Old Joe Clark," "Grey Eagle," "Bill Cheatem," and "Sally Goodin." Pauley stopped entering contests in 2014.

All musicians have active and inactive repertoires. Tunes in Dale's active column are old favorites easily pulled from memory and fiddled. The second batch is his inactive repertoire, a long list of titles not easily conjured without some prompting—an anecdote or a suggested bit of melody from someone ("whistle a few notes of that"). Inactive titles are tunes fiddlers may have known well but seldom play now. Dale Pauley's inactive repertoire includes tunes that he has essentially forgotten, such as "Durham's Reel" and "Waltz of the Winds," but also includes tunes that he can play now but no longer enjoys, such as "Boil the Cabbage Down" and the dreaded "Orange Blossom Special." Tunes drift in and out of one's active repertoire, and, in a comfortable fiddle session with competent colleagues, a player may suddenly bring forth a long-forgotten "inactive" tune with the mere mention of its title or a comment about someone who played it.

A preliminary list in Pauley's active repertoire reminds us of his love of pop music of the 1920s into the 1960s, especially waltzes and "songs" for dancing. Pauley's waltz repertoire is deep and interesting. One of the traditional beliefs, or stereotypes, about central Missouri (Little Dixie region) fiddlers is that they play many more waltzes than the typical fiddler of other regions, and Dale's on-command list of some sixty waltzes proves the stereotype. Dale's active repertoire is quite extensive, once a list is articulated. His inactive tune is far more extensive.

While one might predict that Dale Pauley can play "Arizona Waltz," he rarely plays this and says it was rare in Arizona when he lived there (perhaps at least in part because the tune is relatively new and traces to a Hollywood movie?).[22]

Pauley does not like to play tunes in a session unless he feels he plays them well. But another fiddler may start a forgotten or unfamiliar tune, and by the time the melody is passed around to him, Dale often is fiddling along or ready to take a solo. If Dale likes it, he plays it.

These days, Dale's main opportunities for making music are sessions as well as the occasional concert or program. He does his own violin setup and basic repair on the kitchen table. He has a useful folk remedy for helping keep moisture in his violins during winter's low humidity, a small piece of tinfoil stuffed with some cotton, to which water is added.

A Tuesday-Night Jam Session, and Nuances of Jam-Session Etiquette

Around 1990 Bud Wyatt, Walter Spene, Ivan Crane, Arch Petree, and Ron Boyer started a Tuesday-night fiddle session, invitation only, rotating among the members' homes in Columbia and Centralia. In the early years, they usually convened at Ivan Crane's house, a bachelor who, as Bud Wyatt recalls, "lived alone and had no problems" in terms of being able to welcome musicians into his house.[23] Wyatt and Petree lived in Centralia, Spene and Crane in Columbia, Boyer in Hallsville. All except Ron Boyer played fiddle as well as guitar, and they took turns seconding each other's fiddling. The guitar seconding was both open-chord as well as closed-chord playing.

Sessions begin at seven, with a break for "dessert," and wrap up around nine. After Dale and Mary Ruth Pauley moved back to Columbia in 1999, Dale was invited to join, and Dale brought in Bobby Joe Caldwell. The group began to jokingly call themselves "the 9-1-1 band" because the three principal fiddlers, Wyatt, Caldwell, and Pauley, had undergone open-heart surgery. In time, others were invited to join the group, and the session expanded to include invited members Brad Roby (guitar), Kathy Gordon (bass), Heinrich Leonhard (guitar, mandolin, fiddle), and Howard Marshall (fiddle, guitar, mandolin).

Bud Wyatt's grandson Matt Wyatt is a periodic drop-in musician, as was Centralia mandolinist Harold Barnes. Others sometimes attended by invitation, such as Hal Sappington, a fiddler born in south Boone County and retired engineering professor at Central Missouri State University; keyboard player Betty Glaab; and fiddlers Richard Shewmaker, Sharon Graf (Springfield, Illinois), Bob Hagan, Anthony Wilson (a Texas/Contest Style fiddler from Decatur, Texas, who periodically resides in the area while working construction), Will Scherer, and Charlie Walden. Hillis Crowell attends occasionally when we meet at a home with a piano. Once a person is invited and attends, he or she has a standing invitation to return, notwithstanding an occasional guest who turns out to be incompatible with the session.

The music tends to be a mix of old-time/bluegrass, and swing, with ample waltzes and two-steps. The session is violin-centric but occasionally someone will sing an old country song.

The session has unwritten rules and customs, like all jam sessions, across all genres. What may appear to be a freewheeling frolic has an underlying structure. Mutual respect, support, and common courtesy guarantee a good time for all.[24] Like most fiddle sessions, one fiddler will start a tune and (ordinarily) is allowed to finish it, too.

A conspicuous nuance in this session that differs from most sessions is that, as music goes around the circle with each fiddler playing a tune, other fiddlers *do not* play along unless invited by the fiddler with a nod, glance, or comment, for example, to invite someone to play twin (harmony) on a particular tune. That detail contrasts with most other session etiquette customs. For instance, in many Missouri old-time and bluegrass sessions, the fiddler who starts a tune—perhaps after playing it one time through—passes the tune to the next fiddler on his or her left, and that fiddler is thereby invited to take a solo. Pauley also likes the tune to end after a few minutes; if other players play a tune three or four or more times, after it ends Dale might smile and joke, "Don't wear it out!"[25]

At a session at the Bud and Mary Wyatt house, Centralia, February 2016. *Left to right*: Heinrich Leonhard (guitar), Dale Pauley (violin), Harold Barnes (mandolin), Kathy Gordon (bass), Brad Roby (guitar), Bud Wyatt (violin), and Will Scherer (violin, back to camera). In late 2021, members who attend regularly include Leonhard, Pauley, Gordon, and Howard Marshall. (Photo by Howard Marshall)

Another custom in Missouri, familiar in Appalachian-type sessions and Irish music, is a pattern in which everyone plays the melody just as soon as a tune starts. In Missouri the all-join-in tradition is uncomfortable if not frustrating to some fiddlers, and Pauley is among Missouri fiddlers of my acquaintance (especially of older generations) who dislike it tremendously when other fiddlers jump in on his solo tune. The all-jump-in pattern seems to derive from fiddle-camp teaching circles and folk festivals. At many sessions in Missouri, the two approaches seem to battle each other (one fiddler plays and then passes the tune; a tune starts, and everyone immediately plays the melody together), and these sessions are unsatisfactory and have caused some sessions to cease being held.

The Tuesday sessions are brought to a close by playing "Amazing Grace" together—in this instance, "all join in"—after which Dale lowers his violin and declares, "We're done playing now."

Listen to track 12 on the companion CD to hear Dale Pauley's version of "Marchéta."

During "Weiser week" in Weiser, Idaho, Musial Wolfe (Booneville, Missouri) plays piano at a jam session of musicians playing for dancers during breakfast time in the American Legion hall. At the festival there is a great deal of music of many varieties being played beyond the National Oldtime Fiddlers' Contest itself. (Photo by Sharon Graf, June 2005)

Traditions Tested: Fiddle Contests in the 1980s and 1990s

7

It's all matter of opinion, that's what it is.
—Guy Craighead (1984), in George Mazurak,
"He's Still Playing Around," *Fulton Sun Gazette,* October 13, 1984

In the 1960s and 1970s, the social and cultural movements of the Folk Music Revival helped nourish revitalization of contests and creation of fiddlers' associations. There was resistance to change among many in the old-time fiddling community who saw the old contest styles start to crumble into secondary status among a new crop of highly skilled "contest fiddlers."

Old-time fiddling and bluegrass contests had been held in Missouri because they were familiar and genres preferred by most fiddlers, but the attractions of what John Griffin calls "Tex-a-fied" Contest Style fiddling and accompaniment—foreshadowed by the popularity of jazz and swing in the 1920s, 1930s, and 1940s—had arrived.[1] And just as important was the role of western swing and jazz backup-guitar styles with their many jazz chords in closed positions up and down the neck.

What was seldom recognized was that, while the swinging music was attractive, the idiosyncrasies and distinctive varieties of old-time and square-dance music somehow became less valued *in contests* than fiddling that showed hot licks, advanced technical expertise, debts to classical violin training, and professional-level performance. Perhaps the most telling change in contests was the end of the expectation that one's contest tunes be "danceable"; contest fiddling was and is essentially listening music for seated audiences.[2] But this criticism about contest fiddling is often overstressed, because competitions have always encouraged polish and perfection with little regard to whether anyone can dance to it.

The year 1979 was a pivotal one for the Missouri contest landscape. Nixa held its thirty-first annual state contest but was experiencing difficulties. Attempts to create annual state contests in Osage Beach and Graham fizzled. The Missouri Old-Time Fiddlers' Association and the Midwest Fiddlers' Association from the 1960s had evaporated. A new organization, the Missouri Fiddlers and Country Music Association (1974), sponsored contests but was essentially a St. Louis metro-area group. Bluegrass organizations such as the Society for the Preservation of Blue Grass Music of America (Kirksville), Tri-State Bluegrass Association (Kahoka), and Missouri Area Bluegrass Committee (St. Louis) sometimes sponsored contests but were focused on developing festivals and concerts. Were contests going away, or coming back stronger?

The Missouri State Old Time Fiddlers Association

In 1979, several young musicians in Columbia, students at the University of Missouri and habitués of the Chez coffeehouse, put on a state fiddle contest as a preview of a new organization they were planning to establish called the Missouri State Old Time Fiddlers Association. Like most other fiddlers' associations, the group evolved when a few friends became interested in contests. MSOTFA would become a prominent and influential organization in all things fiddling—and especially contests.[3]

The founders were Charlie Walden, Chris Germain, Bill Shull, Spencer Galloway, and Bob Hagan, savvy about politics and red tape.[4] They formalized the group through the Secretary of State's Office and obtained 501(c)(3) nonprofit corporation status, paving the way for grants and tax relief. The group obtained the imprimatur of Governor Joseph P. Teasdale, declaring the MSOTFA contest to be *the* state fiddle contest; "sanctioned by the Governor" invested the MSOTFA contest with added cachet.

Bob Hagan of Columbia getting ready to fiddle in a Fourth of July contest in Bunceton, 2014. Bob discontinued participation in MSOTFA in the mid-1980s and shifted his musical energies to fiddle, guitar, and mandolin and singing in Ron Lutz's "Rooster Creek Show." Around 2012, Hagan began taking part in fiddle contests again. (Photo by Howard Marshall)

MSOTFA's success was recognized widely, and the organization received a prestigious Missouri Arts Award from the Missouri Arts Council in 1989. MSOTFA leaders advised organizations in other states on establishing, administering, and judging fiddle contests.[5] In the mid-1990s, during a time of proliferation of contests and increasing changes in contests, Bill Shull authored two manuals to help administrators and improve the quality of adjudication, *Guide to Running a Fiddle Contest* and *Guide to Judging a Fiddle Contest.* Among the rules supported by MSOTFA in this early period were rules that stated that nonresidents could not compete in MSOTFA's state contest, that the number of accompanists could not exceed two, and that judges would be seated in front of the stage in view of audience and contestants.

In September 1979, the group organized a Missouri State Fiddling Championship, held in the auditorium at Hickman High School in Columbia. Twenty-seven players entered. Pete McMahan won the Open Division and won again in 1980 and 1981.[6] Joe Grable from Dearborn won the Senior Division. The contest was cosponsored by the city council and enjoyed grant funds from the Missouri Arts Council. Columbia was a good place for the new state contest, a region with a robust contest community and the principal city on Interstate 70 between St. Louis and Kansas City, with newspapers, television stations, two colleges, and the state university (with journalism students on the lookout for topics to meet assignments). In 1979, Andy Maykuth wrote a newspaper article about the new state contest and caught the event's pleasures and characters:

> Taylor McBaine's tapping feet and bobbing head keep time to his rousing rendition of "Marmaduke's Hornpipe." The smile never leaves his face.
>
> In the audience, a wave of fans, synchronized with McBaine's foot-tapping, moves the warm air in Hickman High School Auditorium. Gray-haired heads sway with the tune. They, too, smile at the fiddling Columbian.
>
> In a flurry of deft notes, McBaine finishes the tune, and the crowd cheers its approval. Tucking the fiddle under his arms, he strides off stage, still smiling.
>
> The scene was repeated for five hours the night of Sept. 8 as 27 of Missouri's top fiddlers tried to impress three judges. Only, most of the audience didn't know it was missing the real show.
>
> Near the backstage entrance, in the school's foyer, Jake Hockemeyer sits on a stone bench. He adjusts the straw cowboy hat on his bald head and rosins the bow.
>
> A left-handed fiddler with a right-handed fiddle, he begins to saw, and a nearby guitarist joins in.
>
> Nearby, a young fiddler and his accompanists lean close together, attempting to polish a contest tune. They're trying to coordinate a difficult lick, but the fiddler is frustrated. He shakes his head and starts over.
>
> Down the hall, the mood is buoyant. A group of musicians has formed a circle around two younger fiddlers who are performing a jig for their amused colleagues. A crowd gathers, clapping and hooting as the pair falls to the floor, exhausted.
>
> The ash of Pete McMahan's Camel dangles precariously, but he's in no position to take the cigarette out of his mouth. He is the central character of a backstage jam session.
>
> The 60-year-old Harrisburg tire salesman is an animated fiddler, dipping and jerking with the hoedown, his right foot patting the floor.
>
> Spectators crowd around McMahan . . . . An arms-length from his 160-year-old fiddle, the crowd leans closer to hear the mellow strains.

"Yes, yes," says one man.

"All right. He's got it together tonight," another whispers.

McMahan yanks the finishing stroke, emitting a wisp of white rosin dust. The small group hoots.

The other musicians go on to search for new partners. McMahan goes on to win first place in the championship.

The competition on stage is of secondary importance. . . . The atmosphere is stilted on stage; perfection and skill are the objectives.

Backstage, though, the fiddlers relax. Old, proven fiddlers jam with novices, imparting some of their skill to the younger generation. The fiddlers talk about what they've done since the last contest.

"That's where the best music is, and that's where fiddlers have the best time," McBaine says. "It's just like when you go to a party—people begin dancing and having a good time."

Another old-time fiddler, 75-year-old Lena Hughes, agrees. "A jam session's better than a contest."

Although she is an avid contestant—she has more than 50 trophies—the backstage sessions are what keep her coming back.

She compares the contest's festivity to the informal hoedowns of her childhood on a farm near Ludlow.

"We'd fill our yard with people and have a fish fry. Just fill the yard," she says.

"A bunch of fiddlers used to come in, and us kids would just sit around and listen. That's how I learned, and from my dad. Of course, I'm not the fiddler he was."

McMahan says, "I do it as a hobby and just to meet the people."

And then there's Clarence "Doc" Winingear. At 78, the retired Fulton farmer was the championship's oldest contestant. He's moving a little slower these days, and his fiddle—a 1722 Italian model—remained in its case until it was his turn to perform.

"I just crave it," he says, flashing a wry smile.[7]

Maykuth's article follows a long skein of enthusiastic, atmospheric features and photo essays about old-time fiddle contests and fiddlers, connecting back to many similar stories that helped fuel a previous golden age of fiddle contests in the 1920s.

MSOTFA's state championship was held for several years at Hickman High. By 1982, the association had become official with 501(c)(3) tax status and received wide recognition. In 1983, the contest included more entrants, with seven in the Senior Division and twenty in the Open Division. Inclusion of a Junior Division for younger fiddlers was not yet part of the contest.

In 1985, the contest was held in two locations, the preliminary round in Nifong Park in connection with the city's Fall Heritage Festival and the finals held in Assembly Hall on the Stephens College campus. The Nifong Park location gave the contest assistance from the city's Department of Parks and Recreation and broader exposure to the general public. Around 1990, the contest moved to Sedalia and became an event sponsored by the Missouri State Fair each August. The fair connection

Hickman High School student John Murdock won the Junior Division at the September 1979 state contest in Columbia. Murdock was one of the sharpest of the youngsters who launched into old-time fiddling in the 1970s and one of the youngsters taken under Taylor McBaine's wing. Before long, "Jock" Murdock became McBaine's prize pupil. After graduating, Murdock enrolled in the university and became a resident of the Chez coffeehouse. (Courtesy of Spencer Galloway)

furthered the impression that this was Missouri's most important fiddling competition. By 2002, MSOTFA leadership had recast a small but important part of their advertising; they stopped billing the contest as "old-time" and began calling it the "Missouri State Fair Fiddling Contest."

Like other groups, the Missouri State Old Time Fiddlers Association promoted fiddlers' conventions, too. These events were popular with fans of fiddle music who were not "contest fiddlers" or who did not attend contests. Conventions included jam sessions, a carry-in dinner, and square dancing, and most were situated in small towns in outstate Missouri rather than large towns and cities. A number were held in locations such as senior citizen centers and town halls in Potosi, Tina, Slater, and Montgomery City, as well as the Catholic parish hall in the north Missouri town of Wein.[8]

Fiddlers' conventions were an old tradition in Missouri that MSOTFA included in their menu of events. Many of the big fiddle contests of the 1920s, and many later, included a hospitable gathering of fiddlers and families as an adjunct to the competition. The "State of the Ozarks" fiddlers' convention in the Branson area, led by Bob Walsh and others, drew hundreds of fans and fiddlers. The dance community was also busy that year. Old-time dances and basket dinners were being held in the village hall in Tina in Carroll County one Saturday a month, events that welcomed visiting musicians to sit in with regulars such as Johnny Bruce and Lena Hughes.[9] Contra dances and square dances were held around the state, featuring a bullpen of rotating fiddle bands and dance callers. There were numerous regular jam sessions, and the bluegrass associations were quite active.

A general "Missouri style" of old-time fiddling in contests was brought to a zenith by champions such as Daniel Boone Jones, George Morris, Ed Tharp, Charlie Cook, Cleo Persinger, Taylor McBaine, Leroy Canaday, Pete McMahan, Nolan Boone, Dean Johnston, Warren Helton, Cecil Goforth, Lee Stoneking, Gene and Henry Wells, Jake Hockemeyer, and Kelly Jones (among others), and younger fiddlers such as John Griffin, Charlie Walden, and Travis Inman. This Missouri style evolved principally in the central Missouri region on both sides of the Missouri River. By 1980, the general style of those fiddlers—broadly similar but with individual characteristics—was familiar at contests throughout North America to such an extent that it often was simply called "Missouri style" by outsiders. Of course, there are other styles crucial in Missouri's fiddle heritage, but that was Missouri's peak contest style until the late 1980s.

Left to right: Pete McMahan, Gene Wells, and Jake Hockemeyer after the annual Paris Old Threshers contest in 1974. (Photo by Howard Marshall)

Listen to track 13 on the companion CD to hear Gene Wells's version of "Sally Goodin."

"Weiser"—Carnegie Hall meets Woodstock—remains a contest attracting competitors and tastemakers chiefly from the Pacific Northwest region. One reason is the long-term effect of numerous violin teachers in the region comfortable with fiddling who concentrated on teaching their classical and Suzuki students "fiddling" techniques and the dozen or so contest versions of tunes that succeed in contests. Many (but not all) violin teachers (fiddle teachers, too), instructional materials, fiddle camps, Internet sites, and cyberspace communities have come to value Contest Style fiddling over the "old-time" music around them that in many cases is their historic regional cultural heritage. Impeccable bowing, intonation, and performance values, and a small contest repertoire, were replacing the community's inherited fiddle and dance music. Some teachers and students seem to have one goal: winning fiddle contests. Teachers rehearse students for the pressure and environment at contests, helping them get their tunes played inside the time limit, preparing them for the stage, and having them absorb classic recordings of the giants of Contest Style. Seven-time Weiser champion Megan Lynch Chowning puts it well: "We started teaching competition rather than teaching music."[10]

Proponents of Contest Style are as enthusiastic about their music as are fans of old-time and bluegrass. Jim Wood of Tennessee, a successful Contest Style fiddler, has judged contests and counseled students on strategies with which to bring home the bacon. Wood says that all fiddlers should compete in contests—"the best training ground imaginable"—and expresses the feeling of many players devoted to Contest Style.

> Contest-style fiddling in many ways represents the apex of traditional folk music. It demands of its practitioners a technical command of the violin on par with all but the most pyrotechnical classical repertory, and it requires a keen sense of melodic invention and structural development akin to the best of jazz. In addition, one must marry a deep connection with the contest fiddle tradition to an implacable commitment to developing one's own unique musical voice. Finally, from a psychological standpoint, one must possess an unabashed desire to sound impressive, be willing to take risks, and want to win. It is not for the faint of heart; the very word "contest" implies the competitive spirit.[11]

Contest Style teachers and students often work from the same books and instructional materials, and they concentrate on "clean" playing and controlled improvisation.[12] Extra bits executed in the moment in front of the microphone may be exciting to the player; critics and contest judges may hear them as unwanted or even irritating. Extra bits and new ideas take time to become accepted into the aesthetic of traditional music, which essentially is an aesthetic that honors custom, heritage, and comfortable patterns over innovations and changes that are perceived as painting too far outside tradition's borders.

Fiddlers who compete at Weiser do best who play clear, clean, perfect music, whether anyone in the audience would square-dance to it or not. Many of the modern

Contest Style champions and top players become teachers, and the Contest Style and philosophy are perpetuated.[13] Competition rounds can feel like violin recitals, and perhaps that is not inappropriate for an event where fiddle performances are carefully practiced concerts for listening rather than rhythm for dancing.

The sunshine of old-time "Missouri style" contest fiddling that echoed dance traditions drifted to twilight. By around 2000, the old "Missouri style" of Taylor McBaine and Cleo Persinger was no longer winning most contents. Another, different, golden age was evolving that promoted nationalized Contest Style fiddling with western-swing guitar accompaniment. The contest community gradually began to embrace this increasingly nonregional Contest Style exemplified in Benny Thomasson, often credited with developing modern Contest Style in Texas (before moving west to the Seattle area). Thomasson's creative and perfected contest performance style (and those of his colleagues) was becoming a superstyle.

Texas-based Contest Style was encouraged by the National Oldtime Fiddlers' Contest at Weiser, as well as by the influence of a coterie of Contest Style fiddlers across the continent. This thrilling improvisational yet solid style with Texas genes emerged as a global phenomenon following wins by young Mark O'Connor of Seattle at Weiser, beginning in 1979.

Another contest style that became an international one is southern Appalachian contest style. This hard-driving, rhythmic "mountain style," in some instances related to bluegrass fiddling, was comparatively straight in comparison with the fancier western Contest Style. This second style features comparatively spare improvisation (although Appalachian fiddlers make frequent use of scordatura/cross-tuning and crooked tunes). In many Missouri contests, few judges will "understand" unusual or metrically crooked tunes or "appreciate" tunes performed in cross-tunings, and some Missouri contests ban the use of cross-tuned violins.[14]

This Appalachian contest style is popular in Missouri, but players in the so-called Appalachian style (or styles) must be extraordinarily talented to compete successfully with the Texas-based Contest Style that has captured much of the Missouri fiddle-contest community.

By 2001, most of the elder contest legends of the previous generation had retired or passed away. Many old-time contest fiddlers adapted to the Contest Style (Texas style/progressive style), some only partially in order to continue being successful in contests, often by performing "Texas" and "Weiser" repertoire and, in many cases, by performing with Contest Style swing-guitar backup, or at least by dressing up their old-time performances. But many fiddlers did not care to adapt and kept on with what they knew and enjoyed best, trying not to fret if their old-time style was not rewarded by judges. Some popular masters and champions of the once-prevalent Missouri style, like Kelly Jones, retired from the contest platform rather than change with the times. For very young contest fiddlers, the vast majority were pupils of older Contest Style champions; for them, Contest Style fiddling was what they knew.

The success of fiddle contests from the 1980s into the 2000s, substantially aided by the Missouri State Old Time Fiddlers Association, was also due to Missouri Arts

Council grants, to bluegrass festivals that included fiddle contests in their activities, and to support from organizations such as the Missouri Fiddlers and Country Music Association as well as the Missouri Cultural Heritage Center at the University of Missouri and its offshoot, the Missouri Folk Arts Program, and other cultural agencies and funding organizations.

An ambitious contest in Clinton in June 1989 purported to embrace the entire Midwest. Sponsored by the Chamber of Commerce and with advice from Fred Stoneking, Clinton hosted a Midwest National Amateur Fiddler's Contest. "National" in the title meant that fiddlers from anywhere in the nation would be welcome, just as in "National" in the Weiser contest advertising. The contest offered ten places in one division and gave awards to the youngest fiddler, the fiddler traveling the farthest, and the most "pleasant fiddler." Other contests with nationwide ambition in the 1980s included those held at a resort at the Lake of the Ozarks, hosted by the Society for the Preservation of Blue Grass Music of America (until the late 1990s, bluegrass fiddling was still welcome and successful in Missouri fiddle contests).

There were fractures in the fiddle community. Contest Style fiddling and guitar accompaniment were ascending across the United States and Canadian contest landscape and gradually displacing older fiddle styles and repertoires. With a hiatus of Missouri State Old Time Fiddlers Association programs and leadership (except for the state contest in Sedalia), and because of other factors, the golden age of the 1980s and 1990s fizzled out.[15]

Around 2000, another different era or golden age in contest fiddling evolved. This new era is based on growing interest in the Contest Style fiddling and repertoire and on its preference for swing-style guitar accompaniment. The newly dominant Contest Style players preferred more than two accompanists and preferred several guitarists playing western swing, closed-chord backup style. The tacit acceptance of this Contest Style and multiple accompanists by the Missouri State Old Time Fiddlers Association at the state contest in Sedalia can be seen as just as important as the emergence of this exciting fiddle style itself in bringing change to contests and the world of old-time fiddling.

In 2003, as MSOTFA's activities slowed, the *Contest Calendar* as well as other publications and communications ceased, and this was a great loss to the fiddle community and a factor in the decline of the number of contests in Missouri. The absence of the *Contest Calendar*, widely appreciated by fiddlers and fans, is especially striking. For a time, Wyatt Violin Shop in Independence picked up production of the calendar, and Allen Wyatt volunteered to handle administration of the Sedalia contest. The calendar ceased production after several years, however; the most difficult problem was cajoling contest administrators to submit information for the next year's calendar. In the early 2020s, two sources offer incidental information on contests—Cathy Marriott of Ava, Missouri, via her Facebook page, and David Cavins's website, https://www.mofiddledance.com. But contest fiddlers and aficionados no longer have a comprehensive calendar and must now rely on word of mouth, personal connections rare in the time of COVID, and Facebook posts.

Bill Shull

A solid old-time fiddler with an immense repertoire and scholarly knowledge, in the 1980s and 1990s Bill focused on development and administration of the Missouri State Old Time Fiddlers Association. Bill liked to describe himself as "a social fiddler" and said that he "loses on a regular basis" at contests.[16] Charlie Walden spoke of the origins of the association:

> A friend of mine, Bill Shull down in Missouri—he's a real fiddle fanatic in almost a worse way than I am. It was his idea to start it, actually. He asked me to be the president, and I have been ever since we started, in about 1979. Basically, our goal was to provide information to people who wanted to run contests, because as you go around to contests, you find that people will pick the local Pork Queen and local music store owner and the high school principal to be the judges, and you get a less than desirable result from their judging. Plus, they can be run kind of squirrelly, if you've never run a fiddle contest and you don't have a clue. It makes it so that fiddlers won't come back and it won't encourage them to perform. We wanted to encourage the fiddlers we knew to perform, as one of the means of maintaining the tradition—you've got to get people out so they play and meet other local fiddlers and that sort of thing.
>
> So that's why we started it, to kind of help people run contests. And it just kind of blossomed. We didn't realize there would be such a big interest in it among the local fiddlers. And then we started putting out recordings, again as another means of encouraging people to play the older music. So we picked a handful of fiddlers initially, I think Pete and Taylor, and we put out a few recordings of Cyril Stinnett after his death, unfortunately. Again, to get people to hear more than one style of fiddle music, but we wanted to encourage our regional style, and our regional repertoire. That was the most important thing to us.[17]

Shull was born in Independence in 1950, graduated from high school in 1968, attended the University of Missouri in Columbia, and graduated with a bachelor's degree in English in 1974. He went to law school at the university and in 1979 took his juris doctor degree and was admitted to the Missouri Bar. He began practice in Warrensburg in the office of Legal Aid of Western Missouri and continues as the program's managing attorney. Bill's wife, Margaret, plays violin in the Warrensburg civic orchestra (as did Bill) and helped administer some of the state contests in Sedalia.

That decade that Bill spent in Columbia aligned with the burst of interest in old-time music and fiddling in the late sixties and through the seventies. Bill frequented the Chez coffeehouse, playing old-time banjo and fiddle and rubbing elbows with the many other youthful enthusiasts of the Folk Music Revival.

At a time when the college town's young musicians were digging into classic 78-rpm records of southern Appalachian music, Bill helped lead the trend to care about *Missouri* fiddling. Early on, he understood the value of transcribing the music of local fiddlers and wrote out tunes played by legends he visited such as Lyman Enloe, Cyril Stinnett, and Jake Hockemeyer. With Charlie Walden, Bill became a mentee of R. P. Christeson, Taylor McBaine, Pete McMahan, Enloe, Stinnett, Hockemeyer, and others. Shull was especially interested in Lyman Enloe and published a book of transcriptions of some of Enloe's distinctive tunes.[18] Shull accumulated a library of books, recordings, articles, photos, and ephemera and was among fiddlers who value music-reading ability and knowledge of music theory. After a dozen-plus years away from the Sedalia state contest, during which Allen Wyatt handled the event, in 2014 Bill returned to administering the event, until his death in June 2022, and, in most years since, Charlie has served as emcee.

Bill Shull at a MSOTFA old-time dance and fiddlers' convention, Tina, 1984. (Photo by Howard Marshall)

The Missouri State Old Time Fiddlers Association developed publications, including a newsletter-journal, and issued archival recordings on cassette, some of them reissues of out-of-print LP records of popular fiddlers. Many of these materials are accessible online. One of the association's contributions was the *Contest Calendar*, which immediately became an essential guide for musicians and fans. The first issue in 1982 listed twenty-four contests from March to November, and MSOTFA secretary Bob Hagan wrote: "The Missouri State Old Time Fiddlers Association is a newly formed organization with several goals, among which are: organizing fiddle contests statewide and providing a forum for the expression of views and opinions regarding contest rules, procedures and judging."

Among the many interesting projects of the Missouri State Old Time Fiddlers Association was development of a special fiddle contest in Jefferson City to commemorate the historic contests aired live over WOS-AM radio in the 1920s and early 1930s. Bill Shull and Charlie Walden located a number of musicians who had participated in those earlier contests and invited them to participate in 1984 in the WOS Radio Reunion fiddle contest, along with numerous other fiddlers from across the state. The WOS broadcasts beamed live from the dome of the state capitol, and the 1984 "reunion" was held in the capitol rotunda. The event was a success and helped demonstrate the association's interest in documenting the heritage of Missouri fiddling and fiddlers.

Taking a sample year, the 1989 *MSOTFA Contest Calendar* listed some forty-seven Missouri contests, including the Midwest National Amateur Fiddler's Contest in Clinton, the Mid-America Old Time Fiddle Championship in Bethel, and the annual Land of Mark Twain Fiddle Championships in Hannibal. An additional contest was organized after the calendar was mailed, the Ashlock Invitational Fiddle Contest, an event "more an exhibition than a contest" developed by Walden and Missouri Cultural Heritage Center staffer Julie Youmans in cooperation with KOPN 89.5 FM in Columbia.[19] The radio station occupied the room that was formerly the Ashlock Violin Shop. The 1989 calendar also listed four national contests in neighboring states, the World Series of Fiddling in Langley, Oklahoma; the Mid-America Old Time Fiddle Championship in Avoca, Iowa; the National Fiddlers' Convention and Championships in Mountain View, Arkansas; and the Walnut Valley Festival in Winfield, Kansas. There were contests that did not advertise beyond their communities, so they did not appear in the calendar. Several towns held onetime contests, but many hosting contests with annual fish fries, parish picnics, county fairs, homecomings, and other festivals. The year 1989 was a good time for contests and typical of the era from the mid-eighties into the late 1990s. Producing the *Contest Calendar* required a great deal of time and effort. According to Shull:

> Somewhere around February, I would get mailers out to the contest sponsors, encouraging early submission of their contest information. I would then "calendar" all the dates, catch the date/time conflicts, and call both sponsors and put them in touch with each other to see what could be worked out. That resulted in contests shifting dates and times so that more fiddlers would be able to attend both contests. I also attended the Missouri Association of Fairs annual meetings in January for several years and conducted the "round-table" on fiddle contests. Local fair board reps would attend, and I'd distribute a lot of written info to take back to their fair boards to explain the benefits of their fair having a contest. This resulted in a number of new contests being created.[20]
>
> The calendar was a huge deal for the contests because we kept a very careful list of all the fiddlers' addresses, and had each contest try to get a list of the entrants and then send them to us to add to the database. We charged a minimal amount to be in the Calendar ($10 or so) and saved the contest administrators hours of work and postage. In return, we required that contests not charge an entry fee, AND, if they changed a date or cancelled a contest, that they would pay us the cost of doing a mailing to the entire list. The result of that was that the contests stopped charging

any entry fee, which was huge for the fiddlers. We only had to ban two contests from the Calendar in the entire time—Boone County Fair, and a place up in Independence. Those rules were of great service to the fiddlers.[21]

In 1985, the *MSOTFA Journal* was started, with essays, biographies, transcriptions, discussions, contest results, and archival documentation. For a time, there was a "Fiddle Doctor" column by luthier John Griffin, a "Possum Corner" by MSOTFA president Walden, and guest articles. Shull and Walden authored important articles and books in a variety of other places, too, such as the *Devil's Box*.[22] An archive was set up in the State Historical Society of Missouri, where materials are curated and made available to researchers. Later, the journal was renamed *MSOTFA Quarterly* and, finally, *MSOTFA Annual*.

Bill and Charlie encouraged young fiddlers in a number of ways. As Shull recalled, "We gave out free MSOTFA cassettes to any junior that promised to learn at least two tunes from each cassette."[23] In the mideighties, MSOTFA helped inaugurate the Bethel Youth Fiddle Camp, among the first such camps in the United States. Bill and Charlie, along with administrator Jeanne Adams, played key roles. Seasoned fiddlers were hired to teach, such as Bob Holt, Vesta Johnson, Taylor McBaine, Johnny Bruce, Dwight Lamb, Kelly Jones, Pete McMahan, John T. White, Jim Lansford, and Travis Inman. Collaboration and support were provided by the Historic Bethel Communal Colony organization, along with the Missouri Cultural Heritage Center at the University of Missouri. Grants from the Missouri Arts Council were obtained and continue to provide funding, and modest student fees assist with covering costs.

Campers learn fiddling and guitar backup, and they also learn to square dance under the guidance of callers such as Edna Mae Davis and her daughter Cathy Davis (now Cathy Marriott) of Ava, Steve Young, and others. While mostly Missourians, young Bethel camp fiddlers came to Bethel from other states, such as John and Jason Shaw of Lincoln, Nebraska, who were star pupils of Pete McMahan and Johnny Bruce and went on to become influential musicians and champions.[24] Guitar-backup instruction taught players such as Alvie Dooms, Floyd Kemp, Jim Lindsey, John G. Stewart, and Kenny Applebee. On Saturday, the final day, a Mid-America Old Time Fiddle Championship used to be held (first in 1985), followed by a square dance with instructors, pupils, and guest fiddlers. Old-time piano backup (with electronic keyboard) is encouraged at Bethel, reflecting the piano's historic importance in the fiddle community. Bethel continues in the 2020s, and some of the current fiddle teachers, such as Angie Lennie (Ottumwa, Iowa) and John Williams, were students as youngsters. The Saturday fiddle contest is no longer held.

The Missouri State Old Time Fiddlers Association was effective and served the many fans and musicians. In 1987, Bill Shull and Charlie Walden joined with Bob Walsh and others to secure the "fiddle" as Missouri's official state musical instrument.

In 1994, Bill organized a series of profiles of Missouri fiddlers for two issues of the *Old-Time Herald*. Several authors contributed pieces, and Bill wrote profiles and an article on contests, summarizing their history and popularity in Missouri and noting that there were some two hundred active contest fiddlers in Missouri at the time. Bill articulated some of the tensions, contradictions, and problems in competitions. Contests "tend to perpetuate some of the existing fiddle tradition. On the other hand, the very nature of contests encourages newness, creativity, and daring. To separate yourself from the pack and walk away with a prize, you frequently need to innovate." "The 'winning' style of fiddling in Missouri is, as in all states, a matter of the tastes of the typical complement of three judges." "Most contest judges in Missouri try to listen for quality in the fiddling, rather than working to bring the scoring within strict guidelines of style." "Fiddle contests are criticized by many people for accentuating and rewarding small repertoires and showy, 'non-traditional' fiddling. On the other hand, in modern times when square-dancing and music-oriented house parties are no longer social staples, contests are one of the most effective means of perpetuating the individual art of fiddling."[25]

By the mid-1990s, the contest arena was becoming increasingly murky, when new and old contest fiddling and guitar styles and attitudes came more into conflict with each other. Questions of sportsmanship, fairness of adjudication, and the knotty issue of how many accompanists should be allowed onstage were discussed among of fans, administrators, and musicians. The divide between old-time and bluegrass fiddling and accompaniment and Contest Style fiddling and accompaniment was becoming more evident.

In 1994, an unsigned "Issues" column on sportsmanship appeared in *MSOTFA Quarterly*. This was a time when most Missouri contests were still dominated by old-time fiddlers such as Johnny Bruce, Leroy Canaday, John Griffin, Travis Inman, Kelly Jones, Taylor McBaine, Pete McMahan, Geoff Seitz, and Charlie Walden. But the writing was on the wall: a group of mostly younger fiddlers playing Texas-based Contest Style with closed-chord swing-guitar accompaniment in contests (led by Junior Marriott, Billy Ward, and a few others) were seeing their brand of fiddle music become increasingly successful in contents, with fiddlers such as Katie Benyo, Gunner Byrd, Amy LeGrand, Kyle Link, Cody Marriott, Levi Roden, Liesl Schoenberger, Alita and Lucas Stoneking, Taylor Sullivan, Darren Tapscott, Priscilla and Stephanie Westgate, and Matt Wyatt. They typically brought onstage more than two accompanists (usually two, sometimes three, guitar players), despite most contests' well-known two-accompanist rule, setting the stage for debates, confrontations, and questions about matters of decorum and sportsmanship. It must be added that, in my view, perhaps only a few of the younger Contest Style fiddlers were conscious of the fact that they were, in effect, part of the movement to promote Contest Style fiddling and accompaniment at the expense of old-time Missouri fiddling and other legacy styles.

The anonymous 1994 *MSOTFA Quarterly* essay on sportsmanship mentioned above was a response to the growing tensions in the contest community and encapsulated much of the wide-ranging debate over the rise of the dominance of the Texas-based Contest Style and accompaniment.

> Nobody says that when you don't place in a contest you have to like it. And if you want to romp and stomp a little outside the auditorium or tent after the contest, that's your privilege. A little loud talk never hurt anybody much; in fact, some of the funniest remarks I've heard have come from sore losers (one fiddler said he didn't mind losing, "he just didn't like being judged by guys that couldn't even *tune* a fiddle"). Fiddlers are generally not a placid or mealy-mouthed lot, and if they were, I wouldn't want to be fiddling. Maybe I'm odd, but I happen to appreciate and condone the behavioral patterns of drunken hillbillies (being one myself). On the other hand, before you show your butt in front of the whole crowd, please consider the following points:
>
> 1. Did you really *listen* to the fiddlers who beat you, or did you just assume they sounded like they did the last time you heard them (i.e., two or three years ago)? People get better on the fiddle (and some of them do it amazingly fast). Or did you just *figure* that because some kid was only fourteen years old, he couldn't really play the fiddle?[26]
>
> 2. How long has it been since you listened to yourself on tape? Some guys prance around as if they sounded like a combination of Benny Thomasson and Big Howdy [Howdy Forrester] on a dry day; yet when the rest of us listen to them, we don't quite see the connection. Even if you generally play well, you might have had an exceptional experience (off day, bad microphone, worse accompanist, etc.).
>
> 3. Did you consider who the judges are? You may have a few hot licks down pat (or think you do), but the guys judging the contest may have been listening to, accompanying, appreciating, and playing fiddle for years. Even if they can't beat you head-on in a contest, they may have a much better perspective on fiddling as a whole than you do.
>
> 4. Do you cherish the notion that you're being "rawhided" because you're new to the contest circuit, because you're not in the right "group", because you play the wrong "style," because you're too old or two young, or something of the sort? For that matter, why not just blame it on your dirty jeans or the fact that your hat wasn't on straight?
>
> For parting advice, let me say that the roughest guys (and the best fiddlers) I've ever known knew one thing well, and that was how to take a whipping in style. They don't leave before the prizes are given out, storm off the stage, or insult the judges, their fellow contestants, the contest promoters, or the crowd. It's a matter of individual character, and each fiddle has to decide how they'll stack up in that category.[27]

While these issues are old and probably unsolvable, that anonymous essay could not quiet resentments among some MSOTFA members and others, and it did not shed much light on the crux of the situation in 1994: older Missouri contest fiddle and accompaniment styles were being increasingly threatened if not swamped by the wave of Texas-based Contest Style. One doubts whether many people took time to read carefully or contemplate that unsigned essay. The contest turf continued in a state of uninformed or misinformed debate and general confusion.

In 1996, a column by Bill Shull in the *MSOTFA Annual* presented his insights as a fiddler, contest administrator, and scholar of fiddle history. This excellent 1996 essay points to cracks in the shifting world of contests across North America and provides a good basis for thoughtful discussion of the quite opaque subjects of contest style, authenticity, and contest adjudication:

> A constant question at modern fiddle contests is the extent to which the contest administrator or judges will try to determine scoring based, in part, on a competitor's fiddle "style." In Missouri, this usually translates into a question of what is the "old-time" fiddle style (as opposed to "Texas," "progressive," "bluegrass" or other styles). Many fiddlers claim the high ground in this controversy, believing that their own style is "old-time" and that many of the other fiddlers are playing in some bogus, non-traditional, or otherwise illegitimate manner.
>
> Of course, there are a few bright lines in this analysis. When fiddlers stray so far from the original tune that you can't tell what tune they're playing, when the "licks" overcome and obliterate the melody, and when a fiddler is playing downright trash, most judges can spot it instantly and score accordingly. Similarly, when violinists with no idea about fiddle time, structure, drive, and tone are competing, the judges usually recognize this, and, appropriately, won't score them.
>
> Waltzes in particular are problematic. Many fiddlers will play a very straightforward breakdown and tune of choice but render their waltz in a much more sophisticated or technically complex manner (triplets, slides, "Chubby Wise licks," and so on). And these guys, in my observation, are the ones that seem the most outraged when somebody playing a more progressive breakdown wins the contest.
>
> What it gets down to is whether MSOTFA should try to enforce some stylistic agenda. The problem with such an idea is that it runs counter to the natural process of development within musical traditions. It also contradicts a primary artistic principle: that is, that good musicians will gravitate to their own conception of what their music should be. And, after all, it is those "good" musicians that keep filling a prosperous and popular part of traditional music.
>
> In our view, all a fiddle organization should do is make available a lot of traditional, regional music so that it's there for the learning. If kids or new fiddlers want to learn something else, so be it. And when they play a new tune, or an old tune in a new style, and play it right they ought to win.
>
> Of course, given that every fiddler and his dog have different understandings of what "playing it right" means, this all adds up to a real headache for the judges. What MSOTFA will continue to encourage is the use of experienced fiddlers as judges and encourage those judges to base their evaluations of the fiddlers on musical merit, not personality, showmanship, or other irrelevant factors.[28]

"If kids or new fiddlers want to learn something else, so be it" says it well and bluntly. With the help of others, the Missouri State Old Time Fiddlers Association kept the state contest in Sedalia going. Over time, apart from the state-fair contest, there was a reduction in their activities. In May 1993, Charlie Walden moved to Evanston, Illinois, and his interests and activities broadened. Bill Shull grew busier in his law practice and with other responsibilities. In the later 1990s, with MSOTFA generally in hiatus, and as elders such as Taylor McBaine and Pete McMahan grew grayer and their influence diminished, the new generation of Contest Style fiddlers and swing-guitar accompanists stepped up to the microphone and almost completely took over Missouri contests.

Time has shown that it was folly for the "old-time" contest community to attempt to stem the tide of modern Contest Style in fiddle contests, and time has shown that there continue to be talented young old-time fiddlers and accompanists on the contest scene.

Fiddler Clifford Hill has judged contests for many years and in 2016 contemplated the new prevalence of Texas/Contest Style: "If the Texas [style] guys aren't there, it's a very small contest."[29]

Old-time fiddler H. K. Silvey, from Theodosia, and Traditional Arts Apprenticeship Program master teacher, talks about the ups and downs of fiddle contests, backstage at the Downtown Branson contest, August 2010. In 2020, Jim Nelson produced a CD of Silvey's fiddling for the Field Recorders' Collective. (Photo by Howard Marshall)

Branson, the country music and tourist mecca, held fiddle contests through the years. As different leadership sought to continue the event, around 2000 "Historic Downtown Branson" was one of the groups that received advice from MSOTFA leadership. At the seventeenth annual contest in August 2004, Branson acknowledged both "Texas style" (Contest Style) and "old-time style" by offering separate divisions for each. Fiddlers with the versatility to play both styles had to decide which division to enter. At the registration table, guide sheets were distributed to fiddlers to help them decide which division to enter. Bill Shull wrote the guide and distributed it at the registration table. The sheet presented Bill's thinking on how Texas style (Contest Style) differs from others, and he sought to clarify things and help contestants decide whether to enroll in the Texas-Style Division or the Old-Time Division:

> The following elements are commonly, although not always, found in performances of "Texas/Contest" style fiddling:
>
> 1. Slower tempo, or very "up" tempo (HOT); does not have to be danceable;
> 2. Emphasis on downbeat ("tied triplet" feel, or "swing feel");
> 3. Melodic development/variation;
> 4. Chromaticism ("accidentals" or "blue notes");
> 5. Bow "catches" and other bowing innovations;
> 6. Accompaniment—"sock style" closed chords, use of multiple guitars, including tenor guitar. Uses a walking chord line, use of diminished chords/passing chords.

An experienced fiddler or guitarist could recognize his or her amount of "Texas style" from Bill's guidelines. Fiddlers decided which division to enter. The contest offered significant prize money and drew contest fiddlers from Oregon, Louisiana, Kansas, Oklahoma, and Montana in addition to Missouri. In essence, the elite, versatile contest fiddlers signed up for and divvied up top places in the Old-Time Division as well as the Open Texas-Style Division. Fiddlers clearly playing old-time styles went home at the bottom of the rankings.

There were arguments and complaints after the winners were announced, but the Branson contest continued for a time. The event continued to favor Contest Style; there was little space among the top winners for old-time style players. In 2004, judges were Fred Stoneking, Junior Marriott, and Matt Wyatt—a strong panel. Fred Stoneking was vociferous in denouncing the incursions of Contest Style in what were *advertised* as old-time fiddle contests, and he had a good point. The 2004 Branson contest was among the last contests with active participation by Shull and Walden of the Missouri State Old Time Fiddlers Association. After several years, the Branson contest moved from locations such as a schoolhouse or the bank of Lake Taneycomo to country music–themed tourism facilities; it also got a new name that played on the old contest.

Most recently in Branson, the event was held in an impressive hotel and country music complex and administered by Cathy and Junior Marriott, along with Bill Lennon. The contest was renamed the Branson Fiddle Festival & Mid-America Fiddlers Championship Contest and included workshops and square dancing.[30] Contest Style fiddlers that year included the Bistodeau sisters from Minnesota (Deena and Sedra); Alita Stoneking and her husband, Tom Weisgerber; Eischen Harkins; Bubba Hopkins (who won the grand championship); Billy Ward; and Cody Marriott. By 2010, many people felt that Branson had become one of the better contests in the country. In

2019, due to lack of funding and support, the Branson contest was canceled. With the shadow of the COVID-19 pandemic that would discourage some from participating, it has not resumed.

At the Branson contest in 2010, old-time fiddling and square dancing was provided by fiddler Liz Amos from Pennsylvania (a Bob Holt student and gifted player), guitarist Steve Hall (St. Louis), and clawhammer banjoist Hugh Strawn (Springfield). The banjo has all but disappeared from fiddle contests in Missouri and most western states, especially old-time and bluegrass five-string banjo. (Photo by Howard Marshall)

Much of the credit for the golden age of fiddle contests from the 1980s through the 1990s goes to those young people in the 1970s—and particularly to the Missouri State Old Time Fiddlers Association.

Charlie Walden fiddles a set as a featured performer with guitarist John G. Stewart at the Frontier Folklife Festival in St. Louis, 1984. (Missouri Cultural Heritage Center photo)

Charlie Walden

"Charlie Walden was a breath of fresh air coming through the Missouri contest fiddling scene in the mid-1970s. He was one of only a few young fiddlers competing at that time, but his age didn't prevent him from garnering both contest prize money and respect from the older fiddlers. Charlie has an unselfconsciously traditional style of fiddling and he also exhibits great technique," according to Bill Shul.[31] Walden is one of Missouri's best-known fiddlers and an eloquent advocate for making the music accessible—and keeping it fun. Like his colleague Bill Shull, Charlie is musically sophisticated and highly educated. Walden was born in Rockport in Atchison County in 1957, a farm town near the Missouri River in the northwest corner of Missouri near Iowa and Nebraska. The family moved to St. Joseph and Jefferson City before settling in Hallsville, just north of Columbia. Walden recalls that his family was not a musical one.

In the Hallsville public schools, Charlie was a bright student and excelled in the school band, playing tuba, learning other instruments, and writing sheet-music parts for various instruments. His interest in fiddle music came thanks to Betty White, who was Charlie's seventh-grade English teacher and happened to be married to old-time fiddler John T. White. At fourteen, Charlie bought an old fiddle from John White and began "noodling around." (At the time, Walden owned a mandolin and guitar.) "I sat in my bedroom and scraped and scratched for months until I could finally play a tune. I don't know why I got into it really. Perhaps it was teenage boredom."[32] Walden is left-handed but taught himself to play right-handed and reads and transcribes fiddle music.[33]

His first exposure to other fiddlers was at the Boone County Fair. "I went down to the county fair one night and they were having a fiddle contest. There were all these old men up there playing the fiddle. There weren't any young people playing the fiddle at that time around where I lived at all. And I got to know this one old boy, his name was Taylor McBaine."[34] Walden developed quickly as a fiddler and contest performer and launched a long and successful career that would include teaching, scholarship, writing, recording, fiddle contesting, and all-around advocacy of old-time fiddling and the old-timers who make the music. Like some of his mentors and fiddle heroes, Charlie can pick up a violin and play anything that catches his interest, across genres and styles.

Walden discovered the Chez coffeehouse while in high school and became part of the banjo-and-fiddle crowd there in the early 1970s. He met other young musicians such as Chris Germain and Bill Shull, as well as Spencer Galloway, John Murdock, Marc Rennard, Jim Ruth, and Bob Atchison. But it was meeting elder masters of Missouri fiddling, collectors, and experts in fiddle and dance history, such as McBaine, R. P. Christeson, and Virgil Smith, that fired Charlie's imagination. As he and Christeson became friends, Christeson, a collector of violins, sorted through his music room and presented Charlie with a superior violin (his favorite until Christopher Germain built one for him in 1995).

Charlie's first mentors included McBaine and McMahan, and he learned tunes from Cyril Stinnett and Dwight Lamb (Iowa). Charlie writes of his experiences with Stinnett and talks about the dour bachelor farmer in an *Old-Time Herald* article.[35] Walden was also interested in the fiddling of Boone County champ Cleo Persinger, who had passed away before Walden got into fiddling, but Charlie listened to well-circulated recordings of Persinger.

In 1974, Walden entered his first contest and caught a permanent case of fiddle-contest fever. Charlie played the venerable square-dance tune "Ragtime Annie" and played it too fast. Taylor McBaine noticed the problem and offered to give Charlie lessons. A gregarious man who enjoyed helping young people, McBaine was a perfect teacher. Charlie met with McBaine and learned tunes and technique as well as picking up anecdotes about fiddlers and fiddling. McBaine "played like all those Missouri fiddlers. They played a kind of in-your-face style of hoedown fiddle. All of them I ever met play real loud with a lot of bow. They use alternating or saw-stroke bow to play probably eighty percent of any given tune, and they just use a few connecting slurs to get their bow turned around the way they want it to go."[36]

A year later, in 1975, Charlie placed in a contest for the first time, taking fifth, and in 1976 he took third place in the US Bicentennial contest in Graham. This was a turning point, because at Graham he met more masters as well as impressing judges Cyril Stinnett, Dwight Lamb, and Lonnie Robertson. Charlie took his master's degree in industrial technical education at the University of Missouri in 1984. Walden won the annual contest held at the Missouri State Fair in 1987.[37]

Walden mastered the bowing styles of masters like McBaine and Pete McMahan and explains it all in fiddle camps and workshops.

> "Missouri fiddlers bow a lot when they play," Walden explains. "There is a lot of alternate bowing or saw stroke employed, which makes the notes sound separated and makes the music sound lively and energetic. Missouri fiddlers want to hear every note come out clearly and in tune." Slowly but surely Walden mastered this idiosyncratic style. He learned how to present each note distinctly, so the melody could be heard even at tempos fast enough to push the dancers around the floor. He learned the Missouri repertoire, which was heavy on Scotch-Irish jigs and reels but also included more waltzes than other regions. Soon Walden was playing house parties, dances, and fiddle contests, winning his fair share of the latter.[38]

In a *Fiddler Magazine* interview from 1996, when Charlie was twenty-nine, he said:

> [McMahan] lived in Harrisburg, which was about twenty miles due west of where I was living. So it was pretty easy to go over and see him, particularly when I turned sixteen and had a car I could drive around. So he was probably my next biggest influence, and he was a really great fiddler. He's still living, and he still plays real well. He's kind of become like my second father in a way. I really have a deep respect

> for Pete and I feel very close to him. But he got around a lot. He was kind of the first guy who introduced me to music outside of Missouri. In the early '60s he had played at Weiser and had gotten invited to judge a lot of contests, and so he knew a lot of tunes that weren't necessarily indigenous to Missouri. He was kind of in the circle of big contest fiddlers in the early '60s. The contests were starting to get big and fiddlers were starting to drive all over Hell's half-acre to play in all these different contests. So he knew a lot of tunes that really weren't played around Missouri, like "Tom and Jerry" and some of these big contest tunes that were starting to become real popular in the early '60s. This is all pre-O'Connor [Mark O'Connor's rise to domination of national contest fiddling], when there was still old-time Texas fiddling, too.[39]

Walden's third major influence was Cyril Stinnett, and Stinnett had a different style from McMahan and McBaine. Walden mentions three main old-time styles in Missouri and speaks about Stinnett in the Roberts interview:

> Yeah, I'd say there are probably three ways you hear the fiddle played. The first one I was exposed to, as I was telling you, like with Taylor and Pete. That's kind of the central Missouri, or Little Dixie style of playing. It's notey, and a lot of alternate bows, and real loud. You know, they make a cloud of rosin dust when they play. It's good dance music. Cyril, on the other hand, he was probably the third big influence on my playing after Taylor and Pete. When I heard him play, I was just enthralled. I think my dad took me up to some contest, I was probably about seventeen, up in northwest Missouri, and Cyril was there. He was this little unassuming-looking guy with striped overalls on and real kind of piercing eyes, real small stature, and when he put the fiddle under his chin backwards, you know left-handed, it was just incredible what the guy could do. He was so smooth and so clean. His playing was really unbelievable. And it was so straight-ahead, too.
>
> The amazing thing about him was he could take a melody, like say "Cumberland Gap." I don't consider it to be a particularly complex tune. It's good rhythmically most of the time when you hear it, but not melodically interesting. He could take a tune like that and just fill in all the gaps in a way that you just think, "Man, that's how that tune goes." He could take any tune and make it his, and you wouldn't want to hear it any other way once you'd hear him play it. Any other way of playing it sounded sick after you heard him do it. He and Pete both, I guess, are the ones, by hearing them, encouraged me to learn so many tunes. Cyril probably knew 400 tunes that he could just whip off—and they were hard tunes, you know, they weren't just there so he'd have quantity. They were great tunes, he had worked them out and he could play them all real well.[40]

Unlike many of his peers, Walden was not attracted to the classic 1920s commercial records of southern fiddlers and string bands that meant so much to players such as Spencer Galloway and Rob Golan. He was more attracted to the 1960s and 1970s

LPs of players like Tommy Jackson, Howdy Forrester, and Kenny Baker. Charlie was interested in those and many other fiddlers, but from the beginning he zeroed in on fiddling in central and north Missouri and did not waver in his dedication. In later years, Walden expanded his interests, playing swing fiddle after the example of Johnny Gimble, playing jazz like Kansas City's Claude Williams, and moving into "Ottawa Valley–style" Canadian fiddling.

R. P. Christeson's research and personality appealed to Walden. Christeson helped Charlie appreciate collecting and the scholarly sides of the fiddle community. Walden plays numerous tunes from Christeson's *Old-Time Fiddler's Repertory* tune books; he contributed tunes and assisted with production of the second volume. "R. P. had the impression that no one was interested in the genuine old-time style—even then he was disturbed by what he heard at fiddle contests—the modern influence. But Christeson's salty opinions served a purpose: 'He was very outspoken. I really like him for that because he helped me by the way he felt so strongly about what he was doing. I felt I should feel strongly about what I was doing. If you're going to maintain the tradition, you have to define the genre you're going to play, and play that.'"[41]

Walden's first commercial recording was a 1987 cassette, *Traditional Fiddle Music of Missouri*, a project announcing a very focused young fiddler with a scholarly bent. Tunes included those learned in person from Stinnett and Virgil Smith, as well as tunes from Christeson's books and Christenson's own fiddling. The tune annotations offer information and where a tune might be found in Christeson's books. Walden includes his own composition for his daughter, "Jesse's Quadrille," recorded in 1981 at Christeson's house in Auxvasse by Barry Bergey (then of the Missouri Friends of the Folk Arts).

In the 1980s, Walden helped organize Missouri's first fiddle camp, at Bethel, as well as MSOTFA's state fiddle contest. He continued to be interested in Bethel and the state contest after moving to Evanston, Illinois, in 1993. In Evanston, Charlie married Patt Plunkett. They had met at a Chicago Barn Dance Company dance that Walden traveled to Chicago to fiddle for; Patt was the guest keyboard accompanist.[42]

In 1994, Walden issued another Marimac cassette, *Patt & Possum: Hoe-Downs, Hornpipes & Hokum*, in which he plays standards of the Missouri repertoire—"Forked Deer," "Grey Eagle," "Polk County Breakdown," and "Angus Campbell"—and stirs in some less common tunes he learned from Stinnett, Bob Holt, Pete McMahan, and others, such as "Turkey in the Pea Patch" and Cleo Persinger's "Dundee Hornpipe." Walden presents his version of the exhibition piece "Listen to the Mockingbird," proving that this great tune (banned by fiddle contests in the 1950s) is still played and played well. The project reflects Walden's 1970s nickname, "Possum." With Patt's keyboard work, "Patt and Possum" enjoy a career as a duo, traveling across the continent and to Europe and Australia. Recently, Walden began documenting their trips to contests, jam sessions, fiddle camps, and conventions in a *Fiddler Magazine* series called "Travels with Charlie."[43]

Charlie developed other documentary projects, such as an informal cassette from around 1997 titled *64 Essential Fiddle Tunes for Dances, Contests, and Jamming*, his list of sine qua non tunes. The companion CD gives listeners samples, played straight and well, from "A & E Waltz" to "Woodchopper's Hornpipe." The CD is a major statement of old-time Missouri fiddling.[44]

Now That's a Good Tune reached the finals for the Grammy Awards in two categories (Best Album Notes; Best Documentary Album) in 1989. Walden was a key figure in developing the project, helped select fiddlers and tunes, and helped write text for the sixty-four-page booklet insert in the double-LP album. At thirty, he was the youngest fiddler on the project. In addition to "Soldier's Joy" and "Bill Katon's Tune" (a.k.a. "Old Jeff City"), Charlie plays "Marmaduke's Hornpipe" and "Old Rugged Cross" with second and harmony fiddle by Pete McMahan.

It is common to move back and forth between genres, and in the early 1990s Walden performed with a bluegrass band, the Chip Kickers (John Roach, banjo; Kyle Brown, Dobro; Lowell Appling, guitar; and Forrest Rose, bass). After the brief career of the Chip Kickers, he fiddled in a swing and country band with Brown, Rose, and Mike Powers called the Pole Cats.

Walden is a prolific author and interested in producing recordings to keep the music accessible. His *Dance around Molly* features Plunkett on keyboard and Chris Germain playing clawhammer banjo on a batch of "Show-Me State" standards.[45] Charlie's research, field recordings, and writings have added to our appreciation and understanding of Missouri fiddling and fiddlers. Charlie remains a contest fiddler and in recent years has become a familiar figure in some of the Canadian competitions. Just as with most fiddlers, he has misgivings about the contest world, but, at the same time, he is drawn to the excitement, challenge, and social elements of the contest environment:

> I guess the only comment I'd make is that I like playing contests. I just think they're a lot of fun, and in Missouri that's like the main place left to play fiddle in public, at a contest where fiddlers will congregate, because there aren't many dances left other than the kind of urban contra dance scene, there isn't much of a dance scene left in the rural hinterlands. Yeah, I like contests. The only thing I see that's bad about contests, and it seems to be even getting worse, is the whole creation of this national contest style that's just choking out any regional difference in the way people play. And it seems to be even getting worse now—the threat on any kind of local styles is even more intense.
>
> In Missouri, we've really made a big effort to, I won't say discriminate against people who play that way [in the national contest style], but we try to favor the traditional way of playing, our local traditional way of playing. And it's worked pretty well until recently. It seems like anything, you can only do it so long. As a lot of the older fiddlers die off or become too feeble to play, this more modern style starts to creep in. But it's still not as bad as it is in some parts of the country, where basically all you'll hear is kind of "hot" fiddle, you won't hear any local styles at all. Although they've done a good job out East, like in West Virginia and some places like that I

> think they're keeping their local tradition alive. So it's not like it's totally taken over the whole country, but it's just kind of sad to see all the older ways of playing go completely by the board, and all the tunes with them. With that style [the national contest style] of playing, there's a very limited repertoire of tunes. I mean you could count them on a couple of people's fingers, the tunes you'll hear at a contest where that style of playing is preeminent.[46]

Walden also plays mandolin and guitar and teaches technique on the Internet and in his publication *Charlie Walden's Chord Patterns & Arpeggios for Fiddle and Mandolin*. He plays backup guitar (both old-time and swing style) for Travis Inman on Inman's 2012 *Missouri Fiddler* CD and discusses guitar accompaniment in the Roberts *Fiddler Magazine* interview, articulating distinctions between swing backup (sock rhythm, closed chords) and old-time backup (open chords) in fiddle contests:

> Well, I don't like too much complexity, especially on a hoedown, when I'm playing a square dance tune. I don't like it to get too complicated. I generally don't like sock rhythm for hoedowns, unless I'm playing something I want to make intentionally sound swingy. If I'm playing in a contest, for instance, and a guitar player is backing me up, I'd rather hear open chords, I think, than sock-style rhythm. I do like a moving bass line, but it has to be one that moves on the beat. Rather than a quick bass run or something like that, I don't care for, because I like the on-beat to really keep pumping, and if someone gets too choppy with their bass runs, it kind of detracts from the rhythm.
>
> But now on waltzes, that's a different story. I like lots of chords on waltzes, and I like to get with a guitar player who can play a lot of minor 7th chords and stuff like that on a waltz. I like a waltz that has twenty-five chords in it, and I like to hear all the passing chords. It's kind of hard to find a guitar player you can convince to play cowboy chords on a hoe-down and play like Joe Pass on a waltz, but that's the kind of thing I like. Because with a lot of simple waltzes, it really changes them into real pieces of music when you get all those chords working behind them.[47]

Walden posts recordings and videos of fiddlers, fiddle contests, and Bethel Youth Fiddle Camp on YouTube. There is a measure of nostalgia in his recollections of his early days in Missouri fiddling, a sense of loss as time changes things. "I feel fortunate that I was able to experience the tail-end of an era of fiddle playing and old-time dancing which is fading fast."[48] Charlie created "tune-a-day" videos on YouTube ("366 Fiddle Tunes Project"—one tune a day, plus one more for leap years).[49] He offers online tune transcriptions and instructional videos in addition to a live *Possum's Big Fiddle Show* and other programs, and gives lessons via Skype. In 2021–22, Walden is a master in the Missouri Traditional Arts Apprenticeship Program, working with fiddler Thomas Coriell of St. Louis, and in 2022 will be a master in the Illinois apprenticeship program to work with fiddler Aaron Albrecht of Springfield.[50]

Listen to track 14 on the companion CD to hear Charlie Walden's version of "Angus Campbell."

Thomas Coriell at a jam session after the Mokane fiddle contest, 2019. Coriell, from St. Louis, is Charlie Walden's apprentice in the Traditional Arts Apprenticeship Program, 2021–22, and plays left-handed on right-handed instruments (violin, mandolin, guitar). Thomas's repertoire focuses on old-time tunes particularly from Cyril Stinnett, Jake Hockemeyer, Dwight Lamb, Cecil Goforth, Kathy Summers, and Walden (all left-handed fiddlers). In 2021, Coriell competed in the annual Walnut Valley national championships in Winfield, Kansas, and played Stinnett's version of "Brilliancy," "Shamus O'Brien," and "Waiting for the Robert E. Lee." (Photo by Howard Marshall)

Listen to track 15 on the companion CD to hear Thomas Coriell's version of "A & E Waltz."

John Griffin

John Griffin is one of Missouri's most knowledgeable and strongest fiddlers. As Travis Inman recalled, "John Griffin played smooth as butter. He was the smoothest fiddler I ever heard. I don't feel he got the credit he deserved."[51]

Griffin was born 1953 in Pensacola, Florida, where his father, Harry Griffin, was a US Naval aviator. The family moved from Fairfax, Virginia, to Columbia in 1966 when, after retiring from the US Navy, his father began teaching courses in Naval ROTC at the university. Harry Griffin played guitar and called square dances, and Harry's father, John, played fiddle and banjo.

Griffin describes himself as self-taught, beginning at eighteen when he was a freshman at the University of Missouri in Columbia. The first tune he worked out was "Bill Cheatem," a demanding tune to play well. John learned from taking part in

John Griffin with Pete McMahan at a Traditional Arts Apprenticeship Program lesson in 1989 at Pete's home in Harrisburg. Griffin was a quick student and devoted to McMahan's music and views on fiddling. (Photo by Howard Marshall)

sessions and listening in particular to Art Galbraith, Pete McMahan, Cyril Stinnett, and R. P. Christeson. He also enjoyed recordings of a range of fiddlers playing different styles of old-time and Contest Style, such as Buddy Thomas, Norman Blake, the Fuzzy Mountain String Band, Benny Thomasson, and Clark Kessinger. He loved Chubby Wise's interpretation of waltzes, and Griffin's favorite is "Gypsy Waltz." He plays rare dance-tune types such as cotillions, marches, and quadrilles as well as a number of tunes in scordatura (chorded fiddle) and learned tunes from Christeson's *Old-Time Fiddlers Repertory* books. John plays guitar, mandolin, and bass in addition to violin, and his favorite accompaniment for fiddling is piano and reed organ.

In the late 1980s, Griffin was chosen by Pete McMahan to study in the Traditional Arts Apprenticeship Program, and this was one of the program's most successful partnerships. John maintained McMahan's violins and, in some instances, helped him sell violins and bows. Many younger fiddlers have tried to learn McMahan's bowing style, but John Griffin is one of only several people of my acquaintance who succeeded. Griffin describes his style as "traditional old-time," and he "goes for tone and content rather than just playing fast."[52]

John entered his first contest in 1974 in Quincy, Illinois, three years after taking up fiddle music, and took third place. He has won first or placed high in numerous contests in Missouri, including second and third in the state contest and first at the annual contest in Boonville. Boonville, held in March, was the season opener and featured many familiar names during this period. Emceed by Cecil Windsor, there were fourteen entries in the Open Division in 1983, and Griffin won first place. Griffin played "Sleepy-Eyed Joe" and "Country Waltz" in the preliminary round and "Woodchopper's Breakdown" ("Hornpipe") in the finals.[53] Griffin stopped competing in contests in the late 1990s.

After Griffin graduated from the university in 1975 in wildlife conservation, he decided to learn to make violins. As a teenager, he was interested in how violins were made: "His mother had brought home two fiddles she had bought. One had been turned into a planter. 'I got real interested in, well, how do you fix fiddles without ruining them?' he recalls, 'There's some kind of science here, and it's a very obscure science.'"[54] In 1975, John and his wife, Sherri, moved to Mount Vernon, Illinois, where John apprenticed for two and a half years with Robert Tipple, paying Tipple ten dollars a week.[55] Then he returned to Missouri and took jobs in law enforcement in Perryville and Fayette. In 1983 he became a conservation agent (game warden) with the Missouri Department of Conservation and moved to the Millersburg area to serve his base in Callaway County.

John retired from the Conservation Department in 2002 to give full attention to violin making and repair and to develop Old Standard Wood, a business specializing in sales and production of old-growth Adirondack spruce and tone woods such as curly maple. These valuable and scarce woods are prized by musical instrument makers, including Gilchrist mandolins, Collings guitars and mandolins, and Martin and Eastman guitars, as well as Columbia's Mid-Missouri Mandolin Company.[56] Griffin searches throughout North America and Central America for the best old-growth logs, demonstrating that instruments can be built today with wood that equals the quality of wood in the pre–World War II era of instruments made by firms such as Martin and Gibson.[57] John's father served as the bookkeeper, and Jim Ruth continues to be employed as head sawyer and office manager. Lee Nigh, who worked for Griffin years ago, is now an established violin maker in Fulton.

Like his mentor, Pete McMahan, Griffin has strong opinions when it comes to what is, and what is not, old-time fiddle music and how to manage the matter in contests billed as "old-time"; no subjects in this book are more complicated or controversial than these.

In the early 1990s, Griffin decided to inaugurate a new state contest that he hoped could steer things back to the customary old-time Missouri pattern and performance styles. Griffin had been unhappy with incursions of Texas/Contest Style fiddling—what he calls "Tex-a-fied" and "whoop-de-do fiddling."[58] Located in the Columbia-Fulton area, John knew contests and contest fiddlers and participated both as contestant and as judge. For several years in the nineties, Griffin held what he termed the Missouri State Traditional Fiddle Contest on the courthouse square in Fulton in connection with the town's annual summer festival. Griffin's regulations spelled out the customary two-accompanist rule and that judges would reward fiddlers who played "old-time" style and repertoire. With judges he could

John Griffin with red spruce (Adirondack spruce) logs at Old Standard Wood, November 2013. Griffin spends months each year, searching for correct and available old-growth trees. (Courtesy of John Griffin)

rely on to support the contest's goals, fiddlers playing old-time rather than Contest Style did well.[59]

Griffin's contests were successful in fostering Missouri old-time fiddle styles and repertoire, even while they frustrated competitors performing Texas-based Contest Style. But various conditions (including lack of continued support by the town festival administration) led to the demise of his contest. A few years later, John reflected on contests generally: "I don't think contests have done much for fiddling. I don't think it's done anything good for fiddling. If they had judges that had as their object to further traditional fiddling . . . that would be good, but they won't do that. Traditional fiddling will never beat bluegrass or Texas style or any of that; it can't compete with the crowd and with the judges. That was always real disappointing. Really discouraging."[60] Griffin's absence from the contest community left a noticeable gap.

Listen to track 16 on the companion CD to hear John Griffin's version of "Woodchopper's Hornpipe."

Junior Marriott

Junior Marriott became one of Missouri's most influential contest fiddlers in the 2000s. He has been a force in the contest world since his teenage years in the 1980s, playing backup guitar and helping judge as well as reeling in trophies. Missouri's most vigorous advocate of Texas contest fiddle and guitar-backup styles, Marriott held the lantern high, and others followed.

B. E. Marriott Jr., born in Stover in 1966, graduated from Morgan County R-1 High School. He is one of numerous musicians in Missouri with some Native

American ancestry. Junior is a horse trainer and breeds coon dogs. He and his wife, Cathy Davis Marriott, operate a music business in Ava, where Junior takes care of repairs and sales and specializes in vintage Gibson guitars (favored by most Contest Style guitarists in Texas and the West). He gives lessons and is widely known as an outstanding teacher. Marriott occasionally fiddles for dances in the Ava area. Cathy is a master Ozark jig dancer and square dancer and helps organize events such as the annual Bob Holt Jig Dancing Competition at the Ozark Heritage Festival in West Plains.[61] They often assist organizations in contest administration and judging.

Junior began playing rhythm guitar for his father, Bunney E. Marriott, and by nine was playing upright bass as well. At fourteen, Junior began playing fiddle and in 1983 at sixteen won the Missouri State Fiddle Championship for the first of numerous times. As Charlie Walden and Julie Youmans noted in 1989, "The young fiddler has set himself apart from the crowd by leaning in the direction of the nationally-popular progressive style of contest fiddling. Marriott has been especially influenced by an Oklahoma fiddler, Ace Sewell. While he plays this more modern style of fiddling with great prowess, it sometimes yields mixed results at more conservative Missouri old-time contests. Undaunted, Marriott continues to develop his playing and is without question among the best fiddlers in the Show-Me State."[62]

Junior also gained experience playing other kinds of music. Jim Sumner had a country band that played dances in California at the 87 Club. Junior played his first gigs with the Sumner band, which included fiddler Goodson Marriott, Junior's uncle. Junior is left-handed but plays right-handed.

Early on, Junior absorbed a range of old-time fiddle music in Missouri. At contests, Marriott came into contact with champions, listening and learning particularly from Pete McMahan. In addition, through wide-ranging travels to fiddlers' conventions and contests, Marriott met and learned from Texas– and Oklahoma–Contest Style champions such as Sewell, Dick Barrett, Herman Johnson, Dale Morris Jr., and Terry Morris. Marriott points to Sewell as his principal mentor. At the same time, Marriott continued to learn the Missouri old-time style and repertoire of McMahan as well as others and is adept at both styles.

Growing up in the Stover area in Morgan County, Marriott was fortunate in terms of fiddle music. Three notable and influential players lived nearby, and Junior could play music and learn from them—Kelly Jones (nine years older) and Travis Inman (three years older). This mighty trio of contest champions won so often that they were known simply as "the Stover boys" or, as Bill Shull wrote in 1994, "the Stover connection":

> Stover, Missouri, is a micro-dot on the Missouri page of the *Rand-McNally Road Atlas*; but three of its 600 or so townspeople are among the top fiddlers in the Midwest. [They] all possess fiddling skills which can make grown men shout and cry, grown women cry and shout, and little children shut up and listen. Kelly is the oldest of the three, and has served as something of a mentor to the others, but Travis and Junior have innate talents that supersede any kind of teaching.[63]

Junior Marriott at John Griffin's Missouri State Traditional Fiddle Contest in Fulton during the town's Kingdom Days festival, June 1993. (Photo by Howard Marshall)

As a teenager, Marriott was attracted to western swing–influenced Texas and Oklahoma Contest style and repertoire and its community of musicians. Marriott's surprise victory in the 1983 state contest in Columbia was a milestone. In the Hickman High School auditorium, Junior shocked the crowd by besting champion old-time-style players. With a straight-chord guitar backup, Junior played "Arkansas Traveler," "Martin's Waltz," and "Angus Campbell" and, in the callback round, "Fiddler's Dream." Marriott has won or ranked high in virtually every contest he has entered, from small-town fish fries to major regional and national competitions. According to Spencer Galloway:

> This was the year Junior Marriott just surprised everybody and won it. I remember we were standing in the parking lot listening—they had sound piped out there. We were listening, and Bill Shull says, "He's won this contest!" And used to be, you'd go

> to a fiddle contest and see Junior Marriott and you'd say, well there's *one* I can beat. Then all of a sudden, he just got *really* good. And it was sort of like Robert Johnson at the crossroads at midnight.[64]

Junior is a popular backup guitarist in contests and jam sessions, generously helping children and beginners, fellow champions, and older fiddlers who may be past their prime. He can provide the style of backup that a fiddler prefers, whether western-swing and Texas Contest closed-chord backup or old-time open-chord guitar style. This is a mark of a savvy contest accompanist: providing the kind of accompaniment that fits the fiddler.

Marriott and other premier contest fiddlers have the ability to adjust their performance by dialing up or dialing down their playing to better suit the perceived likes of the judges. When a contest appears to favor older Missouri styles, they can play "Tom and Jerry" and sound like Pete McMahan; with judges favoring Texas music, they can play a tune from Benny Thomasson, Ace Sewell, or Dick Barrett.

Junior has won state championships in Kansas and Arkansas in addition to a number of wins at the Missouri state contest in Sedalia. He has done well in other major competitions such as the annual Grand Lake Fiddle Festival in Oklahoma, the Walnut Valley Old Time Fiddle Championships in Kansas, and the Grand Masters Fiddle Championships in Nashville. Junior's sons, Cody, Tanner, and Preston, are also successful contest fiddlers.

Marriott serves as a judge when invited and has been on panels at contests from small local affairs to the state contest in Sedalia, the Arkansas State Championship, the Grand Masters in Nashville, Grand Lake National Fiddle Fest in Grove (Oklahoma), Rocky Mountain championships in Denver, and the Texas state contest in Hallettsville—major contests where Marriott has competed successfully as well as judged. Judging in Texas offers more than a room and gas money; Texas is the Xanadu of modern Contest Style fiddling.

Marriott has taught extensively, helping beginners grasp the rudiments and showing seasoned players how to improve their technique and versions of contest tunes. He presents fiddle and guitar workshops and helps audiences learn about his approach to playing in contests, as well as playing different styles of backup guitar.

Junior has composed several tunes, including "Uncle Dan," "Snake Creek" (a breakdown to honor a creek in Morgan County), "Heather's Waltz" for his daughter, and "Cathy's Waltz" for his wife. His composition "Uncle Dan" has passages that remind us of Tommy Jackson's "Cherokee Shuffle" as well as "Lost Indian," a reflection of the process of composition in which new tunes can suggest strains reminiscent of other tunes. "Snake Creek" and "Heather's Waltz" are on Marriott's *Snake Creek* cassette along with contest pieces such as "Canadian Waltz," "Dusty Miller, "Sally Goodin," "Tom and Jerry," "Hell among the Yearlings," and "Sally Johnson"—big numbers in the nationwide Contest Style repertoire. Also on the *Snake Creek* project is a recording of the Canadian tune "Woodchopper's Reel" (a.k.a. "Woodchopper's Hornpipe") that was a favorite contest piece of Cyril Stinnett, Jake Hockemeyer, and others of the previous generation. Junior learned it at a music party honoring Taylor McBaine at Debbie and Steve Young's house near Harrisburg around 1990. Debbie, who had been playing backup piano for the fiddling, played "Woodchopper's" from the Christeson's 1973 *Old-Time Fiddler's Repertory*, and Junior absorbed it on the spot.

Cody Marriott, one of Junior's sons, is a Contest Style champion who plays other styles, too, and is an excellent guitar accompanist. Here, Cody and Travis Inman play some twin fiddle pieces to entertain the audience at the Versailles Applefest contest in 2010. Matt Wyatt is on guitar. (Photo by Howard Marshall)

Listen to track 17 on the companion CD to hear Junior Marriott's "Uncle Dan."

Kelly Jones, promotional portrait while working with Lee Mace's Ozark Opry in the mid-1960s. (Courtesy of LeRoy Haslag)

Kelly Jones, Uncompromising Champion 8

Whatever come *before* me, I just wanted to learn it, so I could play it the best I could play it.

—Kelly Jones

For many years, Kelly Jones was a leader among the aristocracy of contest fiddlers, while at the same time working as a semiprofessional musician in bluegrass and country music shows. Versatility and professionalism are key ingredients in Jones's long career. For many years, Jones was "the fiddler" at the Missouri State Fair, where thousands of strolling fairgoers saw him fiddling informally on the porch of the Administration Building with his friend and guitar accompanist Wes Brown or fiddling on the concert stage as the "on-call" fiddler for featured bluegrass and country bands.

Born in 1947, Kelly Jones grew up on the family farm near Nevada in Vernon County, rolling agricultural landscape south of Kansas City along the Kansas border. The family came to Vernon County from Kentucky in the nineteenth century. Kelly's mother's family were Murphys, largely of Irish background, in the Metz community north of Nevada; his mother's mother was one-quarter Cherokee Indian. Kelly's father was Robert Lester (Skeeter) Jones, a fiddler, and the Joneses were English and Irish. Kelly was named for his paternal grandmother, Isabelle Kelly (Mrs. Oscar H. Jones).[1]

As a child, Kelly was "dragged to dances," and the music seeped in. His father, Lester, was a well-known fiddler, with "a good bow" (good bowing). "He had good *timing*. He wasn't a real *intricate* player, you know. He didn't use his little finger a lot, you know. His *timing* was there for the *dancers*. He's the one they always wanted to play for the *dances*. He had some *life* in the music." At fifteen, Kelly began learning to play fiddle music. Unlike many other aspiring fiddlers, he did not play guitar accompaniment. He did play some mandolin, which is tuned the same as standard violin tuning. Kelly started playing for dances his junior year in high school. Under Lester's tutelage, Kelly learned the foundation repertoire of tunes such as "Soldier's Joy," "Mississippi Sawyer," "Arkansas Traveler," "Eighth of January," and "Ragtime Annie." Lester Jones had learned a number of fiddle melodies by listening to his father, Oscar, whistle the tunes. Lester Jones's favorite tunes included "Grey Eagle," "Coming Down from Denver" (from Dean Johnston), and "the old waltzes."[2]

Another favorite of Lester Jones's and a pillar of Missouri fiddling was "Tennessee Wagner," which he had heard Tom Massie fiddle on the Vernon County courthouse square on Saturday market days in Nevada. Massie had won numerous contests, including the 1925 state championship aired over WOS Radio.[3] Lester Jones thought Massie had the best "Tennessee Wagner" he had ever heard. Another old standby Kelly learned from his father is the tune with a thousand names usually called "Lead Out" (LEED-out); Lester called it "Blue Jay."

Lester Jones enjoyed violins and had a dozen or more at any given time. Lester's first violin was an "old black fiddle" of unknown age or pedigree, and his favorite was an old "no-name" European shop violin he played at dances; the latter instrument would become his son Kelly's "number one." When a violin needed repairs beyond his own expertise, Lester took it to Louis Lackey in nearby Nevada.

Kelly Jones's favorite violin is the one his father, Lester, played, a gift from a friend who had found the old instrument in his attic. "And Dad took it, and it needed some work, so he fixed it up and it sounded pretty good, he said. It's a *tubby fiddle*, basically." Apropos for a musician who approaches every aspect of performance with studied care, Jones never uses cheap violin strings; it makes a difference. Kelly typically used a European bow of Pernambuco wood, but recently began playing Glasser bows of braided carbon fiber. Jones uses a shoulder rest for his violin, to help keep it in position. (Photo by Howard Marshall, 2015)

Kelly absorbed his father's interest in acoustics and the mysteries of what makes one violin better than another. To test carrying power and tone, Kelly would play a tune on a violin in the barn, and his father would listen at a distance. "Dad always had a bunch of fiddles, and he was always fooling with them. And he'd have me play them and he'd go down to the barn and listen at how far they'd *carry*, you know. We'd listen to see what (violin) was *good*."

Kelly fiddled his first dances during his junior year in high school at the Chat and Chew, a dance hall with a livestock auction barn attached on one side of the building and a "beer joint" (restaurant) on the other. Lester Jones had played dances there for years, and they typically comprised a violin or two (or three), two guitars, a bass, and a drum kit. The Chat and Chew had an old upright piano, usually out of tune and seldom played. "It was just a good country dance, you know, the squares, and circles and round dances, waltzes." Dean Johnston, the Lamar fiddler, often sat with the band, and Kelly picked up technique and tunes from him. Kelly also enjoyed the fiddling of area players such as Herman (Sac River) Jones (no relation), Andy Beaty, and Earl Ball from Humansville.

When he heard Nashville fiddler Howdy Forrester with Roy Acuff and the Smoky Mountain Boys on Grand Ole Opry radio broadcasts, Kelly Jones was immediately drawn to Forrester's playing:

> I got hung up on Howdy *Forrester*, and I bought his records and I thought he was the greatest—and he *was*. It was that *style*. He had a *hornpipe style*. But he was so *far* over my *head*, you know, when I was a kid—and still *is*. But that's what I *worked on*—those tunes off his first two albums.
>
> I'd be milking the cows, you know, and Roy Acuff would come on the Grand Ole *Opry*, you know, on the radio—and I would *run* to the house and turn the tape recorder on. I taped *everything* that Howdy played, that Roy'd have him play, specials, you know. Taped everything live that I could, then got the albums, ordered them through the Ernest Tubb Record Shop. Those first albums, they were just *perfect*. You couldn't ask for better fiddlin'. He done the "High Level Hornpipe," you know, and the "Doc Harris hornpipe," B-flat things, you know, just perfect. "Leather Britches" is one of the best—he'd go up in the third position and play it. Because he was a violinist, really, and he could go up there and play it just *perfect*.
>
> I met him one time. I was at Fort Rucker, Alabama, in the Army, and I got a weekend pass to go to Nashville—to go the Opry. I wanted to *see* it. I caught him in the alleyway behind the Ryman, there and got to talk to him just a little bit, you know. And I told him I wanted to be a fiddle player, and all that. *His* advice was, "Son," he said, "being a *side man*—you're not going to make it, you know. You need to be more than a side man." Of course, he was into being a booking agent then. But he said, side man—that wasn't the place to be.
>
> So, I worked and worked on that stuff [Howdy Forrester tunes and technique]. It was a little *above* everything else, you know—more *technical*, you know. You couldn't find anybody that knew the *chords* to them, then. *Now days*, you know, they got it all *wrote out* and they know how to do it. Anyway, I fooled with it for quite a while.[4]

The search for Forrester records led Kelly to mail-order catalogs, where he found interesting records, including those of Canadian fiddlers. He appreciated influential professionals. "*Kenny Baker* was the bluegrass player. *Johnny Gimble* was the swing fiddler. *Benny Martin* was great—he had his own thing. All of them have their certain style of licks." But Kelly's favorite remained Howdy Forrester.

In the fall of 1965, senior year at Nevada High School, Kelly Jones boarded a Greyhound bus and traveled south to Nixa to enter his first old-time fiddle contest. With Kirk Powell as guitar second (rules allowed one accompanist), Jones won first in the Junior Division, which was being promoted as the Annual Missouri State Old Fiddlers Contest. Kelly prepared well and included as his "tune of choice" Howdy

Forrester's "Pretty Polly Ann" from Forrester's *Fiddlin' Country Style* LP, a tune in scordatura (cross-tuning). Kelly competed at Nixa a number of times, graduating from the Juniors to the Open Division (at this contest, seventeen and over). A dozen years after his 1965 contest debut at Nixa, Jones took second at Nixa; first place went to his mentor, Dean Johnston.

After graduating from high school and working in radio and TV repair, Kelly inquired about a job with Lee Mace's *Ozark Opry* in Osage Beach. By this time, the *Ozark Opry* had become the premier country music show in the growing tourism in the Lake of the Ozarks region. Mace drove to Nevada and auditioned Jones and Jones got the job. He rehearsed with the cast in the fall of 1965 and began performing in the show when the new season opened in the spring of 1966. Working with entrepreneur Lee Mace, a master of stagecraft and entertaining people, Jones gained experience performing in front of live audiences, learning the art of being an ensemble member, and "selling himself" as an entertainer.[5]

A Career Begins and Is Interrupted by Vietnam

When he turned eighteen in 1966, Jones registered for the draft and in short order received his draft notice. This was a year of President Johnson's heavy escalation of American forces in the growing war in South Vietnam. Kelly decided to let the government draft him into the US Army, which meant that his term of service would be the minimum, two years. When Lee Mace heard that Kelly was being drafted, he and others counseled him to avoid going. Mace had a plan to keep Kelly at the opry: Kelly, who had no great desire to join the Army, would travel to his draft-induction physical examination wearing a back brace and appearing to walk with difficulty, with the expectation that a "4-F" medical waiver would be granted.[6] "Lee wanted me to stay and play on the Opry. He said, wear this, a back brace, and maybe they'll kick you out and you can stay and *play the fiddle*. It didn't work. They didn't care. I had flat feet too, and they didn't care. They was taking them right and left."

Kelly's experience growing up on a farm, learning to operate and maintain equipment, as well as vocational agriculture high school classes stood him in good stead in the Army. He scored high on the mechanical aptitude test in boot camp at Fort Leonard Wood. While most new soldiers were assigned to infantry to fill the swelling numbers headed to Vietnam, Kelly was sent to Aviation School and after training at Fort Rucker qualified for helicopter and fixed-wing aircraft maintenance. "So, they sent me to Vietnam, of course—on January the *eighth*! Eighth of January [a fiddle tune]! Anyway, I went to basic training down at Fort Leonard Wood. I didn't take my fiddle. But from then on, I had my fiddle with me, strapped to my back after that, never left my fiddle. It went to Vietnam, and I played a lot over there."

Jones was assigned to the Twenty-Fifth Infantry Division's Aviation Battalion at Cu Chi.[7] At first, he drove cargo trucks hauling supplies to combat areas. "But then it got to the point where the trucks were upside down, and burning, and all that, and I went to the C.O. and said, 'My M.O.S. [military occupational specialty], you know, is chopper maintenance,' and anyway they put me on the flight field. And all I had to do was fix choppers. They'd go out and fly all day and get shot at, and get holes in the choppers, and come back, and I'd work on them at night." He was promoted to ground-crew chief, maintaining Bell H-13 observation helicopters known as "bubble-gum machines." When he was offered the excitement and likely promotions of combat as a machine-gun door gunner on "Hughey" helicopters, ferrying troops into and out of combat, Jones wryly remembers, "I said, *naw*, I don't want to do *that*."

Word got around that Spec 4 Jones played the fiddle. He was reassigned to special services (the Army's entertainment branch) in Saigon. For his remaining six months, Kelly played in a unit that had a jazz band, blues band, and country band. The country band consisted of an electric guitarist, a drummer, a fiddler (he amplified his violin with a DeArmond pickup), and singers. "We went all over Vietnam, playing. We'd play and sit on some rocks, sometimes, or we'd play in a nice NCO Club or Officers Club. One day we went out on the Seventh Fleet [in the South China Sea] and they let us down from a chopper, you know, and let us and all our equipment down on the deck of the destroyer and we played right *there*. I couldn't keep my bow on the strings, the wind was blowing so hard. They wanted a show out there, so we went."

Kelly found much to appreciate in the Army. He seems neither proud of his Vietnam service nor critical of the politics behind the war. "If it wasn't for the music [getting back home to the *Ozark Opry*], I'd have stayed in, and I'd have done a career, I think, because it was okay."

Back to the Ozarks, and Beyond

Jones was released from the Army on the eighth of January 1968. He rented an apartment in Osage Beach, where the *Ozark Opry* was based. Lee Mace had his fiddler back. Back with the opry, Kelly met his future wife, Shirley Bradhurst, a singer in the cast. Shirley's family was from Stover, but she was born in California when her father moved there for work; when her father retired, the Bradhursts moved to Stover and bought a farm.

A year later, Kelly won an audition with Nashville star Judy Lynn, who had moved to Las Vegas, the first country music show to set up headquarters there. Judy Lynn and her band toured casino ballrooms in Las Vegas, Reno, and Lake Tahoe. "In Vegas, we played the Strip. I started work at Caesar's Palace. And then we played The Flamingo, and The Sahara, and all that. We'd go to Reno for three weeks, and then we'd go to Tahoe for three weeks and play Harrah's Club, just running around the circuit." Kelly traveled back to Stover during breaks in the schedule. Lynn began to contract for "one-nighter" shows throughout the United States, Canada, and Europe. "A good deal, though. I enjoyed it. I was bus driver, fiddle player, concessionaire, and band manager." Jones stayed from 1970 to 1980, when Lynn retired from show business.

Kelly and Shirley were married in Reno in 1970 (Shirley sang with the Judy Lynn cast for a time), and, thinking ahead, they set up a permanent home back in Missouri. After their son, Robert, was born, Shirley and Robert moved to Stover. Once Robert was old enough, Shirley attended Central Missouri State University in Warrensburg, graduated with general education credentials, and began a thirty-two-year career teaching school in nearby Cole Camp. In Stover, Kelly began performing at the Lake of the Ozarks with *Denny Hilton's Country Shindig* and the Starworld Showroom—and got back into contests.

In 1975, Jones issued *Authentic Old-Time Fiddle Tunes*, tracing his interest in the breadth of fiddle music and in presenting some hallmarks of the repertoire. Kelly is accompanied by Kansas City's Bluegrass Association (Jim McGreevy, John Bennett, Chuck Stearman, and Don Montgomery), and the project includes old standards he learned from his father and other favorites, such as "Arkansas Traveler," "Forked Deer," "Fisher's Hornpipe," and "Stoney Point."

When asked about his style, Kelly Jones is uninterested in parsing the fine points. "Just a variety of things I've picked up. I always wanted to *work*—and I tried to learn a little bit of everything. I didn't get stuck in a rut, so to speak. I wasn't just a contest player, I wasn't just a show player, or wasn't just a dance player, or just a bluegrass player. Whatever come *before* me, I just wanted to learn it, so I could play it the best I could play it, you know."

Kelly played shows for five years with Nashville fiddler Bobby Hicks. Kelly says Dale Potter, the influential Missouri fiddler in Nashville who recorded with Hank Williams and others, showed young fiddlers, including Hicks and Jones, about double-stops and triple-stops that became essential in country music and swing. Another skill of the opry fiddler and session artist is "twin fiddle," in which one player has the melody and the other player plays a harmony line above or below the melody.

Kelly is particular about double-stops, befitting a longtime professional. Also, he wants the melody fiddler to play a clear, simple lead line, to which Kelly overlays a closely worked-out "twin" or harmony part; he does not like to "wing it."[8]

Kelly is on call to play in backup groups for Nashville stars on tour. "With Leroy [Van Dyke] and whoever we're going to back up, they send me the tape—they'll send me Moe Bandy's tapes, or Gene Watson's tapes, you know, I just learn them. Whatever they require. Anyway, *I just like to play the music*. I'm not set in a certain thing. I don't play jazz—I don't understand it that well, I haven't been around it."

The decade from 1970 to 1980 that Kelly spent in Las Vegas with the Judy Lynn organization increased his professionalism and understanding of what it takes to work in the business. While working in Vegas, Jones finally learned to read violin music and learned the "Nashville number system" of playing from chord charts:

> In Las Vegas, they hired a *conductor*. And we had—I say we—I learned a *little* bit so I could read a simple melody line. And I forgot all I learned. Because I never had taken any lessons, it was always playing *by ear*. [I learned to read music] so I could get through the charts, you know.
>
> The stuff I've been around, like when I went to work with Judy Lynn, Bobby Hicks was there. And I learned a lot of stuff [with Hicks], a lot of that harmony stuff, you know. There was a lot of stuff to learn. The violin section—we had three violins [Hicks, Jones, and third players who came and went]. We had three fiddles, and you had to learn your parts. She had the great fiddlers before that—she had Buddy Spicher, she had Tommy Williams, even Roger Miller played fiddle way back when, before I was there. It was a good deal. Ten years of good fiddling. I ended up being band manager.
>
> Like that *fiddle album*, you know [*Authentic Old-Time Fiddle Tunes*], I took a lot of it out of the *One Thousand Fiddle Tunes* book but I changed the endings and the intros to suit *me*. But a lot of it's note-for-note, you know, whether it's "Cincinnati Hornpipe" or "Witch of the Wave Reel"—the first tune in that book. That's basically out of that *book*. I got hung up on hornpipes, that style, because Howdy Forrester was a hornpipe player too. And I just learned enough to follow the melody line.

At another juncture, Kelly performed from 2000 to 2006 with banjoist Lonnie Hoppers in New Union. Kelly's ability to play tunes like "Pike County Breakdown" at blazing tempos came in handy. Hoppers's band in its various iterations included mandolinists D. G. Lynch and Larry Sledge, fiddlers Jamie Haage and Dale Hopkins, bassist Bill Wolfe, and guitarists Bob Lovett and flat-picking legend Dan Crary. Jones performed with New Union at bluegrass festivals, in concerts at theaters and shopping malls, and in a segment of the RFD-TV cable show *The Cumberland Highlanders*. Jones also appeared in the 2004 public television program *Lonnie Hoppers, Bluegrass Musician*, produced by *Ozarks Watch Video* magazine. Jones also performed with Hoppers at festivals at Silver Dollar City and at the Shepherd of the Hills in Branson, as well as at the Ozark Folk Festival in Mountain View. Kelly was the fiddler on Lonnie's CD *Lifetime Harvest* (2005). To Hoppers, Kelly was the ideal fiddler and band member, a player with maturity, versatility, taste, and "chops." According to Lonnie: "He's slick. He gets what I call a big *Kenny Baker tone*. I just compare everybody to Kenny, for several reasons, you know, because I recorded several tunes with Bill Monroe and Kenny."[9]

In 2001, Jones issued a self-produced compilation CD, *Through the Years, Volume 1*, developed at the request of fans who heard his performances for several years at the Missouri State Fair in Sedalia, with guitarist Wes Brown of Florence, Missouri. The CD is a sampling of Kelly's fiddling from the 1970s into 2000, with a variety of accompaniment, fiddle styles, and genres of music and includes fan favorites, from "Devil's Dream," "South," and "Dardanella" to "Cripple Creek," "Jerusalem Ridge," and "Alabama Jubilee."[10]

Kelly Jones and Wes Brown (guitar) at a Kingdom Days fiddle contest, Fulton, June 1993. (Photo by Howard Marshall)

The Contest Game

To many people in Missouri, it is not Kelly's professional stage career in Las Vegas or his session and guest appearances that made him famous, but his successful negotiation of the rocky terrain of the old-time fiddle contest. From the 1970s through the 1990s, Jones won practically every contest he entered, whether a modest affair at a fish fry or a statewide event competing against other A-list champions.

Kelly's articulate, perfectionist performances struck some listeners as too perfect, too smooth, too professional. Jones was so skilled that R. P. Christeson assumed he was a classical violinist. "Kelly Jones, from Nevada, Missouri. Here is a violinist playing fiddle tunes. This guy is smooth. He is smooth as ice. Glass. He plays old-time pieces."[11] This is the sort of comment Kelly Jones ignored. Three decades later, in the 2020s, it is common to see contest fiddlers with classical violin training.

At a contest at Hillbilly Days in the town park in Laurie in the late 1970s, Kelly ran up against the occasional prejudice among some judges against fiddlers who perform at an exceptionally high level who also happen to have professional career experience. One of the judges that day was a well-known contest player, music-store owner, and one of the older fiddlers who possessed classical violin skills.

> Down here at Laurie, Missouri, at Hillbilly Days, behind the Pizza Hut in the little park they have down there. Anyway, I played in it, and I didn't even place, didn't get nothin' out of it. And one of the judges was Henry Thompson. And I saw Henry coming out after it was over, and I stopped and asked him, 'Henry? What I gotta do to place in this fiddle contest?' And he looked at me and said, "Kelly, I'll tell you what: You're just *too good*." And that's all he told me. Kinda funny. Contests, I didn't take them too serious. I didn't get into the *politics* and didn't worry about anything else.

Perhaps what Henry Thompson was trying to say is that, in his mind, fiddle contests should be open only to amateurs—although that probably does not quite get at the issue. One of the false assumptions in allowing only "amateur" players is that the music will somehow be more traditional or local or "old-time." A few contests tried, mostly in vain, to ban "professional" musicians from contests, but little attempt was made to articulate a reason.

> What's the opposite of professional? Amateur. You can have an amateur contest or a professional contest. Yes, I can see, I made my money being a professional *player*, and if they want to put a rule in there that professionals cannot play, *fine*. I won't play. They didn't do that—but they *said that*. But that's just people [certain judges, administrators] that listen to the [fiddlers] that weren't professional players and they didn't like it, you know, and they didn't want it to happen. It's *just people*. I see that all the time. It's everywhere.

No clear rule has been formulated for use in fiddle contests. And a person can change professions. And anyway, since 1990, Jones's principal means of making a living has been his "day job" as a US postal clerk.

Another issue in the contest game for state events is whether contestants should be residents. The state contest at Sedalia requires residency, thus excluding interesting and competitive fiddling from elsewhere—like those big 1960s contests at Lexington and Salisbury. The Sedalia rule is argued on an annual basis. Jones is among those who would like to see contests open to anyone, but he accepts rules that are clear and followed. "A deal you get into, you gotta be a *resident* of Missouri, to play the Missouri [state contest]. That's all right, whatever the *rule is*, but I don't see the point. Why not branch out and let somebody new come in."

From the 1970s into the 1990s, Kelly Jones dominated the state championship and other contests. He quietly retired from the arena around 2000. He retired from contests in part because, in the 1990s, the tastes of top competitors, audiences, and most judges had changed in a way he did not care for; Contest Style (Texas/progressive) more and more consumed and altered Missouri old-time fiddle contests. Jones was faithful to his roots and would not compromise; he would not perform in the currently popular national Contest Style simply to win more trophies. "Oh, yeah, I thought about it. A lot [of contest fiddlers] went to the progressive style, and I wasn't a progressive fiddler. And I thought—not much sense of playing if that's what they [judges] are looking for. Because I always played for the *judges*, you know. And it changed. And I thought, well, I can always play in the senior division." Kelly's comment about the Senior Division is trenchant; in the 1990s and 2000s, all but one or two Senior Division contestants in Missouri contests (typically age sixty and up) were older fiddlers whose styles were old-time Missouri styles or bluegrass styles. That comfortable space in contests for older old-time fiddlers is fast eroding. In the 2020s, as influential, younger Texas-style champions age into the Senior Divisions, the Senior Divisions in Missouri contests are likely to be dominated by progressive/Texas-style contest fiddling with its swing-guitar accompaniment.

Teacher

Another side of Kelly Jones is his effectiveness as a teacher and mentor. Jones taught several years at the Bethel Youth Fiddle Camp, including 1986 (the camp's first year). In the 1980s, he served as a master in the Missouri Traditional Arts Apprenticeship Program—his pupil: Travis Inman. This partnership was unusually keen. Inman was a younger man, from Cole Camp, and already a prominent contest fiddler. As a teenager, Inman had gone to Jones to learn more about guitar playing and fiddle backup and then, in his twenties in the mid-1980s, became Jones's apprentice. Their lessons in 1988–89 consisted in large part of the master working through advanced techniques as the younger player sought increased mastery. Travis Inman had already won the state contest at Sedalia three times (1986, 1987, and 1988) before his apprenticeship. Kelly won in 1989 and the next two years, and then Inman continued a long run of state titles.

Jones teaches by ear and phrase by phrase. First, Inman needed to know the melody by heart. In many cases, Inman knew the outline of a tune and came to Kelly to improve, complete, and polish. Jones often pulled out a recording he considered admirable, and they would listen and then work through the tune one phrase at a time. Jones would play a phrase (a measure or more), repeating the phrase and checking notes or bowing until the student got it. He would stop at any point, go over, and improve things if a questionable element crept into the student's playing. Kelly then would move to the next phrase, until the tune was all pulled together.[12]

Sometimes Jones would go to his massive files and retrieve sheet music when he wanted to explain how what was given in print compared to the tune as played in oral tradition. In some cases, Jones considered the "original" published sheet music to be the benchmark to work from or compare with. In many cases, no trustworthy print version exists. It is understood that when a melody in oral tradition happens to be written down and published, it was copied down as the listener heard it fiddled at a fleeting moment in time. And sometimes it is possible to find the first known publication of a composed fiddle tune in books, archives, and online—like "Red Wing"—should a fiddler want to perform a composed tune as its author published it.

Chance encounters with younger players provided opportunities for them. While performing in Columbia on New Year's Eve at a First Night concert in December 2008, drawing together several fiddlers, Kelly Jones sat next to teenager Sadie Currey. Sadie was able to closely observe and hear Jones, and, after the show, Kelly demonstrated some techniques, such as how to play "sixth" two-note chords. Jones explained that it was Missouri fiddler Dale Potter who pioneered double- and triple-stops in Nashville in the late 1940s and taught those techniques to Bobby Hicks and other famous fiddlers. Currey, who performed with her family band, KurreyKorn, in 2015, completed studies at the Berklee College of Music in Boston and moved to Los Angeles to pursue a career in music.

For many years, Jones has operated a violin shop, doing repairs and deals. He ferrets out violins and bows at auctions, flea markets, and yard sales, as well as on the Internet. He says he has every violin bow he ever found and has discovered valuable old bows in cheap cases with cheap old fiddles. He sells violins on Internet auction sites and makes periodic trips with vintage instruments to sell to collectors at the Dallas International Guitar Festival.

Until the COVID-19 pandemic, Kelly continued to work as an on-call fiddler for touring country music stars, such as Rex Allen Jr. and Leroy Van Dyke and with Jane Accurso's Columbia bands. In 2022, as pandemic conditions allow, such performances are beginning to resume. He keeps handy some crowd-pleasers for spots in a show when he is invited to step up to the microphone and play a "special"—tried-and-true blockbusters such as "Orange Blossom Special," "Down Yonder," and "El Comanchero." When invited to play a favorite tune, Kelly usually plays "Missouri Waltz," his favorite for contests. "I always play Missouri Waltz. It's a *money* maker."[13]

Listen to track 18 on the companion CD to hear Kelly Jones's version of "Forked Deer."

Billy Ward turns it loose onstage in the Grand National Division at Weiser, with swinging guitar backup by Joey McKenzie (Texas), Rex Gillentine (Texas), and Justin Branum (Tennessee; *back to camera*). Ward is a veteran in Branson-area shows and oprys and among Missouri's leading contest fiddlers who favor the improvisational Texas-derived competition fiddle style. He is known for creative, extended versions of breakdowns and lush waltzes. (Photo by Howard Marshall, June 2010)

Fiddle Contests from the 2000s Forward 9

All right, let's see you play *this*!

—John Hartford, *John Hartford's Old Time Fiddling ("Trying to Teach My Hands to Do What I Hear in My Head")* (1998)

The good times for Texas-based contest fiddling and guitar accompaniment ("Contest Style") began to pick up speed in Missouri (and other midwestern states) around 2000. The shift was prefigured by Junior Marriott's surprise win performing Texas Contest Style in the 1983 state contest in Columbia. This was perhaps the first major contest in Missouri where a contestant took first place playing a style other than old-time or bluegrass. Change is the law of the universe.

Meet Me at the Fair

The 2001 contest at the state fair was another pivotal event, although few people realized it at the time. The Contest Style fiddlers' and guitarists' long campaign to use more than two accompanists was finally won.[1] During registration in 2001, fiddlers who had been lobbying to change the two-accompanist rule again entreated MSOTFA administration to allow more than two accompanists, and this time it worked, and Contest Style fiddlers proceeded to bring three or even four accompanists to the microphone. Another old rule was bent that year, too: a fiddler from Kansas was allowed to compete despite the Missouri-residents-only rule. There was some immediate blowback to allowing more than two accompanists and permitting a nonresident to compete; several musicians declared that they would not return, and another walked away in disgust before the contest started. It took time for the ramifications of the voided two-accompanist rule to take effect in the fiddle community, as the news made its way around the state. As for the nonresident rule, on that matter the debate continues.[2]

MSOTFA leadership and some fiddlers at Sedalia continued to finesse rules for several more years, but the association's implicit approval of fiddlers using more than two accompanists was a signal that advocates of Contest Style fiddling (with its several swing-guitar backups) had prevailed.[3] With MSOTFA's apparent endorsement of Contest Style fiddling and three guitar backups, in fairly short order Contest Style guitar backup and fiddling, performed expertly by a small entourage of proponents led by champions such as Junior Marriott, Alita Stoneking, and Matt Wyatt, began to prevail at most Missouri contests, just as Contest Style was becoming more dominant across the United States and Canada.

As so often with change, the cherished older thing can look like nostalgia and can be seen by adherents as unfortunately superseded by the new thing. It happened when Mozart played London. It happened when Charlie Parker hit New York and when Dylan went electric.

Contest Style is, of course, a legitimate, traditional art form too, even if it may no longer be grounded in a specific, physical folk community, ethnic group, or geographic region. Like other genres and customs once tied to place (or stereotyped that way), such as bluegrass, Contest Style fiddle and guitar music is now international.[4]

After 2001 and the following few years, few contest administrators were interested in or able to stick to their long-standing two-accompanist-only rule. Perplexed by the confusions and testy debates over the two-guitar-accompanist rule as well the impossibly opaque declarations about "old-time" versus "Contest Style," and without help from the Missouri State Old Time Fiddlers Association, a number of event boards and sponsors grew weary of the disharmony and canceled contests that had been popular in their towns for many years.

Rules have always been a quagmire, whether in old-time fiddle skills or Olympic sports. The debate over accompanists is not likely to go away, but a sort of equilibrium has set in. People gradually learned what to expect if they traveled to the state contest in Sedalia. Old-time-style fiddlers, fans, and judges who came to Sedalia grew accustomed to Contest Style fiddlers with several swing-style guitar seconds capturing most of the limelight.[5] By 2019, the state contest was virtually owned by fiddlers and accompanists playing Contest Style with skill; only the most authoritative and convincing fiddlers in other styles had much of a chance of reaching the winners' podium (unless there were too few Contest Style players in the contest that day).

Many fans and musicians did not realize it, but the issue of how many accompanists a fiddler may have in a contest turned out to be more important than fussing over whether fiddlers were playing old-time or Contest Style or, perhaps, whether nonresidents could compete in the state contest.

It may seem trivial—three rather than one or two backups. But this is central to the discussion of "old-time" compared to "Contest Style" fiddling, because sock-chord swing-guitar accompaniment is crucial to Contest Style. And it is generally the Contest Style players who insist on three (or more) guitar backups playing Texas/western-swing style. The overall effect was that of a full band.

By 2020, in Missouri contests, the Senior Division became the only division where few fiddlers playing something other than Contest Style were able to rank high in the standings. Administrators at some contests try to keep it old-time in the winnings, such as at Mokane and Stovall's Grove, but experience shows that it is not possible, practical, or fair to expect judges to award scores on the basis of what style one plays. In spite of whether they prefer old-time or bluegrass or Contest Style, most judges will strive to award the most points to fiddlers who simply play better that day.

In 2014, after a dozen years, Allen Wyatt returned administration of the state-fair contest back to Bill Shull and Charlie Walden. Allen had done well and kept the contest going, taking the job seriously and looking for ways to improve the event. Allen's wife, Cheri, tended the registration table, and occasionally their son Matt was able

Allen Wyatt administered the state contest at the state fair in Sedalia in 2006; here, with his judging panel. *Left to right*: Junior Marriott, Clifford Hill, and Sharon Graf (Springfield, IL), Wyatt. (Photo by Howard Marshall)

to take part in the contest. The Wyatt Violin Shop contributed substantial time and finances to see the Sedalia contest endure.

Bill and Charlie became active in the contest again, Bill handling administration and Charlie serving as emcee or helping judge. In 2014, the rule change that occurred in 2001 allowing three accompanists appeared on the Internet under "Official Contest Rules": "Each contestant will be allowed no more than three accompanists."[6] At the 2016 state-fair contest, in his emcee's welcome to the audience, Charlie read the backup rule by saying, "Each contestant will typically be allowed no more than two accompanists with three being the absolute maximum." He went on to read, "Recognized styles of play could include Missouri Old-Time, traditional Oklahoma/Texas/Western, Eastern Old-Timey, Canadian Old-Time, Bluegrass and traditional Celtic fiddle styles. Classical, jazz, blues, hot swing and various modern styles of play will not be permitted. Excessive improvisation is not encouraged and can result in point deduction." Two of the seven entrants in the Open Division used three accompanists.

From 2014 until Bill Shull's death in June 2022, the state-fair competition in Sedalia continued to be administered by Shull and Walden and remains a prime occasion for many people in the fiddle community. Opinions linger about perennial issues: For instance, should fiddlers from other states be allowed to enter? Should a person serve as a judge if his or her family members are competing in the contest? May professionals or even quasi-professionals such as "Branson fiddlers" and "opry fiddlers" compete?[7]

At the 2018 Sedalia contest, there were fifteen in the Junior Division (up to age sixteen), fourteen in the Open (any age may compete), and six or seven in the Senior Division (age sixty and up).[8] The judges were Mickey Soltys (Illinois), Tricia Spencer (Kansas), and Travis Inman, all seasoned fiddlers respected in the community. Shull handled administration, Walden emceed, and Cathy Marriott was scorekeeper. MSOTFA leadership has endeavored to bring in judges such as Soltys and Spencer from Kansas, to add perspective, particularly perspective from experienced fiddlers who are not advocates of Contest Style. MSOTFA also invites judges to fiddle a tune or play backup for a fiddler at the microphone before the contest, an excellent device employed by many contests to show everyone that the judges are musicians themselves. While being able to perform on fiddle or a backup instrument is not a requirement for judges, being able to do so is considered important by some people. The state contest was held in 2019, canceled in 2020 due to the COVID-19 pandemic, and returned in 2021.

In former times, children and young teens seldom competed in fiddle contests, although they were always welcome as accompanists. A few competed, but youngsters typically had to enroll in the Open Division ("any age"), and that discouraged all but the most skilled and determined. Before the 1980s and 1990s, most contests had an Open Division (open to any age) and, if budget allowed, a Senior Division (typically for those aged sixty or sixty-five and older). Youngsters would enter the Open Division in contests, and many did well; by age fifteen or sixteen, many fiddlers are already skilled, experienced, and successful contest performers.

From the late 1970s forward, there was an influx of young and very young fiddlers in contests. Most competed more as an adventure, to please a parent or a music teacher, or to just have fun. There had always been young contestants, but they were few and clearly prodigies, such as Mike Hartgrove in the 1960s.

In the 1970s, the Suzuki violin method was bringing many youngsters to the violin/fiddle. Part of the appeal of Suzuki is that it stresses ear training (listening carefully) and learning by doing—just like old-time fiddling. Suzuki kids were encouraged to play fiddle tunes!

The 1970s surge of interest in the fiddle brought forward more, but youngsters began coming to contests in increasing numbers in the 1980s. Perhaps the biggest factor in the new emphasis on rewarding youngsters and encouraging them to compete in fiddle contests was the fiddle-camp movement of the 1980s. Junior fiddlers became a force to be reckoned with in competitions across the United States and Canada. Precocious children and teenagers were no longer unusual in contests, and at last a discrete division of competition was formalized for them. Most competitions had established a Junior Division by 1990.

Allen Wyatt, for many years a participant in (as guitar accompanist) and administrator of contests, watched with interest as the juniors grew in numbers and influence. As contests began including a Junior Division in the 1990s, the division "blossomed. Teachers started the spread and before long you started seeing crowded Junior divisions in fiddle contests. So, by the end of the '90s it really picked up and continued thru the 2000s."[9]

No longer an afterthought or a bit of entertainment or an excuse for a proud parent to push a child onstage, the Junior Division became part of and a substantial influence in the fiddle-contest landscape. Major contests with numerous contestants followed Weiser's lead by creating additional age-specific divisions (for example, "pee-wee," "junior-junior," and so forth).

The Junior Division became very competitive, as impressive and sometimes more impressive than the other divisions. Most of the top juniors were pupils of top fiddlers in the Open and Senior Divisions. At the national contests in Weiser, the number of entries in the several youth divisions far outnumber all other age divisions, and many juniors are competitive with the best older champions.[10] In most contests, young fiddlers continue to have the choice of signing up for an age-specific division or signing up for the Open Division. Exceptionally skilled (or daring) youngsters enter the Open Division to try their luck, and perhaps for the status of doing well there or for the typically bigger purse to be won. Other contests require fiddlers to play in their age divisions, a requirement intended to encourage more youngsters, but which also has the side effect of keeping precocious youngsters from "beating" and "showing up" their elders or teachers.

The Missouri Traditional Fiddle and Dance Network

The Missouri Traditional Fiddle and Dance Network, founded in 2001, an informal group, was concerned about the ebb of old-time square dances and the increasing influence of Contest Style fiddling and guitar accompaniment in contests (considered by many to be generally unsuitable for old-time square dancing). They wanted to help promoters keep contests going, developing lists of fiddlers to receive mailings (the MSOTFA *Contest Calendar* was no longer produced), guidelines to send to promoters, and lists of qualified judges.

Their idea was "to develop and promote educational programs and family-oriented community events to understand, celebrate, and help perpetuate traditional Missouri music and dance." Dances eventually became their focus. The network was interested not in creating another fiddlers' association, defining old-time, or setting up new rules for contests, but rather in trying to support long-familiar customs.

Several contests that were folding were kept going for a year or two more, such as those at the Paris Old Threshers Festival, the Callaway County Fair, and the Boone County Fair in Columbia. The group helped organize a short-lived but successful contest at the annual Fayette Freeze-Off festival (ice cream was the specialty), a town that had seen many contests through the generations.[11]

It was a time of confusion about rules and the appropriateness of Contest Style in contests advertised as old-time. Several contests were on their last legs due to the aging population of administrators. Paris administrators canceled their annual contest, expressing the concern that some of the Contest Style fiddlers and accompanists had become argumentative and disrespectful of the event; the Missouri Traditional Fiddle and Dance Network tried to help the Paris administration keep their contest going, but efforts failed after two more years and Paris was canceled after the 2001 event. Other contests discontinued (some were briefly revived) included Boonville (Missouri Valley Old Threshers Festival), Columbia (Boone County Fair), Fulton (Callaway County Fair), Marshall (Saline County Fair), Odessa (Puddle Jumper Days), and Warsaw (Warsaw Jubilee Days). After several years of attempted resuscitation of the Boone County Fair contest, the fair board dropped their famous contest. Network members gathered at the fair to hold jam sessions next to the building where the contest was held in its final years.

The network helped develop several new contests (some with jam sessions and square dancing) in towns such as Macon, Laddonia, and Fayette. These attracted fiddlers of various styles, but the events did not garner local support and failed to continue. Macon went well. Laddonia suffered from unfocused management and poor judging.

Among the network's successful events—for musicians and fans at least—was a Taylor McBaine Memorial Old-Time Fiddlers Contest developed for the Fall Heritage Festival in Columbia's Nifong Park in September 2002. McBaine was often remembered as a chief of Boone County fiddlers, and his gentlemanly demeanor and meticulous fiddling exemplified what many people admired in Missouri fiddling.[12] The contest was held for several years.

Another event, the Pete McMahan Memorial Fiddlers Reunion, Contest, and Barn Dance, was held in Harrisburg (McMahan's longtime home) in March 2002. As at the Taylor McBaine event, network members created a photo exhibition around the honoree's life and fiddling career. The event was cosponsored with the Harrisburg Lions Club and included square-dance instruction and calling by Steve Young and Ray Thebeau and clog-dancing instruction by Ellie Grace. Refreshments and dinner were available. The contest judges were Vesta Johnson, Gary Watson, and John T. White; the emcee was Chris Canote. Old trophies were donated by Sarah McMahan and refurbished with new brass labels, and all of the fiddlers were allowed to pick up whichever of the renewed trophies they wanted. After the contest, there was dancing; Thebeau brought some of his square-dance group from Ste. Genevieve. In 2003, Young, Thebeau, and the Rev. Howard Hartung (Macon) did the square-dance instruction and calling; contest judges were Thebeau, Lynn Wells, and White.

In July 2003, the group administered an "old-time fiddlers reunion, contest, and barn dance" at the Boone County Fair in Columbia. This contest had been discontinued by the Fair Board in 2001, partly due to lack of knowledgeable leadership and partly due to an argument that broke out between Forrest Rose (a *Columbia Daily Tribune* columnist and bass player) and one or two of the Contest Style contest fiddlers—a fierce argument bringing into the open the problems and resentments brewing over fiddle-contest rules and the growing influences of Texas-based Contest Style fiddling and backup.

For several years the network organized events for Columbia's Fall Heritage Festival as well as the city's First Night Festival on New Year's Eve. At the 2003 First Night event, eight fiddlers took turns playing an exhibition set of favorite tunes and then played for square dancing: Steve Head, Kelly Jones, Billy Lee, Howard Marshall, Lynn Wells, John T. White, John Williams, and Matt Wyatt. Some chose to play well-honed contest pieces, and others offered familiar square-dance tunes or rare tunes. The dancing started out with a cake walk, then a children's square dance taught by Steve Young, and then others joined in.

The Missouri Traditional Fiddle and Dance Network experimented with other programs for the Boone County Fair. In 2006, there was a "Fiddler's Frolics" in the building where the contest had been held, as a kind of fiddlers reunion and jam session. Several local fiddlers were invited to perform a set of their favorite tunes—Bobby Joe Caldwell, Nate Kemperman, Howard Marshall, Dale Pauley, John White, and Bud Wyatt. There was square dancing in front of the stage while each fiddler performed his or her set, with Jim Thaxter calling. Invited accompanists included guitarists Ron Ray, Kenny Applebee, and Brad Roby, along with Kathy Gordon (bass). The following year, in July 2007, another Fiddler's Frolics was hosted at the fair, featuring fiddlers Joel Chrisman, Joe Hinkebein, Dale Pauley, Lynn Wells, Kenny Applebee, Howard Marshall, John White, Mike Wells, Bryan Biswell, Clayton Beall, Jessie Applebee, and Kyle Pudenz.

In 2003, the group inaugurated a monthly dance at Hallsville. John and Betty White lived there and arranged for the network to rent a small community building. The events included an open jam session catering to beginners and youngsters, followed by a carry-in dinner, and dancing from around seven p.m. until the dancers and musicians decided it was time to go home. A wide variety of fiddlers and backup musicians played for the dances. The dances started with a Virginia reel (a traditional "ice breaker" and "get-acquainted" line dance) and included round dancing (waltzes, polkas, schottisches) as well as square dancing. Each set of square dancers had its own caller, and Steve Young shepherded the square dances. When the Youngs, cofounders of the dance, moved to Winigan (Steve's family farm), Columbia caller Jim Thaxter stepped in. Virtually any musician playing any instrument was welcome to sit in with the band. Several fiddlers took turns anchoring the band, and several accompanists were regulars and helped guarantee a solid rhythm section.

Listen to track 19 on the companion CD to hear Amber Gaddy's version of "Black Sally Goodin."

The Missouri Traditional Fiddle and Dance Network held no formal meetings, did not solicit memberships, and did not seek official status as a voluntary association. The group experimented with a variety of events and hoped that some would become annual events. However, within a few years, support for continuation of printed materials, special events, and hosting contests declined. Today, the network has two elements: a website created by David Cavins—with an events calendar, downloadable tunes, square-dance instruction, sample contest rules and standards,[13] biographies, obituaries, and downloadable music—and the monthly Hallsville jam session,

Amber Gaddy of Columbia heard her first fiddle tunes as a young child from her father and grandfathers, all harmonica players from the rural Missouri and Arkansas Ozarks, and learned to square dance from her mother. While attending Grinnell College in Iowa, she met Missouri Valley fiddler Dwight Lamb, who has been a lifelong friend and mentor. She picked up the fiddle in 2015 to help continue the monthly Hallsville square dances after one of its founders, fiddler John White, passed on. Along with guitar player, luthier, and caller David Cavins, she's been a fixture at contests, dances, and festivals in Missouri since 2001. (Photo by Howard Marshall, 2021; fiddler John Williams rear)

potluck dinner, and dance, now under the leadership of Cavins, Amber Gaddy, Bill Foley, and Don and Melinda Schindler (whose three children are musicians and were John White pupils). Callers include Cavins, Thaxter, Gaddy, Rhett Hartman, and others. Guest musicians sit in with the *orchestre du jour*. Health precautions resulting from the COVID-19 pandemic forced the temporary closing of the Hallsville dances, but open-air jam sessions in the town park began to be held in the summer of 2021, and in 2022 the event resumed indoors.

John Williams

John P. Williams, born in 1982, is an old-time fiddler from the "Little Dixie" region of north-central Missouri, Pete McMahan's last apprentice. "My hero and mentor since childhood. There's not anyone that could hold a candle to or draw a bow in the same league as Big Mac."[14] Williams is carrying on McMahan's fiddling as an instructor at the Bethel Youth Fiddle Camp and in the Traditional Arts Apprenticeship Program, as well as by example in sessions, public programs, and contests. John lives on the family farm near Madison, where he and his wife, Jullia, reconstructed the house of his grandfather. John works at a home and construction supply store in Moberly, fifteen miles west. As a child, he was inspired to play violin by his maternal grandmother, Charlotte Winfree Utterback of Paris, and later, his maternal great-grandfather, Henry Utterback of Middle Grove, and was taken to fiddle contests and festivals. His first memories of fiddle music are from contests in Paris and Bethel.[15]

> I've lived the majority of my life in rural Monroe County on the family farm and am a third-generation caretaker of beautiful pastures, woods, and creeks. Tradition, craftsmanship, and community have all been at the core of how I was raised. I spent many summers helping my paternal grandfather build wooden wheels, carriages, wagons, buggies, and carts from the ground up with raw materials. We would fell white oak trees in the woods on our property for my mother to build white oak baskets. I spent many evenings watching my Dad forge pieces of metal into useful tools. This may not have been a typical childhood experience for someone born in the 1980s, but I wouldn't trade a second of those experiences.[16]

When John was seven, his grandmother Utterback bought his first violin (a quarter-size Suzuki instrument), and his parents, Tammy and Preston, began driving him to Moberly for Suzuki lessons with Emily Bowers; they worked together for about a year. Bowers liked fiddle music and, at their lessons, added time to work on a fiddle tune, using transcriptions in John's copy of Craig Duncan's *Deluxe Fiddling Method*.[17] Among tunes they worked on were family favorites and typical tunes for beginners, like "Golden Slippers" and "Red Wing," "Boil the Cabbage Down" and "Tennessee Waltz." When John outgrew the quarter-size violin, his parents obtained a half-size for him, and then a three-quarter-size violin. "My first full-size was one that my Grandma Charlotte had purchased at a yard sale from Dr. Warbritton (a physician in Paris and neighbor) for $90, made by J. A. (Jim) Gilmore of Jefferson City."[18]

After a year with Emily Bowers, Williams took Suzuki for six years with Moberly teacher Barbara Geisendorfer. Eventually, John became more interested in fiddle music and began working on his own, with help from his mother, who accompanied him on piano. John learned tunes in the Christeson tune books and learned tunes by ear from cassette recordings and LP records. To help catch the fiddling, John slowed down LPs with jars of pennies "to slow down the platter (be sure to tune down when destroying vintage stereo equipment)."[19]

In the middle 1990s, Williams began getting involved in jam sessions and meeting with Pete McMahan and other fiddlers:

> One particular get-together sticks with me. In 1994, there was an all-day jam and square dance in Wein, Missouri. All of the big Missouri fiddlers were there, and I was finally getting to a point to where I could sit in on a few tunes and play. My

hard work was starting to pay off! Up until this weekend, I really didn't have any *connections* with the inner sanctum of the music I so loved, and I had only really jammed with kids my own age. The "old guys" (or so I thought, as I'm that age now) started to take this punk kid seriously and a few patient ones took me under their wing. I had finally made my connections into the group that I had so admired for the entirety of my childhood.

Dr. Howard Marshall, Bill Shull, and Charlie Walden are the three individuals that stand out the most. Their eagerness to share their advice, knowledge, and resources was similar to what I encountered in my Dad's blacksmith shop. I was constantly getting new cassettes and sheet music in the mail from those three and still do to this day. Howard and I have put tens of thousands of miles on his vehicles over the years traveling around the country, including driving the Lewis and Clark Trail to Seattle all the way to Voyager Records two days after my high school graduation.[20]

John was enrolled in the Bethel fiddle camp in 1991, his first time away from home. "I was able to study under my heroes I'd watched play on stage and spend the week with children my own age with the same hobby. What wasn't there to like? I didn't miss a year until I graduated from high school. I can't possibly put into words how much the camp has shaped my fiddling, outlook, and circle of lifelong friends."[21] His instructors at Bethel included Bob Holt, Vesta Johnson, Dwight Lamb, Taylor McBaine, Fred Stoneking, Johnny Bruce, Herman Johnson (from Oklahoma), and Pete McMahan.

John Williams took first place in the Open Division at Stovall's Grove in May 2013. First-place winners in each age division received an artistic commemorative cedar plaque made by Sue Ann Storm. John has played different violins through the years. (Photo by Howard Marshall)

In June 1997, at fifteen, Williams attended a new fiddle camp inaugurated in West Plains. He had begun reading about fiddling, and the *Devil's Box* published an article about the West Plains camp and ensuing fiddle contest.[22]

At the Minnesota State Contest in Cotton in 1998, John impressed the judges by performing Pete McMahan's tunes with great success, taking second in the competitive Junior Division. He played so much like Pete that fiddler Leroy Blom of Wisconsin, an old friend of Pete's, affectionately called John "Pete junior."[23] "This is, without doubt, the most pivotal and influential part of my childhood that shaped my path as a fiddler. Pete was known all over the country for his inimitable drive, phrasing of a tune, personal touches, and beautiful, but abrasive double stops. He was the guy to try to beat at a contest, though it was doubtful you'd ever succeed. If you were competing against Pete, you were better off just playing your heart out and hoping for second place, at best."[24] Tunes John worked on with Pete were a mix of old standards and challenging contest pieces, such as "Bill Cheatem," "Rachel," "Old Indiana," "Sugar in the Gourd," "Burt County Breakdown," "Oklahoma Redbird," "Hell amongst the Yearlings," "Ragtime Annie," "Clyde Durst's Tune," "Virginia Darling," and "Rose of My Heart."

As Pete's health was deteriorating in the summer of 1998, John continued visiting him at his nursing home. The visits became important connections for McMahan.

Williams's approach to teaching follows McMahan's. He does not teach with printed tunes but teaches by ear. John says that it is easier for pupils to commit tunes to memory when they use their ears rather than their eyes. Like McMahan, John has the technical knowledge to tell students the specific notes he is playing and does so when it helps a student having trouble learning by ear.[25] John begins most students with a Missouri tune from McMahan called "Ford One Step" ("easy to teach, it's all memorable patterns") and the old standard "Maggie," old-time two-step couple-dance tunes, moderate in tempo.[26] John recommends students access digital files and computer programs or a cell-phone application to slow tunes down (and maintain concert pitch) to help them learn. Bethel camp encourages students to record lessons for later study, and Williams gives students a copy of his *Monroe County Influences* CD and other recordings.[27]

In 2014 Williams was selected to teach in the apprenticeship program, and his first student was Bob Cathey.[28] His next pupil was Jessie Applebee Perrigo (Kenny and Norma Applebee's granddaughter) in 2016, followed by Sophia Cunningham in 2018 and Cynthia Mackey in 2019.

John continued in the fiddler lineup at monthly dances in Hallsville, played occasionally at contra dances in Columbia, and was featured at festivals such as the Big Muddy in Boonville. On hiatus due to the COVID-19 pandemic, some events returned in 2021, and John performed at the Big Muddy in November. How does he feel about the future of old-time fiddling?

> I'm trying to be optimistic about it. But it seems like, [in contests] if it's not perfectly-orchestrated contest style, it's Appalachian Round-Peak style. I like listening to all of

John Williams with Bob Cathey (*right*), his Traditional Arts Apprenticeship Program student, in a program in the Museum of Art and Archaeology at the University of Missouri, April 2016. Cathey is particularly fond of the old railroad "tie hacker tunes" that John learned from Nile Wilson. (Photo by Howard Marshall)

it, but I really feel like what we play [central Missouri style] is dwindling, no matter how hard we're working to keep it going. Everything is so accessible now, too. Everybody wants to play like they're at Clifftop, or they want to play like they're at Weiser. They don't want to play like they're at the Boone County Fairgrounds.[29]

In 2020, here I am on the family farm in the home my paternal grandparents built with my music-loving and supportive bride. Together we're raising the fourth generation of Williamses here. I love a lot of things about life here: the fiddle contests during the summer months, community jam sessions, informal music parties here at the farm, indoctrinating my students with the "culture" that Missouri fiddling and old-time music brings with it, and obsessively collecting all of the rare old-time fiddle recordings I can find. There aren't many of us carrying the traditional Missouri fiddling torch nowadays and true regional Missouri fiddling is but a shadow of its former self. I'm hoping that this eagerness to share continues from others within this community, and most of all, I'm hoping to instill the same sense of tradition, community, inclusivity, and willingness-to-share in my daughter.[30]

Listen to track 20 on the companion CD to hear John Williams's version of "Reuben's Ridge."

Richard Shewmaker

Richard Shewmaker is the son of John Shewmaker, an attorney who as a young man in the 1960s was a leader of the folk music and dance revival in St. Louis. Born in St. Louis in 1992, Richard came with his family to Columbia when his mother, Leone, took a position in the public schools. Richard caught the old-time banjo fever, soon followed by a case of the old-time fiddle bug. He was a quick study. John and Leone took Richard to dances and music parties in the St. Louis area, where he was exposed to fiddlers such as Geoff Seitz, of St. Louis. In Columbia, Richard was exposed to fiddle sessions and contests.

Richard began learning clawhammer banjo at thirteen with the help of Leela Grace, who showed him the basics and ignited his passion for the instrument. With the help of an instructional video by David Holt, and sundry albums of older Appalachian masters, such as Tommy Jarrell, Wade Ward, and Kyle Creed, and younger players such as Adam Hurt and St. Louis's Dave Landreth, Shewmaker began playing with other musicians. Jim Ruth, the dean of Missouri clawhammer players, took Richard under his wing.

Hallsville dances became important in Richard's musical journey, where he got to know more musicians and gained experience playing fiddle and banjo for square dancing.[31] Richard also came to old-time fiddle club sessions at the Boone County Historical Society museum in Nifong Park in Columbia, where he met fiddlers of the older generations such as Bobby Joe Caldwell, Bob Hagan, Clifford Hill, Dale Pauley, and Bud Wyatt. In 2007, Richard attended Bethel fiddle camp and studied with Vesta Johnson, Steve Hall, Dwight Lamb, Angie Lennie, and John White. Richard says of fiddle camp, "I did not learn so much at Bethel, due to lack of skill, but it left a great impression on me."[32] One of the memories he has from that time was sitting with Vesta Johnson while she taught him "Ragtime Annie" and showed him how to cross the strings with the bow in a way that gives the music smoothness and continuity.

Richard mastered a variety of old-time styles on both fiddle and five-string banjo. In his fiddling, he moved with apparent ease between the world of classical violin lessons and performing in the Rockbridge High School Orchestra and hanging out with old-time and contest fiddlers.

Shewmaker began competing in fiddle contests at sixteen in 2008 and became interested in the culture, people, and history behind the "fiddling" in the competitions. Richard was hesitant about entering contests but knew contests were where a lot of fiddlers gather and an important tradition in the fiddle community in Missouri. He made quite an impression. One of his first contests was in Tracy at the Platte County Fair in July 2008, where he competed in the Open Division and did well, to the surprise of those who had not heard him before. In the results, Richard won first place, followed by Joe Fedrizzi, Gunner Byrd, Tess Stephens, Katie Benyo, and Mike Fraser. The year 2009 was a busy time for contests. In March, Richard competed at Troy, where he won first in the Junior Division playing "Irish Cobbler," "Over the Waves," and "Marmaduke's Hornpipe." Among other contests that year, Richard also competed successfully at St. Charles, Boonesboro, the Missouri State Fair contest (where he

Richard Shewmaker at the Hallsville dance, October 2013. (Photo by Jean A. Fugate-Besalke)

won the Junior Division), and Boonville's Missouri Valley Steam Engine Association Fiddle Contest.

In 2009, Wilbur Foss invited Richard to compete in the National Invitational Division at the Great Plains Championships in Yankton, South Dakota. The weekend festival and contest, which includes a live radio broadcast on Friday night, dancing, and jam sessions, is a highlight of the year for many fiddlers and fans in the region. Yankton included Missourians through the years.[33] Shewmaker played well. In round one Saturday night he played "Bennett's Reel," "Cowboy Waltz," and "Bradley's Rag" (a McMahan tune in B-flat from Callaway County radio fiddler Seth Bradley), and in the finals on Sunday afternoon "Marmaduke's Hornpipe," "Stars and Stripes Waltz," and "Whistling Rufus"; he won sixth place.[34]

Richard also attended fiddlers' conventions with his parents to the east of Missouri, such as the Appalachian String Band Festival at Clifftop, West Virginia, where he took part in sessions in a variety of styles, including jamming with Missouri fiddlers such as Joe Hinkebein, Geoff Seitz, and Charlie Walden. Richard traveled to Clifftop in 2009, 2011, and 2015. In 2009, he played in the band contest with the band Fever in the South (Bryan Smith, Geoff Seitz, and Shewmaker, violins; John Hatton, guitar; Susan Sterngold, five-string banjo; Mike Resnick, mandolin), and they played "Molly Put the Kettle On" but did not place. That same year, Richard played "Marmaduke's Hornpipe" in the Clifftop contest but did not make the finals. Among other adventures, Richard and his father attended Pinewoods Camp in

Open Division winners at annual Platte County Fair in Tracy, July 2008. *Left to right*: second place, Joe Fedrizzi (Dearborn); third place, Gunner Byrd (Independence); fourth, Tess Stephens (Independence); fifth, Katie Benyo (Kansas City); sixth, Mike Fraser (Kansas City); and first, Richard Shewmaker (Columbia). (Photo by Howard Marshall)

Massachusetts, where Richard enrolled for Early Music Week and the English Dance Musicians Workshop.

After graduating from high school, Richard chose college at Truman State University in Kirksville, a progressive liberal arts institution. He played violin in the orchestra as a music and violin performance major and became part of a circle of youngsters enthusiastic about old-time fiddling. With Anthony Bodnar (Collinsville, Illinois) and Aaron Albrecht (Edwardsville, Illinois), Richard formed a trio, traveling to festivals, jam sessions, and fiddle contests together (all three play guitar as well as fiddle and accompany each other). With Bodnar and Albrecht, Shewmaker continued to be active in contests through his college years. Richard was also a welcome addition to weekly Tuesday-night private jam sessions in Columbia, where he swapped tunes with Dale Pauley and Bud Wyatt (and others) and learned tunes. In addition to contests, Shewmaker traveled to some of the region's major conventions of fiddlers. At the annual event near Wagoner, Oklahoma, at the Western Hills resort in February 2010, Shewmaker moved from tentative listener at the back of a session circle to being invited up to the middle of the session.

Shewmaker has a scholarly inclination and ear that help him analyze music and write transcriptions. While in college, he documented and analyzed the Hallsville dance and spoke at the annual conference of the Missouri Folklore Society. Shewmaker graduated cum laude in English from Truman State in 2017. In 2018, Richard and Anthony Bodnar signed up for training to teach English as a foreign language, completed certification in France, and in 2019 moved to Mexico to teach English to Mexican students planning careers in the United States.

Listen to track 21 on the companion CD to hear Richard Shewmaker's version of "Brenda's Reel."

Trustin Baker

Trustin Baker is a young contest champion and member of an award-winning family bluegrass band. Baker was born in Poplar Bluff in 1999 and has lived since then in the Birch Tree area. Trustin's family history goes back to John H. W. Baker, born in Tennessee in 1815. The family includes numerous musicians and fiddlers, including Trustin's great-great-great-grandfather D. A. Baker and great-great-grandfather Everett Bradshaw. Like many pioneer families in the Missouri Ozarks, Trustin's family background "is mainly Irish and Cherokee."[35]

D. A. Baker, Trustin Baker's great-great-grandfather (*third from left in the white shirt*) and other contestants at a fiddle contest during the Carter County centennial festival in Van Buren, 1959. The woman in "pioneer dress" and bonnet is Frona Williams, known as "Aunt Frona" and a fiddler. (Photo courtesy of Trustin Baker)

Members of the Baker family have been active in rodeos. "I started out rodeoing when I was very young. I rode sheep and rode in the World Finals in Fort Worth, TX. [He won belt buckles] For steer riding when I was nine. My Grandpa, Dad and Uncles all rode bulls and I grew up watching them."

Trustin's parents, Shawn and Carrie, recognized his enthusiasm and arranged lessons with Junior Marriott. Trustin recalls that Marriott was particularly helpful in learning advanced bowing techniques as well as introducing him to contest-style fiddling. "He was very helpful. I would try and learn tunes on my own [and then] he would critique them and show me what I had wrong. Sometimes he would teach me different variations and show me new licks to add to them." "I have tons of fiddling CDs that I like to listen to. *Touch of Texas* by Terry Morris is one if my favorite Contest Style fiddling CDs.[36] I have Arthur Smith, Pete McMahan, Lyman Enloe CDs that I like too. I listen to fiddlers online too like Cyril Stinnett and others. One of my other favorites is Kenny Baker. There are so many others that I enjoy listening to."

While some other kids his age he met at contests were learning to play old-time Missouri styles, Trustin had an instinct for the more swingy Contest Style and for bluegrass. Interviewed at the annual Callaway County fair, when he won third place in the Open Division in 2012 at thirteen, Baker said, "I like playing western songs the best because you get to improvise a lot."[37]

In addition to working with Marriott, Baker took lessons from Texas fiddler Ricky Boen when Boen was a member of the Sons of the Pioneers (2004–14) and working in Branson-area country music shows. Baker also took several online Skype lessons with Matt Hartz, a multitime national champion and instructor in Boise, Idaho.

Shawn and Carrie encouraged Trustin's interest in bluegrass music, gospel, and country music. Musicians, they decided to form a family band with their three children, and in 2010 Trustin began traveling around the country with the Baker Family Band, to festivals and concerts, performing bluegrass, classic country, and gospel music, as well as taking part in fiddle contests.[38] Trustin has been the fiddler and five-string banjo player, and his younger sister, Carina, plays mandolin and sings, while his younger brother, Elijah, plays upright bass, guitar, and fiddle; their mother, Carrie, is the band's guitarist and bassist. The siblings learned to play all the instruments in the band, and Corina and Elijah also play violin and are competitive contest fiddlers. In 2017, the Baker Family competed in the NBC television program *America's Got Talent*, advancing through two rounds before being eliminated in the "judge cuts" by the celebrity judges. Gaining more exposure, the band has appeared on TV and radio programs as well as festivals.

The family operates the Music Barn, a music venue in Mountain View, Missouri. Trustin Baker graduated from the Alpha and Omega homeschool program. He learned to auctioneer from his father and is pursuing a career in music with the Baker Family Band and making trips to fiddle contests.

Carina Baker (mandolin) and her brother, Trustin Baker (violin), in a Baker Family Band performance, 2020. (Website image, www.bakerfamilyband.com)

As a youngster, Trustin Baker started out strong at contests and became a respected champion. While still a teenager, his competition skills developed to the point that he moved into the Open Divisions to compete against older and more seasoned fiddlers and established champions—and became a frequent top finisher or winner. From 2011 through 2014, he won the Junior Division at the state contest held at the Missouri State Fair in Sedalia. He set his sights on the national contest arena and has become a prominent player and rhythm guitarist for other fiddlers. He won prestigious competitions such as the Junior Division at the National Oldtime Fiddlers' Contest in Weiser in 2013 (the Junior Division is extraordinarily competitive at Weiser) and in 2013 the Junior Division at the Grand Masters in Nashville. Entering Open Divisions, Baker won the Arkansas state fiddle contest in 2016, the Tennessee state championship in 2017, and the Great Lakes Fiddle Championship. In 2016 and 2019, Trustin won the nonresident "Gone to Texas" division at the Texas state championships at Hallettsville, a division attracting numerous champions from other states.

Listen to track 22 on the companion CD to hear Trustin Baker's version of "Grey Eagle."

Roger Netherton

Roger Netherton of St. Louis describes himself on his website as "a folk, old-time, and swing violinist," and he is one of Missouri's more creative young fiddlers and multi-instrumentalists.[39] Roger is known for his devotion to fiddling for contra dances, success in fiddle contests, and appearances in campground sessions and onstage at festivals such as those at Clifftop, West Virginia; Battleground, Indiana; and Winfield, Kansas.

Netherton was born in Fairfax, Virginia, in 1996. At age three he moved to St. Louis with his parents, Robin and Dana, who are native St. Louisans; she is a freelance editor, and he is an independent management consultant. Roger had classical training and began studying old-time fiddling. He had the good fortune to have supportive parents who took an active interest in helping Roger explore the various corners and genres of the fiddling world, taking him to jam sessions, dances, concerts, workshops, festivals, contests, and St. Louis Folk School events. Robin often records and photographs his performances, helps maintain a website, and posts information and videos to Internet sites such as YouTube.

A key element in his early success was the support of guitar accompanists such as Roy Farwell and keyboard player Rich Egan, who often perform with Netherton. Geoff Seitz met Roger early in the lad's exploration of fiddling:

> Roger is one of those rare, talented people who pick up a musical instrument and in short time is not only playing it well, but playing it better than most. I met Roger when he was a middle school kid. His mother, Robin, brought him into my violin shop. He played his fiddle for me and it was, to say the least, very impressive. Since that time, Roger has continued to get better and better, winning fiddle contests, playing outstanding concerts, and being a fan favorite at square and contra dances. He does all of this with grace and humility, never putting on airs, just a class act. For years, I have organized a fiddler's showcase at our St. Louis concert hall, The Focal Point. The concert usually features three fine fiddlers and me. One year I asked

Roger to be one of the featured fiddlers. I would say he stole the show that night. It was the talk of the town for months afterwards.[40]

In November 2020, Netherton wrote some comments about his experiences:

Although I listened to certain fiddlers a lot via CD player (Geoff Seitz, Rhys Jones, Bob Walters, Pete McMahan), I didn't spend very much time learning in person from anyone. Most of my development came from playing in jam sessions and for dances and listening to CDs.

I believe that in order to learn a style, listening to it is just as important as practicing it. As a teen I would listen quite obsessively to one old-time CD or another, often fixating for multiple days on certain tracks that I just couldn't get enough of, before moving on to something else.

I did have the occasional breakthrough when attending fiddle workshops—I learned the "pulse" bowing technique from a workshop taught by Matt Wyatt.[41]

Roger Netherton. (Courtesy of Robin Netherton)

Netherton's repertory is substantial and broad. Like many fiddlers who read music, he pulls tunes from books, but he learns most of his repertoire from listening, not reading. He plays interesting versions of classics from Missouri and the Midwest, such as "Old Jeff City" ("Katon's Reel," "Katon's Hornpipe") and tunes associated with Nebraska's Bob Walters, worked up with personal touches and variations.

Roger's participation in fiddle contests was, like everyone else's, a learning experience. By 2012, he was gaining a reputation. Already a solid old-time fiddler and rapidly learning tunes and techniques, Roger was unfamiliar to most of the Missouri contest fiddlers outside the St. Louis area. At a May 2012 contest at a community festival in Hermann, to the surprise of some of the old guard, the reserved teenager took second place in the Open Division, behind Junior Marriott and just ahead of John Williams. Netherton could have entered the Junior Division but chose to try his luck among some of Missouri's nameplate contest champions. It was clear that the usual winners were going to need to make room for Roger Netherton.

In August that year, Robin took Roger on a three-day excursion to three of the better-known hard-core Missouri contests. They chose well, taking in annual contests of long history and different character—the Montgomery County Old Threshers Festival contest in Montgomery City (administered by the Missouri Fiddlers and Country Music Association, with their rules), St. James (administered by Karen Roskowske and a local group, with their rules), and the Missouri state championships at the state fair in Sedalia (with their rules).

Roger entered these contests and did well, generally playing in an Appalachian style. His manner of performance (sitting down and for some tunes playing solo) and some of the tunes he played were not known to the other fiddlers and audiences. He sometimes played a tune solo because he was unfamiliar with the available backup guitarists, but also because he knew they were unfamiliar with his tune or his version of a tune. As Robin recalls, "Three days, three festivals, three fiddle contests, four prizes—but overall, Roger decided he has a lot more fun playing at dances and jams."[42] As he says:

> I have always enjoyed playing for contra dances, for a myriad of reasons. For one, I love watching the dancers enjoying themselves. I enjoy playing the music itself, of course, but I especially enjoy being able to express the tune in different ways during the many repetitions that occur during an 8 or 10-minute dance (given that these fiddle tunes usually only last thirty seconds before repeating). And as I've grown and developed as a contra dance musician, I have become fascinated with learning different ways to change the energy level and dynamic contour of the music to elevate the experience of the dancers.[43]

My impression of seeing Roger fiddle in those contests was that most of the other fiddlers were impressed with his technical skills but somewhat curious and critical of his eclecticism and apparent focus on what, back in 2012, they were hearing as "Appalachian" fiddling rather than "Missouri" fiddling or "contest fiddling."

Netherton might have done what others do in preparing for competitions by choosing tunes that are popular and "winners" in Missouri and practicing to perfection. However, to win first place in a contest such as the state-fair contest could mean adjusting his performance style and arrangements (as well as, perhaps, tune selection) in order to compete with the familiar repertoire and styles of established fiddlers. All contest fiddlers go through that process to some extent, but such changes do not seem to be part of Netherton's approach to playing the fiddle.

The national and international festivals where all styles are welcome and campground jam sessions are the rule became Roger's favorites. At festivals such as Clifftop and Winfield, Roger began competing in the youth division, working his way to the winners' limelight, and then moved into the adult division. On his fifth journey to the Walnut Valley Festival in Winfield, Kansas, in September 2016, Netherton won all the marbles by taking first place in the highly competitive Old-Time Fiddle adult division. In previous trips to Winfield, Roger had taken second or third place. At Winfield there are two rounds of competition. In the preliminary round in 2016, Roger played "Highlander's Farwell," "Ookpik Waltz," and "Polecat Blues" and, in the finals, "Smith's Reel" and "Blue Moon Waltz." When the results were announced and he came back onstage to treat the crowd with further music, he played "Chips and Sauce" and "Tippin' Back the Corn." His championship prizes included a trophy, a check for $275, a Heinrich Gill X-5 violin, a yellow Winfield ball cap, sunglasses, and a swag bag of festival memorabilia.[44]

After high school, Netherton came to Columbia for college at the University of Missouri with a scholarship to study mathematics and statistics and graduated with honors in 2017. He is employed as a data analyst at a St. Louis company. Roger performs with a variety of bands and accompanists and travels extensively to fiddle for contra and square dances. Among his current groups are Roger and the Nethertones, with West Virginia friends Rachel Eddy, Hunter Walker, and Alex Lacquement; Run Down Boots; the Hot Club of St. Louis (Joe Park, guitar; Paul Davis, rhythm guitar; and Guy Cantonwine, upright bass); and the Triplets of Grubville swing trio.

Roger's 2018 CD, *Roger Netherton*, features a number of unusual tunes, such as "John Stenson's No. 2" (popularized by Cathy Barton and Dave Para at their Big Muddy Festivals), midwestern tunes such as "Ol' Bob" (from Garry Harrison), intriguing interpretations of old standards such as an unusual version of "Durang's Hornpipe," and his composition "Blue Moon Waltz."[45] The style can be generally called Appalachian style, with clawhammer banjo backup and overall feel of the music, but Netherton has his own distinctive style that gives his fiddling something extra. A two-fiddles-only track with Rachel Eddy presents a version of the Kentucky tune (often attributed to Ed Haley) "Half Past Four," exhibiting the intricacies and beauties of two fiddles unaccompanied.

During the COVID-19 pandemic, Netherton presented informal one-man concerts on YouTube, playing a range of tunes on violin, guitar, and mandolin and discussing their history. In the live programs, Netherton responds to viewers' and listeners' comments in real time.

Listen to track 23 on the companion CD to hear Roger Netherton's version of "Tippin' Back the Corn."

Othello Smith and his brother Cloyd Smith (banjo) after a day's work hewing railroad ties, 1930s, near Cole Camp, Missouri. As a child, Travis Inman drew inspiration to learn to play fiddle music from watching and listening to his Uncle Othello. (Courtesy of Dianne Peck)

Travis Inman— "I Try to Play it Clean" 10

Ask Travis how he got interested in playing the fiddle, and he'd warn you, "It's a tale that'll take all night to tell." My great-aunt, Kate Swearngin, a Cherokee Indian woman, was the Oklahoma state champion back in the 1920s. My dad played the fiddle, and so did my uncles, and all kinds of relatives are musicians of one kind or another."

—Instructor profile, Bethel Youth Fiddle Camp, 2016

Travis Inman followed in the footsteps of his mentors, Kelly Jones and Pete McMahan, and took his turn as one of Missouri's most compelling and successful contest fiddlers. Inman enjoyed a good run, four decades as an elite contest fiddler and holder of thirteen state titles. Travis won so many trophies that he lost count when the pile passed two hundred. He was a fiddler who succeeded in the contest world while staying true to his roots in old-time Missouri fiddling.[1]

The Inmans came to American from northern England. "And how they got their name, they claim that they were inn-keepers and prize fighters. That's how they got their name." Among the first in his family to emigrate from England were brothers Shadrach, Meshach, and Abednego Inman. "Just like the ones [names] in the Bible. And I'm not so sure which one, but one of 'em was traveling with Daniel Boone and I think it was Shadrach. Was travelin' with Daniel Boone and he got it in the head with a tommy hawk. And that was the end of *him*. So, the other two brothers came on up around Nixa, Missouri. There's a bunch of Inmans in Springfield, and some of 'em spell it Inman and some of 'em spell it Inmon."

Born in America, Travis's grandfather was Isaac Luther (Jack) Inman, part English and part Irish. "He was a little, wiry Irishman. He was incredibly good with horses and mules." Jack's wife, Travis's paternal grandmother, was Orpha Sidebottom Inman, from the Eldon, Missouri, area. Travis said that Jack Inman was a tough man, and Travis saw some of that toughness in his father, Bob Inman; they were not large or tall men, but "very well put together" and "very strong."[2] Jack Inman's father was Golden Abriel (G. A.) Inman, recalled by family members as a "the best brawler in Arkansas" in the nineteenth century.[3] G. A. Inman was reared in Poplar Bluff in southeast Missouri and lived in Arkansas before moving to Eldon, Missouri. "I don't know what he did over there—I think he was a tailor, making soldiers' uniforms in a factory. Then he moved to Cole Camp and then had his family there, and that's where my dad come from. So I was raised right there in that Cole Camp and Stover area."

Travis's father, Robert Forest (Bob) Inman, was born in Eldon and settled on a farm on Indian Creek in Benton County, six miles south of Cole Camp. His mother was Hazel Brown Inman.[4] Travis was born Kelly Travis Inman in April 1963. Cole Camp was founded by old-stock Missourians and by the Civil War had become a decidedly German settlement mostly of Lutherans and Low German speakers. The German community was faithful to the Union during the Civil War amid prevailing prosecession communities around them, and after the war the old "southern" population was generally replaced in commercial, landowning, and political influence by the German American families who had the luck of being on the winning side. Cole Camp was famed for its cornet bands and music, and today German dancing and music are revived at *Maifest* and *sangerfest* celebrations. "Wilkommen" graces downtown signs.

Travis's mother's people were Swearngins, Cherokee people in Tahlequah, near the reservation in northeastern Oklahoma.[5] His great-aunt Kate Swearngin is said to have been an Oklahoma state champion in the 1920s and lived on the reservation.[6] Kate's brothers John W. and Jim Swearngin came to Benton County in central Missouri, John settling near Lincoln (where his son "Doc" was born and reared)[7] and Jim in the Cole Camp area.

> The Swearngins, they all played music, played square dances. I remember going down to Uncle John's and Uncle Doc's when I was a kid and listening to them play old fiddle tunes that you never hear anymore.[8] We had these gatherings when I was a kid where everyone would come over on a Friday night, and the women would bring pies and cakes and all kinds of snacks, and the musicians would start playing along before dark, and play until two or three in the morning. There was no alcohol or anything like that. Everyone just swapped stories, swapped songs and swapped recipes.[9]

First, We Learned to Play Backup

Travis (born in April 1963) started playing guitar at seven, "trying to learn chords," so he could accompany his father's fiddling at music parties and play hymns in church services. "I played for Dad, you know, he was a three-fingered fiddle player. He had that pinky finger [left hand, his chording hand] crippled in a motorcycle accident in France in World War Two, and never could use his little finger."[10] What guitar backup style did Travis play for his dad?

> I just played open, straight chords, that's all we knew. Dad had an old Gibson guitar, I think it was a J-50. I learned to play on that. Dad would go to church and play his fiddle, and I'd sit there and play guitar with him. I was just a little feller. Sister played the piano. We played old gospel hymns, and we did more upbeat type stuff like "I Saw the Light" and that sort of stuff.
>
> And Dad would go to people's houses and entertain. He'd entertain at the nursing homes. He'd play fiddle tunes like "Soldier's Joy" and "Ragtime Annie" and "Rubber Dolly" and stuff that you could play with three fingers that you could kinda get through. His waltzes were pretty ragged because he couldn't use his pinky finger. But he did all right with it. We'd entertain around locally, y'know. We'd go to a pie supper.

Mrs. Inman became a devout Pentecostal, and church leaders did not approve of dancing. "Dad wouldn't play a square dance. He was a religious man. He was a part-time Pentecostal preacher. Him and Mom was very much against dances. They had done it in their earlier years, and then when they got older they got into *church* and they were like, y'know, it was totally different. I was raised up in a real religious household, . . . they was going this-a-way, and I went *errrr*. I was drinkin' beer, and gettin' in trouble in school—aw, *man*."

Travis Inman began playing fiddle music at twelve. At twenty-five in 1987, he won first place in the Open Division at the Saline County Fair in Marshall, Missouri. For many years the Marshall contest was a major competition and attracted numerous top-drawer contestants. (Photo by Howard Marshall)

It is not surprising that church leaders criticized fiddlers and fiddle music for the inappropriate behavior that took place at dances. Things could get crossways at a dance, yet dances were entertainment and many people's sole occasion to leave work behind, get cleaned up, and go out and enjoy themselves. Stories about trouble at dance halls seem humorous today; people like to tell them deadpan. How bad could things get, though?

Y'know, yeah, they had that dance hall over there east of Cole Camp, and I told ya that my uncle [Othello Smith] and his brother was playin' out there—he was my uncle by marriage, it was my mother's sister's husband. He played out there, him and his brother—they was *old-time* fiddlers, played "Dance around Molly" and all them old tunes *just as good as you could play 'em.* On what tunes they played, they played 'em *good.* His name was *Othello Smith* and his brother's name was *Phillip.* And Othello, he talked with that ree'al heel'billy slang ree'al bad. He was a little bitty ol' guy, just about that tall. He walked like this [gesture: limp] because he had a horse fall on him when he was younger, and broke his leg and one leg was about that much shorter than the other 'un [gestures two to three inches with hand].

And he called his brother "Fee'lip"—he said, "Me and '*fee*'lip' was playin' over there at that *Crocker* at Crocker one night, and we's settin' there in the doorway a-playin," and he said, "they've got into it outside there, and," he said, "that one guy just fired up a chain saw and cut the other un's arm off. And after that they called the place 'the chain saw inn.'"[11]

The Allure of the Contest Scene

In 1974 Bob Inman took his eleven-year-old son to see some fiddle playing at a contest in the community building at Warsaw, a few miles south of Cole Camp.[12] Held in conjunction with the annual heritage festival, Warsaw paid good prize money and drew top contest fiddlers such as Dean Johnston, Lee Stoneking, and Kelly Jones. Excited by the competition and inspired by "real fiddlers" he saw perform, Travis made up his mind to become a fiddler, too.

Learning was easier said than done. His father owned several violins and did his own repairs, but he was particular about his violins and bows and did not like anyone handling them. "If Dad caught you touching a fiddle of his, he'd thrash you. So, I waited until my mom was outside hanging laundry one day, and I climbed up and looked in the cabinets and found an old fiddle that he taken apart. It had no keys and no strings. I rummaged around in dad's spare parts and found the keys and put strings on. But I didn't have any idea how to tune it. I had to get dad's fiddle out of its case to find out how to tune it. And I used his bow and started sawing."

Travis began going over to his uncle Othello Smith's dairy farm, near the Inman farm, and Othello taught him some basic tunes. Travis would go over after school to help milk cows and do chores, and then, after supper, "the fiddle would come out" and Othello would play for Travis. Three months later, Travis entered the Junior Division in the next Warsaw contest and won first place. It wasn't until then that he worked up the nerve to tell his father what he had been up to. "Dad just flat out didn't believe me. I had to get the fiddle out and play the tunes for him," the tunes he played in the contest. "You only had to play three tunes in the competition. It was a good thing, because that's all I knew."[13]

Travis's parents had a record player, and he began learning tunes from LPs by laying quarters on the arm above the needle in order to slow a record down enough for him to catch the notes. He listened especially close to Tommy Jackson square-dance LPs from Nashville. The youngster also learned tunes from Sac River Jones, who lived in the area. "Sac was an awful fine fiddle player, an old-time dance fiddler. When I was growin' up down in there, there was a lot of good fiddle players living up in those hills, you know, dance fiddlers."

Another influence was Virgil Burns. "Virgil was a monster fiddle player. [His wife] didn't like him playin'—so he didn't own a fiddle. One time he went to a fiddle contest in Cole Camp years ago, when I was a small boy, and he got up there, and he borrowed somebody's fiddle, and wound up playin', and won the contest on a borrowed fiddle. That's what kind of a good player he was. He died when I was in my early twenties, and I never got to spend the time with him that I really wanted to." Another fiddler was Milton Taylor, a local veterinarian. "Milton played a few fiddle tunes on the fiddle, and when I was a little bitty boy, I used to go over and listen to Milton fiddle. And Milton played the old 'Blue Mule,' and he played it in C. And the only people I ever heard play that was him and my great-uncles, the Swearngins."[14]

Travis spoke about some interesting contests he attended as a child:

> They had a fiddle contest years ago up at Cole Camp [in the American Legion fall], where they had a bunch of people, trucking companies, that got together and they had a fiddle contest. Each trucker had to pick a fiddle player to represent them in a fiddle contest. And then the trucking company would wind up gettin' whatever prizes they got [if their fiddler placed in the prize money]. I was just about that tall. If you knew a good fiddle player somewhere, you'd want him to represent them in the fiddle contest.
>
> And then, they had another one there, at the American Legion, several years later, and I was *bigger*. And there was a fiddle player come from Boonville, that Musial Wolfe knew, and he was the first man I ever heard play "Orange Blossom Special." And I thought he did an exceptionally good job on it.
>
> Did you ever hear of Dickie Philips? He played that fiddle on his *lap*, and could *bow* that fiddle, layin' it down and playin' it flat on his lap, and he *just eat it up*. He played jazz and everything. One of the finest fiddle players you'd ever hear. He's been dead for years. He learned to play it like that when he was a little bitty kid and never did change it. But he went to Warsaw to a contest at Jubilee Days, in the late seventies, and you know what kind of fiddlers they had down *there*, they *all* come out. I think first place was maybe a hundred bucks. And the damn thing lasted half the night. He showed up down there and was gonna play [in the contest], and they wouldn't let him *play*. They would not let him play, because the *rules* were *then* that you had to *stand up* and put the fiddle *under the chin*. And that was in the Missouri rules. You had to be able to stand up and hold the fiddle under your chin.[15] They wouldn't let him in the contest, but they had him come out and *entertain*. And, boy, Dad's sittin' there with me and he said, "If that guy had *entered* it, there ain't nobody else'd had a *chance*. He was head and shoulders above everybody else." Old fella. *Man*, he could play a *fiddle*.

As Travis began developing his repertoire, he decided to concentrate on a comparatively small number of tunes instead of trying to learn everything.

> I learned just a few tunes and tried to really clean 'em up and play 'em *right.* Rather than learn to play a hundred and fifty or two hundred of 'em and to just run through 'em. There's a lot of guys like that. I don't really understand that—trying to learn every tune you can. I guess it's okay, but I'd rather play a few and play 'em *right*—get the parts right, get the right *chord changes* there, y'know. That was always *my* thing. I'm interested in all them old tunes but I never sat down and tried to learn *every* fiddle tune that was out there. I tried to pick out *classics.* Like these here [tunes on the Jake Hockemeyer 1965 fish fry tape] and try to learn the classic tunes and try to play them really well—something that you could play in a fiddle contest and actually do well with.
>
> You wouldn't want to play something like "Cripple Creek" in a contest, or "Boil them Cabbage." You want to play something that's got some *meat and potatoes* to it. So I tried to learn those classics and polish 'em up and do *well* with 'em.
>
> It seems like, as time goes on, if you don't play those tunes, you *lose 'em.* I know I've lost a lot of 'em. But now I know that if can *hear* 'em again, if I hear a little bit of it, I can play it, you know. It'll come right back real fast. I can learn a tune the same way. I can hear a tune and sit down and *play it* right back to you, but then, by the time I walk out that door, I've forgotten it. It comes easy but it goes easy if you *don't play* it for a while, get it in there [in your memory].

Kelly Jones was a great help to Travis as he was learning as a teenager. Travis's father would drive him over to Stover to Jones's home. Jones was a welcoming, patient teacher and had much to offer. Jones was meticulous in his own playing and conveyed that concern for working out "correct" and effective versions of tunes. As recalled in his interview with Amber Gaddy, at Travis's first visit, "Travis played his newest tune, 'Flop-Eared Mule,' for Kelly. Kelly played it back to him, and just 'played the fire out of it.' Travis went home with stars in his eyes and a promise of lessons. He says 'If it wasn't for him, I wouldn't have become the fiddler I am. Because he showed me technique.'"[16] Decades later, Travis would again study with Jones, in the Missouri Traditional Arts Apprenticeship Program.

Herman Johnson, the perfectionist Oklahoma champion, was another important mentor. "Herman Johnson, he was one of those kinds of players, that, when he played a tune, you could hear it—it literally rang in your head a week or two after you heard him play it."

> Years ago, back in 1979 or 1980, there was a man and woman in Warsaw, Woodrow and Alma Ferguson. They played music at Silver Dollar City, had a family band. I knew him real well since I was a little kid. So when my dad passed away, he and

Alma came up to the house one night, while my mother was livin' out there on the farm, south of Cole Camp. And Woodrow wanted to give me a *horse*. And it was a stallion, and I used to go up there and ride it on his farm, it was a really nice horse. And him and his wife asked my mother if they could *give* me that horse. He had a lot of horses and a lot of big farms that he leased. Momma said, "We can't let you folks give him a *horse*, that just wouldn't be right," and she didn't have the extra money to buy the horse from them, so I didn't get the *horse*.[17]

They said, "We're going to Mountain View, Arkansas, and we'd like to take Travis with us, would you let him?" And I was only sixteen at the time. Mother said, "Yeah, you could take him down there, and expose him to that *fiddle playing*." Well, when we got to Mountain View, *Herman* was down there. So that was the first I had met Herman, that was probably about 1979. And boy was I impressed. He was playing *good*. He was in his sixties. He would stand up there and take requests on stage and play 'em just like he was in a contest. And never miss *nothin'*. [After Herman Johnson's performance, Travis introduced himself.] And I got to crowdin' him a little bit, and asking him to show me stuff, an' he'd say, "Well, pull that chair right over here by me." So I'd get as close to him as I could, and watch him. We exchanged phone numbers and we got to be best friends. He'd call me and ask me if I was going to be somewhere [at a contest] and I'd do him the same way, and that's how I got acquainted with him. Super guy.

Herman wasn't really a *Texas style* fiddler player. He wasn't *old-time*, but he was kind of—as Junior Marriott's dad, ol' Bunney Marriott said, he was a "duke's mixture." But I called him a *contest style fiddler*. He was the only fiddle player to play at Weiser ever to beat Mark O'Connor. He was unbelievable. Like Larry Franklin said on the "Devil's Box" collection of Texas fiddling: "I knew when Herman Johnson come to Texas [to a contest] that we was in real trouble."

Herman Johnson was a "monster swing fiddler" and specialized in Bob Wills and the Texas Playboys songs and dance tunes. Listening to Herman play swing one night, Inman realized that he needed to go home and learn to play swing and "do it right. I liked everything he did." But Travis did not learn by asking Herman Johnson to break tunes apart into phrases. In learning tunes and technique from Johnson, Travis would record Johnson on a cassette recorder. "And I'd have him to play it real slow, just take a tune and play it *draggy* slow. And then I'd take it home and work on it. And the next time I'd see him, I'd hit him for something else." Visiting with Johnson at various events, including fiddlers' conventions at the Western Hills resort in northeastern Oklahoma near Wagoner, where Texas and Oklahoma fiddling and swing were dominant, whetted Travis's appetite for swing fiddle. The jam sessions there were exciting, filling every hallway, nook, and cranny, and fiddlers such as Oklahoma champions J. C. Broughton and Monte and Dave Gaylord frequented the weekend events. Travis learned "Jumping the Strings" (composed by Byron Berline) from Herman Johnson there one year. Arkansas swing fiddler Frankie Kelly was a regular at Wagoner as well as at fiddlers' conventions at Compton Ridge Campground near Branson, where Inman was a regular. Known for his waltz compositions, Inman plays several Frankie Kelly tunes, such as "Eva Anne's Waltz."

In 1998, in album notes for Inman's *Championship Fiddling* (similar to the title of Herman Johnson's first LP), Johnson wrote, "He has the ability to play anything from the very simple to the most difficult tunes with a most pleasing style. His style is of a tonal beauty and melodic accuracy that comes from dedication and hard work."[18]

Travis won major competitions in Missouri as well in other states. "Boy, going to them fiddle contests, that was really icing on the cake. When I was growing up, up there on the farm, I was a kid. There wasn't any way of getting any money unless you worked out in the *hay*—you know, puttin' up hay and back then it was bucking square bales. And we was always needing money."

In September 1979, at fifteen or sixteen, Travis hitched a ride to the state contest in Columbia. Held in the Hickman High School auditorium, this was the first state competition of the Missouri State Oldtime Fiddlers' Association. Pete McMahan took first in the hotly contested Open Division, followed by Jake Hockemeyer and other familiar champions—including a fresh new face on the big stage, Travis Inman. Inman won fourth place, a landmark in his career.

> They didn't have a junior division at that time in the state contest, just open and senior. I didn't have no way to get there, Dad had just passed away and we lived way back out there south of Cole Camp on a gravel road. And boy it was hot still—September. So, I took off walking up that road with my fiddle case. I had a jar of drinking water, and there was a lady lived out there, she picked me up and gave me a ride to Cole Camp. And I got to Cole Camp, I got out there on the blacktop, started thumbin' a ride. And I caught a ride all the way to Columbia [c. 80 miles away]. Pete won the contest and he had that *gold cup* [a large brass traveling loving cup]. And I was standing there licking my chops and thinking, boy, I sure would like to have one of them gold cups.

It was a few years before Inman brought home the state-contest cup, a traveling trophy engraved with the names of winners and years. If a fiddler won three years in a row, he or she could keep the cup, but otherwise it was brought back to the contest each year. Names on the cup—Pete McMahan three years in a row, then Jake Hockemeyer in 1982, and Junior Marriott won for the first time in 1983 (Inman came in third in 1983). "Then Pete took it back from Junior" in 1984, and then "Junior took it back from Pete" in 1985. In 1986, the contest moved to the Columbia Fall Heritage Festival in Nifong Park. "And I showed up in '86 playing 'High Level Hornpipe' in B-flat. I had it nice, a salted-down version of it that I thought would work, and it *did*. I got the *cup* that year and took it home. And then I wound up winning it in '87 and '88 and kept it. And I've still got it, and it's probably my most cherished trophy that I have."[19]

Inman kept some fifty trophies in a storage unit; around 2010, he took the rest of his two-hundred-plus trophies to Bill Shull's home in Warrensburg so that Shull could recycle them for future contests that he administers. (Photo courtesy of Travis Inman)

Travis alluded to how contests often attracted several top-level fiddlers who all could have won first place. They were well acquainted, and any one of four or five people could win a contest on any given day. Often at contests those top players would kind of "switch it around." When Travis was a young man, the gang of the older predictable winners in the Open Division included names such as Pete McMahan, Jake Hockemeyer, and Cyril Stinnett. Audiences did not seem to mind, because they clearly were top contenders. When Travis Inman was himself taking home championship trophies in the later 1980s and 1990s, the predictable winners in the Open Division at most contests would include, besides Inman, names such as McMahan, Charlie Walden, John Griffin, and Junior Marriott.

Most fiddlers accepted the results of the judging with a good attitude, even though they may be disappointed not to rank higher. Some fiddlers had volatile personalities and could take it personally if the "wrong" fiddler won. At Clinton the year Inman won first place, he beat Ace Sewell, an Oklahoma champion. "And, boy, Ace was mad. And he was drunk. And he was gonna whup me—he was gonna give me a butt-whuppin' right there on the square. And ol' Bill Kearns, standin' right there, turned around and looked and he said, 'Ace, you touch that boy and I'll kick your ass all over this place.' And he [Sewell] didn't do nothin' either! I'll never forget that. He went *on* [Sewell], he decided that he wasn't gonna mess with Mister Kearns. I miss that ol' boy, and I miss Bill Eddy, too."[20]

Inman remembers his favorite contests as the state competitions developed by the Missouri State Old Time Fiddlers Association in its early years in the 1980s when the contest was still held in Columbia. Champions like McMahan, Hockemeyer, and McBaine were there, and Texas style/Contest Style had not yet become the winning style in Missouri. "I'll be honest with you, I went to a lot of 'em. I won a lot of 'em and lost a lot of 'em. But I think the most important contest, to *me—not no more—* but back when they was holding it in *Columbia*, the Missouri state fiddle championship, to me was the most prestigious contest that I ever played in. Back when they had the cup in it. I really think it was. Bill Shull and Charlie Walden did it *right*. I loved it when they'd come down for the contest [the old masters that Travis looked up to]. You know, you give Taylor [McBaine] a good day, and he'd clean your plow for ya. He was *dangerous* even when he was *old*."

Inman competed in the state contest in Tennessee at Clarksville and the bigger "Tennessee Valley" contest in Athens, Alabama. Both contests have drawn fiddlers from Missouri through the years, including Pete McMahan and Matt Wyatt. Both contests have also seen the displacement of old-time and bluegrass fiddle styles by Contest Style. Travis was invited in the early 2000s to the Great Plains Championships at Yankton, South Dakota, winning first place in the National Invitational Division fall contest both times he entered, 2004 and 2005.

> You know, I went down to Tennessee and won the state contest down there, in '87, I believe it was. And then I went back, I got invited back to *judge*. Charlie Butler was runnin' it. So Herman [Johnson] and I went back down there, I think it was in '88, and me and Charlie and Herman judged it. Brandon Apple won it that year—boy out of Arkansas—and I think Randy Howard [Nashville, TN] might have got second. I can't remember—it's been too long; as they say, too much water under the bridge. And, then, I went to *Athens*—played there three years ago (2016). I didn't play well, I didn't have a good day. I think if I'd have had, I would've won it. As many fiddlers as they had, I wound up winning third place. I just didn't play good. You know how you have off-days and you just can't find your *butt*? That's the way it was that day.
>
> What do I think of today's Missouri fiddle contests? I guess I'll just tell you my honest opinion about it. Well, when the fiddlers' association went *out* [MSOTFA went on hiatus in the 1990s], they don't pay the good money that they used to have, y'know. So most generally, the money's a hundred or a hundred and fifty dollars at best. Then, you gotta *deal with* all these people who are pure Texas style fiddle players. And *then*, that's not so bad, but [now] the *judges* are Texas style or oriented, too, they *lean toward* Texas style. So your straight, old-time fiddle player, he's just kind of left out there, shakin' his head. So that's basically what's happened to the state contest in Sedalia] I know that's why Kelly quit, and that's why I quit, and Levi, he don't

care nothin' about fiddle contests. Since then, Bill Shull has taken over running the Sedalia contest again and, in my opinion, things are back on the level now.[21]

Travis Inman was a fiddler who saw it all, won hundreds of contests, and saw the times change the style of fiddling that gets the most rewards at contests. Travis Inman got the most enjoyment not in contests but in "gettin' together and having a jam."

Well, I'll tell ya what. Back in the eighties, back when the Association was big, we used to drive all the way from Stover plumb up to Montgomery City—where Virgil [Smith] lived—for seventy-five bucks, and never thought nothin' about it. We never thought nothin' about the money. It wasn't *about the money in those days*. It was about the prestige of going and kicking somebody's *butt*. That's what it was *about*.[22]

Well, I mean, the way gas is now, yeah, you *have* to look at the money. I can't afford to drive that half-ton pickup truck plumb across the state for seventy-five bucks—I'll be in debt when I get home. But back then, we didn't care. It wasn't about the money, back then, you know, gas was probably eighty-nine cents a gallon, and we thought, boy, *if Pete's up there*, we gotta go up there and *kick his butt*. And I know he probably thought the same thing. And Kelly was the same way back then.

We didn't try to dodge each other. *Now*, people [fiddlers] try to *dodge* somebody—"Well, so-and-so's gonna go over *there*, so we don't want to go over there, we'll go this one over *here*. That wasn't the way it was in the eighties, we went to every one we could go to, because we loved the *challenge* of gettin' up there dukin' it *out*. It wasn't about the money. But it's changed, it's all changed.

Boy, *Pete was good*, he was hard to *beat* in them days. And when you beat him, you'd *done* something.

Let me tell ya a story. I'll make it quick. When I was starting to play the fiddle contests, and we would go out and play the *breakdowns*, once in a blue moon we could beat Pete in a fiddle contest. But normally he would win. And when I started out, he'd beat ya eighty-five percent of the time.

Well, I could play good breakdowns, but *waltzes* wasn't my forte *then*. And I told my mother—my dad had already passed away—I said, "I'm gonna have to start doin' something *different* if I'm gonna keep *doin'* this, because it ain't worth my *time* if I keep goin' the way I'm goin'."

She said, "Well, what're you gonna do?" And I said, "Well, I'm gonna have to learn to play *waltzes* better than *he* does." Well, he played them B-flat waltzes and I mean he just *ate 'em up*.

Well, so I told Mother, she asked me what I wanted for Christmas. And I said, "I'll tell ya what I want for Christmas, I want to go and pick out about eight or ten of them 33 rpm LPs from *Weiser*, and I'm gonna learn a bunch of them high-powered waltzes and start playin' 'em in contests."[23] Well, they *weren't old-time* waltzes and they weren't played up to what they call dance speed, either. They were strictly *fiddle contest pieces*. And that's where that "Memory Waltz" came from and

> the "Yellow Rose" and a bunch of them I used to play all the time, "50 Years Ago Waltz," "Rosebuds of Avamore."
>
> So once I learned a bunch of them waltzes and polished 'em up and got the right *chord changes* behind 'em, it started revolving around the *other* way—I got to winning a lot more. And then *Junior* started learning 'em too.

Weiser LPs were recorded by Don Cedarstrom in Boise. American Heritage record company in Caldwell, Idaho, founded by Loyd Wanzer, put out several LPs of fiddlers who were popular at the Weiser contests, including Wanzer, Harold Allen, Bill Long, and others.[24] Travis Inman learned "White Rose Waltz" from Nebraska fiddler (relocated in Oregon) Harold Allen, on his 1960s LP *Waltz Around.* Allen composed "Red Fox Waltz," a favorite among Missouri fiddlers. Another of the big "Weiser waltzes" are Howdy Forrester's "Memory Waltz" and "Yellow Rose Waltz" that Travis learned from a Texas Shorty 45-rpm record.[25]

Kelly Jones is one whose waltzes were a vital ingredient in contest success. Unlike Travis, rather that working on complicated waltzes, Kelly Jones chose comparatively spare waltzes and likes old favorites that most people (and judges) recognize, such as "Over the Waves"—and he plays them to perfection.

> Kelly never played *hard waltzes.* He'd play something like "Missouri Waltz" or "Waltz of the Wind"—which is an old Hank Williams song. He'd play something simple and just play it gorgeously *beautiful.* He would play the real pretty stuff, but he played simple stuff on the waltzes. And he was very smart for *doin' that,* because it sure lessens your chances for a *mistake.* But—if you're not making a mistake once in a while, you're not *playin'.* So we tried to learn the hardest stuff we could. So anyway, that's how it changed [Travis's success in contests].

"Finally, Branson just got *so Texas,* that there was never any way to win it unless you played Texas style." Did he ever travel to Weiser for the National Oldtime Fiddlers' Contest? "No. I always thought Weiser might've been just a little too far from my house."[26]

Inman decided to try his luck at a well-advertised fiddle contest at Dixon Mounds, an Illinois State Museum archaeological site and public park near Lewistown. Nile Wilson, Charlie Walden, and others from Missouri attended. Inman thought about what that contest might be like and tried to prepare accordingly:

> They had a big fiddle contest up there and it paid good money. And Wes Brown was playing guitar for us then. Wes was a *killer* guitar player. And Kelly was playin' fiddle contests strong back then, so me and Kelly rode up with Wes in Wes's car. And I knew there was gonna be some hellacious fiddlin' there that day, and I thought, damn, I sure would like to win that money, 'cause it was a good *purse.* I got up there, and Charlie Walden was one of the *judges.* And I thought, ahhh, that was gonna make it a lot easier. Charlie knows what he's listening to. So I played "High

Level Hornpipe," "Garfield's Hornpipe" (a.k.a. "Blue Water Hornpipe") and "Ozark Mountain Waltz," all of 'em in B-flat. *Won it.* First round, they didn't have a second round, didn't even have call backs. Played one round, *done.* Went home. That was a good 'un. It was a long ways from the *house*, but like I say, back then we didn't care how far we had to drive and the money really didn't matter that much. It was like, you was just goin' and *beatin'* somebody.

The mention of what keys work best in competitions brings out strong views. Many contest fiddlers carefully sort their contest repertoire into sets of tunes in different keys, which may help convey to judges one's versatility (and taste). To some extent the choice depends on the quality of the contest itself, the expected competition that day, and the sophistication of the judges. If the judges were unaware of the difficulty of playing hornpipes in B-flat or F, for example, one might decide to just rip off a hot square-dance tune in a "simple" key like G or D. Inman, however, prefers to play the tough B-flat tunes whenever possible—Howdy Forrester's "High Level Hornpipe," for instance, which only elite players play well. Inman felt that B-flat tunes are better in contests, in most cases, as they are difficult, and even the best performers run the chance of blundering in a complicated passage in hornpipes like "High Level," "Golden Eagle," or "Blue Water."[27] Now and then, Travis would change things up and play his three tunes in his round in the same key. One year to win at the state fair at Sedalia, he played "Hell among the Yearlings," "Country Waltz," and "Woodchopper's Hornpipe": "D chord tunes. I thought they might work if you played 'em *really clean*, and it worked."

Inman's typical selections for a contest round included breakdowns such as "Angus Campbell," "Grey Eagle, "Tom and Jerry," "Bill Cheatem," "Jack of Diamonds," "Sally Goodin," "Jack Danielson's Reel," "Boil the Cabbage Down,"[28] "Fiddler's Dream," "Bitter Creek," "Sugar Tree Stomp," "Hooker's Hornpipe," "Leather Britches," "Fiddler's Dream," "Woodchopper's Reel" (a.k.a. "Woodchopper's Hornpipe"), "Tennessee Wagner," or "Garfield's Hornpipe" (a.k.a. "Blue Water Hornpipe").[29] For the waltz, Travis typically presented "Fifty Years Ago Waltz," "Martin's Waltz," "Wednesday Night Waltz," "Memory Waltz," "Blackhawk Waltz" (G; a.k.a. "Cabri Waltz" and "Capri Waltz"),[30] "Clark's Waltz," "The A Waltz" (a.k.a. "Charlie Cook's A Waltz"), "Festival Waltz," "Yellow Rose Waltz," or "Rosebuds of Avamore."[31] For his tune of choice, Inman sometimes played "Peacock Rag," "Pig Ankle Rag," "Red Apple Rag," or "Cotton Patch Rag." As swing gained influence in contests, Travis began to play swing tunes such as "Sweet Georgia Brown" rather than a rag.[32]

In 1984, Inman participated in the WOS Reunion to celebrate the legendary fiddle contests broadcast over WOS-AM in Jefferson City in the 1920s and early 1930s. The event was held in the state capitol rotunda in Jefferson City and included fiddlers and accompanists who had been in original WOS contests.[33] Travis won first place in the Open Division (Cecil Goforth, second; Henry Thompson, third), and Pete McMahan won first in the Seniors. In Columbia in 1989, Inman took part in the Cope Ashlock Invitational Fiddle Contest, a mock competition that aired live over KOPN 89.5 FM.

The Apprentice Becomes the Master

Inman was an instructor for years at the Bethel Fiddle Camp and in the Traditional Arts Apprenticeship Program and gave private lessons. The lessons and teaching method he absorbed from Kelly Jones stayed with him. "That's the way I teach students today."

In 1989, Travis was Jones's apprentice in the TAAP program. The program usually requires that the pupil have at least the rudiments of playing a violin in hand. First, student and teacher discuss what tune is to be tried and worked on, which implies a fiddle tune that both people know or that the teacher knows and knows the student wants to learn.

Back in the 1970s when Inman learned from Jones, Jones would first play a fiddle tune through in its entirety and then slow down the tune and repeat it carefully. He would then ask Travis to play it or any parts of it he had a grip on. He then would work on troublesome patches—going phrase by phrase: play it for Travis, listen to Travis play it back, make suggestions, "and repeat." Then the phrases were pulled together, resulting in the whole tune.

In the TAAP program, students are expected to record lessons so they can study the recordings before the next lesson. Ear training is very important, and Jones urges students to listen, to use their ears more than their eyes. Rote replication of a teacher's version of a tune is not encouraged, but often this is a useful first step toward the student internalizing the music and technique and then, as it matures, evolving their own interpretation that, at best, is both a quotation of the taught melody and a personal expression. "I teach Levi Roden that way. I'll play him a phrase [a few notes] and make him play it back to me. And if he messes it up, I'll make him go back and do it again. And we'll do that over an' over an' over an' over, if it takes him fifty times. But it never does, he gets it about the third time through. He gets it *quick*." Inman's students in the TAAP program included Roden, Clayton Beall, Olivia and Carlie Cunningham, Brett Dudenhoeffer, Amanda Murphree-Roberts, and Liz Kehl.

Levi Roden

Levi Roden of Purdy, in southwest Missouri's Barry County, born in 1982, started lessons with Travis Inman in 1993. Roden became fascinated with fiddling at age eleven. His great-grandfather Dick Roden gave him a violin, and Levi's real inspiration was seeing Travis in 1993 at a hootenanny in a country schoolhouse in McDowell, a few miles east of Purdy. Levi and his father, Steve, had attended some of the hoots there, which featured bluegrass bands and country singers; they enjoyed the shows, but the music did not interest Levi. Hearing Travis warm up in the back, getting ready to play when his turn came, hit Levi like a lightning bolt. Steve and Levi introduced themselves to Travis, and within a short time Steve began driving Levi to Travis's house for fiddle lessons.[34]

The fiddle music Roden heard before meeting Inman was mainly the contest-oriented fiddling of Herman Johnson and others. "It was great, but it was all contest fiddling, and that's it." There seemed to no one around Purdy playing old-time fiddle. Levi's grandfather Leroy Harris played the guitar. After getting started with Inman in 1993, Steve took Levi to the Bethel fiddle camp some three hundred miles away in northern Missouri. Levi then apprenticed with Inman in the TAAP program in 1996 and 1997. An "ear musician" and quick learner, Roden proved an able student and became a contest champion in his own right. Long after their TAAP lessons, Roden continues to learn from Inman, and they continue to get together to play.

In May 2019, Travis invited me to a jam session in Steve Roden's machine shed with Travis, Levi Roden, and their cousins Andy Harris (guitar) and Rick Harris (bass). Levi and the Harrises play in a country music and gospel band. When I asked Travis what the fiddling would be like, he said, "There won't be no Texas fiddling at this jam session. It'll be old-time fiddle tunes that day!"[35]

Levi Roden at a jam session in Steve Roden's machine shed, Purdy, Missouri. (Photo by Howard Marshall, May 2019)

Inman remembered square dances at Ava and how Bob Holt played ultrafast in order to please the dancers there. Travis played for an Ava dance once. "Play 'Boil the Cabbage Down' and the sweat just drippin' off ya, and an old man standin' in front of me [gesturing at Travis] and goin' 'faster, faster!' Hell, he looked like he was about to have a stroke. Finally, I told that one old man, 'I'll tell ya what, have you ever heard of Lee Stoneking?' I said, 'You need to take a listen to some of his music. Ain't nobody played any more square dances than he did. Lee Stoneking never got in a *hurry*.'"[36]

Listen to track 24 on the companion CD to hear Levi Roden's version of "Stony Point."

Levi talked about going to Bethel as a teenager in the 1990s and the square dances in the evening led by Edna Mae Davis and her Ava group. Campers played for dancers in the evenings, often alongside instructors. Bob Holt was an instructor at the time, and Roden, a young fiddler playing a lot of Texas style, was uncomfortable with Holt's ultrafast hoedown tempo.

> *Roden*: "I couldn't stand it because they played so stinkin' fast. I mean it was *fast*—nine hundred miles an hour for nine hours."
>
> *Inman*: "You know, Bob Holt would have been an awfully good fiddler if he'd have played about half that fast."[37]
>
> *Roden*: Another thing I didn't ever understand. For a square dance, they would play *one tune* for about an hour. That got old to me real quick, y'know. I remember, Bob Holt was up there and he would sit there with his left hand on the knee and he'd sit there like this forever. Played with just the tip of the bow, too. Hours, hours.[38]

Olivia Cunningham was Inman's student in the TAAP program in 2011–12, as was her younger sister Carlie, Inman's apprentice in 2015–16.[39] Olivia Cunningham of Fulton (the family has a livestock and horse farm near Millersburg) had played at Hallsville dances, taking a turn as lead fiddler. A confident youngster, Olivia had no problem providing the rhythm and music to keep the dancers happy. The Cunningham sisters were active at contests, too, doing well in the Junior Division. The girls' parents, Cammie and Gary Cunningham, administered fiddle contests in Callaway County until the COVID-19 pandemic put them on hiatus in 2020.

I asked Cammie Cunningham, mother of the four Cunningham girls, about their years studying fiddle with Travis Inman and also about their summer weeks at Bethel Fiddle Camp.

As Cammie explained, "Olivia and then Carlie began classical violin when they were three and three and a half. Sophia began when she was four. By the time Olivia was ten she was beginning to lose interest in classical music, so I bought a fiddle tunes book thinking this might keep her interest. Her violin teacher encouraged the fiddle playing alongside the classical instruction. Since Olivia and Carlie were reading music, they just picked a tune from tune books and learned it by listening and reading the music." In 2008, the Cunninghams heard about the youth fiddle camp at Bethel. "Olivia and Carlie attended that June. Sophia came a few years later when she was old enough. Marta started playing violin when she turned five. She didn't have the formal instruction like the other three had but learned at home; the girls taught her fiddle tunes."[40]

Angus Campbell

as played by Travis Inman 2012

transcribed by Sharon Graf

Travis Inman's "Angus Campbell," a hornpipe composed by J. Scott Skinner for his *Harp and Claymore* (1904) and popular in Britain, Ireland, and Canada; it has been a frequent contest piece in central and north Missouri from the 1960s to the present time. (Transcription by Sharon Graf)

On the TAAP application with Olivia, Travis listed tunes he proposed to teach, several of which she already knew but needed help improving, Missouri standards, favorites of Inman's, and tunes Olivia asked that they work on. Some are titles chosen for contests. The tunes were "Fifty Years Ago Waltz" ("Anniversary Waltz"), "Swearngen's Hornpipe," "Clark's Waltz," "Back in Old Arkansas,"[41] "Wednesday Night Waltz," "Bill Cheatem," "Grey Eagle," "Kiss Me Waltz,"[42] "Cowboy Waltz," "Hooker's Hornpipe," "Gypsy Hornpipe" (from Kelly Jones, Cyril Stinnett, and Casey Jones), "Mississippi Sawyer," "Red Apple Rag," and "Ragtime Annie." On the sampler tape with their application, the tunes are, from Inman, "Fifty Years Ago Waltz," "Miss McLeod's Reel," and "Granny Will Your Dog Bite," and, for Cunningham, "Down Home Rag" (from Vesta Johnson at Bethel fiddle camp), an untitled waltz, and "Whisky before Breakfast."

Travis Inman with Olivia Cunningham in the Traditional Arts Apprenticeship Program at Inman's home in Sedalia. Olivia and her sister Carlie studied with Inman and have been active at square dances and fiddle contests. (Photo by Howard Marshall, April 2012)

Among elements in fiddling that Inman stresses are the importance of getting "drive," old-time phrasing, character, and accent into one's playing. Travis asked Olivia to "snap it up," make her playing more like "fiddling" than like repetitious rote learning. This is sometimes difficult for classical players and essential if one is to become a fiddler as well as a classical violinist. As most pupils do, Olivia asked Travis what is "the right way" to play a certain passage or tune. Travis would show her the notes and play it through, but was careful to repeat the truism that there is no "right way" in this music. Perhaps because Inman was a contest fiddler for so many years, his style exhibited elements of Contest Style in versions of standard tunes. It is hard to avoid doing that. Thus, by teaching his Contest Style versions of tunes, students learned a contest style but one related to the older Little Dixie Missouri style.

Liz Kehl was Travis Inman's student in the TAAP program in 2015. Here, Liz plays her round in a contest at the Trails End Days festival in Sedalia, April 2015, "Angus Campbell," "Clark's Waltz," and "River Road Two-Step" (learned from Inman); her guitar accompanists were Inman (*left*) and Junior Marriott. (Photo by Howard Marshall)

Liz Kehl of Smithton (b. 1982) played viola in the Lee's Summit school program and won honors in state school contests. After marrying and having children, her family moved to her husband's family farm in southeast Pettis County. While in college at Missouri State University in Springfield, Liz played violin and guitar for church and attended fiddle contests, where she met Travis Inman. Liz decided to enter a contest in Bunceton and played "Fort Smith," "Ashoken Farewell," and "Irish Washerwoman."

> Travis came up to me while I was warming up and asked where I was from and if I needed an accompanist. I said yes, and we practiced some. Junior Marriott and Travis both accompanied that contest performance, if memory serves me correctly. After my performance, Travis asked me if I would be interested in some fiddle lessons. I agreed, and we exchanged information. He taught me a couple of lessons before bringing up the TAAP program. I chose to apply for the program because at that time affording lessons would have been very difficult. I was very interested in expanding my musical training to incorporate fiddling.[43]

One of the tunes Liz worked on was "Marmaduke's Hornpipe," a classic Missouri tune with Civil War history long popular in fiddle contests. "In this particular tune, he taught me a 'lick' in 'Marmaduke's Hornpipe' that was handed down to him from his Uncle Othello. I really enjoyed playing this, because it was something I hadn't heard, even in fiddle contests. Travis taught me the uncommon tunes, not the 'standards' often heard repeatedly in contests today. I remember learning 'Gilsaw,' 'Marmaduke's Hornpipe,' 'Rachel,' and others that are not often heard in contests these days. This is what fiddling and TAAP is all about." Liz continues performing on viola in school programs and special occasions, plays fiddle in local jam sessions and postcontest sessions, and gives lessons in both classical violin and old-time fiddling.

Travis Inman retired after almost twenty years of employment at a corporate dog-food processing factory, where he was a jack-of-all-trades, maintaining equipment, driving forklifts and trucks, and pushing buttons on computerized machines.

For many years, Travis played dances and country music shows in Missouri, Kansas, and Oklahoma, in places such as the Truman Lake Opry at Warsaw, the Moose Lodge at Sedalia, and the Treasure Lake RV Park at Branson, where patrons enjoy buffet dinners and dancing. He played weekly senior-citizen dances with a country band at the Saline County fairgrounds at Marshall. Musicians in these bands are seldom more than part-time, often older or retired, and personnel continually changes; they do not play this music for money, although pay at the end of the evening is welcome.

Several years ago, Travis quit competing in contests but helped judge or emcee when asked. He continued recording and reissued his earlier records (see the discography) and continued offering fiddle lessons.

Travis Inman's enthusiasm for making music did not abate, and he never stopped learning. Thinking back to tunes he felt he still needed to polish up, Travis said he planned to sit down and work out Pete McMahan's "Turkey Knob," a tune Pete learned from a Clark Kessinger LP back in the 1970s and used to good effect in contests.[44] "I'm still workin' on it. *Pete*? That old rascal was hard to beat." You and Pete both, Travis. Travis Inman died in February 2022.

Travis grew up listening to the great fiddlers who defined Missouri fiddling. And that influence was always evident in his playing even after he developed his own contest style which for the most part was unlike the prevailing Weiser-derived style. He was his own man and played the way his instincts led him. And damn, what good instincts he had.[45]

Listen to track 25 on the companion CD to hear Travis Inman's version of "Jack Danielson's Reel."

Lee Stoneking, *Missouri Old-Time Fiddlin'* album cover (*verso*).
(Courtesy of Lee Stoneking)

The Stonekings

11

I grew up listening to these fiddles all day and all night and all morning and at noon and every time in between. Many nights I'd fall asleep to the sound of fiddles and wake up to find my dad still a-playing. Or maybe he'd go to sleep himself and get up early and start all over again.

—Fred Stoneking (1996), "Fiddles! Fiddles! Fiddles!"

Certain families seem to exude music, born to it, sustaining and freshening the rivers of tradition. The Stoneking family is one of those and famous for its fiddlers—three in particular, Lee Stoneking, Lee's son Fred, and Fred's daughter Alita. Their experiences represent much of the continuing evolution of fiddle and dance music through the past century. They enjoyed keeping older family tunes in their active repertoires, and, creative people in different generations, each had personal interpretations of fiddle music. Lee played old-time fiddle (and loved swing, too). Fred came along in the 1950s when bluegrass music was growing, and his style and repertoire reflected that. Alita came into fiddling as a young girl in the 1990s as Texas-based Contest Style was increasing in popularity, and she is a nationally prominent contest fiddler.

Lee Stoneking and daughter Judy Vanderville (five-string banjo), Clinton, November 1975. The violin is one of twenty-five he built (including one with wood salvaged from a door from the demolished 1837 Henry County courthouse). (Photo by Howard Marshall)

Lee Stoneking, "Old Smoothie"

Lee Roy Stoneking was a mainstay on the Missouri fiddle scene.[1] From Chilhowee in Johnson County, his family farmed the rolling landscape of hills and prairies in the upper Osage Plains, technically bordering the Ozark Plateau but more like west-central and western Missouri in cultural heritage and geography. Lee's family was a familiar blend from pioneer times of Scottish, Irish, and English settlers with some Cherokee ancestry.

Lee Stoneking began as a youngster playing rhythm guitar and old-time brush-stroke banjo accompaniment for his father, uncles, and other fiddlers in jam sessions at home, dances, and picnics. Lee learned to play fiddle tunes in the manner of his father. Frank came to Missouri from West Virginia and had four other fiddling uncles, Jake, Price, George, and John Stoneking, although Lee preferred to play square-dance tunes at a slower pace than theirs. Lee's first fiddle tune was "Soldier's Joy." His mother, Mary Ellen, played fiddle, piano, reed organ, and a version of old-time brush-stroke parlor banjo (which she taught the children).

Lee caught tunes at house parties, picnics, and dances and from listening to records and radio programs and hearing new tunes at fiddle contests. He did not consider himself a contest fiddler, but Lee Stoneking competed in many contests in Missouri and beyond, such as the Great Plains championships in Yankton, South Dakota. He made lasting friends at Yankton, and his self-produced LP records sold well there. Some of the tunes Lee played at Yankton, such as "Echoes of the Ozarks" and "Old Indiana," went into the Great Plains regional repertoire. Yankton contest administrator Wilbur Foss's cassettes recorded at the contests included Stoneking's "Willott's Hornpipe," "Turkey in the Straw," and "Echoes of the Ozarks."[2] A good entertainer, Lee would sometimes play well-known fiddle tunes such as "Turkey in the Straw" wearing gloves, and then while holding the violin behind his back and between his legs.

When I visited Lee Stoneking in 1975, recording some fiddle tunes accompanied by his daughter Judy, the conversation ranged widely. One of the topics was the differences between old-time and bluegrass fiddling. Lee had just played a standard of the bluegrass repertoire, "Gold Rush" (albeit not as fast as usually played), and a crossover breakdown, "Sally Goodin."[3] Fred Suse, the Stonekings' son-in-law and neighbor in Clinton, turned to me (the stranger) and asked, "How do you separate bluegrass music from the other?" Mrs. Stoneking emphatically remarked: "Easy! I can. By the *sound* of it. Bluegrass is good listening music, but this is *dancing*! This is *smooth*, you can dance to it. If you got any rhythm in your body you can dance to this. I've tried to dance to bluegrass and I've tried to dance to *this*, and this I can *do*. *Real* good." We all added other comments—bluegrass is "show music"; bluegrass is popular in fiddle contests. But Mrs. Stoneking struck the central point, and Lee added, "I'll tell you one thing about bluegrass music, I think it's a *beautiful sound*, but they *chop it up* an awful lot. Whereas the old-time music is a little smoother, it isn't chopped up as much."

What is the most popular fiddle tune for square dancing in and around Henry County? "'Bill Cheatem's' awful good. And *used* to be, 'Wagner' was a good one, and 'Turkey in the Straw' is an awful good one." Lee characterized his style, inherited in part from his father, Frank, as "listening music." Known as a smooth, clean fiddler, one can hear why on his 1970s LPs.[4]

About a year after my 1975 visit, Stoneking had moved to Appleton City and recorded self-produced LPs of his fiddling in a Warrensburg studio, with backup by his sons Nelson (guitar, banjo) and Bobby (guitar, bass), *Missouri Old Time Fiddlin'* and *Rainbow of Fiddle Tunes*. They were sold at contests, dances, and Silver Dollar City performances as well as by word of mouth. In 1985, Lee was recorded by Brad Leftwich and Linda Higginbotham, with their bandmate Kenny Jackson. Brad and Linda performed at the Mountain Folks Music Festival at Silver Dollar City from 1982 to 1986, and, during their stays in Missouri, they met and recorded fiddlers and old-time musicians in the Arkansas-Oklahoma-Missouri area. They met Fred Stoneking at one of the Silver Dollar City festivals, and Fred suggested they visit his father, Lee.

In 2014, the Field Recorders Collective issued music from the Leftwich-Higginbotham 1985 recordings, *Lee Stoneking: Missouri Fiddling and Banjo Playing*. This recording presents a strong sampling of Lee's diverse and interesting repertoire. Brad and Linda's narrative, "A Visit with Lee Stoneking," gives insight into the Stoneking family's fiddle and banjo traditions. The project includes examples of Lee's up-picking five-string banjo playing. Many of the tunes are family tunes and localized Missouri tunes. There are also pop tunes and titles important in the fiddle-contest environment, such as "Sally Goodin," "Bitter Creek," and "Sally Johnson," as well as bluegrass classics like "Big Sandy River" and "Oklahoma Redbird." For Lee's fans and neighbors from old German-speaking families in his region of Missouri, there are a few schottisches and his own compositions, such as "Rolling Stone Breakdown" and "My Dream Waltz." He also adds the much-requested "Orange Blossom Special." And, as with most fiddlers of his generation, Stoneking includes a Protestant hymn familiar to most fiddlers and virtually all his fans, "What a Friend We Have in Jesus." There are rare tunes and interesting versions of standards such as "Fisher's Hornpipe" played in G followed by the more common key of D.[5]

Tracking Down a Tune: "Echoes of the Ozarks"

Lee Stoneking helped popularize a swingy country rag called "Echoes of the Ozarks." The tune appears to have been composed in the 1930s by Ishmael (Ozark Red) Loveall of Linn Creek (Camden County). It is probable that fiddlers who played it such as Stoneking, Lyman Enloe, and Art Galbraith heard Red Loveall at fiddle contests as well as on radio programs on Springfield's KWTO-AM.[6] Loveall's title for "Echoes of the Ozarks" may have been "Echoes of the Hills," which is the title Lyman Enloe remembered from a 1939 fiddle contest in Bagnell, where he heard Loveall play it. In the 1980s, Bob Holt helped spread the tune. Pete McMahan helped further spread the tune as "Echoes of the Ozarks" and played it in B-flat (rather than D or G). McMahan often said he learned the tune from Lee Stoneking but decided to work out a version in B-flat.

In the 1950s, Columbia swing fiddler Luther Caldwell played a more ragtime-sounding version of "Echoes of the Ozarks" under the title "Traveling Back to Dixie," which he had learned from Ed Tharp. A transcription appeared in 1940 in Ira Ford's

Echoes of the Ozarks

Lee Stoneking
trans. by Brad Leftwich

Lee Stoneking's "Echoes of the Ozarks," 1985. (Transcription by Brad Leftwich)

Traditional Music of America, and in 1973 Christeson published a transcription of Bill Driver's 1940s version.[7] It is possible that Ford, living in the Branson-Nevada area of southwest Missouri in the 1930s at the time his book was coming together, heard Red Loveall or perhaps even Lee Stoneking play it. The "Echoes of the Ozarks"/"Echoes of the Hills" melody may go back to a pre–Civil War minstrel song, or perhaps a cakewalk; it is reminiscent of country rags of the early 1900s.

Lee Stoneking's setting is admirable in part because he lets the music breathe, and lilt, and makes it so danceable. As he played it, it was more suitable as a two-step than a square dance. No doubt the use of the word "Ozarks" in the title, rather than the word "Hills," adds to the appeal of the tune.

Listen to track 26 on the companion CD to hear Lee Stoneking's version of "Echoes of the Ozarks."

Bud Wyatt listens intently as Fred Stoneking emphasizes a point in a conversation at a Fourth of July picnic and fiddle contest in Boonesboro, 2007. (Photo by Kay Allen)

Fred Stoneking, Family Historian and Raconteur

Lee's son Fred Stoneking was an outspoken and proud fiddler who promoted old-time fiddle music. Like his father, Fred's early exposure to fiddle and dance music was in music parties and dances at homes in rural communities such as Urich, Chilhowee, Blairstown, Deepwater, and other places in Henry County.

The farm near Chilhowee was a subsistence farm with row crops (corn, wheat), beef cattle, hogs, a few dairy cows (for the milk, cream, and butter), plow horses, a chicken house, a smokehouse for hams and bacons, and a garden. All the youngsters did farmwork as soon as they were big enough to handle the chores and labor. By the age of ten, Fred was plowing fields behind a team of workhorses. Rural electricity reached the farm in 1948.

Fred was an eloquent narrator of stories from and about the old days and growing up on an old-fashioned farm in a large family well stocked with fiddlers, banjo players, dancers, and singers. His own words, from interviews with Gordon McCann and Mark Wilson, give us a zestful sense of his experiences as he looked back over the years.[8]

Fred became well known widely through festival appearances, including national events such as the University of Chicago Folk Festival and the Festival of American Fiddle Tunes in Port Townsend, Washington. He performed semiprofessionally at Silver Dollar City with various bands, including the Horse Creek Band. He taught at fiddle camps, won fiddle contests, made recordings, and was a magnetic presence at fiddlers' conventions in Oklahoma, Arkansas, and Cape Fair and Compton Ridge in the Branson area of Missouri.

The Horse Creek Band, Silver Dollar City, 1979. This popular bluegrass and country band continues to be led by mandolinist Larry Sledge (a mentee of Bill Monroe). *Left to right*: Arkie Phillips (bass), Ike Fry (jig dancer), Sledge, Butch Gregory (guitar), unidentified (guitar), and Fred Stoneking. (Courtesy of Fred Stoneking, Mark Wilson, and Gordon McCann)

[Horse Creek Band] It was unique in that we never played a set show—it was all requests and everything was by ear. Each of us knew exactly what we could do. It'd all be: "Who knows such and such song?" "I do." "Well, start her off." Boy, that would keep you on your toes, because you never knew what you were going to play. I don't think we hardly ever had to turn down anyone's request. It was all country and old-time with some bluegrass and a lot of gospel thrown in: George Jones, Ernest Tubb, and so on. We didn't have a female singer, so we really couldn't do Kitty Wells stuff, but that didn't keep some of us from trying. Ha! Ha!

That was just when Branson was beginning to build up, though it was absolutely nothing compared to what's it like now. One of the main reasons I don't work with the fiddle down in that area anymore is the traffic. I used to get off work at Silver Dollar City and I was supposed to drive a mile and a half down to the Shepherd of the Hills theatre, where they had me playing "Fiddlin' Jake." It would take me a full hour to drive a mile and a half—it would have been quicker if I could have walked.[9]

As Paul Roberts writes in reviewing *Saddle Old Spike*, "Great family and fiddling anecdotes just pour out of the guy, and he vividly brings to life the sort of close, warm, old-fashioned extended family that is so often the matrix for a strong musical tradition."[10]

I was born way back in the prehistoric days of 1933. I was the youngest of four kids that my mom and dad had before they separated way back yonder. Then my dad married a woman that already had three girls. One of them was the exact same age of me, so we were raised as twins. And then my dad and my stepmother had six more kids. Boy, I'll have to stop and think just how many brothers and sisters I had, because my mom had three more children with her next husband. Well, however many it was, we all got along great. We had a great big long kitchen table, with a big long bench up one side and another big bench down the other. Dad sat at one end and Mom at the other. They'd hand the plates all around and there'd be one big stew kettle sitting in the middle of the table. Generally it was beans, cornbread and green onions. Dad would lift the pan off the stew kettle, and he'd ask, "OK, who wants beans?" And it was, "Me, me, me, me, me, me" up and down that table.

Then there were the butchering days they were always a lot of fun. Two of my uncles and Dad would always butcher together. Sometimes they'd butcher six or seven hogs, which would be an all-day job, but they always had a threshing crew there to help. They had three big vats and my job was to keep that fire a-woofing all day. You'd grind them old cracklings up and sprinkle them in cornbread—gosh, that was good. Boy, them's good days; I feel sorry that my kids missed out on some of those times. I could do everything in the world to try to get them to relive those days, but it'd be impossible—that part of the system is all gone now. You can't even churn butter no more because the cream ain't to be found. All the chickens is caged up—there's hardly anybody that's got chickens and chicken houses any more.[11]

This kind of music just runs in our family. My nationality is Irish, Scottish and English—and I've heard that way back somewheres we were court musicians with a coat of arms. Anyway, my mom was a decent fiddle player and her father was a banjo player too. My granddad on my dad's side of the family was named Frank Burgess Stoneking and he always said that he was The Best Stoneking Fiddle Player. But Granddad had four other brothers and each of them claimed to be The Best Fiddle Player as well—I don't know how they worked that out between them.

Coming down to my dad's generation he had four brothers and all them boys played the fiddle. Even my aunts could saw you something on a fiddle. But every last one of them played the piano and those old pump organs for rhythm and could pound on banjos. As to me, all my brothers play fiddles, all of them play guitars and all of them play banjos. And that's pretty much true of my sisters too. And it seems like that they all married people that played, too. At the last Stoneking Reunion, there were so many strings there, it was like we had our own Bluegrass festival.

So you might consider that I was simply raised with the fiddle.

Square dances used to be very common in that part of the country. Just a bunch of old farmers would get together to have a dance in their homes. They would dance in two rooms and you'd always play right in the doorway. And they'd always bring the food out when they'd take a break. Boy, that was so good. Everything was made right there in the skillets on an old wood stove.

Dad used to play a square dance a week in the little old town in Urich, over in central Missouri. There was enough room in there to have seven sets and each set had its own caller. One set might be doing "divide your own ladies, gents go haw"[12] and another one might have been doing the grapevine twist. A lot of times the caller would dance in his own set, just yelling out the calls. Anytime I could get away from playing and had a chance to square dance, I always wanted to dance in the set where my uncle Young was calling, because he had a good sharp voice that would cut through the air like a pocketknife, and he would sing his calls all the way through, from start to finish. That just made it all livelier. There ain't nobody to do anything like that nowadays. Instead, there'll be one man standing up there with a microphone yelling for ten or fifteen sets—and using records, by gosh.[13]

There's another little town called Deepwater that had two little dance halls and many a Saturday night, me and some of my brothers would play in one place and maybe Dad, one of my uncles and my other brother would play right across the street, and the people would just drift back and forth between us. Of course, sometimes there'd be trouble. Now, my dad wasn't a nonsense type of guy and he didn't like drunks breathing on him. This one old boy had walked in a dance when the set had already started and that made him mad. He put his hand around the neck of Dad's fiddle and said, "If I can't dance, there'd ain't nobody gonna dance." Naturally, that stopped it. Dad just set the fiddle down quietly and pulled out a pocket knife out of his pocket and went, "Clip!"—he snipped off a hunk of the man's ear. He said, "Now, you get away from here and don't bother me no more." And that solved that problem.[14]

Fred learned the family repertoire in a seamless reiteration of his father's fiddle style. People would tell Fred that he sounded just like Lee. As Gordon McCann recalls, as Fred got older, "Fred got tired of sounding just like his dad. 'I play like *Fred*,' he would say."[15]

Drafted into the Army during the Korean War in the early 1950s, Fred was a corporal in the paratroopers. Like other musicians in the service, Fred somehow was able to keep a violin with him. In 1952, Lee Stoneking recorded fiddle tunes on a home wire recorder, and Fred's sister Bertie arranged to have the wires transferred onto one-off 78-rpm discs and mailed them to Fred in Korea. Fred played the recording of Lee fiddling "Echoes of the Ozarks" so much that the needle wore out the grooves in the thin cardboard-backed records.

> Sometimes I used to hear so much music [in my head], it'd begin to drive me up the wall. But when I was over in Korea in 1952, I really missed it. My dad and my twin sister Bertie got hold of all old wire recorder, made some recordings and took them some place to be changed into records. They must have been made out of cardboard or something, because they were soft and real thin. Of course, it took a month for me to get them and the salt air must have gotten to them during the trip over to Korea for they were wrinkled very badly. We had a little old cheap record player that was broken but its sound still worked. So I used to turn the record around myself with my finger, round and round and round. I'd get her going up and down the hills on one of them warped little records. Bertie talked to me a little bit between the tunes and sometimes she would sound like Donald Duck and sometimes she'd sound like a gruff-talking old man. But every once in a while, it'd sound just like my sister Bertie. And, directly, you could get that record turning just right and that old fiddling would come out just as plain as day. Boy, the hairs would stand up on my arms to hear it. I absolutely whirled those records around so many times that I eventually wore them clear out.[16]

After the war, Fred worked on a ranch in California and then moved to Wyoming, then Arizona, and returned to Clinton around 1965. He found work as a welding foreman and retired around 1983. He was proud of his Army service and enjoyed comparing experiences with others who had served in the military.

By the time Fred began competing in contests in the 1960s, he was developing his own versions of tunes he had learned from his father and was incorporating fiddle tunes in his repertoire that his father didn't play. And Fred stuck to the old-time style when some contest fiddlers in Missouri began to adapt to or adopt other styles. Old-time fiddling proved to be compatible with bluegrass music, but Fred's old-time style did not jell with emerging contest fiddle styles generated in Texas and the West.

Contests

Fred Stoneking loved fiddle contests. Contests are gathering places and reunions. And he made his mark. As a youngster, he served as his father's accompanist and advocated for the old-time, straight-chord guitar style. At contests Fred was recruited so often to play backup guitar for top fiddlers—Pete McMahan, Jake Hockemeyer,

Cyril Stinnett, Gene Wells, and others—that his own fiddle performances were not always recognized for their quality. Too many people thought of him as a guitarist rather than a fiddler. Fred deserved more limelight as a fiddler than he received until late in his life. Guitar players often stop playing backup for fiddlers (or try to stop) once they embrace the fiddle, but Fred continued to serve as a backup when asked to do so.[17]

Stoneking was adamant about keeping alive old-time straight-chord guitar accompaniment that was under pressure by modern Contest Style's swing and closed-chord jazz-derived backup. Fred's backup guitar behind Pete McMahan is on instructive display on two of Pete McMahan's LPs from the 1970s, *Missouri Fiddlin'* and *Missouri Fiddlin' No. 3*.[18] Fred talked about playing guitar for McMahan and other contest fiddlers in an interview with Gordon McCann for *Saddle Old Spike*:

> The man that taught me more on the fiddle and done me more good than anyone else is . . . Pete McMahan. Pete has the best expression with his bow that you ever heard and the most solid time. I played rhythm for him for many years, all over the place. Pete Mac would call me up, "Fred, let's go to such and such place," you know. And Pete was always good about paying his rhythm people. Some fiddlers used to just take us for granted, but Pete always paid twenty percent of his winnings to his rhythm. And after that got ahold, I played for another great fiddle player, Cleo Persinger, and for Jake Hockemeyer . . . who's the finest left-handed fiddle player I ever heard. And I played for the Wells boys. Many times I made more money with the guitar than I did the fiddle. I could always get in the money [playing fiddle in contests], but winning came slow for me. But I could always do pretty well with my guitar.[19]

Travis Inman, a younger man competing in Open Divisions with Fred, remembered, "Fred had the best 'Bill Cheatem' I ever heard. McMahan did too, but I tell ya what. Fred played 'Bill Cheatem' one time in a fiddle contest. And I just stood there and wondered how in the hell are we gonna beat *that*! And we didn't either, he *won* it that day."[20] And more people began to appreciate Fred's old-time fiddling as he moved into the Senior Division in the 1990s (by then, the Open Division was beginning to be dominated by Contest Style). Moreover, his reputation as a fiddler with rare tunes (and wry anecdotes) was circulating across the nation in festival appearances and commercial recordings.[21] Fred could count on winning or placing high in just about any contest he chose to enter.

> I've played guitar and banjo all my life and have been to absolutely hundreds of contests. I used to play with my grandfather, Frank Burgess Stoneking, when I was seven years old. But he played so terrible fast—way too fast for a learner. Boy, I remember them black snappy eyes looking at me when I'd done something wrong or I was lagging a little bit. But Grandpa was a great fiddler, and so was Uncle Jake and Uncle John and Uncle George and Uncle Price—all of them.

> But I didn't get real serious about my own fiddling until the early sixties. I was playing rhythm for my dad at a contest and he won a hundred-dollar first place and he did it in about ten minutes. I thought to myself, "Boy, how easy!" So I started really practicing, and finally, I won my first fiddling contest in 1966 at a little town called Lamont. I won a first place ribbon and a brand new twenty dollar bill.
>
> I beat my Dad in that contest and nowadays it's happening to me. Both of my children have turned out to be real good fiddlers. Alita and Luke have both have won Missouri Junior Champions. The first time Alita beat me, she actually cried. She said, "Here, Dad, you won this trophy; I didn't." I didn't see it like that because I know when I'm beat. So I told her, "Now, Alita, don't you feel bad—you beat me fair and square. I was trying my best to win and it just tickles me to death to have one of my kids beat me doing something that I'm trying my best to do. So whenever you do win, you'd earned it. From now on, whatever the judges award you, you walk right up there just as proud as you can be, whether it's for first or last place."
>
> Now I have been beat by the best and I have been beat by the worst. Whatever happens, I've never opened my mouth to complain, because I think that's senseless. But some people take it all so seriously. My dad and I were fortunate enough to have been invited to the North American Championship Invitational up in Nebraska. Well, one so-called "famous fiddler" drove all the way up there, but when he saw who else was there, he turned around and drove all the way home. Then another so-called "famous fiddler" showed up and, after he paid his fees, told the people running the contest that, since he always furnished one of the judges, they could stop looking for anyone else. He'd brought his own judge up from his state free of charge. Needless to say, his judge didn't get to judge that particular contest.

Fred Stoneking liked all kinds of music. But when the chips were down and the focus on him, in a fiddle contest, teaching at a camp, or with an arts council administrator or tune collector, he was all business about the importance of one's family and regional traditions. On numerous occasions, Fred would be sure that Alita, an outstanding guitar accompanist, was going to play it "straight" or "old-time" when they got up to a microphone.

Fred's *Saddle Old Spike* is an important project. Most of the tunes come from Lee and other family members, such as "Muddy Weather," "Saddle Old Spike," and "Honey Creek Special," but his broad repertoire is well represented.[22]

> You know that tune I call "The Honey Creek Special"? Well, Honey Creek was a little old draw up by my dad's farm. The bridge across it was pretty long and had real rickety boards on it. So if you heard a Model A coming across that old clattery bridge, you knew that it was either coming to see the old bachelor that lived near us or coming to our house. Nine out of ten times, it was coming up for fiddling. So we got to considering that bridge a special kind of bridge on account that it would let us know that someone was coming to our house. So the Honey Creek Special let us know that we're gonna have company in about fifteen minutes.

"Adrian's Reel" is among unusual tunes played by Lee Stoneking, Fred Stoneking, Lonnie Robertson, and Pete McMahan. Stoneking's "Adrian's Reel," a compelling performance at a contest in Boonville in 1977, is on the companion CD that accompanies *"Play Me Something Quick and Devilish."* Among other commercial recordings are "In Old Arkansas" and "Blackberry Waltz" on Rounder Records compilations.[23]

Fred Stoneking worked on and set up Travis Inman's Pfretzschner violin (*left*) and Levi Roden's Guarnerius model violin; one of Stoneking's calling cards was rounding off the bottom corners of fingerboards. Fred had watched his father repair and build violins and learned from other luthiers as well. He enjoyed talking about violin bows and violin history and insisted on calling the instruments fiddles rather than violins. (Photo by Howard Marshall, 2019)

Like most artisans, Fred evolved his own techniques for certain tasks. As his friend and fellow luthier Darrell Friend recalls, Stoneking made slides for violin bow frogs out of guitar picks and altered tools he acquired to suit his preferences. He enjoyed re-hairing bows (an odious chore for most luthiers), meticulously counting out 125 strands of fresh horsehair and then adding 5 more strands to replace any hairs that could break or come loose in a new hair job. Fred said he liked fiddles that "talked to you."[24]

Listen to track 27 on the companion CD to hear Fred Stoneking's version of "Buzzard in a Pea Patch."

Fred Stoneking demonstrates fiddle sticks (beating the straws) with his daughter Alita. In this traditional way for a fiddler to have some extra rhythm, a colleague drums on the violin strings while the tune is played, using anything from broom straws to lengths of cattail or prairie-dock stems, knitting and crochet needles, various kinds of wire, pencils, barbecue skewers, and chopsticks. Fred learned fiddle sticks from his father and uncles. (Photo by Mark Wilson, 1996)

Alita Stoneking, Carry It On

Alita Stoneking (b. 1980) has been a dedicated contest champion for many years, and the family old-time fiddle legacy is in capable hands. Alita can sound like her father and grandfather when the occasion presents itself, but her forte is a personal and creative style forged to meet the needs and expectations of the modern fiddle-contest arena.

Fred recognized the values and advantages of encouraging young learners to know music theory, read violin music, and acquire some standard violin habits and provided violin lessons for Alita and her younger brother, Luke, when they were children in Springfield.[25] The combination of some good violin skills and the children's nonstop immersion in fiddle music paid off. Both youngsters developed rapidly and began to take part in contests, jam sessions, and other events.

Alita mastered the family music and old-time guitar accompaniment of her father, Fred, and her energies then tilted toward absorbing Texas-based Contest Style and its concomitant swing-style closed-chord guitar backup. Respecting her roots, Alita "has drawn on that feel, along with influences from Major Franklin, Norman and Vernon Solomon, Dick Barrett, Terry Morris, and Orville Burns, among others."[26] She was fortunate as well to be part of a crew of like-minded, talented young contest fiddlers performing the Texas-based style—especially Bubba Hopkins (a champion multi-instrumentalist and fiddle teacher from Spavinaw, Oklahoma), Matt Wyatt, Billy Ward, Levi Roden, Cody Marriott, and Cody's father, Junior Marriott. This group of skilled Contest Style performers became a force to be contended with at fiddle contests from the later 1990s onward, not unlike creative improvisers such as Joe Venuti, Cecil Brower, and Spade Cooley, who helped develop jazz and western swing.[27]

Fred and Alita traveled to numerous contests, festivals, and fiddlers' conventions together. Among these were their trip as featured artists at the Festival of American Fiddle Tunes in Port Townsend, Washington, and contests such as Wilbur Foss's Great Plains Championships in South Dakota, the Branson contest, Jana Jae's Grove, Oklahoma contests, Rocky Mountain championships in Denver, and the annual Hallettsville, Texas, contest.

Alita Stoneking spoke of male prejudice against women in fiddling:

> My experience as a female musician is 100% different than for others. I am not sexist, and will not make this sexist but what I can honestly tell you is that I had to work very hard to make a name for myself as a female fiddler. My dad was always super proud of me and supported me but there were MANY Missouri musicians that didn't think I "belonged." Even more than the other fiddlers, there was the crowd that followed the contests as well.
>
> I can't tell you how many hundreds of times I was told, "that's pretty good for a girl," or "fiddling is for boys." I left many contests when I was younger in tears from rude remarks about being a young girl fiddler. In my "age group" there weren't really any other girls that were playing. I can really only think of Matt Wyatt and perhaps John Williams of being in the same age category. I once even had a man tell me that I should put a dollar bill in my fiddle and then throw it away—and whoever found it would at least have a dollar! That was the fiddle my dad made for me! Can you imagine?!?!?
>
> I truly think it was all of those experiences as a teenager and even into my early 20's that has made me a strong player. Now, I'm known to be a female fiddler that plays like a boy! I'm so proud of that! I didn't want to be "good for a girl," I just wanted to be me and enjoy music![28]

Alita has won numerous Missouri contests, including the state championship at the state fair in Sedalia in 2001 and again in 2007, a contest she has also helped judge. Since moving to Minnesota, she and her husband, Tom, have become a familiar team in major fiddle contests as competitors and judges, from the Mississippi River to California.

Alita's *Born to Play* is a nice sampling of her fiddling, with guitar accompaniment by Tom Weisgerber. The track list includes contest pieces such as "Dusty Miller," "Old South Waltz," and "Fort Smith"; Texas-style jam session tunes such as "George Booker," "Shortenin' Bread," and "Caledonian Laddie"; as well as some Stoneking

Alita and Fred Stoneking with Gordon McCann (*right*) at Fred's house, Springfield, Missouri, 1996. (Photo by Mark Wilson)

family tunes inherited from her father, Fred, and grandfather Lee, such as "Sugar in the Gourd" and "Echoes of the Ozarks." Alita plays a violin Fred built for her on the *Born to Play* CD.

Born to Play includes several 1800s hornpipes in the flat keys that appear in Cole's 1940 tune book, played by fiddlers of generations past, like Casey Jones, George Morris, and Cyril Stinnett. These are complex yet driving hornpipes as Alita plays them—"Morpeth's Hornpipe," "Sans Succi Hornpipe," and "Holmes' Hornpipe," tunes some of the more skilled contest fiddlers play. These tunes are on a jam-session tape as played by the Texas champion Benny Thomasson, from a Dallas session recorded in 1967 (cassette copies of which have circulated among interested fiddlers for many years). Videos of Alita and Tom Weisgerber as contestants and guitar accompanists at major championships are available on YouTube. Alita's recordings include two additional CDs, *Alita Stoneking* and, with her father, *Late Night Jam*.

Alita offers an interesting case of a brilliantly talented young woman who can perform the old inherited tunes equally well with today's Texas-derived Contest Style repertoire. She has won many fiddle titles across the nation and is a favorite guitar accompanist. It is good to know that, while Alita may enjoy Contest Style, she is proud to carry on the old-time fiddle music of her family, sharing the old repertoire and old stories along with the new.

Alita and Tom

In 2009, Alita married Tom Weisgerber of St. Peter, Minnesota, a fiddle-contest champion and multi-instrumentalist. They met on the contest circuit. Tom is a well-known master and has competed in national and regional contests since his teenage years. In the 1980s, Weisgerber became acquainted with Pete McMahan at Minnesota state contests at Cotton, and McMahan was impressed by his taste and drive. Pete showed Tom some things, and Tom taught Pete some fine tunes, including "Carnival Waltz" and "Ostinelli Hornpipe," both popular and demanding contest pieces. McMahan stated often that Tom Weisgerber "had the best 'Tom and Jerry' of anybody in the country."[29]

Tom and Alita are popular fiddle teachers, giving private lessons, teaching at workshops and fiddle camps, and mentoring young musicians. They are regular top finishers at contests such as the Texas state contest in Hallettsville (where they win or place high in the "Gone to Texas" division for nonresidents), Weiser, and Denver. They put in their turns as judges and serve as backup guitarists for other fiddlers. They accompany each other when their turns come to play their round at the microphone. Tom and Alita often vie for the same honors in contests, and they make formidable competition, and welcome participants, wherever they go.

Today, Alita Stoneking works in the aerospace industry and enjoys the "quiet life here in Minnesota. I enjoy fishing a lot and gardening. My husband and I also enjoy buying, repairing, and selling instruments just as my dad did. When he died, he willed all of his tools to Tom to carry on the tradition and Tom has become a fine luthier."[30]

Listen to track 28 on the companion CD to hear Alita Stoneking's version of "Dusty Miller."

"The Jam Session," 1989 lithograph by Ron Raymer, a Hallmark Cards artist and banjo designer in Kansas City. Ron captured the good vibrations of a typical jam session at a bluegrass festival (based on Herman Smith's festivals at Knob Noster in the 1970s and 1980s). *First row, left to right*: Gary Russell (bowler hat, guitar), Jewell Barnett (beer-can hat, guitar), Ethan Shaffer (legs crossed, guitar), and Wayne Loveall (guitar). *Middle row*: Harley Bonham (mandolin), Charlie Vanzant (Dobro), Ron Raymer (banjo), Larry Robinson (guitar, at Raymer's left elbow), Larry Willis (behind Raymer, dark shirt, guitar), and Robert Collins (banjo, behind Raymer). *Back row, left to right*: Don Montgomery (bass), Lyman Enloe (violin), Jim McGreevy (banjo), Mae Burlison (vocal), Jack Burlison (guitar), and Gerry and Velma Mulkey. (Courtesy of Ron Raymer, October 2016)

Bluegrass Festivals

12

Come in and sit down, stranger. Get out your fiddle and have a tune with us.[1]
—campground greeting often heard at festivals

The history of bluegrass music and bluegrass fiddling appears in *Fiddler's Dream* and *"Play Me Something Quick and Devilish."* We turn now to focus on bluegrass festivals, which arose in the 1960s. Festivals were a key factor in the spread and popularity of bluegrass as it found its footing as more than a subset of country music or folk music.

The term "bluegrass" did not catch on until the 1950s.[2] Many people assumed bluegrass was old music dusted off, but it was a newly made and distinct genre. Pioneers whose commercial records were essential listening in the 1960s included Bill Monroe, Flatt and Scruggs, the Dillards, the Stanley Brothers, and others. The Country Gentlemen's 1961 LP *Sing & Play Folksongs & Bluegrass* and the 1963 *Folk Session Inside* included topical ballads and folksongs from revivalist folksingers of the time as well as archival collections.

Is There any Difference between Bluegrass Fiddling and Old-Time Fiddling?

Old-time fiddling and bluegrass fiddling are genres of traditional or folk fiddling. They differ in interesting ways, and differences may be subtle and unnoticed by casual listeners. Old-time fiddling began as instrumental dance music hundreds of years ago; old-time has numerous substyles. Bluegrass fiddling evolved from old-time and swing music in the 1940s and is largely concert and jam-session music for audiences to listen to, not dance to; the fiddle is not the center of attention but a role instrument in an ensemble, and bluegrass music includes singing. Bluegrass also has substyles. I think that is a reasonable, if debatable, summary of the main differences.

In bluegrass, a fiddler needs to shift from essentially a soloist in front of dancers or a fiddle-contest microphone to being a role player in an ensemble. He or she spends a lot of time playing backup and only plays a solo (a break) during a song or when the set list calls for an old-time fiddle tune. Other instruments are given breaks, and sometimes breaks are divided between the fiddler and the mandolinist, banjoist, guitarist, or Dobro player. In bluegrass, many fans consider banjo the most important instrument, not violin.

Some fiddlers play both bluegrass and old-time, and some are strict devotees of one kind and say they do not play the other. Dick Logan preferred not to label his style and played both styles. Leroy Canaday, Warren Helton, Dean Johnston,

Billy Lee, Pete McMahan, and Taylor McBaine played numerous tunes from the bluegrass repertoire but thought of themselves as old-time fiddlers. So, yes, it is complicated.

Newell Looney, Shepherd of the Hills theater, ca. 1979. Looney (1916–1982), from Billings, was interested in old-time fiddling and bluegrass and performed in country music shows in the Branson and Silver Dollar City area. His principal work was with the Horse Creek Band, and he appears on *Ozark Mountain Music Recorded Live* and on *Lonnie Hoppers and Friends: Pickin' for Fun*. (Courtesy of Larry Sledge)

A bluegrass fiddler needs to provide all kinds of background, support, and periodic melody lines in band performances. Such devices as kickoffs, fills, chops, shuffles, turnarounds, and tune endings support and add accent, rhythm, harmony, and depth to the band and to support the singing. A kickoff is a formulaic measure (or more) for starting a tune or song (think of "four potatoes"); a fill is a brief bit of melody popped in between phrases; chops are quick, percussive strikes of the bow on the strings to add accent, typically stopped two-note muffled chords on the second and fourth beats, usually applied close to the frog; shuffles are melodic and rhythmic incidentals in accompaniment; turnarounds are formulaic melodic passages at the end of a phrase; tune endings (tags, caps) are formulaic signals that a tune or song is concluding (think "shave and a haircut, two bits"). These skills are important in bluegrass, swing, and country music.

Most bluegrass fiddlers in the formative years from the 1940s into the 1960s came out of old-time square-dance fiddling and swing fiddling. Those who were versatile and enjoyed swing and pop music tended to make the transition to the requirements of the bluegrass band more easily. Old-time hoedown fiddlers who did care to adapt to the requirements of bluegrass may simply have rejected bluegrass music altogether. Some old-time fiddlers make the transition to bluegrass fiddle, while others do not. Some, like Lyman Enloe, find a middle way. Enloe was an old-time fiddler who enjoyed being in a bluegrass band and jamming at bluegrass festivals, but he did not adopt bluegrass licks, backup, and an ensemble role. He got along just fine. Perhaps intention is key. Do you want to lead a band playing for dances, or do you want to be a role player in a bluegrass band?

Both the bluegrass and the old-time fiddling communities have fans who are basically preservationists. We may not like the changes, but it is helpful to remember that fiddling of any kind continues to change and that the heart of fiddling stays much the same. More and more fiddlers across these genres are coming into the music with classical training (often also with Suzuki) and formal education. It is not helpful to overstress those points, because bluegrass has always benefited from ideas across the genres, from transitional old-time fiddlers like Clayton McMichen and Arthur Smith to swing, blues, and jazz players like Chubby Wise and Dale Potter, as well as to later stars such as Kenny Baker, Vassar Clements, Stuart Duncan, and Blaine Sprouse, as well as today's tastemakers like Michael Cleveland, to name only a few.[3]

Festivals!

In the 1960s bluegrass found its most significant platform, the multiday outdoor festival with camping facilities. Festivals are essentially pop-up villages of people who journey to the events to celebrate and share. The villages' values and customs are passed on to newcomers and beginners in all sorts of ways, from learning how to listen to and understand the intricacies of a bluegrass ensemble to learning the crucial unwritten folk laws that govern sessions. Workshops add much, giving audiences a golden opportunity to learn from the experts.

The Bluegrass Society was a popular band in the Ozarks in the 1960s that included Army personnel stationed at Fort Leonard Wood. They performed songs from the folk and country repertoire such as "Gentle Annie" and "Wildwood Flower" and bluegrass and old-time fiddle standards such as "Grey Eagle," "Fisher's Hornpipe," "Sugar in the Gourd," and "Billy in the Low Ground." *Left to right*: Bob Simpson, an Army man from California (bass), Hope Weston from Virginia (guitar), Harry Gilbert from central Missouri (fiddle), Frank Jones (Richland, banjo), and Don Weston (Hope's husband, an Army psychiatrist, from Virginia, guitar). They released *Fireside Grass* in 1969.

The first bluegrass festival to feature on-site camping was hosted by Carlton Haney in Fincastle, Virginia, in 1965, on Labor Day weekend. Like the Newport Folk Festival, it was a multiday event with a theme, in this case bluegrass music and its pater familias, Bill Monroe.[4] In 1967 Bill Monroe created a festival on the leafy, rolling landscape on the brim of the southern Indiana hamlet of Bean Blossom. Bean Blossom became a global pilgrimage site for fans, musicians, and record companies, a template for bluegrass festivals everywhere.[5]

Bean Blossom blossomed. Monroe said "y'all come," and we did, in droves, young and old from every walk of life and the four corners of the planet. This mass of humanity perplexed Monroe, but the businessman and promoter in him saw the importance of welcoming everyone—everyone who behaved. Many of his fans were college students and urbanites from places far beyond Kentucky or Tennessee.[6] Fans who made vacation plans to include a festival never forgot the experience. For many people, pulling out the camping gear and servicing the VW bus or motor home was part of an annual ritual. Exposure to famous musicians, jam sessions, like-minded new friends, and storytelling enriched lives as well as music. Inherent in the experience is transmission of a culture that exists foremost in oral (and aural) traditions and in real-time watching, listening, and participating.

In the late 1960s and into the 1970s, massive rock-and-roll festivals got out of hand—freaks and drugs colliding with bikers and booze, for instance—and bluegrass festivals nearly died out. Two overhyped bluegrass festivals in Missouri (Sedalia; north of Eminence) attracted far too many patrons and veered into becoming Woodstock and Altamont calamities. Promoters started to set rules and include "No Drugs or Alcohol" in advertising and campground posters. Not quite sure what to make of the long-hairs and hippie chicks, at Bean Blossom Monroe required them to set up camp away from the main festival grounds and stage area, and thus was founded an ongoing if temporary community called "Hippie Hill."

Bluegrass festivals that survived shifted into family-friendly campouts with concessions, comfort facilities, and proper management.[7] Also, a number of festivals

At Bean Blossom in June 1972, three bluegrass fiddle stars get their photo taken. *Left to right*: Tex Logan, Kenny Baker, and Paul Warren. (Photo by Howard Marshall)

succeeded in part because they were scattered across the map and became an annual round of destinations. More than one festival in the same town in the same month was not sustainable, so, studying listings in *Bluegrass Unlimited* and regional newsletters, administrators could schedule events so as not to compete with others. Many festivals landed on holiday weekends, but competing festivals could survive if they were far enough apart geographically to still draw fans and major performers.

Campground, Back Forty Bluegrass Festival, Saturday afternoon, May 22, 2015. Members of the Missouri River Band warm up for a show onstage, with friends and family gathering around while steaks finish on the grill for an early supper. (Photo by Russell D. Ravert)

Thayne Bradford became a central figure in the bluegrass music community in St. Louis. Here, he performs with the River Bend Bluegrass Band in June 2019 (Kris Shewmake on banjo). Bradford, a multi-instrumentalist who started out in rock and roll, also performs with bands in other genres, such as country, swing, Celtic, and Creole music. (Facebook)

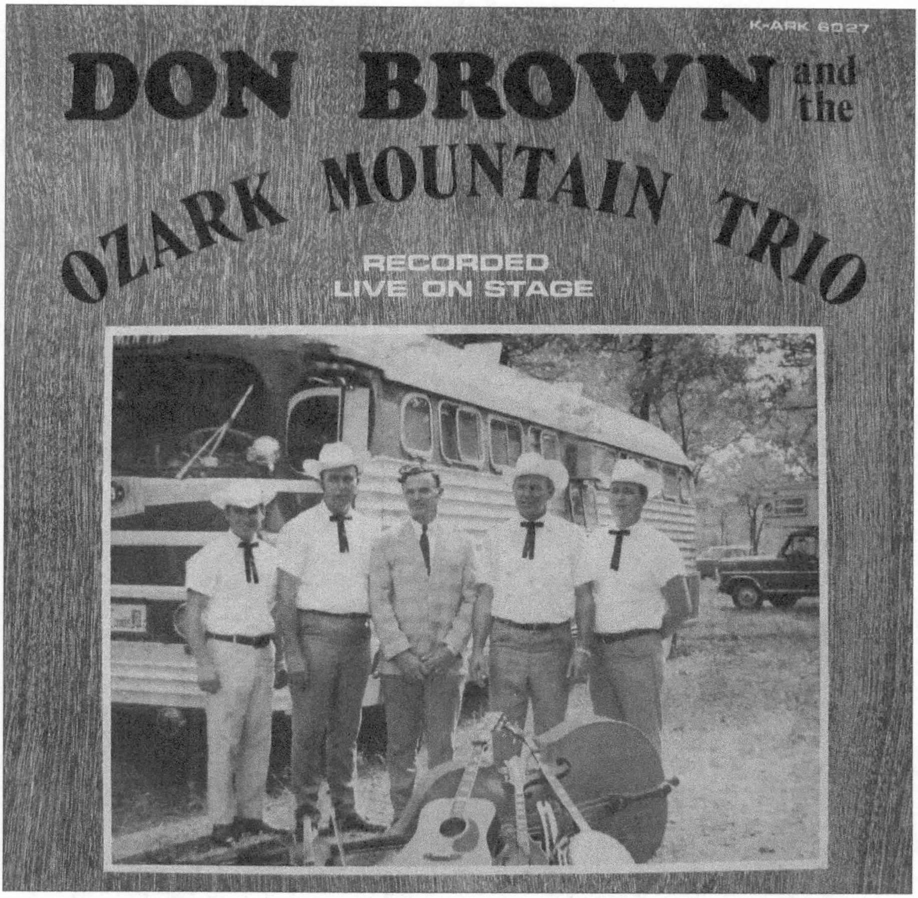

Don Brown and the Ozark Mountain Trio. *Left to right*: Bobby Puckett (violin), Don Brown (mandolin), Cecil Blankenship (bass), Ray Gore (guitar), and Herman Beck (banjo). In 1970, the group won the band contest at Bill Monroe's Bean Blossom festival. Puckett, from southern Illinois, performed with top regional bluegrass bands, such as Don Brown's, Dub Crouch and the Bluegrass Rounders, Bill Box and the Dixie Drifters, and the Bluegrass Patriots. He authored bluegrass instrumentals named after Missouri festivals, such as "Eminence" and "Van Buren Reel." (LP cover art, *Recorded Live on Stage*)

Mike Hartgrove, a Career with the Fiddle

"My job is bluegrass fiddling, but my hobby is Missouri fiddling."[8] Mike Hartgrove went from audacious wunderkind to award-winning professional, touring the world with the Bluegrass Cardinals, IIIrd Tyme Out, Doyle Lawson and Quicksilver, and the Lonesome River Band. And he remains a Missouri farm boy at heart. Many have the dream, but Hartgrove lives it.

Born in 1955 in Shelbina, as a child Hartgrove was fascinated with Earl Scruggs's bluegrass banjo music he heard on the radio and records and learned to pick banjo like Scruggs. He was interested in fiddle music, impressed with Leroy Canaday's bluegrass fiddling and names other influences, including Lyman Enloe, Jake Hockemeyer, Taylor McBaine, Pete McMahan, Cleo Persinger, and Cyril Stinnett. These were central and north Missouri fiddlers who played in that region's hard-driving, articulate, clean style.

Mike's father, Kenny Hartgrove, played guitar, banjo, and some fiddle music. Square-dance fiddler John White of Shelbina helped get Mike started playing old-time fiddle at dances and music parties. At their first meeting, Kenny brought Mike to one of the dances at the rural Lilly Dale schoolhouse near Clarence. White remembered that Kenny "asked if Mike, who was just beginning to learn to play banjo, could sit in with the band. We said yes. I showed him what little I knew about backing up square dance tunes and he was off to the races. Working with Mike and his dad was like teaching ducks to swim. You just showed them the water and got out of the way."[9] Hartgrove also took several classical violin lessons with Ed Harding in Mexico, Missouri (and then in Paris, Missouri), and learned to read printed music.[10]

Mike Hartgrove, with Sammy Shelor and Brandon Rickman at a Lonesome River Band set at the Starvy Creek festival, September 2013. (Photo by Jean A. Fugate-Besalke)

Mike studied Tommy Jackson's fiddle LPs and country records by Nashville singers such as Ray Price, whose band featured powerful fiddling by Jackson, Johnny Gimble, and Buddy Spicher. Like many musicians of his generation, Mike also listened to records by Flatt and Scruggs, with fiddler Paul Warren, one of the old-time fiddlers who transitioned into bluegrass.

As Mike noted in *Bluegrass Now*, "'There were a lot of good old-time fiddlers in Missouri.' 'It's a great place for fiddlers, and Dale Potter was from Puxico, Mo.,' he adds, as if that fact alone says it all—which, for fiddlers, it pretty much does."[11] Mike developed rapidly as a fiddler and proved to be competitive with champions such as Persinger, Canaday, McMahan, Stinnett, and Hockemeyer. In those days, young fiddlers had to earn their stripes: "I feel so lucky, these heroes made you work at it."[12]

Off to Nashville

Mike's parents encouraged him to consider a career in music. After graduating high school at nineteen in 1974, he moved to Nashville. The move was challenging for a young, untried musician, alone, on a meager budget, but the decision had a pragmatic element. A friend of his father had a construction business, and Mike knew he would have a job and could room at his father's friend's home. Mike loaded his pickup truck and headed for Music City, USA. He got acquainted and began finding his way through jam sessions, the crucibles and mixing bowls for musicians. Mike appeared on the Grand Ole Opry as a guest with Moe Bandy, worked as a staff fiddler at Opryland amusement park, and performed with George Jones at the Possum Holler Club.

In 1973, Hartgrove competed in the Grand Masters Fiddle Championship in Nashville. He signed up, but he had no accompanist. Listening to Mike warm up, Jerry Thomasson and Ralph McCraw offered their services. Jerry was a son of Texas champion Benny Thomasson and played backup on tenor guitar; McCraw was champion Herman Johnson's longtime guitar second. The youngster had the good luck of competing with two of the best accompanists in the nation and fiddled big titles in the modern contest repertory, "Tom and Jerry," "Dusty Miller," and "Yellow Rose Waltz."[13]

In 1979, Hartgrove joined the Bluegrass Cardinals, known for their interpretation of classic bluegrass harmony singing and instrumentals. In 1981 Hartgrove moved to San Antonio, Texas, where he played for several years with country music star Moe Bandy. While living in San Antonio, Mike took violin lessons from a Vienna-trained classical teacher, Fred Schade (a protégé of Fritz Kreisler), and learned much, such as playing in second, third, fourth, and fifth positions up the violin neck. Eventually, Schade began to insist that Mike focus exclusively on classical violin; Mike resisted the idea, and the classical lessons ended.

Hartgrove enjoyed performing with the Moe Bandy show but missed playing bluegrass. Watching *Austin City Limits* on TV, he saw Kenny Baker playing fiddle with Bill Monroe and decided that bluegrass would be his focus. He moved back to Nashville and continued working in the country music industry, exploring opportunities and resuming periodic jobs with the Bluegrass Cardinals. Mike visited professional fiddlers such as Tommy Jackson and Benny Martin. Hartgrove points to Tommy Jackson as his biggest early influence, beyond his Missouri mentors, Cyril Stinnett, Jake Hockemeyer, and Pete McMahan.

In 1975, Mike found Jackson's telephone number through the musicians' union. He phoned Jackson, and Jackson invited him to his house, where Hartgrove spent an afternoon visiting about fiddling. Among comments Jackson made, as he fiddled, was that he achieved his famous "bell-like" tone by fingering notes with the meaty part of his forefingers, rather than fingertips.[14] Mike became acquainted with Norman Blake, Vassar Clements, Benny Martin, and Kenny Baker at places like the Old Time Picking Parlor, a music shop where musicians gathered and where impromptu sessions took place. Hartgrove often spoke on the telephone with Baker, who appreciated Mike's interest. Sometimes Mike would play a bit of a tune over the phone, asking Baker how to work out the bowing or phrasing. Hartgrove also listened to recordings of swing and jazz players Stéphane Grappelli and Stuff Smith.

Mike recalls an afternoon with the innovative fiddler Benny Martin and says he learned more in two or three hours than he could have in years on his own.[15] Martin showed Mike how he conceived of and executed creative, influential solos on records with Don Reno and Red Smiley, Flatt and Scruggs, and Bill Monroe. Hartgrove spent time as a sideman with fiddler Tommy Williams, who had performed with Bill Monroe as well as Nashville groups on the Grand Ole Opry, on the *Hee Haw* television show, and at the Possum Holler Club.[16] This was an opportunity to learn techniques for playing harmony fiddle (twin fiddle). In good twin fiddling, there is no room for out-of-pitch playing; the slightest discordant note jumps out in glaring contrast with the other fiddler.

> "We had tunes like 'Monroe's Hornpipe,' 'Wheel Hoss,' and 'Roanoke' worked up with this country band," he recalls. "I remember Bill Monroe coming down to this club, and we played those three songs. Tommy had played Bill's music and had also worked with Judy Lynn in Las Vegas with Bobby Hicks, so he and Bobby were good friends. Anyway, Bill came in the club one day, and the next week he came in and brought his mandolin and got up on stage. That's the first time I had ever known Bill to be on stage with electric instruments and drums," Mike smiles. "He enjoyed it because we had the songs worked out pretty much note for note like they were on his recordings."[17]

A Working Professional

Hartgrove moved to North Carolina and joined the Lonesome River Band in 2001 and continues to tour and record with the award-winning group.[18] For years the band has appeared at Missouri's Starvy Creek festival, where Mike sees old friends and fans. Brandon Rickman, another Missourian who plays bluegrass music professionally, was the band's guitarist for many years.[19]

Bluegrass bands follow a custom set in the 1940s for "an old fiddle tune" at some point in a performance. This gives the fiddler a chance to strut his or her stuff, play a hot breakdown or smooth waltz, reminding one and all of the origins of fiddle music in dancing. Mike learns new fiddle tunes and enjoys going back to "the gold mine" of recordings of fiddlers like Cyril Stinnett and Benny Thomasson and working out tunes. He respects the "wild stuff" played by some bluegrass fiddlers today but says, "You can play the modern stuff, but you need to keep it in the context of tradition."[20]

And that is perhaps the toughest part of being a bluegrass musician today: keeping it in the context of tradition.

Drew Beisswenger includes Mike Hartgrove's "Pretty Red Wing" in his tune book *The World's Hottest Fiddlers.*[21] Mike plans to produce an album that represents the breadth of his experience, echoes his Missouri roots, and has the texture and feeling of an informal music party rather than a studio production.

When he settled in Albemarle, North Carolina, Mike discovered that there were few violin shops nearby. He started collecting cheap fiddles needing repairs and studied violin repair and violin-making manuals and books and started working on instruments.[22] In Missouri he had picked up repair tips from Jesse Sims, such as using apple vinegar in a syringe to loosen glue to help remove a violin top. Mike met luthier Kurt Widenhouse in Belmont, North Carolina, and began visiting the shop to learn techniques of repair and setup. Widenhouse began sending instruments to him for repair and setup. Eventually, Mike opened a music store/fiddle shop.

A Nashville bluegrass business agent and longtime friend and fan states, "Both Mike's noting and bowing are about as precise and smooth as you'll ever see and he's one of the best players around. What's especially impressive . . . is his appreciation

Five Miles Out Of Town

as played by Mike Hartgrove

Transcribed by Amber Gaddy

"Five Miles Out of Town," by Mike Hartgrove, February 2021. A tune of north Missouri and Iowa provenance popularized by Cyril Stinnett, it is printed in Christeson's 1973 *Old-Time Fiddler's Repertory* as played by Des Moines fiddler Frame Davis in the 1960s.

of the history of the old tunes and the tremendous concern he has in seeking out the most authentic version of the melody as it was played."[23] Realizing he is approaching senior status, Hartgrove still has goals he started out with as a teenager in the 1960s. "The most important thing is to keep learning. I think as an older player, it's easy to get in a rut. There are so many young guys out there now. You've got to keep practicing and learning."[24]

Mike teaches and feels that he works most effectively with young people who have Suzuki training or classical lessons and can read music, but who are not "locked into" classical violin technique.[25] He uses the Christeson books and Missouri recordings to convey the essence of old-time fiddling, adhering to bowing styles of Missouri masters.

Listen to track 29 on the companion CD to hear Mike Hartgrove's version of "Five Miles Out of Town."

Henley (Gene) Dykes (*left*) with the Barrier Brothers bluegrass band in the 1960s. Dykes toured extensively to festivals in the Midwest and South and played radio shows and oprys. When Dykes joined the Barriers, they changed the band name to the Barrier Brothers and the Ozark Mountain Boys; Dykes was the only Ozarker. A versatile and smooth fiddler, he was comfortable playing the old-time fiddle standards as well as the popular bluegrass repertoire and fiddle-contest favorites.

One of Missouri's first bluegrass festivals was organized in Eminence in 1970 by Carl Seaman and his son Kenny, a banjoist and singer. In the Ozark Mountains of Shannon County, Eminence was a logical outgrowth of Carl Seaman's 1960s Riverways Opry (later the Current River Opry), which brought in package tours of stars from Nashville. "The festival draws all sorts of people—country folks, long-haired kids from the city, all kinds," said Kenny Seaman. "We've had a Ph.D. from New York playing alongside a fellow who's never been out of Shannon County. We get musicians from all over, but some of the best old-time fiddlers are from right around here. Some of them are gone now, and I could kick myself because I didn't get them down on tape."[26]

At the Billings Street Fair and Cattle Show in Christian County, a 1960s photo of an ad hoc bluegrass band of friends. *Left to right*: Arlie Booker (banjo), Jack Day (bass), Harold Rowden (guitar), Burl Copeland (mandolin), Mona Jones (guitar), Ralph Withers (guitar), and Charles Calton (violin). (Courtesy of Annette Calton Wood)

In 1974, *Billboard* noticed the popularity of festivals and mentioned Herman Smith's Jamboree Park in Missouri:

> The remarkable boom in American rural music is exemplified in the two-state Kansas and Missouri area where about 40 bluegrass festivals, virtually all of them held outdoors in defiance of chiggers and mosquitoes, have been successfully presented since April.
>
> A good example of the craze was last week's Herman Smith Fourth Annual Bluegrass Festival at Knob Noster, Mo., on U.S. 50, in which 1,500 persons participated.
>
> "It's good, clean, family fun," he says. "Why, I read where a lot of rock bands get $50,000—$80,000 a night. And we draw nicer, better-behaved crowds."
>
> "No Alcohol" signs are posted at the festivals, but law officers overlook the patrons sprawled on the grass sipping beer. Rarely is marijuana encountered.[27]

While many were held in bucolic, rural settings, festivals were also held on college campuses and in cities. Some were sponsored by folk-music clubs, and some were developed by agencies such as the National Park Service (in St. Louis) and the Missouri Department of Natural Resources and Missouri Department of Conservation at state parks and public recreation areas. One good but short-lived festival in the 1980s was held in the livestock arena on the campus of the University of Missouri in Columbia.

Dixon: Bluegrass Pickin' Time

In 1969, an experiment by Bill and Mona Jones to bring musicians together for an informal show and jam session became one of Missouri's biggest, best-known, and longest-running bluegrass festivals. Bill and Mona were inspired to create a festival after their first trip to Bill Monroe's festival in Bean Blossom. Among others helping create the Dixon festival included musicians Burl Copeland, Lonnie Dunn, Jim Orchard, and Harold Rowden.

The first festival the Joneses hosted took place over Labor Day weekend in 1969 at a community center near Dixon, a small railroad town in Pulaski County. Jim Orchard, a good friend who also attended the Bean Blossom festivals, a respected musician, band leader, and popular stage personality (see *Fiddler's Dream*), became the festival's emcee. As the event grew, more space was needed, and in 1981 the event was situated in a photogenic thirteen-acre tract on a gentle oak-shaded hillside on the Jones family farm north of Dixon in the upper Ozarks, within reasonable drive from St. Louis, Springfield, Columbia, and Kansas City. The Labor Day festival proved to be a success. In May 1981, Bill and Mona created a sister festival for the Memorial Day holiday, and both events were known as Bluegrass Pickin' Time.

Bill Jones, a mail carrier and farmer, was the festival's Mister Fix-It, doing much of the organizing and campground management, trash hauling, and problem solving—while saving time to perform with the band he and Mona headed, the Bluegrass Travelers. More than once, Bill brought his old Farmall H tractor out and pulled motor homes and campers out of mud holes when a heavy rain came. The "bluegrass park" was continually improved, including indoor shower-and-bathroom facilities and spaces with electricity for the many large motor homes that eventually grew to outnumber the old-style "campers." Many fans and band members drove their motor homes and campers to the park a week ahead of festival time to secure a favorite campsite.

Mona Jones, "First Lady of Missouri Bluegrass"

Mona Jones (1937–2020) started playing guitar in the mid-1940s with a Silvertone archtop, learning chords to Hank Williams songs such as "Lovesick Blues" in the Wheeler community on the Gasconade River in central Pulaski County. Mona's style was the traditional straight-chord (open-chord) guitar accompaniment, played with a flat pick (plectrum). When she took a melody break on a tune like "Wildwood Flower," she kept it simple and in the manner of the Carter Family, whose 1928 recording of the old folksong was (and continues to be) much loved and copied.[28]

Bill and Mona Jones and the Bluegrass Travelers at a bluegrass festival in Centralia, Missouri, 1974. *Left to right*: Garvin Lee, Kenny Cantrell, Mona Jones, Bill Jones, and Carol Jones. (Photo by Howard Marshall)

Mona and Bill Jones had settled in Dixon in 1953. Mona was at Eileen Withers's beauty shop with her younger sister, Joanne, one day, when they were invited to Eileen's house. There was a guitar there. Ralph and Eileen and the Jones sisters started singing with the Witherses, and Ralph asked if they wanted to sing at a revival coming to their church. Mona's brother Burl Copeland decided to join in, and others did too. Ralph, Carol, Burl, and Bill played for a while. "So all this began with just getting a haircut."[29]

Bill and Mona founded their band, the Bluegrass Travelers, which in time included their daughter, Carol, and the band appeared at many festivals as well as their own Bluegrass Pickin' Time. A typical Bluegrass Travelers performance included Mona stepping out to the mike and taking a guitar solo to start "Wildwood Flower." In the early days of bluegrass, soloing on "Wildwood Flower" was a way for a female guitarist to find some limelight. Mona Jones used to joke, "Nobody ever said I played like a girl." Mona was one of few women who took leadership roles in bluegrass bands.

Mona received one of many accolades in June 2017 at the Pioneers of Missouri Bluegrass Concert and Awards, at the Barn, a country music venue near Dixon. In May 2018, an event was held in Rolla, Missouri, to honor Mona Jones and the Jones family's Bluegrass Pickin' Time festival. On the campus of the Missouri University of Science and Technology, the concert and program of reminiscing was sponsored by the State Historical Society of Missouri, where Mona Jones established a collection of bluegrass materials.[30] The emcee was bluegrass radio deejay, magazine publisher, and university professor Wayne Bledsoe. The concert included old bluegrass-picking friends and young admirers, such as Jimmie Allison and the Bluegrass Rounders, Jimmy Orchard and the Ozark Bluegrass Boys, and Mona with a current version of the Bluegrass Travelers. The musicians in these bands on that day in 2018 represented the many musicians at the Dixon festivals. Mona was in good form and spoke of her life in the Ozarks: "I was born a little country girl, bare-footed, and didn't have nothin'."

There were famous and up-and-coming bluegrass bands as well as local bands in the schedule at Dixon festivals. The Bluegrass Travelers hosted, performed in the lineup, and generally made themselves available. Bill played bass and emceed the group, Mona played guitar and sang, and their daughter, Carol, played guitar and sang. A number of banjo players, mandolinists, and fiddlers performed with the group through the years as members moved on or retired. As with most "classic" bluegrass bands, they sang in harmony parts and included at least one gospel number in each set.[31] Their LPs represent traditional bluegrass in repertoire and the ebullient "sound" of capable regional bands.

Bands become identified with certain festivals. One of these is the Bluegrass Five, one of Missouri's long-running groups, founded by Harold Rowden, who began singing and playing bluegrass guitar in the 1950s. Rowden's band in various configurations became a fixture at Dixon and at other festivals in the region.[32] Personnel shifted from time to time, but the core was Rowden and several musicians in the Dixon-Meta-Vienna area.

Joe Wieneman, from Eldon, has played bluegrass mandolin, guitar, and fiddle since the late 1970s and is a familiar presence at festivals. Joe started out with Gateway Bluegrass, a family band, and moved to other touring Midwest groups, including Down the Road, Bill and Mona Jones's Bluegrass Travelers, Rural Roots, Frank Ray and Cedar Hill, Rosa Stringworks, the Bluegrass Five, and Ironweed Bluegrass Band. Joe is an original member of Rhonda Vincent and the Rage in 1995–96. Known for his mandolin and guitar playing, Wieneman is also a fine bluegrass fiddler and baritone singer.

The Dixon festival included concerts by featured bands (typically including one or more "national" bands as well as regional and local groups), workshops by band members, jam sessions throughout the campground, and Sunday-morning gospel music. A small food stand morphed into a diner, with meals and coffee from morning until late at night when the last of the bands finished onstage. The stage, in front of an acre or so where fans watched concerts in folding chairs and lawn chairs, changed over time from a basic stage with a basic PA system and lighting into a professional-quality stage with current equipment and a greenroom backstage with chairs, snacks, and beverages, where bands could tune, make last-minute scribbles on set sheets, dust off boots, and get ready to perform. Bill Jones allowed people to set up sales booths and "tape tables" for recordings, memorabilia, and various other items.

By advertising their event as off-limits to drugs and alcoholic beverages, the Joneses generally avoided disruptions of the kind that plagued certain other bluegrass festivals.[33] There was also a dress code, insisting that booked bands perform in what the Joneses deemed appropriate costumes. If a band chose suits and ties and cowboy boots, that was fine; if they chose boots, jeans, and cowboy shirts—or overalls—those had to be clean and presentable. (See *Fiddler's Dream* for discussion of apparel and hats in bluegrass music.) There would be no shorts or T-shirts here. Bill's dress code extended to the campgrounds, where "decent" and "appropriate" attire was expected.

Bill Jones banned electrified musical instruments and amplifiers when such devices were beginning to be seen at other festivals. Jim Orchard remembers one year when a guest band set up onstage with amplified instruments: "There was a group got on stage and was playing their first tune, and Bill showed up. He just stared out onto the stage and pretty soon he said, 'That's an *omp* [amp], we don't allow *omps* around here'—and he went and got the amp and carried it backstage."[34] The community continues to be divided over the use of electrically amplified instruments. Such maxims as "Keep it close to the ground," "Don't get above your raisin'," or "Bill" (Monroe) or "Earl" (Scruggs) "played it that way" are part of the patois of bluegrass.

Concessionaires were welcomed if they were unobtrusive and fitted the festival's conservative tone, but sellers had to pass muster with the Joneses. For a dozen years or so, an older gentleman whose hobby was making leather belts for friends set up a small tent and offered his goods. Clyde and Nora Jones ("Promoters of Bluegrass," Tulsa, Oklahoma), who loved the festival, parked their motor home along the south edge of the concert area (the only ones allowed to do so) and set up tables to sell recordings from booked bands and others and to distribute flyers for other festivals. And most festivals have a "music store" for on-the-spot sales of new instruments or accoutrements. Some purveyors of instruments, strings, and accessories consider festivals to be an offshoot of their core business.

Some friends and mainstays of Missouri bluegrass get together for some tunes on the porch at Frank Ray's music concession at the Dixon bluegrass festival, September 2004. *Left to right*: Joe Wieneman (mandolin), Lisa Fritchey Jones (bass), Dave Maravilla (guitar), and Allen Jones (banjo). (Photo by Howard Marshall, September 2004)

Newton, Kansas, luthier Russ Morton set up his "store" on tables in front of his camper in an area near the restaurant, with violins and bows and various necessities for sale. Morton would do a violin bow re-hairing job when a fiddler was in need and occasionally perform a bit of emergency violin repair.[35] A number of fiddlers found their next, better, violin at Morton's tables, and others were given a generous deal on a "beginner" fiddle outfit. Russ Morton was interested in helping children get started playing and helped parents acquire quality but affordable instruments. Russ's grandson Andrew Morton is one of many who grew up at festivals like Dixon, and today Andrew is among the region's best-known bluegrass fiddlers.[36]

For several years, Dixon included an old-time fiddle contest, but these were phased out by the 2000s, just as they had been at most other bluegrass festivals. Old-time fiddling and bluegrass fiddling differed but were generally compatible at the festival. Some bluegrass bands featured fiddlers playing an old-time style (versus modern bluegrass styles). Old-time fiddlers interested in becoming full-on bluegrass fiddlers were few in the 1960s and 1970s, so most of the fiddlers who came for the contest were old-time "contest fiddlers" such as Jake Hockemeyer.

The final day of the festivals, Sunday, after the gospel music in the morning and as people were preparing to leave the park, the stage was opened to anyone who wanted to come up and join various band members in the grand finale jam session emceed by Jim Orchard. The last song was always "Will the Circle Be Unbroken."[37]

Fiddlers were engaged in many of the jam sessions in the Dixon campgrounds. Several prominent fiddlers who did not perform onstage developed jam sessions in the campground that became sought-after chances for learners and fans to hear fiddle music. Fiddlers who were jam-session regulars included Billy Lee, Herbie Johnston, Dale Sullivan, Shorty Miller, Clifford Hill, Jim Brake, and Earl Ball. Not focused just on bluegrass, fiddle sessions included old-time as well as a few western swing tunes, Hank Williams classics, and other evergreens in the broad folk-music repertoire. While the habit ebbed during Dixon's final years, some of the paid musicians in booked bands enjoyed sitting in on the fiddle sessions and meeting local players.

Bluegrass Pickin' Time flourished in the late sixties to eighties period of growth for bluegrass festivals and then gradually waned. Some bands brought a more contemporary sound to the music and were welcomed. Midnight Flight's fiddler Gerald Jones (who plays bluegrass fiddle with substantial references to the innovative, swing-influenced Benny Martin) recalls being part of a younger, more contemporary sounding band:

> We did have the feeling of bluegrass, but we kind of developed a style where we brought in something that wasn't real true and traditional. And Bill [Jones] had always told us, "Boys, you're kinda swaying to the side now, you got to keep 'er down that road, now. You got a good *sound*, but you're kinda going to the left or going to the right. Keep 'er down the straight and narrow road of the tradition and that'll get you there [success] someday."

Midnight Flight had begun painting outside the lines Bill Monroe engraved in marble decades before. Later, Midnight Flight kept their music so solid, "classic," and "correct" that they continued to be a Dixon festival favorite throughout the festival's life span.

At Dixon, classic bluegrass was nourished and highlighted in the program, even while something a little different was sometimes heard out in the campground jam sessions. Periodically, an unusual instrument or unique performer would be welcomed in the band lineup, to offer bits of variation and audience appeal. Unusual instruments—unusual for bluegrass—such as accordion and harmonica could be heard in novelty acts or comedy routines. In addition, the Dixon stage welcomed jig dancers and often asked dancers to come onstage and dance to a hot instrumental.

Bill and Mona Jones retired and sold the park in 2006. Its final year was 2009. There were attempts by new owners to keep the event going and open the park in the off-season, but the park was closed in 2013. Closing Dixon sent ripples of disappointment across the Midwest; a family reunion had folded. "The Dixon festival. It's come and gone; precious memories."[38]

As people began to realize the impact of the loss of Dixon, the cornerstone festival, other festivals began to fortify their events to take up the slack, such as Silver Dollar City's events, the Vincent family's Sally Mountain festivals, Jefferson City's January indoor festivals, the Starvy Creek festival, and the Back Forty Bluegrass festival near Curryville. Several excellent new festivals cropped up, such as the Bootheel Bluegrass Festival (at Fruitland, 2005) and Arcadia Valley Mountain Music Festival (on the courthouse square in Ironton, developed by George Portz and featuring a fiddle contest). In addition, a number of community festivals with broader folk-music interests, such as Hootin' an' Hollerin' at Gainesville, include bookings of bluegrass.

Members of the Sally Mountain Show at the Tri-State Bluegrass Association's fall indoor festival, Hannibal, 1988. *Left to right*: Carolyn Vincent (bass), Rhonda Vincent (violin), and Johnny Vincent (banjo). (Photo by Howard Marshall)

Johnny and Carolyn Vincent and family founded a major festival at their Sally Mountain Park, west of Queen City in northern Missouri's Schuyler County.[39] Their daughter, Rhonda, is a well-known professional bluegrass mandolinist, fiddler, singer, bandleader, and songwriter. She is part of the sixth generation in the family in north Missouri. Rhonda competed successfully in fiddle contests in the 1970s and 1980s. Dissatisfied by the contest scene, Rhonda decided to concentrate on her mandolin playing, singing, and song composition, eventually moving to Nashville in 1980 and winning awards. She later moved back to Missouri. Her band, the Rage, was originally spelled "Raje" for the first names of the band's first members—Rhonda, Allen Jones (Dixon, banjo), Joe Wieneman (Eldon, guitar), and Irl Hees (Eldon, bass; most people thought his name was spelled "Earl"). In time, the band name was changed to "Rage."[40] "Sally Mountain" is an apt name for the Vincent family band and their festival. "Mountain" reflected their music and connections to bluegrass and country music in the southeastern United States as well as their family roots in Kentucky. When bluegrass festivals became popular, the Vincents purchased some sixty acres of timbered hills in the Sally Mountain area and built the site.

Lisa Ray performing with Frank Ray and Cedar Hill at the International Bluegrass Music Association convention, Nashville, 2006. As a young girl, she encountered prejudice toward females playing fiddle music. "I've had a lot of trouble with the menfolk. A lot of them thought females shouldn't be playing instruments at all." Lisa's career includes work with the Horse Creek Band at Silver Dollar City near Branson ("And they never had a female fiddler before"). (Photo by Benton Naylor)

Michael Smartt and Roger Matthews, "Fiddle and Banjo." The fiddle-and-banjo duo is a venerable tradition from the days of minstrelsy. Several years ago, Roger launched Fiddle and Banjo, in the manner of the unaccompanied duets made famous by bluegrass pioneers Earl Scruggs and fiddler Paul Warren. When Roger's fiddle partner Clyde Williams (a.k.a. Dan O'Day) moved to North Carolina in 2018, Michael Smartt took up the fiddle duties. (October 22, 2016; courtesy of Matthews)

The Starvy Creek Bluegrass Festival is situated near Conway (Webster County), Missouri, and became one of Missouri's most popular festivals.

> Starvy Greek Bluegrass Festivals started in 1986 as a way for Don & Bobbie Day to share their love of bluegrass music with others. What started out as a small get-together has grown into huge twice-a-year bluegrass events. The Days, along with many relatives and friends, host a festival the first weekend in July and the third weekend of September. They are passionate about bringing top bluegrass acts to Starvy Creek and are strict with rules so all fans have a fun and memorable experience. They work hard to make sure that the park, facilities, bands and food is the best it can be.

Starvy Creek is a branch of the Niangua River and a few miles north of the festival park.

Back Forty Bluegrass, near Curryville in northeast Missouri, was founded by the Turnbull family (bluegrass fans and musicians) in 1996. The Turnbulls helped fill the gap left by the demise of major festivals in their general region, such as those at Kahoka and Hannibal hosted for decades by the Tri-State Bluegrass Association (TSBA). In addition, thanks to schedulings in late May and August, Curryville also helps fill the gap left by Dixon's cancellation. "Back Forty" is an apt name for the festival, on rolling acreage on the Turnbull farm. "Back forty" is a folk expression that refers to a land parcel that is remote, undeveloped, or unused and often inaccessible from the road at the "front" of a farm.

From the beginnings of bluegrass music under the baton of Bill Monroe in the 1940s until his death in 1996, Monroe and his Bluegrass Boys set the standard for the music. Many of his numerous band members through the decades went on to lead their own bands and become influential in the history of bluegrass. Monroe's presence, the Indiana festival he founded during the Folk Music Revival in the 1960s, and the influence of his classic recordings continue. At Monroe's annual festival in Bean Blossom, Indiana, June 1972. (Photo by Howard Marshall)

Bluegrass Clubs

The importance of voluntary associations in launching and supporting bluegrass festivals and grassroots events of any kind cannot be overstated, just as with fiddle contests. Bluegrass clubs were incubators for bands as well as individuals. Musicians who become acquainted, hit it off socially, and notice others' similar musical interests often sort themselves into bands.

In the St. Louis region of eastern Missouri and southwestern Illinois, the Missouri Area Bluegrass Committee (MABC) was organized in 1970 and created festivals, often featuring a fiddle contest along with the standard fare of concerts, workshops, and jam sessions. Jeff and Adena Cook were active in the group's creation, and Jeff hosted a weekly AM radio bluegrass show. The MABC continues to host basket dinners, concerts, and jam sessions and promotes festivals in the region, such as their annual wintertime indoor festival at Eureka.

The Kansas City metro area is perhaps Missouri's most bluegrass-active city. The Kansas City Area Bluegrass Music Club was founded in 1970 and grew out of the informal 1960s "Kansas City old-time fiddlers club." The fiddle-club meetings and

Grass Cuttin' Time in Missouri was produced in St. Louis by Jeff and Adena Cook with the Missouri Area Bluegrass Committee in 1970. The album included Rich Orchard, Frank Ray, and the Ramblin' Bluegrass Boys (Stan Wagganer, fiddle); Don Brown, Norman Ford, and the Ozark Mountain Trio (Brown, mandolin); Dub Crouch and the Bluegrass Rounders; Ken Seaman and the Current River Drifters (Clark Weaver, fiddle); Jeff Cook and the Mississippi Valley Ramblers (Bob Wagganer, fiddle); and Rod Moag and Howard (Rusty) Marshall.

sessions were vital for young people learning about and coming into bluegrass music. Among regulars were fiddlers Andy Beaty, Ed Davis, Larry Ellis, Lyman Enloe, Ed Hamilton, "Long" John Journagin, and Dutch Noah. Jim McGreevy recalls that the club's meetings and sessions were especially good opportunities for newcomers to learn how to play proper accompaniment for fiddlers. The club met at the Iron Workers Local No. 10 union hall at Forty-Seventh and Prospect and was conceived as an informal branch of Cleo Persinger's Mid-West Fiddlers' Association.

While fiddlers performed sets of tunes onstage at old-time fiddle-club meetings, bluegrassers like Audrey Belt (Lyman Enloe's daughter), John Bennett, Jerry Justice, Jim McGreevy, Chuck Stearman, and others got together in the back and played and

Bluegrass Association promotional photo. *Left to right, front*: John Bennett, Jim McGreevy, Lyman Enloe, and Don Montgomery; *rear*: Chuck Stearman and Audrey Enloe Belt. Instruments with visible brand names are Gibson "Granada" model Mastertone banjo, Gibson F-5 mandolin, and Martin D-18 guitar. (Courtesy of Jim McGreevy)

sang bluegrass music. In a 2017 program at the Kansas City Area Bluegrass Music Club on the history of bluegrass in Kansas City, McGreevy recalled, with a touch of droll humor, how the group changed from fiddle club to bluegrass club:

> We would get off in a back room somewhere and play a little *bluegrass*. Some of the people in the audience began to request that we come up and play on stage. Can you believe it—they got sick and tired of *nothing but fiddle tunes*! But they actually requested that we break the monotony a little bit and come up and sing a song. And others followed in that pursuit, like The Original Collins Brothers. So that didn't set too well with the old-time fiddlers—understandably, because it *was* the old-time fiddlers club, not the singers and pickers club, you know. So, they didn't take a liking to our singing too much, you know, and pretty soon that club [old-time fiddlers club] dissolved.[41]

As the fiddle club dissolved, some members and others formed the Kansas City Area Bluegrass Music Club. What had been almost entirely sessions of fiddle tunes widened its appeal by opening up to bluegrass bands and singers. Some disharmony ensued, but most of the old-time fiddlers joined the new group and the few disgruntled fiddlers who disliked the pickin' and singin' found other groups to join. The Kansas City Area Bluegrass Club meets the first Friday evening of the month, October through May, when the club adjourns for the summer bluegrass festival and vacation season. For years the group met in rented fellowship halls of Protestant churches. There is a registration table where memberships may be opened or renewed, and a "tape table" with T-shirts and bumper stickers, cassettes and CDs. At six people begin to gather, and several church members who are cooks open the kitchen for sandwiches and desserts (with proceeds going to the church). A concert of invited bands begins at seven on the fellowship-hall stage, and, at some point, donations are invited from the audience. Open jam sessions commence in adjacent rooms, "open" jams in the sense that anyone is welcome to sit in. This is bluegrass, so there are guitars, banjos, mandolins, basses, Dobros, violins, and incidental other instruments (a snare drum may appear, played quietly with brushes, and a frequent participant plays hammered dulcimer), and people sing bluegrass and country songs. The concert ends around ten, the last jam melts away by ten thirty, and the spaces are tidied by a gentleman from the church who turns out the lights and closes up.

Left to right: Lyman Enloe (violin), Donna Rose Nichols (guitar), and Rusty Dutton (guitar) at Silver Dollar City, ca. 1986. This Ozarks-themed amusement park has programmed bluegrass music and old-time fiddling and hosted old-time and bluegrass festivals since its founding in 1960. (Courtesy of Rusty Dutton)

Rusty Dutton, a Lyman Enloe Understudy

Robert (Rusty) Dutton (1933–2022) was born in Independence and grew up on a farm near Butler. He described his parents as English in background. His mother taught him guitar at age nine, with a "Gene Autry" guitar one of his older brothers had left when he went into the Army during World War II.[42] Dutton started playing fiddle around age eleven, after seeing a fiddler and tenor-banjo duo performing old-time fiddle tunes on the town square.

> I asked them if I could join them and was invited to get my guitar out. We played for the better part of the afternoon when the fiddler asked me how I would like to play square dances with him. I said "my mother would NEVER let me do that." Then he asked who my mother was. She was a telephone switchboard operator in Butler and he knew her. So, I took him to meet with my mother and, to my surprise, she agreed to allow me to accompany him. After a few dances, he decided I needed to learn some tunes on the fiddle in order to spell him occasionally. The first tunes that he taught me were "Rag Time Annie," "Chinky Pin," [a.k.a. "Lead Out"], "Mississippi Sawyer," and "Soldiers Joy," for square dances, and "Four Leaf Clover" for a round dance. I simply cannot remember his name, even though I played square dances with him for a year or so. I do remember a Missouri square dance fiddler name of Brick Harris, and his son Lyle Harris. I went to school with Lyle and he played fiddle at dances also. Another fine fiddler that I admired was Herby Hellwig who lived on a farm south of Butler. He had agreed to teach me fiddling but unfortunately, he was killed in a car accident in his early twenties before I really got to know him.[43]

At sixteen, Dutton was playing lead guitar in a country band. In 1952 he enlisted in the Air Force and while stationed in California met a fellow airman, Del Reeves, and they formed a country band, with Dutton playing electric guitar (Del Reeves went on to fame as a country singer after the service). Transferred to Elmendorf air base in Alaska, Dutton played electric guitar in a country band there. Released from active duty as a sergeant after four years, he moved to Kansas City and played in country and bluegrass bands such as Bill Deckard and His Western Aires, the Jimmy Dallas Road Show, the Bluegrass Brigade, Heartland Express (with the Griffin sisters Lela and Leta and Lela's husband, Len Peeples), and the Singing Gaylords (based in Oklahoma). In 1979 and into the 1980s, Dutton played banjo and fiddle in the Bluegrass Brigade.

Beginning in 1982, Rusty was tutored and mentored by Lyman Enloe. Enloe was known to be hesitant to take on fiddle students, and few people had the opportunity to work with him.[44] Dutton admired Lyman's technique, especially his elegant bowing, and hoped to learn some of Lyman's Missouri tunes. Enloe did violin repair, too, and Dutton absorbed repair skills by watching him work. Dutton traveled the central Midwest as a traveling salesmen in 1982 and occasionally stopped at flea markets; he found a "beautiful old amber fiddle" at a flea market near Sedalia. Rusty took the violin to Lyman, who fixed it up. Rusty continued to take violins to Lyman to look over and repair, and "he began to come out of his shell a little and finally agreed to let me tape-record him playing some of his tunes. I started playing guitar for him on the recordings and that led to his teaching me some of his tunes and bowing styles." While watching Enloe work on violins, Dutton was asking questions and eventually started working on violins, "understudying his fiddle repair secrets." After Enloe's death, Dutton inherited Enloe's tools and other equipment. "We retired to Tucson and I moved all of that equipment out there with us, joined the Arizona Old Time Fiddlers' Association and I have been doing fiddle repair work for a lot of the fiddlers in this area ever since."[45]

Dutton traveled with Enloe to perform at festivals such as the University of Chicago Folk Festival in 1986 and the National Folk Festival in 1990 (in Johnstown, Pennsylvania, that year), often adding harmony fiddle to Enloe's melody. At festivals where Kenny Baker was performing with Bill Monroe's band, Enloe and Dutton enjoyed sessions with Baker in the campgrounds.[46] Enloe appreciated Dutton's interest in the old, unusual fiddle tunes and allowed Dutton to record them extensively and learn them.

Dutton retired in 1998 as national sales manager of ACME Products manufacturing company, and he and his wife, Dory, moved to Tucson, Arizona, in 2001, where they had spent winters. In Tucson, Rusty performed with a bluegrass band and a gospel music group and gave fiddle lessons for the Catalina Fiddle Club. He focused on helping students learn some of the old-time tunes that cross over into bluegrass, such as "Arkansas Traveler," "Back Up and Push," "Bill Cheatem," "Billy in the Lowground," "Blackberry Blossom," "Liberty," "Sally Goodin," "Soldier's Joy," and a favorite waltz in Missouri, "Shamus O'Brien." Rusty Dutton signed letters and emails "Rusty Dutton. Tucson Fiddler. Native of Missouri. Lifetime Musician."

> I was once told at about 50 years of age, that I should quit and let the new breed of musicians take over. I told him the day I quit playing music is when they bring a casket up on the stage, put me in it and carry me off. Lyman always told me "never quit playing because if you do, you'll get old!" I still play the authentic old time fiddle tunes in the way they were taught to me but I have to admit that it requires a lot more practice than it used to.[47]

Based in Kirksville, Missouri, the Society for the Preservation of Blue Grass Music of America (SPBGMA) was organized by mandolinist and promoter Chuck Stearman after trips with Jim McGreevy to Bill Monroe's Bean Blossom festival in June 1969 and 1973. Driving back to Missouri in 1973, McGreevy and Stearman were commiserating on the lack of bluegrass associations in Missouri, and Stearman decided to develop one.[48] Stearman loved old-time fiddling and early bluegrass fiddling and was known as one of the region's best mandolin players.[49] Chuck conceived of SPBGMA as one that would speak to and for the midwestern states as well as for the nation, and their forte was bluegrass festivals. SPBGMA ("spig-muh") continues to

Jeana Martin Faris of the Bluegrass Martins family band of Jefferson City is a young star who grew up in the festival community. The band performs widely and is featured at Silver Dollar City. In this photo, Jeana performs with the Bluegrass Martins at the SPBGMA Bluegrass Music Awards and bluegrass festival at the Capitol Plaza Hotel in Jefferson City, January 2006. (Photo by Benton Naylor)

host indoor bluegrass festivals and industry conventions in the winter, with award ceremonies for performers and bands. The first was held in St. Joseph in 1973, and, after two years, the winter festival moved to the Lake of the Ozarks and, in 1999, settled in Jefferson City.

SPBGMA hosted a National Fiddler's Contest in a convention hotel at the Lake of the Ozarks in 1983 (it later moved to the Ozark Folk Center in Mountain View, Arkansas). Fiddlers from many states competed in the 1983 contest. Randy Howard of Georgia, a gifted professional in Nashville, won the Open Division. Ken Sloan, from Mena, Arkansas, won the Seniors. It is notable that emphasis in these contests especially in the Open Division was not bluegrass or old-time fiddling, however. Most of the top finishers performed some variant of modern Contest Style and repertoire—which helps explain why the SPBGMA contest died out after several years; some bluegrass musicians and fans were not pleased with the intrusion of Texas/Contest Style into bluegrass and old-time music.[50]

Chuck Stearman wanted to keep bluegrass authentic (in his view of authenticity) and separate in the public mind from folk music and rock and roll. He disliked "newgrass" and progressive bluegrass, disliked electrified instruments in bluegrass, and disliked modern country music.

> The reason I started SPBGMA was to set a standard for bluegrass music and to educate the public about what bluegrass music really is. People were confused about ten

years ago with the rock scene and the folk scene, and bluegrass music was starting to be intermingled with this. People thought if a rock band had a banjo or a fiddle, they played bluegrass music. I am offended when people call that bluegrass. [We wanted to] keep them [festivals] clean and with a family atmosphere and bring in real bluegrass music for the weekend. I think we've been successful.[51]

Another group to take a conservative position was the Tri-State Bluegrass Association, formed in 1978 (the three states being Missouri, Iowa, and Illinois), "to promote the education and enjoyment of traditional and Bluegrass music and preserve the folk traditions from which this music has developed." Based in the farm town of Kahoka in Missouri's northeast corner, the group had personal connections with Bill Monroe, John Hartford, Kenny Baker, Benny Martin, and other celebrities. The group held festivals (some with fiddle contests) in their region. The Tri-State Bluegrass Association and Delbert Spray, its leader, are discussed in *Fiddler's Dream*.[52] Kahoka festivals included an open-microphone "fiddler's frolic" Friday night, and fiddlers from featured bands took turns playing tunes alongside local fiddlers; some exciting impromptu fiddling took place, as "campground fiddlers" found themselves standing next to Kenny Baker or Benny Martin. For a number of years, the association sponsored indoor winter events in November and February in a hotel in Hannibal and in some years a hotel across the Mississippi in Quincy, Illinois. The TSBA continues to produce an annual bluegrass festival calendar and band guide under the editorship of Delbert and Erma Spray's daughter, Pat Davidson.

For several years, a major fiddle contest was held by the Tri-State Bluegrass Association at an indoor festival in a Hannibal hotel. Open Division winners, 1989, *left to right*: Kirk Brandenberger, Brad Kennedy, Pete McMahan, Johnny Bruce, Patty Chandler, and Dick Vance (Jamestown, NY). (Photo by Howard Marshall)

The Heart of the Ozarks Bluegrass Association was organized in 1980 by Ethel Willard, Gary Due, Lemuel Adkisson, Kevin Dunlap, Norma and Junior Stubbs (who donated thirteen acres of land to create "HOBA park"), and others, and the event continues largely through the efforts of Randall and Teresa Romans and their family. Like other associations, HOBA has a typical administrative structure, with a president, vice president, treasurer, and advisory board. They held their first festival (with a band contest) in 1982. Teresa Romans writes that HOBA was "the brainchild" of Ethel Willard, a West Plains elementary schoolteacher who, with her husband, traveled to the bluegrass festivals in the summers. Teresa Romans spoke of the importance of volunteers: "A lot of folks have helped HOBA to grow from a seed into a great organization run solely by volunteers with a beautiful bluegrass park."[53] HOBA draws participation primarily from the Ozarks region along the southern Missouri and northern Arkansas region. HOBA park has camping sites, electrical service for motor homes, a cook shack, plumbed comfort stations, landscaping, a covered stage with a PA system, and other necessaries for festival crowds. HOBA sponsors festivals in June and September, modest in size, but booking a "name" band in addition to local performers. Its site and administrators exude a welcoming spirit and relaxed hospitality.[54]

There is a Greater Ozarks Bluegrass Society in the Springfield area. The group was founded in 2011 by Clyde Williams ("Dan O'Day") and others, and its theme announces their territory and echoes other associations: "To preserve, and promote the bluegrass and traditional music of the Ozarks through education and exposure, so as to maximize the understanding and appreciation of the music form."[55] A valuable innovation by the leadership is a scholarship program for young musicians, in honor of the late mandolin builder John Wynn.

In 1990 the Kansas City metro area saw a new association, the Heart of America Bluegrass and Old-time Music Club (HABOT). They followed the customary pattern of meetings and festivals with invited bands onstage and jam sessions. HABOT is located in North Kansas City at the North Cross United Methodist Church, and its founders included Daryl Cline, Bill Blackburn, and Byron Jones.

The newest group to become active is the Missouri Bluegrass Preservation Association, organized in 2016 by C. J. Lewandowski (the Po' Ramblin' Boys) with Janice Martin (the Bluegrass Martins) and others. They hold reunions of musicians and fans and initiated a program to give recognition to people who were part of the evolution of bluegrass in Missouri. Each year (until the COVID-19 pandemic) the group hosted a banquet, concert, and ceremony to present selected founders with an award naming them Pioneers of Missouri Bluegrass. The first award went to Ray Gore (of Don Brown and the Ozark Mountain Trio) in January 2017. The awards read, in part: "Without this elite first generation of bluegrass pioneers the state of Missouri would not have our treasured music. We humbly present this pioneer award as a token of our gratitude, whereas you are a vital part of Missouri history." Lewandowski, a professional bluegrass musician from Grubville, Missouri, now in Nashville, collects and conserves materials related to Missouri bluegrass history and advocates for the classic early bluegrass sounds.[56] The existence of this new group and their presentation of "pioneer awards" suggest that the 1960s, the era of bluegrass music's great expansion, is now thought of as history by younger generations. The early adopters of bluegrass who once were creative youngsters are now tribal elders.

Gerald Jones in one of his trademark fedoras and with his favorite violin, an E. Martin "Amati" model made in Markneukirchen, Germany, in the early 1900s. Jones is among bluegrass musicians who prefer to perform in "Sunday clothes" in the tradition of Bill Monroe's band Flatt and Scruggs and other bluegrass pioneers. Rolla, Missouri, 2006. (Courtesy of Gerald Jones)

Gerald Jones: "It's Not the Notes You Put In. It's the Notes You Leave Out"

Gerald Jones of Salem is one of Missouri's best-known and most versatile bluegrass fiddlers—not quite old enough to qualify as a pioneer but old enough to be called "the old man" by today's bandmates. Gerald was born in Terre Haute, Indiana, in 1957. He started classical violin lessons at age seven and played in the school orchestra through high school. The Indiana Old-Time Fiddler's Association held regular sessions, and, as a teenager, Gerald became acquainted with fiddlers such as Gene Wilhite. From nearby Brazil (Indiana), Wilhite was a fine left-handed fiddler, a state champion, and one of the first Indiana old-time fiddlers to embrace both bluegrass and the "Weiser" Contest Style emerging in the 1970s.[57] Gerald Jones learned a lot of music and technique playing monthly dances with Wilhite and other musicians.

In 1971, Gerald's father, Ralph, a guitar player, took Gerald and his younger brother Daryl (learning to play guitar) to Monroe's Bean Blossom festival, some ninety miles east of Terre Haute. There, Gerald heard Kenny Baker performing with Monroe's band and was captivated by Baker's brilliance. Jones listened to Baker in backstage late-night jam sessions and found a Baker LP at a tape table—the impeccable 1969 LP *Portrait of a Bluegrass Fiddler*, a foundation recording for bluegrass fiddlers. The Bean Blossom experience inspired Gerald to teach himself tunes and work out fiddle "licks," using the "drop-the-needle method."[58]

Gerald also listened to recordings of Paul Warren, the fiddler with Lester Flatt and Earl Scruggs and the Foggy Mountain Boys and a master of straight-ahead old-time "hoedown fiddling" that fitted well in bluegrass. Jones began listening to the brilliant improviser and stylist Benny Martin, whose music remains a palpable thread in Jones's fiddle style. Martin was a master of the bow and often commented, in words that speak volumes, that he'd rather have a good bow and a cheap fiddle than a million-dollar fiddle and a cheap bow.

It was from Benny Martin that Gerald absorbed much of the backup fiddling devices needed in bluegrass bands. Kenny Baker, on the other hand, did not play backup fiddle as commonly understood. "Baker was a fiddler who never stopped. If you ever watched, Baker, he didn't *chop*, he didn't do nuthin, he *played constantly*. Sometimes he was over-riding the other ones, but he never did believe in choppin' or nuthin'. He was always playing runs, scales, trills, and stuff."[59] Studying performance styles and repertoires of these fiddlers, and others such as Chubby Wise and Mac Magaha, gave Jones the versatility to be welcomed in any band or jam session.[60]

For a time, Jones participated in contests, but he decided that the music he enjoyed the most was being the fiddler in a bluegrass band and being part of the lively festival network. After he graduated from high school in Terre Haute in 1975, in 1976 he joined the Downstate Ramblers, a southern Illinois bluegrass band. Around 1980, the Downstate Ramblers loaded up their van and traveled to Eminence, Missouri, site of an early, influential bluegrass festival. The band performed at Eminence, and it was there that Gerald met his future wife, Tina.

Midnight Flight, 2006. *Left to right*: Kevin Shults (mandolin, Columbia), Roger Matthews (banjo, Springfield), Gerald Jones (fiddle), Andy Dye (bass, Dixon), and Jimmy Allison (guitar, Rolla), at the annual Threshermen's Bluegrass Festival in Pontiac, Illinois. Bands typically have a "set sheet" of tunes for a performance in easy view, in this case a yellow pad next to the microphone. (Courtesy of Gerald Jones)

Gerald performed with the Downstate Ramblers until 1985, doing shows at festivals such as those hosted by the Tri-State Bluegrass Association, Society for Preservation of Bluegrass Music of America, and Missouri Area Bluegrass Committee as well as appearing at Bean Blossom in 1979. The Ramblers recorded five albums and played forty to fifty weekends a year, traveling in a converted 1955 GMC Greyhound Scenicruiser bus. "That was some fun times."[61] During his many travels to Missouri festivals, Jones was able to hear and play tunes with Lyman Enloe, another of Jones's inspirations, and recalls Enloe's excellent phrasing: "To me he was as smooth as Kenny Baker."[62] The Downstate Ramblers were featured at the SPBGMA awards show in Nashville in 1984, where they won three awards—Entertaining Bluegrass Band of the Year, Instrumental Group of the Year, and Fiddle Performer of the Year.

Formed in 1992, Midnight Flight was a crowd favorite at festivals such as the Dixon Bluegrass Pickin' Time, and its original members included Roger Matthews,

Jimmy Allison, Earnie Bishop, Frank Ellis, Nancy Bishop, and Nancy Cardwell Erdos. Jones joined in 1993. Midnight Flight toured and recorded and presented itself in an old-style format, grouped around one microphone, rather than the modern rock-and-roll band arrangement in a line across the stage with separate microphones for each player. In 2007, the band broke up, and in 2009 Gerald joined Men of the Week, headed by C. J. Lewandowski. Men of the Week was named 2010 SPBGMA Midwest Traditional Bluegrass Band of the Year, and Jones was Midwest Fiddle Performer of the Year. In his fifties, Gerald was the elder statesman in Men of the Week and enjoyed the role of mentor. In 2010, Men of the Week changed personnel as members moved to new locations; this is how it is in the music business—bands form, become seasoned and get recognition, and then things change. For many years, Jones has held down a "day job" at US Foods in Salem.

Gerald Jones's principal band for several years was the Missouri River Band. Jones is the senior member and affectionately called "the old man." At the Back Forty Bluegrass Festival near Curryville, May 2015. *Left to right*: Jeremy Boling (Kansas City), John Trew (Bolivar), Darrell Turnbull (Curryville), Dale Collins (Blue Springs), and Gerald Jones. (Photo by Russell D. Ravert)

Jones presents workshops at festivals, particularly encouraging learners and passing on ideas about being a bluegrass musician as well as teaching tunes and technique.

> First, I would tell everyone who was in attendance that the fiddle parts you play in a band are to be a complement of a musical experience that blends all the instruments and vocals together in a song that the crowd will enjoy and remember.

Second, I would talk about that there is a time for you to shine and show the audience what you can do in an instrumental break or ride in a song on the fiddle. You need to play the melody line first and then as the song progresses add your own musical improvs, but when you are doing backup fiddlin' you are there to add licks and phrasing, which enhances your personal feeling to the song. You do not want to override the notes but be there with just the right complementary notes.

Third, I would show the different licks and fiddle fills that I had learned that can be adapted in a song to give it a fuller feeling. Showing that one lick can be changed around, and you can use it in a song that is in a different key from what you knew it in.

Fourth, ask for any questions that a fiddler was having trouble with, like bowing techniques, double stops, melodies, when to play notes and not to play notes.

Finally, I would always tell them this, "Music from the heart brings comfort to your soul." Just enjoy the musical experience of friends in a late-night jam or on stage in a band that will make long lasting memories.[63]

A fiddler steeped in old-time and country music as well as classic bluegrass, Gerald Jones's backup fiddling for singers is on display on several CDs, including those by banjo player, fiddler, and country music vocalist in Salem Terry Cunningham (Terry's father, Jack, was a well-known fiddler). Jones continues to be a familiar presence at bluegrass festivals and fiddlers' conventions, where he can be found deep into a hot jam session late into the night.

Listen to track 30 on the companion CD to hear Gerald Jones's version of "Buck Snort."

Bob Walsh of Cape Fair gives a group fiddle lesson to Maddox family youngsters (Springfield) during a mid-1980s Traditional Arts Apprenticeship Program staff site visit. The guitar accompanist is Walsh's longtime colleague Joe Brayfield of Hollister. Walsh encouraged learners to get the basics and then develop their own individual styles; he was fond of saying, "Two crows don't sound alike when they're cawing." (Photo, Missouri Cultural Heritage Center)

How Learning Has Changed, and How it Hasn't

13

The MANUAL will not make a virtuoso out of anyone. . . . With its help, you can *teach yourself.*

—Pete Seeger, *How to Play the Five-String Banjo*

Listen to the old fiddlers and steep yourselves in their music. If you don't have access to "source" musicians, read and learn as much as you can from those who did, as well as from recordings. . . . All art begins with imitation; and, like all good artists, you will absorb the music and eventually put your own stamp on it. But before you can do that you have to listen—and keep listening.

—Julie Henigan, "Listening to the Tradition" (2009)

The hubs and spokes of the wheels of learning have been numerous. New hubs and spokes were added from the 1970s on, innovations in ways to be an old-time fiddler. Suzuki violin, formal apprenticeship programs, fiddle camps, and cyberspace changed things, yet in some ways little changed.

Few if any musicians are truly self-taught. And now, rather than seeking out a fiddler willing to share and teach, or listening to records and radio, learners can call up the digital universe. Global knowledge and experts are there at the tap of a computer key, smartphone app, or commands to a robot, anytime, day or night. All that is welcome, surely. Music gotten from person-to-person physical interaction in fiddle camps and apprenticeships is not over. Timeless, emotionally satisfying, the experience of sitting by people doing things we wish to do like them is forever. The rewards of "ear" music, human interaction, and "learning by heart" are not passé.

Ironically, some of the fiddle camps that sprouted in the 1980s inadvertently or purposely encouraged young learners to learn modern Contest Style, even in places where Contest Style was not traditional and where it usurped local and ethnic styles and repertoires. Fiddle camps and arts council programs supported local and regional traditions, but the kids who could play "Tom and Jerry" like the champions won contests and some teachers helped them achieve that.

Old-time square-dance styles were recognized as historically valid, but in many places without active square dances, the dance fiddling yielded marked share to the dressed-up Contest Style—listening music for audiences more than music for dancing. The sinews that held fiddling and dancing together gradually weakened, although exceptional youngsters could (and can) do it all.

Farnum Family Bluegrass Band, *left to right*: Matthew, Hannah, Tricia, Norm, Benjamin, and Maggie. Hannah Farnum's violin in this photo is a Gliga Gama Elite that was her prize (along with the carbon-fiber bow) for winning third place in the Walnut Valley Old-Time Fiddle Championship in Winfield, Kansas, in 2012 at age fifteen. Hannah occasionally uses an iSolo wireless microphone system on her violin. (Photo by Blaine & Janae Photography, courtesy of Norm Farnum Family)

Hannah Farnum: The Next Generation Steps Up

"I only play by ear."[1] Hannah Farnum is a welcome exception to the belief that many if not most young fiddlers today learn tunes from sheet music and have had classical violin training or at least Suzuki violin. Not so for Hannah; she is an ear musician.

Born in 1997, Hannah is part of a musical family and among young female fiddlers building reputations in the flourishing realm of semiprofessional and professional family bluegrass and gospel bands. Her father, Norm Farnum, came to the Ozarks in the 1970s from California's San Fernando Valley and landed a career in country music, establishing himself in Branson and Silver Dollar City. Norm organized the family band in 2004 with his wife, Tricia, and today the band includes Matthew (mandolin), Benjamin (guitar, mandolin), and Maggie (bass, violin), along with Norm (banjo), Tricia (piano, pennywhistle), and Hannah. They travel extensively to present their music at fairs and festivals and perform in church services and other family-friendly events. They currently host "Ozark Mountain Friday Nights" shows at the New Testament Christian Church in Reeds Spring and frequently include guest appearances by local artists.[2]

Hannah began learning fiddle at age six in 2003 and took more than ten years of lessons from Texas state champion and Branson-area pro Ricky Boen. Formerly with the Sons of the Pioneers, Boen was her earliest mentor and inspiration. Hannah also had classes with Irish master fiddlers Brian Conway and Randall Bays at the O'Flaherty Irish Music Retreat in Midland, Texas, in 2009 and 2011. She also learned from Junior Marriott and soaks up fiddle music on YouTube from fiddlers such as Kenny Baker, Michael Cleveland, Stuart Duncan, Patti Kusturok, and Benny Thomasson (all masters in different styles, from bluegrass to Canadian to Texas contest fiddling). Hannah characterizes her fiddle style as "predominantly Texas style with healthy doses of Irish and Bluegrass influences." Hannah's CD *A Time to Fiddle* was recorded when she was fifteen and offers a good sampler of her repertoire and range of interests.[3]

When the band's performance schedule allows, Hannah competes in fiddle contests. Among the highly competitive contests, in addition to her third-place wins at Winfield (2012, 2021), she won fourth place in the Open Division at the Missouri state contest in Sedalia in 2017. She does not think of herself as a contest fiddler, but enjoys the events and opportunities to visit with other fiddlers and musicians.

In 2019, "on a whim," Hannah posted a live fiddle session on her Facebook page. She was joined by her elder brother Benjamin, and the experiment soon gained fans and followers as they developed an ongoing series of informal "Fiddlin' Friday at Five" concerts from home via Facebook Live. The relaxed, engaging program attracts viewers from around the globe. Benjamin provides solid, sparkling backup and takes solos on his Martin D-15 mahogany dreadnought guitar. On his cell phone between tunes, Benjamin reads comments and responds verbally to viewers and fans, many of whom make requests that Hannah typically plays on the spot or says she will play on a future Friday. Since starting the series, Hannah has learned upward of two hundred fiddle tunes requested by listeners and has a "growing list of tunes to work up."

Listen to track 31 on the companion CD to hear Hannah Farnum's version of "Amelia's Waltz."

Try This at Home

As children we take in music by ear—"Happy Birthday," "Mary Had a Little Lamb," "Frère Jacques," "Pop Goes the Weasel," "Jingle Bells." We hear radio and records, play in school bands, go to festivals, watch TV, cruise the Internet. And we teach each other. Taylor McBaine told me fifty years ago, rare cases notwithstanding, that if a person can whistle or hum a tune, whether it's "Happy Birthday" or "Soldier's Joy," that person is capable of learning to play that tune.

In this chapter, we are looking at the experiences and careers of several fiddlers, different in their development and all sharing much as they pull music from and contribute to the banks of music around them. They represent different generations and overlapping ways of learning, but started out as children with guidance from fiddle masters and, in some cases, classical violin training, too. Kathy Summers, a fifth-generation fiddler "born into the music," learned by watching and listening. David Scrivner was a pupil of Bob Holt, a legendary square-dance fiddler whose repertoire and influences ranged far beyond home. Leisl Schoenberger started with classical violin, became interested in fiddling and a successful contest fiddler as a youngster, and teaches classical violin in a university in upstate New York. Matt Wyatt, a fourth generation of Wyatt fiddlers, added classical violin skills and advanced "fiddle" skills by ear in an apprenticeship program.

There is an old question: How is that some people just seem so gifted even as children, Mozarts of fiddling? Is it "nature or nurture" that accounts for the genius? Does musical ability "run in the family"? On all that, the jury is still out. It is not a competition between nature and nurture; it is nature *and* nurture. Becoming a musician includes both elements in our formation as individuals.[4]

Ed Sutherland gives a fiddle lesson to Herbie Johnston in Norwood, ca. 1975. "When Herbie told Ed he was also taking piano lessons, Ed responded, 'Well, you'll never make a fiddler then.' Herbie said he thought, 'I'll show that old man!' And he did." (Courtesy of Laine Sutherland; Sutherland, July 21, 2018)

The route to expertise in just about anything starts with a seasoned maker who welcomes young people to the mysteries of making. I say "expertise," because certainly one can learn the basics in just about anything from diligent study through schools, books, and cyberspace. But mastery takes more than ambition and concentration; it takes willingness to work with a teacher, and in that relationship come the "trade secrets," details, and inspiration.

Apprenticeship is a time-honored path for traditional arts, just as with many other skills. Many young fiddlers in this book applied for and won partnerships with a master fiddler in the Traditional Arts Apprenticeship Program.[5] But that kind of formal apprenticeship began only in the 1980s. Before that, aspiring fiddlers sought out willing teachers on their own, and this is still a prevailing path for learners—finding someone to learn from whose fiddling is appealing, listen, copy, take in and learn as much as possible, and become part of the fiddle community. The old advice is still good advice: just get around fiddlers, get acquainted, and hang out.

By the time the apprenticeship program and Bethel fiddle camp were inaugurated in the 1980s, attitudes toward women and girls in fiddling had changed a good deal, but old biases do die hard.

Pete McMahan's crotchety side was sometimes on display in his attitude about women in music. For most of his life, Pete disliked seeing girls and women play the fiddle or participate even as backups. He may have considered fiddling men's work, and he may have seen women as potential competition in contests. Forrest Rose, who accompanied Pete on bass in contests in the 1980s and 1990s, reminded me of a contest we attended at Tebbetts in Callaway County. There, on a hot, sunny July afternoon, was a young woman from St. Louis, whose apparel surprised the audience mostly of older folks and farm families—short shorts and a bikini top. To McMahan's consternation, she won a prize in the contest. His comment to several of us standing by the stage was "If they're going to have a butt-shakin' contest, they oughta *call it* a butt-shakin' contest."[6]

Bass player Kathy Gordon of Columbia, a stalwart of the fiddle and dance community, recalls McMahan's conflicting opinions of women playing this music. Around 1995, Kathy brought her bass to one session hosted at the Boone County Historical Society museum in Columbia's Nifong Park. McMahan was the chief fiddler and center of attention. He started most of the tunes, took requests, and, with a nod or comment, passed the baton to other fiddlers in the circle when their turns came to start a tune and when he wanted to let them have a turn at the tune. Other fiddlers and accompanists gathered around in concentric circles (experienced musicians close by him, others fanned out beyond the core), in keeping with jam-session etiquette in this community. "In the mid-nineties I was learning to play the bass and began bringing it to the Nifong sessions. Pete made it clear he didn't think much of women playing the bass. He did tolerate me though and eventually I learned his tunes. I can still see him and Priscilla Westgate [one of his teenage pupils] sitting knee-to-knee playing together. He was patiently teaching her the tunes, so his discomfort with women playing was overshadowed by his desire to pass on the music. We were lucky to have him."[7]

Mandolinist and hunting-dog breeder Frankie Lonberger of Kirksville, at a session at Jim Lindsey's farm near Newark, remembered Pete working with Priscilla and Stephanie Westgate at the Bethel Youth Fiddle Camp. Pete was working on a tune with one of the sisters for the contest that weekend, and Pete said, "Honey, let me tell you something. Them judges don't care how fast or how slow you play, but how *clear the notes are*."[8] His encouraging, patient lessons at fiddle camps in the eighties and nineties and with the Westgate sisters suggest a more mellow and empathic Pete McMahan. By Pete's later years in the late 1990s, it was evident that times had changed, and so had Pete. More girls than boys were into fiddle music, and most were classical violin or Suzuki students—a new force in bluegrass festivals and contests. By the 2000s, more girls than boys were competing in fiddle contests.

Kathy Summers, Conserving Family Heritage

Kathy Summers of Bourbon, Missouri, comes from a long line of family fiddlers. She is lucky that way, and knows it. In Kathy's case, the line reaches back to Ireland in the nineteenth century. Born in 1956, Kathy's maiden name was Bryan. Her husband, Howard Summers, a fiddler, passed away, and Kathy lives with their four children on a working farm between Bourbon and Sullivan in Crawford County in the upper Ozarks. Previous generations of Bryans go back to William and Mary O'Bryan, who came to America from Ireland around 1845 and eventually settled in Pennsylvania. "They dropped the *O* to make it just Bryan." She thinks of herself an "Irish" Missourian.

Kathy's paternal grandfather, Joe Bryan, brought his family to Missouri from southern Illinois to farm in 1915; they thought the climate would be more comfortable west of the Mississippi. Joe Bryan's father was John Bryan, who played cello; Smith Bryan, Joe's grandfather, was a fiddler (Jacob Bryan was Joe's great-grandfather). The family version of "Billy in the Low Land" ("Billy in the Low Ground") was passed down to Kathy.[9] Kathy's father, Delbert Bryan, played guitar for fiddlers.

At seven, Kathy began playing guitar, chording for her grandfather Joe Bryan. She watched him play and wanted to play fiddle, too. At thirteen, Bryan began teaching her fiddle; he was left-handed, and Kathy is left-handed.[10]

> So, when I got to be about twelve, thirteen years old, why, they handed me the fiddle and (it was) right-handed. Like I picked guitar right-handed, and I could play (fiddle) a little bit, I could stagger through a song a little bit right-handed *now*, because it's not the noting that's difficult for me, it's the *bow* action.
>
> I'm a natural left-handed fiddler that, I guess, is hereditary from Grandpa being a left-handed fiddle player. But with my efforts to play right-handed, I kind of gave up on it, and threw it aside. My father, who was probably the biggest lover of music in our family, and never gave up on anybody, he'd set the fiddle out on the table when he'd get the guitar out and sit around after supper, singing.
>
> And one day, I was running through the house, and he was singing "Preacher and the Bear"—if anybody (here) ever heard of such a song, as a kid that was one of the

favorite tunes I loved to hear Dad sing. So . . . I thought, "I'll just grab that up and when it comes time for somebody to play a break on it, and put it in my *left hand* and just start playing like Grandpa does. And it was kind of like a *lightning* bolt, or a gift, I picked it up and staggered through the tune, and my grandpa's eyes lit up he was like, he said, "Well, after school every day now, I know what we're gonna be doing." He said, "I'm not going to be here long, but I'm gonna pass on these *tunes* to *you*." So, I'm an accidental natural-born fiddler player.

I met Kathy around 1983 at a dance and fiddlers' convention at the senior center in Potosi, sponsored by the Missouri Fiddlers and Country Music Association. For many years, Kathy played in a band with Stanley O'Neal at all kinds of events and played a little bit of everything—old-time, Hank Williams classics, 1940s–'60s crossover country music, bluegrass. After O'Neal died, Kathy began performing with guitarists such as Larry O'Neal, Bob Skaggs, Darrol Roskowske, and Chris Case (she and Chris currently perform as a duo called the C&S Folk Company). Summers is keenly aware of the importance of skilled backup guitar at contests, and others who "seconded" for her include the late Gene Stephens (Fulton), who played a snappy, modified closed-chord accompaniment style he had learned in the 1940s, and Jim Nelson (St. Louis), a master of old-time open-chord backup style.

Kathy Summers and guitar accompanist Chris Case at the Montgomery County Old Threshers Festival fiddle contest, administered by the Missouri Fiddlers and Country Music Association, Montgomery City, 2018. Kathy took first in the Open Division, and Chris won best accompanist. Summers plays a Barcus-Berry electric violin at dances and events with country groups with electric instruments. Kathy likes the electric because it can also be played in acoustic mode. (Photo by Howard Marshall)

Left-handed fiddler Cecil Goforth sometimes joins her at community-center dances as an added fiddler. "As Cecil Goforth said one time when he was playing there with us, and the guy with the electric guitar and the guy with the steel guitar kept crankin' up *louder*, and we fiddlers couldn't *get* louder. And Cecil looked over at Stanley, and he said, 'Loud isn't always good, is it?' Loud isn't necessarily better! Sometimes less is *more*." Examples of Kathy's favorite "two-step" country songs for dances and shows are "Hillbilly Fever's Back in Town," "Moonlight on the Colorado," and the Hank Williams's classic "Why Should We Try Anymore." When the band plays these songs, Kathy sings and enjoys the fiddle "kickoffs" and solos.

Her contest pieces include "Rutland's Reel," "New Broom" (from Gene Goforth), her grandfather's version of "Billy in the Low Land," "Bill Cheatem" (her favorite contest tune), "Oklahoma Red Bird" and "Rayland's Reel" (from Lyman Enloe), "Cattle in the Cane" (Cecil and Gene Goforth called it "Cattle in the Corn"), and "Rabbit [a.k.a. Turkey or Buzzard] in the Pea Patch." Kathy puts together her contest rounds with an eye to the judges and the audience. For waltzes, Kathy often performs "Curtains of Night" (from a Carter Family 78-rpm record) and "Ookpik Waltz" (a.k.a. "Canadian Waltz," composed by western Canadian fiddler Frankie Rodgers in the 1960s). She is fond of waltzes with moody, minor passages. Like a lot of contest fiddlers, Kathy tends to perform a certain number of well-honed tunes, although her repertoire is extensive. But beyond that, "I just play what I like and try to put feeling in it."[11]

Kathy places high or wins first place in the group of old-time fiddle contests she respects and attends, such as those at Stovall's Grove and Montgomery City run by the Missouri Fiddlers and Country Music Association. Another contest she frequents is the annual contest at Mokane, where administrators Cammie and Gary Cunningham keep to "old-time" rules. She loves the competition of a contest and the camaraderie of meeting and hearing other fiddlers.

Summers is interested in fiddle history and admires players who keep old tunes alive. In 2016, Kathy recorded a CD called *Good Old Fiddle Tunes* with Darrol Roskowske, and it includes the old breakdown "Stony Point" and a family tune, "O'Bryan's Jig," handed down from her Irish immigrant ancestors through her grandfather Joe Bryan. She also learns tunes from Internet videos, such as "Teardrop Waltz," a Canadian tune credited to Métis fiddler Reg Bouvette that she learned from a Casey Willis teaching video on YouTube.

In 2013, Summers was an instructor in a fiddle camp in Jefferson City organized by fiddle teacher Robin Freeland. Kathy is a careful, gentle teacher with a ready smile. She favors relatively simple melodies for beginners and taught tunes such as "Boil the Cabbage Down" and "Mamma Don't 'Low No Fiddling around Here." As Kathy says about "Preacher and the Bear," "Now that's a very simple tune—but sometimes, if people would stop and think, it's easier to play two or three notes than try and throw the whole musical alphabet at a young person starting out. They need to learn the mechanics of the simplest tune you can find, and learn how to coordinate the bow and play it. That's what made the difference in me going ahead and playing it." Kathy

Kathy Summers with guitarist Bob Skaggs at the November 2013 annual conference of the Missouri Folklore Society, where Kathy and Bob were featured guests and performed at the banquet. (Photo by Howard Marshall)

succeeded in passing the family fiddling tradition on to her children. "At one time I had our four children started on the fiddle and Hattie and Myra still play well, and couple of the grandkids are interested and started, but I think I kinda burned them out on it when they were little before they really got the bug."[12]

Listen to track 32 on the companion CD to hear Kathy Summers's version of "Wink the Other Eye."

In the 1960s, 1970s, and 1980s, the granite wall that had stood between classical violin teaching and performance and folk fiddling began to show cracks. Some classical violin teachers began to allow or encourage young scholars to give fiddling a go. As jazz writer Nat Hentoff said, paraphrasing Thelonious Monk, "There are some things they can't teach you in the conservatory."[13] With the growth of the Suzuki method, things were more inclusive and accessible for violinists intrigued by fiddling and, especially, fiddle contests. Contests were perhaps a key; I recall occasions when young classical players told me that their violin teachers did not like old-time fiddling but encouraged them to sign up for contests because fiddle contests are a way to gain experience performing in front of audiences and adjudicators.

In the culture of old-time fiddlers of former times, the experience was usually more Zen than anything else. Confronted with questions such as "What note is that?" or "Can you play that really slow so I can get it?" the old-time fiddler may try to accommodate, but the tradition is based on listening and watching more than on such detailed direction. One has to ingrain the skills, of course, but once this is done, the process becomes as much intuition as it does rote practice and analysis.

Eventually, the pupil may come to fiddling, unlocking the mind to peace; somehow the mind lets go the impediments to music making—self-doubt, fear of criticism, competitive urges, jealousy, anger, regret, embarrassment.

Phases in musicians' journeys are similar, no matter what brand. A learner has an early period of exposure, discovery, experimentation, and acquiring beginner's skills. Then comes the journeyman period of becoming part of the fiddling community and its venues. Eventually, there comes one's "mature period," when a musician finds his or her niche, whether as a player in jam sessions, in a band, or standing tall in the contest arena. Then comes the artist's "late period," when, like Beethoven or Jake Hockemeyer, old age catches up; the inscrutable incursions of decline take their toll—loss of hearing, arthritis, memory loss—and, now in the "Senior Division," this is when the artist may (or may not) finally enjoy the respect of a village elder.

Liesl Schoenberger's 1996 CD is titled *Classic Fiddle*. The project was recorded in Nashville and produced by Buddy Spicher and nicely represents Schoenberger's fiddle repertoire and style as a young fiddler with classical training, and shortly before she left Cape Girardeau to pursue studies in violin at the Indiana University in Bloomington.

Liesl Schoenberger, a Classical Violinist in the Fiddle Community

"I started playing the violin at the age of 2½ years on a wee 1/32 size violin," in Southeast Missouri State University's Suzuki program.[14] Liesl then studied violin at St. Louis Community Music Program from ages five to nine. From nine to eighteen, she made weekly trips from Cape Girardeau to Bloomington, Indiana, to study violin with pedagogue Mimi Sweig in Indiana University's String Academy,[15] and graduated from Notre Dame Regional High School in Cape Girardeau.

Liesl was interested in all kinds of music, and her piano teacher, Beverly Reece, encouraged her to explore fiddling; Liesl's first tune was "Turkey in the Straw." Schoenberger entered her first contest at nine in Cape Girardeau and soon became a popular and successful player at contests. In 1996, Liesl won the highly competitive Junior Division at the state-fair contest in Sedalia.

While exposed to a wide variety of contest fiddlers, such as her early mentor George Portz, most of the tunes in Liesl's contest rounds were drawn from Stacy Phillips's transcriptions of Mark O'Connor's contest pieces.[16] Leisl continued playing fiddle music right alongside her classical violin training. Her favorite contests were those administered by her friends George and Kathy Porter in southern Illinois and eastern Missouri.

Liesl graduated from Indiana University's Jacobs School of Music in 2008 with bachelor's and master's degrees in violin performance before continuing on to the Yale School of Music for an artist diploma. Liesl is currently pursuing a doctor of music at the New England Conservatory in Boston. She taught at Dartmouth College, the University of New Hampshire, Saint Anselm College, and Southeast Missouri State. Today, Liesl Schoenberger Doty is an assistant professor in the Crane School of Music at SUNY-Potsdam and performs with the Boston-based chamber orchestra A Far Cry and a crossover duo with her husband, bassist Karl Doty. A YouTube video from 2016 features Liesl and Karl playing a fiddle set during a show in Minnesota, "Draggin' the Bow," "Gardenia Waltz," and "I Don't Love Nobody."

While in college in Indiana, on visits back home Schoenberger competed in fiddle contests. Liesl consistently took honors at contests and in 1996 won the Junior Division at Sedalia. She also competed in the Indiana state fiddle championships and was a three-time winner of the Governor's Cup before becoming an adjudicator at the contest. Liesl has recorded three CDs on her label, *Classic Fiddle, Amazing Grace of the Fiddler's Touch*, and *Say Old Man*.

Classic Fiddle was recorded in Nashville with Buddy Spicher (producer, mandolin), David Greer (lead guitar), Bill Rehrig (rhythm guitar), and Roger Spencer (bass). Tracks include Liesl's tour-de-force versions of "Tom and Jerry," "Canadian Waltz," "Turkey in the Straw," "Forty Years Ago Waltz," "Limerock," "Draggin' the Bow," "Hell among the Yearlings," and "Ashoken Farewell," along with something different—"Millionaire's Hoedown." "Millionaire's Hoedown" was composed in 1965 by violinist, teacher, and composer Herman Clebanoff and is a classical violinist's take on old-time fiddling, beginning with a saw-stroke "potatoes" intro and a medley of creative variations on "Devil's Dream" and "Turkey in the Straw." Liesl is among professional classical violinists and music teachers whose tastes and inclinations embrace traditional fiddle music, and she is advancing broader appreciation of both genres in her school programs, workshops, concerts, and career as a professor at SUNY-Potsdam.

Listen to track 33 on the companion CD to hear Liesl Schoenberger's version of "Forty Years Ago Waltz."

David Scrivner, a Bob Holt Student

David Scrivner of Springfield emerged as a leader of a storied public jam session in the hamlet of McClurg in the southwest Missouri Ozarks.[17] While known as a Bob Holt acolyte and dance fiddler, Scrivner's interests range beyond his training; his repertoire includes songs from Art Galbraith and a number of tunes associated with "hornpipe fiddlers" of former generations such as Cyril Stinnett and Bob Walters.[18]

Scrivner grew up in Mansfield and played music in the Mansfield and Ava area, small towns a half hour's drive apart and some two hours east of Springfield. The area enjoys a reputation for traditional music. David was born in 1982 and began learning to play mandolin in 1988 at six, taking lessons from Charlotte Blackwell at the Blackwells' music shop in Seymour, where Scrivner and other pupils played in a band they called the Diamonds in the Rough.[19] "My journey with music had begun, and my dad . . . was living his deferred musical dreams through me. I was never particularly excited about practicing, but by the time I was in eighth grade, I had taken lessons on mandolin, bass fiddle, guitar, bluegrass banjo, and Dobro."[20]

In addition to lessons in Seymour, David played mandolin at gatherings with his father's brothers, who had formed a band as high school students in Ava in the 1950s. Variously known as the Scrivner Brothers Band or the Ozark Mountaineers, they performed in the Ava area and appeared on the Mountain Grove radio station. No family function was complete without music. David's mandolin skills proved helpful when he gravitated to the fiddle.

David's introduction to fiddle music was not entirely exciting. In his younger years, he enjoyed playing mandolin at home, but did not like performing in the student band. Then he heard about Bob Holt and fiddle camp.

> When I was in eighth grade, a girl in my class, Erica Spyres, who played classical violin, told me excitedly that she was taking fiddle lessons from a man I had never heard of in Ava: Bob Holt. She was excited about a fiddle camp she was going to be attending in Bethel, Missouri, and since I had recently started playing fiddle, she thought I should go. Knowing this was another thing my dad would push me into without giving me a choice, I resolved to keep it a secret from him so I wouldn't

have to go. Fortunately (though it seemed incredibly unfortunate to me at the time), her mother spoke to my mother about it, and when my mom told my dad, it was all but decided. I was going to fiddle camp. Having grown up around Ava, my dad knew that Bob was a legend, and he wanted me to learn anything I could from him.

David Scrivner has fiddled the Saturday-night square dances at the Ozark Heritage Music Festival in West Plains for some twenty years and is a lynchpin in jam circles at fiddlers' conventions in Harrison, Arkansas. In West Plains in June 2018, his seconds were Nathan Lee McAlister (Neosho, clawhammer banjo) and Joel Hinds (Willow Springs, guitar), who are also fiddlers. (Photo by Howard Marshall)

David's dad took him to Bob Holt for fiddle lessons. A shy teenager, Scrivner was at first intimidated by Holt, a man of strong opinions and forceful personality, and David worked hard to meet Holt's expectations and gain his respect. The lessons at Holt's dairy farm were ostensibly for an hour but inevitably turned into visits and storytelling that lasted well into the evening. David came to appreciate Bob Holt's approach to passing on his music: "I didn't realize it then, but now I'm convinced that it was part of his philosophy that learning to play traditional Ozarks fiddle music meant, really, learning the Ozarks culture and heritage." David also points to the importance of having friends his age who were into fiddling and learning from the same taskmaster, Bob Holt—such as Erica Spyres and Travis Bentley—and they learned tunes from each other.

Scrivner became close friends with Alvie Dooms. "Alvie's role in my development as a fiddle player is probably at least as significant as Bob's." As pleasant and agreeable as Holt was stern and brusque, Dooms taught David a great deal about music and Ozarks life. Old enough to be David's grandfather, Alvie began playing guitar backup for fiddlers when he was ten years old, played in bluegrass bands and dance bands, and was a stringed instrument collector, repairman, trader, and expert on violin history. Dooms was Holt's favorite guitarist for decades. While in high school, David was invited by Dooms to perform with him at festivals and fiddlers' conventions at Clifftop, West Virginia; Ashville, North Carolina; Berthoud, Colorado; and other places. Holt and Dooms helped instill in Scrivner an appreciation for the depth of old-time fiddling and the history behind the tunes.

Bob Holt honed his teaching through years of experience teaching youngsters at his farm, in the Traditional Arts Apprenticeship Program, and at Bethel fiddle camp, as well as workshops at festivals. A lesson with Bob included fiddling a tune very slowly while the student recorded it on a cassette tape (to practice with at home), and then he played the tune at what he termed "medium" tempo—which at the time seemed quite fast to his students. Students also listened to Bob in sessions and playing for the Ava square dancers at the blazing speed for which he was known. Naturally enough, pupils such as Scrivner, Bentley, Liz Amos, and Ashley Hull Forrest became Bob Holt fast-tempo fiddlers. Bob's "medium" would be normal square-dance speed for most old-time fiddlers.[21] Holt's cruising speed for square dancers was 140 beats per minute, and sometimes beyond. Scrivner points out that other Ozark fiddlers played square-dance tunes fast, too, such as Lonnie Robertson and Bill Bilyeu.[22]

"He [Bob Holt] was very aware of it [his fast tempo] and emphasized turning the tune we had learned at a slow pace into a tune that sounded right when playing it faster." Scrivner recalls that "the nerve-wracking part" of learning from Bob Holt was going back to Bob's farm and hoping he could adequately play the tunes he was supposed to be practicing, learning, and making "danceable." In four or five years of lessons with Holt, Scrivner rarely felt that he was getting the bowing right and making the tunes danceable. Scrivner recalls Holt's "line," the dry remark heard so often by his students: "'Well, you got the notes.'—Which means you don't have the *tune* at all."

Scrivner's Hangin' around the Kitchen CD features Alvie Dooms and Karen Kraft, who played "drop-thumb" old-time banjo, recorded during David's trips home to Missouri while in graduate school in Dallas, Texas. Karen Kraft was from Colorado. She had embarked on a bicycle trip to the East Coast and had a flat tire in Mountain Grove, Missouri, where "a gentleman named Paul Mansker offered her a home-cooked meal with himself and his wife. She stayed with them for a while and ended up staying in the area permanently. At the time, I think she brought a harmonica with her on her bike, but he taught her how to play banjo. It's a pretty incredible story, and it completely fit her personality."

In the project, David presents an interesting and varied set, mostly Missouri and Midwest tunes. Many are regional and local melodies seldom recorded. They

David Scrivener's *Hanging around the Kitchen* features old-time banjo by Karen Kraft and straight-chord guitar accompaniment by Alvie Dooms. The album was recorded in Kraft's kitchen.

include "Hangin' around the Kitchen" (Lyman Enloe's title for "Richmond Polka" or "Richmond Cotillion"),[23] "Tulsa Hop" (popularized by Bob Walsh), "Doc Brown's Dream" (composed by country physician Doc Brown and associated with Art Galbraith and Lonnie Robertson),[24] "Fisher's Hornpipe" (in the key of F), "Vee Latty's B-flat Waltz" (from the central Missouri radio fiddler and contest champion), "Rachel" (from Bob Holt, who played Tommy Jackson's version in the 1950s), "Dusty Miller," "Sally in the Garden," "Good-bye, My Honey—I'm Gone" (associated with the Ozarks), "Golden Slippers," "Pig Ankle Rag," "Hell agin' the Barn Door" (from Dwight Lamb), "Jesse Polka," "Bonaparte Crossing the Rhine," "I Don't Love Nobody" (from Tommy Jackson, Doc Roberts, and Bob Holt), "Granny Will Your Dog Bite," and "Stars and Stripes Waltz" (Vee Latty). We also hear David's versions of Cyril Stinnett's "Old Countryman's Reel," "Purcell's Reel," "Salty River Reel," "St. Joe Hornpipe" (from Dwight Lamb), and "Old Parnell," tunes also played by Ozark fiddlers such as Lonnie Robertson. Several tracks include fiddle and banjo harmony lines "twinning" with the melody.

David became a fiddle teacher at such places as the Ozark Mountain Music fiddle camp in Branson. At this camp, "Alvie liked me to play fiddle while he taught the kids how to play guitar rhythm to a fiddle. I helped him in a similar way as a part of the Traditional Arts Apprenticeship Program. Those experiences gave me firsthand experience learning about Alvie's rhythm techniques." While he may not think of himself as a contest fiddler, Scrivner occasionally competes; in 2019, he won first place in his first contest, the Arkansas state contest.

Scrivner graduated from Mansfield High; took his bachelor's degree in English, philosophy, and religion at the College of the Ozarks in 2005; and earned his master's at the University of Dallas in 2009. For a number of years, he taught English courses at the College of the Ozarks. He is employed writing marketing proposals for a firm in Springfield. Dances and jam sessions remain his favorite music venues.

For years, Scrivner was a fixture at the community jam sessions held in the town park in Mansfield (the Mansfield Jamboree, organized in part by Scrivner's parents) and festivals with square dancing such as the annual Hootin' an' Hollerin' in Gainesville, and he continues to be a leader at the McClurg Monday-night sessions, where a potluck dinner and socializing are essential parts of the evening.

McClurg Monday Nights: "No Drinking and No Dirty Talking"

The McClurg session began decades ago with a chance visit by Bob Walsh. Walsh was a Missouri Department of Conservation agent whose Monday-night rounds during deer season included stopping to check hunting licenses at the McClurg general store and post office in Taney County, where hunters gathered to play music after the twilight close of hunting hours. Like other sensible fiddlers whose habits were supported by earning a living, Walsh always had a violin stowed in his car or truck.[25] Walsh was a popular character, storyteller, and fiddler. Deer-season Monday nights at the store evolved, and word spread about the music, food, and dancing. As Scrivner puts it, "It just happened, because the culture was just that you got together with people and you played music. And that's still pretty much what it is."[26]

After Walsh died in 1990, the session's anchor was shared by Bob Holt and Jim Beeler, who called most of the tunes and informally served as leaders of the jam circle. Beeler would be the principal fiddler for an hour or two, and then Holt would take over. Sitting next to Holt and endeavoring to play any and every tune that Holt passed to him was a great learning experience, "like an apprenticeship." In fact, David Scrivner was Bob Holt's last student in the Missouri Traditional Arts Apprenticeship Program. Now it is David's turn to be the de facto session leader.

In addition to Scrivner, regulars in recent years included Dooms, Noel Scott (guitar), Gordon McCann (guitar), Glen Dale Robertson (banjo), Steve Assenmacher (bass), Toni Giardina (guitar, vocals), and Junior Lawrence (who attended the first McClurg session). Others drop in from time to time, such as fiddlers H. K. Silvey, Luke Cormier (Art Galbraith's great-grandson), Jeremy Myers, Brett Dudenhoeffer (Travis Inman's TAAP apprentice in 2013, who is in the Finley River Boys bluegrass band), Joel Hinds, and Aaron Albrecht.[27] In 2020, the COVID-19 pandemic began to take a toll on McClurg, and since then the group moved outside during fair weather to the tractor shed behind the store, so people can maintain social distancing. Members plan to resume "when the vaccines have made the COVID-19 no longer a threat or weather is warm enough to resume outdoor playing."[28]

David is featured in a 2017 *Kansas City Star* article about McClurg, with a video that went viral, and on *The Today Show* on NBC television in May 2017. Fiddle tunes in the video include "Soldier's Joy," "Coming Down from Denver," and a Kentucky tune, "Martha Campbell," and, in addition to Scrivner, musicians that night included Joel Hinds (violin), banjoist J. R. Johnston (Norwood), and Alvie Dooms.[29] People jig danced while the fiddlers fiddled.[30]

> I love the people here and coming out on Monday nights and playing tunes with them.
>
> This where I really learned, basically. I took lessons, but this is where I really learned what it's supposed to be. I feel like this is genuine Ozark traditional fiddle music, and it's really important to keep alive because it's really unique, and it is part of the Ozark culture that is not influenced by mass media, trends of the day. It's just music. And we just do it for fun. We don't do it to impress anybody. It's our thing and it's what we do, and I think that preserving it is preserving a heritage and a way of life that is largely gone in America.

McClurg is an example of the music parties and jam sessions that are crucial to traditions of the music community and endurance of homemade fiddle and dance music. McClurg manages to survive, thanks in part to its exceedingly remote location (not isolated, just remote) and loyal individuals who keep the event going. Most reporters, writers, and curious visitors from outside the community tend to overromanticize venues like the McClurg session (as well as the people there), but that is how journalistic writing about and popular depictions of such music and musicians in these cultural landscapes have always been. And yes, local people who are regulars at the McClurg session may romanticize it, too.

Asked why he does all this fiddling, Scrivner concludes by saying, "It's about the *community of people*. And it's about this jam we go to every Monday—McClurg."[31]

Listen to track 34 on the companion CD to hear David Scrivner's version of "Sally in the Garden."

Say Old Man—Can You Play the Fiddle? Cover for Matt Wyatt's self-produced 1995 cassette, recorded in Fenton when Matt was sixteen, the year he studied with Gene Goforth and attended Dale Morris's fiddle camp in Arkansas.

Matt Wyatt, Man with a Mission

"Matt went to a fiddle contest with his grandpa and that was what really started it all."[32] Matt Wyatt is one of the more influential and versatile fiddlers in contemporary Missouri. Since childhood, Matt seems to have been driven to explore and, in many cases, master all the varieties of violin music he heard. A creative and inquisitive turn of mind led him on to venture into everything from old-time fiddle tunes, classical violin in school orchestras, bluegrass and country bands, the contest stage, and jazz and western swing to building his own violin shop and teaching studio. An uncommonly supportive family helped make it all happen.

Born in Independence in February 1979, Matt's parents, Allen and Cheri Tietjens Wyatt, moved around Missouri when Matt was a child. A Navy veteran, Allen began a long career with the Social Security Administration in Kansas City in 1979. As he gained promotions, the family moved to new places (for many years, in St. Louis), and eventually Allen was again posted to the Kansas City office, where he retired in 2006. Matt is the fifth generation of his Wyatt line in Missouri, and there have been numerous musicians and fiddlers in the family. Matt's father, Allen, plays guitar and fiddle, as does Matt's grandfather Charles A. (Bud) Wyatt Jr. (Centralia), and as did Matt's great-grandfather Charles A. Wyatt Sr. Charles A. Wyatt Sr.'s grandfather John Wyatt moved to Missouri from Richmond, Kentucky, in 1885 with his son, Robert. "Our ancestry is uncertain but I have heard Grandpa mention Scotch-Irish." John Wyatt's wife (Charles A. Wyatt Sr.'s grandmother) was a Cherokee woman named Rebecca Dinsmore.[33]

Four generations of fiddlers, *left to right*: Allen D. Wyatt, Allen's son Matthew J. Wyatt, Matt's great-grandfather Charles A. Wyatt, and Matt's grandfather Charles A. (Bud) Wyatt Jr. (1931–2022). In Fenton, ca. 1995. (Courtesy of Matt Wyatt)

> I was always interested in fiddle music and some of my earliest memories are of my great-grandpa and also my grandpa playing the fiddle. I was about six when I tried to hold a fiddle. When I was ten, I started in the school orchestra—four kids being taught by a piano teacher! It was during that year, while traveling back and forth from Kansas City to St. Louis to see relatives, we stopped in Columbia. My Grampa Bud was there and I remember him introducing me to Taylor McBaine at a fiddle contest. Taylor said, "So, I hear you like to play the fiddle?" He promptly handed me his fiddle and said, "Play me a tune!" I had only started, and was trying to learn "Ashoken Farewell" off the television. I met Carolyn Eschbach [St. Louis] at that contest. She lived near us in Fenton and offered to give me lessons. That was my start on fiddling.

Matt took classical violin from Rockwood School District teachers in Fenton and participated in the high school orchestra. At the same time, he was picking up fiddling by ear from family members, Carolyn Eschbach, and others at jam sessions. Coming along after the 1970s spread of Suzuki method, living in the St. Louis metro area (Fenton) with classical violin teachers, and when some of the prejudice against "fiddling" among classical musicians was becoming less of an obstacle for classical students interested in old-time fiddling, Matt was able to learn classical and "folk" music at the same time. Most youngsters choose one of these paths, but Matt liked both and was accepted as a leader of his school orchestra, while on weekends he was playing "old-time" fiddle music and learning the fiddle-contest game.[34] According to Allen Wyatt:

> When Matt was barely 11 years old in 1990, he played at his first fiddle contest in Centralia, at the Anchor Festival. He only knew a few songs but had been so inspired by older fiddlers (Pete McMahan, Taylor McBaine, Gene Goforth, and his Grampa Bud). He participated and held his own. There were only two divisions at this contest—Open and Senior. It was rare to see young fiddlers and when they were around most times they competed in the Adult divisions. Those rules started to change through the '90s. Many times, when there were Junior divisions, it was a handful of kids like Matt, Alita Stoneking, Justin Branum, Darren Tapscott, and a

few more. I remember thinking back then that it would be nice (and good for the future of fiddling) if there was a way to get more kids to participate in contests.

By the mid-'90s, things started changing. Mainly with teachers. You were real lucky if you could get around and learn from the Old Masters (Pete McMahan, Gene Goforth, Taylor McBaine, etc.). There were even some younger teachers like Junior Marriott who started teaching in the '90s and had great influence. Kids like Matt, Alita, John Williams, and others started advancing fast.

Camps like Bethel began to spring up. This got lots of kids started and kept them going. Private [classical] teachers started promoting fiddling and participating in contests. Christa Scott (Pleasant Hill) used to make hitting fiddle contests part of her training for students. I remember in the mid-'90s, she brought a van full of her students to the contest in Marshall. Carolyn Eschbach (St. Louis) was another teacher that had lots of influence. Teachers started the spread and before long you started seeing crowded Junior divisions in fiddle contests. So, by the end of the '90s it really picked up and continued thru the 2000s.[35]

"Fiddle contests were always about learning, seeing friends and fellow musicians with the same interests, and an audience that loved hearing the music they used to dance to." In his teens, Matt did well, winning or placing high in the Junior Division (typically age sixteen and below) and also beginning to win in the Open Division (typically open to any age). He was an imaginative and, as I remember, a somewhat restless young musician who had an agenda and sought out master contest fiddlers in Missouri—and Texas and Alabama. Matt became fascinated by the Texas-based contest fiddle styles that were becoming prominent. Junior Marriott, a master of Contest Style, gave Matt a cassette tape of Texas champion Terry Morris, which led Matt to begin searching for more Texas contest fiddling.[36] Becoming a champion in Missouri was not easy, because of the many formidable contest fiddlers across the state—older champions who carried on the older contest styles, and now there was Matt's own general age cohort who were performing the Contest Style and repertoire to good effect.

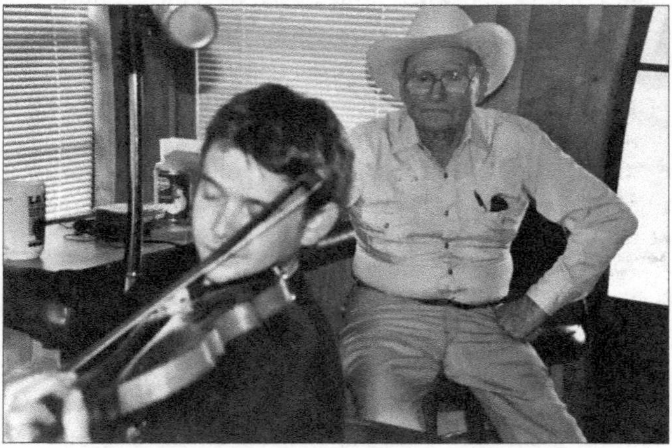

Matt Wyatt with Louis Franklin, one of the legendary Texas contest fiddlers, at Franklin's home in Whitewright, Texas, ca. 1999. (Courtesy of Wyatt)

FORT SMITH

BASED ON LOUIS FRANKLIN AND ORVILLE BURNS

Matt learned "Fort Smith," an old-time Arkansas breakdown, in visits in Texas with Louis Franklin and Orville Burns. In teaching people about fiddlers' bowings, Wyatt uses the tune to illustrate the bowings used by Franklin and Burns in this tune. Recorded by Wyatt on *The Goodbye Waltz* (with guitar backup by Justin Branum). (Transcription by Matt Wyatt)

Wyatt learned backup guitar, helped by his father, Allen, and grandfather Bud. After learning the basics, Matt studied other guitar styles, such as the swing-based closed-chord styles favored by Texas style and western-swing fiddlers and visited such pioneer Texas stylists as Omega Burden.

Wyatt took advantage of every opportunity to increase his fiddling knowledge. One of these was the Bethel fiddle camp. He was a camper for several seasons in his teens, studying with a variety of Bethel instructors. "I learned from everyone." Within a few years, Matt became an instructor.

Matt names a long list of mentors: Missourians Gene Goforth, John Hartford, and Bobby Joe Caldwell, as well as fiddlers from other states such as J. T. Perkins, Randy Howard, Bobby Hicks, Kenny Baker, Buddy Spicher, Herman Johnson, Louis Franklin and his son Larry Franklin, Orville Burns, Randy Elmore, Wes Westmoreland, Carl Hopkins, Dale Morris, Johnny Gimble, and Jim Chancellor. As important as his Bethel experiences, if not more important on a personal level, were in-depth sessions with fiddlers such as these. With Allen's help, Matt traveled to study with J. T. Perkins in Arab, Alabama, and during trips to fiddle contests in Texas, Matt made an effort to visit and learn from Louis Franklin and Orville Burns. Those fiddlers, and others, had heard and met Wyatt at contests and decided to play some music with this obviously dedicated youngster.

Working with Gene Goforth

At the top of the list of experiences for Wyatt was his partnership with Gene Goforth in Missouri's Traditional Arts Apprenticeship Program in 1995 and 1997. Gene Goforth did not consider himself a teacher; he seldom gave any instruction to learners and did not seem to enjoy teaching.[37] But Gene was impressed with Matt Wyatt's cheerful enthusiasm, aptitude, and commitment and agreed to accept Matt as his apprentice.[38] "I spent most of high school learning tunes from Gene and playing on a weekly basis. When I was 15, Gene took me to meet Kenny Baker, and I played on and off stage with Kenny and Josh Graves at a bluegrass festival in Grassy, Missouri."[39]

Some of the tunes Matt learned from Gene, crossing back and forth from Gene's old-time repertoire to his bluegrass repertoire, include a small but interesting sample of Goforth's deep and versatile stock of tunes. In a 1995 lesson, Matt recorded Gene fiddling some longtime Missouri favorites, "Billy in the Low Ground," "I Don't Love Nobody," "Sail Away Ladies," "Rye Straw," "Fisher's Hornpipe" (in F), "Silver Threads among the Gold," "Walking in My Sleep," and "Sally Goodin"; several tunes composed by or associated with Bill Monroe and Kenny Baker, such as "Jerusalem Ridge," "Sushi," "Long Cold Winter," "Old Daingerfield" [*sic*], "Land of Lincoln," "Lonesome Moonlight Waltz," "Ball and Chain Hornpipe," "Little Bitty Acorn in a Great Big Tree," "Festival Waltz," "Mississippi Waltz," "Tom and Jerry," and "Northern White Cloud"; and tunes associated with Howdy Forrester and contests, "Grandmammy Look at Uncle Sam," "Rutland's Reel," "Brilliancy," "Snowflake Reel," and a tune from Canada via Baker, "Blue Mountain Waltz."

Goforth found it difficult to relax in front of a tape recorder or camera. To get the music rolling, Matt would ask Gene to play something Matt knew that Gene played well. Gene would play it and visit about the tune. Bob Skaggs of nearby House Springs (who played bluegrass fiddle as a teenager) was usually available to play guitar for the TAAP lessons, and on some occasions Allen Wyatt played guitar. Matt also played some guitar backup for Gene in the lessons, which helped increase his credibility with his teacher. Goforth was known as extraordinarily "particular" about backup, and very few guitarists measured up to his standard.[40] In 2010, Matt wrote about playing guitar for Gene Goforth:

> Dad and I spent a lot of time at Gene's house and he was really one of those fiddlers that "carried" the rhythm on his own. He was great to play for because his driving rhythm in his bowing and phrasing was hard not to fall in with if a rhythm player was halfway decent! He was very encouraging to other musicians and a patient teacher. I learned a lot about rhythm just playing with Gene. He was the real deal for sure. When I would go over to Gene's to learn tunes, he would show me one or two (fill my brain completely up) and then I would record him solo for a while. He definitely didn't like playing without a rhythm player, so I would end up trying to back him up. He was instrumental in not only my fiddling but my rhythm guitar playing. It was always nice when Dad would go too, because he would play guitar and I could pay better attention to Gene's fiddling! If I played guitar with Gene, I had to concentrate so hard to not mess up that I couldn't hear as much of what he was doing on the fiddle![41]

Matt was also learning from fiddlers such as Pete McMahan.[42] Matt wrote about trying to learn fiddle tunes from two different teachers at the same time:

> I remember it being an interesting learning experience that I didn't understand until much later in life—for instance, when I would learn a tune from Pete and also the same tune from Gene. I would have to keep them straight, because if I played parts Gene taught me, Pete would say "that's wrong," and proceed to show me again or insinuate to try again until I got his nod of approval. What that taught me about Pete was that Pete wanted me to play it like he taught me if I was gonna tell people I learned it from *him*—or he didn't want me playing Gene's stuff! Lol!
>
> And vice versa, but Gene was more open outwardly with me about learning new things and accepting them.
>
> Pete gave me sheet music one time for a few tunes. He told me he could read music a little. This always stuck with me, because of all the stigma there is about fiddlers who are musically literate.[43]

After high school, in 1997 Wyatt set his sights on a career in music and matriculated at Belmont University in Nashville. Belmont's specialties include fields relevant to the burgeoning music business well beyond its country music core. Matt studied jazz violin with Martin Norgaard and performed in the university's symphony orchestra. He graduated in 2001 with a bachelor of fine arts in commercial music performance and jazz studies. Matt made friends and contacts in the industry and formed connections with luthiers and violin shops. He performed on the Grand Ole Opry and toured with the bluegrass and bluegrass gospel band the Sullivan Family, giving him a taste of the life in the business.

Wyatt also continued traveling on the fiddle-contest circuit and during his college years placed high or won in a number of highly competitive contests such as the Tennessee Valley contests at Athens, Alabama; the Grand Masters in Nashville; and state competitions in Tennessee, Mississippi, Arkansas, Kentucky, and Illinois, as well winning as the Missouri state championship in 1999 and 2013. He also tried his luck at the National Oldtime Fiddlers' Contest in Weiser, Idaho, but did not make the finals. Matt went to Texas as often as possible, such as the Texas state contest in Hallettsville and the World Championships at Crockett.

Teacher

Matt began teaching fiddle in high school and has taught dozens of pupils over the past thirty years, serving stints as an instructor at Bethel fiddle camp, Montana Fiddle Camp, the Three Trails camp in Kansas City, and Randy Elmore's camp in Texas, as well as workshops and special programs. On teaching: "Learning from a vast resource of teachers in a wide range of styles has helped me develop a teaching style that not only incorporates traditional techniques and concepts but also teaches a love and respect for music. My goal has been to create an enjoyable environment that inspires students to want to learn and play by incorporating a combination of scale practice through improvisation, learning tunes, compositions, and most of all—listening."[44]

He enjoys sharing what he knows, as well as the give-and-take of wide-ranging discussions of theory and practice. A person with extensive violin training and education who is, at the same time, an ear musician and master of old-time fiddle, bluegrass, Texas-style contest playing, and western swing and jazz, Matt looks comfortable straddling these worlds. He has come to the place in a teacher's life where he wonders about the learning process.

> In fact, only one or two people seemed affected by the stories and music I presented them with. Nothing like when I got the first tape from Junior [tape of Terry Morris] and all I did was listen to that damn thing! I mean obsessively! I would feel drained after talking to people about my inspirations and what I know about the stuff because I think I wanted them to feel the same way. There are people who have the same opportunities we have had, even more so in some ways . . . but they just won't ever get it.

And these further thoughts from Matt could occupy an afternoon's conversation, about his experiences with the complex master Pete McMahan:

> As I made friends with some of the people I respected most I started to realize that my views were skewed because I had all these ideas as to what old-time should be because that is the way I perceived it. Also, because of the things I was told as I learned tunes.

By the time I started understanding how important bowing was, never thinking of it before, Pete [McMahan] was already gone. I worked on tunes of his and actually had the wrong concept to his bowings. I thought I was doing things "just like" he did. I recently listened to some stuff again and realized that it wasn't at all just like him. Pete used to say, "You're not playing the fiddle if you don't make someone pat their foot."

I think it is like Orville Burns said, "You want to hear the influence of the teacher in the student, not the teacher."

On the importance of passing on the stories, history, and hints about the culture and traditions that underpin the saga of fiddle music and musicians, Matt says:

I love it when someone asks me to play a tune, or asks a question about a fiddler, or really wants to learn something more than just a version to play in a contest. Unfortunately that doesn't happen much, but at least the ones interested in a contest have some drive and inspiration.

A lot of people don't know why they are learning at all—maybe they just feel a calling and don't know why yet. All we can do is help them on their journey and give them as many opportunities to learn about the importance of the past as we can. How playing for a square dance can help with phrasing and why, how bowings tie tunes together in different styles; mainly getting recordings in their hands will at least let them discover something when they are ready for it.[45]

I approach beginning students a little different if they are little, like under 7, and quite a bit different if they are adults. But some consistencies are that the main emphasis is *trying to relax*. I show them "correct" ways to hold the bow and instrument, then start them right out with "twinkle" and an A scale.

Then "Cripple Creek," "Faded Love," and such. I like to incorporate notes with the fingerings under them while learning rhythms, and also a tape of everything slow and fast.

But I show them the stuff the old-fashioned way as well. Beginners can learn "Faded Love" and "Liberty" as easy as those classical books teach "Ode to Joy" and Pachelbel's "Canon in D" and accomplish worlds more.[46]

Matt's approach respects the exact versions of old-timers he learned from. But just as they did in their time, Matt knows the importance of one's own interpretation—playing a tune "true to the people you got it from" but then expressing one's own interpretation while keeping the tune intact, danceable, and correct.

Violin Shop

In the 1990s, Allen Wyatt began learning the luthier's art, found books on violin history and luthiery, visited makers and repairmen, accumulated tools, and experimented with simple repair tasks. He moved on to carving and setting violin bridges and bow re-hairing. Clearing an area in the basement in their Fenton home, Allen set up a workbench and began repairing and setting up violins and repairing and re-hairing bows; in 1995 he let it quietly be known that he was in business, even though part-time. This seemed to be a hobby for leisure time, enabling him to take care of his son's violins and bows, but Allen had a long-range plan.

Matt, still in high school, gave fiddle lessons upstairs, helped his father with repairs and research, and began to be interested in swapping and selling bows and violins. He took an after-school job at the Kirkwood music store of Mel Bay Publications, where he reconditioned rental instruments and did repair work.

Little by little, the word got around that Allen was a trustworthy and able workman, and plans for a full-time violin shop took shape. There emerged an enthusiastic circle of musicians who appreciated Allen's careful, judicious approach to the trade and customer relations as well as his skills. And Allen started building violins.[47] In 2003, when Allen was transferred to a new position with the Social Security Administration in the Kansas City office, the family decided to make the transition from a modest word-of-mouth business to a full-service shop in Matt's house in Independence. Allen and Matt formalized their business partnership. The shop (Allen's domain) was in the basement, the upstairs living room was the showroom and public space, and Matt gave lessons in a bedroom.

Bud Wyatt with a violin made "from tree to fiddle" by Allen Wyatt, modeled on an Italian violin by Leandro Bisiach and using aged wood from John Griffin's Old Standard Wood. At right is Bud's "portrait fiddle" ordered from a Chinese firm "in the white," engraved with a portrait of Wyatt on the back and antique words around the bouts by Kansas City artist Ron Raymer, finished and varnished by Allen Wyatt; labeled "To: Charles A. Wyatt, Jr. "Bud" / Inside construction and hand varnish in the workshop / Wyatt Violin Shop Anno 2012 / Kansas City, Mo. / Allen D. Wyatt and Son." (Photo by Howard Marshall, 2018)

Within a few years, Allen and Matt had built up enough business and credibility and opened a new shop in 2006. Matt and Allen attend major stringed instrument auctions, and Matt has developed an online sales business.

The shop handles hundreds of violin, viola, cello, and bass rentals for public schools in Independence, which guarantees a certain amount of business but requires a heavy commitment of time during summers to get the instruments ready for school

Matt and Allen Wyatt, May 2008. (Photo by Howard Marshall)

opening and to service private rentals as well. Allen and Matt order most of these instruments "in the white" (meaning built but not finished) from China and, when received, finish the instruments with Wyatt Shop methods and varnish and do final setup (with their own violin bridges) and complete the instruments for rental or sale. Rental instruments also come from Romania, Germany, and France.

The shop sells fretted instruments as well and at various times has new and used guitars, mandolins, and banjos available. They are authorized dealers for lines made in China called Eastman, Blue Ridge, and the Loar, and the shop specializes in vintage guitars by American makers. The shop deals in violins new and old across a range of quality levels and handles "older reconditioned instruments of German, French, and Italian origin."[48] Matt has a personal interest in violins imported from Germany, especially those of the pre–World War II era from the Markneukirchen and Mittenwald regions.[49] Matt is in charge of sales and customer relations, teaches, and buys and sells violins and bows. Allen handles repairs, with assistance from Matt, and Matt's mother, Cheri, a retired registered nurse, helps with sales, customer relations, bookkeeping, and inventory. Matt's cousin Heath Tietjens joined the staff in 2017.

Matt put together a recording studio, mainly for friends' projects and working out tunes of his own and arranging tunes with his swing ensemble, Swing DeVille. Around 1988, he developed a label, Fiddlesong Music, and the label has issued CDs of Matt with Justin Branum, Matt's fiddle-and-banjo project with Jeff Elsloo, CDs of Lynn Wells and John P. Williams, and CDs of Swing DeVille.[50] "I think music touches people differently and I feel like my job is to keep people interested long enough for them to catch their inspiration—wherever it comes from. Putting regional and even county styles aside, the essence of old-time fiddling is in its predecessors and ultimately based in dance music. Understanding that is the first key."[51]

Listen to track 35 on the companion CD to hear Matt Wyatt's version of "Fort Smith."

"A lot of old-timers are gone and forgotten." Vesta Johnson embodied the spirit of a born teacher dedicated to passing on to others the repertoire, style, and cultural heritage of her native Linn County in north-central Missouri. From childhood in the 1920s on, Vesta experienced the shifts in fiddle music that contribute to our music today—ragtime, swing, country music, contests, radio, sound recordings, bluegrass, TV, the Folk Music Revival, the Internet, and the eventual wide acceptance of women as fiddlers. She did not read music and was taught by ear at camps and home sessions. She believed that if learners have a "good ear," they can grasp music quickly. Attentive listening was crucial to her: "What ain't worth remembering, ain't worth learning." "They got to get it up here first [taps her head]. Once they get it up here they can put it on that fiddle." Vesta Johnson's motto was "keep it old-time." (Photo by Jean A. Fugate-Besalke, October 2013)

Conclusion

Though the great song return no more
There's keen delight in what we have:
The rattle of pebbles on the shore
Under the receding wave.

—W. B. Yeats (1932), "The Nineteenth Century and After"

Traditions are a community's storehouse of practical and comfortable patterns and habits that sustain everyday life. The hallmark of tradition, whether music or architecture or cuisine, is not only constancy but variation. Variation is the key to expressive rendering of anything we do. Rote duplication of received models is boring.

John Kleine of Troy, Missouri, at a festival in Hermann, 2012. Many young fiddlers today share a passion for taking the music forward while tipping their hats to those who came before. (Photo by Kim Carr, https://www.kimcarrphotography.com)

Through habit and a sense of nostalgia, people living through changeful times often feel that the traditional life and work of their communities—the spirit and landscape of their place and time—are quietly crumbling away, rubbed out by forgetfulness, ignorance, the neglect of busy modernity. Those who record, study, and conserve such things as old-time fiddling are constantly reminded that these things are under threat, if not dying out altogether under steamrollers of rude change. But no one wants to see their musical heritage become a dry museum piece. Everything changes, but what is remarkable is not the changes in fiddle technique and repertoire, but, rather, what stays the same as the old heart of music hundreds of years old keeps beating. Fiddling is not dying out, *and*, as an avant-garde artist said, "Each age finds its own technique."[1]

Terms such as "grassification," "Americana," and "jazz grass" are being used by musicians such as Sarah Davis and Mark Atkins-Lieberman, who perform as "Sarah and Mark" from their Columbia base. They enjoy bringing bluegrass fiddle, mandolin, and guitar chops into their interpretations of songs and artists normally outside the bluegrass bin. (Photo by Clintin Davis-Stober, 2019)

Digital Delicatessens

Today, performances and fiddle lessons are available worldwide at the click of the computer button and in "real time" via various digital platforms. YouTube is a place for discovery. Fiddlers who may not be well known in the fiddle-contest world, bluegrass festivals, and the like can make their music available. One example during the COVID-19 pandemic is the videos by Steve Schaffner, in which he plays tunes in a variety of styles at historic sites and conservation areas around Cape Girardeau and environs.[2] We have instant access. We can cherry-pick the tunes we want to capture and hear, avoiding the hassles and delights of negotiating time with a fiddler who may or may not be interested in the stranger's presence and questions.

Will the digital delicatessen of fiddle music mean the end of home cooking? I don't think so. People will always want and need the small-batch, palpable in-person, one-on-one interactions, stories, hospitality, and handshake or hug shared by teacher and learner. In other words, it is the context that matters. Recordings, books, articles, videos, films—all kinds of documentation of today's music and musicians—are essential for the future to hear and see what has come before.

An aspiring fiddler someday may cruise the Internet and come across grainy old videotape of Gene Goforth playing "I Don't Love Nobody" with John Hartford plunking away on his banjo. It was good then, and it is good now. Study, ye student! If future fiddlers frame Gene as retro chic, that's fine. I am certain that, at some point, some young people will wonder, "So, who was Gene Goforth?" and maybe even ask (dare I say it), "Who was John Hartford?" And in its own strange way, the music of past, present, and future will flow on again.

Mike Wells of Franklin with a contest trophy and check, Boonesboro, Missouri. Mike inherits his family's love of fiddling and is a frequent competitor in contests, where he likes to play the old favorite "Marmaduke's Hornpipe." (Photo by Kay Allen, July 2007)

Beyond Mariachi

A great deal of research remains to be done if we are to more fully document and celebrate the spectrum of traditional fiddle music. One topic awaiting future research in archives, libraries, fieldwork, and term papers and dissertations is fiddling traditions of Hispanic and Latino people, particularly in rural and small-town Missouri and across the continent.[3]

Mariachi is the Mexican and Latino music best known to the general public. Like bluegrass and swing, mariachi is an amalgam of traditions in repertoire and performance that emerged in an historic cultural community and region; as it grew, it evolved and took in influences ranging from classical music to pop and rock. Mariachi evolved over a century and a half and predates bluegrass music, jazz, and swing. And, like swing, jazz, and bluegrass, and often in old-time fiddling, mariachi violinists often have classical training as well as folk techniques and repertoire learned by ear.

The Kansas City metropolitan area, including Independence, contains Missouri's largest and best-known Latino community and arguably the largest in the big space between Chicago and Denver and cities in Texas.[4] Kansas City is on Missouri's western border with Kansas, and the increasingly urbanized region includes counties across the line in eastern Kansas. Hispanic and Latino settlement there traces to the 1800s, beginning with traders, pack-train guides, and vaqueros traveling from Spanish colonial New Mexico to Independence after the opening in 1821 of the Santa Fe Trail.[5] Mexican entrepreneurs established businesses and brought families, just like other groups of people, in a pattern familiar in history. Further settlement took place in the wake of the 1911–12 Mexican Revolution. Mexican workers were recruited by railroads to augment labor forces in construction of rail lines, and they settled nearby; many also found employment in steel plants, manufacturing, meatpacking, and seasonal agricultural work.[6] There are substantial and growing numbers of Mexican, Mexican American, and Latino people in small towns and sparsely populated regions with an agribusiness presence nearby, such as confined animal feeding operations in turkey, chicken, and pork production; pet-food factories; meatpacking; and in crops such as cotton and melons.

Kansas City tourism promotes "the Latino Community" in Armourdale (often referred to as the barrio, across the Kansas River in Kansas City, Kansas, near railroad yards), Argentine, and Westside; their website mentions mariachi bands.[7] In Westside at Our Lady of Guadalupe Catholic church, there are both a Hispanic Chamber of Commerce and a cultural agency called the Guadalupe Centers, founded in 1919 by the Roman Catholic Diocese of Kansas City–St. Joseph to serve, assist, and help educate the area's Mexican families in various ways. Among other programs, the centers developed Alta Vista Charter Schools. In the 1990s, documentary research, oral history, and programming in Westside in conjunction with the Guadalupe Centers were developed by Dr. Dana Everts-Boehm of the Missouri Cultural Heritage Center. Her work led to participation of artists and apprentices in the Traditional Arts Apprenticeship Program, and her publication *"¡Qué Viva el Westside!": Mexican Traditional Arts in Kansas City, Missouri* remains an essential overview of a rarely documented cultural scene in modern American life.[8] Mariachi trumpet master Heriberto Lopez Sr., leader of the band "Mariachi Mexico," taught Antonio Sierra Jr. in the Traditional Arts Apprenticeship Program.[9]

In the Latino community in Kansas City's Westside: Avenida Cesar E. Chavez (formerly Twenty-Third Street Trafficway), looking east toward Interstate 35, Union Station, and the Crown Center high-rise district, with the Sheraton Kansas City hotel in distance. On the right is Our Lady of Guadalupe Catholic church. (Photo by Howard Marshall, May 2018)

Paul Anastasio and others have shown that mariachi is a "folk/pop hybrid" of folk music that evolved in the Guadalajara community in the southwestern Mexican state of Jalisco. Anastasio's research and recordings have helped outsiders appreciate mariachi's history. Paul has exhibited and taught fiddle music he learned in Mexico and written articles about the tradition.[10]

Mariachi is popular mostly as entertainment in Mexican restaurants and community weddings, private parties, parades, holidays, and celebrations such as Cinco de Mayo (commemorating the May 5, 1862, Mexican Army victory over France in the Battle of Puebla), Dia de la Independencia (September 16), and Dia de Muertos (Day of the Dead, November 2). Mariachi music is also linked to western swing, country music, and the broader commercial recording industry. Mariachi appeals not only as ebullient and cheerful music but also for the resplendent *charro* (Mexican vaquero) costumes topped off with sombreros. "'Not all people understand Spanish, but they understand the spirit of mariachi music."[11]

Some attention to mariachi is part of schools that incorporate Hispanic and Latino culture into the curriculum. The Guadalupe Centers offer a Mariachi Camp. Some of the instruments are familiar in European and American music—violin, trumpet,

Spanish guitar—while others are Mexican and Latino, such as the *vihuela* (a small, round-back five-string guitar) and the *guitarrón* (*guitarrón mexicano*, a large, deep-bodied, fretless six-string acoustic bass, the principal rhythm in mariachi).

Tess and Maria Cuevas are granddaughters of Teresa Maria Alonzo Cuevas, a mariachi violinist and founder in 1977 of Mariachi Estrella, an all-female band. The family roots are in Guanajuato, and her parents immigrated to Topeka, Kansas, after the Mexican Revolution. Her father took employment with the Santa Fe Railroad. Teresa Maria Alonzo Cuevas had classical violin as a child and played in the high school orchestra in the 1930s. As an adult, she played violin in her Catholic church choir. Mariachi is linked to the church, and groups often perform for Mass. Cuevas's church in Topeka had a Guatemalan priest who loved music, taught "happy songs," and encouraged Cuevas and others to perform, and she accumulated songs from the priest and records and remembered songs she heard as a child.

Tess and Maria began performing as children with their grandmother's band, Mariachi Estrella. While Tess became the main fiddler, both girls took Suzuki and classical violin as children, and their grandmother taught them mariachi violin. Tess's younger sister, Maria, focused on guitar and *vihuela*. The sisters performed with Mariachi Estrella for years, and both graduated from the University of Kansas. According to Tess Cuevas: "Our Mexican American upbringing was very interesting because we felt as if we had two lives. We grew up in a mostly white middle class neighborhood and then every weekend we put on our costumes and makeup and bows, and we were living our double lives as mariachis."[12] After their grandmother, who taught mariachi violin in the Kansas Folk Arts Apprenticeship Program, died in 1993, the sisters formed Maria the Mexican and developed careers in music. They worked out music that honors their grandmother's mariachi heritage, with vocals in Spanish and songs of their grandmother's, and the music blends in contemporary American genres of popular music. The Cuevases find the resulting music difficult to categorize, describing it as "influenced by mariachi music . . . a hybrid of Mexican folklore and Rock," "Americana Soul & Mexican Groove," and "Americana soul and Mexican blues."[13] Their ensemble is a modern one, with guitars both electric and acoustic, electric bass guitar, keyboard, drums, and occasionally trumpet to embellish the mariachi sound when a song requires, and they may add accordion when a *norteño* or Tex-Mex sound is wanted.

The paucity of mariachi fiddlers may compel a band needing a fiddler for a gig to invite a violinist outside the Latino community. Violinist, teacher, and old-time fiddler Katie Benyo has filled in for Tess Cuevas with the band Maria the Mexican. Benyo learned the repertoire from sheet music. "I learned tunes mostly from their grandmother's old written-down music and just improvised based on the 'feel' I was getting from the others I was playing with."[14]

In 2020 the COVID-19 pandemic shuttered most festivals, concerts, fiddle contests, jam sessions, and other events. The precautions and absence of familiar habits of making music together reminds us how social is music. Let us hope that the circle will not permanently be broken.

Researching and writing this book, and preparing the CD that comes with it, has been a pleasurable and challenging journey. I hope that *Keep It Old-Time* will be of interest in the future. I rest my pen, recorder, camera, road maps, and cell phone and welcome others to join the community of people who conserve and write about fiddling and those who carry it on. Bring your tools and add your contributions to document, contemplate, and celebrate the saga. Who knows where the time goes?

> There's a little piece of cornbread laying on the shelf—
> If you want any more, you'll have to sing it yourself.

Hannah and Benjamin Farnum, members of the Farnum Family Band from Galena, host a "Fiddlin' Friday at Five" program on Facebook Live. Hannah shares a variety of fiddle tunes, many of which she has learned at the suggestion of her viewers. Benjamin provides the backup guitar and takes solos as well. Between tunes, he reads viewers' comments on his cell phone and responds to questions and requests in real time. Contemporary digital technology has opened new horizons for performers as well as audiences. (Photo by Tricia Farnum, February 2022)

Notes for the Companion CD

The music CDs with *"Play Me Something Quick and Devilish," Fiddler's Dream*, and *Keep It Old-Time* let us listen to examples of the music and musicians discussed. I chose recordings from home recordings, radio programs, archives, cyberspace uploads, and commercial recordings; a number were provided by musicians or their families. All recordings used with permission. For every player highlighted, there are many others deserving recognition.

Track 1. Henry Wells, "Bill Cheatem," 1969
The great Glasgow southpaw plays one of the big contest tunes. Recorded from a *Tunemasters* weekly television show on KOMU Channel 8 (Columbia), courtesy Musial Wolfe. Host Howard Robertson brought Cleo Persinger, Gene Wells, Henry Wells, and Charlie Jackson the program: "Howdy everybody, welcome to thirty minutes of old-time fiddlin' on The Tunemasters show. Now tonight's the night, the night we've been waiting for, tonight we'll have nothin' on the show but *old-time* fiddle music, and I'm tellin' you, we've got some of the best fiddlers in central Missouri to play for you."

Track 2. Geoff Seitz, "Gravois Creek Pump," 1995
Gravois Creek is a tributary of River des Peres (a tributary of the Mississippi) that passed through the Seitz family truck farm. "There was an old rusted water pump half-buried in the mud at the end of the strawberry field by the creek. My grandfather used it to pump water for irrigation long before my time. I imagined how the pump would've sounded and wrote this tune" (album notes, *The Good Old Days Are Here*). Geoff Seitz (composer; violin), with Jim Nelson (guitar), Dave Landreth (banjo), Curtis Buckhannon (mandolin), Forrest Rose (bass), and Michelle Belanger (dancing).

Track 3. Tom Verdot, "Polka Medley," ca. 2011
Two older polkas, "Lucy Long Polka" and "Jim Crow Polka," on an unpublished promotional CD by the Skirtlifters, who brought to light music from minstrelsy, vaudeville, and early ragtime. Tom Verdot (violin), Clark Buehling (minstrel banjo), and Thom Howard (guitar).

Track 4. The Little Dixie Hoss Hair Pullers, "Jimmy Shank," 1981
The Little Dixie Hoss Hair Pullers was a premier ensemble during the 1970s and early 1980s heyday of the old-time string-band movement. "Jimmy Shank" is a Kentucky breakdown learned from Bruce Greene at a festival in Indiana. Recorded in February 1981 when the Little Dixie Hoss Hair Pullers were featured on KOPN-FM in Columbia as part of the *Old-Time and Bluegrass Music Day* broadcast. A fine time

was had by all. Spencer Galloway and Rob Golan (violins), Jim Ruth (claw-hammer banjo), and Heinrich Leonhard (guitar).

Track 5. Taylor McBaine, "Rachel," 1987

Recorded by Charlie Walden for McBaine's *Boone County Fiddler*. A favorite breakdown of McBaine's and across Missouri. Bowing and arpeggios in the first part are distinctively central Missouri and help define Little Dixie versions. Sometimes associated with or attributed to President Andrew Jackson's wife, Rachel, a Virginian and musician, the melody descends from "St. Louis Quickstep"; other titles include "Texas Quickstep" (Kenny Baker), and many fiddlers learned the tune from Tommy Jackson's 1950s commercial recording. Christeson includes his own version in his second volume and says it was known as "St. Louis Quickstep" in former times in central Missouri. McBaine (violin), John G. Stewart (guitar), and Forrest Rose (bass).

Track 6. Charlie Cook, "Flowers from Heaven," ca. 1958

From a tape recording at a music party in the Columbia area; cassette copy courtesy of Ivan Crane. Composed by Cook, a brilliant old-time and swing player. Several Cook waltzes became specialties of contest fiddlers such as Pete McMahan (who added interesting parts and variations) and Leroy Canaday (see Canaday, *Old Dan Tucker Was a Fine Old Man*, VRCD 353). Art Galbraith's spare version is in Phillips, *Traditional American Fiddle Tunes* (vol. 2, 254) and available on Art's *Simple Pleasures* (Rounder 0157). Charlie Cook died in 1960; recordings are scarce, and too little of his music is remembered outside of central Missouri.

Track 7. Pete McMahan, "Sugar in the Gourd," 1977

A staple of the square-dance repertoire, here played by McMahan who learned it as a child from Clark Atterberry. Jack Deck provides three-finger banjo backup, and Fred Stoneking provides bedrock old-time guitar; reissue, *50 Old-Time Fiddle Gems*.

Track 8. Johnny Bruce, "Leather Britches," 1991

Lena Hughes plays her signature backup banjo for Johnny Bruce on this old favorite. Lena's father taught her banjo when she was a child (ca. 1915) in order to accompany his fiddling. She called her style "double noting" and often tuned her Gibson RB-100 banjo in an open A chord instead of the usual G chord. Recorded by Howard Marshall, February 23, 1991, at the Hughes home in Ludlow, Missouri.

Track 9. Joe Fedrizzi, "Goodnight Waltz," 2021

A favorite waltz often played by Joe's grandfather Joe Grable and played here with assured authority by Fedrizzi. A best-selling 78-rpm record in 1927 by Mississippi's Leake County Revelers, Missouri fiddler Bill Driver's version is notated in Christeson's 1973 tune book. Recorded by John P. Williams in June 2021 at Bethel Youth Fiddle Camp, where Fedrizzi was an instructor. Backup guitar, Kenny Applebee.

Track 10. Dick Logan, "Grape Leaf Rag," 1970

Logan (composer), with his children Paul (five-string banjo), Jane (guitar), and Art (mandolin), a 45-rpm record released in 1971.

Track 11. Cleo Persinger, "Buckeye Reel," ca. 1965

Played by Little Dixie fiddlers of former times such as Daniel Boone Jones, Henry Lee McBaine, Pete McMahan, George Morris, Ed Tharp, and Persinger. Most of his peers called it "Buckley's Reel."[1] "Buckley's Reel" / "Buckley's Favorite-Reel" (a.k.a. "Buckley's Hornpipe") is in collections such as *Howe's 1,000* of 1867, *Ryan's Mammoth* of 1883, and Cole's *One Thousand Fiddle Tunes* of 1940. There is a similar Irish tune, "Buckley's Fancy," in collections such as Krassen's edition of O'Neill's *Music of Ireland.* I believe this was recorded by Jake Hughes at one of his "favorite fiddlers" sessions; courtesy of Hughes, 1975.

Track 12. Dale Pauley, "Marchéta," 2018

"Marchéta" (pronounced Mar-KEE-ta), "A Love Song of Old Mexico," is a sentimental song composed in 1913 by Victor Schertzinger, recorded by singers such as John McCormack (1924), Bing Crosby (1940), Gene Autry (1947), and Al Jolson (1948). The song became popular as theme music in a John Ford 1945 war movie starring John Wayne, *They Were Expendable.* "Marchéta" was a favorite of radio fiddler George Morris, and guitarist N. C. Ficklin (a member of Morris's band) worked out the chord (different fiddlers prefer different chords for this tune). Hillis Crowell, Luther Caldwell, and Dale Pauley learned the melancholy waltz from Morris. Recorded by Kathy Gordon; guitar accompaniment by Caldwell, Heinrich Leonhard, and Brad Roby; bass, Gordon.

Track 13. Gene Wells, "Sally Goodin," 1969

A member of a Howard County fiddle dynasty, Gene offers his take on the venerated "Sally Goodin." See Henry Wells, track 1, for recording information.

Track 14. Charlie Walden, "Angus Campbell," 1983

An evergreen frequently presented dressed up for contest judges. Walden plays his version in the March 1983 fiddle contest in Boonville, with John G. Stewart, guitar. Recorded by the Missouri State Old Time Fiddlers Association and posted on YouTube.

Track 15. Thomas Coriell, "A & E Waltz," 2022

"I learned this tune directly from Charlie Walden, who said he learned it directly from Taylor McBaine." Attributed to fiddler Rusty Modrell of Redmond, Oregon, who popularized it through his many years at the National Oldtime Fiddlers' Contest in Weiser, Idaho; by the 1970s it had spread throughout Missouri, in part via Idaho champion Lloyd Wanzer's *Waltz Wonderland* LP. A favorite waltz among Missouri fiddlers such as Taylor McBaine, Johnny Bruce, and Jake Hockemeyer. Walden has it in his "100 Essential Missouri Fiddle Tunes." Coriell, with Aaron Albrecht, guitar. Recorded by Thomas Coriell, January 2022.

Track 16. John Griffin, "Woodchopper's Hornpipe," 1993

Griffin fiddled this Canadian tune on Pippa Letsky's radio show, *Across the Wide Missouri*, on KOPN 89.5 FM, with Heinrich Leonhard, guitar; courtesy of KOPN. This is a hornpipe played as a breakdown (reel/hoedown), often associated in Missouri with Jake Hockemeyer and Cyril Stinnett, who played it in contests with good results.

Track 17. Junior Marriott, "Uncle Dan," 2004

A smooth Texas-style breakdown from Texas champion Randy Elmore. From the CD *Junior Marriott.*

Track 18. Kelly Jones, "Forked Deer," 1975

A favorite in Missouri, from Jones's immaculate LP *Authentic Old-Time Fiddle Tunes*, accompanied by Kansas City's Bluegrass Association band (Jim McGreevy, five-string banjo; John Bennett, guitar; Chuck Stearman, mandolin; and Don Montgomery, bass).

Track 19. Amber Gaddy, "Black Sally Goodin," 2019

Gaddy learned this intriguing Missouri tune from John White, one of her mentors. White recalled that he may have learned it from Keith Orchard, who taught John some tunes associated with Callaway County fiddler Bill Katon, one of several influential African American fiddlers in central Missouri who performed on WOS-AM radio in the late 1920s and early 1930s (Katon's three-part version as played by Vee Latty is printed in Christeson's 1973 *Old-Time Fiddler's Repertory*). A different, two-part, version was played by Pete McMahan, who learned it from Clark Atterberry and Cleo Persinger; their version is played in cross-tuning ("dischord" tuning), with the E string dropped down to a D note, and with application of left-hand finger plucking (pizzicato) on the retuned E string. Charlie Walden lists "Black Sally Goodin" on his list of "100 Essential Missouri Fiddle Tunes." Recorded by David Cavins; guitar accompaniment, Cavins.

Track 20. John Williams, "Reuben's Ridge," 2019

John P. Williams, with guitarist Robert Mackey, recorded for this project at Williams's farm in Monroe County. A signature Pete McMahan breakdown.

Track 21. Richard Shewmaker, "Brenda's Reel," 2022

Shewmaker has this fine tune from Charlie Walden and Cyril Stinnett. Composed by Toronto fiddler Brian Barron, whose daughter is named Brenda; recorded on his 1959 LP *Old-Tyme Fiddle Jamboree* (Arc Records Arc-503). Also recorded by Nova Scotia fiddler Carl Elliott in 1983. Charlie Walden learned his version directly from

Cyril Stinnett (on Walden's *Draggin' the Bow)*, and Shewmaker reports that Junior Marriott plays a superb version. "It's one of those tunes that has such a good combination of rolling melody and drive that it stands well on its own without much embellishment. It's a tune that captures the essence of North and Central Missouri Fiddling."[2] Recorded by Aaron Albrecht, January 8, 2022; backup guitar by Albrecht.

Track 22. Trustin Baker, "Grey Eagle," 2018

The mighty "Grey Eagle," from Trustin's round in the state contest in Sedalia. Guitar accompaniment by Tad Johnston, Beau Johnston, and Junior Marriott. Available on YouTube, posted by the Missouri State Old Time Fiddlers Association; introduction by emcee Charlie Walden.

Track 23. Roger Netherton, "Tippin' Back the Corn," 2018

On *Roger Netherton*, with Rachel Eddy (guitar), Hunter Walker (clawhammer banjo), and Alex Lacquement (bass). Composed by Jordan Wankoff, an instructor at the Old Town School of Folk Music in Chicago. Roger learned the tune from Chirps Smith's *Down in Little Egypt.*

Track 24. Levi Roden, "Stony Point," 2019

Levi learned this square-dance favorite from Fred Stoneking. Among other titles are "Hop Skip Squirrel," "Wild Horse on Stony Point," and "Pigtown Fling," but when it is presented in fiddle contests, I have only heard it announced as "Stony Point." There is an unrelated Missouri tune called "Stony Hill." Travis Inman, guitar. Recorded by Howard Marshall in Purdy, Missouri.

Track 25. Travis Inman, "Jack Danielson's Reel," 1995

A tune often associated with Bob Walters and Cyril Stinnett. The Walters version is in Christeson's *Old-Time Fiddler's Repertory* (vol. 1) and in Stacy Phillips's volume 1.[3] Stinnett played a sparkling rendition to win his national title at Weiser in 1966 (accompanied on banjo by Lena Hughes), reissued on *Fiddle Classics from the Vaults of County Records and Old Blue Records* (Old Blue OB-709, 2012). Geoff Seitz has it on *Fine as Frog's Hair*, and Charlie Walden fiddles the tune on YouTube videos and includes it in "100 Essential Missouri Fiddle Tunes." From Inman's *Championship Fiddling*, with Fred and Alita Stoneking (guitars) and Forrest Rose (bass).

Track 26. Lee Stoneking, "Echoes of the Ozarks," 1975

With Lee's daughter Judy Stoneking Vanderville (five-string banjo). A favorite in the Midwest, attributed to Ishmael (Ozark Red) Loveall of Bagnell, Missouri, and popularized by Lee and Fred Stoneking as well as swing fiddler Luther Caldwell (who called it "Traveling Back to Dixie") and the Stonekings' friends Lyman Enloe and Pete McMahan. The first known commercial recording may be Fiddlin' Sam Long's 1926 78-rpm record. Geoff Seitz's version is on *Laugh and Grow Fat*. Recorded by Howard Marshall for the Smithsonian Institution at the Stoneking home, 1975.

Track 27. Fred Stoneking, "Buzzard in a Pea Patch," 1996

Grand Ole Opry star Uncle Dave Macon recorded the tune in 1927 as "Rabbit in a Pea Patch"; Vance Randolph lists it by that title in "The Names of Ozark Fiddle Tunes" (1954). Also known as "Turkey in a Pea Patch," the title associated with Kentucky fiddler Buddy Thomas, whose version on his 1973 *Kitty Puss* LP was the source for Fred Stoneking's version. Fred's version is in Beisswenger and McCann's *Ozarks Fiddle Music*. Fred enjoyed using alternate titles; when he played this at the Yankton, South Dakota, Great Plains Championships, he announced it as "Rabbit in the Pea Patch," and in 1999 it appeared on a compilation tape recorded at Yankton, *Top of the Line—Fiddling #56*. Whether the critter in question is a buzzard, rabbit, or turkey is moot; it's a great breakdown. From *Saddle Old Spike* with Fred's daughter Alita Stoneking and Gordon McCann, guitars. Courtesy of Gordon McCann.

Track 28. Alita Stoneking, "Dusty Miller," 2014

A tune central to contest and bluegrass repertoires. Alita's estimable version builds on the traditional tune to dress it up for the competition environment. Guitar by Tom Weisgerber. From *Born to Play*.

Track 29. Mike Hartgrove, "Five Miles Out of Town," 2021

A north Missouri breakdown Hartgrove learned from Cyril Stinnett and Dwight Lamb. Recorded by Mike for this project. Mike plays the tune unaccompanied, recorded over a simple digital "train beat."

Track 30. Gerald Jones, with Midnight Flight, "Buck Snort," 1997

Known as a Lyman Enloe tune. Gerald learned it from Fred Stoneking, who had learned it from Enloe, who recorded "Buck Snort" on Enloe's 1976 *Rugged Road*. Jones exhibits quotations from bluegrass fiddlers such as Benny Martin and Paul Warren. From *The Best of Midnight Flight, Vol. 1* (originally recorded in 1997 for *Takin' Off*).

Track 31. Hannah Farnum, "Amelia's Waltz," 2022

A fine waltz written by New Hampshire contra-dance caller, composer, and pianist Bob McQuillen in 1981. Requested by one of her *Fiddlin' Friday at Five* Facebook Live program listeners, Hannah learned the waltz from a 2019 YouTube video by Canadian champion and teacher Patti Kusturok, from her "365 Days of Fiddle Tunes" series. Recorded January 7, 2022. Hannah and her brother Benjamin, who accompanies her on rhythm guitar, respond to listener comments and play viewers' requests in real time.

Track 32. Kathy Summers, "Wink the Other Eye," 2016

A Kentucky-Tennessee-Missouri square-dance tune associated with Lonnie Robertson and Art Galbraith. The minor chord helps correct the notion that there are few if any minor chords in Ozark fiddling. Commercial recordings include Theron Hale and His Daughters (1928) and Hack's String Band (1931). Alternate titles include Curly Fox's "Wink Your Little Eye" (*Curly Fox and Texas Ruby*). Kathy learned the tune from an Internet service as performed by Seattle's Foghorn Stringband. From Summers's *Good Old Fiddle Tunes* with guitarist Darrol Roskowske of St. James.

Track 33. Liesl Schoenberger, "Forty Years Ago Waltz," 1997

Set in B-flat, challenging and effective. Little is known of its origins; early commercial recordings include a 1949 record by Wade Ray. J. T. Perkins of Alabama helped popularize the waltz at contests and through his 1975 *Fiddle Favorites* LP; Benny Thomasson's 1965 version is on *Texas Hoedown Revisited*.[4] From *Classic Fiddle*, with Buddy Spicher (mandolin), David Grier (lead guitar), Bill Rehrig (rhythm guitar), and Roger Spencer (bass).

Track 34. David Scrivner, "Sally in the Garden," 2007

This southern and midwestern tune nicely represents David's fiddle and banjo duets with Karen Kraft. Karen doubles the melody with David on this tune that, due to extra beats, falls in the "crooked" category. From *Hangin' around the Kitchen*.

Track 35. Matt Wyatt, "Fort Smith," 1998

A breakdown Matt learned in Texas visits with Louis Franklin and Orville Burns. A 1920s record by Luke Highnight's Ozark Strutters is on a 1970 reissue, *Echoes of the Ozarks, Vol. 2*; print versions are in Brody's *Fiddler's Fakebook* and Thede's *Fiddle Book*, and Orville Burns's version is in the *Devil's Box* 31, no. 1 (1997): 37. Origins are unclear; one version has it stemming from the era of the US Army post at Fort Smith, Arkansas, and another suggests it came from Sweden with a musician in Fort Smith named Bottefur (Thede). Recordings include those by Vesta Johnson, H. K. Silvey, and Bob Holt; Charlie Walden lists it in "100 Essential Missouri Fiddle Tunes" and teaches it on YouTube. From *The Goodbye Waltz*; guitar accompaniment by Justin Branum.

Track 36. Howard Marshall, "Sugar Tree Stomp," 2022

A good tune from Fiddlin' Arthur Smith in the 1930s. I learned it from bluegrass fiddler Kenny Baker's version in the late 1960s and from Gene Goforth's version.[5] Heinrich Leonhard, guitar; Kathy Gordon, bass. Recorded by David Cavins in Columbia, Missouri.

Notes

Introduction

1. Examples include Archie Green, *Only a Miner: Studies in Recorded Coal Mining Songs*; Samuel P. Bayard, *Hill Country Tunes: Instrumental Folk Music of Southwestern Pennsylvania*; Edward D. Ives, *Lawrence Doyle: The Farmer-Poet of Prince Edward Island*; and Henry Glassie, *Passing the Time in Ballymenone: Culture and History in an Ulster Community*.

2. Charlie Walden, Traditional Arts Apprenticeship Program celebration and concert, Columbia, Missouri, May 21, 2022.

3. "Newport Folkfest to Draw Scores of Headline Acts."

4. See Howard Marshall, Vivian Williams, and Phil Williams, *Fiddle Seconding Missouri Style, Chords and Bowing Techniques*.

5. Musicologist Chris Goertzen uses the formulation "Texas-derived contest style" in *Southern Fiddlers and Fiddle Contests* in discussing Appalachian and southeastern contest fiddling in comparison with the contest style prevalent in the West. See also Christopher Goertzen, "The Transformation of American Contest Fiddling."

6. Various Artists, *Texas Hoedown* (County 703, 1964; Bartow Riley, Vernon Solomon, Benny Thomasson); Various Artists, *Texas Fiddle Favorites* (County 707, 1965; Major Franklin, Lewis Franklin, Norman Solomon). For Texas-style fiddling, see, for example, Stacy Phillips [Melvin Marshall], *Contest Fiddling*; Gus Garelick, "The Legacy of Benny Thomasson"; and Aaron Smithers, *Curriculum Guide: Texas-Style Fiddling*.

7. Goertzen writes succinct scholarly overviews of the differences in *Southern Fiddlers and Fiddler Contests*, pointing to the purposely more "gritty" style of the Texans in contrast to the more "linear," "virtuosic," and educated style of the Weiser fiddlers from the Pacific Northwest. "In the northwest, Texas style is toned down, mixing with classical timbre" (119). "But overall, one can hear a small but certain difference, a valuing of crystalline timbre [Weiser style] at the expense of aggressive rhythm [Texas fiddlers]" (45).

8. Kenny Hall, July 1975.

9. According to Drew Beisswenger, "I think Texas style is confused by most people with that [expletive] people play in the Southeast and think they are playing 'Texas style.' Modern contest fiddling gives Texas style a bad name. Texas style and Missouri are closely related" (November 11, 2011).

10. To list a dozen or so major contests where Contest Style is on full display and influential globally, add to Hallettsville and Weiser contests such as those at Red Bluff, California; Denver; Crockett, Texas; Nashville; and Athens, Alabama.

11. Jim Wood, "Swinging with Sally Goodin: Jazzy Accompaniment for Contest Fiddling."

12. Other terms include "bar chord," "jazz chord," "swing chord," "sock chord," "chomp-chomp," "Mel Bay chord," "choke chord," and "frog chord."

13. Junior Marriott, August 22, 2010.

14. The Colorado Old Time Fiddlers' Association in Denver, which hosts a major western contest each January, says its mission is to promote "Texas style contest fiddling": "The Colorado Old Time Fiddlers' Association, Inc. ('COTFA') was formed in March of 2002 as a *501(c)(3) non-profit corporation* for the express purpose of promoting, preserving, and educating the

public, throughout the State of Colorado, about the traditional American musical art form of old-time fiddling, with an emphasis on Texas-style contest fiddling" (coloradofiddlers.org). Most groups favoring Texas-derived contest style are more circumspect.

1. The Folk Music Revival of the 1960s and 1970s—and the Fiddle

1. Among works about the Folk Music Revival, and the sixties, see Caroline Bithell and Juniper Hill, *The Oxford Handbook of Music Revival*; Robert S. Cantwell, *When We Were Good: The Folk Revival*; Ronald D. Cohen, *Rainbow Quest: The Folk Music Revival and American Society, 1940–1970*; Jens Lund and R. Serge Denisoff, "The Folk Music Revival and the Counter Culture: Contributions and Contradictions"; David K. Dunaway and Molly Beer, *Singing Out: An Oral History of America's Folk Song Revivals*; Neil Rosenberg, "The Shifting Sands of Folk Authenticity" and "A Folklorist's Exploration of the Folk Revival Metaphor," in *Transforming Tradition: Folk Music Revivals Examined*, ed. Rosenberg; Theodore Roszak, *The Making of a Counter Culture: Reflections on the Technocratic Society and Its Youthful Opposition*; and, a personal favorite, Tom Wolfe's *Electric Kool-Aid Acid Test.*

2. Alan Jabbour, "A Participant-Documentarian in the American Instrumental Folk Music Revival," 123.

3. For example, Cantwell, *When We were Good*, 22ff; and Happy Traum, a folk musician and longtime *Sing Out!* editor and a central contributor in the Greenwich Village scene (who in 1963 was the first to record Dylan's "Blowin' in the Wind"). Traum recognized that young people's interest in folk music was flagging in the late sixties. See Happy Traum, "The Swan Song of Folk Music."

4. Rock initially was of little interest in or threat to the Folk Music Revival or to bluegrass music; that changed in 1964 with the "British Invasion," led by the Beatles.

5. The notion of the Age of Aquarius comes from astrology and, for the counterculture and wider popular culture, became a predicted time of great personal enlightenment, humanity, love, freedom, and antiestablishment politics. "The Age of Aquarius" was the opening song in the 1967 hippie rock musical *Hair* and became a Top 40 hit record by the Fifth Dimension.

6. John Court, Knob Lick Upper 10,000, *Workout!* (Mercury MG 20852, 1963).

7. Pete Seeger, foreword to *Lonesome Traveler: The Life of Lee Hays*, by Doris Willens, xv. Hays, Pete Seeger's colleague, was a leading voice in the early protest movement. See the 1982 reunion film documentary *The Weavers: Wasn't That a Time!* (Warner Brothers) and Brown's film *Pete Seeger: The Power of Song* (Genius Products, 2007). Seeger was among those blacklisted by the House Un-American Activities Committee, and in 1963 he was banned from the television show *Hootenanny*. John Cohen, "The Folksong Revival—a Historical Perspective, Part II," 37. Richard Reuss documents the role of politics and the Red Scare in the revival and related issues in "American Folklore and Left-Wing Politics, 1927–1957." See also Dunaway and Beer, *Singing Out*; Cohen, *Rainbow Quest*; and Cantwell, *When We Were Good.*

8. Belafonte, born in New York City, is Jamaican American; "Banana Boat Song" (RCA Victor 47-6771, 1956), sung in dialect, fueled the fashion for calypso music.

9. "The Eve of Destruction," composed by P. F. Sloan, (McGuire, Dunhill 45-D-4009, 1964); "Ballad of the Green Berets," composed and performed by Sadler (RCA Victor 72-8739, 1966). "Green Berets" is the nickname for US Army Special Forces.

10. "Beatnik" was coined in San Francisco by the hip newspaper columnist Herb Caen in the *San Francisco Chronicle*, April 2, 1958. The same year, the Kingston Trio's "Tom Dooley" topped commercial record charts.

11. A number of bluegrass musicians read the tea leaves, saw the pattern, and began trying to appeal to college audiences with LPs such as *Bluegrass Goes to College* (Hylo Brown and the Timberliners, Starday SLP 204, 1962) and *The Country Cut-Ups Go to College* (Towne House THLP 1000, 1967). The most influential among such albums included Lester Flatt and Earl Scruggs and the Foggy Mountain Boys' 1961 LP, *Foggy Mountain Banjo* (Columbia CS 8364), *Flatt & Scruggs at Carnegie Hall* (Columbia SL 2045, 1963), and *Flatt & Scruggs Recorded Live at Vanderbilt University* (Columbia CS 8934), 1964). As Roger Matthews pointed out, the first bluegrass band to perform at Carnegie Hall was Earl Taylor and the Stoney Mountain Boys in 1959; nodding to the folk revival, their first LP was titled *Folk Songs from the Blue Grass* (United Artists UAL 3049); Matthews, August 17, 2019. Flatt and Scruggs were my favorite in that generation, and other favorites that appealed to young folks and college crowds included the Country Gentlemen and the Greenbrier Boys.

12. *Beatle Country* (Elektra 4006) somehow worked, and the Beatles themselves approved; the group included Harvard students Bob Siggins, Eric Sackheim, and Clay Jackson and Massachusetts Institute of Technology graduate student Ethan Singer. Others such as Joe Val, Everett Lilly, and Jim Field were in the group at times. In addition to Siggins, Field, Val, and Lilly, the Nashville session players, fiddler Buddy Spicher, guitarist Eric Thompson, and Dobroist Craig Wingfield, were hired to add heft to the album.

13. The New Grass Revival's leader, Kentucky fiddler and mandolinist Sam Bush (b. 1952), admired Texas contest fiddlers such as Jim Chancellor as well as bluegrass leaders and had won the Junior Division at the National Oldtime Fiddlers' Contest (Weiser, Idaho) in the 1960s, placed high in grand-masters contests in Nashville in 1970s, and shaped a career in country music as a progressive mandolinist as well as fiddler. The New Grass Revival included Bush, Courtney Johnson (banjo), Curtis Burch (guitar), and John Cowan (electric bass guitar).

14. *Dillinger*, directed by John Milius (American International Pictures, 1973); *The Long Riders*, directed by Walter Hill (United Artists, 1980), featured a saloon band composed of young California pickers Mitch Greenhill (guitar), Bill Bryson (banjo), and Tom Sauber (violin). In *The Outlaw Josey Wales*, directed by Clint Eastwood (Warner Brothers, 1976), a fiddler plays by a campfire for a Texas settlers' dance, and two authentic dance tunes of the Civil War era are in the soundtrack, "Irish Washerwoman" and the couple dance known as "the varsouvienne." In *McCabe and Mrs. Miller*, directed by Robert Altman (Warner Brothers, 1971), all but the 1890s vaudeville and minstrel-stage nonsense song "Ta-ra-ra Boom De-ay!" remain in the repertoires of many fiddlers, although it was still commonly being played in the 1920s and 1930s and remembered into the 1960s as a comic ditty and basis for the theme song for early television's *Howdy Doody Show*. Pete McMahan remembered the tune as one of the first he worked out on the violin as a child in the late 1920s.

15. The four-string tenor guitar occupies a place in fiddle music, especially western swing. Developed in the 1920s and 1930s, it added punchy rhythm to in jazz, swing, and early country music. See Gary Lee Moore, *The Tenor Guitar: Getting Started in Fiddle Backup*; baritone ukulele is a reasonable substitute for a tenor guitar.

16. Harry Smith, *Anthology of American Folk Music* (Folkways FP251, 252, 253), reissued by Smithsonian Folkways in 1997; J. Cohen, "Remembering Harry Smith," *Old-Time Herald* (Spring 1992): 29; Jabbour, *American Fiddle Tunes*.

17. Joe Queenan writes in the *Wall Street Journal*, "In an unnerving sign that the Nostalgia-Industrial-Complex is alive and well, New York City's Carnegie Hall has announced a 2018 series that will allow the public to relive the 1960s. . . . For as a great philosopher once

observed, those who cannot remember the past are condemned to hear 'Puff the Magic Dragon' forever. . . . The Boomers have also been very successful in glossing over the fact that the '60s were basically miserable, with father pitted against son, white pitted against black, young pitted against old. The only fun thing about the '60s was the music. Well, the music and maybe the drugs." "Warning: The '60s Are Breaking Out Again," *Wall Street Journal*, February 18–19, 2017.

18. John Cohen's 1962 film, *That High and Lonesome Sound: The Legacy of Roscoe Holcomb* (reissued by Shanachie Records, 2002; book, CD, DVD, Gottingen: Steidl, 2012). "High, lonesome sound" was coined by Cohen to describe Kentucky banjoist and singer Roscoe Holcomb's edgy, high tenor singing, whom Cohen presented at the first University of Chicago Folk Festival in 1961; the film is a model for documentary filmmakers. See Ray Allen, *Gone to the Country: The New Lost City Ramblers and the Folk Music Revival*; and John Cohen, "The Folk Music Revival—a Historical Perspective, Part I: The Early Years," and "Folk Music Revival, Part II."

19. J. Cohen, "Folk Music Revival, Part I," 30; Gary Reid, "John Cohen"; Bill Friskics-Warren, "John Cohen, Champion of Old-Time Music, Is Dead," *New York Times*, September 17, 2019.

20. J. Cohen, "Folk Music Revival, Part II," 34.

21. Lyle Lofgren, review of *The New Lost City Ramblers: The Early Years, 1958–1962.*

22. *Traditional Dance Tunes* (Kanawha 311, 1968). See Jabbour, "Participant-Documentarian"; and introduction to Rosenberg, *Transforming Tradition*. Alan Jabbour was a Syrian American from Florida and classical violinist, as well as a graduate student in medieval literature at Duke University; Alan taught at the University of California at Los Angeles, became head of the Archive of Folk Song in the Library of Congress, director of the Folk Arts branch of the National Endowment for the Arts, and director of the American Folklife Center (Library of Congress).

23. Alan Jabbour, *Fiddle Tunes Illuminated: 45 Tunes Transcribed and Annotated for Stylistic Study*.

24. Matthew Albani, "From Vietnam to Trump: Protest Songs throughout the Decades."

25. The *Devil's Box* periodical was created in 1969 by Bill Harrison as a function of the Tennessee Valley Old Time Fiddlers' Association (founded in 1967) and edited until its demise in the 2000s by Professor Steve Davis of Emporia State University.

26. For folk festivals, among many solid works, see Ronald Cohen, *A History of Folk Festivals in the United States: Feasts of Musical Celebration*. Rosenberg's *Transforming Tradition* includes discussions of authenticity in the revival and string-band movement.

27. For David Whisnant's critique and observations about interventions into local heritage by outsiders, see *All That is Native and Fine: The Politics of Culture in an American Region*. See also Rosenberg, *Transforming Tradition*.

28. For example, see Melvin N. Artley, "The West Virginia Country Fiddler: An Aspect of the Folk Music Tradition of the United States"; Linda C. Burman-Hall, "Southern American Folk Fiddling: Context and Style"; Richard J. Blaustein, "Traditional Music and Social Change: The Old-Time Fiddlers' Association Movement in the United States"; Earl V. Spielman, "Traditional North American Fiddling: A Methodology for the Historical and Comparative Analytical Style Study of Instrumental Traditions"; Goertzen, "'Billy in the Low Ground': History of an American Instrumental Folk Tune"; Sharon Poulson Graf, "Traditionalization

at the National Oldtime Fiddlers' Contest: Politics, Power, and Authenticity"; Holly Hobbs, "Women of Old-Time Music: Tradition and Change in the Missouri Ozarks"; Bilyeu, "A Comparative Analysis of 'Durang's Hornpipe'"; Judy Mae Warner, "Ozark Old-Time Fiddling"; and James Randolph Ruchala, "Making Round Peak Music: History, Revitalization, and Community."

29. Gus Garelick, "My Encounter with the Folk Police." Kenny Hall fronted the Sweet's Mill String Band in Fresno. Vykki Mende Gray and Kenny Hall, *Kenny Hall's Music Book: Old-Time Music for Fiddle and/or Mandolin.* Garelick contributed a transcription of former Missourian Ron Hughey's "Yellow Gals" in *Fiddler's Dream.*

2. String Bands and College Towns

1. The 1930s spiritual was recorded and promulgated by folklorist/songsters Joe Hickerson, Pete Seeger, and others in the 1950s; first recorded by Hickerson with the Folksmiths (Oberlin College students) on the 1957 Folkways LP *We've Got Some Singing to Do*; the song shifted into a popular folksong through Joan Baez's 1962 setting and soon became a centerpiece of the civil rights movement.

2. Seitz, December 3, 2009.

3. Seitz, December 3, 2009; https://www.seitzviolins.com.

4. Charlie Walden, "Geoff Seitz: The Last of the Great Lemay Fiddlers," 32.

5. Charlie Walden, *Traditional Fiddle Music of Missouri* (Marimac 9011, 1987).

6. For fiddling vis-à-vis blues and early jazz, see Howard Wight Marshall, *"Play Me Something Quick and Devilish": Old-Time Fiddlers in Missouri* and *Fiddler's Dream: Old-Time, Swing, and Bluegrass Music in Twentieth-Century Missouri.*

7. Walden, "Geoff Seitz."

8. See chapter 1 of Marshall, *"Play Me Something Quick and Devilish."*

9. The Broadway play *Grapes of Wrath* was written in 1988 by Frank Galatti as an adaptation of John Steinbeck's classic 1939 novel of the Great Depression. Geoff's "Rose of Sharon" is a different melody from the widely known waltz of the same title made famous by Howdy Forrester in the 1960s and composed by J. Scott Skinner in the 1920s; Rose of Sharon Joad is also a character in Steinbeck's *The Grapes of Wrath* (Thomas Adler, May 25, 2021).

10. *Bob Holt: Dance Fiddling from the Missouri Ozarks* (see discography).

11. Ill-Mo Boys, *Laugh and Grow Fat* (Vigortone, 2001); other recordings include *Timely Old Tunes from the Ill-Mo Boys and Beyond* (Marimac 9020, cassette, 1988) and *Fine as Frog's Hair* (Marimac 9054, 1992, cassette).

12. *The Farmer Wants a Wife* was an American offshoot of an Australian TV production by Freemantle Media North America (Hollywood); it ran from 2007 to 2015.

13. Steve Pokin, "Pokin Around: Farmer Wants a Wife?," *St. Louis Post-Dispatch*, July 5, 2007.

14. Chris King, "String Theory: South City's Geoffrey Seitz Might Sell You a Violin from His Shop. Then Again, He Might Not." The broken violin was one that Geoff's father, Frank, owned and had played.

15. Lisa L. Higgins et al., *Work Is Art; Art Is Work: Interviews with Missouri Luthiers.*

16. Seitz, November 11, 2009.

17. William Powell, "On a String: Violin Maker Geoffrey Seitz," *St. Louis Magazine*, August 22, 2014.

18. Jessica Rapp, "Violin Maker Strikes a Chord with Customers."

19. "Ironclads" ("old standards," "evergreens") are commonplace, popular, favorite, and sometimes universally known old melodies that most people recognize, whatever the style, genre, or even instrument, such as "Happy Birthday" and "Mary Had a Little Lamb"—and fiddle tunes like "Turkey in the Straw" and "Red Wing" beamed from ice cream–truck speakers and sound systems in merry-go-rounds in carnivals and shopping malls.

20. Participants in the revival in these cities have produced valuable memoirs, such as Paul Stamler's wide-ranging article and Barry Bergey's Facebook posts. Stamler has been active in St. Louis since the sixties, helping develop the country/contra-dance community, deejaying folk-music shows on KDHX-FM, working with the Frontier Folklife Festival, and more. Paul J. Stamler, "Freaks and Fiddle Tunes: The Early 1970s Folk Revival in St. Louis."

21. Fullington is mentioned by banjoist R. D. Lunceford in John Salmon, "R. D. Lunceford."

22. In Columbia, Keith was part of a hippie string band called the Migrant Choctaw Underground Cable Confederation, led by Jerome Wheeler and Dan Peek. Keith took summer courses at the Folklore Institute at Indiana University, obtained his PhD, and taught folklore at Northern Arizona University. Through the years, he favorably affected the lives of many students, did contract fieldwork for the Library of Congress (with a research team in Paradise Valley, Nevada), published, and built a reputation as an academic with an understanding of rural life, work, and people. Gillian Bennett, "Keith K. Cunningham (April 1939–April 2013)."

23. See Mike Drayton, "Pearl Sivetts, a Swingin' Missouri Fiddler."

24. Their 1985 recordings were recently issued by the Field Recorders' Collective as *A Visit with Lee Stoneking*.

25. Hobbs, "Women of Old-Time Music"; Bilyeu, "Comparative Analysis of 'Durang's Hornpipe'"; Warner, "Ozark Old-Time Fiddling."

26. Among Henigan's articles and papers are "Art Galbraith, Ozarks Fiddler"; "The McClurg Music Parties: A Living Tradition"; "Play Me Something Quick and Devilish: Bob Holt—Old-Time Square Dance Fiddler"; "Music Parties and Céilís: A Study in Cultural Continuity"; and "Listening to the Tradition," Mel Bay Fiddle Sessions, http://www.fiddlesessions.com, February 2009.

27. For Christeson, among other items, see R. P. Christeson, "Old-Time Fiddling in Missouri: A Workshop"; Howard Wight Marshall, "'King of the Folks': R. P. Christeson and His *Old-Time Repertory*"; Mike Christeson, "Robert Perry Christeson: 'Dean of Missouri Fiddle Music'"; Julia Hager, "Old Time Fiddling: An Interview with R. P. Christeson"; Donald M. Lance, ed., "Reminiscences of R. P. Christeson"; James Olin, Julia Hager, and Barry Bergey, "Old Time Fiddling: An Interview with R. P. Christeson—Part I" and "Old Time Fiddling: An Interview with R. P. Christeson—Part II"; Rebecca B. Schroeder, "The Dean of Missouri Fiddle Music: Remembering R. P. Christeson (1911–1992)"; and Bill Shull, "R. P. Christeson."

28. Howard Wight Marshall, "A Tribute to John Hartford."

29. Hartford, November 15, 2000.

30. Matt Combs, Katie Harford Hogue, and Greg Reisch, comps., *John Hartford's Mammoth Collection of Fiddle Tunes* (the title nods to the 1880s William Bradbury Ryan, *Ryan's Mammoth Collection: 1050 Reels and Jigs, Hornpipes, Clogs, Walk-Arounds, Essences, Strathspeys, Highland Flings and Contra Dances, with Figures, and How to Play Them*); John Hartford, "John Hartford Tune Transcriptions: 'Whoa Mule,' 'Boone County Rag'"; John Hartford, *The Banjo*

according to John Hartford: Licks, Ideas, and Music; Jim Nelson, "John Hartford, Hamilton Ironworks"; Andrew Vaughan, *Pilot of a Steam-Powered Aero-Plane*; and Tony Russell, "John Hartford: Joyously Anarchic Rebel of American Bluegrass Music," *Guardian*, June 11, 2001.

31. An LP was recorded by the group, *The Country's Come to Town* (Madison, WI: Cuca, 1967). Spielman wrote one of the first studies of traditional fiddle music, as well as examinations of fiddle styles, including Texas style; see Spielman, "Traditional North American Fiddling." Tony Russell cites the importance of Spielman's interview with Eck Robertson in *Country Music Originals: The Legends and the Lost*, 3. See also Spielman, "The Texas Fiddling Style." Spielman is among fiddlers who had classical violin lessons during childhood. Spielman moved to Nashville, where, as well as doing session work and producing music, he is a forensic musicologist, helping solve legal problems and issues of intellectual copyright.

32. Moag and I recorded two tracks for the anthology *Grass Cuttin' Time in Missouri*, produced by Jeff Cook in St. Louis for the Missouri Area Friends of Bluegrass (Missouri Area Bluegrass Committee). Martha Louise Hunter, "Volunteer Profile: Rod Moag—Host of 'Country Swing & Rockabilly Jamboree.'"

33. Moag's guitar accompanist was sometimes Kee Groshong, University of Missouri financial officer; Moag, January 28, 2020.

34. Rod Moag's publications include "The History of Early Bluegrass in Texas" and "Bluegrass Music." Recordings include *Rod Moag, the Singin', Pickin' Professor* (Austin: Diploma Disc, 1995); *A-Haa Goes Grass! A Bluegrass Tribute to the Music of Bob Wills* (TexTrax, 2000); and, with Bill C. Malone, *Remember Me: Bill Malone and Rod Moag Play the Music of the Bailes Brothers* (Austin: Hillbilly Dreams 001, 2005). https://www.rodmoag.home.texas.net.

35. Moag, January 12, 2020. Moag resides in Austin in retirement and continues a lifelong hobby of ham radio.

36. https://www.squaredancemissouri.com.

37. "Cotton-Eyed Joe" was recorded by 1920s string bands, revived in the forties by Bob Wills and the Texas Playboys and again thanks to country-tavern line dances in the 1980 Hollywood film (set in Texas) *Urban Cowboy*, directed by James Bridges. For more, see Marshall, pts. 1–2 of "'Where Did You Come from, Where Did You Go?': The Split Personality of 'Cotton-Eyed Joe.'"

38. Claire Buffaut, one of the founders, wrote a history of the group: https://www.mmtd.wordpress.com. Phil and Vivian Williams wrote an overview for musicians at contra dances and square dances, "Playing for Old Time Dances."

39. Unless otherwise indicated, quotes are from an interview with Verdot, February 23, 2019.

40. Goodspeed, *History of Cole, Moniteau, Morgan, Benton, Maries and Osage Counties, Missouri*, 632–43; Marshall, chap. 1, *"Play Me Something Quick and Devilish."* There is an older place named French Village, founded by French Canadian miners in St. Francois County in the old Ste. Genevieve District.

41. Chris Detric, "A Virtuoso of Violins," *Columbia Missourian*, July 5, 2008. Karl Roy was a graduate of the Mittenwald Violin Making School and became director; in his later years he lived parts of the year in New Hampshire, where he taught at the university's violin-making school. Besides many first-class instruments, thousands of copies of Old Master Italian violins were made by various firms in Mittenwald for export to music stores and mail-order firms such as Sears Roebuck and Montgomery Ward, and many of these from the 1880s into the

1920s were bought by Missouri fiddlers and continue in use today. Roy authored *The Violin: Its History and Making*. Nebel specialized in restoration, which he taught Tom Verdot, and was former head of restoration at the Rembert Wurlitzer firm in New York City.

42. https://verdotviolins.com.

43. F. J. Buckley, *The Violinist's Guide*, 23.

44. Krone is from a German American family, is a versatile fiddler, and operates a shop near New Haven; Krone is featured in an exhibition curated by Lisa Higgins et al. at the University of Missouri's Missouri Folk Arts Program, "Work Is Art; Art Is Work: Interviews with Missouri Luthiers" (with video documentary, Columbia, 2007).

45. Scherer, who had moved to Columbia from St. Louis, opened a violin shop in 2013; in 2018, he and his family moved to Louisville, Colorado, where he has a violin shop. For several years, he has been the staff luthier at the summer Rocky Grass festival.

46. Verdot, October 15, 2003, FIDDLE-L Internet discussion group.

47. *A Ragtime Episode* (Fayetteville, AR, SL2004, 2004); Mark Gardner and the Muleskinners, *Songs of the Santa Fe Trail and the Far West* (Native Ground, 1996).

48. Lee Ruth talks about his career and Chez history in Jack Howland, "Discovery Reignites Memories of the Chez at First Presbyterian," *Columbia Missourian*, October 27, 2014. Scott Wilson produced the *Chez Coffeehouse Reunion*, filmed at an October 2006 program featuring former Chez performers (Columbia Access Television), available on YouTube; see also "Return to the Chez: Former Patrons, Performers Reunite at the Relic Café," *Columbia Missourian*, November 6, 2006; and "Musings and Music: Chez Coffeehouse 'Regulars' Reunite to Reflect on Friendship, Folk Tunes," *Columbia Daily Tribune*, November 4, 2006.

49. Spencer Galloway, October 17, 2020.

50. Robert Russell, "Music Promoter Stan Plesser Dies," *Kansas City Star*, September 2, 2011. Plesser's comment that the coffeehouse circuit had passed its peak refers to the beatnik-era originals, not the sixties-era folk clubs that were spreading in the sixties. A favorite Midwest folk duo, Brewer & Shipley was among the groups whose careers were given an early boost at the Vanguard in Kansas City; with the group later finding commercial success in Los Angeles, their song "One Toke over the Line" (from their 1970 LPO, *Tarkio*) was an iconic anthem of the hippie and countercultural era. Other performers at the Vanguard included stand-up comics Pat Paulson and Steve Martin and singer-songwriters John Denver and Glen Frey.

51. I appreciate the assistance of Lyn Wolz with Chez history; a regular and performer for seven years, and informal chef-de-histoire of the lore and history of the coffeehouse, Wolz deposited her archival collection of materials to establish the Chez Coffeehouse Collection (CA 6306) in 2013 in the State Historical Society of Missouri in Columbia.

52. Howland, "Discovery Reignites Memories of the Chez."

53. Galloway, October 17, 2020. The benefit helped the Sound Farm survive some legal difficulties, as Galloway says: "One happy result was that lead singer, Ken Shepard, later owner and proprietor of Crazy Music, never forgot the favor and provided sound, free of charge, for the State Fiddle Contest [administered by the Missouri State Old Time Fiddlers Association; Galloway was an officer] for as long as it remained in Columbia."

54. Dave Para and Cathy Barton Para in Howland, "Discovery Reignites Memories of the Chez." See also Malcolm Smith, "Cathy Barton and Dave Para: Lives on the River."

55. Bill Rogers, May 9, 2019. Crowder came to Columbia from North Carolina between May 1967 and August 1970 to pursue a PhD in sociology. In North Carolina, Crowder had

briefly played guitar as an original member of the Fuzzy Mountain String Band and was part of the Chapel Hill–area string-band revival.

56. "Roots of the Red Clay Ramblers," https://www.earlyblurs.com. A 1973 photo of Dave Crowder with his fellow Fuzzies Vickie Owen, Tom Carter, Sharon Poss, Bill Hicks, and Malcolm Owen, in Tom Carter, "Looking for Henry Reed: Confessions of a Revivalist," 88.

57. Michael Sheward, "Fiddlin' Fiddlers Attract Young and Old Timers," *Columbia Missourian*, April 23, 1972.

58. Galloway, December 17, 2018.

59. Quotes, unless otherwise indicated, are from recorded interviews with Spencer Galloway, December 14, 2017, and December 1, 2018.

60. Ray M. Lawless, *Folksingers and Folksongs in America*; review by Guthrie T. Meade in *Midwest Folklore*; the Ray M. Lawless Collection is in the Archive of Folk Culture, Library of Congress.

61. Galloway, October 11, 2020. In 1969, the Selective Service System began the first of two lotteries, by which eligible young men born between January 1, 1944, and December 31, 1950, were called to military duty (in most cases, this meant orders for Vietnam) according to a number randomly assigned to their birthday. If a low number, one was sure to be headed for boot camp; if a high number, one could breathe easier.

62. Galloway's "Fennario" (a track on Bob Dylan's first LP in 1962 and a 1963 Joan Baez recording) appears on the 1969 *Joint Effort: Recorded Live at the Chez* compilation LP of Chez performers (Century Records 33642); the song is an eighteenth-century Scottish ballad, "The Bonnie Lass O'Fyvie," also known as "Peggy-O" and other titles; see Olive Dame Campbell and Cecil J. Sharp, *English Folk Songs from the Southern Appalachians*. Galloway's version of "Fennario" came from Simon & Garfunkel, who called it "Peggy-O" on their 1964 LP *Wednesday Morning, 3 AM* (Galloway, October 11, 2020).

63. Forrest Rose, "Virtuosos of the Old-Time Sound," *Columbia Daily Tribune*, August 25, 1983.

64. For an overview, see Peter Lippincott and Marget Lippincott, *Traditional Dance in Missouri*.

65. Hockemeyer is featured in chapters 5 and 6 and on the CD for *"Play Me Something Quick and Devilish."* Galloway kept a valuable journal of his experiences as Hockemeyer's pupil.

66. Jake was accompanied by guitarist Russ Orchard, a member of the Rooster Creek Boys who performed on KFAL radio in Fulton. Two stunning tracks from the fish-fry tape are on the companion CD with Howard Wight Marshall et al., *"Now That's a Good Tune": Masters of Traditional Missouri Fiddling*, "Fisher's Hornpipe" and "Marmaduke's Hornpipe." Three tunes by Hockemeyer are on Missouri Friends of the Folk Arts, *I'm Old but I'm Awfully Tough*, "Dance around Molly," "Marmaduke's Hornpipe," and "Coming Down from Denver" (Galloway notes that Hockemeyer was not playing very well the day he was recorded for that project).

67. A different anecdote about this event is in Galloway's notebook from a 1986 lesson with Jake. Frances remarks, "That ain't Jake, he ain't never been that good."

68. Galloway, January 9, 1986.

69. Howard Wight Marshall, "The Swedish Nightingale, 'Jenny Lind Polka,' and American Fiddle Music"; Marshall, chap. 5 of *"Play Me Something Quick and Devilish."*

70. In Galloway's January 9, 1986, TAAP session, Jake explained his view on vibrato: "Good to listen at, but it ain't no good to dance to." Galloway journal.

71. Spencer Galloway, "Missouri Fiddling Styles"; Galloway, "Cleo Persinger, 1909–1971"; "Jake Hockemeyer," *Old-Time Herald*, 16; "Cleo Persinger"; McMillen, "Sound," in *Our Missouri* (Columbia: Missouri Interpretive Materials, 1989).

72. Galloway, December 14, 2017.

73. Bill Rogers, November 12, 2019.

74. Rogers, May 7, 2019, November 12, 2019.

75. Rogers, May 9, 2019. As to his banjo style, he writes: "Well, it's not really Appalachian, though that's the music I tend to play. I learned the way a budding urban player did in the early '60s—the Pete Seeger book and lots of listening to records, especially the New Lost City Ramblers. And of course, later on, Koken. I use my thumb on the inside strings more than most, and don't rely on hammers and pull-offs as much as many players. I learned tunes from fiddle recordings rather than banjo, and that certainly influenced my style. I think it has developed since the early '70s when I came back to Columbia, but not evolved. I never had Jim Ruth's ear, and had to spend a lot of time grinding to learn new tunes. As to my influence, I don't know—other than that Joe Newberry tells me he learned a lot about clawhammer from watching and listening to my playing."

76. Rogers, February 5, 2008, https://www.fiddlehangout.com. "If you listen to his clawhammer, you'll hear at least three distinct styles: his solo approach; with just a fiddle; and with a string band. Each is different; each is superb. Walt is the best string band dance-tune player I've ever heard. It's in his impeccable sense of timing. Everything is syncopated in a way you just don't hear from other players. He is the chordmeister supreme—from his days playing plectrum stuff (on his 5-string) in a Dixieland band."

77. Kyle Creed and Tommy Jarrell were also influential in terms of young Missouri clawhammer aspirants.

78. Walt Koken, May 8, 2012. In the *Old-Time Herald* in 1992, at the University of Missouri, "they awarded Walt a Rhodes Scholarship and 'told me to hit the road,' he said." The magazine did not catch Walt's pun on "Rhodes Scholarship." He was failing courses and dropped out; he mistakenly assumed the magazine would get the joke—"roads scholarship"—not Rhodes Scholarship. (One must be a graduating senior in college with a grade-point average around 3.9 to be considered for a Rhodes and must be recommended by one's college or university.) Alice Gerrard, "Colby Street to New York & Points South: The Highwoods Stringband," 27.

79. See Koken, "Tales from the 'Woods, Part 7: Ithaca," 33; Koken recounts his adventures in a series of articles in *Old-Time Herald* titled "Tales from the 'Woods." The breakthrough Smithsonian festival appearance is recounted, in the context of describing the event, in Koken, "Tales from the 'Woods, Part 4: The Smoke-In." Koken won first place in the Smithsonian's fiddle contest in 1972. See "He Was Just Fiddling," *Bloomington (IN) Courier-Tribune*, June 5, 1972.

80. https://www.mudthumper.com. Koken lives in upstate New York, taking part in sessions, teaching workshops, and performing and recording with Clare Milliner in the Orpheus Supertones (their two banjos are an Orpheum and a Supertone). "We're waiting to catch the wave of the REAL old time music revival, and, as we slowly age in our quest, we're enjoying playing without the headaches of either being constantly on the road or being under the

thumb of an agent or major record label. Old time music is for dancing and its songs are for lifting us above our burdens. Our music gives relief from the everyday burdens of modern life, and an insight into a simpler time, with a glimmer of hope for us all."

81. Ken Mietus, October 10, 2020.

82. The Hoosier Hot Shots was a popular 1930s string band whose 78-rpm records were appreciated in the 1960s and 1970s; the Indiana band favored early jazz and swing music and a good measure of comedy. The group appeared in western movies, and their performing career lasted into the 1970s.

83. Mietus, October 11, 2020. Mietus's musical skills and tastes are eclectic. "Over the years, I have roamed far afield from my roots in folk and old timey music. I started messing around with electric blues guitar in the mid-70's and up until about six years ago performed regularly in a couple of local cover bands. My musical interests are eclectic but I always come back to the old tunes when I need to reconfigure my creative juices."

84. "Down at a festival in Eminence or Salem or somewhere, one time a kid came along and thought he was Doug Dillard" (Galloway, December 14, 2017). See Douglas Dillard et al., *The Bluegrass Banjo Style of Douglas Flint Dillard.*

85. Galloway, October 19, 2020. Kevin Sanders plays clawhammer banjo with the Last Chance Boys in their rendition of "Sandy River Belle" (Craig Keene, violin; Mike Schway, mandolin; and Buddy Ratner, guitar) on *Northwest Regional Folklife Festival, Volume II* (Voyager VRLP 102, 1978). Sanders died in 2004.

86. Galloway, October 25, 2020.

87. Jim Ruth, March 8, 2020.

88. Bill Monroe and the Bluegrass Boys, *Bluegrass Instrumentals* (Decca DL74601, 1965), features Keith on two tracks, "Sailor's Hornpipe" (credited as William Bradford Keith) and "Santa Claus" (credited as Brad Keith). There could be only one Bill in Monroe's band, so Bill called him "Brad."

89. Ruth, March 8, 2020. "Other Side of Baker" is a Sam Bush composition from a 1969 bluegrass instrumental LP by *Poor Richard's Almanac* featuring Bush (violin, mandolin), Alan Munde (banjo), and Wayne Stewart (guitar).

90. Ruth, March 8, 2020. Jim Ruth plays clawhammer banjo on John White's CD *Nine Miles of Dry and Dusty.*

91. Ruth, May 10, 2019.

92. Ruth, March 6, 2019.

93. Ruth, March 29, 2020.

94. Rose, "Virtuosos of the Old-Time Sound." Rose, a newspaper columnist, was also a popular and skilled bass player.

95. Ruth, October 21, 2018.

96. Galloway, October 25, 2020.

97. Jim Ruth, October 11, 2020.

98. Galloway, December 14, 2017.

99. Galloway, October 19, 2020. The fiddle tune "Sally Ann" is an emblem of the southern Appalachian fiddle and clawhammer-banjo repertoire, and versions stemming from Surry County, North Carolina, and players like Tommy Jarrell are popular worldwide; it is a standard of the Galax fiddle contest. "Sail Away Ladies" and "Great Big Taters in the Sandy Land" are related tunes, the former title widely known in Missouri and among bluegrass musicians,

the latter title more widely known in Texas and among contest fiddlers west of the Mississippi. "'Sally Ann' has jokingly been called the Surry County, North Carolina, 'national anthem'" (Andrew Kuntz, *The Fiddler's Companion: A Descriptive Index of North American and British Isles Music for the Folk Violin).*

100. In 1975, the top bands, first through eighth places, were the Shady Mountain Ramblers (Galax); Smokey Valley Boys (Mount Airy, North Carolina); Hot Mud Family (Spring Valley, Ohio); New River Ramblers (Independence, Virginia); Pine Ridge Boys (Mount Airy); Spare Change Boys (Northbridge, Massachusetts); Pine River Boys & Maybelle (Hillsville, Virginia); and the Space City String Band (Huntsville, Alabama).

101. Jim Ruth, Facebook, May 8, 2019.

102. In North Carolina, Rob played violin in the Three Stripped Gears (Mark Abbott, Todd Woerner), and the band issued an LP, *Three Stripped Gears* (Flying Cloud FCOT-0003, 1986); the group is on the compilation LP *Memphis Blues (1927–1939), Volume 2* (Roots Saydisc RL-329, 1970). A 2011 video of Golan fiddling "Dance around Molly" (learned in Missouri) and "Tulsa Waltz" with Mark Abbott (guitar) is available on YouTube.

103. Galloway, October 25, 2020.

104. Galloway, October 25, 2020.

105. Jim Nelson, May 15, 2020.

106. A tape of the Original Mound City String Band, by Paul Stamler, of a 1978 concert at Webster College in St. Louis, intended to become an LP record, is available on CD (Vigortone Records VT-2008, 2020).

107. Jim Olin was a key force in the field recordings and production of the Missouri Friends of the Folk Arts anthology *I'm Old but I'm Awfully Tough*. Bob Abrams also played bluegrass banjo and competed in the banjo contest at Bill Monroe's Bean Blossom festival in 1971.

108. "Sam Long recorded 'Echoes of the Ozarks' in the key of G, instead of B-flat as Jake Hockemeyer and Pete McMahan played it" (Galloway, October 6, 2020). "Corn Dodger Special" is from a 1930s 78-rpm record by the Arkansas Ozarks band George Edgin's Corn Dodgers, titled "Corn Dodger No. 1 Special" (a version of "Cacklin' Hen"). "Corn Dodger No. 1 Special" (Columbia 15754D) was reissued on the anthology *Echoes of the Ozarks* (vol. 3, County Records 503, 1970). Abrams also performed and recorded with Steve Mote: *Bob Abrams & Steve Mote* (St. Louis, no label, 1975), a vinyl album that included "Marmaduke's Hornpipe" and "Yellow Gals."

109. Missouri Corn Dodgers concert at the Indiana Fiddler's Gathering in Battle Ground, 1978; tracks from that concert and the 1975 LP are on the reissue CD called *Old Time String Band Music by the Missouri Corn Dodgers*; a sample of the Corn Dodgers at the Clarksville, Tennessee, fiddlers' convention is on *Tennessee Folk Arts: The Mid-Tennessee Old-Time Fiddler's Championship*. The Missouri Corn Dodgers and other St. Louis–area bands are heard on several compilation CDs of performers at the Indiana Fiddler's Gathering. The County LP mentioned is *Hell Broke Loose in Georgia: Georgia Fiddle Bands, 1927–1934* (1968).

110. The title "Missouri Quickstep" appears in Vance Randolph's 1954 article "The Names of Ozark Fiddle Tunes," but I have not heard an old-time fiddler in Missouri use that title; "Rachel" is the dominant title and has been since Tommy Jackson's commercial 1960 album *Square Dance Festival, Volume 2* (Dot DLP-3331). Among other alternate titles are "Texas Quickstep" as played by bluegrass fiddler Kenny Baker, whose version was popular in Missouri; early recordings as "Texas Quickstep" include Al Clauser and His Oklahoma Outlaws,

reissued on *Hot Western Swing 1937–48* (Krazy Kat KKCD 32, 2004), and the Red-Headed Fiddlers (Red Steely, violin), reissued on *Texas Farewell: Texas Fiddlers, 1922–1930* (County 517, 1969).

111. https://www.chrisbrashear.com; Chris's *Wanderlust* (Copper Creek, 2000). Perfect Strangers included Brashear and bluegrass mainstays Bob Black, Jody Stecher, Peter McLaughlin, and Columbia's Forrest Rose.

112. Paul Fotsch, April 15, 2019.

113. Win Grace, July 14, August 17, 2109.

114. https://www.gracefamilymusic.com. Win Grace and Paul Fotsch divorced in 2009 and continue their careers as solo acts.

115. Win Grace, August 17, 2019.

116. Henigan, "Listening to the Tradition."

3. Pete & Taylor, Two among the Masters

1. McBaine enjoyed being called "Taylor Mac," in part because it emphasized the preferred pronunciation of his name and perhaps because the nickname had a kind of saucy entertainer's vibe.

2. Native American ancestry is not uncommon among Missouri fiddlers, by virtue of the 1830s Trail of Tears that forced families of the Five Civilized Tribes (Cherokee, Chickasaw, Choctaw, Creek, and Seminole) from the southeastern United States across Missouri to Oklahoma's "Indian Territory" government allotments. See Marshall, chap. 8 of *"Play Me Something Quick and Devilish."*

3. Sarah J. Bennett, "The Devil's Instrument," research paper, Art History and Archaeology 142, University of Missouri–Columbia, April 1992. Christian College was renamed Columbia College. Richard McBaine had won the violin, a shop instrument of Bohemian or Bavarian origin, as first prize in a fiddle contest at Christian College in Columbia.

4. This is a tune with many alternate titles, such as "Waiting for the Federals," "Seneca Square Dance," and "Shelby's Mule," which referred to the riding mule ridden by Waverly, Missouri, Confederate general J. O. Shelby (born in Kentucky), with whom many Missourians served during the Civil War. Nile Wilson's title was "Raccoon Tail Has Rings All Around." The title McBaine recalled from childhood is "Hog's Head."

5. Bobby Joe Caldwell, December 12, 2010.

6. Beaudoin, "Fiddler Hums with Age."

7. Thad Hurt (1899–1979) was McBaine's favorite tenor banjoist; a tape of a 1975 jam session including McBaine and Hurt echoes the style of tenor banjo chunk-chunk chording that works well with fiddling (see "Fiddlin' 75," https://www.missourifiddling.bandcamp.com).

8. Taylor McBaine interview with Trudy Balch, November 1985, in Margot Roberson and Howard Marshall, *The Masters: Traditional Arts Apprenticeship Program*, 21. Typical sets were "Butterfly Whirl," "Eight Day Clock," "Texas Star," "Two Gents across the Hall," and "Birdie in the Cage," all still popular a century later.

9. Central and north Missouri were famous for bituminous coal. Farmers often found that their land had coal, and, until the 1950s, many people dug their own sacks of coal out of the seams revealed in banks along roads. Entrepreneurial farmers started their own mines and hired their neighbors' sons as well as numerous European immigrant workers (especially Welsh and Italian). Deep mines eventually closed, with strip mining taking over the

landscape, until strip mining shut down in the 1990s due to the importation of cheaper coal from Wyoming.

10. Pam Lohneiss, "Playing by Heart," *Columbia Missourian*, December 20, 1987. McBaine had the violin Uncle Richard had given him as a child, but it and was in disrepair and unplayable.

11. "Columbian Fiddles Best at Harrisburg Chili Supper," *Columbia Missourian*, January 23, 1967. The chili supper was sponsored by the Harrisburg High School junior class as a fund-raising event. Other winners were second place, Dale Pauley (Columbia); third place, Ernest Brandenberger (Argyle, Iowa); fourth, Lyman Enloe; and fifth place, Jake Hockemeyer. The judges were Cleo Persinger, Wilford Johnson, and Alvin Carruthers.

12. Susan Newstead, "Missouri Legacy."

13. April 18, 1973, fiddle session in Wayne Crane's garage, Columbia (recorded by Dave Crowder; copy courtesy of Jim Ruth). McBaine made similar comments about contests when I recorded him with guitarist Walter Calvin for the Smithsonian Institution in November 1975. In my opinion, the propensity for speedier breakdowns in contests was encouraged by the popularity of ultra-fast bluegrass instrumental music growing popular in the 1950s, as well as the ultra-fast breakdowns on LPs by Nashville's Tommy Jackson (exceptionally popular among old-time fiddlers).

14. McBaine, March 7, 1990.

15. The Down Home Boys, Taylor McBaine with Harold Crane, advertised their program of "homespun music" to be played at the Tiger Kensington retirement center (*Columbia Daily Tribune*, April 14, 1991).

16. In 1975, Taylor was on a short list of Missouri old-time fiddlers I recorded for the Smithsonian Institution's Festival of American Folklife, along with Art Galbraith, Pete McMahan, Glenn Rickman, Cyril Stinnett, Lee Stoneking, and Lonnie Robertson (McMahan and Stinnett were unavailable during this trip to Missouri); at the time, I was director of research at Conner Prairie Pioneer Settlement, an outdoor living history museum in Indiana.

17. *Ballad of the Boonslick* (Boonville, 1982), reissued on CD in 2003, https://www.bartonandpara.com. Cathy spoke of her debt to McBaine and her introduction to Little Dixie–style fiddling in M. Smith, "Cathy Barton and Dave Para." As a banjo accompanist for McBaine, Cathy acquired a loud banjo with a resonator (a Baldwin-Ode), so she could be heard when playing with "loud, driving styles of dance fiddlers like McBaine and McMahan" (34). Also for McBaine, see Cathy Barton, "Taylor McBaine," 23; Roberson and Marshall, *Masters*, 20–21; and Howard Wight Marshall, "In Memory: Taylor Franklin McBaine (1910–1994)."

18. Among his favorite trips was a festival in Libertyville, Illinois, where he performed with Dave and Cathy, "The Masters of Heartland Traditions," hosted by the David Adler Cultural Center.

19. Lois Gandt, *Taylor McBaine, Country Missouri Fiddling; Ballads, Bones and Fiddle Tunes* (video, Columbia: University of Missouri Academic Support Center, 1984); *Taylor McBaine, Contest Fiddler* (University of Missouri Extension Division, Missouri Origins Project, 1981).

20. Missouri State Old Time Fiddlers Association, 2019, digital album, https://www.missourifiddling.com.

21. Cooked squirrel brains in gravy is a dish in some parts of the South and southern Midwest. Among recordings of Chris Germain's composition, which has become traditional

through almost fifty years of oral transmission, is by Bob Bovee and Gail Heil (who knew McBaine) on *For Old Time's Sake* (Jawbone 006). See Kuntz, *Fiddler's Companion*; and Barton, "Taylor McBaine." Germain fiddles his tune in a YouTube video.

22. McBaine, August 8, 1993.

23. Shauna Coon, interview with Taylor McBaine, News 105 (University of Missouri School of Journalism), July 1985 (courtesy of Frank McBaine).

24. Newstead, "Missouri Legacy." "Drive" is the most common term in Missouri; other terms for McBaine and Pete McMahan's drive include "pulse."

25. McBaine, December 12, 1989.

26. McBaine, October 1, 1989.

27. Some fiddlers suggest an orange instead of a tennis ball; others such as Billy Lee suggested imagining you have a glass of water balanced on your right shoulder: "Don't spill the water!" (July 1967).

28. The seventh of Dvořák's 1894 "Humoresques" cycle of piano pieces, often played by violinists as well as fiddlers; Indiana old-time fiddler John D. Summers, in McBaine's generation, fiddled it, as did, I suspect, many others. In the mid-1920s, early talking pictures included a short film of violinist Mischa Elman playing the tune, a movie short that McBaine may have seen in a Columbia theater.

29. Barton and Para, "Taylor McBaine," 23.

30. McBaine's "Marmaduke's Hornpipe" is transcribed in David Brinkman, "'Marmaduke's Hornpipe': A Study of Four Versions."

31. Other titles in McBaine's active repertoire included "Flop-Eared Mule" (in Boone County called "Peach Tree Limb"), "Rachel," "Grey Eagle," "Whisky before Breakfast," "Woodchopper's Reel" (hornpipe), "Rose of Sharon," "Forty Years Ago Waltz," "Devil's Dream," "Run Johnny Run," "I Don't Love Nobody," "Durang's Hornpipe," "Angus Campbell," "Bill Cheatem," "Clark's Waltz," "Lorraine Schottische," "Gold Rush," "Forked Deer," "One Rose," "On the Right Cheek," "Eighth of January," "Sally Goodin," "Mocking Bird Hill," "Wake Up Susie," "Wednesday Night Waltz," "Coming Down from Denver," "Paddy on the Turnpike," "Leesil" (a.k.a. "Lead Out," "Ten Nights in a Bar Room," and others), "Bonaparte Crossing the Rhine," "Sweet Georgia Brown," "Black Velvet Waltz," "Spotted Pony," "Dill Pickles," "Sweet Bunch of Daisies," "Old Hen She Cackled," "Too Young to Marry" (a.k.a. "Lead Out," and others), "Pacific Slope," "Haste to the Wedding," "Irish Washerwoman," "Festival Waltz," "Tom and Jerry," "Rochester Schottische," "Five Foot Two," "Four Leaf Clover," "Darktown Strutter's Ball," "Stone's Rag," "Rickett's Hornpipe," "Arkansas Traveler," "Old Grey Bonnet," "Tennessee Wagner," "Over the Waves," "College Hornpipe," "Billy in the Low Ground," "Goodnight Waltz," "Leather Britches," "Tennessee Waltz," "Peekaboo Waltz," "Cowboy Waltz," "Twinkle Little Star," "Fiddler's Waltz," "Bonaparte's Retreat," "Jenny Lind Polka," "Western Waltz," "Leather Britches," "Kansas City Rag," "Black Velvet Waltz," "South," "The Last Waltz," "Getting Upstairs the Monkey," "Old Rugged Cross," "Waltz of Shannon," "Fiddler's Hornpipe," "The Waltz You Saved for Me," "Stafford Waltz," "Up a Lazy River," "Old Man and Old Woman," "College Hornpipe," "Fisher's Hornpipe," "High Level Hornpipe," "Constitution Hornpipe," "It's a Long Way to Tipperary," and local tunes "Charlie Cook's G Waltz," "Taters" (George Morris's theme tune on his KFRU radio show), "Cotton Blossom," "Parish Hornpipe" (a specialty of Cleo Persinger's), "Garfield's Hornpipe" ("Blue Water Hornpipe"), and "Blackfoot Rag."

32. Drye, February 3, 2021.

33. Marc was also an informal pupil of Pete McMahan's and visited extensively with Art Galbraith, Howe Teague, Carol Hascall, and other fiddlers. Drye's journal, recordings, and photographs constitute a valuable picture of McBaine's music, teaching, and philosophy of life.

34. "Taylor Visits the Hallsville Church" (manuscript), Drye, March 16, 2001.

35. Griffin, "Pete McMahan," 23. I appreciate the assistance of John Griffin, Sarah McMahan, and her daughters. See also Griffin, "Pete McMahan"; "Pete McMahan" in Marshall et al., *"Now That's a Good Tune,"* 40–41; album notes to *50 Old-Time Fiddle Gems*; Howard Wight Marshall, "Pete McMahan Leaves the Stage"; Jody Stecher, "Pete McMahan and Andy de Jarlis Play 'Whisky before Breakfast"; writings of Charlie Walden; and Amy Wastalu, "Don't Fiddle with Tradition," *Columbia Missourian*, November 28, 1990.

36. Galloway, December 14, 2017.

37. *50 Old-Time Fiddle Gems*, reissue of McMahan's *Missouri Fiddlin'* LPs; a fifth album was recorded, but the master tape was lost. Pete was born Preston Belle McMahan but disliked the names Preston and Belle; he insisted on being called "Pete," and when he was old enough to obtain a driver's license, he began signing his first name as Pete and his middle name as Bell.

38. Phil Nussbaum, March 2000.

39. McMahan, May 7, 1992. It is routine for Scotch-Irish people to say they are "Irish," an easy way to explain their heritage to others. McMahan, January 12, 1976; unless otherwise indicated, quotes are from correspondence, interviews, publications, and programs dated July 18, 1975; January 12, 1976; December 17, 1986; February 1989; May 7, May 11, October 12, 1992 (KOPN 89.5 FM radio); March 8, 1993 (KOPN 89.5 FM radio); December 21, 1995; September 24, 1996; and September 17, 18, 19, 1997.

40. For this history, see Marshall, chaps. 3 and 4 in *"Play Me Something Quick and Devilish."*

41. From decades of French ownership of Upper Louisiana, the word "prairie" became dominant from Illinois and Missouri west, generally replacing, at least in earliest times, the term back east of "meadow" or "grassland." There are exceptions, but old-stock Americans of Irish and North British provenance, such as the McMahans, traditionally and before English control, were cattle people, and this inclination carried in pioneer Missouri. In contrast, many of the German-speaking immigrants in pioneer Missouri traditionally were row-crop and cereal farmers who recognized the benefits of the more productive prairie lands.

42. McMahan learned Emmett Heath's "Kentucky Blues" from Heath when Heath fiddled over KFRU radio in the mid-1950s (see Marshall, *Fiddler's Dream*); the tune was also played by Moberly fiddler Frank Reed (later of Overland) on his 1970s private label LP *Ole Tyme Fiddlin'*.

43. "Crystal Stream Waltz" (in F) is a Little Dixie tune favored by Nolan Boone and Jake Hockemeyer as well as Virgil Smith of Montgomery City, who had it from Vee Latty of Millersburg (Latty played it at Virgil's wedding in 1933); Earl Willis (1901–95) of Mineola (Montgomery County) learned it from Vee Latty and took the tune to the Pacific Northwest in the 1930s; and Stuart Williams includes a transcription of it in *Washington State Old Time Fiddlers' Association Newsletter*, February 2013. See also R. P. Christeson, *Old-Time Fiddler's Repertory*, 2:161; Stacy Phillips, *The Phillips Collection of Traditional American Fiddle Tunes*, 1995, 249; and Drew Beisswenger and Gordon McCann, *Ozarks Fiddle Music: 308 Tunes Featuring 30 Legendary Fiddlers with Selections from 50 Other Great Ozarks Fiddlers*, 74. "Stars and Stripes Waltz" (in C) was composed by Vee Latty; McMahan learned it from Daniel Boone Jones

(Callaway County) about 1930; in Christeson, *Old-Time Fiddler's Repertory* (1973), 193; recorded examples include McMahan, *Ozark Mountain Waltz*; and Leroy Canaday, *Old Dan Tucker Was a Fine Old Man.*

44. I thank Linda Danielson and Lew Holt for their generosity in making Danielson's documentary available; see also Oregon Old Time Fiddlers, https://www.ootfa.org. Rea Windsor of Columbia, who grew up in the Mineola area of western Montgomery County, recalled playing accordion accompaniment for Herman Boone in the 1930s in Williamsburg (Windsor, February 18, 2009). Danielson included Earl Willis in her Oregon Old Time Fiddle Project in 1976, and Boone's skill with waltzes is discussed in her interview with Willis (Marshall, chap. 2 of *"Play Me Something Quick and Devilish"*).

45. McMahan, March 8, 1993; December 17, 1986; May 7, October 12, 1992.

46. Harvie Atterberry, February 14, 2019.

47. Edwards Brothers, *An Illustrated Historical Atlas of Callaway County, Missouri, 1876*, 8; *Standard Atlas of Callaway County*, 8 (Township 46N, Range 7W, Section 24, Auxvasse Township); *Plat Book of Callaway County*, 5. Little Tavern Creek continues northeast into Montgomery County near McMahan family farms. Clark's family traces to Michael Mitchell Atterberry, who came to Howard County, Missouri, from Hart County, Kentucky, in 1819 at the age of eight with nine or ten older brothers (some stopped in Illinois, while some later went on to Oklahoma).

48. Harvie Atterberry, February 14, 2019. I appreciate Atterberry's help with family history details and other matters; he is a great-nephew of the legendary fiddler Clark Atterberry and reports that the Atterberrys are "Scot-Irish German."

49. Golda married Theodore (Pete) Carver and lived in Fulton; their son Eddie died in a car wreck as a young man (Harvie Atterberry, February 14, 2019).

50. Harvie Atterberry, July 9, 2005.

51. McMahan et al., *"Now That's a Good Tune,"* 40).

52. "Rye Whisky" is a variant of the seventeenth-century Irish melody "Bacah Buidhe" (on the 2000 Voyager CD *Fiddle Tunes of the Lewis and Clark Era*). I learned the song as a child in the 1940s from a Tex Ritter 78-rpm record. The provenance and authorship of "Ta-ra-ra Boom De-ay!" is unsettled, but the popular melody (with various sets of lyrics) may have first appeared in 1891 in a Boston vaudeville revue called *Tuxedo* by Henry Sayers (Eugene Tomkins and Quincy Kilby, *The History of the Boston Theatre, 1854–1901* [New York: Houghton Mifflin, 1908], 387; "Live Musical Topics," *New York Times*, April 3, 1892, 1). Sheet music for piano sold well and may have been in Pete McMahan's mother's music collection; the song and tune had gone into oral tradition by the 1920s.

53. A transcription of McMahan's "Black Sally Goodin" is in Bill Shull's *Cross-Tuning Your Fiddle: History, Techniques & Transcriptions* (45); Atterberry learned the tune from Katon, and McMahan learned it from Atterberry.

54. Booze and performing music really do not mix well. Irish fiddler, scholar, and writer Caoimhin MacAoidh offers a helpful corrective to timeworn statements from and about fiddlers and other musicians—that they require a few rounds of drinks to loosen up and play well. In a trenchant article, MacAoidh writes, "The forms of music we play are often very strongly associated with drink," and to that he says, "Absolute rubbish!" MacAoidh, "When Folklore Misses the Mark," 46. It is good to report that, at least among musicians of my acquaintance, misuse of alcohol is today the exception rather than commonplace.

55. Sarah McMahan, January 20, 2010.

56. Versions of "Clark's Waltz" were played by Jim Gilmore, Vesta Johnson, Fred Stoneking (obtained from McMahan), and many other Missourians. Fred's father, Lee Roy Stoneking, learned "Clark's Waltz" from McMahan and included it on his 1976 LP, *Rainbow of Fiddle Tunes*; H. K. Silvey of Theodosia (in south Missouri near the Arkansas border) plays the tune on *Traditional Fiddle Music of the Ozarks, Volume Three*, where it is credited to a Lonnie Robertson record and known as "Red Hawk Waltz" (Beisswenger and McCann, *Ozarks Fiddle Music*, 128). Silvey, while born and reared in the Missouri Ozarks near the Arkansas line, is among fiddlers whose style sounds more like central Missouri playing. Gordon McCann's Ozark archives include versions under the "Red Hawk Waltz" title by Red Perriman and Art Galbraith; other recordings include Vesta Johnson's cassette *Indian Creek* and Charlie Walden's *Missouri Fiddle Tunes*, vol. 1.

57. Harvie Atterberry, February 14, 2019. There were white families and black families in Callaway County named Crews and several more families named Kruse (apparently German Americans) as well. On several occasions, fiddler Billy Lee spoke of the title as "Crews Waltz" (spelling not specified), played at dances in the Montgomery County–Warren County area.

58. McMahan, September 18, 1996.

59. Westwood Tharp (Ed Tharp's nephew, Fulton), April 2, 2000; these fiddlers also played "Lightning Hornpipe." Ed Tharp was a coal miner of Cherokee ancestry from Callaway County who had moved to Columbia, recorded by John Hartford in the late 1950s and early 1960s; see Marshall, chap. 8 of *"Play Me Something Quick and Devilish."*

60. McMahan, December 17, 1986.

61. "Marchéta" (pronounced mar-KEE-ta), popularized by George Morris, is little known today but was brought back by Bobby Joe Caldwell and Dale Pauley in the 1990s; Bobby Joe learned it from Hillis Crowell, who had learned it from Morris. "Marchéta" is a 1913 "Love Song of Old Mexico," written by Victor Schertzinger; when played in waltz time, it becomes a beautiful theme. The melody was picked by John Ford for the emotive soundtrack for his 1945 wartime film *They Were Expendable*. The melody is first heard in the robust key of D, when Lieutenant (J. G.) "Rusty" Ryan (John Wayne) attends a hospital dance on Corregidor Island in the Philippines and falls in love with a nurse there (Donna Reed). Much later in the film, as Bataan falls and Corregidor (where his lover is stationed) is being bombed and starved into submission, a touching reprise of the song (now in the moodier key of F) is heard on a radio as Wayne and his mates are getting drunk in a bar, awaiting the inevitable defeat and surrender to the Japanese forces. The tune became a favorite of John Wayne and John Ford; a character actor who played accordion named Danny Borzage, a member of Ford's stock company, was retained on film sets to play mood music to help the cast set the right mood for a scene; "Marchéta" became John Wayne's theme. See YouTube.

62. McMahan's "Morris Hornpipe," from George Morris in the 1950s, is on Pete's 1973 LP and reissued on *50 Old-Time Fiddle Gems*; a similar melody was played by Gene Goforth as "Reveler's Reel" on his 1974 *Strike Up the Bow* LP. McMahan and Goforth were compatriots in the 1960s but parted ways in the 1970s, as Goforth focused on bluegrass and McMahan on contests.

63. The short-lived square-dance craze in this period began in California in opulent ballrooms among movie stars and the wealthy and inspired imitation in some Missouri places. Some of the most popular fiddlers at the "Hollywood" square dances in Los Angeles were people who had migrated from Missouri to find work in the 1930s and 1940s, such as fiddler Earl Willis of Montgomery County; see Marshall, chap. 4 of *Fiddler's Dream*.

64. For the 1917 governor's ball quote, see *St. Louis Post-Dispatch*, January 9, 1917, 1. Some on the planning committee wanted the toddle to be danced, but it was considered passé. Examples of published one-steps include "Swiss Cheese Rag" by A. E. Bohrer (New York, 1913), "Pork and Beans One-Step, Two-Step, Trot" by C. Luckyth Roberts (New York: Jos. W. Stern, 1913), "More Mustard One-Step" by Louis Mentel (Cincinnati, 1914), and L. Wolfe Gilbert and Anatol Friedland's "My Little Dream Girl" (New York: Jos. W. Stern, 1918). The dance and its many varieties were taught in manuals in classes of the day, such as Vivian Dewey, *Tips to Dancers: Good Manners for Ballroom and Dance Hall*; Caroline Walker, *The Modern Dances, How to Dance Them*; and Albert W. Newman, *Dances of To-day*. The one-step is mentioned in David Ewan, *All the Years of American Popular Music*, 313, and other sources on dance history.

65. For a transcription of McMahan's "Ford One Step" by Julie Youmans, see Marshall et al., *"Now That's a Good Tune."* Dance teacher Vivian Dewey in 1918 said: "After a stormy and chaotic period of dance revolution, and constant changing, dancing has one more settled. The one-step and fox-trot have become standardized, and the steps are now sane and practical" (*Tips to Dancers*, 10).

66. "I've Got a Pocketful of Dreams" was sung by Louis Armstrong in the 1937 Bing Crosby movie for Paramount *Sing You Sinners*, and in 1938 Crosby released his own version on a 78-rpm record (Decca 1933, comp. Johnny Burke and James V. Monaco).

67. This material is based on interviews and visits with Hillis Crowell in June and October 2017 and October and November 2019.

68. See Marshall, chap. 8 of *Fiddler's Dream*.

69. Retooling a violin for a left-handed player was explained by luthier Allen Wyatt of Independence: "To truly convert a right-handed fiddle to a left-handed fiddle, the bass bar needs to be moved to other side, peg holes need to be bushed and re-drilled so that the G peg is on the right side of the peg box, etc. Then, the set-up is reversed (new bridge cut for a lefty, sound post moved, etc.). There are subtle things that probably are not changed because they are in the very structure of a violin—like the neck and fingerboard tilt toward the E string side. It would make a passable violin for a lefty if converted. However, the best way is to make a violin left-handed from the start" (Wyatt, October 21, 2019).

70. The raucous nightclub and dance-hall scene, and the likelihood of booze-inspired troubles there, is a steady theme in discussions with older musicians about the post–World War II years (and the previous two decades) and into the 1960s.

71. Crowell, October 15, 2017.

72. Walter Mountjoy, March 19, 2000.

73. Crowell, February 11, 2020. New Year's Eve, the biggest night in the year for dances, guaranteed a bonanza paycheck.

74. Crowell, June 8, 2017. Among those who helped me learn about Charlie Cook are Dale Pauley, Bobby Joe Caldwell, Leroy Canaday, Hillis Crowell, Taylor McBaine, Ivan Crane, Bud Wyatt, Matt Wyatt, and especially Nelda and Knox McCrory.

75. A set of home recordings is available digitally: *Charlie Cook, Boone County Waltz King*.

76. Crowell, June 8, 11, 2017.

77. Leroy Canaday's version of "Charlie Cook's G waltz" (which Canaday learned from Cook at a music party in the 1950s) is on the *Fiddler's Dream* companion CD; McMahan's title for the waltz in A was "Cook's Waltz" (*50 Old-Time Fiddle Gems*).

78. In 1991, McMahan spoke of Cook while performing "Flowers of Heaven" in a public program, but, perhaps unconsciously, Pete reinforced the false notion that Cook couldn't play breakdowns well. McMahan said, "I picked it up from a fiddler down in Boone County, by the

name of Charlie Cook. He was one of the best waltz fiddlers I ever heard—but he couldn't play a hoedown at all. But he could play a waltz and almost make tears come in your eyes, and he made this tune up himself. He called it 'Flowers from Heaven'" (July 3, 1991). Matt Wyatt is among the McMahan pupils who play Cook's "Flowers from Heaven." Wyatt, *Centralia Waltz.*

79. Cook was driving home from Huntsdale (he lived at Rocheport at that time, a few miles away), where he had finished playing a dance. Around ten at night, on the twisting narrow road, his Chevrolet station wagon collided with a Ford sedan carrying four young people; the cars veered into the center line on the crest of a hill. Cook and three of the four young people died. "Four Killed in Head-on Crash Near Here," *Columbia Daily Tribune*, April 19, 1960.

80. Sarah McMahan, February 11, 2011.

81. In my conversations, Sarah McMahan was proud of being Cherokee. Sarah thought the name Ronimous, a familiar Missouri Cherokee name, may once have been spelled "Heronimous" (June 8, 2005).

82. Sarah McMahan, June 8, 2005.

83. Sarah McMahan, January 20, 2010; February 11, 2011. Sarah died in March 2019.

84. From a 1989 TAAP staff site visit when Griffin was McMahan's apprentice (https://www.mofolkarts.missouri.edu).

85. McMahan, March 1992, March 9, 1993. The label in the violin stating it was made in France is incorrect; John Griffin points out that the violin is a "modern Italian from the 1900s" (April 16, 2020). In several conversations with Pete through the years, Pete recalled the cash he paid Journagin in the fiddle deal as $12.50 or $15.00. In 1992, John Griffin bought the violin from McMahan in an arrangement that allowed Pete to keep possession until such time as he was no longer able to play it.

86. Dale Pauley, November 20, 2018.

87. Tim Higgins, "Famed Fiddler Dies at Age 81," *Columbia Daily Tribune*, February 14, 2000; Mikael Lagerblad, "Hall of Fame Fiddler McMahan Dies at 81," *Columbia Missourian*, February 15, 2000; Marshall, "Pete McMahan Leaves the Stage." Pete appears on Marshall et al., *"Now That's a Good Tune"*; and two MSOTFA cassettes, *Ozark Mountain Waltz* and *Kansas City Rag*. He appeared on some South Dakota Old-Time Fiddlers' Association cassettes taped at the Great Plains championships in Yankton ("Dance around Molly," "Grey Eagle," "Fiddler's Dream," and "Missouri Waltz," on *Missouri Old Time Fiddling*, and others); his self-produced albums (a fifth was recorded but the master tape lost) are reissued as *50 Old-Time Fiddle Gems*. Pete performed at the Smithsonian's Festival of American Folklife, the National Folk Festival (Lowell, Massachusetts), the Festival of American Fiddle Tunes (Port Townsend, Washington), and other festivals, and at these appearances McMahan's backup included Charlie Walden (fiddle), guitarist Kenny Applebee, and bassist Forrest Rose, as well as fiddler John Griffin.

4. Voluntary Associations and Fiddle Contests

1. Joe Pfeffer wrote about the "growing revival of the 'folk scene'" in St. Louis in "Guide to Folk Music in the St. Louis Area."

2. Several personal collections of recordings and ephemera were deposited in the State Historical Society of Missouri by fiddlers or family members of departed fiddlers, such as materials from Vernon Clatterbuck (Fulton), Bill Kearns (Slater), Charlie Stallcup (Hannibal), and Billy Craighead (Fulton).

3. Blaustein, "Traditional Music and Social Change," 10ff; Richard J. Blaustein, "Jake and Lena Hughes: Grassroots Promoters of the Old-Time Fiddling Revival in Missouri and the Great Plains Region." A revival musician before becoming an Indiana-trained scholar,

Dr. Blaustein knew Missouri fiddling and provides important insights. See also Richard J. Blaustein, "Grassroots Revitalization of North American and Western European Instrumental Music Traditions from Fiddlers' Associations to Cyberspace," in *Oxford Handbook of Music Revival*, ed. Bithell and Hill, 551–67.

4. As the National Oldtime Fiddlers' Contest and its membership sibling, the National Oldtime Fiddlers' Association, experienced success in the 1960s and 1970s, it tried to influence associations and contests across the country to become associated organizations and use Weiser rules. Efforts to coax contests into the NOTFA mold were rarely successful where there were deep-rooted customs that worked, more or less. The Weiser/NOTFA template fitted better in the West and Pacific Northwest, where the most members lived and where the Weiser/Texas/Contest Style was heavily promoted.

5. Blaustein, "Jake and Lena Hughes," 11.

6. See Frank Maloy, "Canary Waltz as Played by Lena Hughes"; Blaustein, "Jake and Lena Hughes"; Howard Wight Marshall, "Hand-in-Hand: Music and Dance in Central Missouri" and "Missouri's Lena Hughes Passes Away"; Julie Youmans, "Lena Jones Hughes"; Lena Hughes, March 4, 1989 (unless otherwise indicated, other quotes from Hughes are from this visit); and Aaron Zischkale, "Lena Hughes' Rolling Banjo." In November 1974, I recorded Lena for the Smithsonian Institution in Ludlow, while documenting several Missouri fiddlers for the Festival of American Folklife. In the 1970s when I worked at the Library of Congress, I deposited tape recordings from the 1960s, featuring Lena and other Missouri musicians, in the Archive of Folk Culture. Her fiddling of "Forked Deer" and "Red Bird" appears on a sampler LP from the Athens, Alabama, festivals. Hughes plays banjo on *Three Fiddlers from the Show-Me State* with Lyman Enloe, Cyril Stinnett, and Casey Jones; the Athens LP was issued on Davis Unlimited from the Tennessee Valley Old-Time Fiddler's Contest and reissued on CD as *Fiddlers of the Tennessee Valley*.

7. Lena's guitar playing is on *Lena Hughes, Queen of the Guitar Pickers and Her Flat Top Guitar*. Comments by English folk guitarist and composer John Renbourn on Lena Hughes's guitar playing and his search to find the original record in the 1960s in Joel Rose, prod., "The 'Ancient Vibration' of Parlor Music, Revived by Two Generations," NPR, February 6, 2013.

8. *Salisbury Press-Spectator*, June 9, 1967.

9. "Salisbury Old-Time Fiddlers' Contest," *Salisbury Press-Spectator*, August 11, 1967, 9; "Fiddlin' Starts Thursday in Big Contest Here," *Salisbury Press-Spectator*, August 18, 1967, 1.

10. See Sharon Graf, "Oldtime Fiddle Music Gets a Face Lift: The Formation of 'the' National Oldtime Fiddlers' Contest."

11. "'Fiddlin' Includes Wide Variety of Talent, Skill," *Salisbury Press-Spectator*, August 25, 1967, 1.

12. "'Fiddlin' Includes Wide Variety of Talent, Skill," 9; see also "Top Fiddlers Named in Finals Saturday," *Salisbury Press-Spectator*, August 25, 1967, 7.

13. "'Fiddlin' Includes Wide Variety of Talent, Skill," 9; also "Top Fiddlers Named in Finals Saturday," 7.

14. Herman Jones was better known as "Sac River Jones," a popular fiddler from the El Dorado Springs area of Cedar County; the Sac River is a tributary of the Osage River in western Missouri.

15. McMahan, December 17, 1986.

16. "'Fiddlin' Includes Wide Variety of Talent, Skill," 9; see also "Top Fiddlers Named in Finals Saturday," 7. "Of special interest to Chariton Countians were two entries who reached the semi-finals," Bill Shearon of Keytesville and Francis Kepner of Rothville.

17. "Old-Time Fiddlers Contest to Start Here Tomorrow," *Lexington Advertiser-News*, July 31, 1968, 1.

18. "1,500 Hear Fiddlers in Three-Day Contest," *Lexington Advertiser-News*, August 5, 1968, 1. During this time when there were Ladies Divisions, female fiddlers were able to compete in other divisions as well.

19. See Blaustein, "Jake and Lena Hughes"; Barry Bergey, "Sketches of a Fiddle Convention in the Flatlands (1971)"; and Marshall, "Missouri's Lena Hughes Passes Away."

20. A few states established NOTFA branches and had their state contests and their judges "certified" (for example, adhering to National Oldtime Fiddlers' Contest rules) and were part of what everyone hoped could become a big, happy family, but that didn't happen. The Weiser contest was and remains essentially a West and Northwest regional event, with some notable contest fiddlers trekking to Weiser from other states, Canadian provinces, and foreign countries.

21. The August 19, 1968, Boone County Fair contest was won by Dale Pauley of Columbia, playing "Polk County Breakdown," "B-flat Waltz" (a Charlie Cook tune), and "Grey Eagle," with guitar seconds Carl Richardson and Claude Baker to beat out Cleo Persinger, Pete McMahan, and Taylor McBaine. George Tuck, "Fair Climaxed by Fiddles, Horses," *Columbia Missourian*, August 10, 1968, 1.

22. Virginia M. Botts, "The Boone County Fair: 'The Show Window of Boone County,'" manuscript, Columbia, 1970.

23. David Keyes, "Fair Attracts Fiddlers with Cash Prize, Trophy," *Columbia Missourian*, August 4, 1968.

24. Also contributing to the demise of the Boone County Fair contest was its new location; in 1992 the lively, historic fairgrounds and its old frame buildings were abandoned, and the fair moved to a site north of town, with impersonal sheet-metal buildings; the cold, unfriendly "pole barn" metal building was not a hospitable venue, and the new location hurt the contest's attendance and reputation.

25. "Fiddler's Festival Winners Lined Up at East Hills," *St. Joseph Gazette*, September 23, 1971. This is believed to be "Doctor Jimmy Gray," the St. Louis fiddling dentist frequently recalled by John Hartford.

26. Ed Fedrizzi, November 17, 2010; Ed Fedrizzi is the son-in-law of Joe Grable and father of champion fiddler Joe Fedrizzi of Dearborn, Missouri.

27. https://www.mo-fiddlers.com.

28. Vesta Johnson, March 8, 2005. There tends to be disharmony in fiddle clubs and associations when people attend jam sessions and events wanting to sing old country songs; the "fiddlers" are there to play fiddle tune after fiddle tune.

5. Empire Building: Fiddle Contests in the 1960s and 1970s

1. I appreciate the help of Gordon McCann (over many years) in preparing this chapter, as well as a diverse lot such as Ron Adams, Dick Barrett, Charlie Butler, Leroy Canaday, Bob Cathey, Dennis Coelho, Wilbur Foss, Art Galbraith, Spencer Galloway, Cecil Goforth, Gene Goforth, Sharon Graf, Jake and Lena Hughes, Travis Inman, Vesta Johnson, Kelly Jones, Taylor McBaine, Pete McMahan, Margot McMillen, Dale Pauley, Phillips, Richard Shewmaker, Bill Shull, Lee Stoneking, Benny Thomasson, Charlie Walden, Phil and Vivian Williams, and Allen and Matt Wyatt; every fiddler I have known has had an opinion, good or ill, of fiddling competitions.

2. Bill Shull, *Guide to Running a Fiddling Contest.*

3. McGreevy, February 2, 2018.

4. A "parking-lot tale" collected by UCLA graduate student Willie Smyth (*Devil's Box*, ca. 1975).

5. Issues and debates about style will forever be knotted; most count it as a good thing that young musicians are often uncomfortable with the old terms and definitions and come up with their own as they re-create old music: for example, "haunting psychedelic Appalachian folk drone" (photo caption in Sarah Bryan, "Young Old-Time Musicians in North Carolina," 37); this happily reminds me of Dan Peek's advertising the music of our string band in Columbia, Missouri, in the 1960s as "psychedelic old-time music." Discussions of Missouri's many fiddle styles appear throughout *"Play Me Something Quick and Devilish"* and *Fiddler's Dream.*

6. Pauley, June 19, 2018.

7. Donnie Wright (1954–2017) was among young professional country music fiddlers finding success at Nixa contests. Wright's father, Walter, was a country-radio deejay; as a child, Donnie performed on violin and other instruments on radio and television in the Springfield-Nixa-Branson area. Ed McKinney, "Images, Realities, and Cultural Transformations in the Missouri Ozarks, 1920–1960," 177; Wright, September 16, 24, 25, October 4, 2010; obituary, *Springfield News-Leader*, March 18–19, 2017; Wright's recordings include an LP, *The Ozark Mountain Dewers* (Century Records 34657, 1968).

8. "Lloyd Trantham Winner in Nixa Fiddlers Contest," *Springfield Leader-Press*, November 5, 1954, courtesy of Harold Singer, American Legion Post 434.

9. *Nixa Enterprise*, October 10, 1957. On October 17 the paper listed the winners: Earl Morgan of Fair Grove had won the Ozark Grand Champion Fiddler title; second place, Miller McDaniel (Carthage); third place, Kenneth Wilson (Clever); fourth place, Jim (this is probably Jude) Herndon (Nixa); and fifth place, Clyde Hughey (Miller). Earl Morgan would compete successfully in the MFA Oil state fiddle contests a few years later.

10. In 1958 Nixa contest winners were first, Kenneth Wilson (Clever); second, Leslie Haguewood (Nixa); third, Glenn Rickman (Crane); fourth, Earl Morgan (Springfield); and fifth, Clyde Hewly (Hughey) (Miller). *Christian County Republican*, October 30, 1958.

11. "Periman Wins State Champion Fiddler Title," *Nixa Enterprise*, October 16, 1969. A local character, Red Periman claimed to have composed "Orange Blossom Special."

12. Wayne Glenn's *Ozarks' Greatest Hits* offers documentation; photo of the 1969 winners, Childress, Periman, and Wright (455); Periman is shown fiddling in the Golden, Missouri, fiddle contest in 1964 (431), one of the few contest fiddlers documented who seems to have held his violin "down on his chest" as he played.

13. "22nd Annual Missouri State Old Fiddlers Contest," *Nixa Enterprise*, October 11, 1970; "Old Fiddlers Contest Here Saturday Night," *Nixa Enterprise*, October 15, 1970.

14. "23rd Annual Missouri State Old Fiddlers Contest Saturday," *Nixa Enterprise*, September 30, 1971; "Periman Named State Fiddle Winner," *Nixa Enterprise*, October 21, 1971. Second place, Barbara Wilson (Bolivar); third, Mike Lewis (Rocky Comfort). Youngest Fiddler award to "Don Wright, 17."

15. "24th Annual Missouri State Old Fiddlers Contest September 30, 1972," *Nixa Enterprise*, September 28, 1972; again, the contest awarded only three prizes.

16. Announcement, *Nixa Enterprise*, October 14, 1976; "Periman Takes First in Nixa's State Fiddlers Contest," *Nixa Enterprise*, November 4, 1976. Periman's accompanists were daughter Brenda Robbins and her husband, Wade Robbins.

17. *Nixa Enterprise*, September 29, 1977, 1. The 1977 winners: first, Wayne Lawson (Springfield); second, Raymond Thomas (Jenkins); and third, Dennis Essary (Springfield). "Springfieldians Top Winners at Nixa's Fiddlers Contest," *Nixa Enterprise*, October 19, 1977, 1.

18. "31st Annual Missouri State Fiddlers Contest," *Nixa Enterprise*, November 1, 1979; "Johnston Judged Best Fiddler," *Nixa Enterprise*, November 29, 1979. Dean Johnston is featured in *The Masters* booklet *"Now That's a Good Tune"*; Missouri issues of the *Old-Time Herald*; Beisswenger and McCann, *Ozarks Fiddle Music*; and other projects. His "Humansville," "Waldo," and "East Tennessee Blues" are on *"Now That's a Good Tune"*; Beisswenger and McCann include Dean's version of "Chinky Pin" ("Lead Out"), "Crystal Stream Waltz," "Frisky Jim," "Florida Blues," "Lantern in a Ditch," "Turkey Knob," and "Waldo" in Beisswenger and McCann, *Ozarks Fiddle Music*, 73ff. "Frisky Jim," "Crystal Stream Waltz," "Chinky Pin" ("Lead Out"), "Turkey Knob," "Dry Branch," and "Waldo" are on *Traditional Fiddle Music of the Ozarks*, vol. 2, *On the Springfield Plain* (Rounder 0436, 2000).

19. "32nd Annual Missouri State Old Fiddlers Contest," *Nixa Enterprise*, November 22, 1980; 33rd Annual Missouri State Old Fiddlers Contest," *Nixa Enterprise*, November 19, 1981.

20. McCann, November 22, 2010.

21. McCann recorded the contest; McCann, November 22, 2010. Mark Pearman won first in the "over 21" age division, Lynn Wells of Boonesboro took second, and Roger Hale of Billings took third. Other "over 21" contestants included Mike Wells, Billy Ward, Art Galbraith, Wayne Lawson, and Waldo Burke. Shawn Pittman, age thirteen, won the "under 21" division.

22. McCann, November 22, 2010.

23. Breid, August 6, 2018.

24. McCann, November 22, 2010.

25. Lee, November 23, 2001.

26. Randy Smith, FIDDLE-L Internet discussion list, October 14, 2003; translation: park near the stage if you are a judge, in order to make a fast getaway before irate losers or a loser's supporters have a chance to accost you.

27. Seoul Olympics coverage, ABC, February 10, 2018.

28. Wyatt, February 14, 2011, January 24, 2019.

29. Warming up backstage at the Kentucky state fiddle contest some years ago with Shepherdsville, Kentucky, guitarist Ron Adams, I recall being surprised to hear Ron tell me, "Don't play any little tunes." I knew exactly what he meant and complied.

30. Drew Beisswenger, *North American Fiddle Music: A Research and Information Guide*, 143; Bill Shull, "OK, Let's Try It Again: What's 'Old-Time' Music?"

31. Phillips's reference is to his biography, interviews, and analysis of Mark O'Connor's career and influential fiddling, published as *Contest Fiddling*; with transcriptions of O'Connor's contest winners, it is known as "Marks' book."

32. Fred Stoneking, "Fiddles! Fiddles! Fiddles!"

33. Pauley, June 19, 2018.

34. For the history of the MFA Oil Company and the Missouri Farmers Association, see Raymond Young, *Cultivating Cooperation: A History of the Missouri Farmers Association*, 210ff.

35. Courtesy of Leroy Canaday.

36. LeRoy Haslag (1940–2020) was a popular fiddler, playing dances, performing on radio and TV shows with Lee Mace's Ozark Opry, and recording 45-rpm records and LPs. He

performed at MFA Oil's national sales meeting in Memphis, Tennessee, in 1962 and was featured in company publications and newspapers. Haslag was invited to compete in a national contest in Truth or Consequences, New Mexico, in April 1962 but was unable to attend. See Marshall, chap. 5 of *"Play Me Something Quick and Devilish"*; and Howard Wight Marshall, "Live! At the Ozark Opry: An Appreciation of Vaudeville and 'Show Fiddler' LeRoy Haslag."

37. Nell Gross, "Old Fiddlers," *St. Louis Globe-Democrat,* January 21, 1962. The original melody to "Listen to the Mockingbird" is credited to Richard Milburn in 1854, an African American guitarist and street performer in Philadelphia known as "Whistling Dick." Septimus Winner heard Milburn whistle the tune and wrote down the notes. Winner arranged Milburn's music, added lyrics, published the sheet music, and hired Millburn to work in the Winner family's music store. Winner credited Milburn in the first printing. Later editions include Septimus Winner's nom de plume, "Alice Hawthorne" (Winner's mother was a descendant of Nathanial Hawthorne). Typical printings include "The Grave of Hally" ("Listen to the Mocking Bird") (Philadelphia: Lee and Walker, 1865). The ballad was extremely popular as vocal or instrumental music during the American Civil War, a favorite of both sides of the conflict. The sheet music in various editions became one of the three or four best-selling compositions of all time. When Edison cylinder recordings became available in late 1890s, "Listen to the Mocking Bird" was among the first commercial sound recordings to capture wide attention. In addition to "Mocking Bird," Winner's "Whispering Hope" of 1868 is still widely known.

38. Leroy Canaday, August 20, 2002.

39. "The Devil Went Down to Georgia" is also sometimes banned, a song composed and performed by country entertainer and fiddler Charlie Daniels in 1977. It is said that part of the melody was borrowed from "Lonesome Fiddle Blues" by Vassar Clements on his 1975 LP (*Vassar Clements,* Mercury SRM-1-1022), a recording for which Daniels played guitar accompaniment; previously, Clements had fiddled "Lonesome Fiddle Blues" on the Nitty Gritty Dirt Band's influential 1972 LP, *Will the Circle Be Unbroken* (United Artists UAS-9801).

40. A few MFA Oil dealerships continued to sponsor contests, but nothing as ambitious as the state competitions. MFA sponsored a fiddle contest in conjunction with the annual business meeting in Columbia in November 1970, held at the National Guard Armory downtown; winners were Little Dixie–style stalwarts Pete McMahan, Cleo Persinger, Leroy Canaday, Johnny Bruce, and Glen Wells. "MFA Oil Meeting Draws a Large Crowd," *Marshall Democrat-News,* November 10, 1970.

41. Art Logan, https:www.mofiddledance.org, November 29, 2016; website manager David Cavins forwarded the post to me and I followed up. Unless otherwise noted, Art Logan quotes are from May 19, 2017. Art plays mandolin, composes, and sings at sessions such as bluegrass jams at the Fret Shop in Kansas City. His CD *23 and E* includes bluegrass and country songs, instrumentals, and fiddle tunes such as "Clark's Waltz" (from Pete McMahan) and Art's composition "Monegaw Creek," named for a tributary of the Osage River near Appleton City that seems to have been a refuge of the outlaw Younger gang, famed for their alliance with Jesse and Frank James, groups active in the 1850s "border wars" in western Missouri and eastern Kansas Territory; after the war, the James-Younger gang became notorious (or celebrated, depending on one's politics) in popular journalism, local lore, and music. Additional Art Logan references are from April 29 and May 2, 2019.

42. For German heritage in Missouri (more than half of Missourians describe themselves to census takers as German American), see Howard Wight Marshall and James W. Goodrich, eds.,

The German-American Experience in Missouri; Adolf Schroeder, *Missouri Origins: The Landscape of Home, the Survival of German Traditions in Missouri*; Charles van Ravenswaay, *The Arts and Architecture of German Settlements in Missouri: Survey of a Vanishing Culture*; Michael Roark, ed., *French and Germans in the Mississippi Valley: Landscape and Cultural Traditions*; and Marshall, chap. 5 of *"Play Me Something Quick and Devilish."*

43. The knobs at Knob Noster are "two prominent knolls . . . far above the surrounding country, and present a beautiful appearance in the midst of an almost level plain." The odd hills were Native American burial mounds, and treasure hunters and vandals began digging into the knobs in the later 1800s (no treasure was found); Kansas City Historical Co., *History of Johnson County, Missouri*, 489. In Missouri vernacular, a "knob" is a small hill on an otherwise flat prairie landscape; "noster" is Latin for "our," so the place-name Knob Noster (founded 1856, population ca. seventeen hundred) means "our knob." Margot Ford McMillen, *A to Z Missouri: The Dictionary of Missouri Place Names*, 88; Robert L. Ramsay, *Our Storehouse of Missouri Place Names*, 116; Ewing Cockrell, *Cockrell's History of Johnson County, Missouri*, 162; B. Johnson, "Place Names in Six of the West Central Counties of Missouri."

44. The DeArmond firm in Toledo, Ohio, created an affordable electric pickup for guitars in 1939 and later developed a model for violins.

45. Old thresher events became popular in the Midwest in the 1960s and 1970s (often tied to a town centennial or the 1970s US bicentennial era), with displays of antique farm equipment and demonstrations of many kinds, from plowing with draft horses and mules to steam-powered threshing machines, pioneer craft, flea markets and swap meets, and assorted other activities such as country music and bluegrass shows as well as old-time fiddle contests.

46. As mentioned in Marshall, *"Play Me Something Quick and Devilish"* and *Fiddler's Dream*, Logan took third place in the MFA State Championship in Columbia in November 1961.

47. The Gibson Mastertone model RB-250, made from the mid-1950s to 1969 or 1970, is known as a "bow tie" due to the shape of the inlays in the fingerboard.

48. Art and Jane continue to play the instruments; Art also plays an "F-5" model made by Andy Poe in Columbia and performs with "Some Other Brothers" (Art Logan, May 15, 2017).

49. For many years, Bill Monroe harbored ill will toward Scruggs, who, with Lester Flatt, had left Monroe's band to form Lester Flatt and Earl Scruggs and the Foggy Mountain Boys—a hit band competing with Monroe's band. See, for example, Neil V. Rosenberg, *Bluegrass: A History*; and Richard D. Smith, *"Can't You Hear Me Callin'": The Life of Bill Monroe, Father of Bluegrass*. Monroe remained bitter toward Scruggs and did not reconcile with him until 1994.

50. This was the studio where a number of Missouri fiddlers and bluegrass bands recorded self-produced and self-financed 45-rpm and 33½-rpm records in this period; Rimrock was founded in 1961 in Concord, Arkansas, by country music singer and songwriter Wayne Raney and his son Zyndall. Zyndall was the recording engineer and sometimes assisted a session by adding instrumental work. In 1974, Rimrock was bought by Stax Records in Memphis. See *Encyclopedia of Arkansas History and Culture*, s.v. "Rimrock Records," www.encyclopediaofarkansas.net.

51. One possible reason for the lack of fiddlers after year one of Logan's contest could be that the top fiddlers were so good that first year; with many having classical technique and performing fashionable "contest tunes" and Contest Style, other young players with less contesting experience were discouraged and quit trying in contests.

52. Wood Persinger's great-grandfather Joseph Persinger was a Virginian reared by Native Americans who moved to what would become Boone County, Missouri, during territorial times, ca. 1816. Joseph Persinger was a famous hunter and part of a "prestigious family." Robert L. Ramsay, "The Place Names of Boone County, Missouri," 33.

53. David Keyes, "Fair Attracts Fiddlers with Cash Prize, Trophy," *Columbia Missourian*, August 4, 1968; Spencer Galloway, "Cleo Persinger," manuscript, 2001. See also Marshall, *"Play Me Something Quick and Devilish"* and *Fiddler's Dream*.

54. Jim Chancellor, March 23, 2020. "I also remember that Cleo lived in the bottom of two mountains that concealed the morning sun until later in the day. Which I thought was very different and memorable." Chancellor also noted that he was influenced by Persinger that night, as he was by other fiddlers, and that Persinger led him to John Hartford, with whom Chancellor performed and recorded in later years.

55. Persinger's Midway contest drew numerous players from around Missouri, and first place was won by Pete McMahan. "Fiddlin' Champ's Hobby Wins Him State Trophy, Bringing the Total to 60," *Columbia Missourian*, September 14, 1979, A8; see also Carol Davis, "Fiddlers Convene Today," *Clarksville (TN) Leaf-Chronicle*, April 5, 1985, 1.

56. In and around Boone County in Missouri's Little Dixie folk region is the three-part breakdown known variously as "Fiddler's Hoedown," "Black Foot Rag," and "Boone County Rag." When Persinger played the tune at Weiser contests in 1964 and 1965, he called it "Fiddler's Hoedown." Pete McMahan, who learned it from Otto Griggs of Columbia, used the title "Black Foot Rag" as well as "Fiddler's Hoedown," and the only known commercial recording is on McMahan's 1970s LP, reissued on *50 Old-Time Fiddle Gems*. The tune is in Christeson's *Old-Time Fiddler's Repertory* (1984) under the title "The Dead Slave." Walden's transcription of McMahan's version under the title "Fiddler's Hoedown" is downloadable at https://www.charliewalden.com.

57. "Nation's Top Fiddler," *Columbia Daily Tribune*, June 23, 1964, 2. "Cleo Persinger of Route 3 won the national old-time fiddlers title for 1964 Saturday night at Weiser, Idaho. He was one of seven finalists and edged out the defending champion, Loyd Wanzer of Caldwell, Idaho." Following Wanzer were third place, Bill Yohey (McMinnville, Oregon, trophy, $200), and fourth place, Harold Allen (Corvallis, Oregon, trophy, $100).

58. Hartford, November 15, 2000.

59. John Hartford, "John Hartford Tune Transcriptions: 'Coming Down from Denver on a Trip to Galway Here and There,' 'Flannery's Dream.'" Tommy Jackson, *Square Dance Festival* (Dot DLP-3330), is a much-loved LP among fiddlers of my acquaintance. See Kuntz, *Fiddler's Companion*. I recorded Johnny Bruce's admirable version (solo) of "Coming Down from Denver" at his farm in 1988, with the third part that his father and uncle played in the 1930s in Carroll County (on the companion CD with *"Play Me Something Quick and Devilish"*). "Coming Down from Denver" remains important for knowledgeable fiddlers in Missouri and among Charlie Walden's "100 Essential Missouri Fiddle Tunes." There is a third part in "Coming Down from Denver" that some people played (fingered in third position) in the 1930s and 1940s (such as brothers Tyson and Dewey Bruce in central Missouri's Carroll County), but it seems to have been left behind.

60. Harold C. Hopkins, "He Has Fiddled His Way to Eighty-Four Prizes," *Kansas City Star*, November 16, 1947, E14. Hopkins (1922–2014) received his bachelor of journalism at the University of Missouri in 1949 and retired in 1984 after a career in newspaper and

magazine journalism. See also Galloway, "Cleo Persinger, 1909–1971," 25. Persinger also met Fritz Kreisler, and declared Spalding and Kreisler "good old boys." Keyes, "Fair Attracts Fiddlers with Cash Prize, Trophy." Hopkins had mailed his unsolicited article to the *Star*, and it was accepted, giving the aspiring reporter welcome income as well as ensuring a high grade in his article writing class at the university (Harold Hopkins, August 4, 2002). See also Marshall, *"Play Me Something Quick and Devilish."*

61. Persinger and others from this area also played a waltz called "Black Foot Waltz" (the only known commercial recording is by Leroy Canaday on *Old Dan Tucker Was a Fine Old Man*). During the Civil War, there was a group of Confederate guerrilla fighters in Boone and Randolph Counties who operated in the area called the Blackfoot Rangers. A ballad called "The Blackfoot Rangers" circulated in Missouri in the 1800s and appears in Henry M. Belden, ed., *Ballads and Songs Collected by the Missouri Folk-Lore Society*, 354; a version appears on Cathy Barton and Dave Para, *Rebel in the Woods*.

62. Hartford, "John Hartford Tune Transcriptions: 'Whoa Mule,' 'Boone County Rag'"; John Hartford, "John Hartford Tune Transcriptions: 'Darkie's Curly Hair,' 'Knocking at Your Door,' 'Maysville,' 'Better Get Outa My Way.'"

63. Keokuk, Iowa, fiddler Kirk Brandenberger, who participated in bluegrass festivals and contests in Missouri and knew Persinger, recorded Persinger's "Going across the Prairie" on his 1977 LP, *Fiddlin' Around* (St. Louis: Professional Artist Recording 7722-145); Howard Wight Marshall, "Going across the Prairie: A Missouri Fiddle Tune" (transcription by Sharon Graf); Charlie Walden's setting and discussion are on YouTube.

64. *Cleo Persinger: Goin' across the Prairie* (MSOTFA Recordings 007), https://missourifiddling.bandcamp.com.

65. Persinger died of cancer at sixty-two in 1971, just as interest in fiddle playing among young people was gaining momentum. Taylor McBaine, Pete McMahan, Bill Stearns, and Gene Wells served as pallbearers at the funeral.

66. McMahan, May 7, 1992.

67. See Marshall, chap. 7 of *"Play Me Something Quick and Devilish."* Stinnett played the Missouri tunes "Sleepy Joe," "Five Miles Out of Town," and "Canary Waltz"; in other rounds, he played "Sally Goodin" and three Canadian-style hornpipes, "Woodchopper's," "Pacific Slope," and "Bennett's Reel." Recordings of Stinnett, McMahan, Persinger, Hughes, and Art Galbraith at the Weiser contests are in the Williams Tape Archive, donated by Phil and Vivian Williams to the State Historical Society of Missouri in Columbia. Phil uploaded several Stinnett tunes from Weiser on the Voyager website, https://www.voyagerrecords.com. "Bennett's Reel" is sometimes called "The Great Eastern" in Canada and "The Silver Spire" in Irish fiddle music; among outstanding renditions by young Missouri fiddlers today is that of Richard Shewmaker of Columbia.

68. McMahan, December 17, 1986.

69. Shull, *Guide to Running a Fiddling Contest*, writes of the logic of bringing two or more top fiddlers back for a playoff, whether they are technically tied in the scoring or not, as an audience-pleasing device, particularly in hard-fought contests.

70. McMahan, September 18, 1997.

71. For Athens, see Bill Harrison, "History of the Tennessee Valley Old Time Fiddlers' Convention," 1996, https://www.athens.edu/fiddlers/convhist.html. See also Goertzen, *Southern Fiddlers and Fiddle Contests*. For Clarksville, see Stephen F. Davis, "1982 State of Tennessee

Old-Time Fiddlers' Championships"; photo of Pete McMahan on 26. Sorenson played a Yamaha twelve-string guitar strung with six strings.

72. Shull, at the state-fair fiddle contest, August 18, 1996.

73. McMahan, September 24, 1996; Al Cherny, *North American Fiddler Champion Plays Contest Winning Tunes* (1960; reissue, Arc 250, 1965).

74. McMahan, December 21, 1995.

75. McMahan correspondence, July 18, 1975.

76. Ed Carnes, Facebook, 2016.

77. Carnes is a nationally known contest champion from Leitchfield, Kentucky, who works in technology consulting in Nashville. Ed led the revival of, and manages, the prestigious Grand Master Fiddler Championship, in which he instituted a Grand Master Traditional Fiddler Championship division "to recognize fiddlers who play fiddling styles outside the recognized US 'contest' or 'Texas' styles, or Canadian 'contest" styles'" (https://www.grandmasterfiddler.com). As a teenager, Ed knew and competed with McMahan in contests in Kentucky, Tennessee, and Hannibal, Missouri. Carnes, Facebook, January 5, 2016.

78. McBaine, November 25, 1975.

79. Courtesy of Allen Wyatt, January 2011, from a post on Ed Carnes's website referencing Charlie Walden's site, https://www.missourifiddling.com.

80. Typical of some of McMahan's comments, this one could present a complex topic for a graduate seminar; most would debate thinking of Terry Morris as playing too slow, for example, although he may have played slow that day in Memphis to better Randy Howard, who played contest breakdowns "too slow to dance to," as McMahan would say. What is proper tempo for a square-dance tune or waltz varies by region and even from town to town.

81. McMahan, September 18, 1997, August 18, 1996, and other dates; Pete enjoyed retelling this story. In her thesis, "Ozark Old-Time Fiddling," Judy Warner explains and illustrates how "Grey Eagle" is typically rendered in Contest, bluegrass, and Ozark styles.

82. Randy Howard's "Golden Fiddle Waltz" became a global favorite in the 1970s. A piece requiring violinistic skills of a high order, this fine waltz continues to be performed and recorded by top contest fiddlers. Howard was primarily a session fiddler in Nashville, but he was also a successful contest fiddler, where most people heard him, tape-recorded him, and learned his "Golden Fiddle Waltz"; he eventually released a recording of the piece on his 1993 *Survival of the Fiddlest* CD. Among my personal favorite recordings is by Fiddlin' Johnny [John Lardinois], on his CD *Cowboy Legacy* (Makoche Music, 1997). "Slow, dreamy, and filled with double-stops, it is hard to think of a better example of the [Texas] style" (album notes). Howard's championships include the prestigious Union Grove, North Carolina, contest in 1978, where, at eighteen, he bested several famous champions.

83. John Griffin, "Pete McMahan," 24.

84. Bob Cathey, June 7, 2010, restated January 28, 2011; in fact (as Pete knew), "St. Anne's Reel" was often heard in Missouri contests, and he enjoyed playing it at music parties.

85. McMahan, March 8, 1993.

86. McMahan, February 22, 1989.

87. Brad Solon, June 8, 9, 2009.

88. Sharon Graf write about the evolution of "Weiser" as, arguably, the world's biggest and best-known fiddle contest. Graf, "Oldtime Fiddle Music Gets a Face Lift: The Formation of 'the' National Oldtime Fiddlers' Contest" and "Traditionalization at the National Oldtime

Fiddlers' Contest." See also Goertzen, *Southern Fiddlers and Fiddle Contests*, "Balancing Local and National Approaches at American Fiddle Contests," and "Transformation of American Contest Fiddling."

89. Leroy Canaday and LeRoy Haslag were invited to compete at Truth or Consequences in 1962 but could not make the trip. Art Galbraith competed in 1964 and did not make the finals (Galbraith, November 17, 1975).

90. Thomasson was influential in the evolution of today's Contest Style; other influential Texans included Major Franklin, Bryant Houston, and Norman and Vernon Solomon. Chancellor recalled Thomasson as "an incredible innovator" who, with others, took old-time fiddle tunes and "embellished" them; they "feathered the edges" of old tunes, and the tunes became "more of a listening piece than a dancing piece." Josephine Reed, "A Conversation with National Heritage Fellow Texas Shorty," *Art Works* podcast, 2010, National Endowment for the Arts, https://www.nea.gov. For Thomasson's long-form, variation-rich settings, see Pete Martin, *Benny Thomasson Fiddle Transcriptions*; and Garelick, "Legacy of Benny Thomasson."

91. McMahan, September 19, 1997.

92. Phil Williams, December 28, 2013. Viola (Mom) Ruth was a well-known Phoenix, Arizona, dance fiddler, contest champion, tune-book author, and judge; her voice carried authority. Ruth published a tune book in 1947 with square-dance calls and instruction, *Pioneer Western Folk Tunes as Played and Arranged by Viola "Mom" Ruth*. I am reminded of a favorite anecdote about judging. Gene Goforth and his friend Kenny Baker were helping adjudicate the Eureka contest in the late 1980s. On his score sheet, upon hearing a fiddler take off on a tune and drowning the melody in outlandish ornaments, Baker drew a big circle with his pencil and said, "I give that fiddler a big fat zero" (courtesy of Allen Wyatt).

93. The next year, Berline recorded in Los Angeles with the Dillards and two years later worked with Bill Monroe and the Blue Grass Boys; Phil Williams accompanied Berline on bluegrass-style banjo, and Phil's brother Bob played open-chord guitar. Bob, Phil, and Vivian Williams had just met Berline at Missoula. "Byron took us to his hotel room and showed us how he wanted to be backed up. It was *straight 'Missouri' chording*" (Phil Williams, July 16, 2009). Berline played what he called "Oklahoma style," a powerful, driving yet elegant and complex style with palpable veins of both bluegrass, old-time, and the emerging Contest Style.

94. Although Texas Shorty attended the Weiser contest after his elimination at Missoula, he did not compete at Weiser in 1964; he did not compete there until after he retired, in 2004, when he won first place in the Senior Division.

95. The states with the most competitors continue to be Idaho, Oregon, Montana, and Washington, with smaller contingents from other western states such as Arizona, California, and Colorado, and in modern times fiddlers have competed in the contest from countries such as Canada, Japan, Sweden, and France.

96. Other "national" and global fiddle contests have included those in Arkansas (Mountain View), Kansas (Winfield), Union Grove (North Carolina), the International Old-Time Fiddlers Contest (North Dakota), Oklahoma (Grove), National Oldtime Fiddlers' and Step-dancing Contest (Vermont), and National Fiddle Fest (Virginia); the Smithsonian's Festival of American Folklife sponsored national contests. Langley, Oklahoma, held a World Series of Fiddling for several years, and Cortez, Colorado, held a Super Bowl of Fiddling. Branson, Missouri, had a "World Fiddling Championships." The Grand North American Old Time Fiddle Championship has been held in Edmonton, Alberta, since 1981. Crockett, Texas, has hosted a world championship since 1937.

97. In this writer's opinion.

98. Johnson seems to me to be a bridge between old-time and emerging progressive, Texas, and Contest Style. His music was studied by many Missouri fiddlers, and his versions of familiar tunes like "Grey Eagle" and "Billy in the Low Ground" stated the core melodies and presented them with tone, clarity, and perfection that few fiddlers could match. See Jeanine R. Orme, *Herman Johnson, Master Fiddler: 39 Solos by America's Legendary Fiddler*; his LPs are *Champion Fiddlin'* (American Heritage P-120, 1968) and *National Champion* (John's 86-34, 1978). Orme published a learning guide, *The Fiddlin' Workshop*, based on extensive studies with Johnson. As quoted by Andrew Daring, Johnson described his process of becoming a champion in comments much like those of Benny Thomasson and others. "I had to change my style considerably when I began to compete. They had changed their hoedowns quite a lot, fiddlers in the state of Texas. Some of the fiddlers had been doing a lot of work on their tunes, had been building on to them, adding parts. Because they had been having contests a good many years before I started going to them in 1960." Daring, "The Diffusion of Texas Style Fiddling to Non-Fiddlers," https://texasfiddle.pro/the-diffusion-of-texas-style-fiddle-to-non-fiddlers. This mirrors Benny Thomasson's remarks about losing his first contests and going home and working out variations, new parts, and improvisations for his contest tunes (Phillips, *Contest Fiddling*).

99. Vivian Williams, April 25, 2008, https://www.FiddleHangout.com. See also Mark O'Connor, "Remembering 'the Undefeated Champion,' Herman Johnson."

100. For O'Connor, see "My History at Weiser" (https://www.idahobluegrassassociation.org); see also Phillips, *Contest Fiddling*; and Beisswenger, *North American Fiddle Music*, 93, 94.

101. McMahan, September 19, 1997.

102. Phil Williams, January 15, 2014. I judged two of the Junior Divisions in 2005 and attest to the truth in the joke; judges in my panel that year could identify by name what fiddle teachers and tune transcriptions many of the youngsters had worked with.

103. Phil Williams to Karen Penner, National Oldtime Fiddlers' Contest, November 10, 2008 (courtesy of Williams).

104. O'Connor's 1975 LP, *National Junior Champion* (Rounder 0046), was much admired and studied, as fiddlers young and old were rightly impressed with the youngster. Tunes on the LP reflected Mark's contest pieces. Notably, the guitar accompaniment by Charlie Collins (with mandolin by Norman Blake) was *not* today's predominant sock-chord/swing accompaniment style.

105. Phil Williams, June 2009. Vivian and Phil Williams of Seattle attended, competed in, and recorded Weiser contests since 1964.

106. I competed in the Senior Division in 2005, 2006, 2009, 2010, and 2012 and Senior-Senior Division in 2021 (winning first place).

6. Dale Pauley—"Let's Play that Uptown Stuff"

1. Unless otherwise indicated, quotes are from interviews with Dale and Mary Ruth Pauley principally on December 7, 2016, and February 15, 2017. The Tuesday-night fiddle sessions with Dale Pauley (and others) were put on hiatus due to the COVID-19 pandemic of 2020, and in mid-April 2021, year two of the pandemic, we resumed with necessary health precautions. Pauley's "Anniversary Waltz" is included on the CD with *Fiddler's Dream*.

2. "English" in Missouri typically means British Isles Protestant ancestry—Scotch-Irish, Scots, and Welsh in addition to English heritage; the term "Old-Stock American" is frequently

used for this broad group of people who tended to be dominant in the politics and economy of early Missouri. Unlike many Missourians who identify as part of an ethnic population, such as French American, Irish Catholic, African American, German American, or Latino, Dale Pauley's forebears did not retain details of their background; they simply were Americans.

3. The small park is on Ashley Street, adjacent to the Veterans of Foreign Wars Post 280, and now bracketed by the power plant and Interstate 70.

4. Pauley, December 7, 2016.

5. Pauley, December 13, 2016.

6. Dale and Mary Ruth enjoyed the *M*A*S*H* TV show, but Dale says, "It wasn't like that." February 15, 2017.

7. Pauley, December 7, 2016.

8. Pauley, December 7, 2016.

9. Pauley, December 2, 2018; Thompson typically played "Don't Let the Deal Go Down," "Beaumont Rag," and other Texas and Oklahoma contest tunes.

10. Pauley, November 8, 2018.

11. "Dale Pauley Tops Fiddlers; McCowan Takes First Prize" and "Win in Fiddlers Contest," *Columbia Missourian*, August 10, 1961.

12. Pauley, February 15, 2017; for "Marmaduke's," see David Brinkman, "Marmaduke's Hornpipe: A Study of Four Versions"; Howard Wight Marshall, "'Marmaduke's Hornpipe': Speculations on the Life and Times of a Historic Missouri Fiddle Tune"; and Marshall, chap. 6 of *"Play Me Something Quick and Devilish."* For hokum, see *"Play Me Something Quick and Devilish,"* 188ff. Among Internet explanations are those by Casey Willis and Ian Walsh.

13. Lourdes Medrano, "Beards, Fiddlers Entertain at Rodeo Week Contests," *Arizona Daily Star*, February 24, 1986. Bruce Wurst is a music teacher in Phoenix and author of teaching materials such as *The American Fiddle Method.*

14. See Glenda Young, "Super Bowl Fiddle Contest and Country Jamboree," *Bluegrass Unlimited* (1984): 34–38, referenced in Beisswenger, *North American Fiddle Music*, 100.

15. At the July 1987 Cortez contest, Pauley received a NOTFA certificate: "The above-named performer, having fulfilled the requirements of performing in accordance with National Oldtime Fiddlers' Contest rules, and for the purpose of preserving authentic and traditional oldtime fiddling, is hereby acknowledged as a Participating Contestant."

16. Mary Ruth Pauley, December 2, 2018.

17. Mary Ruth Pauley, December 2, 2018.

18. Dale Pauley, December 20, 2016.

19. Composed by Irvin T. Rouse in 1938 to commemorate the celebrated and luxurious Seaboard Line passenger train running from New York to Miami, the tune is scorned by most fiddlers as a boring string of whinkerdinks, but in fact there is something of a nice tune inside all the pyrotechnics and staginess fighting to get out. Everyone except fiddlers seem to think of it as "the fiddlers' national anthem." The commercial recording that started the fashion for "OBS" was Bill Monroe and the Bluegrass Boys' 1942 78-rpm Bluebird record featuring Art Wooten's fiddling, although an excellent earlier recording on Bluebird was by the superb fiddler Tommy Magness with Roy Hall and His Blue Ridge Entertainers in 1938. See Marshall, *"Play Me Something Quick and Devilish"*; and Kuntz, *Fiddler's Companion*.

20. Marshall, *"Play Me Something Quick and Devilish,"* 153. Incidentally, the August 1961 Boone County Fair contest was settled by audience applause, a feature from former times.

21. Dale Pauley, February 13, 2018.

22. Dale Pauley, October 9, 2018. Western movie star and singer Rex Allen composed "Arizona Waltz," recorded it in 1949 (78 rpm, Mercury 6203), and sang it in *The Arizona Cowboy* (directed by R. G. Springsteen, Republic Pictures, 1950). See Phillips, *Traditional American Fiddle Tunes*, 2:238.

23. Bud Wyatt, November 29, 2018.

24. On jam-session etiquette, see, for example, Paul Anastasio, "Order Out of Chaos; or, How to Play in a Group"; Cathy Barton and Dave Para, "Carp Camp: A Singular Jam"; Drew Beisswenger, "Jam Sessions in Southwest Missouri"; Howard Wight Marshall, "Jam Session Etiquette; or, Notes on the Care and Feeding of an American Tradition with Special Reference to Old-Time Fiddling" and throughout *"Play Me Something Quick and Devilish"* and *Fiddler's Dream*; Phillip Nusbaum, "Music and Socializing: The Public Jam Sessions at Warren's Place"; and Vivian Williams, "Jam Session Etiquette."

25. This session custom is markedly different from the Appalachian-derived custom of playing a tune comparatively much longer, and with all the fiddlers playing the melody at once, which helps create what they call a "groove" (see Spencer Galloway remarks about his impressions of the Galax, Virginia, fiddlers' convention in the 1970s in chapter 2).

7. Traditions Tested: Fiddle Contests in the 1980s and 1990s

1. Stacy Phillips: "The roots of the revolution [modern Contest Fiddling] are really in the 1920s and then during the World War II years!" Phillips, "What's Wrong with Fiddle Contest Judging?" As early as 1972, fiddlers and fiddle scholars were calling attention to the rise of the Texas-style fiddle and guitar backup at major contests; see, for example, Vivian Williams, "Some Random Guesses about Why Fiddle Styles Developed the Way They Did in Certain Regions, and What Is Happening Here Now" and "Weiser 1972—a Subjective Summary"; Neil Johnston, "Folk Fiddling, Part I: Which Direction—Preservation or Development?" and "Folk Fiddling, Part II: Which Direction—Preservation or Development?"

2. Among numerous references are, for example, Christeson's "Old-Time Fiddling in Missouri"; and Goertzen, "Transformation of American Contest Fiddling," 107ff.

3. I appreciate assistance from Bill Shull and Charlie Walden in preparing this material.

4. At various stages in the founding years of MSOTFA, Walden worked toward a PhD in robot engineering at the university. Germain graduated and began a career as a violin maker and author. Shull took his law degree at the university and began a career in legal-aid services. Galloway graduated and worked for many years at the *Columbia Daily Tribune*; Hagan, after service in Vietnam as a US Army combat demolitions officer, took a master's degree in sociology at the university and taught classes.

5. Bill Shull helped Gene Rands (a nephew of Missouri fiddler Bill Kearns) and other founders of the Minnesota State Old-Time Fiddlers' Contest in Cotton secure their state government's imprimatur in 1984 in order to prevent other towns, such as Duluth (which held successful fiddle contests), from claiming the state contest. Bill Kearns, August 4, 2009. Kearns helped establish the Minnesota State Contest and secured the judging panel its first year, 1981, Missourians Bill Eddy, Pete McMahan, and Hubert Skidmore. Bill Kearns Collection, Western Historical Manuscript Collection. The Minnesota state contest adopted some Missouri rules, such as allowing no more than two accompanists, but incorporated rules from the National Oldtime Fiddlers' Contest (for example, judges to be sequestered and unable to see contestants perform).

6. “Fiddlin’ Champ’s Hobby Wins Him State Trophy, Bringing the Total to 60,” *Columbia Missourian*, September 14, 1979, A8.

7. Andy Maykuth, “Fiddlin’ around Backstage,” *Columbia Daily Tribune*, September 18, 1979, 55. See also “Fiddlin’ Champ’s Hobby Wins Him State Trophy.” McBaine’s “Amati” violin was a copy from a quality German shop.

8. “Fiddlers Carry on Tradition in Wein,” *Marceline (MO) Press*, May 25, 1995, 1. The article includes interview material with Charlie Walden, Nile Wilson, and thirteen-year-old John Williams, who was learning tunes and technique from Wilson; other fiddlers at Wein in 1995 included Bill Shull and Howard Marshall.

9. See Marshall, “Hand-in-Hand.”

10. Casey L. Penn, “Megan Lynch Chowning: Playing with a Purpose,” *Fiddler Magazine* 22, no. 1 (2015): 24. Lynch Chowning, from Redding, California, works as a teacher and professional fiddler in Nashville. “Megan won a youth division at Weiser at eight and focused thoroughly on mastering the repertoire and perfected style that would win contests ‘when contests were all the rage and genre lines were beginning to blur. She has strong opinions about each phenomenon.’ “She feels both pride and concern over today’s ‘contest scene,’ which she unwittingly helped to create”; many of her students are contest champions.

11. Jim Wood, “A ‘Winning’ Contest Round, Part One,” 33. The article includes a transcription with variations and jazz chords for swing-guitar backup for “Dusty Miller,” a core tune in Contest Style fiddling; he offers a waltz in “A ‘Winning’ Contest Round, Part Two,” 42–43. See also Jim Wood, “A Winning Contest Round for Beginners” and “Play It! The Science of Contest Fiddling,” with transcriptions of three tunes, “Tom and Jerry,” “Rose of Sharon,” and “Beaumont Rag.”

12. For controlled improvisation in jazz (Charlie Parker, Claude Williams) and Contest Style (Terry Morris), articulated by champion Deena Bistodeau in “Texas Style Controlled Improvisation and the American Fiddle Contest,” “Texas Style Controlled Improvisation and the American Fiddle Contest, Part II,” “Texas Style Controlled Improvisation and the American Fiddle Contest, Part III,” “Texas Style Controlled Improvisation and the American Fiddle Contest, Part IV”; and Marshall, chap. 8 of *Fiddler’s Dream*.

13. See Carolyn Osborne, “Contest Fiddling: What Gets Rewarded.”

14. In May 2014, I attended the Stovall’s Grove contest in west St. Louis County; there, Roger Netherton’s contest round was disqualified because he played in cross-tuning. Although many fiddlers agreed that this was a questionable disqualification, the 2014 rules of the contest state, “Standard tuning of strings (E–A–D–G) must be used.” Rules were available online and at the contest registration table.

15. Among ideas to fill the gap with MSOTFA on hiatus, in July 2009, a Mid America Fiddlers’ Association was proposed at a contest in Boonesboro, led by Junior and Cathy Marriott, Lynn Wells, Lynn’s daughter Elisha, and others. Members were enrolled, donations accepted, and plans made for new contests, helping with ongoing contests, and funding lessons; the new association did not gather enough support to become established.

16. Howard Wight Marshall, “Bill Shull.”

17. Rob Roberts, “Missouri Fiddler Charlie ‘Possum’ Walden,” 14.

18. Bill Shull, ed., *“Uncle Pink” and Other Central Missouri Fiddle Tunes from Lyman Enloe.* Shull profiled Enloe, as well as Christeson; see Shull, “Lyman Enloe” and “R. P. Christeson.”

19. The Cope Ashlock Invitational Fiddle Contest was broadcast live. Fiddlers invited to the studio to play contest rounds were Taylor McBaine, Jim Gilmore, Travis Inman, Kelly

Jones, Junior Marriott, Pete McMahan, and Nile Wilson. McBaine was in the hospital and listened from his room. Backups were Forrest Rose (bass), guitarists Wes Brown and Kenny Applebee, and Jack Deck (finger-style five-string banjo); Walden served as emcee. Charlie Walden and Julie Youmans, *Cope Ashlock Invitational Live Radio Fiddling Championship, April 9, 1989.*

20. Shull, November 1, 2020.

21. Shull, November 22, 2020.

22. For example, Shull, *"Uncle Pink"*; Shull, "R. P. Christeson"; Shull, *Cross-Tuning Your Fiddle*; Shull, *Guide to Running a Fiddling Contest*; and Shull, "OK, Let's Try It Again." Drew Beisswenger in *North American Fiddle Music: A Research and Information Guide* notes that Shull speaks to problems of judging contests in terms of old-time versus Texas-style fiddling: "Shull argues that good old-time fiddling should be judged based on musicianship and technique rather than on the 'rusticity' of the music" (143).

23. Shull, February 15, 2021.

24. John and Jason Shaw are skilled guitarists as well as fiddlers and accompany each other in contests; for many years, they have competed regularly in Missouri and midwestern fiddle contests and national events such as the highly competitive National Flat-Picking Championships at the Walnut Valley Festival in Winfield, Kansas (winning first or placing high in the divisions for fiddle and for flat-pick guitar at Winfield).

25. Bill Shull, "Missouri Fiddle Contests," 21.

26. Mark O'Connor was fourteen when he dazzled the fiddling world at contests such as the national contest in Weiser, Idaho.

27. "Issues: Sportsmanship," 5.; the author of the unsigned column was Bill Shull.

28. Shull, "Issues: Fiddle Styles and Contest 'Rules,'" 5, https://www.missourifiddling.com.

29. Hill, August 10, 2016.

30. The new leaders considered naming Branson as the Missouri state championships but decided instead on "Mid-America" championships.

31. Bill Shull, "Charlie Walden." I appreciate Walden's consultation in preparing this material.

32. Marshall et al., "Charlie Walden," in *"Now That's a Good Tune,"* 47.

33. Walden is among fiddlers who consider M. M. Cole's *One Thousand Fiddle Tunes*, a 1940 reprint of the classic *Ryan's Mammoth Collection* (1883), to be the most important tune book in former times.

34. Roberts, "Missouri Fiddler Charlie 'Possum' Walden," 12.

35. Walden, "Cyril Winfield Stinnett: Master of Hornpipe and Hoedown."

36. Roberts, "Missouri Fiddler Charlie 'Possum' Walden," 12.

37. Marshall et al., "Charlie Walden," in *"Now That's a Good Tune,"* 46. The 1987 Sedalia contest was not a Missouri State Old Time Fiddlers Association "state contest," but held the same month.

38. Walden profile, Ozark Heritage Music Festival (West Plains, MO), June 2019.

39. Roberts, "Missouri Fiddler Charlie 'Possum' Walden."

40. Roberts, "Missouri Fiddler Charlie 'Possum' Walden."

41. Marshall et al., "Charlie Walden," in *"Now That's a Good Tune,"* 46.

42. Album notes, *Patt & Possum: Hoe-Downs, Hornpipes & Hokum* (Marimac 5062C, 1994). Patt grew up in Henry County, Illinois; her grandfather Carl Voorhees was a well-known

fiddler. She calls square dances, is a jig dancer, led an Irish band called the Broken Pledge Ceili Band, and accompanies Charlie on ukulele as well as keyboards.

43. For example, Charlie Walden, "Travels with Charlie: Part One: To Shetland—by Rail, by Air, by Sea."

44. Later, an expanded list appeared on Walden's website, "One Hundred Essential Missouri Fiddle Tunes." Walden also plays numerous Ozarks-specific tunes.

45. *Dance around Molly* (Walden, 2016); Walden and Plunkett play "Grey Eagle" on a compilation, *The Young Fogies, Vol. II* (Rounder CD 0369, 1995); Walden plays "Durang's Hornpipe" on a compilation cassette from the 1996 Galax fiddlers' convention, *61st Old Fiddlers' Convention* (Heritage Records HRC-C-173, cassette, 1997).

46. Roberts, "Missouri Fiddler Charlie 'Possum' Walden."

47. Walden and Bill Shull, listening to the complex, fancy waltzes being played in contests by fiddlers such as Junior Marriott and Travis Inman in the 1980s and 1990s, called them "designer waltzes," an apt description.

48. Walden profile, Ozark Heritage Music Festival (West Plains, MO), June 2019.

49. Walden's numerous projects continue to provide strong performances and classic tunes. Among other projects were *Draggin' the Bow* (1996) and, with guitarist Mike Miller, *Possum and Wichita—Old-Time and Hot Fiddling: Recorded Live at the North Central Regional Fiddlers Competition, Hillsdale, Michigan, August 11, 2001* (https://www.charliewalden.com). In 2010, he published a two-volume set, *Missouri Fiddle Tunes*, vol. 1, *Fast and Slow for Learning*, as a learning aid; music CDs of Walden playing the tunes are available online.

50. In 2021, Walden was inducted in the North American Fiddlers' Hall of Fame. He was announced for induction in 2020, but the COVID-19 pandemic caused Walden's induction to be rescheduled; the North American Fiddlers' Hall of Fame is a function of the New York Old Tyme Fiddlers' Association in Redfield, New York (https://www.nysotfa.com).

51. Inman, March 10, 2021.

52. Howard Wight Marshall, "John Griffin."

53. Others in the money in the Open Division at Boonville, March 1983: second place, Taylor McBaine; third, Charlie Walden; fourth, Bob Atchison; fifth, Jim Gilmore; and sixth, Ray (Lynn) Wells. Others were Bill Eddy, Spencer Galloway, Joe Grable, Bob Hagan, Maggie Sprat, Mike Wells, and Musial Wolfe.

54. Martin Northway, "Making Wood Sing: Only the Best Wood Makes the Cut for John Griffin," 27.

55. Jesse Bogan, "From Timber to Tunes," *Columbia Missourian*, November 22, 2001.

56. "Owner John Griffin and his crew scour the forests for precious trees that are in danger of, as John says, 'becoming bug food.' Once John acquires the appropriate permits, he carefully removes these hand-selected and hand-felled trees from their habitat and brings them back to his shop in Fulton, Missouri, perched on the bluffs overlooking Cedar Creek, for processing and drying. John is a conservationist at heart, and accordingly, is committed to the wise use of our natural resources. He believes selectively harvesting dead, fallen or nearly dead trees is essential for the health and longevity of our forests. 'Old Standard Wood specializes in the direct select harvest of Adirondack from deteriorating old-growth stands.'" Griffin, Bedell Guitars website, https://www.bedellguitars.com.

57. Forrest Rose, "Supplier Sets Standard for Instrument Wood," *Columbia Daily Tribune*, July 19, 2003.

58. Griffin, July 18, 2000.

59. In John Griffin's June 1994 Fulton contest, Open Division winners included John T. White (first place), Travis Inman, and Mike Frazier; Senior Division winners included Pete McMahan (first place), Nile Wilson, Virgil Smith, and Howard Marshall.

60. Griffin, July 18, 2000.

61. Cathy's mother was Edna Mae Davis, a square-dance caller in the Ava area who often teamed up at dances with fiddler Bob Holt and guitarist Alvie Dooms as well as teaching at the Bethel Youth Fiddle Camp; her brother was Larry Schuler, a terrific old-time jig dancer who for years was a regular at Bethel Fiddle Camp square dances.

62. Walden and Youmans, *Cope Ashlock Invitational*, 12.

63. See Bill Shull, "The Stover Connection." Marriott, Jones, and Inman became increasingly famous "in the United States."

64. Galloway, December 20, 2017. The Robert Johnson reference is to the famous 1930s Delta blues guitarist, who, according to legend, took his guitar to the crossroads of Highways 49 and 61 in Clarksdale, Mississippi, and was granted astonishing guitar skills by the devil, in exchange for Johnson's soul. Such Faustian deals with the devil are commonplace throughout history. See Barry Lee Pearson and Bill McCulloch, *Robert Johnson: Lost and Found* (Urbana: University of Illinois Press, 2008).

8. Kelly Jones, Uncompromising Champion

1. Kelly Jones's grandfather Oscar H. Jones farmed in the Moundville community in Vernon County. Oscar's father, Lewis C. Jones, was born 1841 in Carroll County and served in the Eighteenth Missouri Infantry of the Union army in the Civil War, fighting at engagements such as Shiloh and Kennesaw Mountain.

2. Unless otherwise noted, quotes from Kelly Jones are from April 11, 2015.

3. Thomas Jasper Massie's father, John W. Massie, was born in Virginia, his mother in Kentucky. Tom was born in Kentucky. After the Civil War, John Massie brought the family to Vernon County. Charlie Walden, "Daniel Boone Jones: Early Radio Fiddler," 5; Marshall, chap. 1 of *"Play Me Something Quick and Devilish."*

4. The Forrester LPs Jones studied are *Fancy Fiddlin' Country Style* (MGM Cub 8008, 1960) and *Fiddlin' Country Style* (United Artists 3295, 1963).

5. For the Ozark Opry and other formative country shows, and fiddlers who made careers as entertainers, see Marshall, *"Play Me Something Quick and Devilish"* and *Fiddler's Dream.*

6. In his youth, Lee Mace had volunteered for the Navy late in World War II. He served four years in the Naval Reserve after the war, and in 1950 he was dismayed to be drafted into the Army to fight in the Korean War. Mace's youthful enthusiasm for war had changed. Joyce Mace: "They told him [Kelly Jones] he shouldn't be drafted right up to the day that he was inducted." Dan William Peek, *Live! At the Ozark Opry*, 27–28.

7. The Twenty-Fifth Infantry base at Cu Chi was built northwest of Saigon and Ton Son Nhut Air Force base, near Highway 1 and strongholds of Vietcong forces; Cu Chi was a difficult location for the Americans in a war that had no front line and contended with a largely guerilla-style opposition. Among sources for Cu Chi, see John H. Hay Jr., chap. 13 of *Vietnam Studies: Tactical and Materiel Innovations.*

8. Kelly Jones, December 31, 2008.

9. Lonnie Hoppers, May 23, 2013.

10. "Dardanella" (Felix Bernard and Johnny Black; New York: McCarthy & Fisher, 1919) was recorded in 1919 by Harry Raderman's Jazz Orchestra; another 1919 recording, by Ben Selvin and His Orchestra, sold five million records. A World War I sentimental song, it is included on Kelly Jones, *Through the Years, Volume 1*, a reissue of a 1985 recording with bluegrass fiddler Gordon Terry.

11. Christeson, "Old-Time Fiddling in Missouri," 6.

12. Travis Inman, May 10, 2019.

13. Jones, January 31, 2007. For "Missouri Waltz" history (composed by a ragtime musician in central Missouri), see Howard Wight Marshall, "Notes about 'Missouri Waltz' by a Missouri Fiddler," and chap. 10 of *"Play Me Something Quick and Devilish."*

9. Fiddle Contests from the 2000s Forward

1. It is not inconsequential that the Missouri old-time contest establishment leadership was being hollowed out by time; the last of the most influential village elders, Pete McMahan died in early 2000.

2. Some state fiddle contests allow nonresidents to compete, and others do not. For states bordering Missouri, only Illinois bans nonresidents. Nonresidents may enter state contests in Iowa, Kansas, Oklahoma, Arkansas, Tennessee, and Kentucky. Nebraska no longer has a state contest.

3. By 2000, most Missouri old-time style contest fiddlers had generally accepted the no-more-than-two-accompanists rule. However, older fiddlers may recall, as I do, debates and arguments at contests in the 1960s, in the heyday of bluegrass bands, when fiddlers sometimes brought an ensemble onstage as accompaniment, which could include a five-string banjo, guitar, mandolin, resophonic guitar, and upright bass. Such ensembles did give the fiddler an advantage, thanks to the power of the group sound, and some people rightly complained that such performances were "a band" rather than "a fiddler." Fiddlers who resented the "band" advantage in those days could be equally frustrated today with fiddlers who bring onstage an ensemble of several guitarists and perhaps a bass as well.

4. Even conservative regional contests such as those at Clifftop, West Virginia, and Galax, Virginia, and big contests in Canada saw the effects of the Contest Style that came from the western United States.

5. Some state fiddlers' associations endorse and promote Texas-style contest fiddling; for example, the mission statement of the Colorado Fiddle Championships in Denver each January, sponsored by the Colorado Old Time Fiddlers' Association, states: "The Colorado Old Time Fiddlers' Association (COTFA) acts to promote and preserve through education and training, the traditional American art form known as old-time fiddling, with a special emphasis of Texas-style fiddling." Contestants may have any number of accompanists. Top five in each division progress from round one on Saturday to round two on Sunday's "Texas Style—Open Division," which is open to "Any age. This is a higher level of competition" (https://www.coloradofiddlers.org).

6. https://www.missourifiddling.com/articles.

7. Despite assumptions, competitions at Missouri's state fair are not restricted to fiddlers who earn money with their music. Missouri State Old Time Fiddlers Association contest rules on the Internet in 2020 state: "No contestant shall be disqualified from competition for the reason that he earns all or a substantial part of his income from playing the fiddle" (https://missourifiddling.com/blog/).

8. I was unable to attend in 2018; I appreciate a letter from Thomas Coriell about the contest (August 27, 2018). Open Division winners: first, Junior Marriott; second, Kyle Link (Lebanon); third, Trustin Baker; fourth, Joe Fedrizzi; fifth, Beau Johnston; sixth, John P. Williams; and seventh, Carina Baker.

9. Allen Wyatt, October 3, 2020.

10. At the National Oldtime Fiddlers' Contest in Weiser, Idaho, there are seven divisions: "National Small Fry (less than 9 years of age), National Junior-Junior (less than 13 years of age), National Junior (less than 18 years of age), National Young Adult (18 to 36 years of age), National Adult (37 to 59 years of age), National Senior (60 to 69 years of age), National Senior-Senior (70 years of age and up), National Grand Champion (open to all regardless of age)" (General Contest Rules Amended August 2018; https://www.fiddlecontest.org).

11. Contestants at the Fayette Freeze-Off represented old-time, bluegrass, and Contest Style, and people respected the rules; in 2004, for example the "Adult Division" (ages sixteen to fifty-five; fiddlers were asked to enter their age division, and there was no "open"), the results were first, Travis Inman; second, Bubba Hopkins (Spavinaw, Oklahoma); third, Cody Marriott; fourth, Junior Marriott; fifth, John P. Williams; and sixth, Lynn Wells.

12. Taylor McBaine died in May 1994.

13. The network's statement on accompaniment in contests: "Up to two accompanists are allowed on stage; fiddlers with more than two will not be scored. Accompanist may not duplicate the melody. Any acoustic instrument suitable for an old-time dance is welcome—for example, piano, guitar, mandolin, banjo (4 or 5 string), cello, reed organ, accordion, tenor guitar, bass. Electronic keyboard, if set in plain piano mode only, is welcome. Contestant may have a second violin as backup, but the second fiddler must play chords or backup (no melody or twin fiddling). Solo fiddling is welcome."

14. John Williams, December 15, 2018.

15. Marshall and Williams, *Fiddling Missouri* (Voyager VRCD344); McMahan and Williams's application for the Traditional Arts Apprenticeship Program; John P. Williams, 2019 biographical essay, "Breathing New Life into Missouri Fiddling: John P. Williams," https://www.Oldtime-Central.com, produced by Rachel Krause, posted to Facebook, 2020.

16. Williams, 2019 biographical essay, "Breathing New Life into Missouri Fiddling." I appreciate John Williams's advice in preparing this profile. Through the years, John has been a welcome part of numerous programs I have presented on the history of fiddle music; we appeared (with Dave Para and Cathy Barton) in 2014 at the Big Muddy Folk Festival in Boonville, Missouri, and other festivals. Over the past decades we have played fiddle together at every imaginable venue, and in a sense I represent a middle generation of Little Dixie and central Missouri fiddlers between John and elders he learned from such as Pete McMahan, Taylor McBaine, and Nile Wilson. The farm where I was born in eastern Randolph County is a few miles from the Williams family farm in next-door Monroe County.

17. Duncan's *Deluxe Fiddling Method* was one of the tune books and tutors that increased in number in the 1970s and 1980s as more learners young and old were receiving Suzuki and classical violin instruction and searching for sources for notated fiddle tunes.

18. Williams, October 2, 2020.

19. Williams, October 2, 2020.

20. Williams, 2019 biographical essay, "Breathing New Life into Missouri Fiddling." In 1999, I invited John to join me in recording a CD in Eureka Springs, Arkansas, *Fiddling Missouri,* with Michael Breid (banjo, guitar, melodeon); this was John's first participation in a

commercial CD. In Seattle, John and I recorded a CD with Vivian and Phil Williams, *Fiddle Tunes of the Lewis & Clark Trail.*

21. Williams, 2019 biographical essay, "Breathing New Life into Missouri Fiddling."

22. Williams, "New Fiddle Camp in the Missouri Ozarks." Organized by Liz Amos (then living in Chicago), instructors were Amos, Bob Holt, Fred Stoneking, Dwight Lamb, Cathy Caspar (Chicago), Barbara Weathers, and Mike Frasier; square dancing was taught, with guitar backup by Alvie Dooms, Jim Nelson, Kenny Applebee, and others. At the end of the week, most of the campers signed up for a fiddle contest in West Plains.

23. Wilbur Foss, the father of the long-running contests at Yankton, South Dakota, wrote to John's parents about meeting John at the September 1999 event; in part, Foss wrote, "April 20, 2000. Dear Mr. and Mrs. Williams, Your son John played in our contest in 1999 and I was very much impressed. He is so polite and gives a very good impression to our fans of old time music. I am sure you are very proud of this young man—and you should be. We hope to have him back some time. Give my regards to John and tell him we enjoyed his music and his image of a fine young American teenager" (courtesy of the Williams family).

24. Williams, 2019 biographical essay, "Breathing New Life into Missouri Fiddling."

25. This bit of instruction only works when the student knows the notes on the violin fingerboard, as many learners today do, having had some Suzuki or classical violin instruction before coming to fiddle camp.

26. McMahan's "Ford One Step" is a Montgomery County tune from the area where McMahan grew up; some fiddlers, such as Bill Katon, used the title "Port One Step." See Christeson, *Old-Time Fiddlers Repertory*, 2:42; the tune is on the *"Now That's a Good Tune"* project as well as McMahan's *Ozark Mountain Waltz* cassette. "When You and I Were Young, Maggie" was published in a book of poems called *Maple Leaves* in 1864 by Canadian poet George W. Johnson; the poem was set to music by James A. Butterfield and was being sung in minstrel shows in the 1870s. The melody has been a staple among fiddlers and is among the most requested "two-steps" at dances; the sheet music is found in countless collections of piano music. For Johnson, see Canadian Songwriters Hall of Fame, https://www.cshf.ca. Jake Hockemeyer's title was "Hams Prairie Round Dance" (for the South Callaway County community).

27. *Monroe County Influences, Vol. 1* with Matt Wyatt, guitar, Jeff Elsoo, five-string banjo; Williams appears on Marshall and Williams, *Fiddling Missouri*; *Fiddle Tunes of the Lewis & Clark Era*; Williams and Mackey, *A Tribute to Lonnie Robertson, Vol. 1*; and *Norma Lou's Waltz.* Williams's version of McMahan's "Gilsaw" is on the companion CD that accompanies Marshall, *Fiddler's Dream.* There are videos of Williams teaching, performing in fiddle contests, and playing in jam sessions on YouTube, Facebook, and other sites in cyberspace.

28. Cathey is featured in Olivia Garrett, "Statewide Program Preserves and Passes on Traditional Folk Arts," *Columbia Missourian*, March 21, 2019.

29. Williams, 2019 biographical essay, "Breathing New Life into Missouri Fiddling."

30. Rachel Krause interview with John Williams, 2019.

31. Richard Shewmaker, February 14, 2021.

32. Shewmaker, February 23, 2021.

33. Missourians at Yankton included W. W. Bone, Bob Brandon, Johnny Bruce, Leroy Canaday, Ray Curbow, Joe Fedrizzi, Ed Grable, Jake Hockemeyer, Travis Inman, Dean

Johnston, Junior Marriott, Howard Marshall, Pete McMahan, Cyril Stinnett, Alita Stoneking, Fred Stoneking, Gene Wells, Lynn Wells, Mike Wells, John Williams, and Matt Wyatt.

34. Others placing in the National Invitational Division: first place, Kevin Blom (Wisconsin, in 2020 living in the Kansas City area); second, Deena Bistodeau (Minnesota); third, Howard Marshall; fourth, Michelle Schettler (Minnesota); fifth, Nate Kemperman (Iowa); sixth, Shewmaker; seventh, Jay Kelly (Nebraska); the judging panel in 2009 consisted of Dwight Lamb, Sharon Graf, and Musial Wolfe. Shewmaker and I played guitar accompaniment for each other in the contest. Shewmaker returned to Yankton in 2010 but arrived after the close of registration and thus unable to compete in the contest.

35. Unless otherwise noted, Baker quotes are from January 13, 2021.

36. Terry Morris, from Fort Worth, was a charismatic, phenomenal champion among a generation of creative young Texas-style fiddlers in the 1970s and 1980s. Morris became aware of the difference between playing the fiddle and "just sawing" when he first heard Benny Thomasson (Cliff Fryer, "Terry Morris"). His arrangements of contest performance tunes continue to be studied by fiddlers inside the Texas/Contest Style and beyond. Morris's "Apple Blossom" "Hot Springs," "Bill Cheatem," "Billy in the Low Ground," "Sally Goodin," "Cattle in the Cane," "Darkie's Dream," "Brilliancy," "Hot Foot," "Westmoreland Hornpipe," and "Dusty Miller" are on the *Touch of Texas* album. Terry's older brother Dale Morris Jr. and father, Dale Morris, are also champion Texas fiddlers.

37. Katherine Cummings, "Youth Keep Fiddling Heritage Going," *Fulton Sun*, August 7, 2012. Open Division winners at Fulton: first, John Williams; second, Lynn Wells; and third, Trustin Baker.

38. https://www.thebakerfamilybluegrasscom. The Baker Family Band has won awards, such as Society for the Preservation of Blue Grass Music in America's Midwest Album of the Year (for *Walking a Straight Path*) and Fiddle Player of the Year (Trustin); CDs available through their website include *Walking a Straight Path*, *If it Ain't Love*, and *Seeing the Invisible: 20/20* (2020). In 2018, Jay Shann of Claremont, Oklahoma, joined the band to play five-string banjo and resophonic ("Dobro") guitar.

39. I appreciate Roger's assistance in this writing, as well as that of his mother, Robin Netherton.

40. Geoff Seitz, November 27, 2020. Netherton learned a version of "Ookpik Waltz" from Seitz's album *The Good Old Days Are Here*.

41. Roger Netherton, November 22, 2020. Roger demonstrates "pulse" bowing in a YouTube video, "Old Time Fiddle Bowing Demo: The Pulse," self-recorded in his dorm room at the University of Missouri, June 2017, and using the tune "Sail Away Ladies." Rachel Eddy likewise teaches "Bow Pulsation" in a YouTube video for MidSouth Folk Sessions, recorded in West Virginia in 2017.

42. Robin Netherton, Facebook.

43. Netherton, November 22, 2020.

44. The Gill X-5 violin was presented by J. J. Hanson, Beautiful Music Violin Shop, Lawrence, Kansas. Gill violins are traditional prizes in junior and adult divisions at Winfield, and this is the fifth Gill violin Netherton has won there. The Heinrich Gill firm was founded in the 1950s in Bubenreuth, in the famous violin-making Bavarian region of Germany.

45. *Roger Netherton* is available at https://www.rogernetherton.com.

10. Travis InMan—"I Try to Play it Clean"

1. Unless otherwise noted, Travis Inman quotations come from an interview by Howard Marshall and Margot McMillen in Wheatland, Missouri, May 10, 2019. I appreciate Inman's help, in preparing this chapter, and help from his cousin Diane Peck.

2. Inman, April 10, 2011.

3. Inman, March 10, 2011.

4. Hazel Inman's mother's maiden name was Della Swearngin. Memorial notes, Hazel Lucille Inman, https://www.findagrave.com.

5. Tahlequah is the location of tribal headquarters of the Cherokee Nation. Travis Inman notes that the name is spelled in various ways, with most spellings as "Swearingin" and "Swearingen," but Travis's branch spells the name "Swearngin." Some family members spell the name "Swanigan." Travis's Swearngin branch of the family "are not on the Dawes Rolls [the Oklahoma tribal headquarters' roster of officially sanctioned Cherokee names], because they didn't make it that far; they escaped from the Trail of Tears somewhere in northern Arkansas and moved north into Missouri. Kate apparently died on the reservation in Oklahoma in the 1950s" (Amber Gaddy interview, April 12, 2012).

6. See N. Julian Castro, "From the Tennessee River to Tahlequah: A Brief History of Cherokee Fiddling," *Chronicles of Oklahoma* 67, no. 4 (2009–10): 400. Castro mentions Travis Inman in the West Plains Ozark Heritage Festival online promotion from the 2006 event: "Travis Inman, a renowned, award-winning fiddle player, came from a family steeped in the tradition of performers such as John 'Doc' Swearingen [sic.] and Kate Swearingen; the latter was the Oklahoma state fiddling champion in the 1920s."

7. The obituary for John D. Swearngin Jr. (1940–2011), called "Doc," is available via the Davis-Miller Funeral Home, Lincoln, Missouri. Doc Swearngin was born in Warsaw, Missouri.

8. Gaddy interview with Inman, April 12, 2012. Inman's composition "John Swearngin's Hornpipe" is named for his great-uncle.

9. Performer profile, Old-Time Music Ozark Heritage Festival, West Plains, June 2008.

10. Robert F. Inman served as a private first class in the US Army in World War II.

11. Crockerville ("Crocker" in local usage) was an unincorporated hamlet east of Cole Camp in Benton County; there is a town called Crocker in the Ozarks west of Dixon (Pulaski County). The exact details of the chain-saw incident are not known to this writer.

12. It may have been 1975, and Travis's first contest at Warsaw the following year may have been 1976; such details are often unclear in oral tradition. In oral history, the location and the event are more important to people than the precise date of the event.

13. Performer profile, Old-Time Music Ozark Heritage Festival, West Plains, June 2008. This contest was the 1975 Warsaw Jubilee Days contest. Travis fiddled "Boil the Cabbage Down," "Maple Leaf Waltz" (learned from an LP of waltzes), and "Old Joe Clark" and won first in the Junior Division.

14. Gaddy interview. Inman learned "Billy in the Low Ground" from Virgil Burns, whose wife was a Cherokee woman from Oklahoma; their farm was about ten miles from the Inman family's farm. An Uncle Dave Macon song, "Old Blue Mule" was recorded by Lonnie Robertson, Art Galbraith, Bob Holt, Glenn Rickman, and others in the Ozarks; I recorded Rickman, of Crane, Missouri, fiddling it in 1975 in a visit for the Smithsonian's Festival of American Folklife. Gordon McCann recorded Rickman playing the tune in 1980, and it is transcribed in Beisswenger and McCann, *Ozarks Fiddle Music*, 112.

15. That rule may have appeared in Warsaw rules, but I have not encountered it elsewhere (nor in Warsaw contests in which I participated). Richard (Dickie) Phillips (1920–91, Sedalia, Pettis County) began playing fiddle at age four by holding the violin in his lap and bowing left-handed. He performed professionally, playing guitar with such nationally popular bands as Spike Jones and his City Slickers, for country star Tex Williams, in orchestras for Pat Boone, and on the Arthur Godfrey TV show; his unorthodox method of playing guitar has been likened to playing piano. Phillips was also a well-known pedal-steel guitar player in country music.

16. Gaddy interview.

17. As Jim McGreevy recalls, Woodrow and his three daughters performed at Silver Dollar City before 1978. "The girls were all pretty good musicians—probably played more than just one instrument, and sang very well. I guess Woody was the fiddler." One of the daughters married Arkansas fiddler Cotton Combs (McGreevy, January 31, 2021).

18. Inman, *Championship Fiddling* (1998). Herman Johnson's two influential LPs are *Champion Fiddlin* (American Heritage P-120, 1968, the year of his first national championship at Weiser) and *National Champion* (John's Music 86-34, 1978); for transcriptions and a CD, see Orme, *Herman Johnson, Master Fiddler*.

19. Inman learned "High Level Hornpipe" as a teenager from Canadian fiddler Graham Townsend's LP *Championship Fiddle Favorites* (1964, 1969); Inman, May 19, 2019. Most fiddlers of my acquaintance point to Howdy Forrester's records as their source.

20. Bill Kearns was a tall, stout railroad brakeman; a genial fellow, Bill could appear intimidating under the right circumstances; Kearns and his friend Bill Eddy (both from Slater, Missouri) were solid old-time fiddlers of the older generation, from Saline County, and frequent contest participants and judges.

21. Marshall interviews with Inman, May 10, 2019, March 10, 2021.

22. At most contests in Missouri in the 2020s, the purse is similar to the purse fifty years ago; prize money has seldom kept up with inflation. By custom in Missouri, fiddlers give their accompanists 20 percent of whatever amount of money they win (however many accompanists there are, the 20 percent is divided among them).

23. "Weiser records" is shorthand for the compilation LP records produced in the 1960s and 1970s of contestants at the National Oldtime Fiddlers' Contest in Weiser, some of whom were excellent waltz players. "Memory Waltz" was composed by Nashville fiddler Howdy Forrester and played by numerous fiddlers at Weiser and across the continent; "Yellow Rose Waltz" was popularized by Texas Shorty (Jim Chancellor) on a 45-rpm record (Goldenbow GO-1016-2, ca. 1960). Among Charlie Walden's videos posted on YouTube are Kelly Jones playing "Memory Waltz" at Bethel Youth Fiddle Camp in 1988 and Travis Inman playing "Yellow Rose Waltz" at Bethel in 2014.

24. Vivian Williams, March 3, 2021.

25. Inman, May 19, 2019, March 3, 2021. Harold Allen, *Waltz Around* (American Heritage AH-401-506). "Yellow Rose Waltz" does not appear on any of the LP records produced by the National Oldtime Fiddlers' Contest itself from 1966 to 1979 (Vivian Williams, February 5, 2021).

26. Inman said that he would have liked to go to Weiser, a three-day trip by automobile and some seventeen hundred miles, after he turned sixty in 2023 (when he would have qualified for the Senior Division).

27. "Blue Water Hornpipe" is the regional folk title for this tune; its title in tune books is "Garfield's Hornpipe" or "President Garfield's Hornpipe." Named in honor of President James A. Garfield (assassinated in 1883), this great tune was composed by Harry Carlton and published in 1883 in *Ryan's Mammoth Collection* (137) and repeated verbatim in Cole's *1000 Fiddle Tunes* in 1940 (101); it is in Charlie Walden's list of "100 Essential Missouri Fiddle Tunes." Stinnett helped popularize the "Garfield's" title in the 1960s; among some fiddlers, whether one uses the "Blue Water" or "Garfield's" title indicates the fiddler's source for knowing the tune; if one uses "Blue Water," it is most likely that the fiddler is principally an ear musician.

28. "Boil the Cabbage Down" is a common square-dance tune that is usually considered too simplistic to impress judges, but some contest fiddlers have made a point of evolving the old chestnut into a highly improvised, extended, and complex piece—with "meat and potatoes"—that can charm judges.

29. Inman announced the tune in contests as "Garfield's Hornpipe" in case judges are not aware of its regional title, "Blue Water Hornpipe."

30. The original title is "Cabri Waltz," a Canadian tune named for the town in Saskatchewan; the title is often mistaken as "Capri Waltz," and "Blackhawk Waltz" is an alternate title in the folk process of shifting tune titles. Joe Pancerzewski's "Cabri Waltz" is on the 1972 Voyager LP *The Fiddling Engineer* (VRLP 302), and Pete McMahan's version, mistakenly titled "Capri Waltz," is reissued on McMahan's *50 Old-Time Fiddle Gems.*

31. "Rosebuds of Avamore" is one of the region's alternate titles for a fine waltz called "The Rosebud of Allenvale" by Scottish fiddler and composer J. Scott Skinner in the 1920s; sometimes fiddlers use Howdy Forrester's title for it, "Rose of Sharon."

32. In former times, a fiddler might play a schottische, polka, or jig as the tune of choice, but rags have become more dominant (with the occasional polka) as one's tune of choice, with their potential for display of improvisational jazzy and swingy performance. In the 2020s, the only time a schottische, march, air, or a jig is apt to be heard is when a contest fiddler decides to make an "old-time" statement and let the score sheets be hanged.

33. Walden, "Radiophone WOS and WOS Radio Reunion and Fiddling Championship."

34. Inman, March 10, 2021.

35. Inman, April 14, 2019.

36. Inman, May 19, 2019.

37. Bob Holt did not habitually fiddle that fast in his younger years; when he lived in Iowa, he played bluegrass and country music. Later, in Ava, Missouri, he played faster to please square dancers there, and he was typecast in the 1980s as an ultrafast "Ozark" fiddler by arts councils, festivals, collectors, and program agencies; Bob went along with the typecasting, and many young fiddlers learned from Bob and adopted his speedy tempos.

38. Holt's sitting position helped him endure long square dances at Bethel, made longer than usual because fiddle campers were being taught to square dance with the seasoned dancers. Bob Holt had a time limit of seven minutes for a square dance, which he would enforce when the occasion called for doing so. He would lay his wristwatch on the floor between his feet and keep track. When five or six minutes elapsed, Bob would begin giving the square-dance caller focused stares and nods, and these physical motions signaled the caller that the dance was reaching his time limit and that he would be winding down the tune when the time reached seven minutes.

39. Sophia Cunningham was an apprentice of John Williams in the Traditional Arts Apprenticeship Program in 2017–18. Among articles about the Cunningham girls, who are

homeschooled, are Katherine Cummings, "Youth Keep Fiddling Heritage Going," *Fulton Sun*, August 7, 2012; "Fiddling Sisters Are Four of a Kind," *Fulton Sun*, June 28, 2015; and Helen Wilbers, "Cunningham Sisters Learn to Play Fiddle Together," *Fulton Sun*, August 24, 2017

40. Cammie Cunningham, February 7, 2021. The tune book the Cunningham girls have is David Brody's *Fiddler's Fakebook*.

41. A Frankie Kelly waltz popularized by Lee Stoneking and Fred Stoneking; Kelly's chord progressions in his waltzes are sometimes complex and include key changes; as Travis said, "It goes into netherland" (May 19, 2019).

42. An old tune that was dressed up and popularized by Kenny Baker on Bill Monroe's 1972 *Uncle Pen* (Decca DL7-5438) and frequently played in Missouri fiddle contests by Taylor McBaine, whose version was admirable.

43. Liz Kehl, February 18, 2021. "I have four children. My oldest two were born in Springfield, and the younger two in Sedalia, around the time I was studying with Travis."

44. Inman, June 19, 2020. The recording is the 1971 LP *The Legend of Clark Kessinger* (County 773). Fred Stoneking also played a sterling version of this great tune.

45. Jim Ruth, February 8, 2022.

11. The Stonekings

1. Some of this material comes from Howard Wight Marshall, "An Evening with Lee Roy Stoneking, with a Few Unexpurgated and Incomplete Comments on Field Recording Traditional Artists during the Heyday of the Folk Festival and Fiddlers' Contest Revival" (based on my visit and recording in 1975 for the Smithsonian Institution).

2. Wilbur Foss referred to Lee Stoneking as "old smoothie." Various Artists, *Missouri Old-Time Fiddling*. Lee Stoneking's "Willott's Hornpipe" is also on this cassette, and he appears on another Wilbur Foss tape, *Jarle Foss and His Friends*.

3. "The Gold Rush" was a popular number coauthored in 1968 by Byron Berline and Bill Monroe (the title was Monroe's; Eddie Collins, "Gold Rush"); later issued by Kenny Baker on his *Master Fiddler* LP, the instrumental is essential in the bluegrass repertoire. See also Neil V. Rosenberg and Charles Wolfe, in *The Music of Bill Monroe*, 158.

4. Brad Leftwich and Linda Higginbotham, in documents with *Lee Stoneking: Missouri Fiddling and Banjo Playing from the Collection of Linda Higginbotham and Brad Leftwich*.

5. "Fisher's Hornpipe" was often played in the key of G by fiddlers of earlier generations; in central and northern Missouri, it is often played in F.

6. For Loveall, see Marshall, chap. 4 of *Fiddler's Dream*; a sample of his fiddling is on the companion CD that accompanies that book. By the later 1940s, Red Loveall had moved to San Francisco, where he flourished as a swing fiddler on radio and television and recording with country singers such as Rusty Draper (from Kirksville, Missouri).

7. Ira W. Ford, *Traditional Music of America*, 123; Christeson, *Old-Time Fiddler's Repertory*, 1:178; other book settings include Beisswenger and McCann, *Ozarks Fiddle Music*, 90 (from Fiddlin' Sam Long, 1926). Brad Leftwich (violin) and Dan Gellert (banjo) have Lee Stoneking's version on *A Moment in Time*; Geoff Seitz's version is on the Ill-Mo Boys, *Laugh and Grow Fat*.

8. Published as "Fiddles! Fiddles! Fiddles!" in *Saddle Old Spike* album notes.

9. Stoneking, "Fiddles! Fiddles! Fiddles!" Fred moved to Reeds Spring when his wife, Evelyn, needed more courses to obtain her nursing degree at College of the Ozarks in Point Lookout, and, without a job, he found the fiddler position with the Horse Creek Band. The

Stonekings moved to Springfield in the mid-1980s, then to Bolivar in 2006 to retire in what he considered a slower-paced, more family-friendly town.

10. Paul Roberts, "Recollections of a Missouri Country Fiddler," review of Fred Stoneking, *Saddle Old Spike: Fiddle Music from Missouri*.

11. Stoneking, "Fiddles! Fiddles! Fiddles!"

12. In driving horses and mules, "gee" and "haw" are spoken instructions from the driver for turning, "gee" for right, "haw" for commanding a left turn.

13. Stoneking, "Fiddles! Fiddles! Fiddles!" To be fair, there continue to be square dances in which each set of dancers has its one caller (one of the members of the set).

14. Stoneking, "Fiddles! Fiddles! Fiddles!" Travis Inman had a version of this story (from Fred) and recalls that the club, known for its fights, was known as "the bloody bucket."

15. McCann, September 14, 2020.

16. Stoneking, "Fiddles! Fiddles! Fiddles!" The discs may have been made of shellac, coated on one side of hard brown paper and engraved with the music.

17. I have often heard (and spoken), watching a fiddler perform who is (or was) better known as a guitar accompanist, comments such as "Too bad he wants to play the fiddle—he was a great guitar backup."

18. McMahan, *Missouri Fiddlin'*; *Missouri Fiddlin' No. 3* (with Jack Deck, five-string banjo), reissued on *50 Old-Time Fiddle Gems*. Here Stoneking plays a Martin D-18 guitar.

19. Fred Stoneking, "Recollections of a Missouri Country Fiddler," album notes, to *Saddle Old Spike*. For Stoneking, also Kim Lansford, "Endless Memories: Remembering Fred Stoneking, 1933–2009."

20. Inman, May 19, 2019.

21. For example, see Various Artists, *Missouri Old Time Fiddling*; Stoneking, *Saddle Old Spike*; Various Artists, *Traditional Fiddle Music of the Ozarks*; Various Artists, *Art of Traditional Fiddle*; and Beisswenger and McCann, *Ozarks Fiddle Music*.

22. "Muddy Weather" has an alternate title unsuitable for this publication; "Saddle Old Spike" is an alternate title for a tune usually called "Saddle Old Kate" that appears in Randolph, "Names of Ozark Fiddle Tunes." Drew Beisswenger in Beisswenger and McCann, *Ozarks Fiddle Music*, 126, suggests the tune bears comparison to another Ozarks tune called "Little Home to Go To" (popularized by Bob Holt and others). Honey Creek is a tributary of the South Fork of the Blackwater River in southern Johnson and Lafayette Counties; the Blackwater joins the Lamine River, which empties into the Missouri River west of Boonville.

23. "In Old Arkansas," *Traditional Fiddle Music of the Ozarks, Volume Two: On the Springfield Plain*; "Blackberry Waltz," *The Art of Traditional Fiddle*.

24. Darrel Friend, March 6, 2021.

25. Lucas (Luke) Stoneking is a talented fiddler and competed in contests as a youngster.

26. Colorado Fiddle Championships (Rocky Mountain Fiddle Championships, Denver), 2010 judges' profiles, https://www.coloradofiddlers.org/judges.

27. See Marshall, chap. 8 of *Fiddler's Dream*.

28. Alita Stoneking, November 1, 2020.

29. For example, McMahan, September 17, 1997. Pete wrote album notes for Weisgerber's 1990 cassette *Solitaire*: "I have known Tom Weisgerber for several years and listened to his fiddling improve over those years. And today he is one of the finest fiddlers I have ever heard. His bow movement is incredibly smooth and every note clean, clear and distinct with beautiful

phrasing and those are the credentials of a Top Notch fiddler. I have been associated with Old Time fiddling all of my 72 years and have never heard anyone any better at fiddling than Tom is. So put this tape into your player, turn it on and sit back and listen to and enjoy music that few people ever have the pleasure of hearing to come from a fiddle. Tom is one of the all-time Greats.—Pete McMahan, Harrisburg, MO."

30. Alita Stoneking, November 2, 2020.

12. Bluegrass Festivals

1. A paraphrase of the campground greeting often heard at bluegrass festivals. "Music" means musical instrument in this context. I have attended the majority of the bluegrass festivals noted in this book (including Bean Blossom). I am indebted to Jim McGreevy for his editorial assistance and for sharing his knowledge of the history of Missouri bluegrass.

2. The generic term "bluegrass" appears in print in 1956. Rosenberg, *Bluegrass: A History*, 12–13; Thomas Adler, July 18, 2021.

3. Chubby Wise was arguably the most influential of the pioneering fiddlers with Monroe's band. Paul Shelasky makes a good case for Wise in "Getting Started in Bluegrass Fiddle," noting that "the hallmark" of Chubby Wise, the first fiddler with Bill Monroe's formative Blue Grass Boys, was "his tone; [and] he played relatively few notes in his solos and his backup, but he made each note count in a concise statement of the melody." For Kenny Baker, perhaps the fiddler best known today, see David Brody, *Kenny Baker Fiddle*.

4. Rosenberg, chap. 7 of *Bluegrass: A History*; Art Menius, "Camp Spring Today: Will There Be a Tomorrow?," 30. See also L. Mayne Smith, "First Bluegrass Festival Honors Bill Monroe," 9.

5. Thomas A. Adler documents the story of Bean Blossom and how festivals function in society as "special cultural space(s) devoted to vernacular music" in *Bean Blossom: The Brown County Jamboree and Bill Monroe's Bluegrass Festivals*, xix, ff.

6. "My hippie fans know when the music is played right. And the college kids are my biggest audience" (Bill Monroe in "Pickin' and Singin,'" *Newsweek*, June 29, 1970, quoted in Lund and Denisoff, "Folk Music Revival and the Counter Culture," 402). Robert O. Gardner discusses bluegrass festivals in terms of sociological and anthropological issues in *The Portable Community: Place and Displacement in Bluegrass Festival Life*.

7. The "Ozark Music Festival" in July 1974 at Sedalia was widely reported on radio and television news as out of control; some three hundred thousand people showed up. It was held on the state fair's racetrack grounds, with its large grandstand; there were thousands of attendees; a Hare Krishna group dancing, chanting, raising tents (and soliciting donations), a novelty to the majority of Missouri festivalgoers; fans and band members playing instruments under shade trees; hippies climbing trees, smoking joints, cavorting; numerous dogs; some skinny dipping in the state-fair pond; rock bands such as Eagles, Bruce Springsteen, REO Speedwagon, Jefferson Starship, and Lynyrd Skynyrd as well as bluegrass bands and quasi-bluegrass crossover bands such as the Nitty Gritty Dirt Band and the Earl Scruggs Revue; and a sea of trash and piles of beer cans littering the fairgrounds. The town Chamber of Commerce set up a telephone Citizens Hotline for people who felt the need to alert the sheriff's department as trouble flared. See *Sedalia Democrat*, July 21, 1974, "ocean of youth" photo story; July 22 article, "Clean-Up Underway; Senate Probe Is Set." This is the festival that nearly drove bluegrass festivals out of business.

8. Hartgrove, June 5, 2019.

9. John T. White, February 22, 2015.

10. Ed Harding was especially helpful in teaching Hartgrove bowing techniques. Hartgrove, February 22, 2015; Nancy Cardwell, "Mike Hartgrove: IIIrd Tyme Out's Secret Ingredient on Fiddle," 21.

11. Cardwell, "Mike Hartgrove," 21. From southeast Missouri, Dale Potter (1929–66) was an influential professional in Nashville and helped pioneer double-stop fiddling in bluegrass and country music; see Marshall, chap. 8 of *Fiddler's Dream.*

12. Hartgrove, February 2, 2021.

13. Hartgrove, February 22, 2015. Hartgrove did not place in the top ten; first place went to Dick Barrett; second, J. T. Perkins; third, Herman Johnson; Thomasson, tenth place.

14. Hartgrove, November 19, 2010. At that time, Jackson played a 1924 Roth violin. For Jackson, see Marshall, chap. 1 of *Fiddler's Dream.*

15. Hartgrove, June 5, 2019.

16. Tommy Williams played twin fiddling with Kenny Baker on the Grand Ole Opry, and Williams appears on the influential LP *Bill Monroe's Uncle Pen* (MCA DL7-5348, 1972);

17. Cardwell, "Mike Hartgrove," 30.

18. For IIIrd Tyme Out when Hartgrove was with the band, see Geoffrey Himes, "IIIrd Tyme Out." See also Geoffrey Himes, "Lonesome River Band"; and Derek Halsey, "Escaping Floods, Working on Buses, and Keeping the Downbeat in Bluegrass Music: The Lonesome River Band Celebrates 35 Years." In 2021, Lonesome River Band personnel are Sammy Shelor (banjo), Mike Hartgrove, Cameron Keller (bass), Jesse Smathers (guitar), and Adam Miller (mandolin) (https://www.lonesomeriverband.com).

19. For Rickman, see Halsey, "Escaping Floods."

20. Hartgrove, November 19, 2010.

21. Drew Beisswenger, *The World's Hottest Fiddlers*, 41. See also for Hartgrove, Ivan M. Tribe, *The Stonemans: An Appalachian Family and the Music That Shaped Their Lives*, 222; and Bill Malone, *Country Music USA*, 459.

22. Hartgrove's favorite violin book is the Sacconi study of Stradivari's techniques. Simone Sacconi was an Italian maker who moved to New York City in 1931 to work for the Emil Herman shop and then Rembert Wurlitzer, specializing in restoration of Old Master instruments. In 1972, Sacconi published *I Segreti di Stradivari* (The secrets of Stradivari). Franco Feroldi and Maya Randolph, *From Violinmaking to Music: The Life and Work of Simone Fernando Sacconi.*

23. Cardwell, "Mike Hartgrove," 30.

24. Cardwell, "Mike Hartgrove," 31.

25. In his teaching, Hartgrove uses Michael Allen, Robert Gillespie, and Pamela Tellejohn Hayes, *Essential Elements for Strings: Violin Book 1* and *Violin Book 2.*

26. Jim Creighton, "In Shannon County, Almost Any Day Is Country Music Day," *St. Louis Post-Dispatch*, April 22, 1973, 4, 6. The PhD from New York was Rod Moag (see Marshall, chap. 7 of *Fiddler's Dream*). Kenny Seaman (1942–2021) led a popular bluegrass band, the Current River Drifters, and moved to Colorado in 1975 where he continued to be a musician and band leader. Gary Reid, "Kenny Eugene 'Ken' Seaman."

27. "Bluegrass Combos Await Bash at Uncle Penn's Pickin' Place," 42.

28. "Wildwood Flower" is an all-time country music hit song, recorded in 1928 in Bristol, Tennessee, by the Carter Family from southwest Virginia; their 78 on Victor sold hundreds

of thousands of copies and has been covered countless times in various music styles. Maybelle Carter played guitar, and her thumb-brush technique is called "the Carter lick" or the "Carter scratch." Mona Jones played Maybelle's guitar solo with a flat pick and achieved an identical sound.

29. Mona Jones, October 27, 2017.

30. The program drew a large crowd and was developed by the State Historical Society of Missouri, Rolla branch, staffers Kathleen Seale and Carole Goggin; the program was videotaped for the Historical Society archives. Mona Jones's "bluegrass papers" (Dixon festival memorabilia, recordings, photographs, posters) are archived as the Mona Darlene Jones Collection, State Historical Society of Missouri, Rolla; other collections there include donations by Wayne Bledsoe, Jim Orchard, Jimmie Allison, and C. J. Lewandowski. See "Rolla Research Center Builds Bluegrass Collection, Sponsors Life Performance in April 2017."

31. For an overview of the importance of gospel music, see Howard Wight Marshall, "Keep on the Sunny Side of Life: Pattern and Religious Expression in Bluegrass Gospel Music."

32. Rowden and the band appeared at the Kahoka festival in 1979; the Bluegrass Five at that time included Ralph Withers (guitar), Burl Copeland (mandolin), Daryl Tunink (banjo), Dale Officer (bass), and Newell Robertson (Dobro); their "So Happy I'll Be" is on the sampler LP from that event, Various Artists, *Live! From the Kahoka Festival of Bluegrass Music.*

33. "Yes, Bill Jones did patrol his grounds religiously, but did it in a non-confrontational way, so long as he didn't find anything going on that violated his policies. He did throw a few people out for drinking, and some men even for wearing Bermuda shorts to the festival! To be fair, the entrance sign did say that drinking was not permitted, and that violators would be ejected from the grounds. Nothing in print on the sign said anything about Bermuda shorts or ladies wearing short-shorts, however the paper flyers put out at various sites (such as those distributed by Clyde and Nora Jones) did say that dress should be 'appropriate.' As I recall, the term 'appropriate' was never defined in print" (Ed McKinney, December 4, 2013).

34. Jim Orchard in the video documentary *Bluegrass Pickin' Time.*

35. Christina Collison, "'The Fiddle Man' Makes a Comeback," *Fulton Sun*, January 19, 2003.

36. Andrew Morton lives in Springfield and works in public school special education; bands he has performed with include Brightwater Junction and Casey and the Atta-Boys.

37. "Will the Circle Be Unbroken" as we know it today is based on a Carter Family 78-rpm record, their version of a 1907 Protestant hymn composed by Ada Habershon and Charles Gabriel. The lyrics evoke nostalgia and longing for loved ones. The Carter Family's song was given new vigor during the 1970s when it was featured on the influential 1972 Nitty Gritty Dirt Band project (*Will the Circle Be Unbroken*) featuring among other early country stars Mother Maybelle Carter (an LP set that introduced country and bluegrass music to a huge new audience).

38. Jim Orchard, May 20, 2018.

39. For Rhonda Vincent, see, for example, Ralph Berrier Jr., "Rhonda Vincent"; Jon Weisberger, "Rhonda Vincent"; Caroline Wright, "How to Raise a Great Musician"; and Marshall, chap. 1 of *"Play Me Something Quick and Devilish"* and "Rhonda Vincent and Missouri's Old-Time and Bluegrass Crossroads."

40. Hees, Wieneman, and Jones can be heard together with other Missouri bluegrass legends on *The Missouri Session: A Studio Jam Session with Years of Memories*. In 2021 the lineup

in the Rage included a Missouri banjo player, Aaron McDaris, who has been with Rhonda's band since 2009. Bill Conger, "Aaron McDaris: All about the Banjo."

41. In addition to the Collins family, others helping found the Kansas City Area Bluegrass Club included Pappy Reese, Dale McIntosh, and Nelly Shaw (Jim McGreevy, January 6, 2017).

42. In the 1930s, Sears Roebuck catalogs sold small acoustic guitars called the "Gene Autry Round-Up" guitar, endorsed by Autry, the famed Singing Cowboy, recording artist, and star of western movies whose syndicated radio performances on Chicago's WLS and his weekly Melody Ranch radio shows were heard across the nation. The guitars, inexpensive but quality built, were made by the Harmony factory and marketed under Harmony's "Supertone" label.

43. Rusty Dutton, "A Bio of My Musical Life: By Robert L. 'Rusty' Dutton, a Missouri Old Time Fiddler," November 19, 2016 (manuscript); "Chinky Pin" (a folk spelling of "chinquapin," a member of the white oak tree family) is one of several alternate titles in Missouri for the tune generally known today as "Lead Out" (thanks to Tommy Jackson's widely popular recordings and performances in the 1950s and 1960s). Clark Kessinger recorded a 78-rpm record with the title "Chinquapin" in 1929. Some thirty alternate titles for this familiar reel appear in my archives; originally from mid-eighteenth-century Scotland, other titles in Missouri include "My Love Is but a Lassie" (Cyril Stinnett), "Too Young to Marry," "Leesil" (Taylor McBaine), "Hog Head" (Nile Wilson), "Blue Jay" (Thomas Jasper Massie, per Kelly Jones), "Love Somebody" (Cecil Goforth, Dean Johnston), "Sledge Hammer" (Amos Bishop, per his grandson Earl Ball), "Step Light Ladies" (Sam Lindsey, per his son Jim Lindsey), "Raymondville," and Lyman Enloe's title, "Ten Nights in a Bar Room" (on Enloe's *Fiddle Tunes I Recall* recording). This tune bears no resemblance to the Appalachian region tune "Chinquapin Hunting." Lyle Harris (1933–2011), son of fiddler Brickey (Brick) Harris of Butler, was an A-list jazz guitarist and teacher (as well as a fiddler) in Columbia.

44. Rusty Dutton and Dan Grotewohl are the only formal Enloe students I am aware of. As a teenager, Dan Grotewohl lived near Enloe's neighborhood and appears in material about Enloe in Marshall, chap. 11 of *Fiddler's Dream.* Dutton plays banjo backup for Lyman Enloe on *Now That's a Good Tune.*

45. Dutton, "A Bio of My Years with Missouri Master Fiddler Lyman Enloe, by Rusty Dutton" (manuscript). Dutton also wrote, at my request, "A Bio of My Musical Life: By Robert L. 'Rusty' Dutton, a Missouri Old Time Fiddler."

46. Kenny Baker and Lyman Enloe were friends for many years, and the Enloes visited at Baker's home on trips to Nashville to attend the Grand Ole Opry. Inez Calton suggested the title "Festival Waltz" for Baker's famous composition. In the 1970s, Inez and Charles Calton (from the Conway, Missouri, area) formed a popular family bluegrass band with their nine children, the Calton Family, and they performed at many bluegrass festivals as well as Silver Dollar City; their 1976 LP (with Jim Bunch, banjo) is *The Calton Family: The Old and New.*

47. Dutton, "A Bio of My Musical Life: By Robert L. 'Rusty' Dutton, a Missouri Old Time Fiddler."

48. McGreevy, "Chuck Stearman, the Man from SPBGMA"; Ed West, "An Interview with Chuck Stearman—Bluegrass Society Founder"; Arlie Metheny, "Jim McGreevy."

49. From the Kansas City area, Stearman played mandolin in the formative group the Bluegrass Association, with Jim McGreevy (banjo), John Bennett (guitar), Don Montgomery (bass), Audrey Enloe Belt, and old-time fiddler Lyman Enloe.

50. SPBGMA's National Fiddler's Contest, 1983: Open Division winners: first, Randy Howard (Georgia); second, Dan Kelly (Pennsylvania); third, Ed Carnes (Kentucky); fourth, Mark Ralph (Kentucky); fifth, Monte Gaylord (Oklahoma); sixth, Billy Ward (Forsyth, MO); seventh, Jerry Hodge (Arkansas); eighth, Wayne Massengale (Arkansas); ninth, Allison Krauss (Illinois); and tenth, Jack Weeks (Georgia). Senior Division (age sixty-two and older): first, Ken Sloan (Arkansas); second, Faye Green (Arkansas); third, Boyd Long (Texas); fourth, Lennis Francis (Kentucky); fifth, Dick Vance (New York); sixth, Lee Townsend (New York); seventh, Archie Smothers (Illinois); eighth, Hank Ayers (Arkansas); ninth, Jack Roebuck (Oklahoma); and tenth, Bob Hastings (Arkansas). In later SPBGMA contests, Missouri fiddlers such as Junior Marriott won prizes.

51. West, "Interview with Chuck Stearman."

52. See Marshall, chap. 10 of *Fiddler's Dream*, for pioneer bluegrass fiddler Delbert Spray (1923–2001), thought to have been the first to perform bluegrass music in Japan, during Spray's service in the Army in 1945 in postwar Tokyo.

53. Teresa Romans, December 21, 2016.

54. Ed McKinney, December 2, 2016.

55. Greater Ozarks Bluegrass Society, https://www.gobluegrass.org.

56. Lewandowski grew up going to the Dixon festivals and was mentored by pioneer St. Louis banjo player and band leader Dub Crouch. Don Brown, Jim Orchard, and Frank Ray taught C. J. to play mandolin in the classic Bill Monroe style. Lewandowski performed at festivals with several bands, including Men of the Week, and the Karl Shiflett & Big Country Show. In 2017, C. J. broke into the elite with his band the Po' Ramblin' Boys, and their recordings have won national awards.

57. Wilhite traveled to the National Oldtime Fiddlers' Contest in Weiser in the 1970s, placing in the top ten, and helped judge several divisions. Gene Wilhite's "Geno Waltz" appears on the sampler LP *National Oldtime Fiddler's Contest and Folk Music Festival* (Weiser ID, Century LP, 1973); his "Tom and Jerry" is on *South Dakota Fiddling Contest, 1978* (Yankton, SD, Wilbur Foss).

58. Jones, May 26, June 30, 2006, March 29, 2015.

59. Gerald Jones, March 28, 2015.

60. Much is known about Baker, Benny Martin, and Chubby Wise but less about Mac Magaha; a fiddler who loved to entertain, for many years Magaha performed and recorded with Don Reno and Red Smiley and the Tennessee Cutups (and coauthored with Reno a hit bluegrass song, "I Know You're Married, but I Love You Still"), before performing for many more years as the jolly, smiling jig-dancing fiddler on television shows and recordings with Porter Wagoner and his Wagonmasters band and appearing often with various other groups at the Opryland theme park. Magaha's stage antics perhaps detracted from the audience's ability to notice his outstanding fiddle work.

61. Gerald Jones, November 10, 2010.

62. Jones, February 17, 2021.

63. Jones, February 17, 2021.

13. How Learning Has Changed, and How It Hasn't

1. Hannah Farnum, February 6, 2022. I appreciate assistance from Hannah and her parents, Norm and Tricia, in preparing this text.

2. https://farnumfamily.org/album/1678616/a-time-to-fiddle.

3. "'A Time to Fiddle' features an assortment of Texas-style breakdowns, waltzes, and rags—with a wee bit of Irish thrown in for good measure!" (https://www.farnumfamily.org).

4. Science confirms that a propensity for making music is a heritable genetic trait and hard-wired in our brains, but experience (a better term than nurture) is crucial, too. David J. Linden, *Unique: The New Science of Human Individuality* (review, Robin Marantz Henig, *New York Times*, November 1, 2020); see also Cynthia Garcia Coll, Elaine L. Bearer, and Richard M. Lerner, *Nature and Nurture: The Complex Interplay of Genetic and Environmental Influences on Human Behavior and Development* (New York: Psychology Press, 2014).

5. See Lisa L. Higgins, "Missouri Folk Arts Program," *Museum Magazine*, 11–12; Jim McCarty, "30 Years of Traditions: Apprenticeship Program Creates Folk Artist Hall of Fame"; and Roberson and Marshall, *Masters*.

6. Rose, March 21, 2000. This occasion has gone into oral tradition, and tellers offer different specific details and even locations of the contest.

7. Gordon, January 13, 2019; Priscilla Westgate and younger sister Stephanie were young classical violinists taking fiddle lessons with McMahan in the mid-1990s (also younger brother J. T.); both were adept pupils, competing successfully in contests. Pete applied with the girls for the Traditional Arts Apprenticeship Program, but their applications were denied.

8. Lonberger, March 5, 2005.

9. Summers, May 29, 2010, February 19, 2021.

10. Unless otherwise noted, Kathy Summers quotes are from a recording I made during a program about fiddling and her career (with Bob Skaggs, guitar) at the Missouri Folklore Society annual conference, Potosi, November 8, 2013.

11. Summers, May 29, 2017.

12. Summers, November 25, 2013.

13. Hentoff, *American Music Is*, 245.

14. Schoenberger, *Classic Fiddle* album notes. I appreciate Schoenberger's courtesy in this writing and in providing me with her fiddle CDs.

15. Schoenberger, February 23, 2021, https://www.jacobsacademy.indiana.edu.

16. Phillips, *Contest Fiddling*.

17. I appreciate David Scrivner's help and edits in preparing this material. Unless otherwise noted, quotes are from Scrivner, December 16, 2020.

18. Old-time fiddlers in the Ozarks region generally play few tunes in F or B-flat, and fewer tunes learned from tune books, in comparison with fiddlers to the north; Scrivner is an exception in this regard, as are so-called Ozark fiddlers like Henry Thompson, H. K. Silvey, and Lonnie Robertson, whose fiddle styles fit nicely with central and north Missouri fiddling.

19. Scrivner played in the group for six years, even after starting fiddle with Bob Holt.

20. Ben Smith and David Osban, "David Scrivner: Interview + Tunes." Unless otherwise indicated, Scrivner quotes are from this interview.

21. Holt also played country music and bluegrass, which is famous for fast tempos. For Holt, see, for example, Julie Henigan, "Play Me Something Quick and Devilish"; material in *Bob Holt: Dance Fiddling from the Missouri Ozarks*; and Marshall, *"Play Me Something Quick and Devilish"* ("Ninth of January" is on the accompanying companion CD) and *Fiddler's Dream*.

22. Nashville stars such as Clark Kessinger, Fiddlin' Arthur Smith, and Tommy Jackson played ultrafast square-dance breakdowns, and their commercial recordings from the late 1920s

into the 1960s were admired by Missouri old-time and bluegrass fiddlers, especially Tommy Jackson's "square dances without calls" 45s and LPs in the 1950s and 1960s; other big tunes in Missouri old-time and bluegrass connected to Jackson include "Bitter Creek" (a contest powerhouse), "Acorn Hill Breakdown," "Polk County Breakdown," "Snowflake Reel," "14 Days in Georgia," "Cherokee Shuffle," and—a favorite dance tune of Bob Holt's—"Tomahawk."

23. "Richmond Cotillion" is among tunes popularized by West Virginia fiddler Clark Kessinger, and the Kessinger Brothers, under the title "Richmond Polka" on a 1929 78-rpm record by the Kessinger Brothers (Brunswick 309), reissued on *The Kessinger Brothers: Done Gone* (Goldenlane Records, 2013); a 1960s version by Kessinger when he came out of retirement during the Folk Music Revival is on the Folkways 1966 LP *Old Time Country Music* (Folkways FA 2336; Smithsonian Folkways reissue on CD, 2014); other reissues are available. The first commercial recording was probably a 1927 78 (Challenge 407) by Frank Neal and His Boys (a pseudonym for DaCosta Wolz's Southern Broadcasters). Other titles include "Plaza Polka," used in 1950s recordings by Canadian fiddlers Don Messer, Andy DeJarlis, Graham Townsend, and Patti Kusturok, and American fiddler Howdy Forrester also used this title. Other titles include "Robert E. Lee Swing," "Stonewall Jackson," "Rocky Road to Dublin" (not the Irish slip jig), "Richmond," "Sally Put a Bug on Me," and "Redman's Reel" (in Ford, *Traditional Music of America*, 116). The tune appears unnamed as "Breakdown #9" in Christeson, *Old-Time Fiddler's Repertory* (1973, 68). When I worked at the Library of Congress in the late 1970s and early 1980s, I remember Alan Jabbour fiddling the tune as "Too Young to Marry," as did several Virginia-area fiddlers of my recollection at that time, by this and other titles. Lyman Enloe's version is included in the documentary double-LP album *Now That's a Good Tune*. Enloe learned the tune from the Clark Kessinger record ("Richmond Polka"), but forgot the title and began calling it "Hanging around the Kitchen ('til the Cook Comes Home)" (*Now That's a Good Tune*). David Scrivner notes that the tune was recorded by Ozark fiddler Bill Bilyeu in 1941 as "Aunt Kay" (or "Aunt Katy"). A cotillion is a colonial-era dance-tune type related to the minuet; a cotillion is also a term for a dance event.

24. "Doc Brown's Dream" was the title Bob Holt and other fiddlers used for "McCraw Ford," a tune put together and titled as "McCraw Ford" by Doc Brown, a country doctor who lived in Stafford (Greene County). McCraw Ford was a low-water crossing on the James River east of Springfield. See Marshall, chap. 3 of *"Play Me Quick and Devilish."* Art Galbraith learned it as a young man and taught the tune to Lonnie Robertson; Galbraith has it on his *Dixie Blossoms* LP. Bob Holt's version as "Doc Brown's Dream" is on *Bob Holt: Got a Little Home to Go To*. There is a photo of McCraw Ford in Marshall, *"Play Me Something Quick and Devilish"* (92). It is believed that the physician in question was William McF. Brown; "Dr. William McF. Brown is a member of a family of doctors in this and adjoining counties. He graduated in 1885 and after practicing for many years in Strafford removed to Springfield about 1910" (Jonathan Fairbanks and Clyde Edwin Tuck, *Past and Present of Greene County, Missouri*, 1040); Missouri State Archives death records indicate William McFarland Brown (1861–1921).

25. Bob Walsh, born in West Eminence in 1929, founded the State of the Ozarks Fiddlers' Association, taught young fiddlers for many years privately and in the Traditional Arts Apprenticeship Program, hosted fiddlers' conventions at his farm near Cape Fair that later were held at Compton Ridge Campground near Branson, lobbied the state legislature to name the fiddle as Missouri's state musical instrument in 1987, and is featured in Marshall et al., *"Now That's a*

Good Tune." Bob Walsh's grandfather Mitchell Walsh came to the Ozarks from County Cork, Ireland, in 1843 and brought his violin with him, the violin that Bob learned to play as a child; Bob donated the violin to the Missouri State Museum in Jefferson City.

26. Scrivner, interview; Caitlyn McConnell, "Ozarks Alive: Time Capsule of Old-Time, Ozarks Fiddling," KMSU 91.1 FM radio (Springfield), November 11, 2020, https://www.ozarksalive.com. Regarding Monday nights, Scrivner cites Noel Scott, who was at the McClurg session in October 1983, recalling that Mondays were chosen to suit the schedule of Jim Beeler, a dispatcher for the Taney County sheriff's office, who played fiddle and sometimes strummed banjo for Bob Holt at square dances.

27. A YouTube viewer comment: "Amazing music. The guy on the fiddle at 3:51 [David Scrivner] used to be my English professor. He's a skilled musician and teacher!" (YouTube, February 2, 2016).

28. Jennifer Moore wrote about McClurg during the COVID-19 hiatus, "Quieted by the Pandemic, Mountain Music Is in Jeopardy," *New York Times*, February 4, 2021, A13. The store and other property were purchased by Tom Peters, dean of Missouri State University Libraries, Springfield (a fan and scholar of Ozark music), thus the future of the session appears to be secure. "Missouri Fiddling on FaceBook," January 25, 2022. See also Jeremy Myers, "McClurg: The Ozark Tradition Lives On."

29. J. R. Johnston (1929–2019) was an old-time basic-strum banjo player whose rhythm was impeccable and taste spot-on for fiddle backup, welcome in sessions at bluegrass festivals as well as among old-time fiddlers; J. R.'s son, Herbie, is a top-drawer bluegrass fiddler and performs with several bands such as Possum Trot.

30. Donald Bradley, "Old Mountain Music Gets New Life," *Kansas City Star*, February 23, 2017 (video by Keith Myers), on YouTube; Harry Smith, "Tiny Town Keeps Music of Ozarks Alive," *The Today Show* (NBC television, May 2017). See also Zach Smith, "Monday Night in McClurg"; and Jennifer Moore, "In the Ozarks, the Pandemic Threatens a Fragile Musical Tradition," *New York Times*, February 3, 2021.

31. Smith and Osban, "David Scrivner: Interview + Tunes."

32. Wyatt Violin Shop, Facebook.

33. "The interesting thing to me is the Native American ancestry. Rebecca Dinsmore was born in Georgia in the 1800s and married John Wyatt in Kentucky" (Matt Wyatt, February 18, 22, 2021). Unless otherwise noted, quotes from Matt Wyatt are from February 18, 2021.

34. Among articles about Matt Wyatt are Diana Lambdin-Meyer, "Fiddling Champ Teams Up with His Woodworker Father," *Kansas City Star*, November 17, 2004, 28.

35. Allen Wyatt, October 3, 2020.

36. "Terry Morris tapes" from the 1980s remain compelling statements of the art, among the "best" recordings ever made of fiddle music across all genres.

37. Gene's father, Richard (Dink) Goforth, refused to teach his sons to play the fiddle. "He never would show me nothing, no way. He said, 'there it is, go learn it, on your own, and if you learn you done it *yourself*.' If you *learn* it, okay, if not, too bad, you know" (Marshall interview, November 11, 1987).

38. When the TAAP program was new in the mid-1980s, I asked Gene Goforth if he would be interested in teaching in the program, but teaching did not interest him in the least; in retrospect, he may have been waiting for a worthy pupil—Matt Wyatt.

39. Matt Wyatt, August 29, 2006. For Goforth, among many sources, see John Hartford's anecdotal fiddle project *Hamilton Ironworks* and Goforth's *Eminence Breakdown*; the

documentary recording and booklet Marshall et al., *"Now That's a Good Tune"*; Marshall, "Done Gone: Gene Goforth, 1921–2002"; and Marshall, *"Play Me Something Quick and Devilish."*

40. Gene Goforth also appreciated and acknowledged the guitar accompaniment of Al Murphy of Iowa City, Iowa (also a fine fiddler), whose backup (along with banjoist Bob Black) appears on the *Now That's a Good Tune* recordings I made of them in a motel room in Hannibal, Missouri, in November 1987.

41. Matt Wyatt, August 20, 2010.

42. Gene Goforth and Pete McMahan were friends in the 1960s and sometimes went to sessions where both played tunes together (as a recording in my files proves); however, they parted company when Gene focused on bluegrass bands and bluegrass festivals and Pete focused on fiddle contests.

43. Matt Wyatt, February 3, 2021.

44. Matt Wyatt, August 29, 2006.

45. Matt Wyatt, August 15, 2007.

46. Matt Wyatt, September 6, 2003. "I introduce students to musicianship early on" (February 18, 2021).

47. "#10—It is the only one that I am a little happy with. The others are like a progression of sorts. I had to learn by doing. After I am done with one, I can see what I need to do on the next one, or where I went wrong. But by then it is too late to correct. So, I start again by making a brand-new mold for #11. I started it today" (Allen Wyatt, May 3, 2005). Wyatt presented a program on his violin-making experiences in a session on violin making in Missouri at the annual conference of the Missouri Folklore Society, Hannibal, October 1998; he presented "The Factory Strad in Missouri" at the Missouri Folklore Society conference, Kansas City, 2008.

48. Brochure, https://www.wyattviolin.com. Among articles about the Wyatt shop are Phoebe Yao, "The Violin Merchant," *Globe*, January 28, 2004, https://www.chsglobe.com/23865/features/the-violin-merchant/.

49. Markneukirchen is in the German state of Saxony, close to the border with the Bohemian region of the Czech Republic; falling in East Germany during Germany's split during the post–World War II era, the violin-making business there was almost extinguished; however, following German reunification in 1990, the Markneukirchen trade was rejuvenated. Mittenwald is a municipality in the Garmisch-Partenkirchen in the Bavarian Alps south of Munich; as part of the former West Germany, violin making in Mittenwald continued to flourish. (Courtesy of Sean Franzel, February 25, 2021.) See Bruce Babbitt, *Markneukirchen Violins and Bows from Saxon and Bohemian Musikwinkel: Late 19th Century and Early 20th Century.* "[Winkel] loosely translates into 'corner,' as in a little corner of the world. The Musikwinkel is a small area where Lower Saxony meets Bohemia and many of the world's musical instruments came from here. Also, the families of CF Martin and Wurlitzer among others" (Babbitt, February 18, 2021).

50. Fiddlesong projects include Matt Wyatt, *Centralia Waltz*, the title tune of which is Matt's composition; Matt Wyatt and Justin Branum, *The Good-Bye Waltz*, the title tune of which is Matt's composition; Jeff Elsloo and Matt Wyatt, *Banjo & Fiddle*; Lynn Wells, *Mainline Missouri Fiddling*; John P. Williams, *Monroe County Influences, Vol. 1*; and Swing Deville, *Western Swing DeVille* and *Salt Up the Dance Floor*.

51. Matt Wyatt, August 15, 2007.

Conclusion

1. William Wright, "Jackson Pollock, an Interview," 1950, https://www.homepages.neiu.edu.

2. Schaffner is director of the Southeast Music Academy in the Department of Music at Southeast Missouri University; his video series is called "Fiddlin' around Cape Girardeau."

3. For one standard distinction: "Hispanic refers to individuals who are Spanish-speaking or have a background in a Spanish-speaking country. Latino refers to those who are from or have a background in a Latin American country. These terms encompass culture, ethnicity, and identity and are rooted in shared cultures and not racial categories" (Google). I appreciate the assistance of Joe Palmer, Katie Benyo, and Tess and Maria Cuevas in preparing these comments, as well as the 1993 publication on the Kansas City Mexican and Latino scene by my colleague Dana Everts-Boehm at the University of Missouri Cultural Heritage Center. In 2017–18, folklorist Thomas Grant Richardson conducted research in rural and small-town northern Missouri for the Missouri Folk Arts Program (Lisa L. Higgins, "Missouri Folk Arts Program"). Among Richardson's findings are Mexican and Mexican American traditional arts; the survey did not document fiddle music. Debbie Bailey, October 8, 2018; T. Grant Richardson, March 2, 2019.

4. "Hispanic," "Latino/Latina," "Mexican American," and "Chicano" are terms often used interchangeably by members of the community as well as by outsiders. "Chicano" is sometimes an alternate for "Mexican American." Distinctions among these terms can be subtle and puzzling to outsiders, and opinions vary as to which is preferable. "Hispanic" and "Latino" have been most often used in Missouri and favored by politicians such as the Westside's US congressman for the Fifth District Emanuel Cleaver II.

5. Mexico became independent from Spain on September 21, 1821; following the Mexican-American War (1846–48), the Treaty of Guadalupe Hidalgo in 1848 ceded Mexican territory in the Southwest to the United States; New Mexico became a US territory in 1848 and a state in 1912. See, for example, Dana Everts-Boehm, *"¡Qué Viva el Westside!": Mexican Traditional Arts in Kansas City, Missouri*. In Kansas, permanent settlement began after Missouri.

6. For Kansas, see Judith Ann Fincher Laird, *Argentine, Kansas: The Evolution of a Mexican-American Community, 1905–1940*; Daniel Serda, "Finding Latin Roots: Hispanic Heritage in Kansas City"; and "Mexican Americans in Kansas," *Kansapedia* (Kansas Historical Society online encyclopedia), https://www.kshs.org. For Missouri, see Ann Rynearson, "Hiding within the Melting Pot: Mexican-Americans in St. Louis"; Theresa L. Torres, "The Kansas City Westside: Home of the Shrine of Our Lady of Guadalupe," in *The Paradox of Latina Leadership in the Catholic Church: Las Guadalupanas of Kansas City*, 27–53; John J. Green and Elizabeth Barham, *Latinos in Missouri*; Andreas M. Dominguez, "A Latino Presence in the Heartland: Challenges and Opportunities"; Everts-Boehm, *"¡Qué Viva el Westside!"*; and Bryan Winston, "Mexican Migrants in Urban Missouri: Social Welfare Institutions and Racial Boundaries in Kansas City and St. Louis, 1915–1940."

7. https://www.visitkc.com.

8. Everts-Boehm, *"¡Qué Viva el Westside!"* After the Missouri Cultural Heritage Center's demise in 1993, the folk arts program was transferred to the Museum of Art and Archaeology.

9. Everts-Boehm, *"¡Qué Viva el Westside!,"* 2.

10. Paul Anastasio, "The Music of Mexico's Tierra Caliente: A Renaissance." Another genre, *norteño*, emphasizes accordions and *bajo sexto* (a thick twelve-stringed guitar) and is less

common than mariachi in Missouri. For mariachi, see Everts-Boehm, "*¡Qué Viva el Westside!,*" 6–8; Daniel Sheehy, *Mariachi Music in America: Experiencing Music, Expressing Culture*; and Patricia Greathouse, *Mariachi*.

11. *KC Hispanic News*, April 26, 2018, 5.

12. Tess Cuevas, May 15, 2018.

13. Timothy Finn, "Drawing on Their Roots," *Kansas City Star* February 12, 2014; Crystale Lampitt interview with Maria Cuevas, "Behind the Spotlight," KMCI-TV, Kansas City (https://www.kshb.com), May 1, 2017; Stephen Hill, "Blood Harmony: Sisters Blend Mariachi Roots and Pop in Maria the Mexican"; recordings include *Moon Colored Jade* (private label, 2013); Michelle Bacon, "Maria the Mexican: A Career Driven by Tradition," *Bridge*, April 5, 2018, https://www.bridge909.org.

14. Katie Benyo, April 29, May 2, 2018.

Notes for Companion CD

1. There are other "Buckley's"; Phil Rice's 1858 five-string banjo tutor includes "Buckley's Best Reel" (*Phil Rice's Correct Method for the Banjo, with or without a Master*), named after the composer and minstrel musician Fred Buckley; in his banjo instructor of 1868, Buckley includes the tune as "Buckley's Hornpipe" (reissue, Tim Twiss, *Early American Banjo*).

2. Shewmaker, February 9, 2022.

3. Phillips, *Phillips Collection of Traditional American Fiddle Tunes*.

4. I appreciate Vivian Williams's help documenting the tune, February 29, 2021. The Wade Ray 1947 recording is the earliest known (Capitol 40205). Ray, from Indiana, performed on Pappy Cheshire radio shows in St. Louis; retired in Sparta, Illinois; and was a popular figure in the country music and fiddle scene until his death in 1998. Fiddlers at Weiser in the 1970s, such as Bill Long and Harold Allen, helped position "Forty Years Ago Waltz" in the repertoires of top contest fiddlers.

5. Baker's "Sugar Tree Stomp" is on his County Records compilation LP (*Master Fiddler*, County 2705, 1968); Baker's version begins with the low part rather than the high part as on Arthur Smith's original 78-rpm record in 1937 Bluebird B6927-B). Tommy Jackson's, Howdy Forrester's, and Paul Warren's versions follow Smith's pattern; Jackson, *Swing Your Partner* (Dot DLP 25454, 1962); Forrester's version is on his 1983 LP with Baker, *Red Apple Rag* (County 784, 1983); among bluegrass versions recently is Michael Cleveland on *Let 'Er Go, Boys* (Rounder 11661-0561-2, 2006).

Selected Bibliography

Interviews

Interview materials include informal conversations, email exchanges, letters, telephone calls, and recorded interviews.

Albrecht, Aaron. June 10, 2018; June 4, October 13, 2019.
Atchison, Bob. November 15, December 11, 2018.
Atterberry, Harvie. July 9, 2005; February 14, March 20, 2019.
Babbitt, Bruce. February 18, 202.
Bailey, Debbie. January 24, 2012; October 8, 2018.
Baker, Trustin. January 13, 14, 25, 2021.
Ball, Earl. December 6, 2007; February 18, 2008.
Barrett, Dick. September 10, 2005.
Barton, Cathy. November 19, 2018.
Beisswenger, Drew. March 27, 2006; November 12, 2011; February 21, 2012.
Benedict, Sue Ann (McMahan). February 13, 2019.
Benyo, Katie, April 29, May 2, 2018; August 1, 2020.
Branum, Justin. March 11, 2010.
Breid, Michael (Arkansas Red). August 6, 2018.
Buffington, Beau. September 22, October 6, 11, 2019.
Burlison, Jack. March 2, 12, 15, 2018; June 16, 2020.
Caldwell, Bobby Joe. April 4, 2007; November 4, 2010.
Canaday, Leroy. October 6, December 9, 2000; February 15, March 10, 2001; August 20, 2002.
Carter, Tom. April 16, 2019.
Cathey, Bob. June 7, 2010; January 28, 2011.
Chancellor, Jim. March 23, 2020.
Chandler, Patty Morrow. October 9, 2007.
Chase, Amos. September 22, 2000.
Christeson, R. P. August 21, 1982; December 1985; December 22, 1986; December 13, 1987.
Clatterbuck, Vernon. May 1, 2002.
Coelho, Dennis. June 30, July 5, 6, 9, 11, 18, 28, 2017.
Colbert, Van. June 5, 2017.
Coriell, Thomas. August 27, 2018.
Cormier, Luke. June 6, 15, August 4, November 1, 2016; April 17, June 27, July 3, 2017; February 19, March 29, April 6, October 9, 2018.
Craighead, Billy. June 29, 2013; January 30, 2018; February 3, 13, 2021.
Crowell, Hillis. June 8, June 15, October 15, 2017; October 6, 10, 11, 23, 2019.
Cuevas, Tess. May 15, May 31, 2018.
Cunningham, Cammie. February 7, 2021.
Cunningham, Keith. May 16, 2008.

Davidson, Patricia Spray. March 19, April 1, 2, 201.
Davis, Sarah. December 20, 2020.
Drayton, Mike. October 1982; December 22, 2003; May 2006; August 24, 2009.
Dutton, Rusty. February 16, 2015; August 15, October 7, September 29, November 4, 18, 19, December 2, 2016; July 1, 29, 2017; April 5, 2019; February 6, 2020; January 2, 5, April 4, 2021.
Enloe, Lyman. November 22, 1986.
Fedrizzi, Ed. March 23, 24, 2021.
Foss, Wilbur. Foss, September 20, 1992.
Fotsch, Paul. April 15, 22, 2019.
Franzel, Sean. September 11, 2018.
Fraser, Mike. May 14, 2022.
Frederick, Lynn. November 6, 26, 2014.
Friend, Bythel. September 20, 26, 2006.
Friend, Derrell P. March 6, 2021.
Gaddy, Amber. May 5, 2012.
Galbraith, Art. April 17, 1968; March 17, 1969 (DeMaire recording); June 24, November 17, 1975; June 24, 1977; April 29, 1982; December 1989.
Galloway, Spencer. December 14, 20, 2017; November 29, December 1, 2018; October 6, 17, 25, 26, 2020.
Garelick, Gus. November 24, December 18, 2009; January 10, 2010; May 19, 2015; May 18, 2017.
Gilmore, Jim. July 15, 1987.
Golan, Rob. October 27, 28, November 2, 4, 2020.
Gordon, Kathy. January 13, 2019.
Grace, Win (née Horner). April 15, July 17, August 4, August 17, 2019.
Graf, Sharon. July 8, 2019; September 12, 2020.
Griffin, John. May 6, 1994; April 18, 2000; April 16, 2020; January 27, 2021.
Hagan, Bob. October 16, 2014; October 22, 2018; April 12, 2019.
Hall, Kenny. July 4, 1974.
Hartford, John. March 29, April 17, July 4, 17, 19, November 14, 15, 2000.
Hartgrove, Mike. February 14, 2000; April 30, May 8, 13, 27, 2015; October 20, 2016; August 14, 16, 2017; May 5, 2019; January 27, February 1, 2, 15, March 13, 2021.
Haslag, LeRoy. November 13, 2004; September 9, 14, 22, 2010.
Head, Steve. January 7, 2004.
Hopkins, Harold. August 4, 2002.
Hoppers, Lonnie. May 23, June 17, 2013; October 13, 2014; February 16, 21, 26, March 29, April 24, June 23, 2015; April 1, 2016; November 3, 2018.
Inman, Travis. April 10, 2011; April 12 (interview by Amber Gaddy), 13, 30, May 1, 2012; June 22, 2015; March 14, 15, December 14, 2017; January 12, April 14, 28, May 10, September 7, 2019; January 25, June 19, July 30, 2020; March 3, April 13, 2021.
Johnson, Vesta. June 1988 [TAAP site visit], March 8, 2005; June 7, 2019 (interview with Margot McMillen).

Jones, Gerald. June 7, 2006; November 19, 2007; November 10, 2010; December 31, 2014; March 21, 28, 29, May 22, August 11, 2015; February 14, 2017; January 2, December 23, 2020; February 17, March 3, 2021.

Jones, Kelly. June 16, 1988; December 31, 2003; January 8, 2007; December 31, 2008; April 11, 2015; October 30, 2020; April 20, 2021.

Jones, Mona. October 21, 2017; May 20, 2018; April 13, 2019.

Kehl, Liz. February 9, 18, 2021.

Koken, Walt. January 2, 2009; April 12, May 8, 12, 2012.

Krassen, Miles. September 3, 2019.

Krone, Greg. August 29, 2018.

Lansford, Kim. August 23, 2020.

Lee, Billy. January 28, 1989; May 15, 2001; January 3, 2002; January 25, 2004.

Leftwich, Brad. November 17, 22, 25, 2014; June 1, 26, 2016.

Lewandowski, C. J. December 8, 2016; December 12, 2017; March 1, 2018.

Logan, Art. November 29, December 2, 3, 2016; May 15, 2017; September 5, 6, 20, 2018; April 29, May 2, 2019.

Lonberger, Frankie. March 5, 2015.

Lutz, Ron. May 8, 2003; October 5, 2010.

Matthews, Roger. August 17, 2019; July 2, 2020; January 26, 2001.

McBaine, Taylor. November 17, 1975; October 1, December 12, 1989; February 9, March 7, 17, 1990; May 16, 1992; August 8, 1993.

McCann, Gordon. February 24, 2005; November 22, 2010; September 20, October 9, 29, November 3, 2014; January 12, June 20, 2015; March 21, July 5, 2016; October 18, November 9, 10, 2017; September 14, 2020.

McGreevy, Jim. March 14, 23, July 5, 2015; January 6, March 2, June 25, 2017; February 2, October 30, 2018; January 21, 29, February 8, 9, 12, 12, 23, March 2, 18, December 16, 2020; January 21, 31, 2021.

McKinney, Ed. September 2005; March 8, 2007; February 21, 2008; October 26, 2010; December 4, 2013; June 10, 12, 14, 2015; December 2, 3, 2016; December 11, 2018; September 22, 2019; June 26, 2020.

McMahan, Pete. November 1975; January 12, October 12, 1976; February 15, 1980; December 17, 1986; December 26, 1988; February 22, 23, 1989; March 15, April 17, 1991; March, May 7, October 12, December 1992; February 2, March 7, 8, 11, October 12, 1993; December 21, 1995; January 20, August 19, September 23, 24 (Jen Stoeker interview), 1996; September 11, 18–19, 25, 1997.

McMahan, Sarah. November 22, 2001; June 8, 2005; January 20, 2010; February 11, 2011.

Mietus, Ken. October 10, 11, 13, 18, 2020.

Moag, Rod. March 1, 2017; December 14, 2019; January 12, 14, 28, 2020.

Mountjoy, Walter. March 19, 2000.

Muhrer, Darryl. September 15, November 6, 28, 2019.

Nelson, Jim. March 16, June 17, 2015.

Netherton, Robin. November 23, 25, 2020.

Netherton, Roger. July 29, November 22, 27, 2020; May 6, 2021.

Newberry, Joe. July 1, 13, 2020.

Nusbaum, Phil. March 31, 2000.
Orchard, Jim. June 6, 11, 16, 28, 2015; May 20, 2018.
Para, Dave. May 15, August 18, 2009; April 20, 2010; August 18, October 20, 21, November 19, 2018; February 1, 2020.
Pauley, Dale. November 19, 2009; April 29, 2013; April 15, 2014; June 23, October 11, December 7, 20, 2016; October 9, 10, 30, November 8, 20, 29, December 18, 2018; May 14, 2019.
Pauley, Mary Ruth. November 29, 2018.
Peck, Dianne. January 2004; August 7, 2012; July 10, 2019.
Peek, Dan William. May 13, September 22, 2010; January 5, 2015; April 24, October 27, November 12, 13, 16, 2018.
Phillips, Stacy. July 11, 12, 13, 17, 2017.
Ray, Frank. January 6, December 14, 2019.
Ray, Ron. November 14, December 3, 2018.
Richardson, T. Grant. March 2, 2019.
Rinzler, Ralph. July 5, 1975.
Robertson, Lonnie. November 1975.
Rogers, Bill. February 5, 2008 (FiddleHangout.Com), March 7, 2013; May 7, November 12, 2019.
Romans, Teresa. December 21, 2016.
Rose, Forrest. March 21, 2000.
Ruth, Jim. December 31, 2004; April 2, November 21, December 16, 2016; March 25, 2017; October 21, 22, 2018; January 14, 20, May 10, September 12, 13, 2019; February 4, March 29, 2020; January 4, February 21, 2021.
Schoenberger Doty, Liesl. February 23, 2021.
Scrivner, David. December 11, 16, 2020.
Seaman, Kenny. June 15, 20, July 11, 2015.
Seitz, Geoff. November 3, 11, December 3, 2009; February 6, 2012; July 7, 19, 2017; July 17, 22, August 3, November 23, 27, 2020.
Shewmaker, John. November 14, 2018.
Shewmaker, Richard. April 28, 2016; June 9, 2017; April 4, 10, 16, May 13, 2019; February 23, 2021.
Shull, Bill. August 18, 1996; August 2004; September 23, 24, October 10, 2013; December 19, 2014; December 14, 2017; November 1, 2, 6, 22, 2020; February 15, 2021.
Silvey, H. K. September 20, 2014.
Skaggs, Bob. May 7, 2008; November 19, 2010; November 8, 2013; February 5, 2016; January 15, 2019.
Smith, Roosevelt (Sonny). November 22, 2002.
Smith, Virgil. December 3, 2001.
Solon, Brad. June 8, 9, 2009.
Spray, Delbert. November 17, 1990.
Stallcup, Charlie. October 14, 1990.
Stecker, Jenn. September 24, 1996.
Stoneking, Alita [Alita Stoneking Weisgerber]. November 1, 6, 2020.
Stoneking, Lee Roy. November 17, 1975.

Summers, Kathy. April 25, May 29, 2010; November 8, 2013; September 2, 2018; February 19, 22, 2021.
Sutherland, Laine. November 10, 17, 2017; January 19, March 25, June 1, July 21, 26, 2018.
Tharp, Westwood. April 2, 2000.
Turner, John T. November 1, 2015; November 2018.
Verdot, Tom. February 23, March 11, 2019; January 21, 2020; February 27, 2021.
Walden, Charlie. June 3, 2016 (Facebook); July 27, December 31, 2018; October 2, 2020.
Williams, John P., Jr. June 10, 16, August 25, 1998; November 7, 1999; August 22, 2000; May 25, 2016; December 15, 2018 (Facebook); October 2, 3, 2020.
Williams, Phil. March 31, 2008; June 23, November 2, 29, 2009;, May 27, July 15, December 28, 2013; January 15, 2014.
Williams, Phil, and Vivian Williams. June 16, 2005; June 26, July 16, 2009.
Williams, Stuart. June 1, 19, October 2, 6, 16, 2015.
Williams, Vivian. June 22, 2006; January 4, 2007; December 1, 2009; August 5, 2011; June 27, 2019; September 12, 2020; February 5, March 2021.
Wilson, Mark. October 1, 3, 2020.
Windsor, Rea. February 18, 2009.
Wolfe, Musial. November 25, 1994; March 5, May 6, 1997 (Carrie J. Watson interview).
Wood, Annette Calton. January 24, 2021.
Wyatt, Allen. August 26, 2000; March 11, 2008; June 16, 2009; January 12, August 20, 2010; January 22, 2011; August 5, 2014; April 26, 28, 2018; February 19, 2021.
Wyatt, Bud [Charles]. November 29, 2018.
Wyatt, Matt. November 1, 2002; July 1, September 6, 2003; August 29, 2006; August 13, 15, 2007; March 31, 2008; October 2, 2010; February 14, May 9, August 20, 2011; January 24, 2019; September 14, 2020; February 3, 18, 22, 2021.

Other Sources

This list is intended as a guide for readers. It is not exhaustive, but a selection of pertinent works as well as personal favorites. Additional references appear in the endnotes.

Adam, E. [Ernst] F. *Old-Time Fiddlers' Favorite Barn Dance Tunes for the Violin*. 1927. Reissued as *Mel Bay's Old Time Fiddle Solos*. Pacific, MO: Mel Bay, 1977.
Adler, Thomas A. *Bean Blossom: The Brown County Jamboree and Bill Monroe's Bluegrass Festival*. Urbana: University of Illinois Press, 2011.
Albani, Matthew. "From Vietnam to Trump: Protest Songs throughout the Decades." *Billboard*, November 23, 2016.
Allen, Michael, Robert Gillespie, and Pamela Tellejohn Hayes. *Essential Elements for Strings: Violin Book 1*. 2002. Reprint, New York: Hal Leonard, 2012.
———. *Essential Elements for Strings: Violin Book 2*. New York: Hal Leonard, 2003.
Allen, Ray. *Gone to the Country: The New Lost City Ramblers and the Folk Music Revival*. Urbana: University of Illinois Press, 2010.
Anastasio, Paul. "The Music of Mexico's Tierra Caliente: A Renaissance." *American String Teacher* (May 2004): 60–65.

———. "Order Out of Chaos; or, How to Play in a Group." *Fiddler Magazine* 8, no. 3 (2001): 40–41.

———. "The Remarkable Music of Mexico's Terra Caliente: An Update." *Fiddler Magazine* 25, no. 4 (2018–19): 19.

Artley, Melvin N. "The West Virginia Country Fiddler: An Aspect of the Folk Music Tradition of the United States." PhD diss., Chicago Musical College, 1955.

Babbitt, Bruce. *Markneukirchen Violins and Bows from Saxon and Bohemian Musikwinkel: Late 19th Century and Early 20th Century*. Delaware, OH: Babbitt, 2014.

Barton, Cathy. "The Hammer Sisters." *Big Muddy Soundings* (April 2001): 3.

———. "Old-Time Music in Missouri." *Old-Time Herald* 4, no. 5 (2007): 10–11.

———. "Taylor McBaine." *Old-Time Herald* 4, no. 5 (1994): 23.

Barton, Cathy, and Dave Para. "Carp Camp: A Singular Jam." Paper presented at the Missouri Folklore Society annual conference, Defiance, 2012.

Bayard, Samuel P. *Dance to the Fiddle, March to the Fife: Instrumental Folk Tunes in Pennsylvania*. University Park: Pennsylvania State University Press, 1982.

———. *Hill Country Tunes: Instrumental Folk Music of Southwestern Pennsylvania*. Philadelphia: American Folklore Society, 1944.

Beisswenger, Drew. "Final Notes: Fred Stoneking." *Old-Time Herald* 12, no. 2 (2009–10): 3.

———. "Gordon McCann: The Improbable Ascent of the Ozarks Fiddle Man." *Old-Time Herald* 10, no. 4 (2006): 32–36.

———. "Jam Sessions in Southwest Missouri." https://www.library.missouristate.edu/projects/jamsessions.

———. *North American Fiddle Music: A Research and Information Guide*. New York: Routledge, 2011.

———. *The World's Hottest Fiddlers*. Transcribed by Drew Beisswenger. Pacific, MO: Mel Bay, 2015.

Beisswenger, Drew, and Gordon McCann. *Ozarks Fiddle Music: 308 Tunes Featuring 30 Legendary Fiddlers with Selections from 50 Other Great Ozarks Fiddlers*. Pacific, MO: Mel Bay, 2008.

Belden, Henry M., ed. *Ballads and Songs Collected by the Missouri Folk-Lore Society*. 1940. Reprint, Columbia: University of Missouri Press, 1966.

Bennett, Gillian. "Keith K. Cunningham (April 1939–April 2013)." *Folklore* 124 (2013): 345–47.

Bergey, Barry. "Sketches of a Fiddle Convention in the Flatlands (1971)." *Missouri Friends of the Folk Arts* (St. Louis) (ca. 1973): 1–2.

Bergey, Barry, et al. *I'm Old but I'm Awfully Tough: Traditional Music of the Ozark Region*. New Haven, MO: Missouri Friends of Folk Arts, 1977.

Bernhardt, Jack. "Compton and Newberry." *Bluegrass Unlimited* 54, no. 4 (2019): 26–27.

Berrier, Ralph, Jr. "Rhonda Vincent." *Bluegrass Unlimited* 42, no. 11 (2008): 28–33.

Beuchner, Alan, and Bill Shull. *Thirty Fiddle Tunes from the Manuscript Collections William Sidney Mount*. Columbia, MO, and Stony Brook, NY: Missouri State Old-time Fiddlers' Association and the Museums of Stony Brook, 1995.

Bilyeu, Mark. "A Comparative Analysis of 'Durang's Hornpipe.'" Master's thesis, Missouri State University, 2007.

———, prod. *Ozarks Musical Traditions* [videorecording]. Springfield: Southwest Missouri State University Office of Broadcast Services, 2002.

Bistodeau, Deena. "Texas Style Controlled Improvisation and the American Fiddle Contest." *National Oldtime Fiddler* (October–December 2011): 18–19.

———. "Texas Style Controlled Improvisation and the American Fiddle Contest, Part II." *National Oldtime Fiddler* (January–March 2012): 19–20.

———. "Texas Style Controlled Improvisation and the American Fiddle Contest, Part III." *National Oldtime Fiddler* (Summer 2012): 21–23.

———. "Texas Style Controlled Improvisation and the American Fiddle Contest, Part IV." *National Oldtime Fiddler* (October–December 2012): 20–22.

Bithell, Caroline, and Juniper Hill, eds. *The Oxford Handbook of Music Revival*. New York: Oxford University Press, 2014.

Blaustein, Richard J. "Farewell to Jake Hughes: Some Thoughts on the Passing of a True Country Gentleman." *Devil's Box* 15, no. 1 (1981): 3–5.

———. "Jake and Lena Hughes: Grassroots Promoters of the Old-Time Fiddling Revival in Missouri and the Great Plains Region." *Missouri Folklore Society Journal* 13–14 (1991–92): 1–16.

———. "The Oldtime Fiddler's Association Movement: A Grassroots Folk Revival." *Southern Folklore Quarterly* 51, no. 3 (1994): 199–217.

———. "Rethinking Folk Revivalism: Grass-Roots Preservation and Folk Romanticism." In *Transforming Tradition: Folk Music Revivals Examined*, edited by Neil V. Rosenberg, 259–74. Urbana: University of Illinois Press, 1993.

———. "Traditional Music and Social Change: The Old-Time Fiddlers' Association Movement in the United States." PhD diss., Indiana University, 1975.

———. "Will Success Spoil Old-Time Fiddling and Bluegrass?" *Devil's Box* 17, no. 2 (June 1972): 21–24.

"Bluegrass Combos Await Bash at Uncle Penn's Pickin' Place." *Billboard*, September 21, 1974, 42.

Bovee, Bob. "Vesta Johnson, Missouri's Well-Kept Secret." *Old-Time Herald* 1, no. 8 (2008–9): 8–11.

Brassieur, C. Ray. "Expressions of French Identity in the Mid-Mississippi Valley." PhD diss., University of Missouri, 1999.

———. "Three Characteristics of Missouri French Fiddling: Early, Often, and Toujours." *OldTime Herald* 4, no. 5 (1994): 16.

Breathnach, Breandán. *Folk Music and Dances of Ireland*. 1971. Reprint, Cork: Ossian, 1996.

Brinkman, David. "'Marmaduke's Hornpipe': A Study of Four Versions." *Devil's Box* 23, no. 3 (1989): 14–18.

Brody, David. *The Fiddler's Fakebook*. New York: Oak, 1983.

———. *Kenny Baker Fiddle*. New York: Oak, 1979.

Bryan, Sarah. "Young Old-Time Musicians in North Carolina." *Old-Time Herald* 14, no. 2 (2020): 36–40.

Buckley, F. J. *The Violinist's Guide*. Chicago: The Violinist Publishing Company, 1916.

Burman-Hall, Linda C. "Southern American Folk Fiddle Styles." *Ethnomusicology* 19, no. 1 (1975): 47–65.

———. "Southern American Folk Fiddling: Context and Style." PhD diss., Princeton University, 1973.

Campbell, Olive Dame, and Cecil J. Sharp. *English Folk Songs from the Southern Appalachians*. New York: G. P. Putnam's Sons, 1917.

Cantwell, Robert S. *When We Were Good: The Folk Revival.* Cambridge, MA: Harvard University Press, 1996.

Cardwell, Nancy. "The Fiddle Music of Art Galbraith: An Ozark Family Legacy Passed Down Four Generations." *Bluegrass Unlimited* (1984): 16–19.

———. "Lyman Enloe: A Stylist of the Old-Time Fiddle." *Bluegrass Unlimited* (January 1989): 61–64.

———. "Mike Hartgrove: IIIrd Tyme Out's Secret Ingredient on Fiddle." *Bluegrass Now* (2000): 21–24.

Carter, Thomas. "Looking for Henry Reed: Confessions of a Revivalist." In *Conference on the Collecting and Collections of Southern Traditional Music*, edited by Daniel W. Patterson, 73–89. Southern Folklife Collection. Chapel Hill: University of North Carolina, 1991.

"Carter County Observes Centennial." *Missouri Historical Review* 54, no. 2 (1960): 192.

"Cathy Barton." *Dulcimer Players News* 20, no. 4 (1994–95): 22–25.

Christeson, Mike. "Robert Perry Christeson: 'Dean of Missouri Fiddle Music.'" *Old Settlers Gazette* (Waynesville MO, Old Stage Stop Foundation), Fall 2009, 42–49.

Christeson, R. P. *The Old-Time Fiddlers Repertory*. 2 vols. 1973–84. Reprint, Columbia: University of Missouri Press, 2010.

———. "Old-Time Fiddling in Missouri: A Workshop." *Missouri Folklore Society Journal* 20 (1998): 1–24.

Cockrell, Ewing. *Cockrell's History of Johnson County, Missouri*. Vol. 2. Topeka, KS: Historical, 1918.

Cohen, John. "The Folksong Revival—a Historical Perspective, Part I: The Early Years." *Old-Time Herald* 3, no. 3 (1992): 27–32.

———. "The Folksong Revival—a Historical Perspective, Part II." *Old-Time Herald* 3, no. 4 (1992): 34–40.

Cohen, Ronald D. *A History of Folk Festivals in the United States: Feasts of Musical Celebration*. Lanham, MD: Scarecrow Press, 2008.

———. *Rainbow Quest: The Folk Music Revival and American Society, 1940–1970*. Amherst: University of Massachusetts Press, 2002.

Cole, M. M. *One Thousand Fiddle Tunes*. 1883. Reprint of *Ryan's Mammoth Collection*. Chicago: Cole, 1940.

Combs, Matt, Katie Harford Hogue, and Greg Reisch, comps. *John Hartford's Mammoth Collection of Fiddle Tunes*. Franklin, TN: StuffWorks Press, 2018.

Conger, Bill. "Aaron McDaris: All about the Banjo." *Bluegrass Unlimited* (November 2015): 34–35.

Daring, Andrew. "The Diffusion of Texas Style Fiddling to Non-Fiddlers." https://texasfiddle.pro/the-diffusion-of-texas-style-fiddle-to-non-fiddlers/.

Davis, Stephen F. "1982 State of Tennessee Old-Time Fiddlers' Championships." *Devil's Box* 16, no. 2 (1982): 25–26.

DeRyke, Delores. "American Old-Time Fiddlers' Association." *Devil's Box* 18 (September 1972): 6–7.

———. "So Hell Is Full of Fiddlers—Bet It Won't Be Crowded!" *Western Folklore* 23, no. 3 (1964): 183.

Dewey, Vivian Persis. *Tips to Dancers: Good Manners for Ballroom and Dance Hall.* Kenosha, WI: Dewey, 1918.

Dillard, Douglas, et al. *The Bluegrass Banjo Style of Douglas Flint Dillard.* Hialeah, FL: Almo, 1980.

Dominguez, Andreas M. "A Latino Presence in the Heartland: Challenges and Opportunities." Charles N. Kimball Lecture, Western Historical Manuscript Collection, University of Missouri–Kansas City, April 2003.

Drayton, Mike. "Pearl Sivetts, a Swingin' Missouri Fiddler." http://www.sonic.net/~mdrayton/pearl.

Dunaway, David K., and Molly Beer. *Singing Out: An Oral History of America's Folk Song Revivals.* New York: Oxford University Press, 2010.

Duncan, Craig. *Deluxe Fiddling Method.* Pacific, MO: Mel Bay, 1981.

Edwards Brothers. *An Illustrated Historical Atlas of Callaway County, Missouri, 1876.* Philadelphia, 1876.

———. *An Illustrated Historical Atlas of Montgomery County, Missouri, 1878.* Philadelphia, 1878.

Everts-Boehm, Dana. "Missouri's Traditional Arts Apprenticeship Program and Its Incorporation of Ozarks Craftspeople." *OzarksWatch* 5, no. 2 (1991): 10–11.

———. "Notes from the Field: An Evening in Douglas County." *Tradition* (Missouri Cultural Heritage Center) 7 (1990): 3.

———. *"¡Qué Viva el Westside!": Mexican Traditional Arts in Kansas City, Missouri.* University of Missouri Cultural Heritage Center, Missouri Folk Arts Program, 1993.

———. *"You'll Never Get Ireland in America": Irish Traditional Music and Dance in St. Louis, Missouri.* Columbia: University of Missouri, Missouri Folk Arts Program, 1994.

Ewan, David. *All the Years of American Popular Music.* Englewood Cliffs, NJ: Prentice Hall, 1997.

Ewing, Tom, ed. *Bill Monroe: The Life and Music of the Blue Grass Man.* Urbana: University of Illinois Press, 2018.

———. *The Bill Monroe Reader.* Urbana: University of Illinois Press, 2000.

Fairbanks, Jonathan, and Clyde Edwin Tuck. *Past and Present of Greene County, Missouri.* Vol. 2. Indianapolis: A. W. Bowen, 1915.

Feroldi, Franco, and Maya Randolph. *From Violinmaking to Music: The Life and Work of Simone Fernando Sacconi.* 1972, Cremona, Italy: ACLAP, 1956.

Fleischhauer, Carl, and Neil V. Rosenberg. *Bluegrass Odyssey: A Documentary in Pictures and Words, 1966–86.* Urbana: University of Illinois Press, 2001.

Ford, Ira W. *Traditional Music of America.* New York: E. P. Dutton, 1940.

Fryer, Cliff. "Terry Morris." https://www.texasfiddlemusic.com.

Gaddy, Amber. "Farewell to Jim Lansford." November 1, 2012. https://www.mofiddledance.org.

———. "Lena Hughes, Ludlow, Missouri." Columbia: Missouri Traditional Fiddle and Dance Network. https://mofiddledance.org.

Gage, Allen. "Old-Time Fiddling, a Traditional Folk Art with Four Ozark Musicians." *Bittersweet* 9, no. 3 (1982): 48–64.

Galbraith, Arthur. "Autobiography." Album notes, *Dixie Blossoms.* Somerville, MA: Rounder Records LP 0133, 1980.

———. "Devil's Own Box." *Bittersweet* 9, no. 3 (1982): 58–60.

———. "Devil's Own Instrument." *Ozarks Mountaineer* 25, no. 9 (1977): 21.

———. "Music Parties in the Ozarks." *Ozarks Mountaineer* 28, nos. 6–7 (1980): 35, 50.

Galloway, Spencer. "Cleo Persinger, 1909–1971." *Old-Time Herald* 4, no. 5 (1994): 25.

———. "Grand Old Man of the Opry." *Missouri Old Time Fiddlers' Association Journal* (1985): 10–11.

———. "Missouri Fiddling Styles." In *Old-Time Fiddling: Traditional American Music*, edited by Margot Ford McMillen, 5–6. Columbia: University of Missouri Cultural Heritage Center, 1986.

———. "Sam Long: 'Echoes of the Ozarks.'" *Missouri Old-Time Fiddlers' Association Journal* (1985): 12–13.

Gardner, Robert O. *The Portable Community: Place and Displacement in Bluegrass Festival Life*. New York: Routledge, 2020.

Garelick, Gus. "Fiddling from the 'Show-Me State.'" *Fiddler Magazine* 24, no. 3 (2017): 47–52.

———. "The Legacy of Benny Thomasson." *Fiddler Magazine* 7, no. 1 (2020): 12–16.

———. "My Encounter with the Folk Police." *Fiddler Magazine* 24, no. 2 (2017): 47.

———. "Why I Hate the Cloverdale Fiddle Contest and Go Back Every Year." *Fiddler Magazine* 22, no. 4 (2015–16): 48.

"Gene Wells, 1918–1981." *MSOTFA 1982 Contest Calendar* (Columbia): 7.

Gerrard, Alice. "Colby Street to New York & Points South: The Highwoods Stringband." *Old-Time Herald* 3, no. 4 (1992): 26–33.

Gillespie, Gail. "Blue Flame." Review, *Old-Time Herald* 4, no. 6 (1994–95): 47–48.

Glassie, Henry. *Passing the Time in Ballymenone: Culture and History in an Ulster Community*. Philadelphia: University of Pennsylvania Press, 1982.

Glenn, Wayne. *The Ozarks' Greatest Hits: A Photo History of Music in the Ozarks*. Nixa, MO: Glenn, 2005.

Goertzen, Christopher. "Balancing Local and National Approaches at American Fiddle Contests." *American Music* 14, no. 3 (1996).

———. "'Billy in the Low Ground': History of an American Instrumental Folk Tune." PhD diss., University of Illinois, 1983.

———. *Southern Fiddlers and Fiddle Contests*. Jackson: University Press of Mississippi, 2008.

———. "The Transformation of American Contest Fiddling." *Journal of Musicology* 6, no. 1 (1998): 107–29.

Goldfield, Steve. "Alan Jabbour: Fiddler, Scholar, and Preserver of Tradition." *Fiddler Magazine* 13, no. 3 (2006): 14–20.

Goldsmith, Thomas, ed. *The Bluegrass Reader*. Urbana: University of Illinois Press, 2004.

Goodspeed. *History of Cole, Moniteau, Morgan, Benton, Maries and Osage Counties, Missouri*. Chicago: Goodspeed, 1889.

Gow, Niel. *Part Second of the Complete Repository of Original Scots Tunes, Strathspeys, Jigs and Dances (the Dances Arranged as Medleys in Their Respective Keys for the Harp, or Piano-Forte, Violin and Violoncello &c. Humbly Dedicated to Her Grace the Duchess of Buccleugh by Niel Gow & Sons)*. Edinburgh: Niel Gow and Sons, 1802.

Graf, Sharon Poulson. "Oldtime Fiddle Music Gets a Face Lift: The Formation of 'the' National Oldtime Fiddlers' Contest." *Missouri Folklore Society Journal* 25 (2003): 43–54.

———. "Traditionalization at the National Oldtime Fiddlers' Contest: Politics, Power, and Authenticity." PhD diss., Michigan State University, 1999.

———. "Why Fiddling Is the Perfect Hobby during Quarantine." *Visible Magazine*, October 19, 2020. www.visiblemagazine.com.

Gray, Vykki Mende, and Kenny Hall. *Kenny Hall's Music Book: Old-Time Music for Fiddle and/or Mandolin*. Pacific, MO: Mel Bay, 1999.

Greathouse, Patricia. *Mariachi*. Layton, UT: Gibbs Smith, 2009.

Green, Archie. *Only a Miner: Studies in Recorded Coal Mining Songs*. Urbana: University of Illinois Press, 1972.

———. "Thomas Hart Benton's Folk Musicians." *John Edwards Memorial Foundation Quarterly* 12, no. 42 (1976): 74–90.

Green, John J., and Elizabeth Barham. *Latinos in Missouri*. Occasional Paper Series no. 1. Columbia: Department of Rural Sociology, University of Missouri, 2002.

Griffin, John. "Pete McMahan." *Old-Time Herald* 4, no. 6 (1994–95): 23–24.

Hager, Julia. "Old Time Fiddling: An Interview with R. P. Christeson." *Devil's Box* 10, no. 3 (1976): 14–20.

Haley, Alex. *Roots: The Saga of an American Family*. New York: Doubleday, 1976.

Halsey, Derek. "Escaping Floods, Working on Buses, and Keeping the Downbeat in Bluegrass Music: The Lonesome River Band Celebrates 35 Years." *Bluegrass Unlimited* 52, no. 5 (2017): 16–18.

———. "John Hartford: Still Influencing New Generations Decades Later." *Bluegrass Unlimited* (February 2021): 12–18.

———. "Po' Ramblin' Boys' C. J. Lewandowski Talks Digging into Bluegrass' Rich History." Recording Academy, September 29, 2018. http://www.grammy.com.

Harris, Craig. *Bluegrass, New Grass, Old-Time, and Americana Music*. Gretna, LA: Pelican, 2018.

———. "The Greenbrier Boys." http://www.allmusic.com.

———. "Tracy Schwarz." *Bluegrass Unlimited* (July 2017): 38–40.

Hartford, John. *The Banjo according to John Hartford: Licks, Ideas, and Music*. Instructional video with text, 2 vols. Woodstock, NY: Homespun Tapes, 2004.

———. "Benny Martin: The Genius of Music City, USA." *Fiddler Magazine* 6, no. 3 (1999): 4–11.

———. *John Hartford's Old Time Fiddling ("Trying to Teach My Hands to Do What I Hear in My Head")*. Video, booklet. Los Altos, CA: Fiddler Magazine, ca. 1998.

———. "John Hartford Tune Transcriptions: 'Coming Down from Denver on a Trip to Galway Here and There,' 'Flannery's Dream.'" *Devil's Box* 29, no. 1 (1995): 12–14.

———. "John Hartford Tune Transcriptions: 'Darkie's Curly Hair,' 'Knocking at Your Door,' 'Maysville,' 'Better Get Outa My Way.'" *Devil's Box* 29, no. 4 (1995): 17–19.

———. "John Hartford Tune Transcriptions: 'Hamilton Iron Works.'" *Devil's Box* 32, no. 4 (1998): 53.

———. "John Hartford Tune Transcriptions: 'Whoa Mule,' 'Boone County Rag.'" *Devil's Box* 28, no. 4 (1994): 11–13.

———. "Old-Time Ed Haley Tunes: Garfield's Blackberry Blossom." *Fiddler Magazine* 6, no. 4 (1999–2000): 40.

———. "Old Time Tunes: 'Wolves a-Howlin'.'" *Fiddler Magazine* 4, no. 4 (1997–98): 37.

———. "On the Study of Fiddle Tunes: Reassurance That There Is No Frivolous Design behind This Seemingly 'Goofy' Maneuver." *Fiddler Magazine* 6, no. 2 (1999): 38–40.

———. Preface to *Fiddler's Curse: The Untold Story of Ervin T. Rouse*, by Randy Noles. Frederick, MD: Centerstream, 2007.

Hay, John H., Jr. *Vietnam Studies: Tactical and Materiel Innovations*. Washington, DC: Department of the Army, 1989.

Henderson, Betty Craker. "The McDowell Gold Jubilee: History of a Hootenanny." *Missouri Folklore Society Journal* 27–28 (2005–6): 8–19.

Henigan, Julie. "Art Galbraith, Ozarks Fiddler." *Come for to Sing: Folk Music in Chicago and the Midwest* 9, no. 4 (1983): 26–28. http://www.fiddlesessions.com.

———. "The McClurg Music Parties: A Living Tradition." *Old-Time Herald* 4, no. 5 (1994): 20–22.

———. "Music Parties and Céilís: A Study in Cultural Continuity." Paper presented at the Ozarks Studies Symposium, Missouri State University, West Plains, September 24, 2009.

———. "Ozark Ballads as Story and Song." *Missouri Folklore Society Journal* 27–28 (2005–6): 157–81.

———. "Play Me Something Quick and Devilish: Bob Holt—Old-Time Square Dance Fiddler." *Old-Time Herald* 4, no. 6 (1994–95): 26–30.

———. Review of *Sugar in the Coffee: Pre-revival Dulcimer, Fiddling and Songs from the Missouri Ozarks*. Missouri State Old Time Fiddlers Association MSOTFA 301-C. http://www.mustrad.org.uk/revieews/b_graves.htm.

Hentoff, Nat. *American Music Is*. New York: Da Capo Press, 2004.

Hickerson, Joseph C., comp. *A Bibliography of Fiddling, Fiddle Tunes, and Related Dance Tune Collections in North America*. Washington, DC: Archive of Folk Song, Library of Congress, 1974.

Hicks, Ray. "Portrait of a Fiddler: Billy Lee." *MABC Bluegrass Ramblin's* (June 15, 1972): 14–15.

Higgins, Lisa L. "Missouri Folk Arts Program." *Museum Magazine* 72 (2018): 11–12.

Higgins, Lisa L., et al. *Work Is Art; Art Is Work: Interviews with Missouri Luthiers*. Video. Columbia: Missouri Folk Arts Program, 2007.

Hill, Stephen. "Blood Harmony: Sisters Blend Mariachi Roots and Pop in Maria the Mexican." *Kansas Alumni Magazine* http:/www.kansasalumnimagazine.org.

Himes, Geoffrey. "Lonesome River Band." *Bluegrass Unlimited* 37, no. 6 (2002): 32–36.

———. "IIIrd Tyme Out." *Bluegrass Unlimited* 34, no. 11 (2000): 42–46.

Hobbs, Holly. "Women of Old-Time Music: Tradition and Change in the Missouri Ozarks." Master's thesis, Indiana University, 2003.

———. "Women of Old-Time Music: Tradition and Change in the Missouri Ozarks." *Missouri Folklore Society Journal* 25 (2003): 55–72.

Howe, Elias. *Howe's 1,000 Jigs and Reels, Clog Dances, Contra Dances, Fancy Dances, Hornpipes, Strathspeys, Breakdowns, Irish Dances, Scotch Dances, and More*. 1867. Reprinted as *Mel Bay Presents Howe's 1,000 . . .*, edited by Patrick Sky. Pacific, MO: Mel Bay, 2001.

———. *Musician's Omnibus, Complete; Containing 1500 Pieces of Music for Violin, Flute, Fife, Cornet, Clarionet, Flageolet or any Treble Instrument*. Boston: Howe, 1864.

Hunter, Martha Louis. "Volunteer Profile: Rod Moag—Host of 'Country Swing & Rockabilly Jamboree.'" http://www.koop.org.

Hyland, Deborah. "The Ill-Mo Boys—*Laugh and Grow Fat*" (review). *Folk Fire* (January–February 2000).

"Issues: Sportsmanship." *MSOTFA Quarterly* 1, no. 1 (1994): 5. https://www.missourifiddling.com.

Ives, Edward D. *Lawrence Doyle: The Farmer-Poet of Prince Edward Island*. Orono: University of Maine Press, 1971.

Jabbour, Alan. *American Fiddle Tunes* (1971). Archive of Folk Song, Library of Congress; reissue, Rounder Records, 2000.

———. "Fiddle Music." In *American Folklore: An Encyclopedia*, edited by Jan Brunvand, 253–56. New York: Garland, 1996.

———. *Fiddle Tunes Illuminated: 45 Tunes Transcribed and Annotated for Stylistic Study*. Washington, DC: Jabbour, 2011.

———. "A Participant-Documentarian in the American Instrumental Folk Music Revival." In *Oxford Handbook of Music Revival*, edited by Caroline Bithell and Juniper Hill, 116–34. New York: Oxford University Press, 2014.

"Jake Hockemeyer." *Old-Time Herald* 4, no. 6 (1994–95): 16.

Johnson, Bernice E. "Place Names in Six of the West Central Counties of Missouri." Master's thesis, University of Missouri, 1933.

Johnson, Sherry Anne. "'If You Want to Win, You've Got to Play It Like a Man.'" *Canadian Journal for Traditional Music* 27 (1999–2000): 10–19.

———. "Negotiating Tradition in Ontario Fiddle Contests." PhD diss., York University, 2006.

Johnston, Neil. "Folk Fiddling, Part I: Which Direction—Preservation or Development?" *Seattle Folklore Society Journal* 4, no. 2 (1972): 3–5.

———. "Folk Fiddling, Part II: Which Direction—Preservation or Development?" *Seattle Folklore Society Journal* 4, no. 4 (1973): 13–15.

Kansas City Historical Co. *History of Johnson County, Missouri*. Kansas City: Kansas City Historical, 1881.

Kinder, Rose Marie, and Kristine Lowe-Martin. *Old-Time Fiddling: Hal Sappington*. Warrensburg, MO: Johnson County Historical Society Press, 2012.

King, Chris. "String Theory: South City's Geoffrey Seitz Might Sell You a Violin from His Shop. Then Again, He Might Not." *St. Louis Magazine*, August 31, 2007.

Koken, Walt. "Tales from the 'Woods, Part 4: The Smoke-In." *Old-Time Herald* 13, no. 4 (2012): 22–23.

———. "Tales from the 'Woods, Part 7: Ithaca." *Old-Time Herald* 13, no. 7 (2013): 32–33.

Krassen, Miles. *Appalachian Fiddle*. New York: Oak, 1973.

———. *Clawhammer Banjo*. 1974. Reprint, New York: Music Sales of America 1992.

———. *Masters of Old-Time Fiddling*. New York: Oak, 1983.

———. *O'Neill's Music of Ireland: Over One Thousand Fiddle Tunes*. New York: Oak, 1992.

Krassen, Miles, and Tony DeMarco. *A Trip to Sligo: A Comprehensive Guide to the Art of Irish Fiddling, Sligo Style*. Pittsburgh: Silver Spear, 1978.

Krause, Rachel. "Breathing New Life into Missouri Fiddling: John P. Williams." Oldtime-Central, February 13, 2020. https://www.oldtime-central.com.

Kuntz, Andrew. *The Fiddler's Companion: A Descriptive Index of North American and British Isles Music for the Folk Violin*. https://ibiblio.org/fiddlers/FChomepage.

Laird, Judith Ann Fincher. *Argentine, Kansas: The Evolution of a Mexican-American Community, 1905–1940*. Lawrence: University Press of Kansas, 1975.

Lance, Donald M., ed. "Reminiscences of R. P. Christeson." *Missouri Folklore Society Journal* 20 (1998): 25–36.

Lansford, Kim. "'Boy! He Sure had Some Good Tunes!': The Music of Lonnie Robertson." *Ozarks Mountaineer* (July–August 2012): 38–39.

———. "Endless Memories: Remembering Fred Stoneking, 1933–2009." *Ozarks Mountaineer* 58, no. 1 (January–February 2010).

Lawless, Ray M. *Folksingers and Folksongs in America*. New York: Duell, Sloan, and Pearce, 1960.

Leftwich, Brad. *Round Peak Style Clawhammer Banjo*. Pacific, MO: Mel Bay, 1999.

Letsky, Pippa. *Compendium A–Z: 114 Original Fiddle Tunes by Pippa Letsky*. 2nd ed. www.pippaletsky.com.

———. *Nineteen Tunes for 2009*. www.pippaletsky.com.

Linden, David J. *Unique: The New Science of Human Individuality*. New York: Basic Books, 2020.

Lippincott, Peter, and Marget Lippincott. *Traditional Dance in Missouri*. Vol. 1, *Southern Missouri Jig Dancing*. St. Louis: Childgrove Country Dancers, 1984.

Lofgren, Lyle. Review of *The New Lost City Ramblers: The Early Years, 1958–1962*. *Old-Time Herald* 3, no. 4 (1992): 49.

Lofgren, Lyle, and Elizabeth Lofgren. "Bob Bovee and Gail Heil: For Old Time's Sake." *Old-Time Herald* 9, no. 3 (2004).

Lund, Jens, and R. Serge Denisoff. "The Folk Music Revival and the Counter Culture: Contributions and Contradictions." *Journal of American Folklore* 84, no. 334 (1971): 394–405.

MacAoidh, Caoimhin. "When Folklore Misses the Mark." *Fiddler Magazine* 27, no. 4 (2020–21): 46–47.

Malone, Bill C. *Country Music USA*. Rev. ed. Austin: University of Texas Press, 2002.

Maloy, Frank. "Canary Waltz as Played by Lena Hughes." *Devil's Box* 10, no. 3 (1976): 54–56.

Marshall, Howard Wight. "Alva Lee Hendren Dies at 77." Missouri Traditional Fiddle and Dance Network, March 2007. http://www.mofiddledance.org.

———. "Art Galbraith, 1909–1993." *Devil's Box* 27, no. 3 (1993): 6–8.

———. "Bill Shull." *Old-Time Herald* 4, no. 6 (1994–95): 21–22.

———. "Black Jack David on Wax: Child 200 and Recorded Hillbilly Music." *Keystone Folklore Quarterly* 17, no. 4 (1972): 133–43.

———. "Bluegrass Time in the Show-Me State." *Missouri Historical Review* 112, no. 1 (2017): 25–45.

———. "A Brief Sketch of Violinmaker Walter Boswell of Moberly, Missouri." Manuscript, 2012, rev. 2018, Randolph County Historical Society.

———. "Charlie Stallcup Dies at 101." Missouri Traditional Fiddle and Dance Network, December 2007. http://www.mofiddledance.org.

———. "Chinkapin." *Missouri State Old-Time Fiddlers' Association Journal* (Spring 1994): 3.

———. "A Conversation with Jim McReynolds." *Country Music Magazine* 1, no. 2 (1972).

———. "Country Music Interviews: Lester Flatt." *Country Music Magazine* 1, no. 3 (1972): 51–53.

———. "Cyril Stinnett, Legendary Missouri Fiddler: Home Videos from the Dwight Lamb Collection." *Old-Time Herald* 13, no. 11 (2015): 43–47.

———. "Done Gone: Art Galbraith, 1909–1993." *National Old-Time Fiddler* 10, no. 2 (1993): 1–5.

———. "Done Gone: Gene Goforth, 1921–2002." *Fiddler Magazine* 10, no. 3 (2003): 25–29.

———. "Evansville (Missouri, That Is)." *MSOTFA Journal* (1994): 3.

———. "An Evening with Lee Roy Stoneking, with a Few Unexpurgated and Incomplete Comments on Field Recording Traditional Artists during the Heyday of the Folk Festival and Fiddlers' Contest Revival." Online notes to Brad Leftwich and Linda Higginbotham, *Lee Stoneking: Missouri Fiddling and Banjo Playing*. Ravenna, OH: Field Recorders' Collective FRC 708, 2014. http://www.fieldrecorder.com.

———. "Farewell Bill Eddy." Missouri Traditional Fiddle and Dance Network, August 2010. http://www.mofiddledance.org.

———. *Fiddler's Dream: Old-Time, Swing, and Bluegrass Music in Twentieth-Century Missouri*. Columbia: University of Missouri Press, 2017.

———. "First Tunes." May 21, 2013. www.fiddlingmissouriblogspot.com.

———. *Folk Architecture in Little Dixie: A Regional Culture in Missouri*. Columbia: University of Missouri Press, 1981.

———. "Going across the Prairie: A Missouri Fiddle Tune." *Missouri Prairie Journal* 22, no. 3 (2000): 10–13.

———. "Hal Sappington, Missouri Fiddler" (review). *Old-Time Herald* 13, no. 3 (2012): 50–52.

———. "Hand-in-Hand: Music and Dance in Central Missouri." *Old-Time Herald* 3, no. 2 (1992): 10–13.

———. "Harold Leake, Callaway County Radio Fiddler (1923–2014)." Missouri Traditional Fiddle and Dance Network, June 2014. http://www.mofiddledance.org.

———. "Hornpipes." *Missouri State Old-Time Fiddlers' Association Journal* (Spring 1993): 3.

———. "Howdy Folks! Welcome to Renfro Valley! Modern Folklore in the Kentucky Mountains." *Country Music Foundation Newsletter* 2, no. 3 (1971).

———. "In Memory: Taylor Franklin McBaine (1910–1994)." *Devil's Box* 28, no. 4 (1994): 33–35.

———. "Irish Echoes in Outstate Missouri." *Missouri Historical Review* 100, no. 1 (2005): 40–53.

———. "Jake Hockemeyer and the Legacy of Missouri Traditional Fiddling." *Devil's Box* 32, no. 4 (1997): 14–21.

———. "Jam Session Etiquette; or, Notes on the Care and Feeding of an American Tradition with Special Reference to Old-Time Fiddling." Paper presented at the Missouri Folklore Society Conference, Defiance, 2012.

———. "John Griffin." *Old-Time Herald* 4, no. 6 (1994–95): 22–23.

———. "Johnny Ray Bruce, 1939–1992." *National Old Time Fiddler* 9, no. 8 (1992): 1–3.

———. "Keeping the Tie-Hacker Tunes Alive: Nile Wilson." *Old-Time Herald* 1, no. 4 (1994–95): 24–38.

———. "Keep on the Sunny Side of Life: Pattern and Religious Expression in Bluegrass Gospel Music." *New York Folklore Quarterly* 30, no. 1 (1974): 1–43.

———. "'King of the Folks': R. P. Christeson and His *Old-Time Fiddler's Repertory*." *Old-Time Herald* 13, no. 3 (2012): 22–35.

———. "Leroy Canaday." *Old-Time Herald* 1, no. 4 (1994–95): 17–18.

———. "Live! At the Ozark Opry: An Appreciation of Vaudeville and 'Show Fiddler' LeRoy Haslag." *Old-Time Herald* 12, no. 9 (2011): 24–35.

———. "Lloyd Lalumondier, 1924–2015." Missouri Traditional Fiddle and Dance Network, October 2015. http://www.mofiddledance.org.

———. "Lonnie Robertson, Radio Fiddler, Part One." *Fiddler Magazine* 14, no. 2 (2017): 12–15.

———. "Lonnie Robertson, Radio Fiddler, Part Two." *Fiddler Magazine* 14, no. 3 (2017): 24–25.

———. "Lonnie Robertson, Radio Fiddler, Part Three." *Fiddler Magazine* 14, no. 2 (2017): 25–26.

———. "'Marmaduke's Hornpipe': Speculations on the Life and Times of a Historic Missouri Fiddle Tune." *Missouri Folklore Society Journal* 13–14 (1991–92): 101–22.

———. "Meat Preservation on the Farm in Missouri's 'Little Dixie.'" *Journal of American Folklore* 92, no. 366 (1979): 400–417.

———. "Missouri Fiddle Champion Leroy (Red) Canaday Passes at 88." Missouri Traditional Fiddle and Dance Network, June 2016. http://www.mofiddledance.org.

———. "Missouri's Lena Hughes Passes Away." *Devil's Box* 32, no. 2 (1998): 46–47.

———. "Notes about 'Missouri Waltz' by a Missouri Fiddler." *Fiddle Sessions*, December 2006. http://www.fiddlesessions.com.

———. "Notes en Route: A Fiddle Contest in Southern Colorado." *Fiddler Magazine* 13, no. 1 (2006): 24–27.

———. "Open Up Them Pearly Gates for Me: Pattern and Religious Expression in Bluegrass Gospel Music." *Folklore Forum* 4, no. 1 (1971).

———. "Ozarks Fiddler Ray Curbow of Blue Eye, Missouri, Dies at 79." Missouri Traditional Fiddle and Dance Network, February 2016. http://www.mofiddledance.org.

———. "Pete McMahan Leaves the Stage." *Fiddler Magazine* 7, no. 2 (2000): 21–25.

———. "The Place of Traditional Fiddling in Midwestern Culture." In *Folk Roots: An Exploration of the Folklore and Cultural Traditions of Kansas*, edited by Jennie Chinn, 11–18. Manhattan, KS: University for Man, 1982.

———. "'Play Me Something Quick and Devilish': Adventures in the Documentation and Conservation of Missouri's Heritage of Traditional Fiddle and Dance Music." *Missouri Historical Review* 108, no. 2 (2014): 105–22.

———. *"Play Me Something Quick and Devilish": Old-Time Fiddlers in Missouri*. Columbia: University of Missouri Press, 2012.

———. "Portrait of a Bluegrass Fiddler: Delbert Spray, 1923–2001." *Missouri Folklore Society Newsletter* 26, no. 102 (2002): 7–11.

———. "A Preliminary View of Thomas Jefferson's Fiddle Music." *Fiddler Magazine* 8, no. 2 (2001): 21–25.

———. "Rattlesnake Buttons." *MSOTFA Quarterly* 13, no. 1 (1995): 3.

———. "Remembering Jake Hockemeyer." *MSOTFA Quarterly* 16, no. 1 (1999): 1–2.

———. "Remembering Missouri Fiddler Warren Helton." *Fiddler Magazine* 27, no. 4 (2020–21): 15–17.

———. "Rhonda Vincent and Missouri's Old-Time and Bluegrass Crossroads." *Old-Time Herald* 13, no. 8 (2014): 10–21.

———. "Shelby's Mule." *MSOTFA Journal* 10, no. 2 (1992): 3.

———. "Skilled Fiddler and Local Historian: Thomas Arthur Galbraith (1909–1993)." *Missouri Folklore Society Journal* 13–14 (1991–92): 165–66.

———. "So Long, Nile [Wilson]." Missouri Traditional Fiddle and Dance Network, March 2008. http://www.mofiddledance.org.

———. "The Swedish Nightingale, 'Jenny Lind Polka,' and American Fiddle Music." *Missouri Folklore Society Journal* 24 (2002): 37–68.

———. "That Texas Contest Sound, Take Two." *Old-Time Herald* 1, no. 2 (1987–88): 14–17.

———. "Thomas Arthur Galbraith (1909–1993): An Appreciation." *Old-Time Herald* 3, no. 8 (1993): 126–28.

———. "Toward the Furtherance of Country Music Studies." *John Edwards Memorial Foundation Newsletter* 9, no. 4 (1973).

———. "Traditional Fiddling in Mississippi." In *Festival of American Folklife*. Washington, DC: Smithsonian Institution, 1974.

———. "A Tribute to John Hartford." *Fiddler Magazine* 8, no. 3 (2001): vi.

———. "We Was Just Kids Out of the Hill Country: The Case of the Buchanan Brothers." *Journal of Country Music* 5, no. 2 (1974).

———. "'Where Did You Come from, Where Did You Go?': The Split Personality of 'Cotton-Eyed Joe,' Part One." *Fiddle Sessions*, 2010. http://www.fiddlesessions.com.

———. "'Where Did You Come from, Where Did You Go?': The Split Personality of 'Cotton-Eyed Joe,' Part Two." *Fiddle Sessions*, July 2010. http://www.fiddlesessions.com.

Marshall, Howard Wight, et al. *"Now That's a Good Tune": Masters of Traditional Missouri Fiddling*. Rev. ed. Seattle: Voyager Recordings and Books, 2008.

Marshall, Howard Wight, and James W. Goodrich, eds. *The German-American Experience in Missouri*. Columbia: State Historical Society of Missouri and Missouri Cultural Heritage Center, 1986.

Marshall, Howard, Vivian Williams, and Phil Williams. *Fiddle Seconding Missouri Style, Chords and Bowing Techniques*. Seattle: Voyager Recordings and Books, VR-DVD1001, 2012.

Martin, Pete. *Benny Thomasson Fiddle Transcriptions*. Seattle: Petimar Press, 1997.

Matheny, Arlie. "The Bluegrass Brigade." *Bluegrass Unlimited* (August 1988): 29–32.

———. "Jim McGreevy." *Bluegrass Unlimited* (April 1988): 82–84.

McCann, Gordon. "Art Galbraith." *Old-Time Herald* 4, no. 5 (1994): 24.

———. "Bob Walsh." *Old-Time Herald* 4, no. 5 (1994): 13.

———. "Leonard Smith." *Old-Time Herald* 4, no. 6 (1994–95): 20–21.

———. "Lonnie Robertson." *Old-Time Herald* 4, no. 5 (1994): 12–13.

———. "Missouri Fiddler Lyman Enloe to Receive National Heritage Fellowship." *Devil's Box* 29, no. 3 (1995): 51–52.

McCarty, Jim. "30 Years of Traditions: Apprenticeship Program Creates Folk Artist 'Hall of Fame.'" *Rural Missouri* (July 2015): 18–19.

McCrory, Knox. "Notes on the Harmonica: Toy or Musical Instrument?" *Missouri Folklore Society Journal* 20 (1998): 157–66.

McCullough, Lawrence E. *The Complete Irish Tinwhistle Tutor*. Pittsburgh: Silver Spear, 1976

McDowell, Robert E. "Bones and the Man: Toward a History of Bones Playing." *Journal of American Culture* 5, no. 1 (1982): 38–43.

McGreevy, Jim. "Chuck Stearman, the Man from SPBGMA." *Bluegrass Music News* (Winter 2017): 3.

———. "The Collins Family of Kansas City: A Bluegrass Legacy." *Bluegrass Music News* (Summer 2008): 8–9.

McKinney, Edgar D. "Images, Realities, and Cultural Transformations in the Missouri Ozarks, 1920–1960." PhD diss., University of Missouri, 1990.

McMillen, Margot Ford. *A to Z Missouri: The Dictionary of Missouri Place Names*. Columbia: Pebble, 2014.

———. "Dean Johnston. *Old-Time Herald* 4, no. 6 (1994–95): 18–20.

———, ed. *Old-Time Fiddling: Traditional American Music*. Columbia: University of Missouri Cultural Heritage Center, 1986.

———. *Paris, Tightwad, and Peculiar: Missouri Place Names*. Columbia: University of Missouri Press, 1994.

Meade, Guthrie T. Review of *Folksingers and Folksongs in America*, by Ray McKinley Lawless. *Midwest Folklore* 1, no. 3 (1961): 167–70.

Mendelson, Michael. "A Bibliography of Fiddling in North America." *JEMF Quarterly* 43 (1975–76): 39–41.

Menius, Art. "Camp Spring Today: Will There Be a Tomorrow?" *Bluegrass Unlimited* (May 2015): 30–35.

Metheny, Arlie. "Jim McGreevy." *Bluegrass Unlimited* (April 1988): 82–88.

"Mid-America Old-Time Fiddling Championship and Convention: 1985 Results and Plans for 1986." *Devil's Box* 20, no. 2 (1986): 19–21.

Miller, Dan. "Joey Wieneman, Missouri Mandolin Master." *Bluegrass Unlimited* May 2021: 26–29.

———. Review of *Old Time Fiddle Tune Favorites: 15 Melodies Commonly Played in Jams Written in Tablature and Standard Notation with Sources and History*, by Tristan Scroggins. *Bluegrass Unlimited* (February 2021): 58.

Moag, Rod. "Bluegrass Music." *Handbook of Texas Online*. http://www.tshaonline.org/handbook/online/articles/xbb02, 2014.

———. "The History of Early Bluegrass in Texas." *Journal of Texas Music History* 4, no. 2 (2004): 1–13.

Moore, Gary Lee. *The Tenor Guitar: Getting Started in Fiddle Backup*. 4th ed. Seattle: Okie Boy Books, 1999.
Moore, Tiny, and Merle Haggard. 1982. *Merle Haggard Presents Swinging Texas Fiddlin' by Tiny Moore with Warren Helton and Vernon Solomon: A Study of Traditional and Modern Breakdown and Hoedown Fiddling*. New York: Peer International, 2018.
Morris, W. H. *Old-Time Violin Melodies*. 1927. Reprint, Columbia: Missouri State Old-Time Fiddlers' Association, 1992.
Myers, Jeremy. "McClurg: The Ozark Tradition Lives On." *Ozarks Mountaineer* 59, no. 6 (2011): 13–15.
Nelson, Jim. "Jim and Kim Lansford: Songsters of the Ozarks." *Old-Time Herald* 7, no. 1 (1999): 20–24, 52.
———. Review of *John Hartford, Hamilton Ironworks*. *Old-Time Herald* 8, no. 4 (2002): 48–49.
Newman, Albert W. *Dances of To-day*. Philadelphia: Penn, 1914.
"Newport Folkfest to Draw Scores of Headline Acts." *Billboard*, May 11, 1963, 4.
Nisa, Jeronimo. "Keeping the Tradition Alive in Little Dixie." Master's thesis, University of Missouri, 2008.
Northway, Martin. "Making Wood Sing: Only the Best Wood Makes the Cut for John Griffin." *Rural Missouri* (June 2002).
Nussbaum, Phil. "Music and Socializing: The Public Jam Sessions at Warren's Place." *Mid-America Folklore* 9, no. 3 (1983): 22–36.
O'Connor, Mark. "My History at Weiser." https://www.idahobluegrassassociation.org.
———. "Remembering 'the Undefeated Champion,' Herman Johnson." https://www.deeprootsmag.org.
Olin, James, Julia Hager, and Barry Bergey. "Old Time Fiddling: An Interview with R. P. Christeson—Part I." *Missouri Friends of the Folk Arts Newsletter* 2, no. 2 (1974): 4–6.
———. "Old Time Fiddling: An Interview with R. P. Christeson—Part II." *Missouri Friends of the Folk Arts Newsletter* 2, nos. 3–4 (1974): 2.
O'Neill, Francis. *The Dance Music of Ireland: 1001 Gems*. 1907. Reprint, Dublin: Walton's, 2004.
———. *O'Neill's Music of Ireland: Eighteen Hundred and Fifty Melodies*. 1902. Reprints, New York: Daniel Collins, 1964; Hohokus, NJ: Rock Press, 1977; New York: Oak, 1976 (edited by Miles Krassen).
Orme, Jeanine R. *The Fiddlin' Workshop*. Pacific, MO: Mel Bay, 1995.
———. *Herman Johnson, Master Fiddler: 39 Solos by America's Legendary Fiddler*. Pacific, MO: Mel Bay, 1999.
Osborne, Carolyn. "Contest Fiddling: What Gets Rewarded." *Fiddle Sessions*, February 2009. https://www.fiddlesessions.com.
Patterson, Daniel W., ed. *Sounds of the South: A Report and Selected Papers from a Conference on the Collecting and Collections of Southern Traditional Music*. Southern Folklife Collection. Chapel Hill: University of North Carolina, 1991.
Peek, Dan William. *Live! At the Ozark Opry*. Charleston, SC: History Press, 2010.
Pfeffer, Joseph G., ed. *Frontier Folklife Festival, 1979*. St. Louis: Missouri Friends of the Folk Arts, 1979.
———. "Guide to Folk Music in the St. Louis Area." *MFFA* 1, no. 3 (1973): 1.

Phillips, Stacy [Melvin Marshall]. *Contest Fiddling.* Pacific, MO: Mel Bay, 1983.

———. *The Phillips Collection of Traditional American Fiddle Tunes.* Vol. 1, *Hoedowns, Breakdowns, & Reels.* Pacific, MO: Mel Bay, 1994.

———. *The Phillips Collection of Traditional American Fiddle Tunes.* Vol. 2, *Rags, Blues, Hornpipes, Waltzes, Polkas, Jigs, Etc.* Pacific, MO: Mel Bay, 1995.

———. "What's Wrong with Fiddle Contest Judging?" *Fiddle Sessions,* December 2008. http://www.fiddlesessions.com.

Phillips, Stacy, and Mark O'Connor. *Mark O'Connor: The Championship Years: 1975–1984.* Pacific, MO: Mel Bay, 1991.

Plat Book of Callaway County, Missouri. Rockford, IL: W. W. Hixson, 1930.

Ramsay, Robert L. *Our Storehouse of Missouri Place Names.* Columbia: University of Missouri Press, 1952.

———. "The Place Names of Boone County, Missouri." *Publications of the American Dialect Society* 18, no. 1 (1952).

Randolph, Vance. "The Names of Ozark Fiddle Tunes." *Midwest Folklore* 4, no. 2 (1954): 81–86.

———. *Ozark Folksongs.* 4 vols. 1946. Reprint, Columbia: University of Missouri Press, 1980.

Ransdell, D. R. *Secrets of a Mariachi Violinist.* Tucson: Black Cat Productions, 2016.

Rapp, Jessica. "Violin Maker Strikes a Chord with Customers." *Suburban Journal of Greater St. Louis* (September 3, 2009).

Reid, Gary. "John Cohen." *Bluegrass Unlimited* (November 2019): 8–9.

———. "Kenny Eugene 'Ken' Seaman." *Bluegrass Unlimited* (December 2021): 12–13.

Reuss, Richard A. "American Folklore and Left-Wing Politics 1927–1957." PhD diss., Indiana University, 1971.

Roark, Michael, ed. *French and Germans in the Mississippi Valley: Landscape and Cultural Traditions.* Cape Girardeau: Southeast Missouri State University, Center for Regional History and Cultural Heritage, 1988.

Roberson, Margot, and Howard Marshall. *The Masters: Traditional Arts Apprenticeship Program.* Columbia: University of Missouri Cultural Heritage Center, 1986.

Roberts, Paul. "Recollections of a Missouri Country Fiddler." Review of *Saddle Old Spike: Fiddle Music from Missouri* (Rounder 0881, 1996), by Fred Stoneking. *Musical Traditions Internet Magazine,* September 22, 1997. www.musictrad.org.uk.

Roberts, Rob. "Missouri Fiddler Charlie 'Possum' Walden." *Fiddler Magazine* 3, no. 3 (1996): 12–17.

"Rolla Research Center Builds Bluegrass Collection, Sponsors Life Performance in April 2017." *Missouri Times* 12, no. 3 (2016): 5.

Rosenberg, Neil V. *Bluegrass: A History.* 1985. Reprint, Urbana: University of Illinois Press, 2005.

———. *Bluegrass Generation: A Memoir.* Urbana: University of Illinois Press, 2018.

———, ed. *Transforming Tradition: Folk Music Revivals Examined.* Urbana: University of Illinois Press, 1993.

Rosenberg, Neil V., and Charles K. Wolfe. *The Music of Bill Monroe.* Urbana: University of Illinois Press, 2007.

Roszak, Theodore. *The Making of a Counter Culture: Reflections on the Technocratic Society and Its Youthful Opposition*. 1969. Reprint, Berkeley: University of California Press, 1995.

Roy, Karl. *The Violin: Its History and Making*. Barrington, NH: Roy, 2006.

Ruchala, James Randolph. "Making Round Peak Music: History, Revitalization, and Community." Master's thesis, Brown University, 2011.

Russell, Tony. *Country Music Originals: The Legends and the Lost*. New York: Oxford University Press, 2007.

———. *Rural Rhythm: The Story of Old-Time Country Music 78 Records*. New York: Oxford University Press, 2021.

Ruth, Viola. *Pioneer Western Folk Tunes as Played and Arranged by Viola "Mom" Ruth*. Phoenix: Ruth, 1948.

Ryan, William Bradbury. *Ryan's Mammoth Collection: 1050 Reels and Jigs, Hornpipes, Clogs, Walk-Arounds, Essences, Strathspeys, Highland Flings and Contra Dances, with Figures, and How to Play Them*. Boston: Elias Howe, 1883. Reprinted as *Mel Bay Presents Ryan's Mammoth Collection . . .*, edited by Patrick Sky. Pacific, MO: Mel Bay, 1995.

Rynearson, Ann M. "Hiding within the Melting Pot: Mexican-Americans in St. Louis." PhD diss., Washington University, 1980.

Salmon, John. "R. D. Lunceford." *Banjo Newsletter* (2008). https://www.banjonews.com/2008.

Sandburg, Carl. *The American Songbag*. New York: Harcourt Brace, 1927.

———. *Carl Sandberg's New American Songbag*. New York: Broadcast Music, 1950.

Saunders, Walter V. "Notes & Queries." *Bluegrass Unlimited* (October 2017): 17–19.

Schmidt, Claire. "Vesta Johnson, Award-Winning Old-Time Missouri Fiddler." *Museum Magazine* 63 (2013): 8–9.

Schroeder, Rebecca B. "The Dean of Missouri Fiddle Music: Remembering R. P. Christeson (1911–1992)." *Missouri Folklore Society Journal* 13–14 (1991–92): 157–63.

Schroeder, Adolf E. *Missouri Origins: The Landscape of Home*. Columbia: University of Missouri Extension Division, 1981.

Scruggs, Earl. *Earl Scruggs and the Five-String Banjo*. New York: Peer International, 1968.

Seeger, Pete. *How to Play the 5-String Banjo: A Manual for Beginners*. 3rd ed. 1948. Beacon, NY: Pete Seeger, 1962.

Serda, Daniel. "Finding Latin Roots: Hispanic Heritage in Kansas City." *Kansas Preservation* 33, no. 3 (2011): 8–15.

Sheehy, Daniel. *Mariachi Music in America: Experiencing Music, Expressing Culture*. New York: Oxford University Press, 2006.

Shelasky, Paul. "Getting Started in Bluegrass Fiddle." *Fiddler Magazine* 25, no. 1 (2018): 48.

Shewmaker, Richard. "Hallsville: Conserving Traditional Missouri Music and Dance." Paper presented at Missouri Folklore Society Conference, Kirksville, 2016.

Shull, Bill. "Charlie Walden." *Old-Time Herald* 4, no. 6 (1994–95): 15.

———. *Cross-Tuning Your Fiddle: History, Techniques & Transcriptions*. Pacific, MO: Mel Bay, 1994.

———. "Fiddle Method Reviews—Part 25." *Devil's Box* 33, no. 4 (2000): 20–21.
———. *Guide to Judging a Fiddle Contest.* Columbia: Missouri State Old-Time Fiddlers' Association, 1996.
———. *Guide to Running a Fiddling Contest.* Columbia: Missouri State Old Time Fiddlers Association, 1996.
———. "Lyman Enloe." *Old-Time Herald,* 4, no. 5 (1994): 18.
———. "Mid-America Old-Time Fiddling Championship and Convention: 1985 Results and Plans for 1986." *Devil's Box*, 20, no. 2 (1986): 19–21.
———. "Missouri Fiddle Contests." *Old-Time Herald* 4, no. 6 (1994–95): 21.
———. "OK, Let's Try It Again: What's 'Old-Time' Music?" *Devil's Box* 32, no. 3 (1998): 48–50.
———. "R. P. Christeson." *Old-Time Herald,* 4, no. 5 (1994): 17.
———. "The Stover Connection." *Old-Time Herald* 4, no. 6 (1994–95): 24.
———. "Texas Style Fiddling Is Different from Other Fiddling Styles." Handout, Branson Old Time Fiddle Contest, August 2004.
———, ed. *"Uncle Pink" and Other Central Missouri Fiddle Tunes from Lyman Enloe.* Columbia: Missouri State Old-Time Fiddlers' Association, 1993.
Skillman, Amy. "She Oughta Been a Lady: Women Old-Time Fiddlers in Missouri." *Missouri Folklore Society Journal* 13–14 (1991–92): 123–34.
Skinner, James Scott. *The Harp and Claymore.* Edited by Gavin Greig. 1904. Reprint, Pacific, MO: Mel Bay, 2002.
Smith, Ben, and David Osban. "David Scrivner: Interview + Tunes." Oldtime Central, November 22, 2019. https://oldtime-central.com/david-scrivner.
Smith, Harry, comp. *Anthology of American Folk Music.* Folkways FP251, 252, 253, reissue, Smithsonian Folkways, 1997.
Smith, L. Mayne. "First Bluegrass Festival Honors Bill Monroe." *Sing Out!* 15, no. 6 (1966): 69–69.
Smith, Malcolm. "Cathy Barton and Dave Para: Lives on the River." *Old-Time Herald* 11, no. 4 (2008): 21–39.
Smith, Richard D. *"Can't You Hear Me Callin'": The Life of Bill Monroe, Father of Bluegrass.* New York: Da Capo, 2001.
Smith, Zach. "Monday Night in McClurg." *Rural Missouri* (March 2018): 10–11.
Smithers, Aaron. *Curriculum Guide: Texas-Style Fiddling.* Austin: Texas Folklife, 2013.
Smyth, Willie. "A Parking Lot Tale." *Devil's Box* [ca. 1975].
Spencer, Thomas E., and Stephen F. Davis. "On the Popularity of Old-Time Fiddlers' Contests." *Tennessee Folklore Society Bulletin* 43, no. 1 (1977): 27–32.
Spielman, Earl V. "The Texas Fiddling Style." *Devil's Box* 14 (1980): 24–32.
———. "Traditional North American Fiddling: A Methodology for the Historical and Comparative Analytical Style Study of Instrumental Musical Traditions." PhD diss., University of Wisconsin, 1975.
Stamler, Paul J. "Freaks and Fiddle Tunes: The Early 1970s Folk Revival in St. Louis." *Missouri Folklore Society Journal* 27–28 (2005–6): 18–30.
Standard Atlas of Callaway County, Missouri. Chicago: Ogle, 1919.
State Historical Society of Missouri. "Place Names of Boone County Place Names, 1828–1945." https//:shsmo.org/manuscripts.

Stecher, Jody. "Pete McMahan and Andy de Jarlis Play 'Whisky before Breakfast.'" *Fiddler Magazine* 22, no. 2 (2015): 44–45.
Steinbeck, John. *The Grapes of Wrath*. 1939. Reprint, New York: Penguin, 2006.
Stoneking, Fred. "Fiddles! Fiddles! Fiddles!" Album notes to *Saddle Old Spike: Fiddle Music from Missouri*. Rounder Records CD 0381, 1996.
"Teresa Cuevas." *Kansapedia*. https://www.kshs.org.
Thede, Marion Unger. *The Fiddle Book*. New York: Oak, 1967.
———. "Traditional Fiddling." *Ethnomusicology* 6, no. 1 (1962): 19–24.
Thomas, Emmy. "Covering Lee Ruth." *Columbia Missourian* (*Vox Magazine*), December 4, 2003.
Thompson, Richard. "Frank D. Ray to SPBGMA Hall of Greats." *Bluegrass Today*, December 21, 2018. www.bluegrasstoday.com.
Torres, Theresa L. *The Paradox of Latina Leadership in the Catholic Church: Las Guadalupanas of Kansas City*. New York: Palgrave Macmillan, 2013.
Traum, Happy. "The Swan Song of Folk Music." *Rolling Stone*, May 17, 1969, 7–8.
Tribe, Ivan M. *The Stonemans: An Appalachian Family and the Music That Shaped Their Lives*. Urbana: University of Illinois Press, 1993.
Twiss, Tim. *Early American Banjo*. Pacific, MO: Mel Bay, 2019.
———. *Early American Banjo: Transcriptions from Buckley's Banjo Guide of 1868*. Pacific, MO: Mel Bay, 2019.
Tyler, Paul. "Fiddling." In *The American Midwest: An Interpretive Encyclopedia*, edited by Richard Sisson, Christian Zacher, and Andrew Cayton, 384–86. Bloomington: Indiana University Press, 2007.
Valerio-Jimenez, Omar, Santiago Vaquera-Vasquez, and Claire F. Fox, eds. *The Midwest Latina/o Reader*. Urbana: University of Illinois Press, 2017.
Vallely, Fintan. *The Companion to Irish Traditional Music*. New York: New York University Press, 1999.
van Ravenswaay, Charles. *The Arts and Architecture of German Settlements in Missouri: Survey of a Vanishing Culture*. Columbia: University of Missouri Press, 1977.
Vaughan, Andrew. *Pilot of a Steam-Powered Areo-Plane*. Franklin, TN: Stuffworks Press, 2013.
Via Dolorosa Films. *Mariachi Estrella: Ad Astra Per Aspera*. Topeka: Kansas Humanities Council, n.d.
Vonnegut, Kurt. *A Man without a Country*. 2005. Reprint, New York: Random House, 2007.
Walden, Charlie. "Brief Guide to Fiddling Contests: A Continuing Missouri Tradition." Columbia: Missouri Cultural Heritage Center and Missouri State Old Time Fiddlers Association, [ca. 1984].
———. "Cyril Winfield Stinnett: Master of Hornpipe and Hoedown." *Old-Time Herald* 4, no. 6 (1994–95): 10–11.
———. "Daniel Boone Jones: Early Radio Fiddler." *Missouri Old Time Fiddlers' Association Journal* (1985): 4–16.
———. "Geoff Seitz: The Last of the Great Lemay Fiddlers." *Old-Time Herald* 4, no. 6 (1994–95): 32–34.
———. *Missouri Fiddle Tunes*. Vols. 1–2, *Fast & Slow for Learning*. Evanston, IL: Charlie Walden Music, 2010.

———. "Missouri Old-Time Fiddling Traditions." *Fiddler Magazine* 3, no. 3 (1996): 5–11.

———. "One Hundred Essential Missouri Fiddle Tunes." http://www.missourifiddling.com.

———. "Radiophone WOS and WOS Radio Reunion and Fiddling Championship." http://www.missourifiddling.com.

———. "Travels with Charlie, Part One: To Shetland—by Rail, by Air, by Sea." *Fiddler Magazine* 27, no. 1 (2020): 25–27.

Walden, Charlie, and Julie Youmans. *Cope Ashlock Invitational Live Radio Fiddling Championship, April 9, 1989*. Columbia: University of Missouri Cultural Heritage Center, Missouri State Old Time Fiddlers Association, KOPN 89.5 FM, 1989.

Walker, Caroline. *The Modern Dances, How to Dance Them*. Chicago: Saul Brothers, 1914.

Wallace, Anthony F. "Revitalization Movements." *American Anthropologist* 58 (1956): 264–81.

Warner, Judy Mae. "Ozark Old-Time Fiddling." Master's thesis, University of Arkansas, 2010.

Watson, Carrie J. "Musial Wolfe: A Study in Traditional Music." Research paper, Art History and Archaeology 142, University of Missouri, May 1997.

Webster, Bob. "The John Hartford Fiddle Tune Project, Vol. 1." Review of vol. 1 of *The John Hartford Fiddle Tune Project*, compiled by Matt Combs and Katie Harford Hogue. *Bluegrass Unlimited* (February 2021): 64.

Weisberger, Jon. "Rhonda Vincent." *Bluegrass Unlimited* (April 2000): 38–42.

Wells, Mike. "The Wells Family of Howard County, Missouri." *Old-Time Herald* 4, no. 6 (1994–95): 24–56.

West, Ed. "An Interview with Chuck Stearman—Bluegrass Society Founder." *Country Times* (October 1981): 4–5.

Western Historical Company. *History of Boone County, Missouri*. St. Louis, 1882.

Whisnant, David. *All That Is Native and Fine: The Politics of Culture in an American Region*. Chapel Hill: University of North Carolina Press, 1983.

Willens, Doris. *Lonesome Traveler: The Life of Lee Hays*. 1988. Reprint, Lincoln: University of Nebraska Press, 1993.

Williams, John P., Jr. "New Fiddle Camp in the Missouri Ozarks." *Devil's Box* 32, no. 3 (1998): 43–47.

Williams, Phil, and Vivian Williams. "Playing for Old-Time Dances." http://www.voyagerrecords.com.

Williams, Stuart. "Tune of the Month: Crystal Stream Waltz." *Washington State Old Time Fiddlers' Association Newsletter* (February 2013).

Williams, Vivian T. "Jam Session Etiquette." https://voyagerrecords.com.

———. "Playing for Old Time Dances." https://www.voyagerrecords.com.

———. "Some Random Guesses about Why Fiddle Styles Developed the Way They Did in Certain Regions, and What Is Happening Here Now." *Seattle Folklore Society Journal* 3, no. 3 (1972): 11–13.

———. "So You Think You Can't Play by Ear." https://www.voyagerrecords.com.

———. "Weiser 1972—A Subjective Summary." *Seattle Folklore Society Journal* 3, no. 4 (1972): 6–8.

Williams, Vivian T., and Phil Williams. "Contra and Square Dance Playing." 1998. https://www.voyagerrecords.com, posted 2004.
Winkelman, Donald M. "Fiddleville." *Sing Out!* 17, no. 1 (1967): 16–17.
Winston, Bryan. "Mexican Migrants in Urban Missouri: Social Welfare Institutions and Racial Boundaries in Kansas City and St. Louis, 1915–1940." *Missouri Historical Review* 113, no. 4 (2019): 259–83.
Wolfe, Tom. *The Electric Kool-Aid Acid Test.* 1968. Reprint, New York: Picador, 2008.
Wolz, Lyn A. "Anglo-American Folk Music in Missouri: An Annotated Bibliography." *Missouri Folklore Society Journal* 4 (1982): 51–104.
Wood, Jim. "Play It! The Science of Contest Fiddling." *Devil's Box* 31, no. 2 (1996): 11–20.
———. "A 'Winning' Contest Round, Part One." *Fiddler Magazine* 12, no. 4 (2005–6): 33–35.
———. "A 'Winning' Contest Round, Part Two." *Fiddler Magazine* 13, no. 2 (2006): 41–43.
———. "A Winning Contest Round for Beginners." *Fiddler Magazine* 24, no. 1 (2017–18): 35–36.
Wright, Carolyn. "How to Raise a Great Musician." *Bluegrass Now* (June 2002): 40–44.
Wurst, Bruce. *The American Fiddle Method.* 1998. Pacific, MO: Mel Bay, 2015.
Yeats, William Butler. "The Nineteenth Century and After" [1932]. In *Selected Poems and Two Plays of William Butler Yeats*, edited by M. L. Rosenthal, 128. New York: Collier, 1955.
Youmans, Julie. "Lena Jones Hughes." *Old-Time Herald* 4, no. 5 (1994): 29.
———. "Vesta Wilson Johnson." *Old-Time Herald* 4, no. 6 (1994–95): 22.
———. "Warming the Cold Notes: Style and Boundaries in Old-Time Music." *Missouri Folklore Society Journal* 13–14 (1991–92): 133–49.
Young, Raymond A. *Cultivating Cooperation: A History of the Missouri Farmers Association.* Columbia: University of Missouri Press, 1995.
Zepp, Donald. "Is It Frailing or Is It Clawhammer?" https://www.banjo-l.org.
Zischkale, Aaron. "Lena Hughes' Rolling Banjo." *Old-Time Herald* 14, no. 10 (2018): 12–15.

Selected Discography

Field recordings of Missouri fiddlers are archived in the Library of Congress, Smithsonian Institution (Festival of American Folklife), and Missouri collections at institutions such as the Greene County Library in Springfield, Meyer Library at Missouri State University, and the State Historical Society of Missouri in Columbia. This discography is a sampling of recordings.

Self-produced LP records, primarily by bluegrass bands and old-time fiddlers, became popular in the 1970s. Several studios in Missouri (and one in Arkansas) provided most of recording, mastering, and manufacturing. Most studios left it to artists to devise their own record-label names. These "vanity press" LPs, as well as the self-produced 78- and 45-rpm records that preceded them and the cassette tapes and CDs that followed, were significant in spreading the music and bringing a bit of income to the performers.

The Late, Great Album Note

Researching and writing informational documentary album notes was an essential part of the 1960s embrace of traditional music. The size of the twelve-inch LP record album cover helped make album notes on the back practical and valuable. One could print only limited text on the "liner" itself (the record sleeve), but one could write lengthy essays on the back of the cardboard record jacket, and perhaps even enclose notes inside the album or between the leaves of a double album. Sometimes album notes were extensive, detailed, and extraordinary statements.

Album notes with LPs were an important step in the gradual development of research and documentation of the music and sometimes inspired scholars to develop new research projects. LPs by bands such as the New Lost City Ramblers and the Old Reliable String Band, and documentary projects of the Library of Congress and record companies such as Folkways, included extensive documentation. Just as with jazz LPs, some of the best writing and research on history and performers remain on those dog-eared record jackets that many of us treat like rare books from the Bibliothèque Nationale.

Among the writers and scholars in the sixties into the eighties were Ralph Rinzler, Archie Green, Mike Seeger, Joe Wilson, Vivian and Phil Williams, Mark Wilson, Alan Jabbour, Charlie Faurot, Kerry Blech, Gus Meade, and Brad Leftwich. Writers such as those also provided album notes for the many reissues on LP by firms such as County, and Rounder, of the classic 1920s and 1930s 78-rpm records that were the inspiration and gold mine for young musicians and revival string bands. Bill Monroe's *Bluegrass Instrumentals* album notes by folklorist, scholar, and Smithsonian administrator Ralph Rinzler were detailed and interesting and helped show that album notes could be more than just a track list and puff piece. Many of us became interested in the documentation, history, and stories behind the music through informative and evocative album notes like Ralph's.

In the eighties and early nineties, the cassette tape and then the CD rubbed out the LP record (almost permanently). Nothing much replaced the wonderful old LP album notes and artistic album covers.

The small size of the insert "J cards" that came with cassette tapes, and the slightly larger size of booklet inserts in CD "jewel cases," meant that album notes grew less informative and substantial. Today the CD itself is under challenge from new digital music-delivery systems and cyberspace. Some CDs now have no insert booklet and instead direct customers to an Internet site for downloads if information is actually wanted. With the disappearance of countless magazines, newspapers, and journals as well as the shrinkage of the book market and the hollowing out of our nation's libraries, people's access to information is, many would suggest, reduced in certain ways.

The digital age in this respect has, I think, made access to information and research more difficult, not less. Online results of searches can be untrustworthy, misleading, erroneous, and in some cases so mistaken as to be funny. The mistakes flying through the digital cloud may be taken as fact (if not planted there as counterfeit information). The beginnings of a rejuvenation of the LP record (and, hopefully, album notes) is a positive sign. Time will tell.

Abrams, Bob, and Steve Mote. *Bob Abrams & Steve Mote*. St. Louis: (no label), 1975. (Abrams, violin; Mote, banjo)

Arkansas Red [Michael Breid]. *Front Porch Pickin'*. Eureka Springs, AR: Ozark Red, Ozark Troubadour, 1986 (cassette).

Baker Family Bluegrass Band. *If It Ain't Love*. Birch Tree, MO: private label, 2017.

———. *Seeing the Invisible: 20/20*. Birch Tree, MO: private label, 2020.

Ball, Earl. *Family Favorites*. Humansville, MO: private label, ca. 2003.

The Barrier Brothers and the Ozark Mountain Boys. *Gospel Songs Bluegrass Style*. Phillips 600-082, 1962. (Henley "Gene" Dykes, vocal)

Barton, Cathy, and Dave Para. *Ballad of the Boonslick*. 1982, CD reissue, Barton and Para, www.bartonandpara.com, 2003. (Taylor McBaine, John Murdock, violin)

———. *Carp Fishing in Missouri*. Boonville, MO: Big Canoe Records, 2017. (Taylor McBaine, Cyril Stinnett, Nile Wilson, violin)

———. *Crazy Quilt*. Boonville: Big Canoe Records, 1998.

———. *Living on the River*. Roustabout Records, 2000.

———. *On a Day Like Today*. Folk Legacy FSI-107, 1986.

———. *Rebel in the Woods: Civil War Songs from the Western Border, Vol. 2*. Boonville, MO: Big Canoe Records, 1995.

Barton, Cathy, Dave Para, and Bob Dyer. Boonville, MO: Big Canoe Records, 1993. (Howard Marshall, violin)

Bluegrass Association. *One Tin Soldier*. Independence, MO: Cavern Custom USR 4122, 1973. (Lyman Enloe, violin)

———. *Strings Today . . . and Yesterday*. Independence, MO: Cavern Custom 42419, 1974. (Lyman Enloe, violin)

Bluegrass Brigade. *Festival Favorites*. Bluegrass Brigade Records BBR-84-105, 1984. (Don Montgomery, violin)

———. *Happy I'll Be*. Ozark Opry 00R81-104, 1981. (Don Montgomery, violin)

———. *Little Old Log Cabin*. Kansas City, 2005. (Don Montgomery, violin)

———. *Old Spinning Wheel*. Kansas City, 2011. (Don Montgomery, violin)

———. *Wishful Thinking*. Bluegrass Brigade Records BBR-86-106, 1986. (Don Montgomery, Rusty Dutton, violin)

Bluegrass Five. *Bluegrass from the Missouri Hills*. Professional Artists PAS 7633-97, 1976.

Bluegrass Hoppers. *The Country's Come to Town*. Cuca Records K-1160, 1967. (Rod Moag, mandolin; Don Gale, banjo; Earl Spielman, violin; Jerry Wicentowski, guitar; Charley Taylor, bass)

Bluegrass Society. *Fireside Grass*. Concord, AR: Rimrock, ca. 1969. (Harry Gilbert, violin)

Bovee, Bob, and Gail Heil. *For Old Time's Sake*. Train on the Island Records Tl-12, 1986.

Brashear, Chris. *Kentucky Rose*. chris@chrisbrashear.com, 1992 (cassette).

———. *Wanderlust*. Dog Boy, 1999; Copper Creek, 2000.

Bressler Brothers. *Heroes*. Shan-Co-Mo Records 4001, 1998.

Brown, Don, and Ozark Mountain Trio. *Traditional Bluegrass*. King Bluegrass Records KO-537, 1972. (Gene Goforth, violin)

Bruce, Johnny. *Carroll County Fiddler*. Private label, ca. 1977 (cassette).

Bryan, Cliff. *Got a Little Home to Go To*. Voyager Recordings and Books VRCD 378, 2015.

The Calton Family. *The Old and New*. Professional Artist Recording Studio PAS 7633-12, 1976. (Charles Calton, violin)

Canaday, Leroy. *Old Dan Tucker Was a Fine Old Man: Missouri Fiddler Leroy Canaday*. Voyager Recordings and Books VRCD 353, 2001.

Cedar Hill. *Portrait of a Song*. Hay Holler HH 1377, 2006. (Lisa Ray, violin)

Celebrated Renaissance Band. *Celebrated Renaissance Band: Real Live American Music*. Columbia, MO: Dan William Peek. (recorded in Boston, mid-1960s)

Childgrove Country Dancers. *Face the Creek*. St. Louis: Wildstone Audio CCD 98001, 1998. (Matt Wyatt, Bob Holt, Geoff Seitz, Marc Rennard, Rhys Jones, violin)

Christeson, R. P., ed. *The Old-Time Fiddler's Repertory: Historic Field Recordings of Forty-One Traditional Tunes*. 1976. Reprint, Columbia: University of Missouri Press, 2011.

Collins, Earl. *"That's Earl": Collins Family Fiddling*. Briar Recordings LP 4204, 1975.

Collins Brothers. *Family & Friends*. Kansas City, 1990 (cassette). (Gary Brown, violin)

Cook, Charlie. *Charlie Cook, Boone County Waltz King*. Missouri State Old Time Fiddlers Association, MSOTFA 117, n.d.

County Line. *Sweet Prairie Hay*. Springfield, MO: Grass Mountain Records GM1001, 1975. (Dale Hopkins, violin)

Crouch, Dub, and the Bluegrass Rounders. *Down to Earth Bluegrass*. King Bluegrass Records 750431, 1972 (LP). (Stan and Bob Wagganer, violin)

———. *Footprints in the Snow*. King Bluegrass, 1976. (Bob Wagganer, violin)

———. *Last Train South*. Professional Artist 7433, 1974. (Gene Goforth, violin)

Crouch, Dub, Norman Ford, and the Bluegrass Rounders. *Traditional Bluegrass*. King KB-537, 1975. (Gene Goforth, violin)

Currey, Sadie. *Sadie Caroline*. Columbia, MO: Curreykorn, 2010.

Cyril Stinnett, Legendary Missouri Fiddler: Home Videos from the Dwight Lamb Collection. Canton, SD: Missouri Valley Music, 2013. (DVD)

DeWitt, Deborah, Producer. *Bluegrass Pickin' Time: Through All These Years*. Private label, 2012.

The Dillards. *Back Porch Bluegrass*. Elektra 7232, 1963.

———. *Live! Almost!* Elektra EKL-265, 1964.

———. *Pickin' and Fiddlin'*. Elektra 7285, 1965. (Byron Berline, violin)

Dirt Road Rascals with Hector of Huckleberry Holler. Columbia, MO: private label, 2006. (Warren Elliott, violin)

Draper, Rusty, with Ozark Red Loveall. *Rusty and Red: The Early Recordings of Rusty Draper Featuring Ozark Red Loveall*. British Archive of Country Music CD D334, 2011.

Drifters. *Live from Everywhere*. Kansas City, MO: Driftime Productions DTP001, ca. 1980 (cassette). (Gary Brown, violin)

Ellis, Larry. *Larry Ellis Fiddle CD #1*. Lee's Summit, MO: private label, 2012.

Elsloo, Jeff, and Matt Wyatt. *Banjo & Fiddle*. Fiddlesong Music, 2005.

Enloe, Lyman. *Fiddle Tunes I Recall*. 1973; reissue, County, 1978, County CO-CD-2702 (1993).

———. *Rugged Road*. Society for the Preservation of Blue Grass Music in America, 1976; reissue, Missouri State Old Time Fiddlers Association MSOTFA 004, 1989.

Enloe, Lyman, Casey Jones, and Cyril Stinnett. *Three Fiddlers from the Show-Me State*. County CO-2739-CD, 2005.

The Farmertones. *Old Time Stringband Music*. Lemay, MO: Oceana Productions OP 005, 2008. (Geoff Seitz, Marc Rennard, violin)

The Farnum Family. *A Time to Fiddle: Hannah Farnum with the Farnum Family*. Galena, MO: Farnum Family, n.d.

Foss, Wilbur, prod. *Fiddler's Reunion, 1979*. Vol. 13. Yankton: South Dakota Old Time Fiddlers' Association MC6323 (cassette). (Pete McMahan, W. W. Bone, Gene Wells, violin)

———. *Great Plains Fiddlers—1992*. Yankton: South Dakota Old Time Fiddlers' Association (cassette). (Howard Marshall et al., violin)

———. *Jarle and Wilbur Foss Invite You to Listen to Fiddlers from Nine States*. Vol. 25. Yankton: South Dakota Old Time Fiddlers' Association, n.d. (Pete McMahan, W. W. Bone, et al., violin)

———. *Jarle Foss, Norwegian Emigrant Fiddler and the Fiddling Farmers*. Vol. 14. Yankton: South Dakota Old Time Fiddlers' Association, MC21511, ca. 1979. (Cyril Stinnett, violin)

———. *Jarle Foss and His Friends*. Vol. 8. Yankton: South Dakota Old Time Fiddlers' Association MC6249, ca. 1978. (Lee Stoneking et al., violin)

———. *Missouri Old-Time Fiddling*. Vol. 50. Yankton: South Dakota Old Time Fiddlers' Association, ca. 1990 (cassette). (Pete McMahan, W. W. Bone, Bob Brandon, Cyril Stinnett, Jake Hockemeyer, Lee Stoneking, Dean Johnston, Junior Marriott, Joe Grable, Lynn Wells, Mike Wells, Howard Marshall, Johnny Bruce, Leonard Smith, Gene Wells, violin)

———. *Old Time Fiddling Is What You Hear in Yankton, South Dakota*. Vol. 38. Yankton: South Dakota Old Time Fiddlers' Association, n.d. (cassette). (Pete McMahan, Junior Marriott, Jake Hockemeyer et al., violin)

———. *Top of the Line—Fiddling #56*. Vol. 56. Yankton: South Dakota Old Time Fiddlers' Association, n.d. (cassette). (Dr. W. W. Bone, Johnny Bruce, Joe Grable, Pete McMahan, Howard Marshall, Cyril Stinnett, Fred Stoneking, Gene Wells, Lynn Wells, Mike Wells, Ray Wells, violin)

———. *We Invite You to Listen to Good Old Time Music Makers from Ten States*. Vol. 34. Yankton: Wilbur Foss, WMC21710, ca. 1985. (Pete McMahan et al., violin)

Fraser, Michael. *Fiddles and Forests*. Missouri Department of Conservation, 2003.
———. *Missouri Roads*. Boiler Room Productions and Big Time Productions, 2012.
———. *Standing on the Rock*. Columbia: Pete Szkolka Productions, 2014. (Shortleaf Band)
———. *Voices of the Hills: A Journey to Shannon County*. Missouri Department of Conservation, ca. 2000. (Shortleaf Band)
Galbraith, Art. *Dixie Blossoms*. Rounder Records LP 0133, 1980. Reissue, Musical Traditions Records MTCD509, 2010.
———. *Simple Pleasures: Old-Time Fiddling from the Ozarks*. Rounder LP 0157, n.d.
Gardner, Mark, and the Muleskinners. *Songs of the Santa Fe Trail and the Far West*. Native Ground, 1996. (Tom Verdot, violin)
Goforth, Gene. *Eminence Breakdown*. Rounder Records 0388, 1997.
———. *Strike Up the Bow*. Professional Artists PAS 7433-21, 1974.
Grace, Leela, and Ellie. *Leela and Ellie Grace*. Columbia: Grace Family Music, 2003. (Ellie Grace, violin)
Grace Family. *Dance upon the Earth*. Columbia: Grace Family Music, 1996.
———. *Fifty Miles of Elbow Room*. Columbia: Grace Family Music, 1987. (Paul Fotsch, violin)
Greencorn String Band. *Down in the Cotton and the Cane*. Columbia, MO: private label, 2001. (Dierik Leonhard, Vic Phelps, violin)
Green Side Up. *Green Side Up*. Kansas City: Chapman Studios, 1988 (cassette). (Larry Ellis, violin)
———. *How Does Bluegrass Grow? Green Side Up*. Kansas City: George's Music Service, 1975. (Larry Ellis, violin)
Grotewohl, Dan. *Bear in the Greengrass*. Orchard, 2000.
Harris, Lyle. *For All We Know: A Lyle Harris Reunion*. CDE Ind. CDE1111, 2002.
Hartford, John. *Hamilton Ironworks*. Rounder 0442, 2001.
———. *The Speed of the Old Long Bow*. Rounder 0438, 1998.
Hartford, John, and Bob Carlin. *The Fun of Open Discussion*. Rounder 0320, 1995.
Hartford, John, and Texas Shorty. *Old Sport*. Small Dog a Barkin', 1994. (Jim Chancellor, violin)
Hartford String Band. *Good Old Boys*. Rounder 0462, 1999.
Hascall, Carol. *Spotted Pony*. Cavern Custom, 1975.
Haslag, LeRoy. *Reflections of a Missouri Fiddler*. Private label NR 21420, 2001.
Head, Steve. *32 Acres*. Browning, MO: private label, n.d.
———. *Draggin' the Bow*. Browning, MO: private label, n.d.
Helton, Warren. *Warren Helton: Old Tyme Fiddler*. Vienna, MO: Warren Helton Music, 2014.
Henigan, Julie. *American Stranger*. Waterbug WBG0035, 1997.
Herd, Jim. *Old Time Ozark Fiddling*. Voyager Records VRCD 340, 1999.
Holt, Bob. *Bob Holt: Dance Fiddling from the Missouri Ozarks*. Field Recorders' Collective FRC-721, 2017.
———. *Got a Little Home to Go To*. Rounder CD 0432, 1998.
———. *"Rabbit in the Pea Patch": Traditional South Missouri Dance Tunes*. Self-produced, ca. 1992 (cassette).

———. *The Way I Heard It*. Self-produced, 1993 (cassette).

Hopkins, Dale. *Old'n in the Way*. Reissue CD. Macks Creek, MO: Nearly Famous Records, 2001.

Hoppers, Lonnie. *Lifetime Harvest*. Urbana, IL: Franklin Ridge Records, 2005. (Kelly Jones, violin)

———. *Old Country Church: Instrumentals Featuring Five-String Banjo*. Urbana, MO: Hoppers, 1992; CD reissue, 2000. (Jamie Haage, violin, electric bass; Hoppers, banjo, guitar)

Hoppers, Lonnie, and Dan Crary. *Lonnie Hoppers and Dan Crary and Their American Band*. Pinecastle PRC-CD-100, 2000. (Jamie Haage, Dale Hopkins, violin)

Hoppers, Lonnie, and Friends. *Pickin' for Fun*. Dungeon 2041; reissue, Urbana, IL: Lonnie Hoppers, 1980. (Mark Pearman, David Wilson, Randy Newman, violin)

Hoppers, Lonnie, and New Union. *Grass Hoppin'*. Kirbyville, MO: Haage Studio, 2000. (Jamie Haage, violin)

Horse Creek Band. *Don't Be Ashamed of Your Age*. LGS 101, 1982. (Newell Looney, violin)

———. *Ozark Mountain Music Recorded Live*. Branson: Silver Dollar City LGS-103, 1979. (Newell Looney, violin)

Huck, Joseph B. *The Red Violin*. N.p. Private label, 2009.

Hughes, Lena. *Lena Hughes, Queen of the Guitar Pickers and Her Flat Top Guitar*. Power Records PLR185, ca. 1965; CD reissue, Tompkins Square (2013).

Hughey, Ron. *Country Fiddlin' Ozark Style*. American Heritage AH-402-511, 1973.

Hull, Ashley. *Just for the Fun of It! Fiddle Music from the Ozarks, with Gordon McCann*. Springfield, MO: private label, 2009. (Ashley Hull Forrest, violin)

Ill-Mo Boys. *Fine as Frog's Hair*. Marimac 9054, 1992 (cassette).

———. *Laugh and Grow Fat*. Vigortone, 2001.

———. *Timely Old Tunes from the Ill-Mo Boys and Beyond*. Marimac 9020, 1988 (cassette). (Geoff Seitz, violin)

Inman, Travis. *Championship Fiddling*. Sedalia: private label, 1995.

———. *Championship Fiddling Series II*. Sedalia: private label, 2021.

———. *Missouri Fiddler*. Seattle: Voyager Recordings and Books, VRCD 376, 2012.

———. *Remembering the Championship Years*. 2000. Sedalia, MO: private label, 2021.

Johnson, Ray "Pick." *Tunes I Learned from My Uncle Cleve from Big Spring, Missouri*. Graphic Recording LP GR-1004, ca. 1980.

Johnson, Vesta. *Blue Flame*. Marimac 9057, 1994 (cassette).

———. *Down Home Rag*. Marimac 9017, 1988 (cassette).

———. *Indian Creek*. Kirkwood, MO: private label, 1999 (CD).

———. *Old Liberty*. Kirkwood, MO: private label, 2007.

———. *Vesta Johnson with Steve Hall: North Missouri Dance Fiddling*. Field Recorders' Collective FRC-715, 2015.

———. *Washington Lee Swing*. Kirkwood, MO: self-produced, 2007.

Johnston, Herbie. *Fiddlin' around with Herbie Johnston*. Ca. 1985 (cassette).

Jones, Bill, and the Bluegrass Travelers. *A Beautiful Life*. SPBGMA Bluegrass Records SRS 7933-11, 1977. (Kirk Brandenberger, Keokuk, IA, violin)

———. *Bluegrass Favorites*. SPBGMA Bluegrass Records SRS 7733-03, 1979. (Kirk Brandenberger, violin)

———. *Hymns We Love to Sing—Bluegrass Style*. SPBGMA Bluegrass Records 42511, 1974. (Garvin Lee, violin)

———. *They're Holding Up the Ladder*. Ozark Opry Records 13473, 1982. (Jim Winters, violin)

Jones, Bruce, Dub Crouch, and the Blue Grass Rounders. "Ozark Breakdown." Trepur 18937, 1966 (45 rpm). (Bob Wagganer, composer, violin)

Jones, Casey. *Rocky Road to Jordan*. Missouri State Old Time Fiddlers Association MSOTFA 102, 1992 (cassette).

Jones, Herman ("Sac River"). *Medley of Old Fiddle Tunes and Songs*. El Dorado Springs, MO: GR-1006, n.d.; reissue, Missouri State Old Time Fiddlers Association, 2015.

Jones, Kelly. *Authentic Old-Time Fiddle Tunes*. Independence, MO: Cavern Custom, USR7714, 1975; reissue, Missouri State Old Time Fiddlers Association MSOTFA 006, 1990 (cassette).

———. *"Through the Years," Volume 1*. Private label, 2001.

Jones (Mona) and the Bluegrass Travelers. *Live at Starvy Creek: A Tribute to Bill Jones*. Dixon: Jones, 2009. (Joe Wieneman, violin)

Kelley, Stirling, and Ralph Lee Smith. *Old-Time Harmonica, Bones, and Hickory Leaf Playing*. Troubadour Records 4783, 1977.

Lamb, Dwight. *Joseph Won a Coated Fiddle*. Rounder CD 0429, 1999.

———. *Old Ladies Pickin' Chickens*. Missouri State Old Time Fiddlers Association MSOTFA 201, 1992 (cassette).

———. *Old Time Fiddling 2: Left-Handed Style*. Private label 1227, 1972.

Lansford, Jim, and Kim Lansford. *Minstrel Banjo Styles*. Rounder 0312, 1990. (Jim Lansford, banjo)

———. *Old-Time Fiddling*. Galena, MO: private label, 1989. (Jim Lansford, violin)

Latty, Vee. *Fever in the South*. Missouri State Old Time Fiddlers Association MSOTFA 101, 1992 (cassette).

Lee, Billy. *Up Jumped the Devil*. Voyager Recordings and Books VRCD 357, 2003.

Leftwich, Brad, and Dan Gellert. *A Moment in Time*. Marimac 9038-C, 1993. (Leftwich, violin)

Leftwich, Brad, and Linda Higginbotham. *Lee Stoneking: Missouri Fiddling and Banjo Playing from the Collection of Linda Higginbotham and Brad Leftwich*. Ravenna, OH: Field Recorders' Collective FRC708, 2014.

Letsky, Pippa, and Friends. *Animal Crackers*. 2 vols. www.pippaletsky.com, 2010.

———. *Diamond in the Rough Bluegrass*. Columbia, MO: www.pippaletsky.com, 2008.

———. *Seagulls*. www.pippaletsky.com, n.d.

Letsky, Pippa, and the Strawmen. *At the Corner of a Crossroads*. www.pippaletsky.com, 2013.

———. *Missouricana*. www.pippaletsky.com, 2018.

Link Family. *Stand by Me*. Lebanon, MO: private label, 2003.

Logan Family. "Grape Leaf Rag" (Grape Leaf GS 405), recorded at Rimrock Records, Arkansas, 1970 (45 rpm; comp. Dick Logan). B-side: "Knoxville Girl."

———. "Maggie" (Grape Leaf GS 406), 1970 (45 rpm). B-side: "Your Love Is Like a Flower." (Dick Logan, violin)

Lonesome River Band. *Bridging the Tradition*. Mountain Home Music MH-16502, 2016.
———. *Head on in to Heartache*. Mountain Home Music MH-10332, 2005.
———. *No Turning Back*. Rural Rhythm RHY-1040, 2008.
———. *Outside Looking In*. Mountain Home Music MH-17272, 2019.
———. *Window of Time*. Doobie Shea DS 4006, 2002. (Mike Hartgrove, violin)
Lunceford, R. D. *Old Blue Tick: Traditional Fiddle Tunes from Missouri*. Santa Rosa, CA: Ceilidh Brothers Music, 1997.
Lutz, Ron. *Jack of Diamonds*. Jefferson City, MO: Hot City Productions, 2007.
Mace, Lee, and His Ozark Opry Gang. "Resurrection Morning" / "Someday We'll Know." Starday SEP152A EP, 1960. (Don Russell, violin)
———. "Steppin' in the Straw" / "Ozark Fiddler." Starday SEP152B EP, 1960.
Maria the Mexican. *Moon Colored Jade*. Topeka, KS: private label, 2013. (Tess Cuevas, violin)
Mark Gardner and the Muleskinners. *Songs of the Santa Fe Trail and the Far West*. Native Ground, 1996 (Tom Verdot, violin)
Marriott, Cody. *Cody Marriott*. Ava, MO: private label, 2004.
Marriott, Cody, and Junior Marriott. *Cody & Jr. Marriott*. Ava, MO: private label, 2004.
Marriott, Junior. *Junior Marriott*. Ava, MO: private label, 2004.
———. *Snake Creek*. Missouri State Old Time Fiddlers Association MSOTFA 008, 1998 (cassette).
———. *Vintage*. Ava, MO: Marriott Music, n.d.
———. *Wolves Howlin'*. Ava, MO: Marriott Music, n.d.
Marshall, Howard, and John Williams. *Fiddling Missouri*. Voyager Recordings and Books VRCD 344, 1999.
Marshall, Howard, Phil Williams, and Vivian Williams, prods. *"Now That's a Good Tune": Masters of Traditional Missouri Fiddling*. 1989; rev. ed., Voyager Recordings and Books, 2008.
Marshall, Howard, and Vivian Williams. *Fiddle Seconding Missouri Style, Chords and Bowing Techniques*. Seattle: Voyager Recordings and Books VR-DVD1001, 2012 (instructional DVD with historical commentary).
Marshall, Howard, Vivian Williams, Phil Williams, and John Williams. *Fiddle Tunes of the Lewis and Clark Era*. Voyager Recordings and Books VRCD 358, 2002.
The Martins *Bluegrass Martins: Martin Family). *Christmas*. Jefferson City, 2008.
———. *Cold Lonely Night*. Jefferson City, 2008.
———. *Turn Back the Years*. Jefferson City, 2013.
———. *World of Our Own*. Jefferson City: Aurio Records CD0012, 2011.
McBaine, Taylor. *Boone County Fiddler*. Missouri State Old Time Fiddlers Association MSOTFA 002, 1987 (cassette).
———. *Fiddlin' 75*. Missouri State Old Time Fiddlers Association, 2019; digital album, www.missourifiddling.com.
McCrory, Knox. *Old-Time Tunes on Harmonica*. Columbia, MO: private label, 1997 (cassette).
McMahan, Pete. *50 Old-Time Fiddle Gems*. Reissue of *Missouri Fiddlin'* series (four LPs). Voyager VRCD 366, 2005.
———. *Kansas City Rag*. Reissue of *Missouri Fiddlin' #3*. Missouri State Old Time Fiddlers Association MSOTFA 003, 1989 (cassette).

———. *Missouri Fiddlin'*. Graphic Recording MLP-534, 1972.
———. *Missouri Fiddlin' #2*. Graphic Recording MLP-538, ca. 1976.
———. *Missouri Fiddlin' #3*. Graphic Recording, ca. 1977.
———. *Missouri Fiddlin' #4*. Graphic Recording, ca. 1978.
———. *Ozark Mountain Waltz*. Missouri State Old Time Fiddlers Association 001, 1987 (cassette).
Midnight Flight. *The Best of Midnight Flight, Vol. 1*. Plateau PRCH 1006, n.d. (Gerald Jones, violin)
———. *Fan Favorites*. Plateau PRCH 1006, n.d.
Miller, Shorty. *Fiddling Around*. Camdenton, MO: private label, NQD14381, 1996 (cassette).
Missouri Corn Dodgers. Unlimited DU 33018, 1975; CD reissue, Spring Fed Records, 2011. (Bob Abrams, violin)
Missouri Friends of the Folk Arts. *I'm Old but I'm Awfully Tough: Traditional Music of the Ozark Region*. New Haven, MO: MFFA0001, 1977. (Emanuel Wood, Jake Hockemeyer, Vesta Johnson, Frank Reed, Charlie Pashia, Joe Politte, violin)
Moag, Rod. *A-Haa Goes Grass! A Bluegrass Tribute to the Music of Bob Wills*. Austin, TX: TexTrax, 2000.
———. *The Singin', Pickin' Professor*. Austin, TX: Diploma Disc, 1995.
Moag, Rod, and Bill Malone. *Remember Me: Bill Malone and Rod Moag Play the Music of the Bailes Brothers*. Austin, TX: Hillbilly Dreams 001, 2005.
The Morrow Sisters Band. *Yesterday, Today, and Two Morrows*. Rolla: Rosa Stringworks, ca. 2005 (CD). (Patty Morrow Chandler, violin)
Murphy, Al. *Through the Fields*. New York: Global Village LP 305, 1987.
Myers, Jeremy. *Jeremy in the Briar Patch*. Private label, 2016.
———. *Nail That Catfish to a Tree: Traditional Missouri Old-Time Fiddlin'*. Private label, n.d.
Netherton, Roger. *Roger Netherton*. St. Louis: private label, 2018.
———. *Two Hot Fiddles: Roger Netherton and Trisha Spencer*. St. Louis: private label, 2012.
Newberry, Joe. *Big Medicine: Fever in the South*. Yodel-Ay-Hee 053, 2004.
———. *Joe Newberry and April Verch: Going Home*. AMPED, 2017.
———. *Mike Compton and Joe Newberry-Live*. Self-produced CD, 2012.
Newstead, Susan, Prod. *Missouri Legacy: Fiddlers Plus*. Columbia: KOPN 89.5 FM, 1986 (cassette).
Orchard, Jim. *Front Porch Fiddlin'*. Birch Tree, MO: Orchard, 2003.
———. *Ozarks Fiddlin' from Hartshorn to Low Wassie*. Birch Tree, MO: Orchard, n.d.
Orchard, Jim, and the Ozark Bluegrass Boys. "Longing for the Ozarks" / "Trouble in B." Cherry Records CH 014, 1972. (Odie Mullins, violin)
———. *Old 'Ens an' New 'Ens*. Birch Tree, MO: Orchard, n.d.
Orchard, Jim, and Devin Quick. *Today and Tomorrow*. Birch Tree, MO: Orchard, ca. 1999.
Orchard Brothers. *McHenry Hollow Fiddlin*. Birch Tree, MO: Jim Orchard, 1995. (Jim Orchard, violin)
The Original Mound City String Band. St. Louis: Vigortone Records VT-2008, 2022. (Kevin Kegin, violin)

The Ozark Opry. *Lee Mace's Ozark Opry: On Stage*. Springfield, MO: Century Records 25163/5, ca. 1964.

———. *A Night at Lee Mace's Ozark Opry, Volume 2*. Osage Beach, MO: Lee Mace's Ozark Opry SoN 115591, ca. 1964.

The Ozark Originals. "Please Pass the Biscuits" / "Home Sweet Home." Sure 8100-6262, 1963. (Don Russell, violin)

Perfect Strangers. *Perfect Strangers*. Rebel Records CD 1793, 2003. (Chris Brashear, violin)

Perkins, Bill, and the Midwesterners. *Pickin' at Liberty*. Columbia, MO: Ozark Records 39077, 1978. (Bill "Junior" Perkins, violin)

Persinger, Cleo. *Cleo Persinger: Goin' across the Prairie*. MSOTFA Recordings 007 (https://bandcamp.com, 2018).

Piedmont Melody Makers. *Wonderful World Outside*. Vigortone Records VI-2007, 2017. (Chris Brashear, violin)

The Po' Ramblin' Boys. *Back to the Mountains*. Random Records 064, CD, 2016.

———. *Toil, Tears, and Trouble*. Rounder Records 1166100656, 2019. (C. J. Lewandowski, mandolin)

Potter, Dale. *Dale Potter: World's Champion Country & Western Fiddler, Hoe Down! Volume 1*. Rural Rhythm RRDP 179, 1963 (cassette); reissue, *Dale Potter and Shot Jackson: Twenty Fiddle Favorites*, 1994.

———. *Jazz from the Hills*. 1953, RCA; reissued on CD, with the Country All-Stars. (Dale Potter, violin)

Puckett, Bobby. *Bobby Puckett and Elmer Jones: Just Bobby & Elmer*. Cassette, 1986; CD reissue, Caney, KS: Dawn and Judy Gaff, ca. 1995.

———. "Eminence" / "Squaws along the Illinois." St. Louis: DB 643, 1972 (45 rpm).

———. "Indian Council" / "Van Buren Reel." St. Louis: DB, ca. 1972 (45 rpm).

Quick, Devin, and Jim Orchard. *Today and Tomorrow*. Private label, ca. 1999.

Raggedy Grass String Band. *The Raggedy Grass String Band*. Moberly, MO: Shoestring Tape, 1968 (five-inch reel). (Dan William Peek, banjo; Warren Elliott, violin; Howard "Rusty" Marshall, mandolin, guitar; Bill McIlvain, bass)

Raines, Roy J. *Old Time Fiddlin' Bluegrass Style*. Columbia, MO: A 1 Studio, ca. 1975.

Reed, Frank. *Ole Tyme Fiddlin'*. Frank Reed TS76-922-923, 1976.

Reese, Bud. *Country Get-Together Album*. Kirksville, MO: BR Records BR7181, ca. 1970. (Bobby Joe Caldwell, violin)

Rennard, Marc. *Earthenware*. Tucson: CB Records 0001, 2016.

———. *Old Graveyard Pine (All Covered with Snow)*. St. Louis: Oceana Productions OP006S, 2008.

Robertson, Lonnie. *Country Fiddling*. Caney Mountain CLP-229, ca. 1975.

———. *Fiddle Tune Favorites*. Caney Mountain CLP-228, 1972.

———. *Fiddle Tunes Ozark Style by Lonnie Robertson*. Caney Mountain CLP-232, n.d.

———. *Fiddle Tunes Ozark Style by Lonnie Robertson, Vol. 2*. Caney Mountain CLP-233, n.d.

———. *Home Folks Get Together*. Caney Mountain CEP-211, ca. 1969.

———. *Lonnie's Breakdown: Classic Fiddle Music from Missouri*. Compilation, reissue CD, Rounder 0375, 1996.

———. *Old-Time Fiddle Tunes*. Caney Mountain CLP230, ca. 1976.

———. *Square Dance Fiddlin'*. Caney Mountain CEP-213, ca. 1971.

Robertson, Lonnie, and Thelma Robertson. *Favorite Gospel and Country Songs*. Caney Mountain CLP-231, 1976.
Robertson, Lonnie, Thelma Robertson, and Jarrett Robertson. *Favorite Hymns by the Down Home Folks*. Springfield, MO: Caney Mountain CS-301, ca. 1965. ("Take Up the Cross," "Rank Strangers to Me")
Roden, Levi. *Levi Roden*. Cassville, MO: Trippo 03-050301, 2003.
Russell, Don. "Please Pass the Biscuits" / "Home Sweet Home." Winona: Ozark Originals, MarSure 8100-6262, 1963.
———. "Resurrection Morning" / "Someday We'll Know." Osage Beach: Lee Mace and His Ozark Opry Gang, Starday SEP152A, 1960.
———. "Steppin' in the Straw" / "Ozark Fiddler." Osage Beach: Lee Mace and His Ozark Opry Gang Starday SEP152B, 1960.
Sappington, Hal. *Hal Sappington and Friends: Fiddling*. Warrensburg, MO: private label, 2010.
Schoenberger, Liesl. *Amazing Grace of the Fiddler's Touch*. Sugar Bear Records, ca. 2000 (CD).
———. *Classic Fiddle*. Sugar Bear Records, 1997 (CD).
———. *Say Old Man*. Sugar Bear Records, 2005 (CD).
Schwarz, Tracy. *Learn to Fiddle Country Style*. Folkways FI 8359, 1965.
Scrivner, David, Alvie Dooms, and Karen Kraft. *Hangin' around the Kitchen*. Mansfield, MO: private label, 2007.
Seitz, Geoff. *Common Fiddle Tunes Fast and Slow*. Geoffrey J. Seitz, 1994.
———. *The Good Old Days Are Here*. Oceana Productions OP003, 1995.
Shaw, John, and Jason Shaw. *Flowers from Heaven*. Lincoln, NE: Startracker, 1989 (cassette).
Silvey, H. K. *H. K. Silvey: Fiddling from Ozark County, Missouri*. Field Recorders' Collective FRC-719, 2020.
———. *Traditional Ozarks Fiddlin'*. Gainesville, MO: D&D Studio, n.d. (cassette).
The Skirtlifters (Clarke Buehling & the Skirtlifters). *A Ragtime Episode*. Fayetteville, AR: SL2004, 2004. (Tom Verdot, violin)
———. *Wait for the Wagon*. Fayetteville, AR: SL1998, 1996. (Jim Lansford, violin)
Smith, Leonard. *Fiddle Tunes by Leonard Smith, the One-Armed Fiddler: Mountain Style*. Stark City, MO: Table Rock Records 1020, 1976.
Spike Bones [Darryl Muhrer]. *Bones Meets Jazz*. Chicago: Tones and Bones Productions, 2002.
St. Louis Irish Arts. *St. Louis Irish Arts, Vol. 1*. St. Louis: St. Louis Irish Arts, 1997. (Niall Gannon, Ian Walsh, Kevin Buckley, Alexis Westrich, violin)
State of Tennessee Old-Time Fiddlers' Championships. *1981 State of Tennessee Old-Time Fiddlers' Championships*. Clarksville, 1981. (Pete McMahan, violin)
Stinnett, Cyril. *Cyril Stinnett Plays His Favorite Old Time Fiddle Tunes*. Stinnett Records Slp-234, ca. 1971.
———. *Fiddler's Dream*. Stinnett Records Slp-1012, ca. 1973.
———. *Grey Eagle in C*. Missouri State Old Time Fiddlers Association MSOTFA 103, 1992 (cassette).
———. *Mahoney's Reel*. Missouri State Old Time Fiddlers Association MSOTFA 105, 1992 (cassette).

———. *Plain Old Time Fiddlin'*. Stinnett Records Slp-1013, ca. 1975.

———. *Salty River Reel*. Missouri State Old Time Fiddlers Association MSOTFA 104, 1992 (cassette).

Stoneking, Alita. *Alita Stoneking*. St. Peter, MN: private label, 2014.

———. *Born to Play*. St. Peter, MN: private label, n.d.

Stoneking, Fred. *Saddle Old Spike: Fiddle Music from Missouri*. Rounder 0381, 1996.

Stoneking, Fred, and Alita Stoneking, with Tom Weisgerber. *Late Night Jam*. St. Peter, MN: private label, n.d.

Stoneking, Lee. *A Visit with Lee Stoneking*. Field Recorders' Collective FRC-708, 2015.

Stoneking, Lee, and Sons. *Missouri Old Time Fiddlin'*. Graphic Recording NR11285, ca. 1976.

———. *Rainbow of Fiddle Tunes*. Graphic Recording NR13168, ca. 1976.

Summers, Kathy. *Good Old Fiddle Tunes*. Bourbon, MO: private label, 2016.

Sunny Side Up. *Sunny Side Up*. West Plains, MO: private label, 2004. (Dean Von Allmen, violin)

Swing Deville. *Swing Deville: Salt up the Dance Floor*. www.swingdeville.com, 2010.

———. *Western Swing De Ville*. Fiddlesong Music, 2009. (Matt Wyatt, Justin Branum, violin)

Teague, Howe. *Ozark Memories: Fiddle Tunes by Howe Teague*. OMHT-001, 1986.

———. "Ozark Mountain Fox Chase." Salem, private label, n.d. (45 rpm).

———. *Square Dance Music/Ozark Fiddlin'*. Gold Standard GS-SQ D.LP1, 1964.

Three Stripped Gears. *Three Stripped Gears*. Flying Cloud FCOT-0003, 1986. (Rob Golan, violin)

Various Artists. *24 Fiddle Favorites*. Rural Rhythm Classics RHY-253, 1997. (Dale Potter, violin)

Various Artists. *61st Old Fiddlers' Convention 1996*. Galax, VA: Heritage Records HRC-C-173, 1997 (cassette). (Charlie Walden, violin)

Various Artists. *The American Fogies, Vol. 2*. Rounder CD 1389, 1996. (Jim Lansford, violin)

Various Artists. *Art of Traditional Fiddle*. Rounder 11592, 2001. (Jim Herd, Fred Stoneking, Art Galbraith, Lonnie Robertson, Ray Curbow, Alton Jones, Bob Holt, Howe Teague, violin)

Various Artists. *Banjo Classics from the Vaults of County and Old Blue Records*. Old Blue OB-710, 2012. (Lena Hughes et al.)

Various Artists. *Echoes of the Ozarks, Volume I (Arkansas String Bands, 1927–1930)*. County Records LP 518, 1977; reissue CD, CO-3506, 1986.

Various Artists. *Echoes of the Ozarks, Volume II (Arkansas String Bands, 1927–1930)*. County Records, LP 519, 1977; reissue, CO-3507, 1986.

Various Artists. *Echoes of the Ozarks, Volume III*. County Records LP 520, 1970; reissue CD, CO-3506, 1986.

Various Artists. *Fiddle Classics from the Vaults of County Records and Old Blue Records*. Old Blue OB-709, 2012.

Various Artists. *Fiddlers of the Tennessee Valley*. Ca. 1965; reissue, Spring Fed SFR-DU-33004, ca. 2007. (Lena Hughes, violin)

Various Artists. *Grass Cuttin' Time in Missouri*. St. Louis, Missouri Area Bluegrass Committee MABC-LP101, 1970. (Don Brown, Don Millinger, Bob Wagganer, Stan Wagganer, Clark Weaver, violin)

Various Artists. *Joint Effort: Recorded Live at the Chez.* Columbia: Century Records 33642, 1969.
Various Artists. *Live! From the Kahoka Festival of Bluegrass Music.* Kahoka, MO: Delbert Spray OS16396, ca. 1980. (Gerald Jones, Darrin Vincent, violin)
Various Artists. *Masters of the Folk Violin.* Arhoolie CD 434, 1995. (Claude Williams et al., violin)
Various Artists. *The Missouri Session: A Studio Jam Session with Years of Memories.* Audio Loft TMS-3033-CD, 1990. (Kirk Brandenberger, Larry Ellis, Lyman Enloe, Joe Wieneman, violin)
Various Artists. *National Oldtime Fiddler's Contest, 1996.* Bismarck, ND: Chairmaker's Rush, CD, CF0145D, 1996.
Various Artists. *Northwest Regional Folklife Festival, Volume II.* Voyager VRLP 102, 1978. (Kevin Sanders, banjo)
Various Artists. *Old-Time Fiddler's Repertory.* Columbia: University of Missouri Press, 1976. (Bill Driver, Tony Gilmore, George Helton, Cyril Stinnett, Bob Walters, violin)
Various Artists. *Oldtime Fiddling and Other Folk Music, Weiser, Idaho, 1968.* American Heritage. (Pete McMahan et al., violin)
Various Artists. *Oldtime Fiddling and Other Folk Music, Weiser, Idaho, 1970.* American Heritage. (Cleo Persinger, violin)
Various Artists. *Old-Time Music Ozark Heritage Festival.* West Plains Council on the Arts, ca. 2005. (Colbert Brothers, Kim and Jim Lansford, the Black-Eyed Susies, Jessica Collins, Howard Marshall, Dean Von Allmen, Roger Williams)
Various Artists. *Rural Parlor Guitar: Recordings from 1967–1971.* County CO-CD-2774, n.d. (Lena Hughes et al.)
Various Artists. *Texas Fiddle Favorites.* County 707, 1965. (Major Franklin, Lewis Franklin, Norman Solomon)
Various Artists. *Three Fiddlers from the Show-Me State.* County CO-CD-2739, 2005. (Lyman Enloe, Casey Jones, Cyril Stinnett, violin)
Various Artists. *Traditional Fiddle Music of the Ozarks, Volume One: Along the Eastern Crescent.* Rounder 0435, 1999.
Various Artists. *Traditional Fiddle Music of the Ozarks, Volume Two: On the Springfield Plain.* Rounder 0436, 2000.
Various Artists. *Traditional Fiddle Music of the Ozarks, Volume Three: Down in the Border Counties.* Rounder 0437, 2000.
Various Artists. *The Young Fogies, Vol. II.* Rounder 0369, 1995. (Charlie Walden, violin)
Vincent, Rhonda. *All-American Bluegrass Girl.* Rounder 11661-0580-2, 2006.
———. *Bound for Gloryland,* Rebel Records CD-1692, 1991.
———. "Muleskinner Blues" / "Satisfied." Greentop, MO: private label, 1970 (45 rpm).
———. *Ragin' Live.* Rounder 11661-0553-9, 2005 (DVD).
———. *The Storm Still Rages.* Rounder 11661-0474-2, 2001.
——— [Sally Mountain Gang]. *The Sun Is Coming Up.* Stardust SRLP-1001, 1980.
———. *Taken.* Upper Management UM 001, 2010.
———. *Timeless and True Love.* Rebel Records CD-1697, 1991.
———. *Yesterday and Today, 30 Years of Music (1971–1994).* Lighthouse Records CD1331, 1998.

Von Allmen, Dean. *Country Fiddlin'*. West Plains, MO: private label, 2005.

Wagganer, Bob. *Bluegrass Instrumentals from Missouri*. N.d., ca. 1989; reissue, 2017. (Stan Wagganer, harmony violin)

Walden, Charlie. *Dance around Molly*. Evanston, IL: Charlie Walden, 2016.

———. *Draggin' the Bow*. Missouri State Old Time Fiddlers Association MSOTFA 007, 1996 (cassette).

———. *Missouri Fiddle Tunes*. 2 vols. Evanston, IL: Charlie Walden, 2010.

———. *Patt & Possum: Hoe-Downs, Hornpipes, & Hokum*. Marimac 5062C, 1994 (cassette).

———. *Traditional Fiddle Music of Missouri*. Marimac 9011, 1987 (cassette).

Walsh, Bob. *Old-Time Ozark Fiddlin'*. Archive of the Missouri State Oldtime Fiddlers' Association MSOTFA 107, ca. 1990.

Weeks, Russ. *Just Fiddlin' Around*. Buffalo, MO: Vintage, n.d. (LP).

Wells, Lynn. *Mainline Missouri Fiddling*. Independence, MO: Fiddlesong Music, 2003.

Wells, Lynn, and Pippa Letsky, *Live! At the Cherry Street Artisan*. Boonesboro, MO: private label, 2010.

White, John. *A Little Further Down the Road*. Canton, SD: Missouri Valley Music, 2017.

———. *Memories of Lily Dale: Old Time Music and Dance in Shelby County*. Self-produced CD, 2003.

———. *Missouri Fiddler John White: Nine Miles of Dry and Dusty*. Voyager Recordings and Books VRCD 373, 2007.

Williams, John P. *Monroe County Influences, Vol. 1*. Fiddlesong Music, 2009.

———. *Norma Lou's Waltz*. Madison, MO, 2022.

Williams, John P., and Robert Mackey. *A Tribute to Lonnie Robertson, Vol. 1*. https://johnpwilliams.bandcamp.com/album/a-tribute-to-lonnie-robertson-vol-1, 2019.

Wilson, Nile. *Tie Hacker Hoe-down*. Missouri State Old Time Fiddlers Association MSOTFA 202-CD, 1995.

Wyatt, Matt. *1995 Fiddle Tunes*. Fenton, MO: private label (cassette).

———. *Centralia Waltz*. Independence, MO: Fiddlesong Music, 1998.

———. *Say Old Man—Can You Play the Fiddle?* Fenton, MO: private label, 1995 (cassette).

———. *That's a Plenty, June 1997*. Fenton, MO: private label (cassette).

Wyatt, Matt, and Justin Branum. *The Good-Bye Waltz*. Fiddlesong Music, 2003.

Index

D

G

H

I

L

Y

Z